Landmobile and Marine
Radio Technical Handbook

D1518919

Landmobile and Marine Radio Technical Handbook

by Edward M. Noll

Howard W. Sams & Co., Inc.
A Subsidiary of Macmillan, Inc.
4300 West 62nd Street, Indianapolis, Indiana 46268 U.S.A.

FIRST EDITION
FIRST PRINTING — 1985

International Standard Book Number: 0-672-22427-5
Library of Congress Catalog Card Number: 85-71769

Acquiring editor: *Richard K. Swadley*
Illustrators: *Ralph E. Lund, Jr. and William D. Basham*
Manuscript editor: *Don Herrington*
Compositor: *Central Publishing Company, Indianapolis*

Printed in the United States of America

Contents

CHAPTER 4

Modulation Systems

CHAPTER 5

Digital and Microprocessor Electronics

CHAPTER 6

Test Equipment and Methods

CHAPTER 7

Antenna Systems and Interference

CHAPTER 8

Landmobile Radio Equipment

CHAPTER 9

Repeater, Trunked, and Cellular Radio Systems

CHAPTER 10

Marine Radio and Navigational Systems for Small Craft

Preface

This book is a complete atlas of the commercial two-way radio field. It covers the landmobile (industrial, public safety, and land transportation), marine (radiotelephone and radiotelegraph), and personal radio services. Approximately two million radio stations are licensed in these services.

This book contains updated material from my previous books *General Radiotelephone License Handbook* and *Marine Radiotelegraph License Handbook* as well as all-new material. Here, in this one volume, you will find:

- Two-way radio fundamentals
- Equipment circuit details
- Maintenance and installation data
- Test equipment types and practical usage

Since navigation, radiotelegraphy, and radar remain important facets of a number of radiocommunications systems, these fields are also discussed. In addition, there is coverage of cellular radiotelephones and satellite communications systems.

Landmobile and Marine Radio Technical Handbook has been written for current and prospective two-way radio technicians, operators, and engineers. It can be used as a radiocommunications textbook in community colleges, trade schools, and universities as well as radiomarine and armed forces radio schools. It should be a public library standard and a reference book for all types of two-way radio businesses. In-plant training courses can be organized around its content. A special objective has been to prepare the book as a reference for those electronics persons seeking two-way certification or FCC licensing.

Individual chapters are devoted to:

- Two-way radio services and their frequencies
- Transmission characteristics and emission and modulation classifications
- Solid-state fundamentals as related to transmission circuits presentation
- Modulation systems used in two-way radio services
- Digital and microprocessor circuits
- Test equipment types and usage
- Antenna systems
- Landmobile two-way radio systems and circuits
- Repeater, trunked, and cellular radio systems
- Marine radiotelephone and radiotelegraph equipment
- Direction finders and loran
- Marine radar
- FCC licensing information

Landmobile and Marine Radio Technical Handbook is a very practical presentation. It provides fundamentals along with a comprehension of advanced practices that can make you a more knowledgeable and capable two-way radio technician.

Edward M. Noll

1

Two-Way Radio Services

In the two-way radio services there are three major station classifications — mobile, base, and fixed. A mobile station is one associated with a moving vehicle such as a truck, automobile, boat, or aircraft. A base station, often referred to as a land station, has a fixed position and is used for communicating with one or more mobile stations (and, on occasion, with other base or fixed dispatch stations). The great majority of two-way radio systems come under the base-mobile classification and usually include a single base station and one or more associated mobile stations.

1-1. Fundamental Systems

A fixed station is one in a permanent location used to communicate with other fixed stations. This form of two-way radio is usually referred to as point-to-point communications. Normally, in such services, there are no facilities for communicating with mobile stations. Their principal objective is to convey information between two or more fixed locations. This differs from the base station, which also has a permanent position but is used for the purpose of communicating with mobile stations.

The most common arrangements of two-way radio stations are shown in Fig. 1-1. In the *simplex* arrangement of Fig. 1-1A, the base and mobile units operate on the same frequency (F1). A sequential "on-off" communication is established in which only one station can transmit at a given time, but can be heard by all other stations of the system. Each mobile station can hear both sides of a conversation between the base station and any mobile station. Likewise, communications can be established mobile-to-mobile when the stations are within range. Although not common, a simplex arrangement can also be used in a point-to-point radio system.

In some systems, an inaudible tone signal can be sent out from the base station to the mobiles. Each mobile will then be activated only when its assigned tone frequency is received. As a result the other mobiles will remain shut down and their operators will not be annoyed by chatter not meant for them.

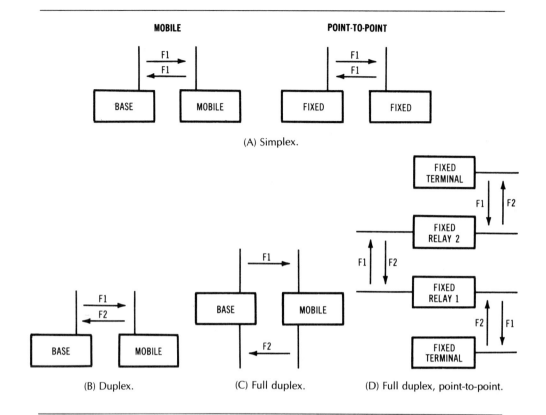

(A) Simplex.

(B) Duplex.

(C) Full duplex.

(D) Full duplex, point-to-point.

Fig. 1-1. Two-way radio systems.

The *duplex* arrangement of Fig. 1-1B is a common two-way radio arrangement. The base station transmits on one frequency (F1), while the mobile stations use a different frequency (F2). In this arrangement the base station can communicate with all mobile stations, but the mobile stations cannot communicate directly with each other. Information to be conveyed between mobile units must be transmitted through the base station. Each mobile station receives only the base-station signal.

Although the duplex arrangement requires two transmitting frequencies (one for the base station and one for the mobile units), it is usually more satisfactory. It is possible to exert better control over the mobile units, and each mobile station is not confused by signals coming from other mobile stations (as with the simplex system).

The duplex arrangement also uses an "on and off" method of transmission. Quite often, frequency F1 is close to frequency F2. In fact, it is customary at each station to use the same antenna for transmitting and receiving. A relay or electronic switch, operating in conjunction with the transmit-receive switching of the station, changes the antenna between the transmitter and the receiver. It is not uncommon for the other segments of the station equipment to be used in both the "receive" and "transmit" positions.

A *full duplex* arrangement is shown in Fig. 1-1C. Operating frequencies F1 and F2 are well-separated; consequently, each station can transmit and receive at the same time. Each transmitter output is isolated and separated in frequency in order not to block the input of its companion receiver. With this arrangement, there can be simultaneous communications between the two stations as in telephone conversations. If more than one mobile station is included, each will usually be on a different transmit frequency. The base station can use the same or different frequencies to establish communications with the different mobile stations.

Full duplex is more common in point-to-point communication services than in mobile systems. In the typical arrangement of four stations shown in Fig. 1-1D, the transmit and receive frequencies of the various fixed stations are staggered, each station receiving on one frequency and transmitting on another. Highly directional antennas are employed, making it possible to establish duplex — and even full duplex — communications with minimum interference between stations. Notice that relay station 1 transmits on F1 and receives on F2, and that relay station 2 transmits on F2 and receives on F1. To permit the use of antenna systems with the highly directional characteristics needed to prevent interference, point-to-point stations are usually assigned frequencies which are in the upper half of the UHF spectum, or in the microwave range.

1-2. Station Assignments and Licensing

Each radio transmitter requires a station license. The transmitter operators do or do not require an operator's license, depending on the radio service they are associated with. For example, in most Maritime and Aviation Services it is necessary that the operator have a license. In fact, an operator's permit is required for practically all radio services that operate below 25 MHz in the Maritime and Aviation Radio Services. Many of the radio services above 25 MHz, including the private Land Mobile Radio Services, do not require an operator's license.

However, a distinction must be made between strictly operation and equipment maintenance. In most cases, the lower-grade operator licenses permit little else than the operation of those controls required in the normal handling of two-way radiocommunications. Adjustments or tests during or coincident with the construction, installation, servicing, or maintenance of a radio transmitter in the Maritime and Aviation Radio Services shall be made by or under the immediate supervision or responsibility of a person holding a commercial radio operator's license, either radiotelephone or radiotelegraph, as may be appropriate for the type of emission employed. Such a licensee is responsible for the proper functioning of the transmitter.

Table 1-1. Major Two-Way Radiotelephony Bands

Medium frequency (MF)	1.6–25 MHz
High frequency (HF)	25–50 MHz
Very high frequency (VHF_1)	108–136 MHz
Very high frequency (VHF_2)	150–174 MHz
Ultrahigh frequency (UHF_1)	450–512 MHz
Ultrahigh frequency (UHF_2)	806–821 MHz
Ultrahigh frequency (UHF_3)	851–866 MHz

The frequency ranges of the major bands used for two-way radio are listed in Table 1-1. The major two-way radio assignments in the medium-frequency (MF) band are police radio, marine, and aviation, although there are some point-to-point relay assignments and a very limited number of landmobile allocations. Because of the great emphasis on small boats, an active portion of the spectrum between 2 and 3 MHz has been allocated to small-ship stations operating in coastal and inland waters. There are numerous aeronautical station assignments, largely for the benefit of air-carrier services (passenger and cargo). Many two-way radio aeronautical assignments, particularly for private aircraft and airport facilities, are made in the VHF_1 band.

The HF spectrum is crowded with mobile assignments. It includes not only the very active Citizens Band, but a moderate pecentage of the private landmobile radio services as well. It is a very active portion of the frequency spectrum insofar as landmobile radio equipment is concerned.

Similar assignments are made in the two VHF bands. The 72–76 MHz band has been allocated largely to operational fixed-station use. Point-to-point relay systems have allocations in this spectrum. In time, most point-to-point allocations and some of the systems now operating on this band will use the superhigh frequency (SHF) and the upper end of the UHF bands. A high degree of stability and freedom from interference can be obtained more readily in the microwave spectrum.

Aeronautical radio facilities dominate the VHF_1 spectrum. The assignments in the VHF_2 spectrum are similar to those of the HF band. Landmobile-radio assignments are predominant. However, aviation radio, railroad radio, and coastal radiomarine allocations are also available.

The allocations on the UHF band are similar to those of the VHF and HF bands. A number of fixed point-to-point allocations are becoming available, particularly at the high-frequency end of the UHF band. This band includes an impressive array of allocations for land vehicle, marine, and aviation facilities. Radionavigational aids (including radar) for aeronautical and marine services are served by UHF and higher microwave frequency assignments. Some mobile radio assignments are also made in the UHF television spectrum between 470 and 890 MHz.

1-3. Active Two-Way Radio Services

Two active two-way radiotelephone services that require the services of a general licensed radiotelephone technician are private aviation and small-boat marine radiotelephone. The FCC is concerned about transmitter adjustments and measurements. Of particular concern are power, frequency, and modulation characteristics. These are factors of concern when the transmitter is initially installed, and when any change is made in the transmitter which may influence these parameters. Technical details are covered in later chapters.

1-3-1. Private Land Mobile Radio Services

Frequencies are allocated for a variety of radio services under the main headings of public safety, special emergency, industrial radio, and land transportation. Most allocations are in the frequency spectra of 25–50 MHz, 150–174 MHz, and 450–512 MHz. Sections in the 806–896 MHz spectrum are increasingly active.

The radio services that come under public safety are local government, police radio, fire radio, highway maintenance, and forestry-conservation. The special emergency radio services provide allocations for medical services, rescue organizations, veterinarians, disaster relief organizations, school buses, beach patrols, isolated area radio service, communications standby, and emergency repair of public communications facilities. The categories that come under the industrial radio services are power, petroleum, forest products, motion picture, relay press, special industrial, business radio, manufacturers, and telephone maintenance. The land transportation radio services include motor carrier, railroad radio, taxicab radio, and automobile emergency.

In the foregoing radio services there are approximately one million authorized stations. This provides some idea of the scope of the technical activities in the private landmobile radio services. Frequency assignments are at a premium, and it is necessary to have local frequency-advisory boards that assist the FCC in making frequency assignments to minimize as much as possible interference among stations.

Technical considerations are covered in detail in Chapter 8. However, the general scope of the material is introduced in the following paragraph under transmitter measurements as taken from Volume V of the FCC Rules and Regulations.

Sec. 90.215 Transmitter measurements.

(a) The licensee of each station shall employ a suitable procedure to determine that the carrier frequency of each transmitter authorized to operate with an output power in excess of two watts is maintained within the tolerance prescribed in Section 90.213. This determination shall be made, and the results entered in the station records in accordance with the following:

(1) When the transmitter is initially installed;

(2) When any change is made in the transmitter which may affect the carrier frequency or its stability.

(b) The licensee of each station shall employ a suitable procedure to determine that each transmitter authorized to operate with an output power in excess of two watts does not exceed the maximum figure specified on the current station authorization. On authorizations stating only the input power to the final radio-frequency stage, the maximum permissible output power is 75% for frequencies below 25 MHz and 60% of the input power for frequencies above 25 MHz. If a non-DC final radio-frequency stage is utilized, then the output power shall not exceed 75% of the input power. This determination shall be made, and the results thereof entered into the station records, in accordance with the following:

(1) When the transmitter is initially installed;

(2) When any change is made in the transmitter which may increase the transmitter power input.

(c) The licensee of each station shall employ a suitable procedure to determine that the modulation of each transmitter, which is authorized to operate with an output power in excess of two watts, does not exceed the limits specified in this part. This determination shall be made and the following results entered in the station records, in accordance with the following:

(1) When the transmitter is initially installed;

(2) When any change is made in the transmitter which may affect the modulation characteristics.

(d) The determinations required by paragraphs (a), (b), and (c) of this section may, at the option of the licensee, be made by a qualified engineering measurement service, in which case the required record entries shall show the name and address of the engineering measurement service as well as the name of the person making the measurements.

(e) In the case of mobile transmitters, the determinations required by paragraphs (a) and (c) of this section may be made at a test or service bench: Provided, That the measurements are made under load conditions equivalent to actual operating conditions; and provided further that after installation in the mobile unit the transmitter is given a routine check to determine that it is capable of being received satisfactorily by an appropriate receiver.

1-3-2. Marine Small-Boat Ship-to-Shore Radio

There are more then 400,000 stations authorized in the radiomarine services. A high percentage of these are compact ship-to-shore and ship-to-ship radiotelephones installed on small commercial and pleasure boats. In fact, any vessel, regardless of size, that is transporting more than six passengers for hire and is navigated in the open seas or any tidewater within the jurisdiction of the United States adjacent or contiguous to the open seas, must be equipped with an acceptable radio installation.

Small marine transceivers are operated in the 2–3 MHz and 156–162 MHz bands. These units are very compact and can be installed conveniently on small commercial and pleasure boats. Key allocations are given in Table 1-2. In the case of the VHF assignments channel designators instead of specific frequencies are indicated.

The call and distress frequency for ship radiotelephone stations in the 2–3 MHz band is 2182 kHz. Channel 16 or 156.8 MHz is the calling and distress frequency for the VHF assignments.

Actual frequency assignments depend on the area in which you operate, and it is the responsibility of dealers and technicians to provide guidance as to appropriate operating frequencies and facilities available in a specific geographic area of interest.

Typical VHF-FM marine transceivers are usually multichannel radios. Some have only a modest number of channels while others include many transmit and receive channels. There are also facilities for weather receive channels as well. Transmit power is the maximum permissible value of 25 watts, although many units have facilities for reducing power in order to minimize interference. Facilities for maintaining a watch on channel 16 are also included.

Presently short-range marine communications take place more frequently on the VHF rather than the MF bands. In fact, a VHF installation is compulsory even though MF equipment is installed on the boat.

The medium-frequency marine radiotelephone employs single-sideband transmission rather than the old double-sideband, amplitude-modulation technique which required a greater operating bandwidth. Single-sideband operation requires only one-half of the emission bandwidth needed by standard amplitude modulation.

A typical 2–4 MHz radiotelephone might include eight or more crystal-controlled channels including the 2182 kHz emergency frequency. Again the selection of crystals for the channels requires guidance from the dealers and radiotelephone technicians of a given area. Assignments depend on the area facilities as well as the possible range of operation of the boat.

The following applies to the adjustment of transmitting apparatus:

Adjustment of Transmitting Apparatus

All adjustments of radio transmitting apparatus in any station subject to this part during or coincident with the installation, servicing, or maintenance of such apparatus which may affect the proper operation of such station, shall be performed by or under the immediate supervision and responsibility of a person holding a general operator license, who shall be responsible for the proper functioning of the station equipment; Provided, however, that:

(a) Only persons holding a radiotelegraph operator license shall perform such functions at radiotelegraph stations transmitting by any type of Morse code;

(b) Only persons holding a license, containing a ship radar endorsement shall perform such functions on radar equipment.

Table 1-2. VHF-FM Channel Designations

Channel Designators	Type of Communications	Points of Communications
16 (Mandatory)	Distress, Safety & Calling	Intership & Ship to Coast
06 (Mandatory)	Intership Safety	Intership
65, 66, 12, 73, 14, 74, 20	Port Operations	Intership & Ship to Coast
13	Navigational	Intership & Ship to Coast
22	Liaison Communications Only With U.S. Coast Guard Ship, Coast, or Aircraft Stations	
07, 09, 10, 11, 18, 19, 79, 80	Commercial	Intership & Ship to Coast
67, 08, 88	Commercial	Intership
09, 68, 69, 71, 78	Noncommercial	Intership & Ship to Coast
70, 72	Noncommercial	Intership
24, 84, 25, 85, 26, 86, 27, 87, 28, 88	Public Correspondence	Ship to Public Coast
162.40 MHz, 162.475 MHz 162.55 MHz	NOAA Weather Service	Ship Receive Only

1-3-3. Ocean-Traveling Vessels

More complex and elaborate radio and navigation installations are required aboard cargo vessels, passenger ships, and tankers that travel the open seas. In addition to the radiotelephone and navigation equipment, radiotelegraph capability is compulsory aboard all passenger ships regardless of size and aboard cargo vessels of 1600 gross tons and higher. Cargo vessels under 1600 gross tons must also have radiotelegraph capability if they are not equipped with a radiotelephone station in compliance with international communications law. Communications on the open seas must often be maintained over great distances, and radiotelegraph communication is often more reliable. It is especially advantageous when trouble or disaster limits the amount of available power or when emergency equipment must be battery powered. Radiotelegraph installations also occupy less frequency space. Fortunately with the advent of solid-state electronics, other modulation techniques can be operated with excellent power efficiency and power requirements. Information can now be transferred in more detail (and faster) when compared to basic Morse code radiotelegraphy.

A variety of other equipment can be found aboard ship; this includes radioteletype and units that can make a direct copy of received code signals. Other facilities are short-range and long-range navigation equipment as well as radar. Satellite navigation and communications has become increasingly popular.

Each vessel must maintain a watch on prescribed distress frequencies. This watch can be an operator or an automatic alarm system that responds to any received distress information. The six distress frequencies and the preferred type of emission for each are:

500 kHz	—	A2 Emission
2182 kHz	—	A3J Emission
8364 kHz	—	Expedient Emission
121.5 MHz	—	A2-A3-A9 Emissions
156.8 MHz	—	F3 Emission
243 MHz	—	A9 Emission

The emission types are: A2, radiotelegraphy; A3, amplitude modulation; and F3, frequency modulation. Emission A9 is a special emission combine.

Frequency bands are set aside for radiomarine communications at several positions in the radio-frequency spectrum. A major frequency band for ocean-going vessels that use radiotelegraphy is 450–535 kHz. In fact, this is a compulsory band and includes the 500-kHz (600 meters) international distress frequency. There is a lower-frequency marine radiotelegraphy band that extends between 90 and 160 kHz. Additional radiomarine activity (both radiotelegraphy and radiotelephony) dominates the following frequencies:

2	–	3.0	MHz
4.1	–	4.45	MHz
6.2	–	6.5	MHz
8.2	–	8.8	MHz
12.3	–	13.2	MHz
16.0	–	17.4	MHz
22.0	–	22.7	MHz

Specific frequencies in these bands are assigned to coastal and shipboard radio stations. Although there is a significant intermingling of signals including radiotelephone, radioteletype, and radiotelegraph, each mode of transmission is distributed loosely in specific segments of a given band. If you have a shortwave receiver that can demodulate code (CW) and sideband signals, you can tune in the activities.

1-3-4. Aviation Radio Services

The aviation radio services set aside portions of the spectrum for radiocommunication and radionavigation facilities for aircraft operators, aeronautical enterprises, and organizations that require radio transmitting facilities for safety purposes and other necessities. The radio stations are allocated on the basis of a number of categories — airborne-aeronautical advisory, aeronautical multicom, aeronautical enroute, aeronautical metropolitan, flight test, flying school, airport, aeronautical utility, aeronautical search and rescue mobile, aeronautical fixed, operational, radio-navigational land, and civil air patrol. Most of these stations require a licensed operator. Insofar as installation and maintenance are concerned a higher grade license is needed.

In general, communications in the aviation services shall be restricted to safe, expeditious, and economical operation of aircraft, and the protection of life and property in the air. There are many electronic aids to aircraft navigation; they can be considered in four general categories of communication, navigation, traffic control, and landing. Most of the modern-day aeronautical radio acitivity occurs in the frequency spectrum between 108 and 136 MHz. Radionavigation uses the spectrum between 108 and 118 MHz; air traffic control uses 118–136 MHz. Spotted throughout the spectrum are frequencies assigned to both aircraft and aeronautical ground stations. For example, in flying a private aircraft you will find the frequencies of the various ground stations given on navigational maps and/or charts. These aeronautical ground stations monitor certain aircraft frequencies, and you can quickly establish contact enroute by setting your aviation radio to an appropriate frequency.

Many aviation radio units have dual-reception capability. Thus it is possible to receive a radionavigational signal and also maintain a two-way radio contact with an aeronautical ground station.

Most modern flying is done via the VHF omnidirectional range stations. These are called *VOR* or *OMNI* stations. In the VHF spectrum there is largely static-free reception, and the bending and false beams of the older lower-frequency radio range stations are not transmitted. A reliable directional pattern can be produced at the higher frequencies.

A typical installation on a small aircraft may be a transmitter and receiver that operate on a frequency indicated by a digital readout. The communicator can be used as a simple transceiver operating on the same frequency. However, duplex operation is also possible by proper settings with the transmit and receive frequencies differing. A strictly navigational receiver can also be included. Its associated meters indicate bearing and right-left positioning of the aircraft with respect to a VOR range station.

A low frequency receiver may also be installed to permit tuning to a low-frequency range station. Many aircraft include a *transponder* which sends out a coded signal. Thus at a ground station the aircraft can be seen and identified on a radar screen. Another addition could be a distance measuring (DME) unit. In operation it sends out an interrogating signal to a special range facility called a *VORTAC* station. The VORTAC station in turn sends back a signal to the aircraft unit that permits the pilot to determine the distance to the VORTAC station.

The frequency of 121.5 MHz is the universal simplex clear channel for use by aircraft in distress or condition of emergency. It is not assigned to aircraft unless other frequencies are assigned and available for normal communications needs. The channel is available as follows:

1. For emergency communications when circumstances beyond the control of a pilot prevent communication between the aircraft and ground stations on other regularly assigned channels.
2. For emergency direction-finding purposes.
3. For establishing air-to-ground contact by aircraft in distress, emergency, or when lost.
4. In connection with search and rescue operations, to provide a common channel for aircraft (either civil or military) not equipped to transmit on 123.1 MHz. This includes communications between aircraft, and between aircraft and ground stations. Stations having the capability should change to 123.1 MHz as soon as practicable.

5. To provide a common frequency for survival communications and survival beacons (emission A2).

6. For air/ground communications between aircraft and ocean vessels for safety purposes when service on other VHF channels is not available.

The frequency 243 MHz is available to survival craft stations which are also equipped to transmit on 121.5 MHz.

Installation, maintenance, and adjustments that influence the radiation from the transmitter must be made by an operator with a general radiotelephone license.

The various aeronautical ground stations must be operated by FCC-licensed operators with the exception of the FAA stations operated by government employees. Also certain landmobile stations to not require an operator; usually such vehicles are associated with an airport control station or other aeronautical ground station which is under the control of a licensed operator. The general operator requirements are:

General Operator Requirements

(a) Except as provided for in FCC rules or as limited on the face of the operator license or permit, all stations in the Aviation Services shall be operated by persons holding any class of commercial radio operator license or permit issued by the Commission: *Provided,* That

(1) Only a person holding a marine operator permit or a third class or higher operator permit shall operate aircraft stations

(i) Utilizing frequencies below 30 MHz not exclusively allocated to the aeronautical mobile service, or

(ii) Utilizing frequencies above 30 MHz not allocated exclusively to aeronautical mobile services and which are assigned for international use; and

(2) Only a person holding a general radiotelephone license shall operate an aircraft station at which the installation is not used solely for telephony, or at which the power is more than 250 watts carrier power or 1,000 watts peak envelope power.

(b) The licensed operator of a land or aeronautical public service station using telephony may permit other persons to transmit or to communicate under his direct supervision and responsibility over the facilities of the station in accordance with the terms of the station license.

Transmitter Adjustments and Tests by Operator

All transmitter adjustments or tests during or coincident with the installation, servicing, or maintenance of a radio station, which may affect the proper operation of such station, shall be made by or under the immediate supervision and responsibility of a person holding a general radiotelephone operator license who shall be responsible for the proper functioning of the station equipment?

1-3-5. Citizens Band (CB) Radio Service

The Citizens Band (CB) Radio Service has had a phenomenal growth, as attested by the millions of transmitters now in operation. A segment of the frequency spectrum has been set aside for the Citizens Band Radio Service to provide a private, short-distance radiocommunications service for the business or personal activities of the licensees. No operator or station license is required.

The Citizens Band Radio Service has many uses. It is particularly attractive because low-cost, efficient equipment is available and almost everyone is eligible for a license. The Citizens Band Radio Service is basically mobile in nature with a majority of installations made in trucks and autos. Travel conditions, highway instructions, and personal exchanges dominate the mobile conversations. There are local activities as well as continuous chatter among trucks and private cars on the interstate highways.

The family base-mobile installation is particularly popular. The base station (still considered a mobile installation in terms of FCC terminology) is installed at home, and a mobile unit is installed in the family car. When one member of the family is shopping or traveling to or from work, that member is able to maintain contact with home. In this manner delays, travel changes, and additional shopping information can be confirmed and arranged via two-way radio. Often the time of departure from one's business or place of employment is quite indefinite. At a reasonable distance from home, a mobile-to-home contact can be made to let the family know said person is on the way home.

Of course, the two-way radio is handy in case of a car breakdown, or other delays. In many localities it is not only possible to call home, but necessary assistance can be obtained by calling a station operated by a garage or service station. Channel 9 has been set aside for the exclusive use in requesting road help or for other emergencies. Citizens Band radio is often quite helpful on long trips because breakdowns on turnpikes often involve considerable delay if you have to await the routine scheduled trip of a repair truck along the highway. Citizens Band operation permits you to obtain a variety of services ahead of time such as lodging, repairs, location and traffic guidance, medical assistance, etc.

Citizens Band radio can be a special boon to a small businessman. Any type of pickup and/or delivery service can derive benefit in terms of reporting delays, breakdowns, changes in routing, and last-minute pickups or deliveries. A fuel-oil delivery service represents only one example of the many businesses that can use CB radio to advantage. Enroute trucks can be informed of call-ins from customers right after they have been completed and while the truck may be in the vicinity of the customer's location. Parts jobbers in the service field use CB to advantage in making their deliveries to retail stores and service shops. Communications can even be maintained between the main store and outlying branches of various types of businesses.

Professional people can use Citizens Band radio for maintaining contact between car and office. Late call-ins or emergencies can be radioed to the doctor as he makes his rounds. Similarly, a veterinarian making his farm calls can keep in touch with his office.

Channel 9 may be used only for emergency communications or for traveler assistance.

CB channel designations and frequencies are as follows:

Channel	Frequency (MHz)	Channel	Frequency (MHz)
1	26.965	13	27.115
2	26.975	14	27.125
3	26.985	15	27.135
4	27.005	16	27.155
5	27.015	17	27.165
6	27.025	18	27.175
7	27.035	19	27.186
8	27.055	20	27.205
		21	27.215
9	27.065	22	27.225
		23	27.255
10	27.075	24	27.235
11	27.085	25	27.245
12	27.105	26	27.265

Channel	Frequency (MHz)	Channel	Frequency (MHz)
27	27.275	34	27.345
28	27.285	35	27.355
29	27.295	36	27.365
30	27.305	37	27.375
31	27.315	38	27.385
32	27.325	39	27.395
33	27.335	40	27.405

You must, at all times and on all channels, give priority to emergency communications.

No station or operator's license is needed. However, a general radio operator license is required for adjustments to radio transmitters during installation, testing, or servicing that may cause the transmitter to operate off frequency, or in a manner which may in other ways violate the rules.

1-4. Station License

Radio transmitters in the two-way radio services may not be operated without a station license. Station license authorization is granted by the FCC. The necessary application form can be requested from the FCC in Washington, DC or from a district office (refer to Chapter 14).

A variety of technical and business information is required to complete the form. The business information requested verifies the eligibility of the applicant and includes a general description of the business and activities and how the radio system is to be employed in that activity. Business addresses must be given as well as the address of the transmitter site and the location of the transmitter control points. Antenna structure, height, and other data must be indicated as well as a description of the possible area in which the station or units of the station normally will be operated. Other technical data including type of service, emission, and maximum input power requested must be shown.

The technician should see to the proper posting of licenses. As an aid to his customers the technician should keep an eye on the expiration dates of the various stations with which he is concerned. He can also keep an eye on license renewal dates, making certain that the station owners renew within two months before the expiration dates.

1-5. Orientation Tips

Much understanding and knowledge can be gained by listening to the activities on the two-way radio bands. Today this can be done at relatively low cost. Shop wisely and you can find bargains in scanners. These operate on the VHF and UHF public-service and landmobile bands. Some scanners also operate on the VHF aviation band.

The beginning or prospective technician soon learns good operating procedures along with the technical problems encountered in maintaining a reliable two-way radio service. You can hear what is going on. Well-planned systems and properly serviced equipment are essential.

Bargains in new general-coverage communication receivers abound. Look through the trade magazines. Fine performing used receivers are available. Shop carefully and choose one that can demodulate AM, sideband, and CW signals. Such a receiver is especially appropriate if your interest lies with the radiomarine services. You can listen to radiotelephone and radiotelegraph operating procedures. If you are a prospective shipboard radiotelegraph operator you can bring up your code-copying speed with practice on a radiotelegraph segment of the marine bands. Tune between 8.36 and 8.45 MHz as well as between 12.5 and 12.7 MHz to sharpen your code ability.

Purchase copies of FCC Volume IV (Marine and Aviation Radio Services) and/or Volume V (Land-Mobile Radio Services). They are really essential to anyone interested in the two-way radio services because of their coverage of FCC technical requirements, frequency assignments, normal and emergency operating procedures, radio law, etc. Refer to appropriate information in Chapter 14.

2

Transmission Characteristics

2-1. Frequencies and Operating Characteristics

Two-way radio, mobile, and point-to-point services are distributed throughout the entire frequency spectrum. The FCC makes frequency assignments in accordance with the services to be rendered and the program characteristics suitable for this service. The radio-frequency spectrum is apportioned into the following subdivisions:

VLF (very low frequency) .... below 30 kHz
LF (low frequency) .... 30 to 300 kHz
MF (medium frequency) .... 300 to 3000 kHz
HF (high frequency) .... 3000 to 30,000 kHz
VHF (very high frequency) .... 30,000 kHz to 300 MHz
UHF (ultrahigh frequency) .... 300 to 3000 MHz
SHF (superhigh frequency) .... 3000 to 30,000 MHz
EHF (extremely high frequency) .... 30,000 to 300,000 MHz

The two lowest-frequency bands and a low-frequency segment of the medium-frequency band are primarily used in the maritime and aeronautical services. Up to 540 kHz, radiotelegraph transmissions are most common. Information is transmitted in the form of the International Morse code, and operators are required to have some form of commercial radiotelegraph license. Airway beacon and other stations that send out navigational signals use sections of this frequency spectrum, and the international distress frequency of 500 kHz (600 meters) is also located here.

In this frequency spectrum, the ground wave (Fig. 2-1) dominates. As a result, a very reliable transmission medium exists, both for short- and medium-distance communications.

If adequate transmitter power and receiver sensitivity are available (along with a large, efficient transmitting antenna), it is possible to establish very reliable long-distance communications. In recent years much experimental work has been done in this frequency spectrum toward developing reliable worldwide communications.   25

Since very low frequencies will penetrate the ocean water more readily than higher-frequency waves, the former can be used for communicating with submarines.

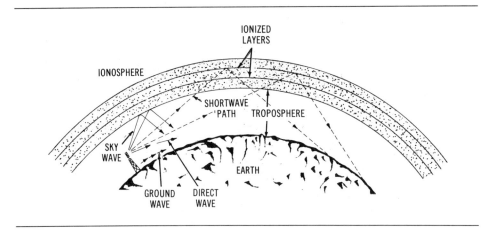

Fig. 2-1. Propagation of radio signals.

In the medium-frequency spectrum between 300 and 3000 kHz, both the ground wave and the sky wave contribute to the net signal delivered to a receiving location. At the low end of the medium-frequency spectrum, the ground wave dominates the sky wave very much. Consequently, reliable ground-wave communications can be established with limited and occasional interference introduced from sky-wave components.

The radio broadcast band (AM) starts at 540 kHz and extends to 1600 kHz. The ground wave serves as a reliable local and regional transmission medium for most of the broadcast band. During the night hours, especially in the winter, strong sky-wave components return to the earth. At varying distances from the transmitter, the ground waves and sky waves may interact, sometimes adding and sometimes subtracting. This can cause fading of the signal. At the high-frequency end of the broadcast band, the ground-wave radiation is reliable over a shorter distance than it is at the low-frequency end. Particularly at night, the local ground-wave components are subject to interference from the sky-wave components originating from other stations on the same frequency but located a substantial distance away.

In this frequency spectrum, atmospheric noises are predominant. Summer transmission is plagued by lightning static, and the winter reception problem is interaction between the ground wave and sky wave.

In the frequency spectrum between 1.6 MHz and 5 MHz, there is a variety of two-way radio assignments. It is here that small-boat radio assignments are made. Small-boat installations must be installed, adjusted, and serviced only by general radio-telephone license holders.

The upper end of the medium-frequency spectrum provides reliable coverage up to 50 or 100 miles and, under proper circumstances, even farther. For most small-boat and aviation two-way radio installations, the desired range is substantially less than 50 miles. Consequently, reliable performance is obtained with compact, low-power, single-sideband equipment.

Atmospheric noises are prevalent, and in mobile installations the problem of ignition interference must be considered. Sky-wave components bounced off the ionized layers sometimes travel a great distance. They then return to the earth at a high signal level and are capable of interfering with more localized communications. In some point-to-point communications systems, sky-wave transmission is advantageous in covering long distances (up to several hundred miles) on a reliable, scheduled basis.

Long-distance point-to-point communications and other services are assigned to the shortwave HF spectrum between 3 and 30 MHz. Various bands of shortwave broadcast stations occupy these frequencies. By using the sky-wave bounce from the ionized layers, these stations make reliable, worldwide communications possible.

The ionization of the various layers above the earth is a continuously shifting process. Careful observation and measurement over a period of years have permitted the development of consistent long-distance performance. These long-distance communications services — by proper choice of frequency, time, power, and directive antenna systems — are able to accurately pinpoint these strong signals to almost all corners of the earth.

Atmospheric static is strong at the low-frequency end of the spectrum, but gradually becomes weaker toward the 30-MHz limit. Conversely, ignition interference increases in intensity toward the high-frequency end of the shortwave spectrum.

Sunspot activities and aurora borealis, along with the consequent magnetic storms, have a decided influence on shortwave performance. Sunspot activities also have been cycled over the years and must be considered in shortwave radio transmission. The level and degree of ionization become a function of sunspot activity, varying from day to night, season to season, and year to year. On occasion, magnetic storms are so intense that all or large segments of the shortwave bands are rendered inoperative.

In addition to the point-to-point communications, many mobile services are crowded in between 25 and 50 MHz, near the high-frequency end of the shortwave spectrum. Also, there are maritime and aviation assignments in this spectrum.

At the high-frequency end of the shortwave spectrum, the direct wave (Fig. 2-1) predominates. The ground wave is attenuated to an insignificant level only a short distance from the transmitter. Sky-wave reflections are more sporadic. Thus, most communications are by way of the direct wave which travels in the immediate atmosphere between transmitter and receiver. The reliability of the direct wave makes this segment of the frequency spectrum ideal for mobile two-way radio systems. With proper facilities and sufficient power output, the reliable maximum range can be extended to 75 miles.

The popular Citizens Band assignments are made in the 27-MHz range. Millions of mobile stations are licensed to operate in this band.

The VHF spectrum extends between 30,000 kHz and 300 MHz. In addition to many other less-publicized services, this segment contains our television and FM broadcast stations. Two frequency bands are used extensively for two-way mobile-radio systems, and a third band is assigned to point-to-point communications. A concentration of aeronautical two-way radio systems and other aircraft and marine navigational services are also assigned space in this frequency spectrum.

Direct-wave propagation (Fig. 2-1) is predominant in this spectrum. The ground wave drops to an insignificant value just a short distance from the transmitting antenna. The sky wave penetrates the atmosphere and the ionized layers before going off into space. In fact, in the VHF and UHF spectrums, guidance and telemetering signals are sent to missiles and satellites.

The lower half of the VHF spectrum is subject to some ionospheric reflection. Intense sunspot activities will result in a dense ionosphere and some reflection of VHF signals. Ignition and other sparking noises are strong at the low end of the VHF band, and gradually decrease toward the high end. Atmospheric noises seldom exist, or if they do, they are very low in intensity. Inherent receiver noises now become significant. In the VHF, UHF, and higher microwave spectra, receiver input-circuit noises are of primary concern. In most receivers, noise from the input stage predominates.

The immediate atmosphere (troposphere) exerts a great influence on the range and reliability of VHF transmissions beyond the horizon. Customarily, we refer to VHF

28

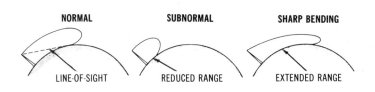

NORMAL   SUBNORMAL   SHARP BENDING

LINE-OF-SIGHT   REDUCED RANGE   EXTENDED RANGE

Fig. 2-2. VHF propagation and tropospheric bending.

and UHF transmission as being line of sight. However, there is some bending of the VHF wave by the atmosphere. This atmospheric bend, or refraction, causes the wave to travel beyond the strictly optical line of sight. How far the wave travels depends on how much it is bent (Fig 2-2). Many meteorological factors influence the degree of bending — barometric pressure, temperature, humidity, and others. Discontinuities such as air-mass layers or temperature inversions in the upper atmosphere exert a great influence on the degree of bending. In fact, under extreme conditions the radio wave is confined in ductlike fashion within these sharp discontinuities. Consequently, it can be propagated hundreds, and even thousands, of miles before returning to the earth.

Although these propagation phenomena are interesting and unusual, routine two-way radiocommunications must be more reliable. Consequently, communication systems are designed on the basis of line-of-sight range, plus a reasonable extension based on an average minimum amount of atmospheric bending. This distance is referred to as the radio-path horizon.

The UHF region between 300 and 3000 MHz represents an extension of the services provided in the VHF spectrum. Similar two-way radio assignments for land, marine, and aviation are made; and UHF television assignments occupy a good slice of this spectrum. Radionavigational aids, including radar, are also assigned here. Assignments for point-to-point microwave relay systems are made at the high-frequency end of the spectrum. In common terminology, that portion above 1000 MHz is called the microwave region.

The range of UHF transmission, in general, is less than that of VHF. However, the UHF wave, being more beam-like, can be reflected sharply by objects. For this reason, in metropolitan areas a UHF two-way radio system is often more satisfactory than its VHF counterpart — the ability of the wave to be reflected permits the signal to be bounced to a mobile unit surrounded by skyscrapers. In suburban and rural areas VHF, because of its greater range, seems to operate better.

The UHF wave, particularly at the high-frequency end, can be packed into a concentrated pencil-like beam by the use of directional antennas. At this high frequency, the physical dimensions of a highly directional antenna are practical. As a result, this end is advantageous in point-to-point communications systems.

For transmission between two fixed points within line of sight, only two terminal stations are needed. If the communications system is to extend along a lengthy right-of-way (oil or natural-gas line, turnpike, railroad line, truck route), intermediate relay stations — either manned or automatic — can be used.

Microwave relay systems are in operation, or are being planned, for many industrial and commercial services. Translators that carry television signals into remote areas use the UHF and microwave spectrums. Studio-transmitter links and remote-pickup equipment operate in the microwave spectrums.

The SHF (superhigh frequency) spectrum extends between 3000 and 30,000 MHz. Radar and microwave relay services are assigned to this sector. However, much developmental work is being conducted here, to duplicate the services rendered in the

UHF and VHF spectra, and some mobile operations are under test or development. Navigational devices in particular can take advantage of the very sharp physical dimensions. Licensing and technical requirements are somewhat more liberal on the many developmental frequencies.

In traveling through the atmosphere, radio (electromagnetic) energy is lost. This is called absorption. At higher frequencies, especially in the microwave spectra, this absorption becomes important. Absorption is significant in precipitation and, in heavy rain, there can be a considerable loss in transmission range, especially in the microwave ranges.

2-2. Types of Emission and Modulation

The FCC classifies three major types of modulation — amplitude modulation (AM), frequency modulation (FM), and pulse modulation (PM). In an AM system, as shown in Fig. 2-3, the information is conveyed by varying the amplitude of the resultant RF wave. An amplitude-modulated resultant wave is developed, formed by three signals — the original carrier, the upper sideband (the carrier plus the modulating frequency), and the lower sideband (the carrier minus the modulating frequency).

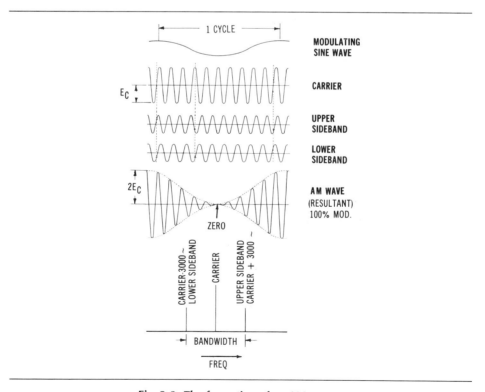

Fig. 2-3. The formation of an AM wave.

It is apparent that the bandwidth occupied by the signal in an amplitude-modulated system is set by the highest modulating frequency. If this frequency is 3000 hertz, the total bandwidth of the pure amplitude-modulated signal will be 6 kHz. If it is 10 kHz, the total bandwidth required will be 20 kHz.

In radio-broadcast systems, the highest audio-frequency component transmitted lies between 8000 and 12,000 hertz (although some of the high-fidelity broadcast stations transmit higher components). Thus, the bandwidth of broadcast stations lies somewhere between 15 and 25 kHz.

In AM broadcasting, the frequency response is generally limited at the receiver. The IF system in an average broadcast receiver is designed to pass audio components up to approximately 5000 Hz, in order to minimize interference between broadcast stations with operating frequencies that are close together. The bandwidth of the average AM broadcast receiver is usually somewhat less than 10 kHz.

The low- and high-frequency audio components are of significance in the transmission of music and other program material. However, in terms of the intelligibility of voice communications, a low-frequency limit between 300 and 350 Hz and a high-frequency limit between 3000 and 4000 Hz are satisfactory.

There are three advantages to confining the frequency response and bandwidth in voice communications. With a narrow bandwidth at the transmitting and receiving ends, the communication is less subject to heterodyne and sideband interference from other stations on the same or adjacent channels. Likewise, the narrowband signal does not radiate as many sidebands capable of interfering with other services on the same or adjacent channels. Moreover, a narrowband receiver minimizes the amount of static and man-made noise that enters, and its inherent noise is usually less than for the wideband type. In summary, a narrowband system conserves the frequency spectrum, minimizes interference, and has a lower noise level.

In voice transmission, few significant frequency components are present above 3000 or 4000 Hz, and if present, they are usually low in amplitude and contribute very little to intelligibility. It is true that these overtones and high-frequency components do determine the quality and individualism of a person's voice. However, the intelligibility is not reduced when these high-frequency components are absent. Hence, most voice communications channels cut off at approximately 2500 to 3500 Hz. By so doing, there is a conservation of the frequency spectrum, along with a reduction in interference, and more economy in equipment.

Voice-frequency components below 300 Hz do determine the bass quality of a human voice, but again, they are not essential if intelligibility is the primary objective. The low-frequency components also contain the bulk of the voice power. Equipment designed for good low-frequency performance must be capable of handling the higher power levels contained in the low-frequency voice components. If these components are eliminated in the modulation process, the available power can be concentrated into the middle-frequency range. This is the range that has the most to do with good intelligibility. The removal of lows permits more effective use of the desired audio range, plus more economical equipment design because low-frequency performance and disturbances need not be considered.

The various types of transmissions and emissions are shown in Table 2-1. Notice that each type of transmission and modulation is given an identifying symbol. For example, regular AM double-sideband, full-carrier emission is given the symbol A3. These symbols are in common usage, particularly throughout all FCC publications. In making a specific AM assignment for voice or other communications, a numerical prefix is often added to indicate the bandwidth assigned. For example, the symbol 6A3 indicates double-sideband amplitude modulation, the highest audio-frequency component being 3000 Hz. The total bandwidth would be 6 kHz.

Table 2-1. Various Types of Transmission and Emission

Type of Modulation of Main Carrier	Type of Transmission	Supplementary Characteristics	Symbol
Amplitude modulation	With no modulation		A0
	Telegraphy without the use of a modulating audio frequency (by on-off keying).		A1
	Telegraphy by the on-off keying of an amplitude-modulating audio frequency or audio frequencies, or by the on-off keying of the modulated emission (special case: an unkeyed emission amplitude modulated).		A2
	Telephony	Double sideband	A3
		Single sideband, full carrier	A3H
		Single sideband, reduced carrier	A3A
		Single sideband, suppressed carrier	A3J
		Two independent sidebands	A3B
	Facsimile (with modulation of main carrier either directly or by a frequency-modulated subcarrier).		A4
	Facsimile	Single sideband, reduced carrier	A4A
	Television	Vestigial sideband	A5C
	Multichannel voice-frequency telegraphy.	Single sideband, reduced carrier	A7A
	Cases not covered by the above, e.g., a combination of telephony and telegraphy.	Two independent sidebands	A9B
Frequency (or Phase) modulation	Telegraphy by frequency-shift keying without the use of a modulating audio frequency: one of two frequencies being emitted at any instant.		F1
	Telegraphy by the on-off keying of a frequency-modulating audio frequency or by the on-off keying of a frequency-modulated emission (special case: an unkeyed emission, frequency modulated).		F2
	Telephony		F3
	Facsimile by direct frequency modulation of the carrier.		F4

Table 2-1—cont. Various Types of Transmission and Emission

Type of Modulation of Main Carrier	Type of Transmission	Supplementary Characteristics	Symbol
	Television	....	F5
	Four-frequency diplex telegraphy	....	F6
	Cases not covered by the above, in which the main carrier is frequency modulated.	....	F9
Pulse modulation	A pulsed carrier without any modulation intended to carry information (e.g., radar).	....	P0
	Telegraphy by the on-off keying of a pulsed carrier without the use of a modulating audio frequency.	....	P1D
	Telegraphy by the on-off keying of a modulating audio frequency or audio frequencies, or by the on-off keying of a modulated pulsed carrier (special case: an unkeyed modulated pulsed carrier).	....	P2
		Audio frequency or audio frequencies modulating the amplitude of the pulses.	P2D
		Audio frequency or audio frequencies modulating the width (or duration) of the pulses.	P2E
		Audio frequency or audio frequencies modulating the phase (or position) of the pulses.	P2F
	Telephony	Amplitude-modulated pulses	P3D
		Width- (or duration-) modulated pulses	P3F
		Phase- (or position-) modulated pulses	P3E
		Code-modulated pulses (after sampling and quantization).	P3G
	Cases not covered by the above in which the main carrier is pulse modulated.	....	P9

2-2-1. Suppressed Carrier

Some voice-communication circuits, both base-mobile and point-to-point, use suppressed-carrier transmission, as shown in Fig. 2-4. In the AM modulation process, the information to be conveyed between two points is contained in either sideband.

The carrier itself is excess baggage — it really contains no useful information. Its presence does simplify receiver design, and the carrier can be put to work in the form of AVC and AFC. However, with appropriate receiver design it can be dispensed with, or at least transmitted at a much reduced level.

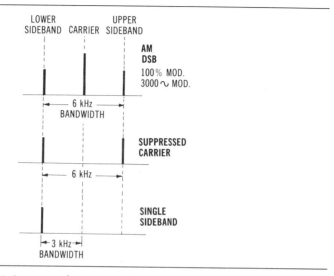

Fig. 2-4. Suppressed-carrier sideband transmission.

In conventional AM systems with 100% modulation, two-thirds of the transmitted power is in the carrier and only one-third in the useful sidebands. For modulation percentages of less than 100% (usually the case except on peaks), the ratio of the power in the carrier to that in the sideband is substantially higher. As a result, a lot of transmitter power is wasted in the formation of the carrier. Furthermore, it is the interaction of carriers and sidebands that sets up the whistles and squeals which hamper communications under crowded conditions. Thus, if the carrier is reduced or suppressed, a source of interference is also removed.

Two other advantages of reduced-carrier transmission are the economies of transmitter design, and the fact that all useful available power can be concentrated into the information-carrying sidebands. Receiver design is more complex because a stable substitute for the carrier must be generated within the receiver.

2-2-2. Single Sideband

Still another form of AM transmission with wide acceptance in marine point-to-point and amateur communications is single-sideband, suppressed carrier (SSB). This type of transmission is symbolized as *A3J*. In single-sideband transmission, not only is the carrier suppressed or reduced substantially, but one sideband is also eliminated. Hence, as shown in Fig. 2-4, the required bandwidth of the signal has been cut in half. The total bandwidth of *3A3J* transmission thus is only 3 kHz.

In addition to the conservation of frequency in the spectrum, single-sideband transmission requires less power and further narrows the bandwidth to reduce interference. In two-way radio systems, single-sideband transmission is used widely in marine radiotelephone and for fixed point-to-point services. However, it can be expected in some, and anticipated in more and more, mobile installations. Radio amateurs have demonstrated its capabilities in mobile installations.

The power-saving feature of single-sideband transmission is obvious when we consider that, with conventional double-sideband 100% amplitude modulation, only one-sixth of the total power is contained in each sideband. Nonetheless, all the information to be conveyed is contained in one of the sidebands. With single-sideband transmission, all the available power of the transmitter can be concentrated into this one sideband. The narrow bandwidth and the absence of a carrier are very important interference-reducing characteristics.

Single-sideband transmission has become increasingly popular for transcontinental and intercontinental communications. It is somewhat less subject to ionospheric variables, and less troubled by selective fading, than other methods of transmission. With selective fading, some frequency segments of a transmitted signal fade more (or less) than others. This condition produces intermodulation distortion in the receiver and results in garbled speech. With only one sideband and a narrow bandwidth, such fading becomes less objectionable.

In many radio services single-sideband transmission is replacing conventional double-sideband amplitude modulation. This changeover has been proceeding on the radio amateur bands for some time. Sideband has almost completely replaced conventional AM on most bands. Some of the fixed commercial services have also used sideband for a number of years. In fact, in some of the commercial services, particularly on the medium-frequency marine band, single sideband has become compulsory and AM is being phased out.

In the 1.605- to 4.000-MHz spectrum, commercial A3 assignments are no longer available. This band was changed over to single sideband on Jan. 1, 1977.

There are three recognized sideband emissions (2.8A3H, 2.8A3A, and 2.8A3J). The 2.8 represents the highest permissible modulating audio frequencies. The 3 refers to the total bandwidth of 3 kHz. The *H*-form of emission refers to one sideband and full carrier. The *A*-form is one sideband and partial carrier, while the *J* authorization refers to one sideband and completely suppressed carrier. In certain portions of the medium-frequency spectrum, the *H*-type will be abolished after a certain cutoff date.

2-2-3. Frequency Modulation

In two-way mobile-radio systems, the use of frequency modulation (FM) has a number of advantages. The ignition systems of moving vehicles are a source of impulse noises, which appear as amplitude variations on the incoming RF signals. When AM transmission is used, noise variations cannot be suppressed entirely because of the hazard of also suppressing the desired amplitude variations of the incoming signals. In a frequency-modulation system, the desired information is in the form of a frequency deviation of the wave. Consequently, any amplitude variation introduced can be reduced almost completely without endangering the desired information carried by the incoming radio signal.

The very nearness of the noise source to the receiver, as in a moving vehicle, makes the frequency-modulation system attractive for mobile communications. In the UHF, VHF, and high HF bands, frequency modulation is the more common form for mobile communications. Although amplitude modulation is used for some services in these spectra, it is much more common in the shortwave and low-frequency half of the high-frequency (HF) band.

In an FM system, as shown in Fig. 2-5, the carrier is *frequency* modulated by the incoming signal. The frequency of the transmitted wave increases sinusoidally during

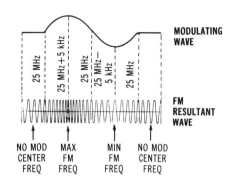

Fig. 2-5. Basic FM wave with a 25-MHz carrier.

the positive alternation of the modulating sine wave. The greatest upward frequency deviation (+ 5 kHz from the carrier) occurs at the positive crest of the modulating wave. As the modulating sine wave swings toward the zero axis, the frequency decreases sinusoidally to the carrier, or center, frequency. On the negative alternation, the frequency of the transmitted wave decreases with respect to the center frequency. The greatest downward swing away from the center frequency occurs at the crest of the negative alternation (− 5 kHz from the center frequency).

The frequency-change limits of the FM wave determine the frequency deviation. In the example shown, the deviation is ±5 kHz. In assigning a channel for FM transmission, the FCC specifies 100% modulation as the maximum deviation permissible for the particular class of station. This maximum frequency deviation corresponds to the 100% modulation limit of an AM wave which, as shown previously in Fig. 2-3, occurs when the wave rises to twice the original carrier amplitude at the positive crest of the modulating wave, and falls to zero at the negative crest.

This maximum FM modulation is not the same for each type of service. The maximum permissible deviation (100% modulation) is ±75 kHz for FM broadcasting stations. For the FM sound signal associated with television broadcasting, it is ±25 kHz. For post two-way FM radio systems, 100% modulation corresponds to ±5 kHz, depending on the station classification.

In an FM system, it might be assumed that the total transmission bandwidth is determined by the maximum deviation of the resultant wave. However, like the AM wave, the FM wave is a composite of the carrier or center frequency and a number of sidebands. Unlike the AM wave, however, which has only one pair of significant sidebands, the FM wave (Fig. 2-6) has one or more pairs of significant sidebands. They are a function of the modulation index which, at the highest modulating frequency, determines the number of pairs and hence the bandwidth of the FM transmission. It is calculated by:

$$\text{Modulation index} = \frac{\text{Deviation}}{\text{Modulating Frequency}}$$

The sideband pairs are separated from the center frequency by the frequency of the modulating wave and by its harmonic multiples (2, 3, 4, 5, etc.). If an FM wave for a given maximum deviation has *three* significant sideband pairs, the total bandwidth is $2 \times 3 \times$ the highest modulating frequency. If the highest modulating frequency is 10 kHz, the total bandwidth required would be 60 kHz ($2 \times 3 \times 10,000$).

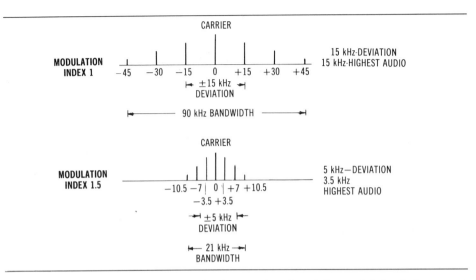

Fig. 2-6. FM sidebands and distribution as a function of the modulation index.

If the highest modulating frequency is reduced to 3 kHz, the total bandwidth required by the FM transmission will be only 18 kHz (2 × 3 × 3000). It is significant, just as in AM practice, that reduction of the highest audio frequency reduces the bandwidth.

In FM broadcasting, particularly for high-fidelity transmission, the highest audio frequency is over 12 kHz. As we learned in communications, the best intelligibility is obtained by limiting the highest audio frequency to 3000 – 4000 Hz. Consequently, the FM wave used for communications can be crowded into a much narrower bandwidth than is required for FM broadcasting.

Another method of reducing the bandwidth of an FM transmission is to reduce the amount of deviation. In an FM system the best noise rejection is obtained with the greatest deviation. For this reason, the narrowband system (NBFM) has a poorer noise rejection. However, the signal-to-noise ratio improves when the highest audio frequency is reduced. Inasmuch as the highest audio frequency for a voice communications service is much lower than required in broadcasting, it is possible to obtain a very fine signal-to-noise ratio despite the much more confined deviation of an NBFM system.

The symbols for FM emission are shown in Table 2-1. The two-way radio assignments are predominantly *F3*. A numerical prefix establishes the permissible bandwidth. For example, *18F3* signifies FM telephony with a total bandwidth of 18 kHz.

Be familiar with some symbols of the other common forms of transmission. Symbol *A1* is given to radiotelegraphy, in which the carrier is interrupted in accordance with a coded message (usually International Morse code). In this form of transmission, the carrier is turned on and off, as shown in Fig. 2-7.

Telegraph speed is often given in bauds. Based on the duration of the shortest code element the baud rate would be the number of these code elements transmitted per second. A Morse code speed of 25 words per minute has a baud rate of 20.

Another form of radiotelegraphy, common on the low- and very low-frequency ship bands, is *A2*. Here the carrier is transmitted continuously, but is modulated by an audio tone in accordance with the coded message. For example, an 800-Hz audio tone could be used. The tone is turned on and off to simulate the dots and dashes (on) and the spaces (off) of the International Morse Code.

Symbols *F1* and *F2* represent methods of sending frequency-modulated coded messages. Numbers 4 and 5 represent facsimile and television transmission, respec-

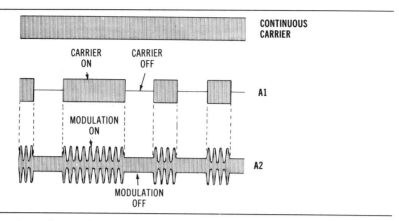

Fig. 2-7. A1 and A2 code transmission — Morse code letter L as an example.

tively. An *A* or *F* prefix is used, depending on whether AM or FM is employed. In television broadcasting, *A5* is used for picture transmission and *F3* for sound.

Various types of pulse modulation can be noted in the last section of the chart. Pulse modulation techniques are used in advanced multiplex, telemetering, and computer data applications. Digital voice communications is a form of pulse transmission.

The baud also specifies rate in the transmission of digital data. In terms of serial data transmission, the baud rate is approximately the number of bits transmitted per second. This includes the actual data bits as well as so-called character-framing bits. For example, in a computer system of 63 characters with an 8-bit interval assigned to each character, the actual rate in bauds would be approximately 500 (63 × 8).

2-3. Signals and Processing

In preparing a radio-frequency signal for transmission there are a number of modulation and processing steps. Most of these procedures will be described in detail in later chapters of the handbook. At this point it is important to become familiar with various signal terms and definitions used within the industry and by the FCC.

The fundamental radio-frequency wave is the *sine-wave*. This sine-wave at the transmit frequency is called the *fundamental* frequency. In the generation process, every attempt is made to form a pure single-frequency sine-wave carrier. In the generation and amplification process harmonic components can be formed. A *harmonic* is a sine-wave component with a frequency that is an integral multiple of the fundamental frequency. The second harmonic of a 600 kHz fundamental is 1200 kHz. The fifth harmonic of a 600 kHz fundamental wave is 3000 kHz.

In the processing of radio-frequency signals in transmitters and receivers, it is often necessary to multiply the signal frequency. In *frequency multiplication* the signal frequency is multiplied by an integral multiple. Such a stage is called a *frequency multiplier*. A times-two multiplier is called a *doubler* and multiplies the incoming frequency by a factor of two. A *tripler* stage would multiply the incoming signal by a factor of three. A 600 kHz signal applied to the input of a tripler would appear at the output with a frequency of 1800 kHz.

Another way of raising or lowering the frequency of a signal is known as *mixing*. In the mixing process two signals are heterodyned and the output is tuned to the sum or difference frequency. This technique is used in both transmitters and receivers. A 6 MHz signal mixed with a 5 MHz signal can be made to develop an output which is either 1 MHz (6 − 5) or 11 MHz (6 + 5).

The mixing process can be used to change over the frequency of a modulated radio-frequency signal in the same way. The entire baseband of modulating information can be changed up or down in frequency. By definition the *baseband* refers to the spectra occupied by a carrier and all the associated modulating frequency components. These modulating components might be formed by a single voice frequency signal or even a number of subcarriers and their individual modulating components as well.

The mixing technique is also used in a process called *frequency translation*. In frequency translation an incoming carrier and its entire baseband is stepped up or down in frequency. An example of this technique is employed by television translators. In this application it could be used to provide television coverage to a small community in a mountain valley. A frequency translator on the mountain top would receive the signal from the television station, translate it directly to a different frequency spectra, and reradiate a signal down into the valley community.

The quality of a received signal is often evaluated in terms of *signal-to-noise ratio*. The signal-to-noise ratio is an amplitude ratio that compares the desired signal with the noise signal. Usually the ratio is given in decibels.

In modern radiocommunication systems many types of information are transmitted in addition to voice frequencies. *Information* refers to the total package that must be conveyed. *Data* transmission is the basic element-by-element means used to convey information. *Data rate* refers to the frequency at which the data elements are conveyed. In an amplification or modulation process the term *bandwidth* is the width of the frequency spectra needed to convey the desired information.

Several types of signals and codes that are used to convey information are analog, digital, binary, ASCII, and Baudot. An *analog* signal is a continuous change of voltage or current representing the changes of a given situation. This might be an audio signal or the changes indicated by a physical variable such as temperature, velocity, rotation, etc. To prevent distortion such a signal must be processed by *linear amplifiers*. A *digital* signal uses discrete voltage levels to convey information and data. Most often there are two levels of voltage representing logic 1 and logic 0. The frequency, spacing, absence and presence of pulses, and other pulse characteristics such as duration and spacing convey the desired information despite the fact that the digital pulse has only two specific voltage levels.

A *binary* signal is a two-level digital signal representing 0 and 1. In the binary system these two numbers can be used to represent any decimal number. Such a signal has a squared-wave pulse waveform.

The *Baudot* code is a five- or six-bit (marks) code that is used to represent 32 or 64 numbers, letters, and symbols. The code is used in radioteletype transmissions. *ASCII* is the abbreviation for American Standard Code for Information Interchange. It is an 8-bit code with one bit used for parity check and seven bits that convey 127 characters

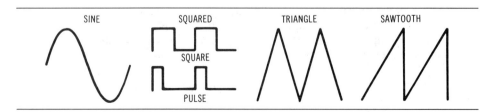

Fig. 2-8. Typical waveforms.

(numbers, letters, and symbols). In addition to the *sine* wave, three other waveform types found in radiocommunications and radiocommunication test equipment are *square, triangle,* and *sawtooth,* as shown in Fig. 2-8. The true square wave and the pulse are basic to the formation of digital signals. They represent the two discrete voltage levels that can be used to represent logic 0 and logic 1. These two waveforms are also common in radiocommunication test instruments. Triangle and sawtooth waves are useful in digital signal processing and are also a part of test instrumentation, especially oscilloscopes.

3

Solid-State Fundamentals

Semiconductor diodes, bipolar transistors, field-effect transistors, and integrated circuits are essential electron devices in modern two-way radio equipment. A knowledge of solid-state fundamentals and circuitry is mandatory if you are to install, tune, and service modern transceivers. A review and expansion of these subjects as related to two-way radio applications are the content of this chapter.

3-1. Semiconductor Theory

It is necessary to delve a bit into atomic theory to understand semiconductor operation. The difference between an insulator and a conductor is related to the number of free electrons. The greater the number of free electrons, the greater the conductivity of the material. These free electrons drift in a random manner throughout the conductor. However, with the application of an electromotive force (EMF), free electrons are made to drift in a given direction, producing a charge motion, or current.

Whether a material is a good conductor or a good insulator depends on its atomic makeup. Each element has its own specific grouping of electrons, both in number and in placement around the nucleus. These electrons may occupy one of several energy bands as shown in Fig. 3-1. Electrons of approximately the same energy level are grouped together in close-spaced orbits. Such a group is referred to as a shell. Shells are spaced a specific distance from the nucleus and contain a specific number of electrons. The number of shells and the number of electrons distinguish one element from another.

Electrons that orbit in shells near the nucleus have a low energy level and are tightly bound. Electrons in the outer shell have a high energy content and are less tightly bound to the atom.

The important electrons of the outer shell are referred to as *valence* electrons. In the makeup of matter there are never more than eight electrons in the outer shell but there may be fewer than eight. When the element has exactly eight electrons it has a high order of stability, and the valence electrons (electrons in the outer shell) are tightly bound to the atom.

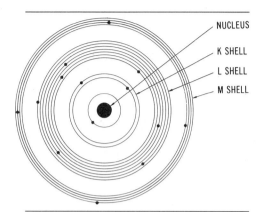

Fig. 3-1. Atomic makeup showing nucleus and energy bands.

Atoms having fewer then eight electrons are less stable and they are more ready to associate with the electrons of the outer shells of neighboring atoms. In general, atoms having shells of five, six, or seven electrons are inclined to borrow additional electrons from other atoms. Atoms with one, two, or three valence electrons are inclined to lose these electrons to other atoms. The interlocking of the valence electrons forms stable molecules of a substance, and under proper conditions, the molecules form crystals.

Two important elements in the makeup of semiconductor diodes and transistors are germanium and silicon. As shown in Fig. 3-2 they have thirty-two and fourteen electrons, respectively. The first and second shells are full with two and eight electrons, respectively. This means that the third shell of the silicon atom contains four electrons.

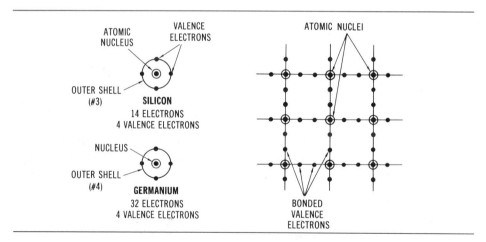

Fig. 3-2. Atomic structure of silicon and germanium.

When the first three shells of an atom are filled they contain two, eight, and eighteen electrons, respectively. In the case of germanium this means that the fourth shell also contains four electrons, making up a total of thirty-two. Therefore, both silicon and germanium have four valence electrons. As shown in Fig. 3-2, such an electron arrangement can, by the sharing of the four valence electrons with nearby atoms, form a stable crystalline structure. A stable crystalline construction acts as an insulator. Its conductivity is very poor because of the tightness with which the valence electrons are bound.

In the construction of semiconductor diodes and transistors the initial step is the developing of highly purified germanium or silicon. These pure elements are referred to as *intrinsic* germanium or silicon crystals. Although the conductivity is poor, such a crystalline construction is not really a perfect insulator because the bonding can be broken with high temperature or appropriate electrical potentials.

In the manufacture of semiconductor devices very minute yet accurate amounts of impurities are added to the intrinsic crystal. These impurities lower the resistivity of the crystal a specific amount. Therefore, a controlled amount of conduction is made possible. Such a crystal with the proper amount of impurity (doping) is called an *extrinsic* semiconductor. It has a conductivity that lies somewhere between the high conductivity of a conductor and the extremely low conductivity of an insulator.

3-1-1. P and N Crystals

Whether a semiconductor crystal is a p-type or n-type depends on the nature of the impurity. When an intrinsic crystal is doped with an element that has five valence electrons instead of four, the impurity atoms are inclined to bond with the intrinsic atoms. In so doing, as shown in Fig. 3-3A, an extra electron exists for every combination of impurity and intrinsic atoms. This free electron is not bonded and will move about in random fashion. This type of crystal is referred to as an *n-type* and the motion of the electrons results in the movements of negatively charged particles. The semiconductor material formed does not have a negative charge because the total number of electrons in the substance equals the total number of protons. It is said, however, to have *electron carriers*.

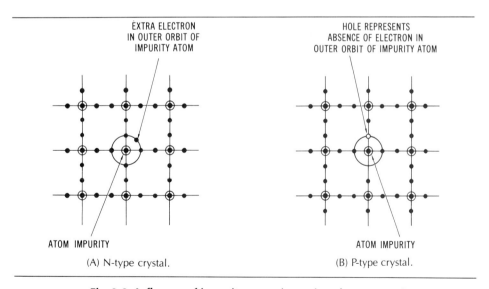

Fig. 3-3. Influence of impurity atoms in semiconductor crystal.

A *p-type* semiconductor is made by doping the intrinsic crystal with an element that has three valence electrons. In this case the three electrons will be bonded with the intrinsic atoms. However, as shown in Fig. 3-3B, at each impurity-intrinsic bond position there will be an electron vacancy. Such an empty charge position, at which there would be an electron if the complete bond had been established, is referred to as a *hole*. It represents the absence of an electron and therefore can be considered as a positive particle. Again this new semiconductor material has no charge because of the balance between electrons and protons.

In a p-type semiconductor material there is always a tendency for an electron from a neighboring atom to move into the empty spot or hole. In this case, there is a hole left in the bonded makeup of the neighboring atom. As a result there are free holes. In the p-type semiconductor the motion of charges throughout the material is a result of the random movement of holes (positive particles) instead of electrons (negative particles). Current that results from the random motion of holes is said to be supported by the motion of so-called *hole carriers*.

In summary, the type of doping of an intrinsic semiconductor material determines whether it becomes a p-type or n-type "extrinsic" semiconductor. The conductivity depends on the amount of doping.

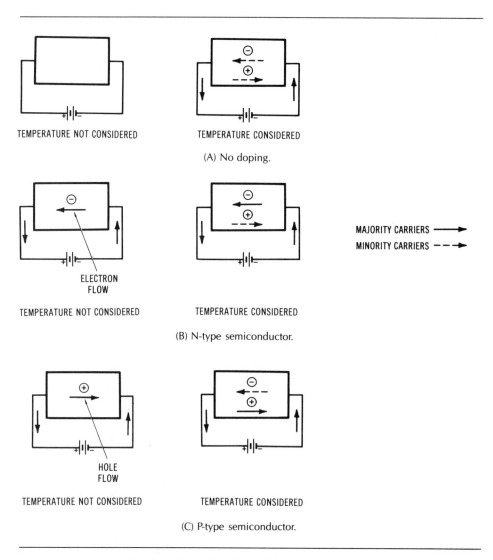

TEMPERATURE NOT CONSIDERED   TEMPERATURE CONSIDERED

(A) No doping.

ELECTRON
FLOW

TEMPERATURE NOT CONSIDERED   TEMPERATURE CONSIDERED

MAJORITY CARRIERS ⟶
MINORITY CARRIERS - - ⟶

(B) N-type semiconductor.

HOLE
FLOW

TEMPERATURE NOT CONSIDERED   TEMPERATURE CONSIDERED

(C) P-type semiconductor.

Fig. 3-4. Charge flow in semiconductor crystals.

Fig. 3-4C demonstrates charge flow in a p-type block. In a p-type block the current carriers are holes or positive particles. As shown, current direction in the external circuit is the same as for the n-type crystal. However, in the block itself it is the motion of holes (opposite from the direction of electron carriers in Fig. 3-4B) that provides the means of positive majority carriers. The temperature breakup of bonds results in some free electrons as well. However, the number of free electrons is substantially less than the number of holes. Consequently, the temperature-caused electron flow is the negative minority carrier conduction in p-type semiconductor material.

Minority current is a problem in the design of semiconductor and transistor circuits. In general there are fewer minority current carriers for silicon than germanium because there is tighter bonding in a silicon crystal. Thus, silicon devices are less temperature sensitive than germanium devices. The higher the doping, the greater the number of electron or hole carriers. Often the current is spoken of as the movement of positive carriers or negative carriers instead of hole carriers or electron carriers, respectively. It is very important to keep in mind that in the case of n-type semiconductor material current is the result of the motion of electrons while in p-type material it is the result of the motion of holes.

The electron or hole carriers can be made to drift in a given direction to produce a current. When a battery is connected to an intrinsic-type crystal, there will be no charge flow if we neglect the influence of temperature. However, temperature does have a substantial influence on charge flow in a semiconductor crystal. Even at room temperature there is some breaking of valence bonds and, consequently, there is a random motion of holes and electrons. Hence, if we want to represent the small amount of current that exists as a result of temperature, it can be indicated as shown at the right in Fig. 3-4A. The higher the temperature, the greater the current that results from the breaking of the valence bonds.

Fig. 3-4B shows the current direction that results from the connection of a source of voltage to an n-type crystal. In the n-type there are electron carriers. Therefore, there will be an electron flow from the negative terminal of the battery through the semiconductor crystal to the positive terminal.

The influence of temperature on the current is shown at the right of Fig. 3-4B. This motion of plus charges is considerably less than the regular motion of electrons in the n-type crystal. Therefore, they are referred to as *minority carriers* while the main flow are *majority carriers*. In the p-type material, holes are the majority carriers, while electrons are the minority carriers.

3-2. Semiconductor Diodes

Semiconductor diodes are manufactured in many forms for a wide variety of applications. The number of types seems almost limitless because of the ease with which characteristics can be controlled by shape, type of material, and degree of doping. Some diodes are used as detectors and others as rectifiers. Special forms are used as voltage regulators, switches, parametric amplifiers and mixers, oscillators, sensors, and voltage-variable capacitors.

3-2-1. The PN Junction

A semiconductor diode is formed by placing p- and n-type segments together to form a solid block of semiconductor material as shown in Fig. 3-5. The point at which the two segments touch is referred to as a pn junction. Such a junction permits current in one direction and blocks current in the opposite direction.

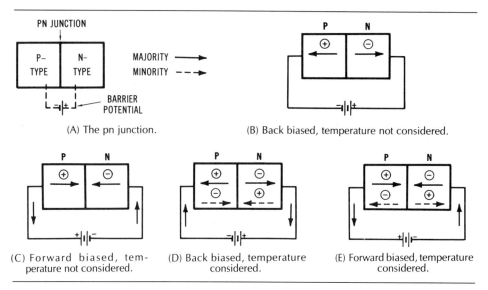

(A) The pn junction.

(B) Back biased, temperature not considered.

(C) Forward biased, temperature not considered.

(D) Back biased, temperature considered.

(E) Forward biased, temperature considered.

Fig. 3-5. The pn junction showing directions of majority and minority carrier movement.

When a pn junction is first formed some of the holes of the p section drift into the n section while some of the free electrons of the n side drift into the p side. Thus, there is some neutralization of holes and electrons. As a result there is a space in the junction area referred to as the *depletion region* in which there are no current carriers (electrons or holes). This neutralization of carriers in the depletion region results in the development of a difference of potential, amounting to a few tenths of a volt between the p and n sections. The developed positive ionic potential on the n side repels any additional movement of holes from the p side, and the negative potential on the p side repels any additional movement of electrons from the n side. This establishes a condition of equilibrium and produces what is referred to as the *barrier potential* (Fig. 3-5A) of a pn junction.

When the diode junction is biased as in Fig. 3-5B, there is no charge flow and the junction is said to be *reverse-* or *back-biased*. When the circuit is connected, the electrons of the n side are attracted to the positive terminal of the battery. The holes of the p side, because they are positive charges, are attracted to the negative terminal of the battery. Due to the movement of current carriers away from the junction, the width of the depletion area is increased and the barrier potential rises to the same value as the applied EMF. The resistance of the diode in this case is very high and no significant external electric charge flows.

The semiconductor junction is said to have a high reverse resistance. Note that the reverse bias is of the same polarity as that which symbolizes the barrier potential of the junction.

If the voltage applied to the pn junction is changed in polarity to that of Fig. 3-5C, the negative potential applied to the n side forces electrons toward the junction while the positive potential applied to the p side forces holes toward the junction. By forcing the majority carriers toward the junction the depletion area is reduced. If the applied EMF is high enough to overcome the very low barrier potential, there will be a continuous exchange of holes and electrons through the junction. The electron carriers of the n side move across the junction into the p side, while the hole carriers in the p side move across the junction into the n side.

The electrons that leave the n side are continuously being replaced by the electrons from the source of voltage. Therefore, there is a continuous current through the junction and the external circuit. The diode resistance in this case is low and it is said that the forward resistance of the semiconductor junction is low. The junction is said to be *forward biased* or biased in the conducting direction. Note that this bias is such that the voltage applied to the p side is positive and that applied to the n side is negative. The forward bias is opposite in polarity to the symbol representing the barrier potential. Therefore, the barrier potential must first be overcome before the diode conducts in the forward direction.

The illustrations of Figs. 3-5D and 3-5E show the influence of temperature on the diode pn junction. When the diode is back biased, the majority carriers are forced away from the junction. However, the minority carriers, which are a result of the breakup of bonds because of temperature, are forced toward the junction. Thus, there is a movement of minority carriers across the junction and there is a small amount of reverse current. The quality of semiconductor diodes is checked by determining the ratio of the reverse to forward resistances.

At a low operating temperature there is little or no current for small values of reverse bias. If the reverse bias voltage becomes excessive, however, there is a wholesale breaking up of the electron bonds and the current rises sharply as shown in Fig. 3-6. This is called the *avalanche* condition. This avalanche of current can become excessive and can destroy the pn junction. In some semiconductor designs the avalanche current is used to advantage.

At a high temperature a significant reverse current begins to flow even at low values of reverse bias, increasing as the back bias is increased. The high temperature conditions are shown by the dashed curve of Fig. 3-6. When the junction is severely overheated, the diode loses its unidirectional characteristic completely, and is no longer capable of operating as a pn junction. In general diodes are rated by the maximum forward average and peak currents, and the peak inverse voltage (PIV).

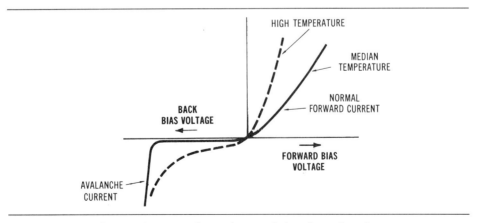

Fig. 3-6. Current-voltage characteristics of a pn junction.

When a diode is forward biased the majority carriers are forced toward the junction. In this case the minority carriers are attracted away from the junction. As a result the minority carriers make no contribution to forward current.

If the temperature effect is neglected, the forward junction current increases with an increase in the forward bias. The current rise is not, however, exactly linear. With

48

the high applied voltage more electron-pair bonds are broken, a higher operating temperature is produced, and the current increase is accelerated. As shown in Fig. 3-6, the higher the operating temperature, the faster the rate of forward current increase with an increase in the applied EMF.

3-2-2. **Special Semiconductor Types**

In addition to the use of semiconductor diodes as rectifiers, mixers, detectors, etc., special types are used for modulators, voltage regulators, and other more specialized applications in two-way radio units. The zener voltage-regulator diode is one such type. Zener diodes are used widely to stabilize the supply voltages of transistor equipment.

The zener diode operates in the avalanche current region of the characteristics curve. This occurs when a high reverse voltage is applied to its pn junction. Both sides of the zener diode junction are heavily doped to obtain a relatively low breakdown voltage. Proper control of the doping sets this breakdown voltage at the desired level. Zener diodes are available with various voltage ratings.

A typical zener diode response is shown in Fig. 3-7. Note that at the avalanche point the current rises sharply. This tremendous current at one specific voltage is the condition that makes the zener diode an excellent voltage regulator. Once the diode is in the avalanche condition, various amounts of current can be drawn through the diode, but the voltage across the diode will remain practically constant. The maximum current is limited, however, by the wattage rating of the diode.

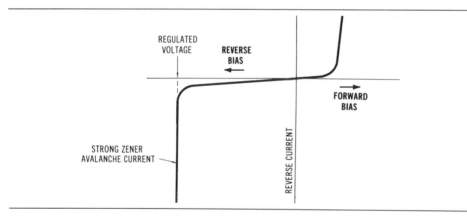

Fig. 3-7. Zener diode characteristics.

Another semiconductor used in modern equipment for both frequency modulation and frequency-control applications is the voltage-variable capacitor, or *varactor*. The voltage-variable capacitor is constructed and doped in a manner that emphasizes the change in capacitance which results from variations in the depletion area of a pn junction. A typical response is shown in Fig. 3-8. By proper selection of an operating point an applied audio voltage can be made to cause the necessary change in capacitance to either frequency- or phase-modulate an RF signal.

In your study of the pn junction you learned that forward bias pushes the hole and electron carriers toward the pn junction and that a high forward current results. With the application of reverse bias, however, the electron and hole carriers are attracted away from the pn junction. The extent of the depletion area that results depends on the amount of back bias. In this mode of operation the depletion area and the pn end segments of the diode take on some of the characteristics of a capacitor. There are positive and negative particles present on the pn end segments just like the accumulation of charges on two capacitor plates. There is an appropriate electric stress between the two charges across the depletion area. Therefore, the depletion area acts as the dielectric of the capacitor.

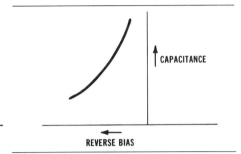

Fig. 3-8. Characteristics of a voltage-variable-capacitance diode.

When the back voltage is changed, the width of the depletion area changes in a like manner. As a result we are changing the effective spacing between the capacitor segments as well as the dielectric characteristics, producing a change in the diode capacitance. This change of capacitance is used to cause frequency modulation in modern communications transmitters. Similarly, the same characteristics may be used in automatic-frequency-control (AFC) circuits of receivers.

A *pin* diode operates as a variable resistance in VHF and higher-frequency circuits. Such a diode has highly doped p and n ends. These ends are separated by a relatively wide and lightly doped junction region.

In operation a DC bias current applied to the diode determines its resistance to the transfer of radio frequencies. When reverse-biased the junction resistance to radio frequencies is high; forward-biased, it is low. In this application the pin diode can be made to operate as a radio-frequency switch. In a suitable circuit, the bias can be made to vary in response to an AGC bias. As a result the resistance to the transfer of a radio-frequency signal can be varied in accordance with the strength of a received signal.

A hot-carrier diode is a sensitive low-noise detector and mixer. It has a low junction capacitance and therefore performs effectively at VHF/UHF frequencies. As a mixer it has a high conversion efficiency and low noise content. The hot-carrier diode has a metal/semiconductor junction and there is a majority carrier flow with the application of even a very weak signal voltage.

3-3. Bipolar Transistor Fundamentals

A bipolar transistor is formed by combining two such pn junctions as shown in Fig. 3-9. The three segments are called *emitter, base*, and *collector*. Transistors come in two basic types, pnp and npn. In operation the junction between the base and the emitter (base-emitter junction or simply *emitter junction*) is forward biased while the junction between the base and the collector (collector-base junction or simply *collector junction*) is reverse biased. Proper biasing of the two types is shown in Figs. 3-10 and 3-11.

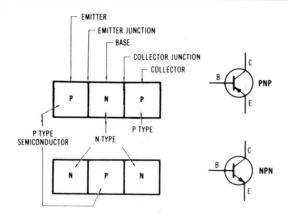

Fig. 3-9. Basic transistor construction and symbols.

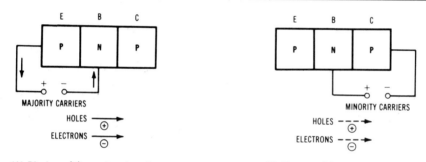

(A) Biasing of the emitter junction.

(B) Biasing of the collector junction.

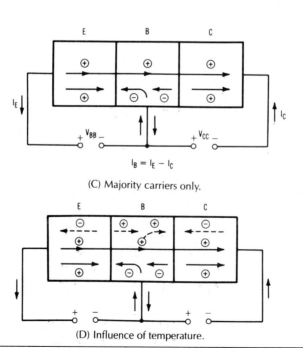

(C) Majority carriers only.

(D) Influence of temperature.

Fig. 3-10. Carrier movement in a pnp transistor.

In operation, the emitter junction is forward biased. As a result there is a base-emitter current. The collector junction is back biased and, if we neglect the influence of the emitter junction, there would be no collector-base current. This would be the case if there were no emitter-junction bias or if the emitter junction were back biased. However, with the emitter junction forward biased, the carrier motion is such that there is a current through the collector junction. In fact, with the emitter junction forward biased and the collector junction back biased, the actual collector current is greater than the base current, and the device functions as an amplifier.

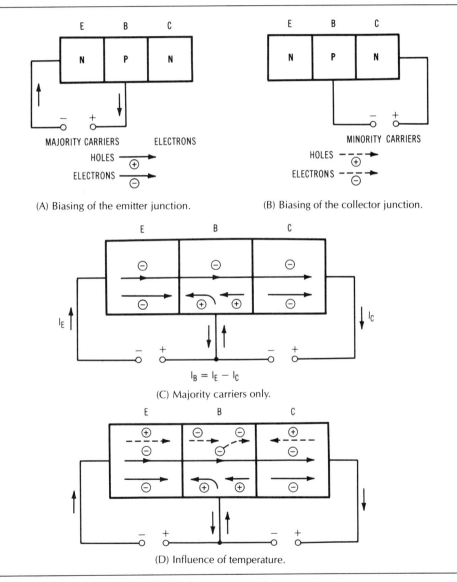

(A) Biasing of the emitter junction.   (B) Biasing of the collector junction.

$I_B = I_E - I_C$

(C) Majority carriers only.

(D) Influence of temperature.

Fig. 3-11. Carrier movement in an npn transistor.

The collector current is a result of the motion of holes through the base and across the collector junction for the pnp transistor; the motion of electrons over a similar path, in the case of an npn transistor.

3-3-1. Majority Carrier Movement

Majority and minority carrier movements are illustrated in Figs. 3-10 and 3-11. In the case of the pnp transistor, Figs. 3-10A and B show the proper biasing of the transistor; the emitter junction is forward biased and the collector junction is back biased. With the two junctions biased correctly the majority carrier flows are illustrated in Fig. 3-10C.

When the emitter junction is forward biased, the electrons of the n-type base move to the emitter junction as do the holes of the p-type emitter. The holes moving across the junction are neutralized by base electrons.

For each electron that neutralizes a hole at the junction there is an electron supplied to the base from the bias source. Likewise at the terminal end of the emitter there must be an electron that leaves and enters the positive terminal of the voltage source. This continuous current through the junction and around the external circuit is referred to as the base-emitter current.

There are more holes injected across the emitter junction, however, than there are electrons to neutralize them. Since the base is very thin, these positive particles diffuse through the base to the collector junction. The holes have a positive charge and at the collector junction they are attracted to the negative potential of the collector. As a result they move through the collector junction into the collector element. The holes arriving in the collector element are neutralized by electrons from the collector supply voltage source. As electrons leave the negative terminal of the power source they must be replaced with electrons from the base element flowing into the positive terminal. This movement of charges is referred to as the collector current.

It is important to recognize that in terms of the base current flow, the emitter-base and collector-base currents are in opposite directions. Also it is important to understand that the hole flow to the collector junction is greater than the hole flow that is neutralized by electrons at the emitter junction. This is the result of a number of transistor characteristics. The emitter and the collector are heavily doped as compared to the base. Thus, there are few electrons in the base to neutralize the holes crossing the emitter junction, leaving many holes for diffusion to the collector junction. The base area is made very thin; therefore, the holes can diffuse quickly between the two junctions.

Note that the difference of potential between collector and emitter (two voltage sources in series) is higher than the base-to-emitter voltage (a single voltage source). Thus, the collector has a greater attraction for the injected holes than does the base.

The emitter current follows two branches. There is a flow (positive particles or holes) across the emitter junction and out of the base element. Another branch diffuses through the base and out of the collector element returning through the external circuit to the emitter. Thus, the emitter current can be stated as:

$$I_E = I_B + I_C$$

The base current then is the difference between the emitter current and the collector current (as shown by the opposite current arrows associated with the external base circuit):

$$I_B = I_E - I_C$$

$$I_C = I_E - I_B$$

Consequently, the collector current is greater than the base current. The ratio of the two currents (I_C and I_B) is known as the DC *beta* or DC current gain:

$$\beta = \frac{I_C}{I_B}$$

The DC beta is an important transistor characteristic. The collector current is less than the emitter current. The ratio of the collector current to the emitter current I_C/I_E is called the transistor *alpha:* It is always somewhat less than unity.

$$\alpha = \frac{I_C}{I_E}$$

As in the case of a single pn junction, the emitter-base current begins only after the barrier potential of the emitter junction is exceeded by the emitter-base forward voltage. In the case of a germanium transistor the barrier potential is approximately 0.2 volt; for a silicon transistor, approximately 0.7 volt. When the emitter junction forward-bias voltage is increased there is a rise in the emitter-base current. There is also a corresponding rise in the collector current. Fundamentally, a transistor is a current amplifier. The collector current follows the change in the base-emitter current.

In the pnp transistor, the more hole carriers that can be propelled across the emitter junction, the greater the collector current. This motion of holes across the emitter junction is related directly to the base-emitter current. Thus, in considering transistor charateristics we often refer to *bias current* instead of *bias voltage.*

3-3-2. Diffusion Current

The movement of the carriers injected into the base (from the emitter junction) to the collector junction is referred to as a diffusion current. There is no difference of potential between the collector and the emitter sides of the base proper. The injected carriers (holes in the case of pnp transistor) appear with high concentration at the emitter junction region. Since there is a mutual repulsion between the charges, the random motion is such that the carriers will diffuse to a region of low concentration from an area of high concentration. In this manner the holes injected into the base diffuse in the direction of the collector junction. Once they arrive at the collector junction they are moved at high velocity in the manner of conventional current because of the difference of potential across this junction.

The thinner the base the shorter the time interval needed for the carriers to diffuse from the emitter to the collector side of the base. Of course, the faster they are pulled through the collector junction the faster they must be replaced by charges from the emitter side. As a result, the higher the collector voltage, the more readily the charges are moved from emitter to collector junctions.

3-3-3. NPN Operation

The operation of an npn transistor is similar to that of a pnp except that the majority carriers are electrons rather than holes. To forward bias the emitter junction of an npn transistor it is necessary to connect the negative terminal of the voltage source to the emitter and the positive terminal to the base as shown in Fig. 3-11A. To reverse bias the collector junction it is necessary to connect the positive terminal of the collector supply voltage to the collector and the negative terminal to the base (Fig. 3-11B).

When the emitter junction is forward biased there is a flow of electron carriers from the n-type emitter and a flow of holes from the p-type base toward the junction (Fig. 3-11C). As a result there are electron carriers injected into the base through the emitter junction. Some of these electron carriers are neutralized by the holes in the base. However, there is again a high ratio of injected negative carriers to base hole carriers. Therefore, electron carriers diffuse through the base to the collector junction. Here they are attracted by the positive potential applied to the collector and they flow through the collector into the output circuit.

Other relations are similar to those of the pnp transistor. The greater the number of electrons diffused to the collector junction in comparison to those neutralized in the base, the higher the current gain of the transistor. As a result the current relations for I_E, I_B, and I_C are identical to those of the pnp transistor. The exception is that the directions of current are opposite. Compare the external current arrows in Figs. 3-10C and 3-11C.

3-3-4. Temperature Effect

The minority currents of a transistor are thermally induced the same as in the simple pn junction. The dashed lines in Figs. 3-10D and 3-11D show the minority currents. In normal operation the emitter junction is forward biased. Therefore, the minority carriers that are present, electrons in the p-type emitter and holes in the n-type base, move away from the junction and the minority current is insignificant and is not considered. Were the emitter junction reverse biased there would be no majority current but there would be some minority current because minority carriers would be repelled toward the junction.

In the normal operation of a transistor the collector junction is reverse biased. As a result the minority carriers, electrons in the p-type collector and holes in the n-type base, are repelled toward the collector junction and there is a minority current. The minority current in the collector circuit when there is zero voltage present at the emitter junction is called the collector cutoff current (I_{CO}).

With normal operation of the transistor and a forward bias applied to the emitter junction there is a resultant collector current. However, there is also this minority collector current which is related to the effects of temperature.

In summary, the total collector current is a result of two components, the majority current (result of either the nonneutralized holes or electrons injected into the base from the emitter) and the minority current (thermal effect). Stated as an equation:

$$I_C = (I_E - I_B) + I_{CO}$$

One of the hazards of minority carrier flow is a distinctive effect called *thermal runaway*. Under certain circuit conditions the minority current can bias the emitter junction. Its direction is such that the emitter junction is forward biased even though no external forward bias is being applied. There will be some collector current through the emitter junction. As the junction is heated there will be more minority carriers formed, and the minority current will increase and place a higher forward bias on the emitter junction. This results in additional collector current and further heating of the junction. The activity multiplies rapidly and the resultant high current and heating can destroy the transistor. Appropriate circuit design can reduce the possibility of thermal runaway.

3

3-4. Transistor Configurations and Operation

The transistor can be connected in three basic transistor configurations. These are common base, common emitter, and common collector (emitter follower). In terms of the method of circuit connection they can be compared approximately with grounded grid, grounded cathode, and grounded plate (cathode follower) vacuum-tube stages. Thus, the collector, base, and emitter can be compared respectively with plate, control grid, and cathode of a vacuum tube (Fig. 3-12). Here the similarity ends, and it is best to consider transistor and vacuum-tube functions separately with only occasional comparisons.

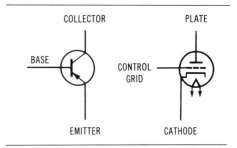

Fig. 3-12. Comparison of transistor and tube elements.

3-4-1. Common-Emitter Circuit

The most popular transistor amplifier configuration is the common-emitter circuit shown in Fig. 3-13. The circuit is shown for both pnp and npn transistors; they differ only with respect to the direction of electron flow and polarity of the bias voltages. Figs. 3-13A and B show the use of two separate bias-voltage sources. Under other circumstances, a single tapped-voltage source can be used as in Figs. 3-13C and D. In this arrangement the proper voltages can be obtained using supply voltage taps or resistive divider arrangements.

Notice the directions of electron flow and make a comparison with I_B, I_C, and I_E currents of Figs. 3-10 and 3-11. The following current relations are of significance:

$$I_C = I_E - I_B$$

In the common-emitter circuit the base current is the input current and it is customary to express collector current as:

$$I_C = \beta I_B$$

It is possible to establish a relation between alpha and beta. For example, expressions for I_C and I_E can be set down in terms of beta. As stated previously, I_C is the product of beta and I_B. An expression for I_E in terms of beta would be as follows:

$$I_E = I_C + I_B = \beta I_B + I_B = I_B(\beta + 1)$$

The equation for alpha can then be set down and appropriate substitutions made to obtain alpha in terms of beta:

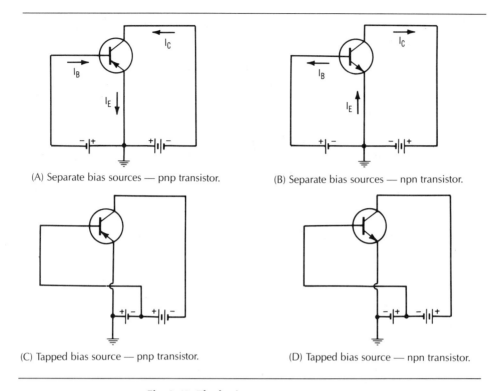

(A) Separate bias sources — pnp transistor.

(B) Separate bias sources — npn transistor.

(C) Tapped bias source — pnp transistor.

(D) Tapped bias source — npn transistor.

Fig. 3-13. The basic common-emitter circuit.

$$\alpha = \frac{I_C}{I_E} = \frac{\beta I_B}{(\beta + 1)I_B} = \frac{\beta}{\beta + 1}$$

It is possible to solve this equation for beta to obtain an expression in terms of alpha:

$$\beta = \frac{\alpha}{1 - \alpha}$$

In practice it is necessary to consider leakage current I_{CO}. Since this component of current flows in the emitter-base circuit through the emitter junction (refer to the current symbols of Fig. 3-14), it is amplified by a factor of beta. As a result the leakage current that flows in the collector circuit of the common-emitter configuration has a value of beta I_{CO}. Therefore, the total collector current is more accurately given with the following expression:

$$I_C = \beta I_B + I_{CO} + \beta I_{CO}$$
$$I_C = \beta I_B + I_{CO}(\beta + 1)$$

The factor I_{CO} which is the result of thermal energy discloses the very significant effect that temperature has on the collector current and operating conditions of a transistor stage. As long as I_{CO} is small in comparison to βI_B it will have only a limited influence on the operating conditions. As heating increases, it is possible that the I_{CO} component will double with each 10-degree rise in temperature.

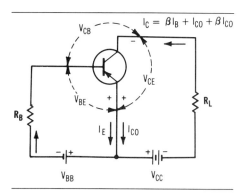

Fig. 3-14. Significant currents and
voltages in common-emitter circuit.

Circuit configurations and bias arrangements are chosen so as to minimize the influence of temperature on the collector current and operating conditions of a transistor stage. When temperature has little influence on the stage it is said to have a high stability factor.

It is also important to give some consideration to the voltage drops around the transistor elements as shown in Fig. 3-14. In a transistor circuit the resistance of the emitter-base junction is very low. Thus, the amount of base-bias current, in the case of the common-emitter circuit, is dependent on the external series resistance (R_B). This resistance is substantially larger than the resistance of the emitter junction. As a result the voltage drop from base to emitter (V_{BE}) is essentially a constant equal to the barrier voltage. In most bias calculations it is practical to substitute 0.7 volt for a silicon transistor and 0.2 volt for a germanium transistor.

The voltage across the collector junction is the difference in potential between the collector and base or V_{CB}. It follows then that the difference of potential between the collector and the emitter (V_{CE}) becomes the sum of the previous voltages or:

$$V_{CE} = V_{CB} + V_{BE}$$

3-4-2. Common-Base Circuit

A fundamental common-base circuit is shown in Fig. 3-15. In this illustration the emitter current is the input current and the collector current is again the output current. Since the emitter current is the sum of the collector and base currents, there can be no current gain in this type of circuit. In fact, the practical current gain approximates the value of alpha or:

$$I_C = \alpha I_E$$

A more exact expression for the collector current must consider the influence of temperature. Therefore:

$$I_C = \alpha I_E + I_{CO}$$

In the case of the common-base circuit the leakage current finds a direct path to the base. Thus, it does not bias the emitter junction as in the case of a common-emitter stage.

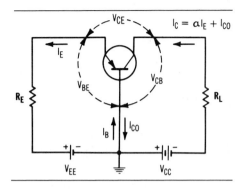

Fig. 3-15. Significant currents and voltages in common-base circuit.

3-4-3. Common-Collector Circuit

The fundamental common-collector circuit is shown in Fig. 3-16. In this arrangement the input current is the base current while the output current is the emitter current. Again the emitter current is the sum of the base and collector currents and, therefore, current gain is possible. The equation for I_E in terms of I_B is derived by assigning a value of αI_E for I_C:

$$I_E = I_B + I_C$$

$$I_E = I_B + \alpha I_E$$

A more exact expression is obtained with the addition of the thermally generated leakage current that is also present in the emitter output circuit.

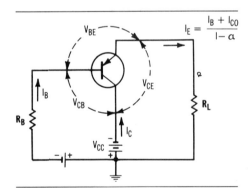

Fig. 3-16. Significant currents and voltages in common-collector circuit.

Solving for I_E:

$$I_E = \frac{I_B + I_{CO}}{1 - \alpha}$$

It must be pointed out that the previous basic equations consider only the direct currents in the three basic circuits. The common-emitter and common-collector circuits are capable of direct-current gain, while the direct-current gain of the common-base amplifier is always less than unity.

3-5. Basic AC Operation

Each transistor configuration (common-emitter, common-base, and common-collector) has different characteristics than the others. Let us now consider each configuration in terms of AC amplification.

3-5-1. Common Emitter

A common-emitter circuit is shown in Fig. 3-17. An applied signal causes a voltage variation across the base resistor, R_B. This, in turn, varies the base current I_B about its operating point bias of 0.2 mA. As a result there will be a corresponding change in the collector current. The collector current change through the load (R_L) develops an output voltage component (E_O).

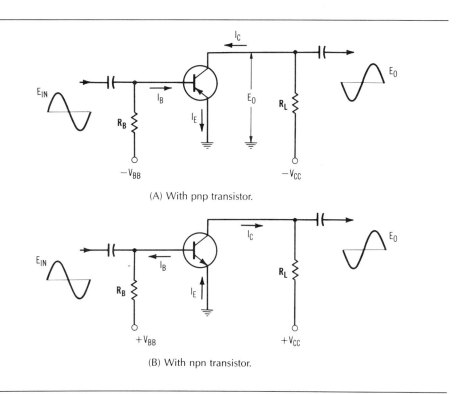

(A) With pnp transistor.

(B) With npn transistor.

Fig. 3-17. Common-emitter circuits.

For a pnp stage (Fig. 3-17A) the positive alternation of the input sine-wave voltage decreases the forward bias and results in a decline in the base current. As a result, fewer positive carriers (holes) are injected into the base, and the collector current declines. With the negative swing of the collector current there is less of a voltage drop across load R_L, and the collector voltage (output voltage) becomes more negative. Hence, the output and input voltages are out of phase.

The negative input alternation provides additional forward bias for the emitter junction. As a result more positive carriers (holes) are injected into the base and there is a rise in the collector current. There follows a swing of the output voltage in the positive direction.

A similar relation exists between output voltage and input voltage for a common-emitter npn amplifier. For the npn circuit (Fig. 3-17B) the positive alternation of the input sine wave increases the forward bias. Consequently more negative carriers (electrons) are injected into the base. As a result there is an increase in collector current. However, the current directions and bias polarities are opposite from those of the pnp type. Therefore, the increase in collector current results in a less positive voltage (negative swing) appearing across the output. Oppositely, for the negative alternation of the input wave there is a decrease in the forward biasing of the emitter junction. Fewer positive carriers (electrons) are injected into the base and there is a resultant decrease in collector current. Now the collector and output voltage swings positive to form the positive alternation of the output wave.

3-5-2. Graphical Analysis

The operation of a common-emitter stage can also be shown graphically as in Fig. 3-18. This drawing is a graphical representation of how the collector current changes with a change in collector voltage. The diagonal line, called the *load line*, drawn across the base current curves shows how the operating point moves as the collector current changes. The slope of this line varies according to the value of the collector load resistor. In this case, a 500-ohm load line is used. The collector supply voltage (V_{CC}) is 20 and the base supply voltage (V_{BB}) is such that the operating-point base current is 0.2 milliampere. Thus, the operating-point collector current and collector voltage are 15 milliamperes and 12.5 volts, respectively. The operating point is so marked on the graph.

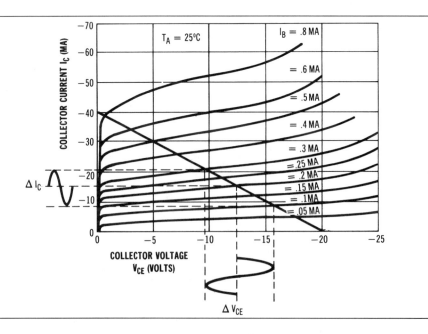

Fig. 3-18. Common-emitter circuit collector characteristics.

The transistor is a pnp type. When a positive input voltage is applied to the base the instantaneous bias is reduced, causing a decrease in the base current; a negative input voltage results in a rise in the base current. Let us assume that the amplitude of the input voltage is such that the base current swings between 0.1 and 0.3 milliampere. Horizontal lines drawn from these two extremes to the collector current line show that the collector current will vary between 8.5 and 20.5 millamperes. The collector current change swings the collector voltage between 9.5 and 16 volts. A value for the current gain is as follows:

$$\text{AC Gain } (h_{fe}) = \frac{\Delta I_C}{\Delta I_B}$$

$$= \frac{20.5 - 8.5}{0.3 - 0.1}$$

$$= 60$$

3-5-3. Common Base

In a common-base circuit, Fig. 3-19, the input and output voltages are in phase. A positive swing of the input increases the forward bias on the pnp emitter junction. Hence, a higher base current results and more positive carriers (holes) are injected into the base. Consequently, the collector current rises and the output voltage becomes less negative (swings positive).

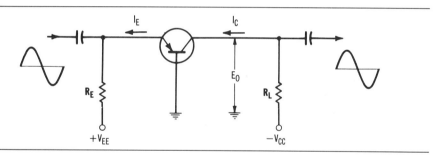

Fig. 3-19. Common-base stage.

During the negative alternation the forward bias decreases and fewer holes are injected into the base. The collector current falls and the output voltage swings negative.

It is to be noted that current gain is not possible with this arrangement because the input current is the emitter current (I_E). However, *voltage* and *power amplification* are possible because the output load resistance R_L is higher than the input resistance.

3-5-4. Common Collector

In the common-collector circuit (Fig. 3-20), a positive alternation of the input wave decreases the forward bias. Again there is a decline in base current, injected holes, and collector current. With the decrease in the emitter current (a result of the decline in the collector current), there will be a positive swing of the emitter and output voltage. Oppositely, the negative alternation of the sine-wave input increases the forward bias and through transistor action the emitter current rises. Consequently, the emitter voltage swings more negative and there is a negative alternation of the output voltage.

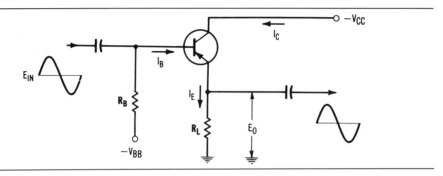

Fig. 3-20. Common-collector stage.

The common-collector stage is capable of *current gain* because the base current is the input current while the emitter output current I_E is the sum of the collector and base currents.

This stage is often referred to as an emitter-follower because the emitter voltage tends to follow the voltage applied to the base.

3-6. Small-Signal Operation

In the amplification of small signals the transistor can be considered to be an essentially linear device. In low-level or small-signal amplifiers the input signal variations are usually between the values of less than one microvolt up to some tens of millivolts. When a transistor is biased correctly and operates within this narrow input signal range, there is no significant distortion and the output and input signals are essentially identical in waveform. This condition applies to RF and IF transistor amplifiers as well as low-level audio and video amplifiers and certain other small-signal amplifiers.

There are six factors of concern in evaluating transistor amplifiers. These are voltage gain (A_v), current gain (A_i), power gain (A_p), input resistance (R_{in}), output resistance (R_{out}), and phase. Some of these factors were discussed briefly in the previous topics. The latter factor of phase was considered; you learned that input voltage and output voltage were in phase for both the common-base and common-collector configurations but out of phase for the common-emitter circuit. The three basic circuit configurations are repeated in Fig. 3-21 which gives special emphasis to the six factors just mentioned. These factors are also related to the actual load R_L placed on the stage as well as input-circuit constants. Each of the first five factors listed will be considered in the following material. The relations apply only over the normal small-signal operating range of a given transistor type.

Common-base and common-emitter circuits are capable of approximately the same *voltage gain* A_v, with the common-base circuit having a slight edge, particularly at higher values of load resistance. The higher the value of the load resistance for either

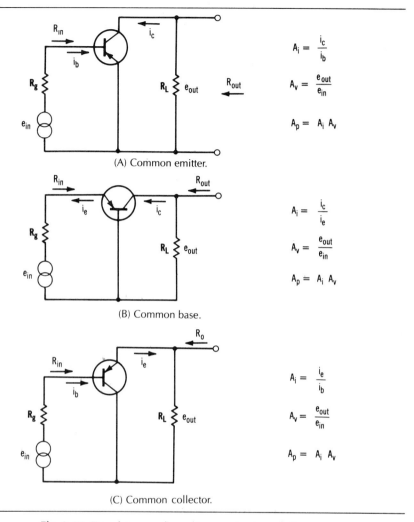

(A) Common emitter.

$$A_i = \frac{i_c}{i_b}$$

$$A_v = \frac{e_{out}}{e_{in}}$$

$$A_p = A_i A_v$$

(B) Common base.

$$A_i = \frac{i_c}{i_e}$$

$$A_v = \frac{e_{out}}{e_{in}}$$

$$A_p = A_i A_v$$

(C) Common collector.

$$A_i = \frac{i_e}{i_b}$$

$$A_v = \frac{e_{out}}{e_{in}}$$

$$A_p = A_i A_v$$

Fig. 3-21. Transistor configurations and gain equations.

type of circuit, the greater the voltage gain. The voltage gain of the common-collector circuit is always less than unity.

The *current gain* (A_i) of common-collector and common-emitter configurations is approximately the same, with the common-collector having a slight edge. Current gain decreases with an increase in load resistance for either type of circuit. The common-base stage has a current gain of less than unity.

The *power gain* (A_p) for all three transistor configurations is the product of the voltage and current gains or:

$$A_p = A_v A_i$$

The common-emitter stage has the highest power gain over the normal range of load resistance. For high values of load resistance, the common-base power exceeds that of a common-collector stage. However, at low values of load resistance, the common-collector stage has a higher power gain than the common-base circuit.

In general the power gains of both common-emitter and common-base circuits increase with a higher value of load resistance, while the power gain decreases with an increase in load resistance in common-collector stages.

The *input resistance* (R_{in}) to any transistor stage is low when compared to the input resistance of field-effect transistors and vacuum-tube circuits. The base-emitter junction is forward biased; thus, it has a low resistance. The *output resistance* (R_{out}) is substantially higher than the input resistance because it is across the reverse-biased collector junction.

The common-collector stage has the highest input resistance. The common-emitter circuit has an intermediate value of input resistance and the common-base circuit the lowest input resistance. The higher the value of the load resistance, the higher the input resistance for a common-collector circuit. The input resistance of the common-base circuit gradually increases with an increase in load resistance while the input resistance of a common-emitter circuit gradually declines.

The use of feedback also influences resistive values. For the popular common-emitter circuit the use of negative feedback increases the input resistance substantially.

The common-base circuit has the highest output resistance and the common-collector stage the lowest. In a small-signal transistor circuit the output resistance is more dependent on the input circuit resistance than the output load resistance. In common-base and common-collector configurations the output resistance increases with an increase in the input or source resistance. This can be understood if you consider that the collector junction is reverse biased and the output conditions are a function of the carriers injected into the base which, in turn, are influenced by the source resistance.

The common-emitter configuration has the intermediate value of output resistance. This resistance decreases with an increase in the source resistance.

3-7. Biasing and Stabilization

If a transistor is to operate in a linear amplifier circuit it must be properly biased and a suitable operating point must be found. The DC operating point depends on bias current, collector voltage, and collector current. Obtaining the desired DC operating point requires the selection of the bias resistors and output load resistor to provide the proper input current and collector voltage.

The stability of a transistor amplifier is very important because if the operating point is allowed to shift with temperature changes, the circuit will introduce unwanted distortion. Besides the undesired effect of distortion, if a circuit is allowed to drift off the normal operating point with a rise in temperature, the physical safety of the transistor is endangered. The transistor could be destroyed by excessive collector current resulting from thermal runaway.

An input signal of a suitable magnitude causes the base current to vary equally on each side of the operating point, thus producing a collector current change and an output voltage variation across the load resistor that is a reasonable copy of the voltage variation of the input signal. A major problem in the design of a transistor amplifier is keeping the DC operating point constant with changes in temperature. The operating point will shift with temperature because of the change in leakage current. This change in collector current can cause a shift in the DC operating point. If the collector cutoff current (I_{co}) value is small in comparison with the normal value of the operating collector current, it has little influence on the DC operating point.

The common-emitter circuit is especially vulnerable to the change in leakage current I_{co}. The leakage current in a common-emitter configuration is effectively multiplied by the factor of beta. However, the common-emitter circuit is used extensively because of other favorable operating characteristics.

The influence of temperature on common-emitter characteristics is shown in Fig. 3-22. The solid curves are for a particular standard operating temperature (usually 25°C). The dashed curves show the influence of an increase in transistor gain and/or leakage current with a rise in temperature.

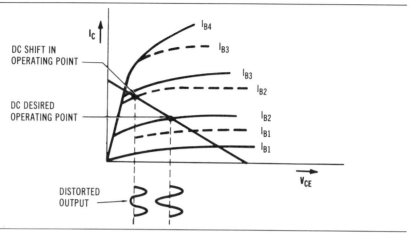

Fig. 3-22. Influence of temperature on common-emitter characteristics and DC operating point.

For a given load resistance, represented by the load line of Fig. 3-22, it should be noted that the DC operating point has been shifted to a higher collector current (I_c) and a lower collector voltage (V_{CE}) when the temperature rises. In fact, for a given base-bias current the operating point has been shifted very near to the knee of the curve. When the operating point shifts to a point which is near the knee of the curve the positive alternation of an input current will become distorted. The increase in temperature, therefore, has caused distortion in the form of a flattening of one alternation of the output wave.

In some cases the operating point can be shifted so that maximum safe transistor currents or power dissipations are exceeded. If the junction temperatures are increased in certain circuits there is also the danger of thermal runaway.

3-7-1. Bias Arrangements

Five typical bipolar transistor bias arrangements are given in Fig. 3-23. In the first arrangement of Fig. 3-23A a bias resistor (R_B) is connected between the supply voltage and the base. The ohmic value of the resistor is selected in accordance with the desired base current. Typical calculations are given later.

In the second arrangement of Fig. 3-23B an emitter resistor (R_E) is added. This resistor improves the bias stability. Now the actual base-bias current is determined by both resistors R_B and R_E.

In the circuit arrangement of Fig. 3-23C, the base resistor R_B is returned to the collector voltage rather than the supply voltage. This factor must be considered in determining the value of the resistor to obtain a specific base-bias current. This circuit is also degenerative and improves the bias stability.

Fig. 3-23D shows perhaps the most common type of biasing. In this case resistors R1 and R_B act as a bias current divider in conjunction with the base-to-emitter resistance of the transistor and resistor R_E (if present). Values for the three resistors are selected to establish good bias stability.

The arrangement in Fig. 3-23E is also common because multiple voltage supplies are common in modern transistor radio equipment. In this arrangement there is a separate emitter voltage supply line that can be used to establish the appropriate base-bias current as determined by the ohmic values of resistors R_B and R_E.

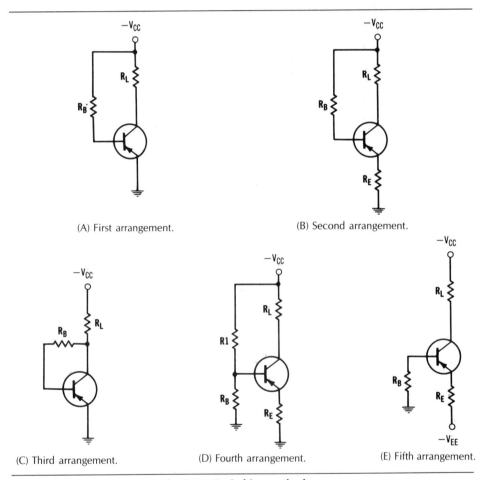

(A) First arrangement.

(B) Second arrangement.

(C) Third arrangement.

(D) Fourth arrangement.

(E) Fifth arrangement.

Fig. 3-23. Basic bias methods.

3-7-2. Simple Bias Calculations

The simple circuit of Fig. 3-24 can be used to demonstrate base bias and other current relations in the common-emitter configuration. If we assume the supply voltage is 20 volts, load resistance 500 ohms, and collector current of 15 milliamperes, it is possible to determine the required value for resistor R_B for proper biasing of the stage.

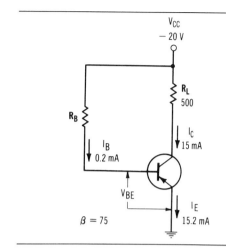

Fig. 3-24. Basic bias circuit.

If the beta of the transistor is 75, the base current can be determined by dividing the collector current by 75 or:

$$\beta = \frac{I_C}{I_B}$$

$$I_B = \frac{I_C}{\beta} = \frac{15}{75} = 0.2 \text{ milliampere}$$

The voltage drop across the base bias resistor (R_B) is the supply voltage minus the constant base-emitter barrier voltage of 0.7 volt. Therefore:

$$R_B = \frac{V_{CC} - V_{BE}}{I_B} = \frac{20 - 0.7}{0.2 \times 10^{-3}} = 96,500$$

This operating point matches that shown previously in Fig. 3-18. It should be stressed that there is some spread in the value of the beta — it could be substantially more or less than 75. Under this condition some adjustment in the ohmic value of R_B is necessary if a desired collector current of 15 milliamperes is obtained. A decrease in the ohmic value of R_B will increase collector current I_C. The emitter current (I_E) is, of course, the sum of the base current plus collector current, or 15.2 mA.

3-7-3. Emitter Stabilization Resistor

The stability of a common-emitter circuit can be improved with the use of an emitter resistor (R_E). Such a circuit is shown in Fig. 3-25A. Since the voltage drop across the emitter resistor is due to the emitter current, the polarity of the voltage would develop a back bias for the base-emitter junction instead of a forward bias. In a fixed bias circuit using an emitter resistor it is still necessary to use some form of base bias.

The use of the emitter resistor, in conjunction with a base-bias circuit, improves the operating point stability because of the degenerative influence of the voltage developed across it. One of the contributing factors to the drift of the DC operating point is the effect of the leakage current as it flows through the emitter junction. If a higher percentage of the leakage current can be bypassed to the base rather than the emitter, the better the operating point stability will be. As shown in the equivalent schematic of Fig. 3-25B, the insertion of a resistor in the emitter circuit does this.

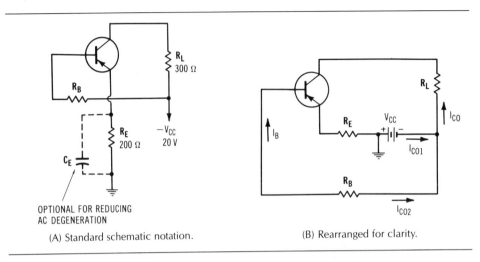

(A) Standard schematic notation.

(B) Rearranged for clarity.

Fig. 3-25. Stabilization of fixed bias with emitter resistor.

The leakage current in emitter resistor R_E is in such a direction that a compensating change will be made in the base-bias current. For example, an attempted rise in the leakage current (as a result of a temperature increase) develops a voltage across the emitter resistor that will decrease the base-bias current and bring about a correcting change in the collector current. The emitter resistor, therefore, exerts a degenerative influence on collector current. The emitter resistor because it is in series with the local resistor is a part of the collector-emitter output circuit.

If an AC signal is being applied to the stage there will be a corresponding AC voltage variation across the emitter resistor. This emitter voltage variation is in phase with the base voltage variation. Since these voltages are in series opposing across the base-emitter junction, the effective input voltage is reduced. This AC degeneration can be reduced with the use of an emitter capacitor (C_E) that bypasses the AC voltage variation around emitter resistor R_E.

The following example demonstrates how the value of R_B can be determined:

The DC load on the collector-emitter circuit is to be 500 ohms. If a sample value of 200 ohms for R_E is used, it is necessary to reduce R_L to 300 ohms to maintain a 500-ohm DC load. Since V_{BE} is very low (0.7 volt), the sum of the voltage drops across R_E and R_B for practical applications equals the supply voltage. For a desired DC operating point of 0.015 ampere, the voltage drop across R_B must have the following value:

$$V_{RB} = V_{CC} - V_{RE}$$
$$= V_{CC} - I_E R_E$$
$$= 20 - (0.015 \times 200)$$
$$V_{RB} = 17 \text{ volts}$$

Knowing the voltage drop across R_B, it is possible to determine the value of the base resistor required:

$$R_B = \frac{V_{RB}}{I_B}$$

$$= \frac{17}{0.0002}$$

$$R_B = 85,000 \text{ ohms}$$

3-7-4. Divider Bias

The most popular form of common-emitter biasing is the current-divider arrangement shown in Fig. 3-26. In this arrangement the divider current separates into two paths after R1; one path is through the base resistor R_B, the second path is through the series combination of the emitter junction and emitter resistor R_E. The current in the second path is the base current. The equivalent circuit (Fig. 3-26B) shows the current paths.

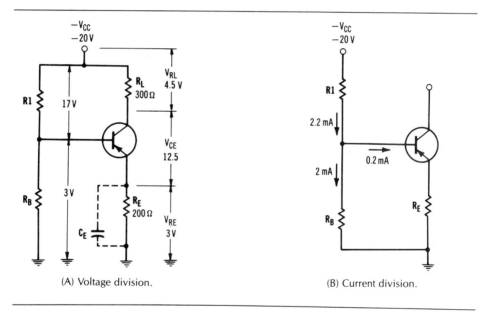

(A) Voltage division.   (B) Current division.

Fig. 3-26. Divider biasing arrangements.

If an emitter current of 0.015 ampere is assumed to be the same as used in the previous example, the voltge drop across R_E will be 3 volts. Since resistor R_B is in parallel with the series combination of the emitter junction and emitter resistor R_E, the voltage drop across R_B must also be 3 volts if the base-emitter junction voltage is not considered. The required voltage drop across R1 will be 17 volts.

The divider bias arrangement permits the design of a highly stable common-emitter stage. The base resistor is kept low. For best stability use a current in resistor R_B that is greater than the DC base-bias current. However, there is a limit to which the value of a base resistor (R_B) can be reduced. The lower the base resistance is, the greater will be the load placed on any signal source.

Next determine the required values of resistors R1 and R_B for establishing the operating point. The desired base-bias current is 0.2 milliampere. Therefore, for good stability ten times this current should be shunted through base resistor R_B. This means that the current in R_B should be 2 milliamperes (Fig. 3-26B). Knowing this and the voltage drop across R_B, it is possible to determine the value of R_B as follows:

$$R_B = \frac{E_{RB}}{I_{RB}}$$

$$= \frac{3}{0.002}$$

$$R_B = 1500 \text{ ohms}$$

All the divider-circuit current is through resistor R1. Therefore, the total current in resistor R1 is 2.2 milliamperes (2 + 0.2). The voltage drop across this resistor is the difference between the supply voltage and the voltage across R_B, or 17 volts (20 − 3). From this information it is possible to obtain the required value for resistor R1:

$$R1 = \frac{E_{R1}}{I_T} = \frac{17}{0.0022} = 7730 \text{ ohms}$$

3-8. Audio Power Amplifiers

Transistor stages can be biased class A, B, or C (Fig. 3-27). In class-A biasing the operating point on the transfer characteristic is such that the input signal swings over the linear portion of the transfer characteristic. Single-ended audio power amplifiers are biased in this manner.

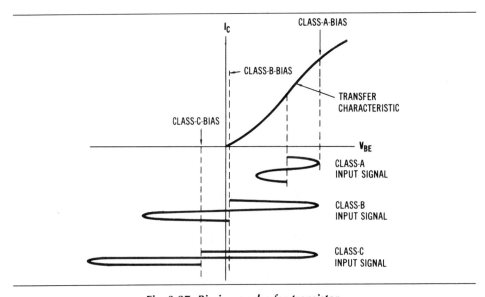

Fig. 3-27. Biasing modes for transistor.

In class-B biasing the stage is biased to cutoff. Of course that cutoff bias is equal to the barrier voltage. This is approximately 0.7 volt for a silicon transistor. Hence for true class-B operation it is necessary that a slight forward bias be employed. Thus for a class-B push-pull audio power amplifier there is a slight forward biasing equal to at least the barrier potential. Quite often an additional small amount of forward biasing is needed to minimize crossover distortion in the output.

When no bias is applied to a transistor stage it is biased class C because there is no collector current. Recall again that a small amount of forward bias is needed to overcome the barrier potential before there is any collector current flow. If desired, additional back biasing can be used if the stage is to be biased even further beyond cutoff. This possibility will be considered in the description of class-C RF amplifier operation.

Two class-A audio power amplifier stages are shown in Fig. 3-28. Inasmuch as the transistor is basically a current amplifier, some input power is needed. Therefore an input transformer is employed to match the output of the succeeding stage to the low-impedance input of the power amplifier. Class-A biasing is accomplished with resistors R1 and R_B. The circuit is temperature stabilized by emitter resistor R_E. This resistor keeps the operating point stabilized. An output transformer of proper turns ratio matches the low-impedance collector output to the low-impedance speaker system.

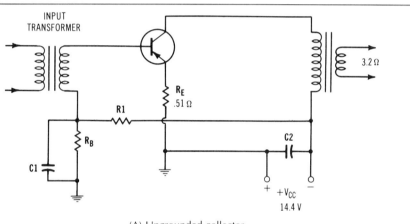

(A) Ungrounded collector.

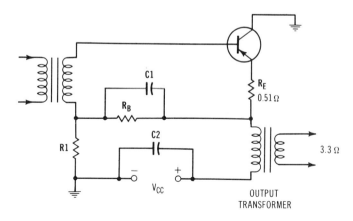

(B) Grounded collector.

Fig. 3-28. Class-A power amplifier showing grounded and ungrounded collector arrangements.

The circuits of Fig. 3-28 show both ungrounded (Fig. 3-28A) and grounded (Fig. 3-28B) collector arrangements. In a typical power transistor, the case of that device is usually connected electrically to the collector. The case, in turn, is often connected to a heat sink or chassis to provide transistor cooling in the form of radiation through the chassis or metallic heat sink that fits over the transistor case. Heat sinks are finned structures that function well as heat radiators. They are usually painted black to increase the efficiency of heat radiation.

If the transistor is used in a circuit that permits the collector to be operated at ground potential, the transistor case itself can be connected directly to the chassis or a grounded metallic heat sink. This manner of connection applies to the circuit arrangement of Fig. 3-28B.

In other circuits the collector cannot be operated at ground potential. In such instances there must be an insulating washer to insulate the case of the transistor from the ground potential of the metallic heat sink. These washers have a low thermal resistance and will conduct the heat from the transistor case to the metallic surface.

The simplified circuit of Fig. 3-29 shows how an appropriate diode (D1) can be used to stabilize the bias of a transistor power stage. In this case the bias is established by resistor R1 and the resistance of the diode. The diode is an effective stabilizer because its constants are chosen to match the characteristics of the base-emitter junction of the transistor. In effect this base-emitter junction itself acts as a diode. When junction characteristics change with heating effects, there is a like change in the characteristics of the bias diode. Thus if the collector current tends to rise as a result of the heating of the base-emitter junction, the change in the characteristics of the external diode will follow and produce a compensating change in the base-bias current in resistor R1. Consequently the operating-point bias is stabilized and is less subject to temperature change.

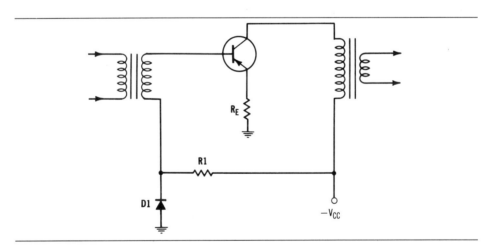

Fig. 3-29. Diode bias stabilization.

A basic push-pull class-B amplifier using bipolar transistors is given in Fig. 3-30. A push-pull stage can be biased class B because one transistor will conduct on the positive alternation of the input wave and the other transistor on the negative alternation. As a result the complete sine wave is reconstructed in the output circuit.

In a theoretical case the class-B stage is biased to cutoff. However, the operating point is usually forward-biased a slight amount from this point to prevent crossover distortion in the output. The biasing arrangement of the circuit shown in Fig. 3-31 shows such an arrangement. The actual bias is determined by resistor R1 and the parallel combination of resistor R_B and the thermistor resistor.

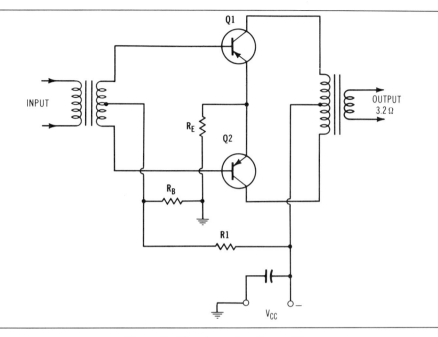

Fig. 3-30. Class-B push-pull amplifier.

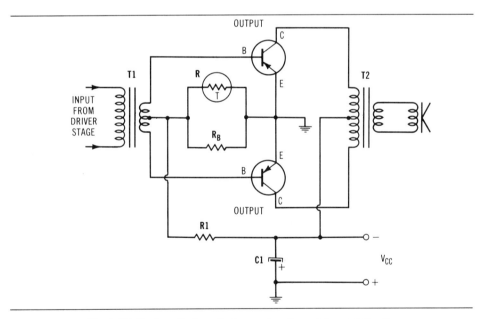

Fig. 3-31. Push-pull class-B stage using thermistor stabilization.

The thermistor is used widely for bias-stabilizing transistor power amplifiers. It has a negative temperature coefficient; that is, its resistance decreases with an increase in temperature. A change in the thermistor resistance causes a lower forward-bias voltage to appear across the base and emitter junction with an increase in temperature. This reduction in forward bias compensates for the increase in conductance of the emitter junction with a rise in temperature.

The amount of temperature compensation is a function of the thermistor characteristic. Quite often the thermistor is placed in parallel with a bias resistor of specific value in order to provide an exact compensation.

3-9. Tuned Transistor Amplifiers

Tuned amplifiers are used extensively in the receiver and transmitter sections of modern radiocommunications equipment. Neutralized and nonneutralized transistor tuned amplifiers are employed. Usually nonneutralized amplifiers are employed in the intermediate-frequency range, while a neutralized amplifier is more likely to be found in the amplification of VHF or UHF signals.

When a tuned amplifier is designed for maximum gain conditions some neutralization is often advisable. Fewer stability problems and other favorable operating conditions are obtained when transistor stages are operated at lower gain. The lower-gain operation is obtained with the use of low-impedance loading at input and output or the use of intentional mismatch. The avoidance of neutralization is desirable from the standpoint of stability and freedom from feedback effects which can vary substantially with temperature.

In the case of the IF amplifiers in a communication receiver the use of relatively low value tuned circuit impedance is not favorable from a standpoint of narrow-bandwidth requirements. However, it is helpful in terms of amplifier stability and AGC operating conditions. As a result an optimum choice must be made. The amplifier design problem becomes less critical with the use of highly selective wave filters that determine the selectivity of the IF system. Consequently, the IF amplifier design can be slanted in favor of stability, and the added bandwidth will not harm the selectivity.

Several basic amplifier circuits as used in IF application are shown in Fig. 3-32. The simplest form of IF amplifier uses a single resonant circuit and a low-impedance untuned secondary winding, matching the output of the first stage to the low-impedance input of the second (Fig. 3-32A). The examples in Figs. 3-32B and C show double-tuned interstage transformers. Fig. 3-32B is the more conventional form, using inductive coupling between primary and secondary resonant circuits.

A more favorable arrangement, as shown in Fig. 3-32C, can be used to establish a good response curve as well as being more effective in blocking out strong off-channel signals. This circuit uses no inductive coupling. A small capacitor (C) provides the mutual coupling element between the two resonant circuits. The secondary inductor is sometimes tapped to permit appropriate match to the next stage, or a low-impedance secondary winding can be used.

The common-emitter stage is the most popular tuned amplifier transistor circuit configuration. It is to be noted that the biasing is similar to that employed in low-frequency audio circuits — a combination of base-divider biasing and emitter stabilization.

Figs. 3-32D and E show two common methods of neutralization used in VHF RF amplifiers and occasionally in high-frequency IF amplifiers. In the arrangement of Fig. 3-32D the inductor is tapped near its low end and operates at RF-ground potential. Therefore an out-of-phase signal is made available between the bottom of the coil and the tap. This signal is fed to the base circuit through a neutralization capacitor (C_N). This out-of-phase component balances out the regenerated component that would cause amplifier oscillation. In Fig. 3-32E the required out-of-phase signal is made available at the secondary winding of the interstage transformer and fed back to the input base circuit through a neutralizing capacitor (C_N).

3

Solid-State Fundamentals   75

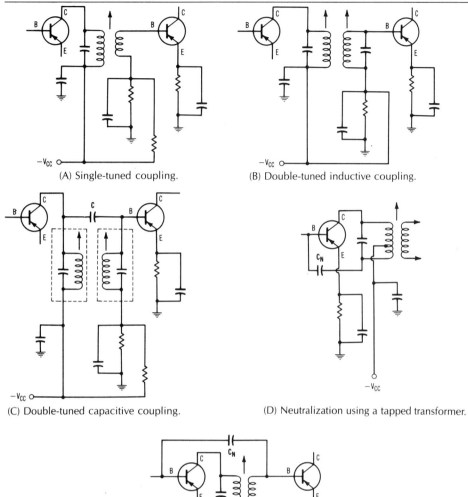

(A) Single-tuned coupling.

(B) Double-tuned inductive coupling.

(C) Double-tuned capacitive coupling.

(D) Neutralization using a tapped transformer.

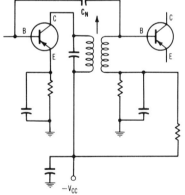

(E) Neutralization using the transformer secondary.

Fig. 3-32. Tuned transistor amplifiers.

An example of a solid-state neutralized RF amplifier is shown in Fig. 3-33A. A double-tuned input resonant circuit contains low-impedance taps for matching the antenna to the base circuit of the transistor. The collector coil is also tapped to provide matching to the succeeding mixer. A low-impedance secondary winding could also be used. A tap on the primary provides the required out-of-phase feedback voltage for neutralization. In this particular RF stage the lower tap on the resonant circuit is at AC and DC ground potential. The pnp transistors in these circuits are biased properly with the application of a positive voltage to the base and emitter circuits.

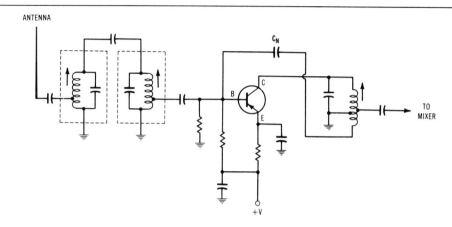

(A) Neutralized stage.

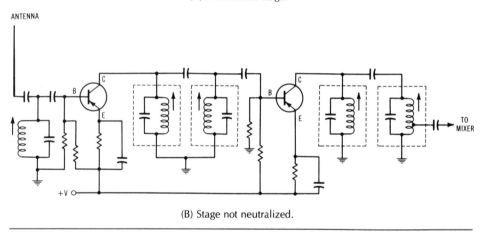

(B) Stage not neutralized.

Fig. 3-33. Basic RF amplifiers.

No neutralization is needed in the two-stage amplifier of Fig. 3-33B. A single tuned-resonant circuit is used for the input coupling. Double tuned transformers link both the first RF stage to the second and the output of the second stage to the mixer. Only the final resonant circuit is tapped to provide matching to the mixer. In configurations of this type sometimes intentional mismatching is employed to improve stability. The use of two stages instead of one develops the required overall gain and selectivity.

3-10. Transmitter Transistor RF Stages

Transistors are used in the RF section of a transmitter as oscillators, buffers, multipliers, and RF power amplifiers. Not all of these stages operate class C in all transmitters. Quite often the low level stages are not operated class C because the advantage of high-efficiency class-C operation is nullified by the need for input driving power. Thus the overall efficiency is no better than that which can be obtained more conveniently with the use of class-A operation. However, in the driver-amplifier and power-amplifier stages of the transistor transmitter, class-C operation is preferable because of the more favorable efficiency obtained in the amplification of high-power signals.

Many low-level stages of the transmitter RF section are similar in circuit arrangement to the transistor tuned amplifiers used in the receiver, with the exception that less forward bias is used. Biasing is more nearly class B than class A. A typical stage is shown in Fig. 3-34. Double-tuned interstage coupling systems are used much less frequently than single-tuned types. Usually a tapped coil, split capacitor, or low impedance link is used to obtain impedance-matched coupling. Toroid transformers are especially popular.

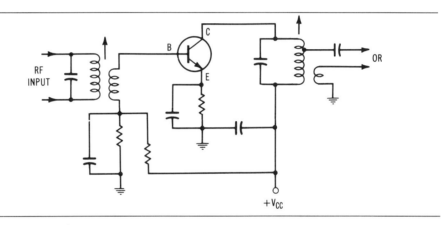

Fig. 3-34. Example of low-level RF amplifier for a transmitter.

3-10-1. Basic Transistor Class-C Amplifier

A transistor operates readily as a class-C amplifier, because with no forward bias applied to its emitter-to-base junction, it is already biased class C. There is no collector current without some forward biasing. As you learned, germanium and silicon transistors require forward bias of approximately 0.2 volt and 0.7 volt, respectively, before there is collector current.

It is apparent from the foregoing that transistors can be class-C biased by simply eliminating the emitter-to-base junction bias as shown in Fig. 3-35. This amount of biasing is only slightly beyond the value of class-B cutoff bias and is used in low-level stages and is common for high-power VHF and UHF power amplifiers.

The circuit arrangement of Fig. 3-36 shows how a simple resistor-capacitor combination in the base circuit permits biasing beyond cutoff. This reduces the angle of the collector current. In the npn stage, the more positive portion of the positive alternation of the input wave forward-biases the junction and produces base current. The direction of the base current is such that the charge placed on capacitor C_B is a back-bias. The emitter-to-base junction is reverse-biased as it should be for class-C operation.

The output current occurs in bursts that replenish the power in the output tank circuit. During the portion of the input wave that biases the emitter-to-base junction in

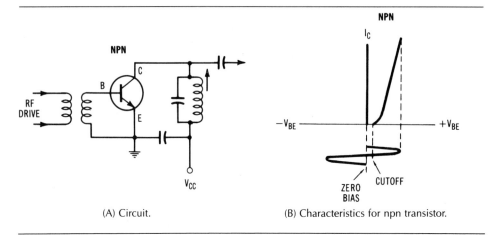

(A) Circuit.

(B) Characteristics for npn transistor.

Fig. 3-35. Basic class-C amplifier.

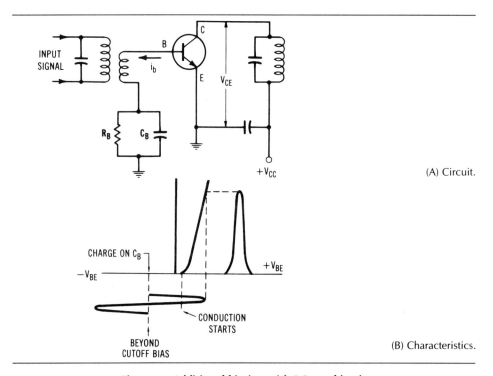

(A) Circuit.

(B) Characteristics.

Fig. 3-36. Additional biasing with RC combination.

the forward direction there is a short interval of collector conduction. At this time the resonant circuit capacitor is charged to its peak value. The oscillatory action in the resonant circuit reconstructs the complete RF cycle.

The Q of the resonant tank is significant. The unloaded Q should be as high as possible to obtain efficient operation of the tank circuit and to obtain maximum transfer of power from the tank to the load. The loaded Q of the tank circuit should be relatively low to permit effective transfer of power, but it must not be too low or the generation of harmonics will be excessive. This is quite a problem in transistor RF power amplifiers because of the inherent low impedance of the transistor. Thus suitable low-impedance resonant circuits and matching arrangements must be employed. Bifilar wound toroidal inductors are often essential.

The low impedance of the transistor has an advantage because neutralization is often not required. Quite often the input impedance itself is very low and, this fact, along with the very low output impedance, reduces the tendency to self-oscillation. However, such a circuit must be protected from parasitic oscillations with appropriate RF chokes.

The pi-network (Fig. 3-37) is used widely in transistor power-amplifier circuits because of its convenient impedance matching capability and good harmonic rejection. It can be found in low- and moderate-power RF stages. For higher-powered stages it is often found in conjunction with other matching elements that ensure a proper match from the extremely low-impedance output of a high-powered transistor RF amplifier.

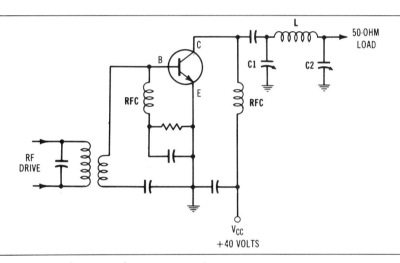

Fig. 3-37. Class-C stage with pi-network output circuit.

The pi-network can provide a proper match to a low-impedance antenna system. The output impedance of the transistor itself is often below this 50-ohm value, and the function of the pi-network is to match the low-impedance output of the transistor stage to the higher impedance of the 50-ohm loading. Note the RF chokes in both the input and output circuits. These prevent the supply voltage source and biasing networks from having an adverse influence on the loading and tuning of the input and output resonant circuits.

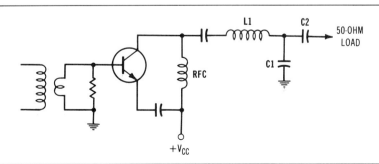

Fig. 3-38. T-network matching.

The T-network tuning arrangement of Fig. 3-38 is also popular in transistor power amplification. Its advantage is its ability to match the very low output impedance of a high-power RF amplifier stage to a significantly higher, but still relatively low, impedance load. The network consists of inductor L1 and capacitors C1 and C2. The network reflects a substantially lower impedance to the output of the transistor than the 50-ohm load into which the circuit must operate.

3-11. RF Oscillators

Fundamentally an oscillator is an amplifier circuit in which the output is linked through a suitable network to its input. The radio-frequency oscillator contains a resonant circuit which determines the frequency of the oscillations generated. To cause oscillation a portion of the output signal that is fed back to the input must be in phase with an input change. Oscillations are sustained when the feedback or loop gain is greater than unity. The loop gain refers to the combined gain of the amplifier and the feedback network. In most oscillators the output variation is out of phase with the input and, to ensure in-phase feedback, the feedback network itself must produce a polarity shift. The manner of obtaining this feedback is the basic difference among the various types of oscillators.

Two basic oscillator types are the *Colpitts* and *Hartley* circuits shown in Fig. 3-39. Although they are used at both high and low radiocommunication frequencies, the Colpitts oscillator is somewhat more popular at the higher frequencies while the Hartley oscillator is more common at lower frequencies. In the Hartley oscillator the coil of the resonant circuit is tapped and usually placed at RF ground potential. This permits a small-amplitude out-of-phase RF voltage to be made available between the bottom of the coil and the tap. This out-of-phase voltage is linked back to the input circuit. In practice the product of the network gain and the gain of the stage is made greater than unity to permit a buildup of the initially weak component and to compensate for circuit losses at the oscillating frequency. Thus, at the start of oscillation the feedback voltage is greater than the input voltage. However, the gain of the stage falls off as the oscillation builds up. In so doing the greater-than-unity feedback causes the signal level to rise until the final maximum-magnitude level is attained. In effect the feedback to the input circuit is of just the proper level to continuously recycle the energy supplied to the resonant circuit and oscillations of constant amplitude are sustained.

The Colpitts oscillator (Fig. 3-39B) differs only in the manner in which the feedback voltage is obtained. In the Colpitts circuit the feedback voltage is picked off at the lower capacitor associated with the resonant circuit. It too provides a 180-degree shift and brings the output back in phase with the input voltage. The fraction of the input voltage that is fed back to the input is a function of the relative reactances of C1 and C2.

It should be noted that the oscillators are forward-biased a certain amount by resistors R1 and R2. Remember that the barrier potential must be overcome before the transistor draws any collector current. Thus with no bias the oscillations would not start. The bias resistors overcome the barrier potential and result in a start of collector current which then builds up to produce continuous oscillation.

A high-stability oscillator is shown in Fig. 3-40. The resonant frequency is determined by inductor L1, capacitor C1, and the combination of capacitors C2 and C3. The latter two capacitors are extremely high values; therefore a relatively low value of inductor L1 is needed to establish a given resonant frequency. The advantage of

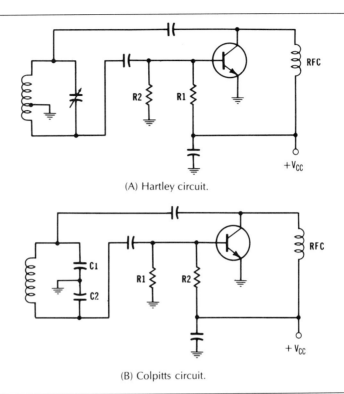

(A) Hartley circuit.

(B) Colpitts circuit.

Fig. 3-39. Basic oscillator circuits.

determining the oscillator frequency with a high C-to-L ratio is the great frequency stability that results. The large-value capacitors are so large in value that changes in transistor and external capacitive components have no significant influence on the operating frequency. The operating frequency is determined by the resonant circuit and not by stray external components.

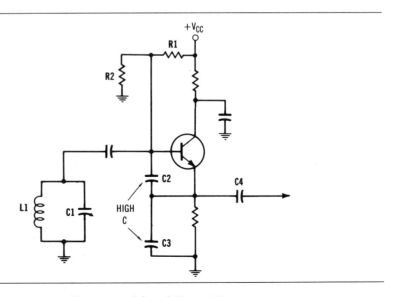

Fig. 3-40. High-stability oscillator.

Minimum loading of the oscillator circuit results when the output is removed from the low-impedance emitter circuit through an appropriate low-value coupling capacitor (C4). Resistors R1 and R2 provide the slight forward bias needed to start oscillations.

3-11-1. Crystal Oscillator

Certain crystalline materials produce a voltage when placed under mechanical stress. One such material is quartz, used in the manufacture of radiocommunication crystals. If the pressure on such a crystal is varied, an alternating voltage will be developed; conversely, when an alternating voltage is applied across the crystal, a physical vibration is set up in it. Quartz crystal vibrates freely, is very stable, and most important, it vibrates at a particular frequency determined by its size and structure.

A quartz crystal, when inserted into an oscillator stage tuned near its natural frequency, will vibrate strongly. In fact, a potential difference, much like the resonant voltage across a tank circuit, will be developed across the crystal. This voltage variation is supplied as feedback to the oscillator base (Fig. 3-41). A similar variation is now set up in the collector tank circuit and is now fed back to the crystal to keep it in mechanical vibration. Inasmuch as the feedback is strongest at the mechanical-resonance frequency of the crystal, the frequency of oscillation is determined by the natural frequency of the crystal.

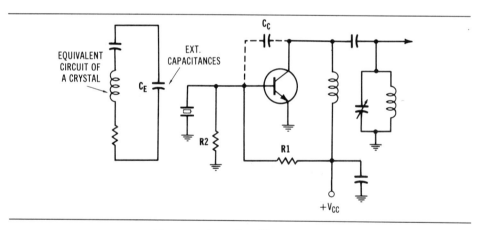

Fig. 3-41. Crystal oscillator circuit.

In fact, the characteristics of the crystal are quite similar to those of a resonant circuit as shown in Fig. 3-41. The crystal is the equivalent of a series resonant circuit having a high inductance and low capacitance. The crystal and the capacitance of its holder, along with the distributed external capacity shunted across the crystal, also form a parallel-resonant circuit. Since the series capacitance of the crystal is low, the external capacitance has only minimum influence on the oscillating frequency.

The feedback between output and input is provided by the collector-to-base capacitance (C_C) of the transistor. In some oscillator circuits, a small amount of external capacitance is connected between collector and base to establish the most favorable feedback condition.

The fundamental resonant frequency of a crystal is a function of its dimension and cut. The higher the frequency of the operation, the smaller the crystal; a very-high-frequency crystal is very small, thin, and fragile. Fortunately crystals can be cut in such a manner that they are able to vibrate in a harmonic mode. Thus it is possible to obtain high-frequency output from a crystal that has lower frequency fundamental dimensions. Such a crystal is much less fragile than one cut for fundamental operation at a very high frequency.

The resonant frequencies of a crystal that correspond to the harmonic vibrations are referred to as *overtone* frequencies rather than harmonic frequencies. This differentiation is made because the overtone frequencies are close, but not exact, integrals of the fundamental frequency.

In general, overtone crystals are sold on the basis of their specific overtone frequency. The most popular overtone crystal is the third-overtone type; less common types are fifth- and seventh-overtone crystals. In a crystal oscillator designed for overtone operation the resonant frequency of the crystal circuit must be tuned to the appropriate overtone crystal frequency. The Q of the crystal at the overtone frequencies is high and good stability of the oscillator is assured. Usually an overtone crystal oscillator has a significantly lower output than that obtained from a fundamental oscillator circuit. Overtone crystals and oscillators are commonly used in communications equipment that is used in the VHF and UHF spectra.

3-11-2. Unijunction Transistor

The unijunction transistor (UJT) functions well as an unusual oscillator capable of generating very short duration low or high frequency pulses. The unijunction transistor consists of an n-type semiconductor bar with a moderately high resistance (Fig. 3-42A). Base 1 and base 2 connections are made at opposite ends of the bar. A small p-type junction is made along the bar and is called an emitter.

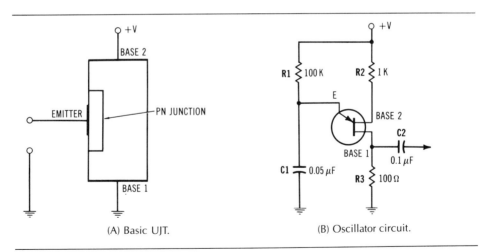

(A) Basic UJT.   (B) Oscillator circuit.

Fig. 3-42. Construction of a UJT and circuit.

Understand that there is a voltage gradient along the bar that becomes progressively more positive from base 1 to base 2. When a voltage applied to the emitter exceeds the voltage gradient at the junction, the pn junction becomes forward-biased and there is a current flow. However, when the conduction holes are injected from the emitter into the bar and the resistance drops between base 1 and emitter, a rapid increase in current is caused over this path.

When the emitter voltage is reduced to below the forward biasing value, the pn junction ceases conduction and the current drops away to zero very quickly.

A typical UJT oscillator circuit is shown in Fig. 3-42B. When the circuit is turned on, capacitor C1 charges toward a positive value through resistor R1. This charging action finally supplies a potential to the emitter which is above the trigger value. Consequently, the unijunction goes into a high current state and a large current is present in the output resistor R3.

The resistance between the emitter and base 1 is now very low. Thus the capacitor is discharged quickly, causing the emitter voltage to drop below the unijunction conduction level. The junction is reverse-biased and the current in output resistor R3 drops very quickly to zero.

The frequency of the unijunction oscillator is determined largely by the time constant of resistor R1 and capacitor C1. This time constant is made very long if a low-frequency pulse train is to be obtained. Lowering the time constant will increase the output frequency. If the duration of the output pulse is to be increased for a given time constant, increase the value of C1 and decrease the value of R1 a like amount. If an adjustable frequency output is desired, resistor R1 can be a fixed resistor and potentiometer combination.

3-12. Field-Effect Transistors

A field-effect transistor (FET) is a three-element device consisting of source, gate, and drain (Fig. 3-43A). It is basically a single-junction (unipolar) device made up of a semiconductor bar (n-type material in the example) into which two facing strips of semiconductor material of the opposite type are diffused.

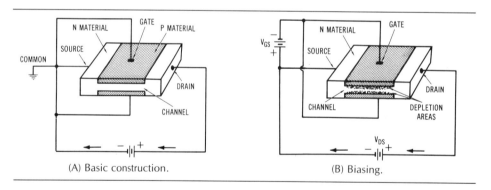

(A) Basic construction.

(B) Biasing.

Fig. 3-43. Construction and biasing of FET.

In FET terminology the bar is called a channel while the element that controls the motion of charges along the channel is known as the gate. The common end of the channel is known as the source while the opposite end is called the drain. When the semiconductor bar is biased as in Fig. 3-43A, there is a motion of electrons from source to drain through the bar or channel. In the fundamental operation of the FET, the gate is able to control this motion of charges along the channel. Let us consider how this is accomplished.

In a practical circuit the gate-to-channel junction is reverse biased, with the source being used as the common connection (Fig. 3-43B). This reverse biasing of the junction causes a depletion region to extend into the channel. The presence of the depletion region in the channel causes an increase in the resistivity of the bar (decrease in conductivity). When the gate bias is increased there is a further penetration of the depletion region, a further rise in the channel resistance, and the motion of charges (drain current) is reduced. If the gate bias voltage is made high enough, the channel or drain current can be reduced to zero, thus producing cutoff.

The basic operation of an FET amplifier, along with a typical circuit and transfer characteristic, is illustrated in Fig. 3-44. An applied audio or other signal causes the gate voltage to vary about the gate bias set by the gate-bias voltage. As the gate voltage varies so does the extent that the depletion region varies back and forth in the channel causing a similar change in the channel resistance. Consequently the gate voltage variation causes a similar variation in the channel or drain current. In fact, as the gate voltage is made to vary with signal, there results a substantial change in the drain current. The actual drain output voltage results from the variation of the drain current in the drain load resistor. The actual voltage gain of the stage is, of course, the ratio of V_O/V_{IN}.

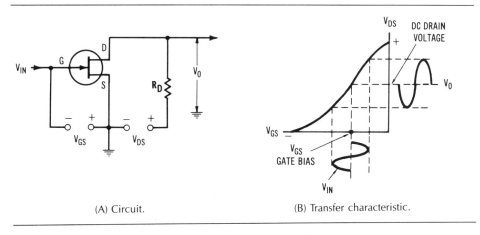

(A) Circuit.   (B) Transfer characteristic.

Fig. 3-44. Basic FET operation.

A positive swing of the gate voltage produces an increase in the drain current. In turn there is a drop in the drain voltage (output voltage swings negative). Conversely the negative alternation of the input voltage decreases the drain current and there is a positive swing of the drain and output voltages. Input and output voltages are said to be of opposite polarity, or out of phase.

In the example the channel was composed of n-type material and therefore the charge carriers (current) were electrons. The gate is composed of hole, or positive, carriers which neutralize some of the electron carriers to produce the depletion region that controls the resistance of the channel. This is known as an n-type junction field-effect transistor.

There are also p-type junction FETs. In this type the current in the channel is the result of the motion of hole charges. The gate has electron carriers and they in turn neutralize the hole carriers to form the depletion region that moves in and out of the channel in accordance with gate-voltage change. Operation is still the same with the channel current being a function of the gate-voltage change. The only difference is that the drain voltage is made negative instead of positive as in the case of the n-type junction FET.

3-12-1. Common-Source Amplifier

The field-effect transistor is basically a voltage amplifier rather than a current amplifier as is the bipolar transistor. There is no significant gate current, and, therefore, the input displays a high impedance to any signal source. The gate circuit responds to an input voltage change rather than an input current change. The output impedance too is moderately high and is higher than that displayed by the usual bipolar transistor.

A practical common-source FET amplifier circuit is given in Fig. 3-45. No external gate bias is necessary. Rather the presence of drain current in source resistor R2 develops the negative gate-to-source DC bias. Resistor R1 can have a high ohmic value because there is no significant gate current. This too aids in keeping the output inpedance high. The resistance of R2 is kept low in value in order to develop the voltage that will bias the transistor stage on the linear portion of its transfer characteristic. Typical values are given for a general purpose small-signal FET.

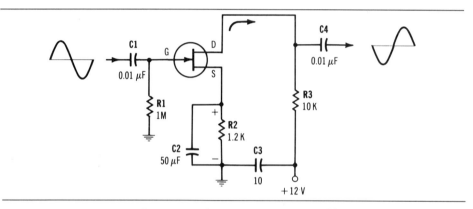

Fig. 3-45. Basic common-source amplifier.

Resistor R3 is the drain load resistor across which the output signal is developed. Its value is selected to maintain the proper DC collector voltage and collector current.

Capacitor C2 prevents an AC voltage from developing across source resistor R2. This AC voltage is degenerative and would reduce the amplifier gain.

3-12-2. Common-Gate Amplifier

In the common-gate configuration (Fig. 3-46) a signal is applied between the source and common, and is removed between the drain and common. The Fig. 3-45 circuit was that of a common-source stage, with the signal being applied to the gate and removed at the drain. The common-gate amplifier is capable of voltage gain but has a current gain that is less than unity. The common-source stage is capable of both voltage and current gain.

The common-gate stage has a very low input impedance and a very much higher output impedance. Therefore it can be used in any circuit where there must be a transformation between low input impedance and high output impedance at the same time there is a possible voltage gain. It is not a particularly common FET circuit although it does have some application in radio-frequency amplifiers.

Component values are approximately the same as those used in the common-source stage of Fig. 3-45. No gate resistor is used. Instead the gate is returned to the

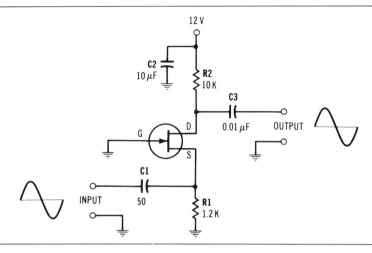

Fig. 3-46. Common-gate amplifier.

common. The signal is applied across the source resistor; this resistance along with the input resistance of the source circuit presents a low impedance to the source of signal. It is necessary to increase the value of the input coupling capacitor because of the much lower input impedance of the common-gate stage. This step maintains the frequency response to a low limit of at least 100 hertz. High-frequency response is well over 20,000 hertz.

When using the common-gate configuration input and output voltages are in phase. In the previous common-source circuit input and output voltages were 180 degrees related. The voltage gain is approximately the same as that obtained with the common-source stage. Maximum undistorted output can be obtained by proper regulation of the resistor R1 and R2 values.

3-12-3. Common-Drain (Source-Follower) Stage

In the *common-drain* configuration the input signal is applied to the gate; the output is removed from the source (Fig. 3-47). The common-drain, or *source-follower*, stage is an effective impedance transformer. The input impedance is very high; output impedance is quite low. Thus the stage is capable of current gain but not voltage gain. In a properly designed stage the output voltage is just slightly less than the input voltage. Such a stage is used mainly in matching a high-impedance source of signal to a low-impedance load. It does so with a minimum loading effect on the source of signal.

The output voltage is in phase with the input voltage. Another advantage of the common-drain stage is its capability of handling a higher input signal level without distortion and, at the same time, placing a very minimum load on the source of the signal.

The practical source-follower stage of Fig. 3-47 uses a general-purpose FET. Resistor R1 in the gate circuit is returned to the junction of resistors R2 and R3. Therefore proper gate bias is applied to the stage and is that voltage developed across resistor R2. Resistors R2 and R3 in combination establish the proper drain voltage and serve as the output load resistance of the circuit.

The stage will operate over a considerable range of audio input signal levels and has a low-frequency response that extends down to at least 100 hertz. High-frequency response extends well above 20,000 hertz.

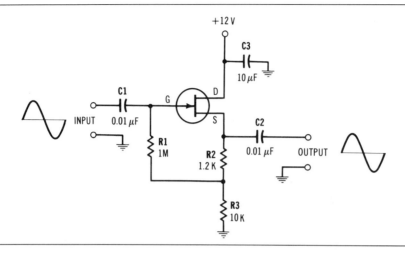

Fig. 3-47. Common-drain stage.

3-12-4. Stabilized Common-Source Amplifier

Two factors have a significant influence on FET bias requirements. One is the production spread, which may be such that the saturation current I_{DSS} may have a ratio of 3-to-1 or higher. Temperature drift is the second factor and involves both the warmup operating-point drift and a shift as the result of change in ambient temperature.

The changes in operating conditions as a result of production spread and temperature are pronounced when external gate bias is used. Self-biasing is much more self-adjusting because a shift in operating-point drain current is compensated for by the change in bias produced by the change of current in the source resistor. Additional operating-point stabilization can be obtained with a further increase in the ohmic value of the source resistor. Normally this would result in an improper bias, but a combination of gate-divider positive bias and a higher value of source bias can be used to set up the required operating point. Refer to Fig. 3-48.

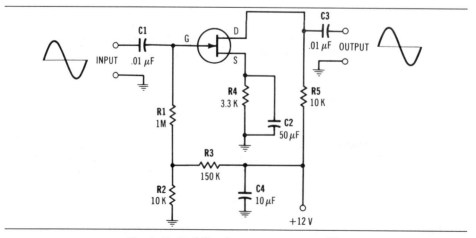

Fig. 3-48. Stabilized common-gate amplifier.

Resistor R4 is increased in value to improve stabilization. However, its ohmic value is too high for obtaining the correct operating bias. Resistors R2 and R3 are added to make appropriate compensation and the combination of the three resistors R2, R3, and R4 establish the correct and stabilized operating bias for the stage. Good stabilization is obtained by increasing the ohmic value of the source resistor three to five times. The ratio of the two resistors (R2 and R3) must then be set to establish correct bias.

3-12-5. Radio-Frequency Amplifier

The field-effect transistor is well suited to radio-frequency applications. A low distortion and a low noise figure that extends up into the VHF and UHF spectra make them ideal for use in radiocommunication receivers. Because of the high-impedance characteristic, simple circuit arrangements can be used.

A principal advantage of the FET in RF service is its low distortion. The field-effect transistor is a square-law device. When a single-frequency RF signal is applied to a square-law amplifier, its nonlinearity is such that three components develop in the output — the fundamental frequency, the second harmonic, and a DC component. The latter is not transferred to the next stage, and the second-harmonic component is so widely separated in frequency from the fundamental that tuned circuits prevent its transfer. Therefore, only the fundamental-frequency signal is conveyed to the next stage. The nature of its characteristics is such that additional higher-order harmonics are not developed. Also, the level of intermodulation distortion is reduced as compared to other devices, because there is less opportunity for the development of spurious beats with other signals.

Low-noise and low-distortion features also make the field-effect transistor an attractive mixer. In an FET mixer the sum or difference frequencies are developed with a minimum of cross-modulation difficulties. Associated circuits, as compared to bipolar transistors, are less complex, and impedance matching and temperature instability are less of a problem.

An example of an unneutralized simple stage is shown in Fig. 3-49A. The circuit is stabilized by shunting an appropriate resistive load across the FET output — either an actual resistor or a low-impedance load. This reduces the stage gain and increases the bandwidth.

Fig. 3-49B is that of a neutralized high-frequency FET amplifier. It has tuned input and output circuits along with an appropriate neutralizing inductor (L_N) that is connected between input and output resonant circuits.

A popular circuit for junction field-effect transistor amplifiers is the cascode arrangement of Fig. 3-49C. This circuit too requires no neutralization. The input stage is connected in a common-source configuration with unity gain; it is followed by a common-gate amplifier. The input stage has a high input impedance and is biased near or at zero. Therefore it provides a suitable load for a high-impedance small-signal source. Most important the input capacitance it presents to any such source is low.

The common-gate stage has a low input impedance. Consequently, a substantial load is placed on the drain circuit of the first stage, and the latter does not operate with gain. The gain is handled by the common-gate output stage which requires no neutralization.

The cascode combination has the gain of a single transistor stage. However, the circuit is unique in that good gain is obtainable, input and output impedance are high, and input and output voltages are in phase. Thus it is a very stable HF, VHF, and UHF amplifier.

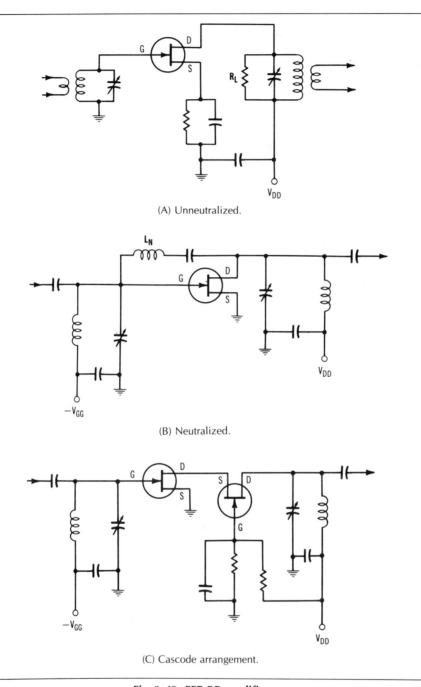

(A) Unneutralized.

(B) Neutralized.

(C) Cascode arrangement.

Fig. 3-49. FET RF amplifiers.

3-13. MOSFET Amplifiers

The structure of the *MOSFET* (metal-oxide semiconductor field-effect transistor) provides some unique characteristics and makes the MOSFET attractive for small-signal and low-noise RF amplifiers and mixers. The characteristics are favorable for use in other high-impedance applications and in chopper and switching circuits. In the structural arrangement (Fig. 3-50A) the gate electrode acts as a control element just as it does in a junction field-effect transistor. However, that control is exerted whether the gate is swinging positive or negative. In the normal operation of a junction type the gate exerts an influence only when the junction is reverse biased.

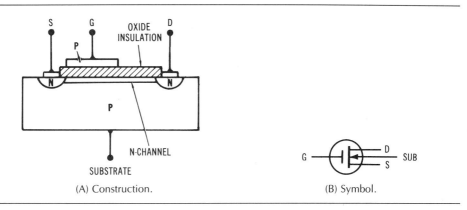

(A) Construction.   (B) Symbol.

Fig. 3-50. Depletion MOSFET.

In the MOSFET construction a thin gate layer is insulated from the semiconductor material that forms the channel by a thin layer of silicon dioxide. The electrical field that results when the gate is biased appropriately influences the active carriers in the source-drain channel. Since there is insulation instead of an actual junction between the gate and channel, the leakage current is very low and is little affected by temperature. A very high input impedance results. The gate and channel, separated by an oxide layer, are in effect the plates of a capacitor.

The arrangement of Fig. 3-50A shows the structure of a depletion-type MOSFET. In this example, the channel material is n-type and there are excess electrons. As the gate is made negative relative to the source, the number of electrons in the channel is depleted (reduced). This action is similar to that of a junction FET. However, during normal operation the gate of a junction FET may not be permitted to swing significantly past zero because the junction will then be forward-biased, thus decreasing the input impedance. The MOSFET has no such limitation. If the metal gate is made to swing past zero there is no increase in input current or decrease in input impedance, and the gate maintains its control of channel conductivity. This can be shown in the characteristic curves of Fig. 3-51. Note that the gate voltage can be made to swing either positive or negative.

A popular type of MOSFET construction is the enhancement-mode arrangement of Fig. 3-52. Note that in its basic structure there appears to be no actual channel between the source and the drain. However, the gate itself does span this region; when a positive bias is applied to the gate, a conduction path between the source and the drain is established. The conductivity of this path is a function of the charge on the gate. In this manner, the magnitude of the drain current is controlled.

The unusual characteristic of the enhancement-type MOSFET is that it is normally cut off (no drain current) until the application of the positive gate voltage. The application of a gate voltage causes the drain-source current to increase. The more positive the gate-source voltage is, the higher is the drain current. This is shown in the characteristic curves of Fig. 3-53.

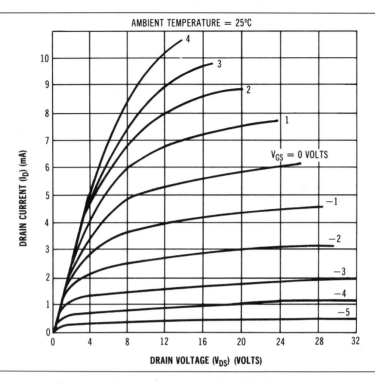

Fig. 3-51. Characteristic curve of a depletion MOSFET.

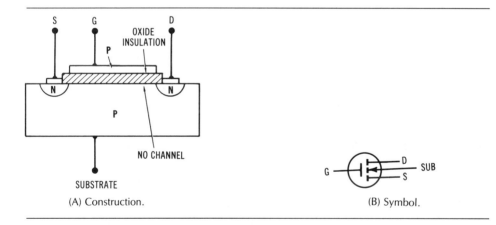

(A) Construction.   (B) Symbol.

Fig. 3-52. Enhancement MOSFET.

The high input impedance is both an advantage and a hazard of the MOSFET device. Since the input impedance is so high, a very tiny current or static charge is able to build up a high voltage on the gate which can possibly damage the device. Thus MOSFETs must be handled carefully and circuit arrangements must be such that excessive charges are kept off the gate. Another way of avoiding this hazard is by using gate-protective diodes built within the device (Fig. 3-54). These diodes are electrically connected between gate and source, bypassing those voltage transients which could damage the device.

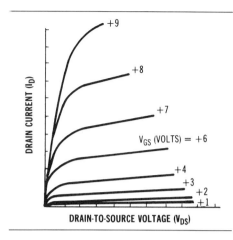

Fig. 3-53. Enhancement MOSFET curves.

The two- or dual-gate arrangement provides a separate gate for signal and for applying an external control bias. The dual-gate configuration can be used conveniently in mixer and other balanced circuit arrangements. The dual-gate plan also makes possible a reduction in feedback capacitance obtained by AC grounding of the second gate. Thus the device can be used favorably in amplifier circuits without neutralization. Local-oscillator feedthrough to the antenna is reduced.

A typical VHF amplifier using a MOSFET transistor is given in Fig. 3-55A. The input signal is applied through an appropriate tuned circuit and matching arrangement to gate 1. An AGC bias voltage is applied to gate 2 and is able to regulate the gain of the RF stage in accordance with the magnitude of the incoming signal. No neutralization is used and, if desired, the output can be matched to a low-impedance load.

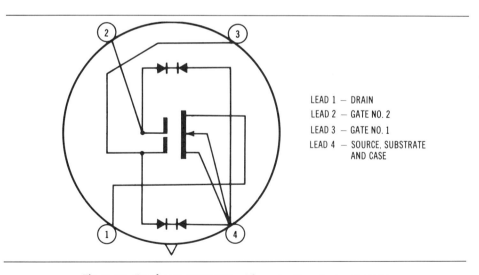

LEAD 1 — DRAIN
LEAD 2 — GATE NO. 2
LEAD 3 — GATE NO. 1
LEAD 4 — SOURCE, SUBSTRATE
              AND CASE

Fig. 3-54. Dual-gate MOSFET with protective diodes (40673).

A dual-gate mixer is shown in Fig. 3-55B. In this circuit, the signal is applied to gate 1 while local-oscillator injection is made via gate 2. Circuit arrangement is simple and compact fine-performing mixers can be constructed around dual-gate MOSFETs. Such circuits are found widely in the receivers of modern radiocommunications equipment.

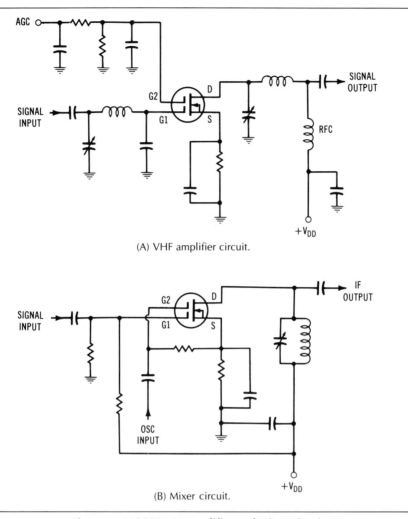

(A) VHF amplifier circuit.

(B) Mixer circuit.

Fig. 3-55. MOSFET RF amplifier and mixer circuits.

3-14. FET Oscillators and Class-C Amplifiers

Field-effect transistors have become common in transmitters and two-way radio transceivers. Their principal uses are likely to be in oscillator, low-level RF amplifier, multiplier, audio, modulator, and demodulator circuits. Of course, applications involving high-powered RF circuits can be anticipated.

Field-effect transistors have characteristics that are ideal for use in the crystal oscillators that appear in transmitters, transmitter test and calibration circuits, and receive sections of two-way transceivers. A high-Q resonant circuit, important in the design of an easy-starting oscillator, is not loaded by an FET.

Either the Pierce or the Miller oscillator can be employed (Fig. 3-56). The Pierce oscillator has the advantage of not requiring any tuning; it can be operated over a wide frequency range simply by plugging in an appropriate crystal. The Miller circuit permits a higher output, and the drain (output) circuit is tunable.

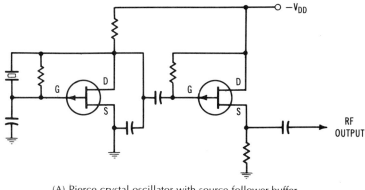

(A) Pierce crystal oscillator with source-follower buffer.

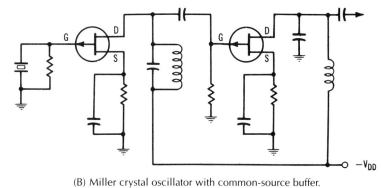

(B) Miller crystal oscillator with common-source buffer.

Fig. 3-56. FET crystal oscillators and buffers.

As a solid-state oscillator, the field-effect transistor is superior to the bipolar type. A bipolar stage has a low impedance and can be troubled with feedback and starting problems if the crystal is not especially active. Also, the bipolar crystal oscillator must be forward-biased slightly or it will not start. In a field-effect circuit, biasing is a matter of control rather than of necessity.

If a low-impedance output is desired, the crystal oscillator can be followed by a source-follower or common-source amplifier. There is a minimum load on the crystal oscillator, and operation is little affected by any load that is connected to the output of the source follower.

A typical FET class-B or class-C amplifier is shown in Fig. 3-57A and B. External bias can be used. Biasing according to class of operation is shown in the transfer characteristic (Fig. 3-57C). For class-A operation the biasing is at the center of the linear portion of the transfer curve. To operate the amplifier class B it is necessary that the level of external bias match the cutoff bias of the transistor. A class-C stage is, of course, biased beyond cutoff.

The input impedance of an FET RF amplifier can be kept at its highest by making certain that the peak of the positive alternation of the input signal does not extend to the near-zero bias level that results in gate current. However, for more convenient and efficient operation and a somewhat lower input impedance, the stage may be operated in such a manner that the gate current is drawn at the peak of the positive alternation. In such an arrangement, one can use gate current to establish the required class-B or class-C operation, using the circuit arrangement of Fig. 3-57B. The direction of the gate current is such that a negative bias is developed on the gate capacitor. With a proper time constant, this capacitor charge remains constant and serves as the DC gate bias for the stage. As mentioned, the input impedance is now lower, and somewhat more input power is required.

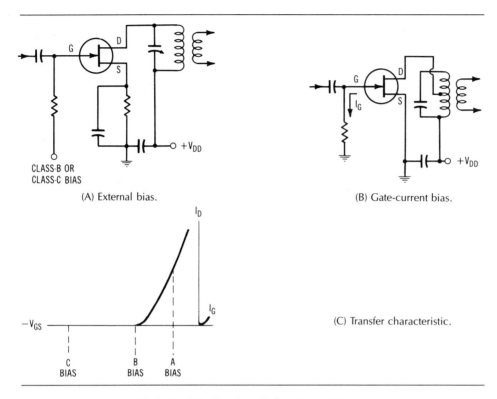

(A) External bias.

(B) Gate-current bias.

(C) Transfer characteristic.

Fig. 3-57. FET class-B and class-C amplifiers.

When the RF excitation is removed from its input, the drain current rises. It is advisable to use a protective source resistor which limits the drain current to a safe value in case RF excitation is lost.

The waveforms, shown in Fig. 3-58, demonstrate the operation of the FET class-C stage. The transistor draws drain current during only part of the positive peak of the input wave. Thus, the drain current is drawn in bursts that supply electrical energy into the drain resonant circuit, charging the capacitor to a high negative value (sharp drop in drain voltage). However, a resonant circuit has a smoothing and energy-storing capability. When the bursts of drain current cease, the charge on the capacitor begins to fall off, and energy is transferred to the coil. After the charge reaches zero, the collapsing field of the coil releases its stored energy back into the tank circuit. The current reverses, and the capacitor is charged to an opposite polarity (positive), even though the drain current has stopped. The magnetic field around the coil is now of opposite polarity. When the capacitor loses its peak charge, the magnetic field again collapses, and a new cycle begins.

Soon after, a new burst of drain current is introduced because of the positive swing of the gate input. Again the capacitor in the drain tank circuit is charged to a maximum negative value, adding energy to the circuit. Although the RF amplifier operates class C and drain current is not present for the full input cycle, a good sine wave is developed across the drain tank circuit when the proper choice of inductance, capacitance, and load has been made. The magnitude of the sine wave depends on the drain supply voltage. Over a substantial range, RF output voltage is a linear function of the drain supply voltage.

The positive peak of the input wave draws a small gate current, which develops a negative charge on the gate capacitor (C_G in Fig. 3-57B). The current is such that the charge placed on the capacitor biases the gate beyond cutoff. Between intervals of gate current, the charge leaks off the capacitor through the gate resistor (R_G). If the time constant of $R_G \times C_G$ is high enough, a reasonably constant bias is maintained during the entire cycle of the input wave. This is equivalent to a DC voltage value that is significantly higher than the cutoff values. Of course, the capacitor is restored to full charge by the gate current at the crest of each positive input wave.

The length of time that drain current exists can be expressed as a number of degrees (angle) out of a full cycle (360 degrees). The angle of the drain current is a function of the desired efficiency, the output level, and the quality of the waveform. Values can occur between 90 and 150 degrees. The gate-current angle is significantly shorter because gate current is present only at the very peak of the RF input wave. This can be seen in the waveforms of Fig. 3-58.

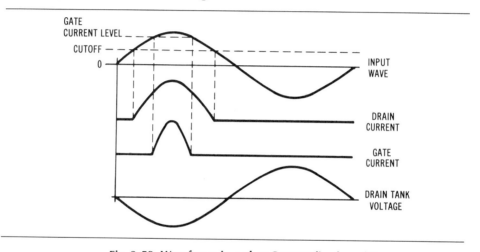

Fig. 3-58. Waveforms in a class-C neutralized amplifier.

3-14-1. VMOS Power FET

The conventional JFET and MOSFET transistors are fundamentally low-power devices. The regular FET is a horizontal-motion device (Fig. 3-59A) because the charge motion along the body or channel flows horizontally from source to drain. This limits the current density, compelling the chip area to be large and the cost high if any significant power capability is to be obtained.

However, this power limitation has been eliminated with the development of the VMOS (vertical metal-oxide semiconductor) field-effect transistor (Fig. 3-59B). The V-groove gate region and associated arrangement of elements permits a vertical motion of charges and a much greater current density is possible. It is an enhancement-mode transistor and requires that the gate and drain both be positive relative to the source if there is to be a motion of charges. Note the characteristics shown in Fig. 3-60. Before there is a drain current the gate voltage must be made positive. At zero volts and negative voltages the drain current is cut off.

In operation the positive gate sets up an n-type channel on both sides of the p-type body. Electrons flow from the source through the n-type channel and the epi (epitaxial) region to the substrate. The substrate serves as the drain connection for the VMOS device. The higher width-to-length of the VMOS channel plus other factors provide a much greater current density and a higher power-handling capability. The power capability is now comparable to that of bipolar devices without some of the disadvantages.

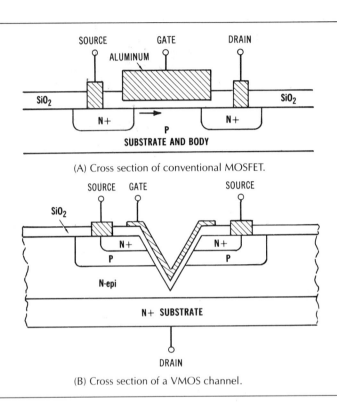

(A) Cross section of conventional MOSFET.

(B) Cross section of a VMOS channel.

Fig. 3-59. Structure of MOSFET and VMOS.

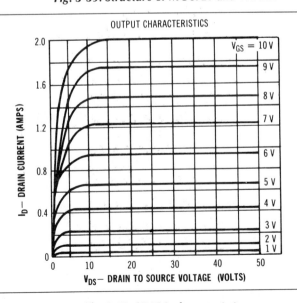

Fig. 3-60. VMOS characteristics.

The VMOS is a high-impedance voltage-driven device that provides good linearity and low distortion. A given device can function well as either a weak- or strong-signal device. As it heats, its characteristic is to draw less current instead of more. Consequently the thermal runaway hazard does not exist. It is not subject to secondary or mismatch breakdown. Furthermore there is no change in input capacity with changes in drive level and frequency.

A VMOS connected in a Pierce crystal-oscillator circuit is shown in Fig. 3-61. A good output is obtained using a 12-volt supply. Higher output can be obtained by increasing the drain voltage to 18–24 volts. The circuit differs from the conventional FET arrangement because the VMOS is an enhancement device and it is necessary to supply a starting bias by way of resistors R1 and R2. The value of resistor R3 can be regulated to control the output level and shape of the output wave. In general the lower the output, the more sinusoidal is the output waveform. The oscillator will operate on fundamental crystals from 1 to 25 MHz and possibly higher with adjustment of component values. A higher output can be obtained by using a resonant drain circuit instead of untuned.

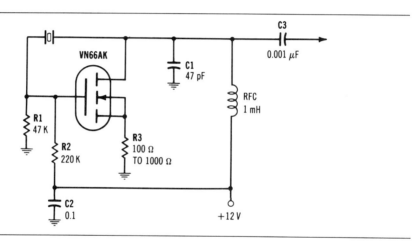

Fig. 3-61. VMOS crystal oscillator.

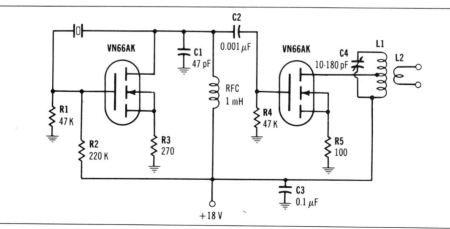

Fig. 3-62. VMOS oscillator-amplifier circuit for HF operation.

A VMOS crystal oscillator and followup class-C amplifier for high-frequency operation is shown in Fig. 3-62. The output of the Pierce crystal oscillator is resistor-capacitor coupled to the gate of the output stage. No DC bias is supplied to this gate. Positive alternations of the signal from the crystal oscillator draw bursts of drain current through the output resonant circuit. A tapped inductor provides an appropriate impedance match to the VMOS output. A low-impedance winding provides matching to an antenna system or followup low impedance load.

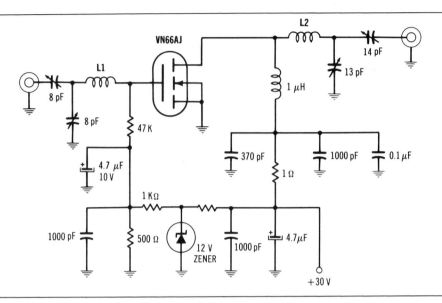

Fig. 3-63. VMOS VHF amplifier.

A typical VMOS VHF amplifier is given in Fig. 3-63. T-networks provide input and output matching from a low-impedance source and into a low-impedance load. The combination capacitive dividers provide impedance matching and, at the same time, in conjunction with the appropriate gate and drain inductors, resonate the input and output circuits to the desired VHF frequency. Supply voltage is applied to the drain through an appropriate 1-µH radio-frequency choke. Optimum biasing for the gate is by way of a 12-volt zener diode that is linked to supply voltage point. An appropriate resistive divider then taps off the voltage required at the gate of the VMOS VHF amplifier.

3-15. Integrated Circuits

Integrated circuits are now being produced in the millions and are found extensively in two-way radio and test equipment. Inside each small package are components numbering from a few to tens of thousands of items. One device may function in a routine way in a simple system; another will perform a complex function in a complex electronic system. Each device may just be a simple amplifier or a complete system.

There are two basic types: linear and digital. Under the linear category are various types of amplifiers (radio-frequency, intermediate-frequency, and audio-frequency), oscillators, modulators and demodulators, waveform generators, special arrays, etc. Linear types will be described in this chapter. There is also a great variety of digital integrated circuits. These will be covered in a later chapter on digital electronics.

There are two basic integrated circuit structures: monolithic and hybrid. The monolithic types are, by far, the more common with the entire integrated circuit completed as a single silicon chip. All circuit components are an inherent part of the structure. All components are inseparable in a continuous array of silicon atoms of proper polarization and differing degrees of impurity. Interconnections between components and connections to the output leads are handled by metalized patterns included in the manufacturing process. Thin wire leads connect the terminals to the pins of the integrated circuit casing, whether they are round, flat pack, or the most common, the dual in-line configuration (Fig. 3-64).

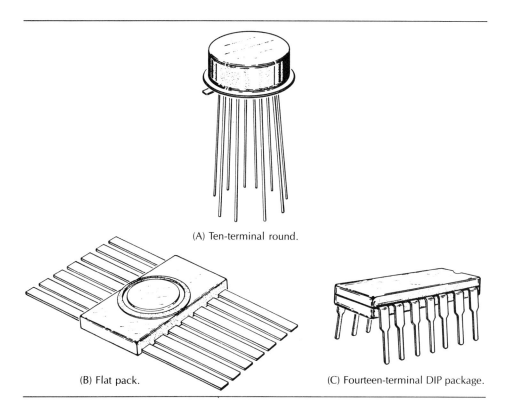

(A) Ten-terminal round.

(B) Flat pack.

(C) Fourteen-terminal DIP package.

Fig. 3-64. Integrated-circuit packages.

The structure of a monolithic IC is built around a single silicon specimen. More than one monolithic device can be incorporated in a single case. Electrical isolation among various devices and components is handled by polarization of the various layers and the deposition of special insulating strata. Isolating dielectric barriers separate individual monolithic components or groups of components both electrically and physically. In a hybrid structure, as the name implies, metallic depositions or wire bonds interconnect very tiny active and discrete components within a small case. A hybrid circuit can contain one or several individual monolithic structures plus discrete components in its design. Integrated circuit fabrication is simply an extension, elaboration, and miniaturization of the basic solid-state techniques. The transistor remains the key device; bipolar, FET, and MOSFET. Processed simultaneously along with these basic devices are diodes and resistors. Also there may be occasional capacitors, coils, and other components.

3-15-1. Differential Amplifiers

The differential amplifier is a key circuit of many ICs. The circuit (Fig. 3-65) is basically an emitter-coupled configuration. It has fine stability and a good rejection of undesired signal components. Being direct coupled, no interstage coupling capacitors are needed, providing a saving in space. Correct differential operation requires that the two collector resistances be identical in both ohmic value and general characteristics. In the fabrication of integrated circuits, these conditions are met quite readily and at low cost as compared to a similar amplifier designed to use discrete circuit components.

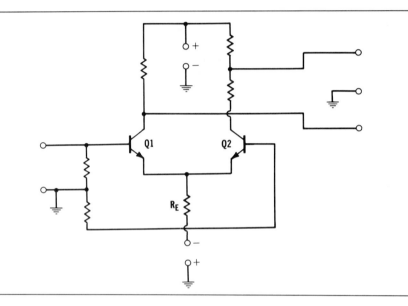

Fig. 3-65. Basic differential amplifier.

In basic operation, the differential amplifier responds to the signal difference that exists between the base inputs, developing equal-amplitude and out-of-phase collector signals. This type of input is called a *differential-mode* input signal.

When two equal-amplitude but same-polarity signals are applied to the base inputs, the AC signals across the common-emitter resistor are subtractive. In a situation of perfect balance, the differential amplifier thus performs in a bridge-like manner and there is no output from collector to collector. A much reduced output signal appears from each collector to common.

In-phase signals at the bases are referred to as common-mode input signals. This is usually in the form of any undesired signal, such as hum and interference components. Thus, another advantage of the differential amplifier is its ability to reject and reduce common-mode signals.

In the differential-mode operation, a signal applied to the base of transistor Q1 (Fig. 3-65) appears at the collector output of transistor Q1 and also across the common-emitter resistor. The latter signal component serves as the input signal for transistor Q2. Consequently, a signal of opposite polarity appears at the collector of transistor Q2. In effect, the differential amplifier acts as a phase splitter, developing two equal-amplitude but opposite-polarity signal components at the output.

The differential amplifier has a high order of DC stability, reducing the influence of supply voltage changes, temperature, etc. Supply voltage variations, in general, create a common-mode type of interference which the differential circuit inherently reduces. Thus, it is a stable DC amplifier and is very practical when designing the multistage circuits that are so common in ICs. Not only does the basic circuit have no need for interstage coupling capacitors, but the emitter bypass is also eliminated.

In the rejection of common-mode signals, one depends on the degenerating effects of the common-emitter resistor. The higher the ohmic value of this resistance is, the greater is the rejection. Such increase is limited by supply voltage requirements and the difficulty involved in including high-value resistors in integrated circuits.

One answer to obtaining high stability and good rejection of common-mode signals is to include a constant-current emitter source composed of an additional active component rather than a high-value resistor. The fundamental arrangement is shown in Fig. 3-66. In this circuit, the combination of the transistor and its low-value emitter resistor acts as the high-resistance constant-current source. The presence of a common-mode signal on the differential transistors affects both voltages and junction resistances. A constant-current source holds the emitter and collector currents constant. In fact, the undesired voltage change appears totally across the constant-current source circuit, which is unbypassed and, therefore, highly degenerative. Thus, the differential gain of the amplifier, in terms of the common mode, is greatly reduced.

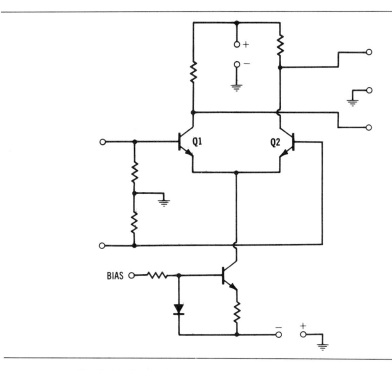

Fig. 3-66. Constant-current source using an active component.

Additionally, diodes in the base circuit of this constant-current source provide temperature compensation. When the characteristics of the base-emitter junction of the constant-current transistor and the diode junction are identical, there is exact compensation. An increase in the conductance of the base-emitter junction results from a rise in temperature. Since the compensating diode junction is physically near the transistor, there follows a similar change in its conductance. As a result, a compensation is made in the base bias, thus keeping the collector-emitter current constant. The basic circuit of Fig. 3-66 is very common in integrated circuits.

3-15-2. Darlington Configuration

The previous differential amplifiers have low input impedances. When a high impedance is required, Darlington circuitry is included in the integrated circuits. An additional transistor is included for each pair as shown in Fig. 3-67.

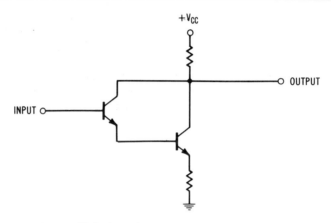

(A) Basic Darlington pair configurations.

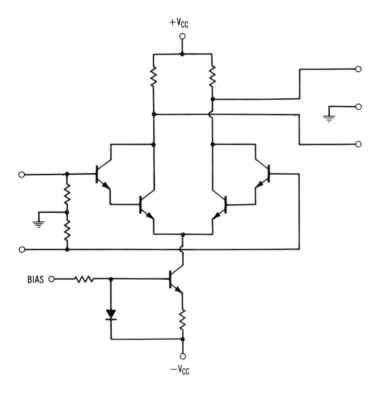

(B) Differential amplifier using Darlington pairs.

Fig. 3-67. Use of Darlington circuits in differential amplifiers.

In the normal operation of a transistor, the emitter junction is forward-biased and conducts. Input resistance is low and approximates the product of beta times the emitter resistance:

$$R_{IN} = \beta R_E$$

To a degree, the input resistance can be increased by increasing the ohmic value of the emitter resistance. There is a resultant sacrifice in gain and a need for a higher supply potential. The Darlington-pair approach is to use the input resistance of a second transistor as the emitter resistance of the first (Fig. 3-67A). The input stage then operates with a highly degenerative emitter circuit and a resultant high input impedance. Both stages contribute an output with a net gain figure that is comparable to that obtained using a single transistor of the same type but operating with a much lower input resistance. Two such identical circuits are needed for the separate inputs of the differential configurations shown in Fig. 3-67B.

The advantages of a differential amplifier match the needs of integrated circuits. The IC fabrication process permits the attainment of exceptional balance because all the components of the circuit are processed simultaneously. They have identical characteristics and can be placed near each other. They display similar temperature coefficients and maintain stable electrical characteristics over a wide temperature range. Good input and output isolation are inherent and no neutralization is required. This is basic to simple feedback systems.

Either no capacitors, or very few, are needed in differential circuitry. Large-value resistors can be avoided, and exact absolute resistor values are not critical, because differential amplifier performance depends mainly on resistance ratios.

The differential amplifier is a versatile configuration, lending itself well for use as an amplifier, oscillator, limiter, modulator, demodulator, mixer, or several other applications. Its ability to emphasize the desired signal and de-emphasize common-mode components was mentioned previously, along with its capability for highly linear amplification.

Differential amplifiers can be operated in various modes. The mode described in the foregoing is referred to as the differential-input differential-output mode.

The differential amplifier has three additional operational modes (Fig. 3-68). In the circuit shown in Fig. 3-68A the signal is applied to the base of transistor Q1 and removed at the collector of transistor Q1. A positive input swing results in a negative swing between the collector of transistor Q1 and common. This is known as the single-ended input, single-ended output, inverting mode.

Fig. 3-68B shows the input at the base of transistor Q1 and the output between the collector of transistor Q2 and common. The input swings positive and so does the collector voltage of transistor Q2. The output and input voltages are in phase. This operation is known as the single-ended input, single-ended output, noninverting mode.

In the final manner of operation (Fig. 3-68C), the input voltage is applied from base to base and the output voltage can be removed from either of the collectors. This is known as differential input, single-ended output mode.

The various modes of operation require that gain be specified in one of three ways. First, differential-voltage gain is the ratio of collector-voltage change to the difference voltage between the two bases. Second, the double-ended differential-voltage gain is the ratio of collector-to-collector voltage change to the base voltage change. Finally, the single-ended differential-voltage gain refers to the ratio of collector-to-common change to the base-voltage change.

The internal schematic of a simple integrated circuit is given in Fig. 3-69. It consists of four transistors and six resistors that can be connected into any desired configuration including a differential amplifier. Separate base inputs are available and all emitters are joined together and connected to pin 4. An external high-value resistor or a constant-current source can be connected to the emitters for stabilizing a differential amplifier.

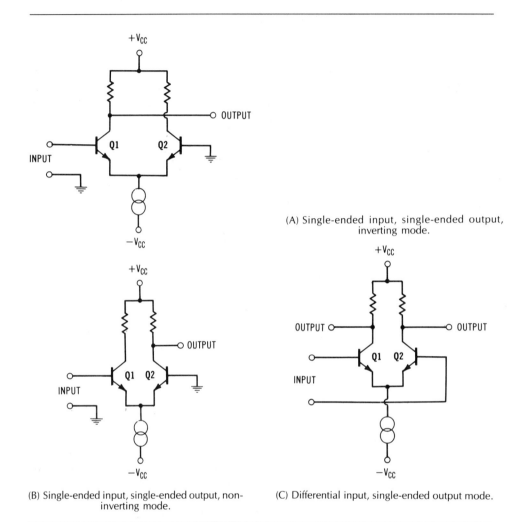

(A) Single-ended input, single-ended output, inverting mode.

(B) Single-ended input, single-ended output, non-inverting mode.

(C) Differential input, single-ended output mode.

Fig. 3-68. Operating modes of a differential amplifier.

The two symbols of Fig. 3-69B indicate the manner in which linear integrated circuits are often represented. The triangular symbolization is the more common and provides a simpler associated schematic diagram with the inputs and output isolated from each other in the resultant schematic layout.

A typical schematic diagram for a differential amplifier using this integrated circuit is given in Fig. 3-70. Base inputs 1 and 2 are paralleled and input signal from an audio generator can be applied. A differential-mode input is obtained by connecting bases 3 and 5 to ground through an appropriate capacitor. The two 1-megohm resistors provide biasing for the four bases. An emitter resistor is connected between pin 4 and ground.

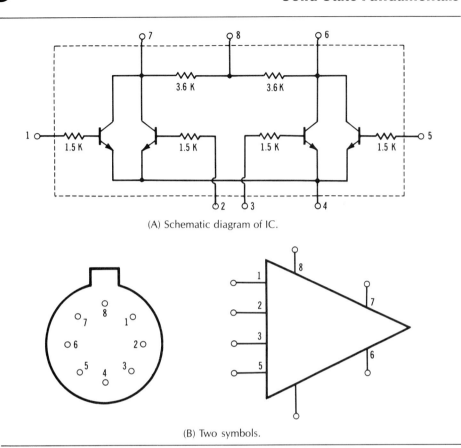

(A) Schematic diagram of IC.

(B) Two symbols.

Fig. 3-69. Integrated circuit and symbols.

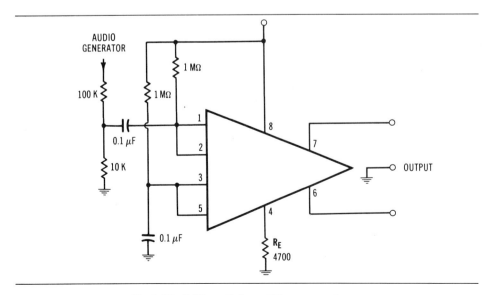

Fig. 3-70. Differential amplifier connections.

A balanced output is obtained between pins 6 and 7. An unbalanced output can be obtained between 6 and common or between 7 and common. The output can be selected depending on whether the differential amplifier is to have an inverted or noninverted output signal.

3-16. Types of Integrated Circuits

An *operational amplifier* is a special form of linear integrated circuit with high DC and AC gain and high stability. Its many applications include digital as well as linear functions. Some of these are signal amplification, waveform generation and shaping, analog-digital conversion, impedance transformation, instrumentation, etc.

When the amplifier no-feedback gain (open-loop gain) is adequate and a feedback system is of correct design, the closed-loop gain and characteristics of the operational amplifier become a function of only the feedback components. Basically the relative ohmic values of two external resistors can be used to set the operating gain for a particular operational amplifier.

The operational amplifier or *op amp* is a multistage affair that includes the popular monolithic differential amplifier as well as other types of amplifiers, level shifting, matching, and voltage regulation stages. A typical operational amplifier is shown in Fig. 3-71. It consists of a pair of differential amplifiers and a cascaded single-ended output stage. The first differential amplifier uses transistors Q1 and Q2 along with constant-current transistor Q6. There is also a temperature-compensating diode (D1). The second amplifier consists of transistors Q3, Q4, Q7, and diode D2.

The feedback circuit of transistor Q5 reduces any common-mode error signal. It does this by evaluating the signal at the emitters of transistors Q3 and Q4. When the second differential amplifier is driven push pull, there should be a zero level at this point, indicating proper operation of both the first differential amplifier and the input system of the second. If an error voltage is present, a correcting voltage is developed across resistor R2 (in the differential collector circuit) by transistor Q5. This same transistor (Q5) also introduces an error bias into the constant-current transistor circuit (Q7) to bring a further reduction in common-mode signal.

The emitter circuit of this important stabilizing transistor (Q5) also supplies a DC error voltage to the base of transistors Q7 and Q9. Common-mode DC stabilization results. For example, a decline in supply voltage reduces the base bias at transistors Q7 and Q9. Since the collector of Q9 is linked to the base of transistor Q10 and to the emitter of transistor Q8, there is a similar change there as well as at the bases of transistors Q3 and Q4. The net result is to produce increases in collector voltages and compensate for the supply voltage decline. The feedback stabilization furnished by transistor Q5 offers excellent common-mode rejection, tolerance to supply voltage change, and high open-loop stability.

The output of the second differential amplifier supplies drive to the base of the emitter-follower transistor (Q8). In turn, transistor Q8 supplies a signal to the base of the single-ended emitter-follower output transistor (Q10). There is a limited amount of signal gain contributed by the output circuit as a result of the *bootstrap* (small amount of positive feedback) from the emitter of transistor Q10 to the emitter of transistor Q9. Therefore, transistor Q9 serves a dual purpose — as a constant-current source for the drive transistor and as a part of the bootstrap. The output system also provides a DC-level shift and the level at terminal 9 now corresponds to the no-signal input level.

The feedback plan of the operational amplifier provides high stability and characteristics that can be, if desired, related directly to the external feedback network. An operational amplifier has additional favorable attributes. The bandwidth of some

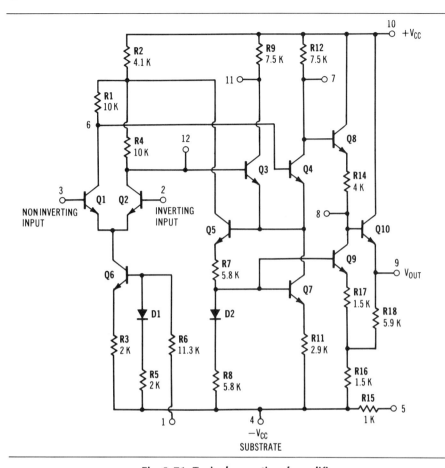

Fig. 3-71. Typical operational amplifier.

extends uniformly from DC up to several hundred megahertz. Common-mode rejection is excellent and there is little DC offset or drift with temperature. If desired, the input impedance of some types can be made very high, and the power input and current requirements made insignificant.

Most operational amplifiers have single-ended outputs and push-pull inputs. There are some operational amplifiers with single-ended inputs, although these are not versatile and may have only a specialized function. An advantage of the differential input in this respect is demonstrated in Fig. 3-72. When signal is applied to one of the differential inputs (Fig. 3-72A), the output is not inverted (same polarity). If the signal is transferred to the second input, an inverted (opposite polarity) signal appears at the output (Fig. 3-72B). In terms of an AC input signal, this means that an input can be selected to produce either an in-phase or an out-of-phase output signal. Ordinarily, the input terminals of operational amplifiers are labeled as either the inverting input (−) or the noninverting input (+).

Equivalent diagrams of inverting and noninverting operational amplifier configurations are given in Fig. 3-73. These are closed-loop equivalents with a portion of the output transferred back to one side of the differential input by way of resistors Z_F and Z_R. Resistor Z_R, of necessity, must include the source impedance as well as bias components when used. Inasmuch as there is a differential input, the DC return path to common from both sides must be equal. Therefore, the ohmic value of resistor R_R must be made equal to the ohmic resistance Z_R and must consider the resistance of the signal source (V_{IN}).

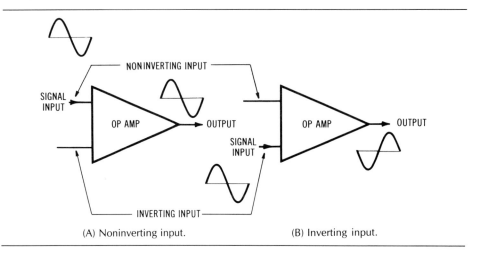

(A) Noninverting input.　　　　　(B) Inverting input.

Fig. 3-72. Operational amplifier inputs.

The input impedance (Z_i) and output impedance Z_o are intrinsic to the operational amplifier. The output generator has a value of A_oV_{IN}. The term A_o is the open-loop differential voltage gain. (The closed-loop gain is lower than this value because of the influence of the feedback.)

The load resistance (R_L) is also shown although it is assumed in this discussion of the basic equivalents that its value is high in comparison to the output impedance of the operational amplifier. Therefore, it can for the moment be neglected.

The closed-loop gain expression is very simple.

$$A_V = \frac{V_{OUT}}{V_{IN}} = \frac{Z_F}{Z_R}$$

Note that the gain of the inverting configuration (Fig. 3-73A) is entirely dependent on the values of the external feedback components. This is true only if certain requirements are met. The open-loop differential voltage gain must be very high. The intrinsic input impedance (Z_i) must be much greater than the value of Z_R and the paralleling feedback components. The intrinsic output impedance (Z_o) must be smaller than the feedback value (Z_F).

Similar operational requirements can be safely assumed for the noninverting configuration (Fig. 3-73B). The signal is applied to the noninverting side while the feedback component must of necessity be applied to the inverted side of the differential input. The basic equation for the closed loop voltage gain is:

$$A_V = \frac{V_{OUT}}{V_{IN}} = \frac{Z_R + Z_F}{Z_R}$$

A knowledge of the configuration equivalents for inverting and noninverting operation permits an easier understanding of an operational equivalent circuit which includes the influence of the output load. This basic equivalent applies to both inverting and noninverting operation (Fig. 3-74). Within the equivalent, the terms Z_{IN}

and Z_{OUT} will have different values for the inverting and the noninverting modes. The values for Z_{IN} and Z_{OUT} take into consideration the values of the feedback components. Even though the expression Z_R is included within the equivalent dashed block, one must make certain that its value includes the influence of the source impedance. For these reasons, the equivalent is appropriate for both configurations of an operational amplifier.

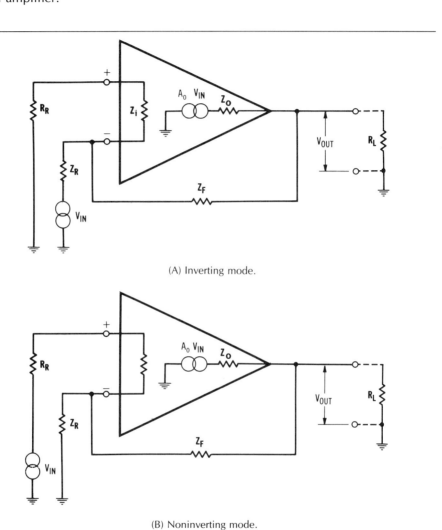

(A) Inverting mode.

(B) Noninverting mode.

Fig. 3-73. Equivalent diagrams of op amp configuration.

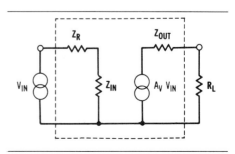

Fig. 3-74. Closed-loop equivalent, including output load.

The voltage of the output generator is the product of the closed-loop voltage gain of the operational amplifier times the input voltage, or $A_V V_{IN}$. This voltage divides between the output impedance and the load. Hence, the output voltage itself becomes:

$$V_{OUT} = A_V V_{IN} \frac{R_L}{R_L + Z_{OUT}}$$

and the stage gain becomes:

$$\text{Voltage gain} = \frac{V_{OUT}}{V_{IN}} = \frac{A_V R_L}{R_L + Z_{OUT}}$$

If the ohmic value of the output impedance (Z_{OUT}) is low in comparison to the ohmic value of the load resistance, there is a further simplification of the equation for voltage gain. For the inverting mode:

$$\text{Voltage gain} = A_V \cong \frac{Z_F}{Z_R}$$

and for the noninverting mode:

$$\text{Voltage gain} = A_V \cong \frac{Z_R + Z_F}{Z_R}$$

In summary, the operational amplifier is a DC and AC amplifier of high stability. It can operate with a low gain or a high gain, depending on the values of three external resistors. In fact, the actual gain of the amplifier depends on external resistance ratios rather than internal components.

The two common input arrangements are shown in Fig. 3-75. The example in Fig. 3-75A shows a noninverting amplifier with the amplified output voltage being of the same polarity as the input. Balanced operation occurs when the input resistances at

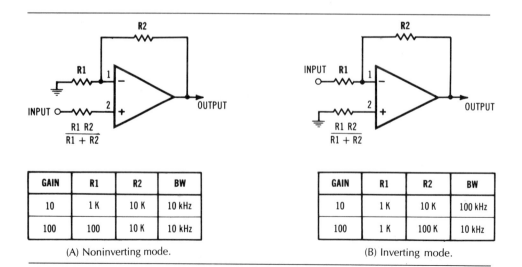

GAIN	R1	R2	BW
10	1 K	10 K	10 kHz
100	100	10 K	10 kHz

(A) Noninverting mode.

GAIN	R1	R2	BW
10	1 K	10 K	100 kHz
100	1 K	100 K	10 kHz

(B) Inverting mode.

Fig. 3-75. Operational amplifier operating modes.

the input terminals are identical. In the calculation of the input resistance it is always necessary to consider the influence of the feedback resistance. In the case of the noninverting amplifier, input 1 resistance is equal to R1. However, signal-input 2 resistance has an ohmic value which must match the parallel combination of resistors R1 and R2.

Typical gain and resistance values are listed in the charts. Note that gain increases when there is a higher ratio between the ohmic values of resistors R2 and R1. This is to be anticipated because there is less feedback. Likewise, the bandwidth is reduced.

To obtain an inverted output as in Fig. 3-75B the signal is applied to the same input as the feedback component. Again the resistance values determine the stage gain. Stage gain approximates the ratio of feedback resistance R2 over the input resistance (R1). This can be verified from the chart by dividing the ohmic value of resistor R1 into that of resistor R2.

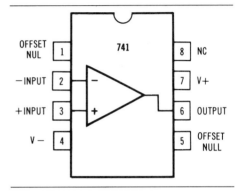

Fig. 3-76. Diagram of the 741 8-pin minidip IC.

Circuits can be built around an 8-pin *minidip* 741 operational amplifier (Fig. 3-76). The actual circuits are given in Fig. 3-77. A split voltage supply consisting of two 6-volt batteries is shown.

Fig. 3-77A shows a noninverting type with the signal being applied to the noninverting or + input of the operational amplifier. A sine wave input will result in a sine wave output of the same phase. The gain of the amplifier will be 10 as determined by resistors R1 and R2. If a positive rise of the DC voltage is applied to the input there will be a positive rise of the DC voltage at the output. A tenth of a volt rise at the input will show up as a 1-volt increase in the output.

Fig. 3-77B is the circuit of an inverting operational amplifier. Now the signal is applied to the inverting or minus input of the operation amplifier. An amplified voltage that is 180 degrees related to the input voltage will appear at the output. Again the gain of the inverting amplifier is determined by resistors R1 and R2.

3-16-1. Audio Power Amplifier IC

Integrated circuit audio power amplifiers are used frequently in two-way radio equipment. An example of such a circuit is given in Fig. 3-78. The internal circuit is given in Fig. 3-78A while the pin-out diagram is shown in Fig. 3-78B. The input stage is a differential amplifier using Darlington pairs to raise the input resistance. In the circuit diagrams of Figs. 3-78C and D, note that the input signal is applied to the noninverting input 3. Pin 2, or the inverting input, is connected to ground. Thus the input amplifier is fed in the differential mode.

The differential-input amplifier is followed by a Darlington-pair power output stage. The simple circuit arrangement of Fig. 3-78C provides a gain of 20. Additional

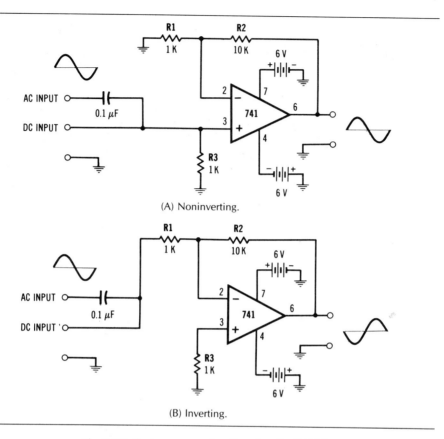

Fig. 3-77. Basic op amp circuits using the 741 IC.

gain can be obtained by connecting external components between pins 1 and 8. The use of the 10-μF capacitor between these two pins in Fig. 3-78D provides the maximum gain of 200. Note for this maximum gain operation that the 10-μF capacitor is connected across the internal 1.35 kΩ resistor which is part of the emitter system of the differential amplifier transistors.

A practical IC audio power amplifier is shown in Fig. 3-79. The feedback network between pins 1 and 8 consists of a resistor and a capacitor. In this manner the actual gain of the stage can be decided and will be something less than the maximum value of 200 depending on the needs of the audio system. A decoupling capacitor (C4) is connected between pin 7 and ground and, in effect, is the supply voltage feed line. High-frequency rolloff is controlled by resistor R3 and capacitor C5.

3-16-2. FM IF Subsystem for Communications

Integrated circuits are available that contain a complete IF system and FM detector along with an audio amplifier and other special circuits in one single chip. Such a unit can serve as a complete receiver subsystem for a communications package. The one shown in Fig. 3-80 includes a three-stage FM IF amplifier/limiter channel, plus individual signal level detectors for each stage. This section is followed by a doubly balanced quadrature FM detector that can be used with either a single-tuned or double-tuned detector coil. The quadrature detector is followed by an audio amplifier with a typical 400-mV output level. The quadrature detector also supplies drive to an

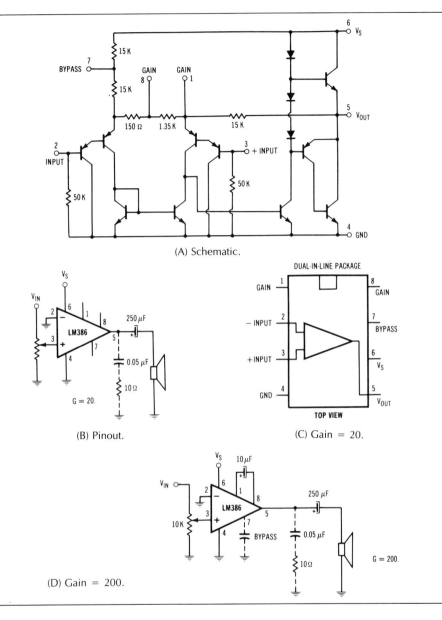

(A) Schematic.

(B) Pinout.

(C) Gain = 20.

(D) Gain = 200.

Fig. 3-78. Audio power amplifier.

automatic-frequency-control amplifier, the output of which can be used to hold the local oscillator on the correct frequency.

The level-detector stages associated with the IF amplifiers supply a signal for a tuning-meter circuit as well as a delayed AGC component for the RF amplifier in the tuner section of the communications receiver. A level detector is also associated with the quadrature detector. It supplies a drive component to the squelch system. The squelch output, in turn, is supplied to the muting stages of the audio amplifier. Such a squelch circuit silences the output of the receiver when there is no incoming signal above a level set by the muting sensitivity control.

Only the IF input and the quadrature detector are tuned. A variety of frequencies

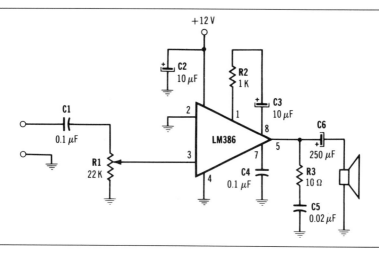

Fig. 3-79. Practical IC audio power amplifier.

for the IF system can be chosen. Values indicated are for a 10.7-MHz intermediate frequency.

A complete circuit for the subsystem as it would be shown on a schematic diagram is given in Fig. 3-81. The various pinouts can be compared to show how the output components are properly attached according to the function that takes place within the integrated circuit chip.

3-16-3. Phase-Locked Loop

The many applications for phase-locked loops (PLL) include frequency multiplication and division, signal conditioning and interference suppression, frequency synthesizers, data synchronizers, tracking filters, decoders, modulators, demodulators, etc.

The basic phase-locked loop (Fig. 3-82) has three main sections — phase comparator, low-pass filter, and voltage-controlled oscillator (VCO) — all connected in a closed-feedback loop. Almost an entire PLL circuit can be included in an integrated circuit. Its major objective and big advantage in many applications is the ability to lock onto the frequency of any applied signal.

To understand the operation of the PLL, let us assume first that the device is not locked onto the incoming signal, even though the two frequencies are reasonably close. The incoming signal and the locally generated signal from the VCO (e_i and e_{osc}) are compared in the phase detector. The output of the phase detector will be a difference or beat frequency (e_x). Since it is low in frequency, output e_x is able to pass through the filter and pass to the voltage-controlled oscillator. The passband of the filter is such that the incoming and VCO components do not pass. The feedback component (e_f) then shifts the frequency of the oscillator and locks it onto the incoming frequency.

Actually, it is a DC voltage that holds the oscillator on frequency because at the moment lock-in occurs, both the input signal and the VCO signal are on the same frequency; thus, the output of the phase detector is zero. If either the incoming signal changes frequency or if the VCO attempts to drift in frequency, there is an instantaneous shift in the phase between the two components in the phase detector. Immediately, there will be a DC output from the phase detector which will be either

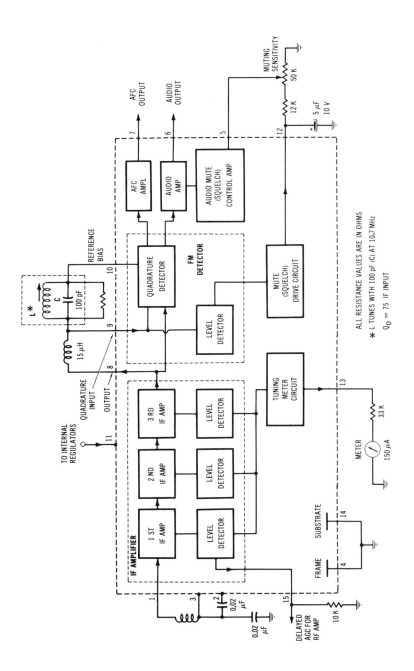

Fig. 3-80. A communications FM IF subsystem.

positive or negative, depending on the direction of the frequency separation. This DC output will cause a frequency-controlled voltage to be immediately applied to the voltage-controlled oscillator (VCO) that will again equalize the two frequencies.

If it is the VCO that attempts to drift in frequency, the DC voltage will prevent it from doing so. If it is the incoming signal that changed in frequency, the DC voltage will cause the VCO to follow that change in frequency. From this it is apparent that the

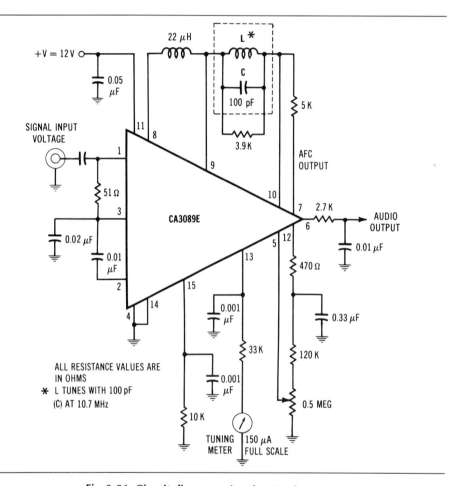

Fig. 3-81. Circuit diagram using the IC subsystem.

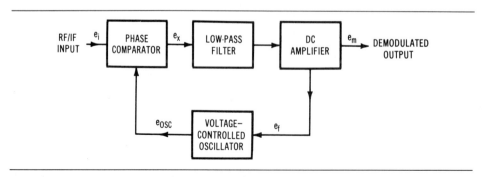

Fig. 3-82. Block diagram of a PLL feedback loop.

phase-locked loop can be made to hold its own frequency precisely or be made to follow the frequency of an applied signal. This action has many attractive attributes in various types of electronic systems.

The range of frequencies over which a PLL can hold a lock is known as the lock-in range of the system. The lock-in range is always greater than the range of frequencies over which the lock can be acquired by the PLL. The range of frequencies over which a lock can be acquired is known as the capture range of the PLL system. Stated another way, when a PLL is attempting to lock in on an incoming signal, it is able to do so if the incoming signal falls within its capture-frequency range. Once the lock is established, the PLL is able to hold a lock over a greater range of frequencies than it needs for capture. That is, the lock range represents a greater bandwidth than the capture range of the PLL system. In practical operation, a lock will occur immediately when the incoming signal falls within the capture range of the PLL system.

The loop filter is very important to the operation of the PLL. It is true that the DC control voltage passes through the filter to the VCO. However, the AC performance of the filter is also important. In fact, the bandwidth of the system performance is established by the loop filter. The bandwidth is selected in accordance with the desired lock-in or hold-in range and the time required to establish lock. Loop bandwidth must be kept narrow to minimize jitter that can be caused by external noise or interference components. However, the loop bandwidth must be adequate to pass desired components and establish an adequate capture range. In all circumstances, the loop bandwidth must be wide enough to accommodate the frequency components that make up the modulation. When used for the demodulation of an FM signal, one understands that the bandwidth should be greater than that required for the demodulation of a narrowband AM signal.

A function block diagram of the Signetics Corporation NE561B PLL integrated circuit is shown in Fig. 3-83. This device is an AM/FM demodulator system. The VCO is an emitter-coupled multivibrator, the frequency of which can be controlled by an external capacitor (C_O). Its output is applied to the phase comparator along with the incoming FM radio-frequency signal. When the VCO and the center frequency of the FM wave are matched, the DC component of the output of the phase comparator is a

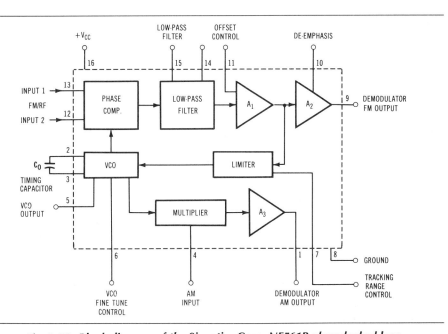

Fig. 3-83. Block diagram of the Signetics Corp. NE561B phase-locked loop.

120

reference zero. If frequencies do not match, an error voltage results which is passed through the filter, a succeeding amplifier and limiter, and back to the VCO.

The demodulated FM signal also passes through the filter amplifiers A_1 and A_2 to the FM output. A de-emphasis network can be attached to terminal 10 if required.

In the demodulation of an AM signal, the signal is applied to the multiplier input. The PLL system sets the VCO on the exact carrier frequency. This VCO component is also applied to the amplifier. Therefore, the multiplier acts as a product detector, and its output frequency is the difference between the AM input signal and the locally generated carrier from the VCO. The demodulated AM signal is increased in level by amplifier A_3 and is recovered at terminal 1 of the device.

A complete external circuit for using the device as an FM demodulator is shown in Fig. 3-84A. The FM signal is applied between terminals 12 and 13. Capacitor C_O determines the VCO frequency. An approximate equation for determining its value is:

$$C_O = \frac{300}{f_O}$$

where,
C_O is the capacitance in picofarads,
f_O is the oscillator frequency in megahertz.

Values for typical intermediate frequencies are given in the chart of Fig. 3-84B. If the VCO is to be used as a tunable local oscillator, this capacitor is made variable.

The values of the series resistor-capacitor combinations connected to terminals 14 and 15 determine the characteristics of the low-pass loop filter. The time constant (tc) of the filter is:

$$tc = C1(R1 + R_{in})$$

where,
R_{in} is the internal impedance and is approximately 6000 ohms.

A practical version of the equation would be:

$$C1 = \frac{1}{2\pi f_h R1}$$

where,
f_h is the desired bandwidth of the filter.

For example, frequency f_h might be 15 kHz for use in an FM receiver.

A capacitor can be used to ground one side of the input to permit the FM signal to be applied single-ended and differential.

Capacitor C_D provides de-emphasis, and its value is based on the time constant:

$$tc = R_D C_D$$

Resistor R_D is 8000 ohms, the output impedance at the de-emphasis terminal. The time constant is whatever value needed for a particular FM demodulator service.

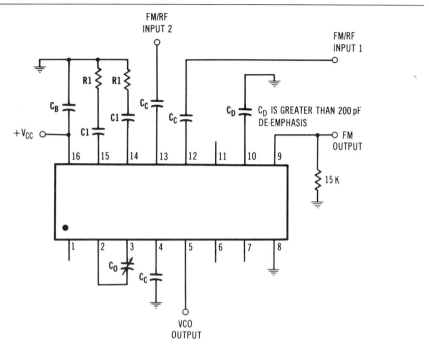

(A) Device and external circuitry.

FREQUENCY	C_0	R1	C1
10.7 MHz	30 pF	100 Ω	1000 pF
4.5 MHz	54 pF	50 Ω	2000 pF
455 kHz	650 pF	0	5000 pF
67 kHz	4600 pF	0	0.01 μF

(B) Component values for typical intermediate frequencies.

Fig. 3-84. An FM PLL demodulator.

3-17. Frequency Synthesizers

Frequency synthesizers are used extensively in setting the transmit and receive frequencies of modern two-way radio equipment. Other key frequencies for both transmit and receive mixing are also generated by the synthesizer system. Usually the synthesizer proper is an integrated circuit connected in a phase-locked loop configuration.

The basic functional plan of a frequency synthesizer is given in Fig. 3-85. In a synthesizer the output of the voltage-controlled oscillator is applied to a frequency divider instead of directly to a phase comparator. By changing the division ratio of the divider, it is possible to set the frequency of the voltage-controlled oscillator on some precise frequency.

In the phase comparator the output of the divider and usually a crystal-controlled reference frequency are compared. A correcting DC voltage at the output of the comparator is applied to the voltage-controlled oscillator and sets it on frequency. This locked frequency when applied to the divider will produce an output that will be identical to the reference frequency applied to the phase comparator.

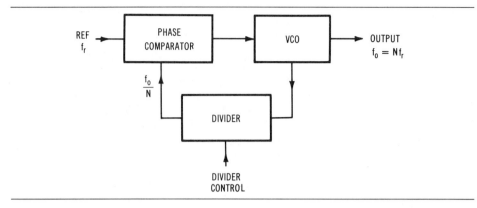

Fig. 3-85. Basic frequency synthesizer.

In operation the output frequency is equal to the product of the divider ratio and the reference frequency. In the example of Fig. 3-85 let us assume that the divider ratio is 10 and the input reference frequency is 1 MHz. As a result the output frequency (f_O) is the product of (10×1) or 10 MHz. This output frequency (f_O) is also applied to the divider and the output of the divider is 1 MHz (10/10). Thus the voltage-controlled oscillator is locked in precisely on the operating frequency of 10 MHz. Any attempted change in the output frequency will set the phase-locked loop into operation, and the DC correcting voltage at the output of the phase comparator will restore the voltage-controlled oscillator frequency to 10 MHz.

How can the frequency of the voltage-controlled oscillator be changed by the divider? Assume that the divider has a control system that establishes a count of 9 instead of 10. This would mean that output frequency f_O now becomes (9×1) or 9 MHz. In this case output frequency f_O is divided by 9 to produce, once again, a 1-MHz component at the output of the divider. This component is again compared with the 1-MHz reference frequency, and the voltage-controlled oscillator is now held precisely on 9 MHz.

This is the basic technique used to establish an array of frequencies for a radio transceiver without the use of an array of crystals. For example, in a modern CB transceiver forty separate divider ratios that can be established with a digital divider control system can be used to precisely set the voltage-controlled oscillator on a specific frequency that will permit operation on a chosen one of the forty possible channels. Changing the channel selector will change the divider ratio in such a manner that operation will now be switched to the new channel specified on the digital channel readout.

The functional plan of a typical 40-channel CB transceiver using a frequency synthesizer is given in Fig. 3-86. Transistors are used throughout except for the integrated circuit that is a part of the phase-lock loop synthesizer and another integrated circuit for the audio output system used on both receive and transmit.

The PLL unit generates three signal components. One of these is the transmit-frequency range and the other two are local oscillator injection components for the dual-conversion receiver.

Two crystal oscillators are used in the PLL frequency synthesizer (Fig. 3-87). The VCO, located near the center of the block diagram, generates a frequency range between 16.27 and 16.71 MHz depending on the selected channel. Its output is applied at that frequency to the first mixer of the receiver. Output also is applied to the transmitter mixer where it combines with the frequency generated by the crystal oscillator. The summation of these two frequencies produces a range of frequencies that falls within the assigned CB radio spectrum between 26.965 and 27.405 MHz.

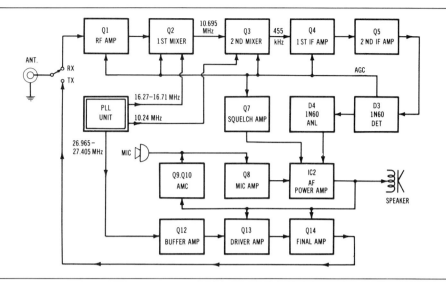

Fig. 3-86. Block diagram of a CB transceiver.

Output is also taken from the VCO and applied to yet another mixer through buffer Q204. In this mixer, the output is compared with a signal generated by a reference crystal oscillator. This oscillator operates on 10.24 MHz and through a 2-to-1 divider develops a 5.12-MHz signal that is applied to tripler T206. Thus, in the mixer, the signal from the voltage-controlled oscillator and the reference crystal oscillator are mixed to produce a difference frequency that falls between 910 and 1350 kHz.

This latter signal is applied to the programmed divider. The actual division depends on the setting of the channel selector switch. The division is such that a 10-kHz signal is removed from the programmed divider. This is applied to the phase

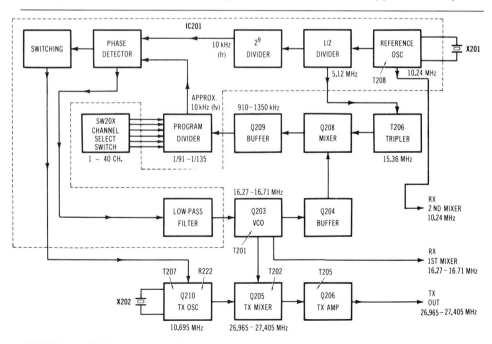

Fig. 3-87. Block diagram of a phase-locked loop synthesizer.

detector (top left in Fig. 3-87). The output of the 2-to-1 divider that follows the reference oscillator is further divided by a factor of 512 (2^9). Thus the 10-kHz reference frequency is also applied to the phase detector.

If there is any drift in phase between the two 10-kHz components there is a pulse excitation to the low-pass filter. The filter acts as a digital-to-analog converter and the generated information is applied to the VCO as a correcting DC voltage. Thus the VCO is held on frequency, and that frequency depends on the setting of the channel selector switch. If the phase detector is inactive there is a special switching circuit that shuts off the 10.695-MHz transmit oscillator so spurious signals will not be radiated by accident or by failure in the PLL circuit.

Note that the output of the PLL unit in Fig. 3-86 is supplied to the buffer-amplifier transistor (Q12) at the bottom left of the diagram. The output of this common-emitter amplifier is applied to a succeeding driver amplifier transistor (Q13). This stage is connected to the final amplifier. Thus it is the combined stages involving transistor Q13 and Q14 that develop the 4-watt output at a low-impedance level for application to antenna receptacle. This is the RF section of the transmitter.

The input microphone amplifier is located at the center (transistor Q8) of Fig. 3-86. Its output is applied through the squelch switching circuit to the integrated circuit audio amplifier modulator. By way of the secondary of a modulation transformer, the audio is applied to the DC supply-voltage to the collector circuits of both the driver amplifier (Q13) and the final amplifier (Q14). Both stages are collector-modulated to obtain full and linear modulation of the RF wave.

Note that the modulating wave at the output of the modulation transformer is also applied to the base of the automatic-modulation-control (Q9) at the lower left. Depending on the strength of the audio, a component is detected and filtered to develop a DC component applied to transistor Q10. It has a loading effect and limits the level of the microphone signal applied to the microphone amplifier. Thus over-modulation is avoided at the same time a high average level of modulation can be maintained.

3-18. Waveform Generators

Waveform generators are used in test equipment, timers, and control circuits. Some of these use the popular 555 timer IC. The timer consists of five basic circuits — two comparators, a bistable flip-flop, a resistive voltage divider, a discharge transistor, and an output stage (Fig. 3-88). The three resistors of the divider are of equal value; the threshold comparator is referenced at two-thirds of the supply voltage, while the trigger comparator is referenced at one-third of the supply voltage. Note that the outputs of the comparators are connected to the bistable flip-flop.

If the trigger voltage applied to the trigger comparator is dropped below one-third of the supply voltage, the comparator changes state and causes the flip-flop to drive the output to its high state.

The threshold input monitors the capacitive voltage of an external RC timing network (Fig. 3-89). When the capacitor voltage of this external circuit exceeds two-thirds of the supply voltage, the threshold comparator resets the flip-flop. In this case the flip-flop now drives the output to its low state. In this condition the discharge transistor is on and the external timing capacitor will be discharged. However, when the capacitor is discharged the comparator awaits another trigger pulse to cause the timing cycle to be repeated.

In a pulse-generator circuit the threshold and trigger inputs are tied together and connected to the external capacitor (C) as shown in the circuit of Fig. 3-89. Note how the external resistors are connected to the supply voltage and present a series path

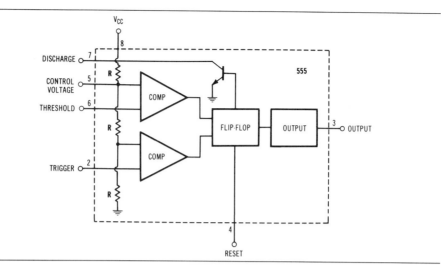

Fig. 3-88. Functional block diagram of the 555 IC timer.

along with the capacitor from the supply voltage to common. The discharge circuit is connected to the junction of the two resistors, while the threshold and trigger connections are made between the junction of the second resistor and the capacitor. A discussion of the timer connected as an astable oscillator follows.

When the power is turned on the capacitor is in a discharge state. However, circuit activities cause the capacitor to charge toward the supply voltage level through resistors R_A and R_B. When the capacitor reaches the threshold level of 2/3 V_{CC}, the output drops low and the voltage on the capacitor discharges through resistor R_B and the discharge transistor of the timer. When the capacitor drops to the level of 1/3 V_{CC}, the trigger comparator triggers, causing the flip-flop to change over and a new charging cycle begins. Thus, the voltage on the capacitor varies between 1/3 V_{CC} and 2/3 V_{CC}. The output voltage at pin 3 is high (value of V_{CC}) during the charging interval and low (0 volts) during the discharge period.

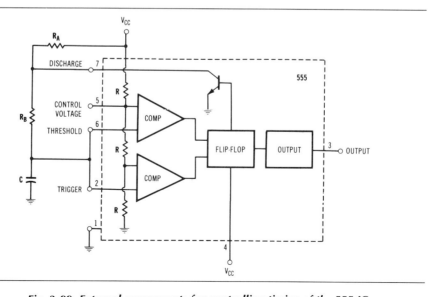

Fig. 3-89. External components for controlling timing of the 555 IC.

A practical value for the discharge period would be:

$$t_{dis} = 0.693R_BC$$

The charging time is longer and has a value of:

$$t_{ch} = 0.693(R_A + R_B)C$$

The total period of the charge and discharge activities becomes:

$$T - t_{ch} + t_{dis} = 0.693 \ (R_A + 2R_B)C$$

The repetition rate or frequency is the reciprocal of the period, or

$$f = \frac{1}{T} = \frac{1.44}{(R_A + 2R_B)C}$$

The graph of Fig. 3-90 shows the relationship among capacitance, frequency of operation, and the quantity $(R_A + 2R_B)$. Can you determine the approximate frequency of operation for the circuit of Fig. 3-91?

The quantity $(R_A + 2R_B)$ is approximately 100 kΩ. The capacitor value is 0.01 microfarad. The 100-kΩ line crosses the 0.01 horizontal line between 1 and 2 thousand hertz. Use the frequency equation to obtain the exact value as follows:

$$f = \frac{1.44}{(.033 \times 10^6 + .066 \times 10^6) .01 \times 10^{-6}} = 1455 \ hertz$$

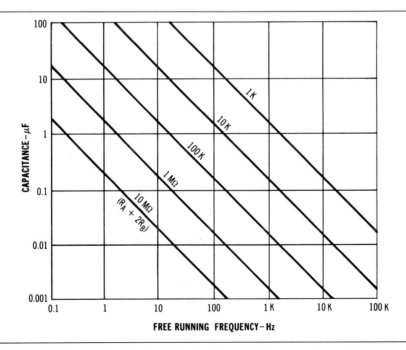

Fig. 3-90. Resistance, capacitance, and frequency relationship.

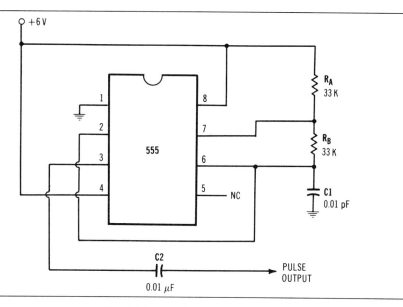

Fig. 3-91. Astable pulse generator.

In the circuit of Fig. 3-91 the pulse-repetition rate and period are determined by resistors R_A, R_B, and capacitor C1. The longer this time constant is, the lower is the frequency of the output pulse. A negative pulse appears at the output and has a duration determined by capacitor C1 and resistor R_B. The time interval between the trailing edge of the pulse and the leading edge of the next is set by the charge time constant of capacitor C1 plus resistors R_A and R_B.

If a shorter duration pulse of the same frequency is to be developed at the output it is necessary to decrease the value of resistor R_B and increase the value of resistor R_A. Thus, by controlling the relative values of the two resistors and the capacitor, a negative pulse of specific duration and repetition rate can be developed at the output.

Many additional solid-state circuits and solid-state devices are covered in the chapters that follow.

4

Modulation Systems

In the two-way radio services two principal forms of modulation are used. These are *frequency modulation* and *amplitude modulation*.. The former (FM) is usually used in the VHF and UHF spectra and is the dominant form of modulation in the private land mobile radio services. The latter form of modulation (AM) is used more widely in the HF region in various radio services and also to some degree in the VHF and UHF region. Conventional double-sideband amplitude modulation is popular in the Citizens Band radio service. Single-sideband amplitude modulation (SSB) is found in the MF and HF marine radio services and other point-to-point services. These modulation systems are introduced in this chapter.

4-1. FM Principles

Frequency modulation has several attractive advantages for radio communication use; it requires no significant audio power and has a very low susceptibility to noise and interference. Since a frequency-modulated wave is employed, the amplitude variations contributed by noise can be limited sharply at the receiver. The ability to eliminate amplitude impulse noise is an important advantage when the equipment must be operated in close proximity to ignition systems and other noise sources, which radiate strong amplitude-varying RF signals. In a similar manner the beat variations (amplitude changes) between two interfering RF signals can be reduced. Thus by using a frequency-modulation system there will be less interference between stations operating on the same or adjacent channels. In FM systems the stronger station dominates the weaker station and pushes it into the background.

It is significant that FM transmission requires a wider emission bandwidth. The emission bandwidth is more than twice the highest modulating frequency. The greater the frequency deviation (higher modulation index), the greater the emission bandwidth for a given modulating frequency. However, bandwidth can be held down by establishing a limit for the highest audio frequency and by using a very low maximum-permissible frequency deviation. In the two-way radio services it is customary to limit the highest modulating audio frequency to 2500 Hz and the maximum deviation to ± 5 kHz.

In an FM system the frequency of the resultant RF wave is made to vary with the modulation. The extent of the frequency change, or deviation, varies with the amplitude of the modulating wave. The rate at which the frequency changes varies with the frequency of the modulating wave.

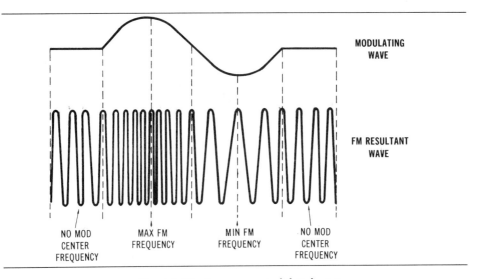

Fig. 4-1. The frequency-modulated wave.

As shown in Fig. 4-1 the actual amplitude of the resultant RF wave remains constant — only its frequency changes with the modulation. This latter characteristic means that any amplitude variations (noise) present in the resultant FM signal can be safely removed because the desired signal information has nothing whatsoever to do with amplitude change. This elimination of undesired amplitude variations is accomplished in the FM receiver.

4-1-1. Direct and Indirect Frequency Modulation

The basic theoretical principle of the frequency-modulation process can be demonstrated with a motor-driven capacitor. If such a capacitor had a linear frequency characteristic and was placed across the tank circuit of an oscillator, the frequency of the oscillator could be made to change with the capacitor rotor rotation. The oscillator frequency would, of course, be minimum when the capacitor plates are meshed fully and maximum when the capacitor plates are entirely out.

If the associated motor rotated the capacitor rotor at the rate of 100 revolutions per second, the frequency of the oscillator would also vary at the 100 cycle-per-second rate. If the motor speed were increased or decreased there would be a similar change in the rate of frequency change. This would be the same as changing the frequency of the modulating wave in a practical FM system.

If the value of the capacitor is reduced, the range over which the frequency of the oscillator could change would be reduced. The lesser deviation would correspond to the application of a weaker modulating wave to the input of a practical FM system.

If it were practical for a rotating motor to follow the complex variations of speech, it could be used to generate an FM wave for a two-way radio system. However, a similar and practical deviation can be accomplished with the use of a transistor stage designed to place a variable capacitance or variable inductance across the tuned circuit of an oscillator. This type of circuit is called a *reactance modulator.*

An FM wave can be formed by varying the phase of an RF wave in accord with the variations of a modulating signal. This technique is used extensively in FM two-way radio systems and the circuit is referred to as an *FM phase modulator.* The source of the signal is usually a crystal oscillator, variable crystal oscillator (VXO), or variable frequency oscillator (VFO).

When an FM wave is formed by deviating the frequency of the oscillator with a reactance device, it is called *direct frequency modulation.* The oscillator can also be any one of the types mentioned previously.

In most FM units the fundamental oscillator operates at a much lower frequency than the assigned transmit channel frequency. A series of multiplier stages then follows the low-frequency oscillator to increase the frequency to the desired transmit channel frequency. As the frequency is multiplied, any deviation of the fundamental oscillator frequency will be increased by a like amount. To obtain a small linear frequency change, the actual oscillator deviation produced by the reactance circuit is quite limited. Assume the 12.95-MHz frequency of an oscillator is deviated by only 350 Hz and there is a multiplication factor of 12. The final transmit frequency will be 155.4 MHz (12 $\times$ 12.95) and the maximum deviation 4200 Hz (12 $\times$ 350). Somewhat greater deviation would result in the maximum permissible value of $\pm$ 5 kHz. From this example it can be seen that frequency-multiplier stages increase the small frequency deviation of the fundamental oscillator to the permissible deviation desired.

Multiplier stages used in an FM transmitter can be conventional class-C amplifiers. The FM wave, which carries the modulating information, is in the form of a changing frequency. There is no danger of distortion because of the nonlinear amplitude characteristic of a class-C stage. The standard AM and sideband modulation methods require linear amplification (after the modulation envelope has been formed) in order to retain the original modulation. In fact, the limiting activity of a class-C stage in terms of amplitude change is used to advantage in an FM system. In the FM process undesired amplitude variations may also occur simultaneously with a desired frequency change. These undesired amplitude variations are eliminated by the class-C multipliers, thus producing a constant amplitude FM signal output.

Very little audio power is necessary in the modulation of an FM wave as compared to a standard AM system. The power in a resultant FM wave remains constant with modulation; it is simply distributed in differing amounts among carrier and sidebands, thus producing changing frequency but a constant amplitude output.

One of the problems with direct frequency modulation (Fig. 4-2A) is the center-frequency stability. It must be held constant to maintain the proper operating stability and prevent distortion. Both the oscillator and associated reactance device must be carefully designed for the most stable operation. A stable crystal oscillator or VFO is needed. An alternative is an AFC system (Fig. 4-2B) that compares the center frequency of the transmitter to some crystal-controlled standard. A DC error voltage is developed at the output of the AFC circuit, and, through the reactance device, it alters the center frequency an amount necessary to correct any frequency drift.

A block diagram of an indirect frequency-modulation system is shown in Fig. 4-2C. In this case the RF carrier is phase modulated (PM). Phase (or angle) modulation, like direct frequency modulation, can be accomplished in a number of ways. Using a suitable correction arrangement, the phase-modulation process can be used to generate a true FM wave.

Most indirect systems use a crystal oscillator or VXO. Thus, the center-frequency stability is good and an AFC circuit is not required. A phase-modulation process is limited in the amount of deviation that can be obtained; however, this is an unimpor-

132

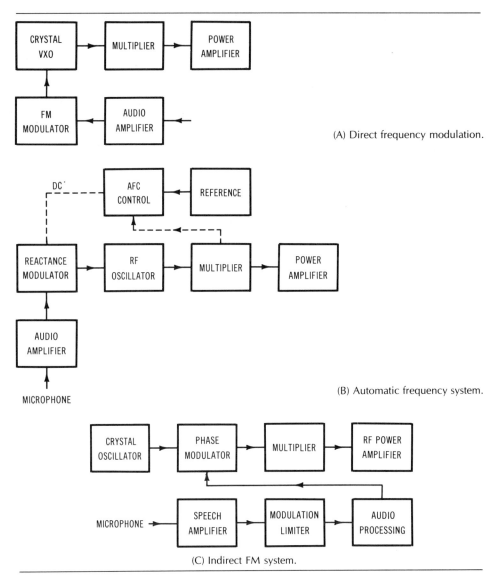

(A) Direct frequency modulation.

(B) Automatic frequency system.

(C) Indirect FM system.

Fig. 4-2. Functional plans of FM systems.

tant consideration in two-way radio systems because they are predominantly narrow-band limited-deviation systems.

In the phase-modulation process used in two-way commercial transmitters, the audio variations continuously vary the phase of the RF carrier wave. They do so by placing a changing reactive component in the path of the RF carrier wave. This produces a changing phase shift. The higher the amplitude of the audio wave, the greater is the phase shift and the more the RF wave is delayed during one alternation. Conversely, on the opposite alternation of the audio wave, the phase shift is of opposite sign and the RF wave is advanced instead of delayed. If the phase modulator speeds up the RF wave, its period is reduced. This means it has a higher frequency as shown at A in Fig. 4-3. If the radio-frequency wave is delayed, its period is increased and it has a lower frequency as shown at B in Fig. 4-3.

In practice the phase shift varies throughout the entire audio cycle reaching the maximum value only at the sine-wave peaks. Positive and negative peaks produce the same phase shift but of opposite sign (lag and lead). The phase shift is zero when the audio wave passes through zero. Therefore, the frequency of the RF wave deviates above and below the carrier value following the amplitude and polarity changes of the audio wave as shown at C in Fig. 4-3.

An increase in the modulating frequency increases the frequency deviation of the carrier. The amount of frequency modulation produced indirectly by phase modulation varies directly with the frequency of the modulating signal.

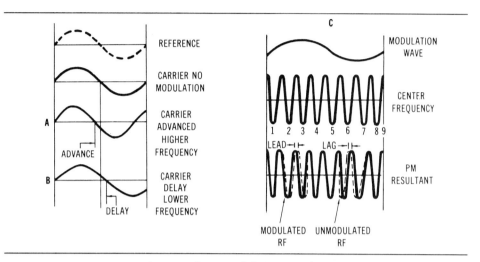

Fig. 4-3. Phase-modulation waveforms.

The amount of frequency deviation produced is relatively small. Usually a low carrier frequency is chosen to be phase modulated. After the FM wave has been generated by the indirect process, it is applied to a series of multipliers. These multipliers increase both the frequency and frequency deviation. As in the direct FM system, the multipliers increase the deviation to the maximum permissible value allowed for a particular service.

There is one fundamental difference between frequency and phase modulation. In a direct FM system, the frequency deviation is constant for a given audio amplitude regardless of the audio frequency. The modulation index formula indicates that a change in audio frequency will cause a change in the modulation index even though the deviation remains fixed:

$$\text{Modulation index} = \frac{\text{frequency deviation}}{\text{modulating frequency}}$$

Thus in a direct FM system the modulation index decreases with modulating frequency, assuming a fixed deviation.

In a phase-modulation process, it is the modulation index that remains constant for a given amplitude regardless of audio frequency. Inasmuch as the modulation index is constant the deviation itself must vary with the audio frequency.

$$\text{Frequency deviation} = \text{modulation index} \times \text{modulating frequency}$$

Actually, the higher the audio frequency of a given amplitude, the greater the frequency deviation when using phase modulation.

It is apparent from the foregoing paragraphs that, in generating a true FM wave using the phase-modulation process, some form of compensating circuit must be used ahead of the modulator. Such a circuit is called a *predistorter* and is inserted between the audio source and the phase modulator.

The predistorter has a response that declines with an increase in frequency. Thus the output of the predistorter at a high audio frequency is less than the output at a lower frequency for the same input amplitude. Its response compensates for the fact that a phase modulator produces a greater deviation for a high-frequency modulating wave than for a lower-frequency one of the same amplitude. The compensation introduced by the predistorter is equal and opposite to that of the modulation process. Therefore, with predistortion it is possible to generate a true FM wave using the phase-modulation process.

In the usual FM two-way radio system there is an essentially narrow-band audio-frequency range, and any necessary predistortion can be handled very simply by proper control of overall amplifier frequency response. The associated modulation limiters and integrators inherently suppress the high-frequency components and prevent them from causing excessive deviation of the center frequency. Thus, it is possible in some cases to handle predistortion without the actual use of a predistorter network.

4-2. Composition of FM Wave

The resultant FM wave, like an AM envelope, is the algebraic summation of a number of individual RF waves. In the FM process, when modulating with a single-frequency tone, a number of sideband pairs are generated according to modulating frequency and deviation. This is unlike the AM process, which generates only a single pair of sidebands when modulation is by a single-frequency tone.

In a standard AM system, the carrier remains constant in amplitude; however, the algebraic addition of the two sidebands and the carrier produces an amplitude-changing resultant (AM envelope). In an FM moduation system the amplitude of the resultant wave remains constant while the amplitude of the carrier changes. The carrier amplitude change is such that when added to the various sideband pairs, a constant amplitude but changing-frequency resultant is produced.

Actually, the ratio of the powers in the sidebands and in the carrier changes with the modulating frequency and deviation. However, the resultant power output is always a constant. In fact, under specific conditions of modulating-wave amplitude and frequency, it is possible that the carrier or center-frequency power can even fall to zero. In this case all of the power is in the sidebands. Under other conditions of frequency modulation, most of the power is in the carrier and only a small amount in the sidebands. In fact, the evaluation of shifts in power and relative changes of amplitude among the sidebands and carrier can be useful in checking the performance of an FM system.

The number of sideband pairs generated in the FM process depends on the modulation index. The emission bandwidth, in turn, depends on the modulation index at the maximum permissible deviation of the highest-frequency modulating wave. Some possible frequency distributions are illustrated in Fig. 4-4.

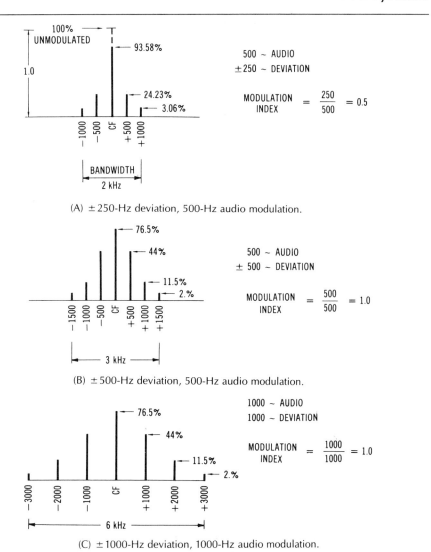

Fig. 4-4. Spectrum distribution of various FM waves.

The wave equations and solutions that result when one RF wave is frequency-modulated by another lower-frequency wave are very complex. Such equations can be solved using *Bessel functions*. Despite the complex solutions, very practical mathematical results can be obtained using a table of Bessel functions. Table 4-1 provides a set of Bessel-function solutions that are applicable to the narrow-band frequency modulation used in two-way radio. The table gives the relative magnitudes of carrier (center frequency) and side frequencies for various modulation indexes. The unity reference represents the magnitude of the carrier when unmodulated. A side-band frequency is considered significant when its magnitude is more than 2% of the magnitude of the unmodulated carrier.

Table 4-1. Bessel Function Chart Applied to Carrier and Side Frequencies of an FM Wave

Modulation Index	Carrier (f_c)	$f_c \pm f_m$	$f_c \pm 2f_m$	$f_c \pm 3f_m$	$f_c \pm 4f_m$	$f_c \pm 5f_m$	$f_c \pm 6f_m$
0	1.00	0					
0.1	0.9975	0.0499					
0.2	0.99	0.0995					
0.3	0.9776	0.1483					
0.4	0.9604	0.1960					
0.5	0.9385	0.2423	0.0306				
0.6	0.912	0.2867	0.437				
0.7	0.8812	0.329	0.0589				
0.8	0.8463	0.3688	0.0758				
0.9	0.8075	0.4059	0.0946				
1.0	0.7652	0.4401	0.1149	0.0196			
1.2	0.6711	0.4983	0.1679	0.0329			
1.4	0.5669	0.5419	0.2073	0.0505			
1.6	0.4554	0.5699	0.257	0.0725			
2.00	0.2239	0.5767	0.3528	0.1289	0.034		
3.00	0.2601	0.3391	0.4861	0.3091	0.1320	0.0430	
4.00	0.3971	0.066	0.3641	0.4302	0.2811	0.1321	
5.00	0.1776	0.3276	0.0466	0.3648	0.3912	0.2611	0.131

For example, when the FM modulation is such that the modulation index is 0.5, the magnitude of the center-frequency component is 93.85% of the unmodulated center-frequency level, the first pair of sidebands has a magnitude that is 24.23% of the unmodulated center frequency value, and, finally, a second sideband pair has a magnitude of 3.06% of the unmodulated center-frequency value and, finally, a second sideband pair has a magnitude of 3.06% of the unmodulated center-frequency value. If the modulating frequency were 500 Hz, there would be a pair of sidebands, one at each side of the center frequency, displaced by 500 cycles. Each sideband, upper and lower, would have a magnitude of 24.33% of the unmodulated carrier value. Further-more, there would be a second pair of sidebands displaced by 1000 cycles (2 × 500) from the center frequency. These frequencies would have a magnitude of 3.06%. A simple spectrum distribution graph (Fig. 4-4A) can be used to illustrate relative magnitudes among the wave components and the required emission bandwidth for transmitting this FM signal.

If we increase the magnitude of the modulating wave and thus cause a greater deviation, the emission bandwidth will increase because an additional significant sideband pair will be transmitted (Fig. 4-4B).

The higher the audio frequency for a given index, the greater the separation between side-frequency pairs of significance, and the greater the required emission bandwidth. Compare the examples in Figs. 4-4B and C.

Collate these graphs with the information given in the Bessel Function table. The results prove that the emission bandwidth increases both with frequency and devia-tion. Therefore, in the narrow-band two-way radio services it is necessary to hold down the emission bandwidth by limiting both the extent of the deviation of the center frequency and the highest permissible audio frequency.

The maximum emission bandwidth assigned to a given radio service is a function of the maximum permissible deviation and the highest modulating frequency. The modulation index for this important operating condition is called the deviation ratio:

$$\text{Deviation ratio} \quad = \quad \frac{\text{maximum permissible deviation}}{\text{highest modulating frequency}}$$

Calculation for the two-way radio deviation of $\pm$ 5 kHz based on a maximum permissible modulation frequency of 2500 Hz becomes:

$$\text{Deviation ratio} \quad = \quad \frac{5000}{2500} \quad = \quad 2$$

4-3. Typical Circuits

In the typical FM transmitter the modulation occurs at a low radio frequency. Narrow-band deviation is the rule, and, consequently, many frequency modulators use a phase-modulator stage to obtain frequency modulation by the indirect means. Other transmitters employ direct frequency modulation of a crystal oscillator using a voltage-variable capacitor diode.

A basic bipolar phase modulator is shown in Fig. 4-5. Such a phase modulator is inserted in the radio-frequency path between the crystal oscillator source and the multiplier section of the transmitter.

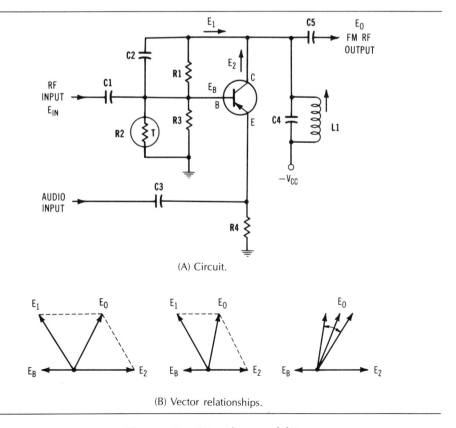

(A) Circuit.

(B) Vector relationships.

Fig. 4-5. Transistor phase modulator.

The input voltage E_{in} follows two paths. One path is through capacitor C1 to the base of the phase modulator. This RF component is labeled E_B in the schematic and associated vector diagram. A second path is coupled to the output circuit by way of capacitors C1 and C2. This component is shown as voltage E_1. The RF component (E_B) supplied to the base appears inverted in the collector circuit of the phase modulator as voltage E_2. Since the transistor provides a polarity reversal, it would seem that the two components E_1 and E_2 present in the collector circuit would be of opposite polarity. However, this is not the case because of the phase-shifting activity of the input capacitors which, along with other component values, have been selected to obtain an appropriate phase relation between the two RF components as shown in the vector diagram. They are neither in phase nor 180° out of phase.

The vector diagram shows a possible relationship between the two components E_1 and E_2. In the output circuit the direct voltage E_1 remains constant in amplitude. Likewise, the RF signal component (E_B) applied to the base is constant. However, the g_m of the stage varies with the applied modulating wave felt at the emitter. Therefore, the output voltage component (E_2) varies in amplitude with the modulating wave. As shown by the vectors, the amplitude of voltage E_2 varies with respect to the constant amplitude of voltage E_1.

The vector diagram of Fig. 4-5B shows how the phase modulation is caused. The net RF output voltage (E_0), or the resultant FM wave, is the vector sum of E_1 and E_2. The resultant voltage changes in phase as the amplitude of the E_2 component varies with the applied audio. The higher the amplitude of the applied audio, the greater the phase deviation and the greater the resultant frequency modulation. The higher the frequency of the applied audio, the more often the angle will swing between the two extremes.

The second vector diagram shows how the output voltage (E_0) has an angle that deviates further from voltage E_2 when the amplitude of E_2 declines.

The third vector diagram shows briefly what happens to the output voltage as the voltage E_2 varies in accordance with the amplitude of the audio input signal. This change in E_2 amplitude causes the angle of E_0 to vary, following the changes of the audio wave. As mentioned, the audio component is applied to the emitter circuit, varying the base-emitter voltage in accordance with the audio modulation. The base-divider bias circuit includes a thermistor (R2) to stabilize the operating point against temperature change.

Transistors can also be used as variable reactance devices. The output capacitance of a transistor, the capacitance of the collector junction (C_0) specifically, can be made to vary quite readily. The collector junction is reverse-biased, and the depletion area of the junction depends on the junction voltage. When a higher reverse voltage is applied to the junction, the depletion area increases and reduces the junction capacitance. An audio signal applied to the base or emitter circuits can cause this capaci-

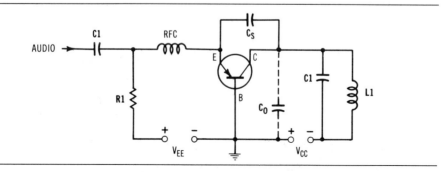

Fig. 4-6. Self-reactance modulator-oscillator system.

tance to change. If the capacitance is shunted across a tuned circuit, there will be a corresponding change in its resonant frequency (Fig. 4-6). The oscillator is connected in a common-base configuration with the small capacitor (C_s) providing the necessary feedback between collector and emitter circuit to sustain self-oscillation. The audio signal is supplied to the emitter, and the resultant change in the collector-to-base voltage will cause the transistor-output capacitance (C_0) to vary and cause a change in the frequency of oscillation. This type of circuit is referred to as a self-reactance FM oscillator.

4-3-1. Voltage-Variable Capacitor

One of the effects of a changing voltage across a semiconductor diode is a change in capacitance. By suitable semiconductor design and doping, the change in capacitance can be emphasized and made to have a capacitance-versus-junction voltage characteristic that will permit it to operate as an efficient voltage-to-frequency converter.

A voltage-variable capacitor (also called a varactor) placed across an oscillator tank circuit as shown in Fig. 4-7 can be used to control or vary the resonant frequency of the tuned circuit. As shown, the modulating voltage is supplied to the diode by way of an isolating RF filter. A voltage source sets the DC bias of the diode at a point on its voltage capacitance transfer characteristic that ensures a linear deviation of the oscillator signal. As the bias point is made to vary with the positive and negative excursions of the modulating wave, there is a corresponding change in diode capacitance, and in the resonant frequency of the tuned circuit with which the diode is associated. A capacitive divider arrangement (capacitor C1 and voltage-variable capacitor D1) may be used to regulate the extent of the capacitance deviation for a given magnitude of audio input signal. Such an adjustment may be used to ensure a linear frequency deviation for a given maximum level of audio input signal.

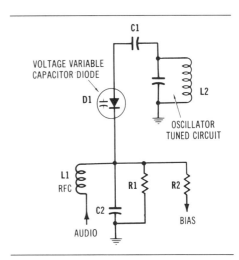

Fig. 4-7. Using a voltage-variable capacitor diode to vary the frequency of a resonant circuit.

The variable-capacitance diode can be used either to frequency- or phase-modulate an RF signal. In the simple phase modulator of Fig. 4-8A the variable-capacitance diode (D1) is a part of a resonant tank circuit that follows the oscillator.

The coupling capacitor (C1) from the oscillator to the resonant circuit has a rather high reactance at the output frequency. Thus, the audio variation that is applied across the voltage-variable capacitor is able to change the resonant frequency of the tank circuit but not the oscillator frequency. However, the change in the resonant frequency causes a change in the phase angle of the RF signal delivered by the oscillator as it is developed across the tank circuit. This is to be anticipated because with a change in the frequency of the tuned circuit away from the frequency of the oscillator, the tuned circuit will present an impedance that now has a reactive component at the oscillator frequency.

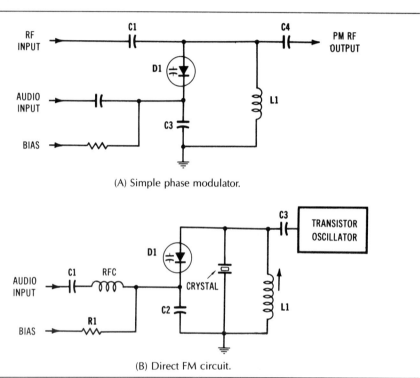

(A) Simple phase modulator.

(B) Direct FM circuit.

Fig. 4-8. Variable-capacitance diode as a phase or frequency modulator.

The unmodulated resonant frequency of the tuned circuit depends on the LC constant and the capacitance contributed by the variable-capacitance diode (at the established DC bias). In the case of no applied modulation the oscillator frequency and the resonant frequency of the tuned circuit are one and the same. However, when an audio signal is applied to the variable-capacitance diode, there will be a corresponding change in the diode capacitance. This will cause the resonant frequency of the tuned circuit to change. In effect the tuned circuit will now present a changing reactive component, and the individual RF cycles will be shifted in phase. As in any form of phase modulator this change in phase will compress and expand the periods of individual RF cycles, and frequency modulation will have been produced by an indirect means.

It is also possible to connect the variable-capacitance diode directly into the crystal circuit of an oscillator as shown in Fig. 4-8B. Often an overtone-crystal oscillator is used. The resonant circuit consists of inductor L1, capacitor C3, and the variable-capacitance diode (D1). An applied audio signal will cause a change in the capacitance, and a limited deviation of the crystal oscillator frequency will result. By using an overtone oscillator, this change in frequency can be made substantial and narrow-band frequency modulation will result. The deviation, of course, can be increased by using succeeding multiplier stages.

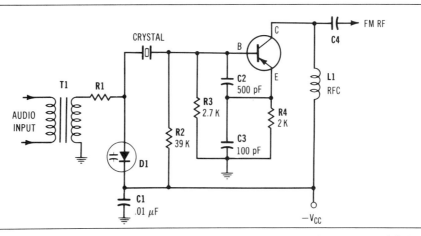

Fig. 4-9. Crystal oscillator with variable-capacitance diode direct-frequency modulation.

    A practical variable-capacitance frequency modulator used in conjunction with a Clapp-type crystal oscillator is shown in Fig. 4-9. The crystal operates in its series-resonant mode. Capacitors C2 and C3 are of high value and act as swamping capacitors. Their values are high enough to swamp out any capacitive changes that may be contributed by the transistor due to heating or other circuit changes.

    The frequency of the oscillator is determined by the resonant characteristics of the crystal and the capacitance added in series by the variable-capacitance diode. In effect, the variable-capacitance diode is adding additional series capacitance to the series-resonant characteristic of the crystal when it is oscillating in its series mode. It is apparent, then, that any changes in the capacitance of D1 with the application of an audio wave will cause a corresponding deviation in the frequency of the crystal oscillator.

    A two-diode phase modulator is shown in Fig. 4-10. The output of the transmitter crystal oscillator is supplied to the resonant input transformer T1; the FM component is derived at the output of resonant transformer T2. The capacitances of diodes D1 and D2 are varied by the voice-frequency components applied to the junction of resistors R1 and R2. A bias divider composed of resistors R3 and R4 set the diode bias for optimum linear deviation.

    A small capacitor (C1) serves as the coupling between the two transformers. This aids in keeping a precise center frequency at the same time the audio variations vary the reactances of the resonant circuits to produce a phase shift of the oscillator frequency.

    The typical FM demodulator also uses a phase-shift principle in the manner in which it recovers the audio information from the received frequency-modulated signal. There are a variety of FM detectors. However, the conventional Foster-Seeley discriminator is basic to these types.

    A basic discriminator circuit is shown in Fig. 4-11A. The operation of a discriminator is based on the phase relationship between two FM RF components that appear at its input. One component is coupled directly by way of capacitor C1 and appears across the discriminator inductor L1. Another RF component is coupled via the flux lines that link the primary and secondary resonant circuits. The secondary IF voltage, when two coupled resonant circuits are employed, differs in phase 90° from the primary voltage and, therefore, is also related by 90° to the IF voltage that has been

142

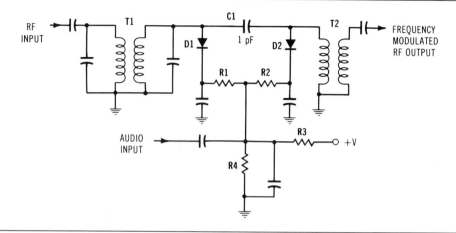

Fig. 4-10. Phase modulator using diodes.

coupled directly across inductor L1. The 90° component is divided into two segments with reference to the secondary tap. One segment appears at the anode of diode D1, and the other appears at the anode of diode D2. In terms of the diode anodes, these two components are 180° apart.

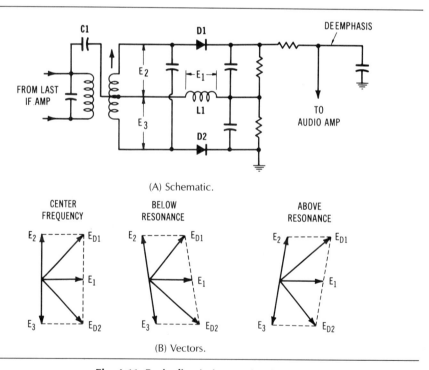

(A) Schematic.

(B) Vectors.

Fig. 4-11. Basic discriminator circuit.

From the discussion, it is apparent diode D1 is excited by two RF signals ($E_1 + E_2$), while diode D2 is excited by a signal component composed of ($E_1 + E_3$). At the frequency to which the discriminator transformer is tuned, these two signal components are of equal amplitude. Therefore, they draw the same peak diode current, and, inasmuch as the diode currents occur in opposite directions in the output circuit, there is no output from the discriminator.

When the IF signal deviates, the signal applied to the discriminator transformer does not remain on one frequency (center frequency). Rather it deviates with the modulation, swinging on each side of the center frequency. An off-resonance frequency applied to the discriminator transformer results in secondary components E_2 and E_3, which lead or lag the direct voltage (E_1) by more or less than 90°. Therefore, when the incoming signal deviates on one side of the center frequency, a higher resultant voltage is applied to diode D1 than to diode D2. Conversely, when the signal swing is on the other side of center frequency, diode D2 is driven by a higher net voltage than diode D1. Refer to the vectors in Fig. 4-11B. When diode D1 draws the higher current, the net output of the discriminator is positive. Conversely, when the diode D2 draws the most current, the net output of the discriminator is negative.

How much positive or how much negative the output swings depends on just how far the incoming signal swings away from the center frequency. Thus, as the incoming FM signal deviates in frequency, the output voltage of the discriminator follows the frequency change, and a conversion is made from frequency change to amplitude change. The greater the deviation of the incoming signal, the greater the voltage range between maximum positive and maximum negative, as developed across the output.

The faster the rate of deviation of the incoming signal, the faster the amplitude change at the output of the discriminator. In this manner, the modulating wave that is present as a frequency change of the incoming signal is converted back to the original amplitude variations of the modulating wave.

4-4. Block Diagram Description

A functional plan of an FM communications transceiver is given in Fig. 4-12. The transmission process begins with the generation of a crystal-controlled signal by the transmitter oscillator shown at the lower left. It is followed by the phase modulator that uses the phase-shift process to indirectly generate a frequency-modulated wave.

The output of the microphone is applied to an audio amplifier and follow-up limiter. It is then applied to a roll-off filter that attenuates the high-frequency audio components sharply, limiting the audio bandwidth to a high of 2500 Hz. The filter is also necessary because of the tendency of a phase-modulation process to result in an FM deviation that is greater at higher frequencies. A present deviation control is located between the limiter and the phase modulator. This control is often factory preset to prevent any deviation greater than ± 5 kHz.

Three multiplier stages follow to obtain a total frequency multiplication of 12. Hence, the crystal-oscillator frequency is $\frac{1}{12}$ of the transmit frequency.

Three RF power amplifiers follow building up the level of the signal to 25 watts output in the example of Fig. 4-12. A high-attenuation low-pass filter follows. Its purpose is to reduce the harmonic output of the transmitter. The output is applied through the push-to-talk relay contacts to the antenna system.

On the receive mode the incoming signal is first applied to an RF amplifier and then to the first mixer. Proper bandwidth and selectivity is set by monolithic crystal filters that are located between the first mixer and the second mixer of the receiver. The bandpass of these crystal filters is only 16–20 kHz wide at the intermediate frequency of 10.7 MHz.

The output of the second mixer is also followed by a critical ceramic filter. It has a bandpass of 16 kHz and excellent skirt selectivity. Therefore, unwanted adjacent

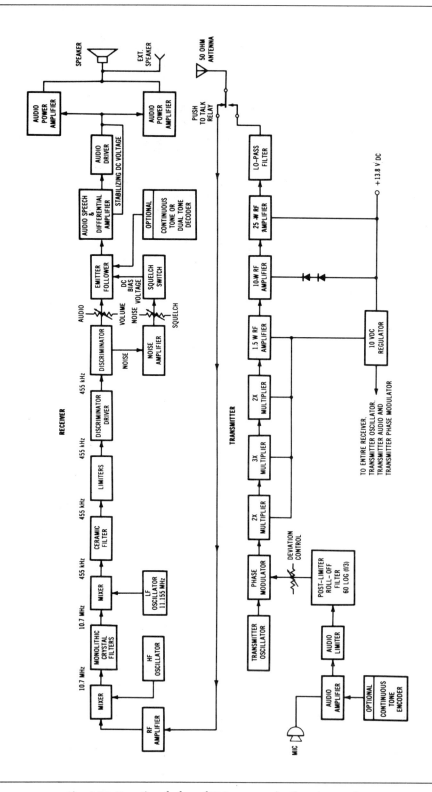

Fig. 4-12. Functional plan of FM communications transceiver.

channel signals are rejected. A series of untuned intermediate-frequency and limiter stages follow to build up the level of the signal. Note that in the communications receiver the gain is handled by the untuned IF amplifier. However, the selectivity is set by the dual-filter arrangement. Therefore, operating constants of the amplifier and limiter stages do not influence the bandpass characteristics of the receiver. A discriminator driver and discriminator follow. The output of the discriminator is applied through the volume control to an emitter follower and a succeeding three-stage audio power amplifier ending in a class-B complementary-symmetry power output stage that drives the speaker.

A noise amplifier and squelch switch provide receiver squelch operation. Thus, the squelch control can be used to cut down on the background noise level when there is no incoming signal. An incoming signal will break the squelch, and the demodulated audio becomes audible.

Many modern FM communications transceivers also employ continuous-tone controlled squelch systems (CTCSS). Such a system prevents the receiver from being activated except when the incoming signal contains a specific low-frequency tone that unsquelches the receiver. Unsquelching will occur only when the incoming tone is of the specific frequency which is used by the base station and other mobile stations of the communications system. Hence, other systems operating on the same channel frequency do not unsquelch the receivers of your own particular system.

4-5. Conventional Amplitude Modulation

In an amplitude-modulating system the radio-frequency wave is made to vary in amplitude in accordance with the audio variations. On the positive crest of the modulating wave the RF cycles at the output of the modulated amplifier (Fig. 4-13) are at maximum. When the modulating wave goes into its negative crest, the RF amplitude is a minimum. The rate at which the RF wave varies in amplitude depends upon the frequency of the modulating wave. The higher the frequency of the modulating wave, the faster the rate at which the RF wave varies in amplitude.

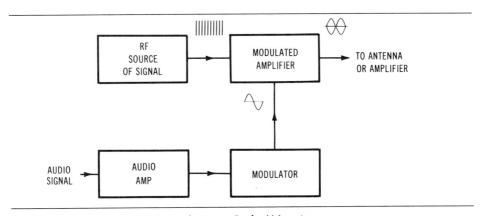

Fig. 4-13. Basic AM system.

A basic AM system is shown in Fig. 4-13. A constant-amplitude radio-frequency wave is applied to one of the inputs of the modulated amplifier. The audio signal through audio amplifier and modulator is also applied to the modulated amplifier. Actually, the modulated wave causes the gain of the modulated amplifier to vary at an audio-frequency rate. Consequently, the degree to which the radio-frequency wave is amplified depends on the modulating wave. Therefore, the output of the modulated amplifier is a series of radio-frequency waves the amplitude of which varies and follows the changes in the modulating wave. Actually, it is a mixing process that takes place. The radio-frequency envelope at the output is the algebraic addition of a carrier of constant amplitude and two sidebands, displaced on each side of the carrier frequency by an amount equal to the frequency of the modulating wave.

If a 30-MHz wave is modulated by a 1000-Hz note, there will be three waves that comprise the modulation envelope. These are the 30-MHz carrier, the upper sideband at 30 MHz plus 1000 Hz, and the lower sideband at 30 MHz minus 1000 Hz. The extent to which the modulation envelope is modulated (depth of modulation) depends on the strength of the modulating wave.

Amplitude modulation is measured in percentages. When the amplitude of the RF voltage swings to twice the unmodulated value at the output of the modulated amplifier during a positive modulating crest and falls to zero on the negative crest, the carrier is said to be 100% modulated. This is shown in Figs. 4-14A and B. Full modulation of the carrier is important in obtaining a good transmission range and maximum demodulated audio at the receiver. For a lower-amplitude audio variation the modulation envelope is not filled out and appears as shown in example C. In actual practice 100% modulation is only obtained during the voice-frequency peaks. At other times the modulation percentage is less than this complete or 100% value. In an amplitude-modulation system it is desirable to maintain as high an average modulation percentage as possible.

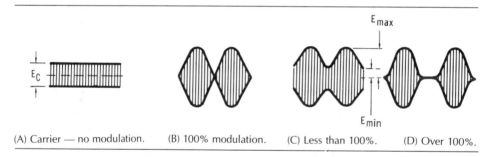

(A) Carrier — no modulation. (B) 100% modulation. (C) Less than 100%. (D) Over 100%.

Fig. 4-14. Modulation percentages.

However, to obtain a linear and undistorted modulation characteristic the transmitter must not be overmodulated as shown in the waveform of Fig 4-14D. Note that on the negative crest the wave flattens off to zero and remains so for a period of time. Thus, the negative and positive crests of the envelope become asymmetrical, and distortion is present. In fact, to prevent distortion the amplitude of the positive crest of the modulated RF sine wave must not be more than twice the amplitude of the unmodulated value. If it exceeds this value, overmodulation is present. A formula often used to calculate modulation percentage is:

$$\% \text{ modulation} = \frac{E_{max} - E_{min}}{2 E_c} \times 100$$

where,

E_{max} is the maximum amplitude of the modulation envelope,
E_{min} is the minimum amplitude of the modulation envelope,
E_c is the amplitude of the unmodulated carrier.

Since a modulating signal is seldom a pure sine wave but rather a combination of various frequencies of differing amplitudes, it is often useful to determine positive and negative modulation percentages separately. Positive modulation refers to the increase in RF cycle amplitude above the unmodulated value; the negative modulation, to the drop in RF cycle amplitude below the unmodulated value. The positive and negative modulation percentage equations are:

$$\text{\% mod. (positive)} = \frac{E_c - E_{min}}{E_c} \times 100$$

$$\text{\% mod. (negative)} = \frac{E_{max} - E_c}{E_c} \times 100$$

Most modulating waves are not of the constant amplitude that maintains 100% modulation continuously. The average during voice modulation is considerably lower, and only on an occasional voice peak does the modulation reach 100%. Nevertheless an AM system must be adjusted so that there will be no overmodulation on voice peaks. Since the voice peaks are only occasional, it is apparent that the average modulation must be lower than 100%. At the same time, for clarity of transmission and range, the average level of modulation should be kept as high as possible. Consequently, two-way radio equipment usually includes special circuits that compress the voice peaks so they do not cause overmodulation and, at the same time, boost up the lower amplitude passages so that they are not too weak.

4-5-1. Carrier and Sideband Power

As mentioned previously, the modulation envelope is a composite waveform. During the modulation each RF cycle differs from the preceding and following ones. They are no longer pure sine waves. This is another way of stating that the resultant signal is no longer composed of a single wave (RF carrier) but, in the case of modulation by a single sine-wave tone, a carrier plus upper and lower sidebands. Actually, the carrier, despite modulation, remains of constant magnitude and frequency. The only difference has been the addition of two sideband components.

The foregoing relationships indicate that the carrier power is unchanged with modulation. Any net addition in power is contributed by the two sidebands.

The instantaneous power of the modulation envelope varies continuously during the modulating cycle. At the peak of the envelope, assuming 100% modulation, the RF voltages are twice as high as during the unmodulated period. This doubling of the voltage represents a fourfold increase in power because the rise in power is equal to the square of the voltage. At the crest of the negative modulation, the resultant envelope falls to zero, and the instantaneous power is zero.

When the power is averaged over the complete sine-wave cycle for 100% modulation, it is 50% higher than the unmodulated carrier power. One hundred percent modulation occurs whenever the amplitude of each sideband is one half the amplitude of the unmodulated carrier as shown in Fig. 4-15. This means that each sideband contains one fourth as much power as the carrier. Since there are two sidebands, they contain one half the power of the carrier.

The modulating information to be transmitted is contained in the sidebands, each of which contains the same information. The carrier itself contains none of the information to be transmitted.

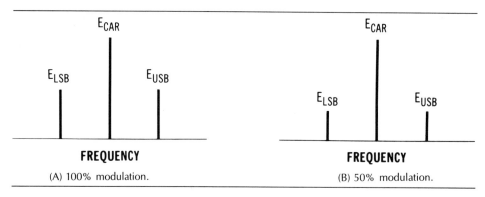

FREQUENCY

(A) 100% modulation.   (B) 50% modulation.

Fig. 4-15. Carrier and sideband voltage levels.

Let us now reconsider the power relationship in terms of the total power output. The total output (envelope power) is the sum of the power contained in the carrier and sidebands or:

$$P_o = P_{car} + P_{usb} + P_{lsb}$$

where,

P_o is the total output (envelope) power,
P_{car} is the power carrier,
P_{usb} is the upper sideband power,
P_{lsb} is the lower sideband power.

Assuming carrier power as unity:

$$P_o = 1 + \frac{1}{4} + \frac{1}{4} = \frac{3}{2}$$

Since the sidebands contain only one-half the power of the carrier, they represent only one third of the total transmitted power. The carrier represents the remaining two thirds.

$$\frac{P_{car}}{P_o} = \frac{1}{3/2} = \frac{2}{3}$$

$$P_{car} = \frac{2}{3} P_o$$

and

$$\frac{P_{sb}}{P_o} = \frac{1/2}{3/2} = \frac{1}{3}$$

$$P_{sb} = \frac{1}{3} P_o$$

It is apparent that amplitude modulation is a rather wasteful method of conveying information via a radio wave. All the information to be sent can be packed into one of the sidebands, representing one sixth of the total transmitted power. The relationship is even more exaggerated for modulation of less than 100% — the prevailing condition in the usual voice communications. An example of 50% modulation is shown in Fig. 4-15B.

For 50% modulation the sideband amplitude is only one quarter the carrier amplitude. Therefore, each sideband contains but one sixteenth the power in the carrier. Hence, the power in both sidebands is only one eighth the carrier power, a very small fraction of the total transmitted power. This relationship proves why a high average-modulation percentage is important in maintaining an effective transmission range and strong audio-frequency components at the receiver.

Efficiency factor is another consideration. Its value is:

$$\text{Efficiency factor} = \frac{\text{RF power output}}{\text{DC input power}}$$

$$= \frac{P_o}{I_c V_c}$$

The DC power input remains constant, whether the carrier is modulated or unmodulated. Likewise, the carrier power output is a constant, and the RF carrier output is supplied by conversion from the power supply of the modulated amplifier.

However, the RF power output increases with modulation. What is the source of this additional power? You learned that the additional power with modulation is contained in the two sidebands. The sidebands are due to introduction of the modulating wave into the supply line via the modulator. Consequently, the RF sideband power is contributed by the audio-output system or modulator.

4-5-2. Modulator Power

With 100% sine-wave modulation, the RF power output of the transmitter is increased by 50%. To make this much additional power available, the audio power output of the modulator must be one half the DC power input to the modulated amplifier. However, since only occasional voice peaks extend to 100% modulation, the average power output of the modulator can be less than 50% of the DC power input.

For 100% modulation, the audio peak voltage must be approximately equal to the supply voltage. Only under this condition will the voltage of the modulated amplifier swing to twice the supply voltage, a necessity for obtaining 100% modulation at the crest of the positive audio cycle. The negative sweep of the same modulating wave reduces the supply voltage to zero to produce the 100% modulated envelope trough.

To produce the desired peak audio voltage at the required power, the audio must be developed across a specific impedance. The impedance seen by the modulator output must equal the DC input resistance to the modulated amplifier. The DC input resistance is related to the DC component of supply current and voltage, or:

$$R_{in} = \frac{V_c}{I_c}$$

The modulation transformer or the output system of the modulator must be designed to match this impedance, just as an audio output transformer must have the proper turns ratio to match the impedance of a speaker voice coil.

4-6. Typical AM Circuits

A bipolar transistor can be amplitude modulated by varying the supply voltage to one of its elements — base, emitter, or collector. However, in modern two-way radio equipment the dominant method is to use collector modulation (Fig. 4-16). The DC collector voltage is made to vary with the modulating signal by inserting the secondary of the modulation transformer in the supply voltage path. The collector voltage of the amplifier is increased or decreased by the audio modulating signal.

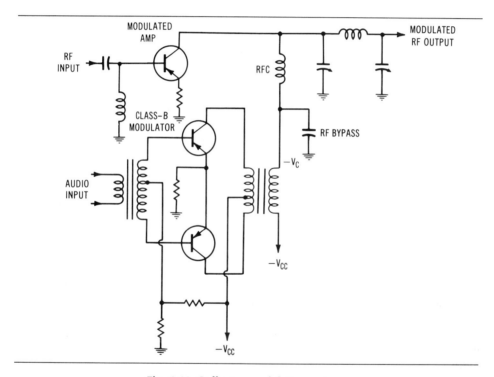

Fig. 4-16. Collector modulation system.

The unmodulated RF carrier is fed to the base of the modulated amplifier. The mixing of the two signals in the modulation process results in the formation of a modulated RF signal across the collector tank circuit. In the modulated RF stage the tank circuit voltage varies linearly with the collector supply voltage; thus, doubling the supply voltage doubles the tank RF voltage over a suitable operating range. If the modulated amplifier is operated from a 12-volt V_{CC} supply, the instantaneous collector supply voltage can be made to vary above and below 12 volts.

If the modulating wave is a pure sine wave, this variation can be symmetrical. In bipolar transistor stages it is quite difficult to obtain absolute and symmetrical full

100% modulation. However, satisfactory and reasonably good amplitude modulation is obtained with a single stage.

The rate of variation of the supply voltage depends on the frequency of the modulating wave; the magnitude of the change depends on the amplitude of that wave. This change in the collector supply voltage becomes a replica of the modulating wave. If the variations on each side of the zero axis of the modulating wave are identical, the average DC collector voltage remains at 12 volts. Likewise, in a perfect bipolar modulation system the DC collector current would also remain constant. This ideal operating characteristic is not always feasible in a simple bipolar modulation system.

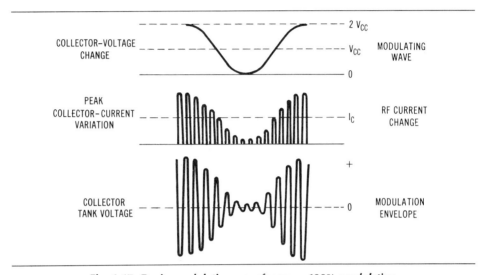

Fig. 4-17. Drain modulation waveforms — 100% modulation.

The influence that a change in the collector voltage has on the operation of the modulated amplifier is shown in the waveforms of Fig. 4-17. As the collector voltage changes in a class-C amplifier, so does the peak collector current drawn for each individual radio-frequency cycle. In fact, the peaks of the latter are a copy of the modulating wave as shown in the second waveform of Fig. 4-17.

The peak collector current, in turn, determines the magnitude of the RF voltage developed across the collector tank circuit. The higher the maximum collector current, the higher will be the amplitude of the corresponding RF voltage. It follows then that the RF collector voltage waveform is also a copy of the modulating wave. In this manner the standard AM envelope is formed.

To develop the desired change in the envelope with full modulation capability, the collector voltage must be made to swing between twice the collector supply voltage and zero. The impedance seen by the modulator output equals the DC resistance of the modulated amplifier input. This DC resistance is quite low because of the low collector voltage and high collector current;

$$R_{in} = \frac{V_{cc}}{I_c}$$

It is this impedance that the output of the modulator (modulation transformer) must match. In so doing the proper load is reflected to the output of the modulator, and it is possible to obtain a high level of modulation with good efficiency.

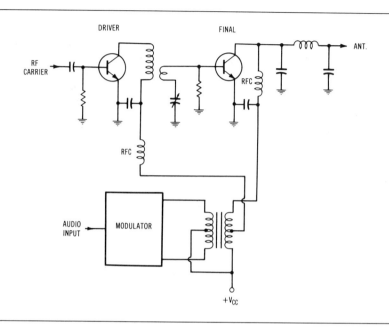

Fig. 4-18. Modulation of final and RF driver.

A more common system of amplitude modulation is that shown in Fig. 4-18. Linear and full 100% modulation is obtained. In this plan both the final and the driver are modulated. This arrangement is of particular help because the driver is then able to supply the necessary additional base drive to the final that can accommodate the 100% modulation peaks. The proper level of modulating wave to the driver to accomplish full modulation capability is set by the tapped position on the secondary of the modulation transformer. Note that the final RF amplifier obtains the full secondary voltage.

4-7. Single-Sideband Modulation

The advantages of single-sideband modulation over standard amplitude modulation are narrower bandwidth, better signal-to-noise ratio, better signal-to-interference ratio, and more efficient use of available power. In standard amplitude modulation, a carrier and two sidebands are transmitted. As previously covered the carrier remains fixed in amplitude and carries none of the modulation, while the two sidebands carry identical modulation information. Thus, it is possible to abandon the carrier and one sideband because all the desired data can be conveyed by the single remaining sideband.

Three specific processes are involved in the generation of a single-sideband signal. In the actual modulation process, the carrier itself must be suppressed, the undesired sideband removed, and the desired sideband converted in frequency and then amplified to a desired power level.

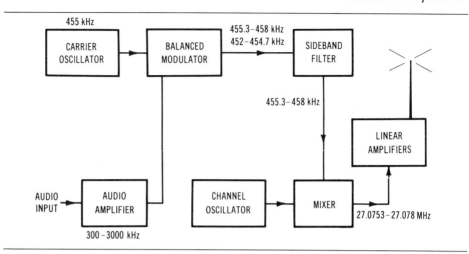

Fig. 4-19. Basic single-sideband transmitter.

A simplified block diagram of a sideband transmitter is shown in Fig. 4-19. A crystal-controlled carrier generator is used to generate the basic carrier. This carrier is passed to a balanced modulator to which the audio signal is also applied. In a balanced circuit arrangement, the carrier is cancelled and two radio-frequency sidebands are generated. If the source of the carrier signal is a 455-kHz component, the sideband spectra for a 300- to 3000-Hz audio range would be as shown at the output of the balanced modulator. The two sideband spectra fall above and below the frequency of the absent carrier.

The second process in the generation of a single-sideband signal is the removal of one sideband. It does not matter which sideband is removed because both carry like information. The choice depends on the basic system design. Sometimes a switching arrangement permits the generation of either one of the sidebands, upper or lower. In the filter method of sideband removal a carefully designed crystal or ceramic filter highly attenuates the sideband that is not to be transmitted (undesired sideband) but passes the desired sideband with a minimum of attenuation. Such filters have a highly selective response and must have a high order of stability.

The sideband signal must now be converted to the transmit frequency band. Inasmuch as it carries modulation, it must be converted in frequency and amplified in strength by linear circuits (harmonic multipliers and class-C amplifiers are not used). So-called linear mixers are used. The channel oscillator frequency component is mixed with the sideband signal and produces an output frequency in the desired transmit band. In fact, the output circuit can be tuned to either a sum or difference frequency depending on whether the desired transmit band is above or below the sideband frequency. In the simplified example of Fig. 4-19, a high-frequency sideband is to be generated on CB channel 10 (27.075 MHz). The sideband spectra entering the mixer from the sideband filter has a frequency range between 455.3 and 458 kHz. When mixed with the channel oscillator frequency of 25.620 MHz, the output-frequency spectra of the mixer, for a 300- to 3000-Hz audio range would be 27.0753 to 27.078 MHz. Note that this is a range of frequencies between 300 and 3000 Hz above the CB channel-10 carrier frequency of 27.075 MHz.

Succeeding stages build up the weak upper-sideband signal present at the output of the mixer to the 12-watt PEP limit set for sideband operation on the Citizens Band. This discussion simplifies the sideband transmission process. An actual single-sideband CB radio incorporates both transmit and receive functions in the sideband generation and demodulation process.

154

4-7-1. Waveform Relationships

A clear understanding of the makeup of various AM waves can be obtained by considering Fig. 4-20. Such knowledge will permit a better understanding of the sideband-modulation envelope that is important when checking and adjusting sideband equipment. As you will recall, the standard AM wave, when modulated by a single sine-wave tone, is a composite of three RF waves, a constant-amplitude carrier, and two side-frequency components, which are above and below the carrier frequency by the frequency of the modulating wave. At 100% modulation, the two side frequencies are one half the amplitude of the carrier.

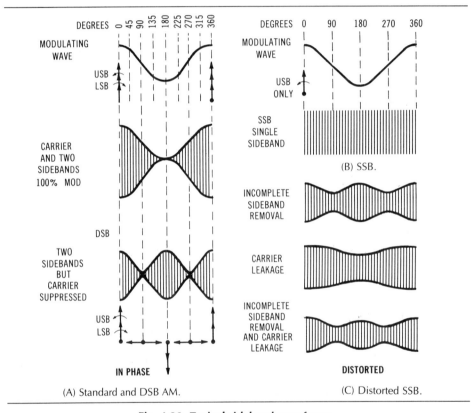

Fig. 4-20. Typical sideband waveforms.

In the vector comparison shown in Fig. 4-20A, all three components are in phase at the crest of the modulation envelope, and the peak amplitude builds up to twice the unmodulated signal value. Since the two side frequencies are not the same and also differ from the carrier frequency, the phase relationship among all three components changes throughout the modulating cycle. Note in Fig. 4-21 that the carrier is established as a zero-reference phase. On the positive crest of the modulating wave, the carrier and both sidebands momentarily are all in phase. Hence, the resultant modulation-envelope signal rises to twice the unmodulated-carrier value. When the modulating sine wave is passing through zero, the two side frequencies are related 90° to the carrier and 180° to each other. Therefore, the side frequencies cancel, and the net amplitude of the amplitude-modulated wave is the same value as its carrier.

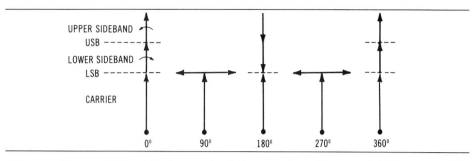

Fig. 4-21. Vector relationships for standard AM wave through one modulating-wave cycle.

On the negative peak of the modulating wave, the two side frequencies are again in phase with each other but 180° out of phase with the carrier. Now there is a complete cancellation, and the net envelope output drops to the zero point of its cycle.

In summary, it is the changing phase relationship among the three components that causes the amplitude variations in their resultant amplitude-modulated envelope. Of course, the intermediate levels of the modulation envelope also depend on the instantaneous phase relationship among the three waves. Actually, the side frequencies when following the amplitude changes of the modulating wave can be considered to rotate vectorially around the zero-reference phase set by the carrier. They rotate in opposite directions, one being above and one being below the carrier frequency.

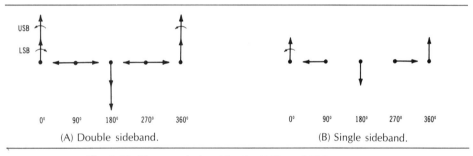

(A) Double sideband.   (B) Single sideband.

Fig. 4-22. Vector relationships for DSB and SSB components.

Consider next the type of resultant modulation envelope obtained when the carrier is suppressed, and the two side frequencies remain (lower part of Fig. 4-20A). As shown in Fig. 4-22A, the side frequency components shift in phase relative to each other. Even though the carrier magnitude is zero, the side frequencies can be considered to revolve in phase with respect to the zero carrier-reference phase. As the modulating wave goes through its cycle, the side frequencies at times become out of phase and at other times exactly in phase during the modulating wave period. Actually, the modulation envelope goes through two cycles during the one cycle of the modulating wave. The peak amplitude of the envelope rises to twice the individual sideband magnitude. It falls to zero when the two vectors are exactly out of phase.

The magnitude and vector relationships for a single-sideband signal are shown in Figs. 4-20B and 4-22B. Now there is only one rotating vector. In fact, only one RF component is generated as the modulating wave goes through its cycle. Hence, a constant-amplitude resultant is produced.

The sideband modulation envelopes are important in assessing the performance of a sideband system. The nature of any distortion on these envelopes points up the various characteristic defects and maladjustments. In fact, the oscilloscope is an important tool for adjusting sideband systems. When the sideband system is functioning properly and is modulated by a single-tone frequency, the output RF wave is of constant amplitude as shown in Fig. 4-20B. If the undesired sideband is not completely removed, there will be a double-frequency ripple on the sideband output waveform as shown in Fig 4-20C. Likewise, if there is carrier leakage into the output, there will also be a frequency variation on the envelope that corresponds to the frequency of the modulating wave. Of course, the combination of the two defects produces the resultant wave shown at the bottom of Fig. 4-20C.

4-7-2. Power Relationships

In addition to the reduced bandwidth compared to that of a double-sideband system, a single-sideband system also conserves power. A mathematical example will prove this saving. A standard AM transmitter with a rated carrier of 4 watts radiates 1 watt per sideband with single tone 100% modulation. The carrier power is 4 watts and the total sideband power is 2 watts. Peak power is, of course, four times the carrier value under this circumstance and reaches 16 watts, because the RF output voltage is twice the unmodulated carrier voltage during 100% modulation peaks. Nevertheless, the sideband power output is only 1 watt.

In order to generate a 12-watt sideband signal using the single-sideband modulation method, the peak envelope power is 12 watts because all of the energy is contained in the transmitted sideband. Furthermore, only half the frequency spectra is required as compared to a double-sideband signal. Consequently, two sideband signals can be made to fit in the same frequency spectrum as a single double-sideband signal. Thus, there is not only conservation of power but also conservation of frequency spectra.

4-7-3. CB Sideband Methods

Some sideband transceivers include both sideband and standard AM capabilities. Most of the circuits are used interchangeably on AM and sideband. Others must be switched in and out as a changeover is made between single sideband and standard amplitude modulation.

A functional diagram of a CB receiver and transmitter is shown in Fig. 4-23. The receive signal is picked up by the antenna and is applied to the mixer through an RF amplifier stage. A local-oscillator signal is derived from a phase-locked loop circuit. The frequency range of the local oscillator injection signal varies between the limits indicated depending on whether upper- or lower-sideband reception is desired. The lower-sideband frequencies are indicated in parentheses. The output of the mixer is applied to the sideband filter (XF), which has a 3-kHz bandwidth. The input to the filter circuit is one of the two frequencies indicated depending on whether upper- or lower-sideband emission is being received.

A multistage IF amplifier builds up the signal and applies it to the product detector. The demodulating frequency for the product detector is also derived from a phase-locked loop circuit. The volume control and an integrated-circuit audio amplifier follow. One of the IF stages as well as the RF amplifier and mixer are under the control of an AGC circuit system.

In the transmission process, the audio signal is derived from the microphone amplifier (integrated circuit) and is applied to the balanced modulator (BM). The level-control circuit is associated with the audio section to maintain a high average modulation level without exceeding the peak level that will produce audio distortion

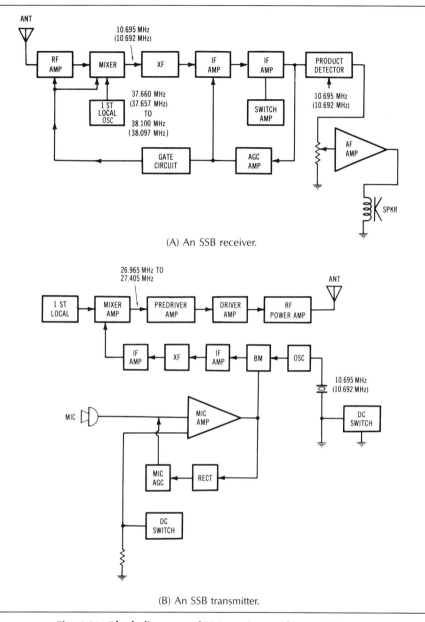

(A) An SSB receiver.

(B) An SSB transmitter.

Fig. 4-23. Block diagrams of SSB receiver and transmitter.

or flat topping in the modulation process. Appropriate switching is also necessary depending on whether the audio system is used for sideband or amplitude modulation.

The carrier signal is derived from an appropriate crystal oscillator, which is a part of the PLL circuit. The frequency of the crystal oscillator is changed by a switch depending on the choice of upper-sideband or lower-sideband emission.

The output of the IF amplifier is applied to the sideband filter and on to a followup IF amplifier that builds up the level of the sideband signal. The function of the balanced modulator is to produce a double-sideband signal without carrier. The followup filter then removes the undesired sideband. Therefore, a single-sideband signal alone is

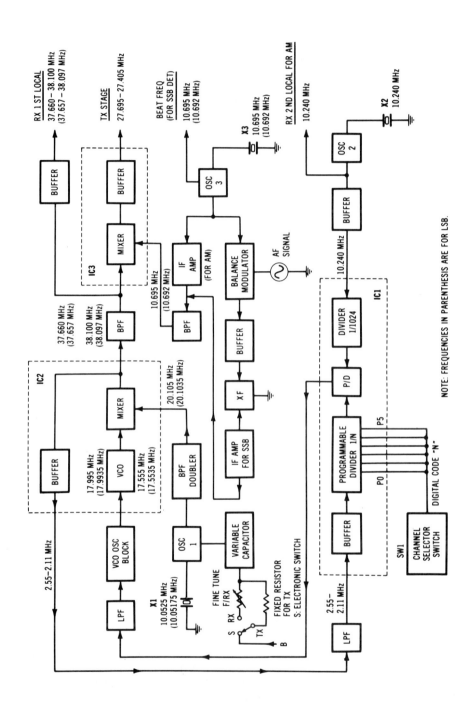

Fig. 4-24. Block diagram of PLL section.

applied to the mixer amplifier. The injection frequency for the mixer amplifier is derived from the PLL circuit.

The output of the mixer is tuned to the difference frequency which falls in the Citizens-Band frequency range. A series of linear RF amplifier stages build up the sideband signal to the 12-watt PEP level before application to the antenna system.

A functional plan of the PLL section of the transceiver is shown in Fig. 4-24. The basic theory of the phase-locked loop was discussed previously. The programmable divider and associated circuits are shown at the bottom; the voltage-controlled oscillator and associated circuits at the top center.

Let us begin with the phase detector (P/D) located at the immediate right of the programmable divider. In this circuit, the output of the programmable divider is compared with a reference signal derived from oscillator No. 2. Oscillator No. 2, at the lower right, operates on 10.240 MHz. The signal is applied through a buffer to a divider chain that has a ratio of 1/1024. Therefore, the frequency applied to the phase detector is 10 kHz. When the CB transceiver is on correct frequency for a given channel, the output of the programmable divider is also 10 kHz.

If there is a frequency differential, the output of the phase detector is applied through a low-pass filter to the frequency control circuit of the voltage-controlled oscillator (VCO). The purpose of the phase detector is to keep the VCO on correct frequency.

The comparison signal is derived from a mixer at the output of the VCO and is applied through a low-pass filter and buffer to the input of the programmable divider. The frequency range of this feedback signal, depending on the channel received, falls between 2.11 and 2.55 MHz. This is the signal frequency applied to the programmable divider. However, the channel selector switch, along with its digital code and LED display, sets the proper divider ratio for a given channel. As a result, the output of the programmable divider, when everything is functioning properly, is 10 kHz. When switching channels, this divider will also change. Meanwhile, an appropriate change is made in the setting of the VCO because of the correcting voltage supplied by the phase detector.

Let us next consider the four signals that are supplied by the PLL circuit. First a transmit frequency must be developed for both AM and sideband operation. Then a local oscillator signal must be generated to permit both sideband and AM mixer activity. A third signal must be developed for use in the sideband detector. The fourth, and final, signal supplied by the PLL circuit is the second local-oscillator frequency for AM demodulation. This transceiver uses single conversion for sideband reception and double conversion for amplitude modulation reception.

Oscillator No. 1 at the middle left in the diagram generates a 10-MHz component that is applied to a doubler and bandpass filter (BPF) and then to a mixer that is a part of the VCO integrated circuit. Since the VCO operates in the 17.5- to 18-MHz range, the sum frequency at the output of the mixer is in the 37- to 38-MHz range as shown in Fig. 4-24. It is applied to another mixer that is a part of integrated circuit IC3.

The third crystal oscillator, shown at the right center, generates a frequency of either 10.692 or 10.695 MHz depending on the selected sideband. For sideband modulation it is applied to the balanced modulator and associated sideband circuits as described previously for Fig. 4-23. This is noted again at the center of Fig. 4-24. The output of the IF amplifier passes through a bandpass filter to the mixer that is a part of integrated circuit IC3. The output of this mixer is tuned to the difference frequency and produces a frequency range between 27.965 and 27.045 MHz, which is the Citizens-Band radio spectra.

The output frequency of the VCO section is that frequency required by the first local-oscillator injection signal. This is shown at the top right in Fig. 4-24. The output oscillator (No. 3) also generates the frequency component that is applied to the product detector for single-sideband demodulation. These three signals shown at the top right are needed for operation for both the transmitter and the receiver for single-sideband operation.

In AM transmission, the same frequency range is required for the transmit mode. Likewise, the same frequency range is required for the first local-oscillator injection. However, to obtain a frequency component for the double-conversion process, still another frequency must be generated. This is supplied by oscillator No. 2 at the bottom right and has a frequency of 10.24 MHz. Note at the right center of Fig. 4-24 that for AM transmission the output of oscillator No. 3 passes through an IF amplifier and goes directly to the bandpass filter and on to the mixer associated with integrated circuit IC3. This generates the basic transmitter frequency range for AM transmission.

4-8. Sideband Circuits

The first step in the generation of a single-sideband signal is the formation of sidebands along with the removal of the carrier. These two objectives can be accomplished simultaneously. Diodes, transistors, and integrated circuits are used in modern balanced-modulator circuits. Considerable help in understanding the operation of a balanced modulator can be gained by first reviewing the operation of a diode as a modulator. The diode is used frequently as an AM detector or demodulator. In this application, the modulated signal is applied to the diode input. By rectifying the radio-frequency cycles, the lower-frequency modulating wave can be recovered in its output circuit.

A diode can be made to operate in the opposite fashion; that is, a weak audio signal and a stronger radio-frequency signal can be supplied to its input. The same nonlinear operation or rectifying action causes sum- and difference-frequency components to be developed in the output circuit. These are the familiar upper- and lower-sideband frequencies. The waveforms shown in Fig. 4-25 demonstrate the mixing or modulation process. When the radio-frequency signal alone is applied to the diode modulator, there is diode current during the positive alternations of the input cycle. Hence, positive bursts of current develop through the load. Inasmuch as the load is a resonant circuit a sine wave is reconstructed in the output. This action is similar to the influence of resonant circuits on the output of class-B or class-C, RF amplifiers.

When an audio wave is applied to the input along with the radio-frequency wave, there is an algebraic summation. The peak amplitudes of the diode current bursts now depend on the net diode anode voltage at the crest of each radio-frequency cycle. This peak voltage varies up and down with the modulating wave. As a result, the peak diode current varies correspondingly. This peak current diode change is comparable to the peak current variation of a modulated class-C amplifier. Again, the resonant circuit, because of its energy storing ability, reconstructs the negative alternation of the output variation, forming the familiar amplitude-modulation envelope.

The input wave is the simple combining of two separate signals — high-frequency radio wave and low-frequency audio wave. The output wave results from nonlinear mixing or heterodyning and is composed of three radio-frequency components — the carrier plus two side frequencies. The audio wave is filtered out by the low impedance of the output circuit.

Diode modulation has poor efficiency. However, at a low signal level, combinations of diodes in a number of circuit arrangements can serve admirably as stable balanced modulators. Diodes have a low order of modulation linearity. Nevertheless, by using a modulating wave of much lower amplitude than the radio-frequency wave (low percentage modulation), a linear output can be obtained (modulation envelope variations correspond faithfully to the modulating wave). By arranging combinations of diode modulators it is possible to generate the sideband frequencies at the same time the radio-frequency carrier itself is suppressed.

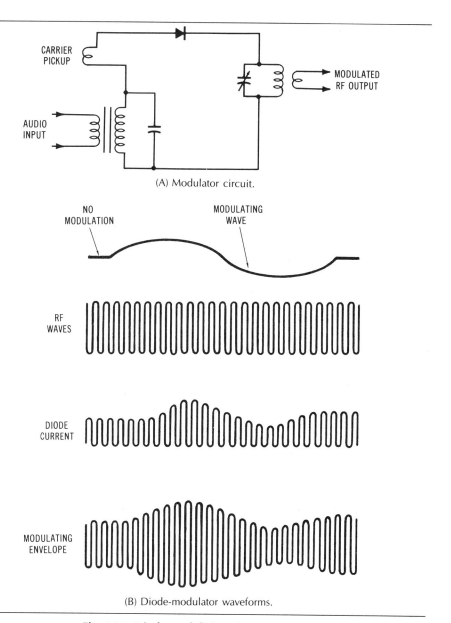

(A) Modulator circuit.

(B) Diode-modulator waveforms.

Fig. 4-25. Diode-modulation circuit operation.

Two basic and common diode balanced modulators are the bridge and ring circuits shown in Figs. 4-26 and 4-27, respectively. Since radio-frequency and audio waves are supplied to the various diodes, modulation takes place. Thus carrier and sideband currents are produced. However, the carrier current components cancel with relation to the output system.

Let us consider the operation of the bridge circuit in Fig. 4-26 when only the radio-frequency carrier is applied. When the radio-frequency cycle swings negative, point A

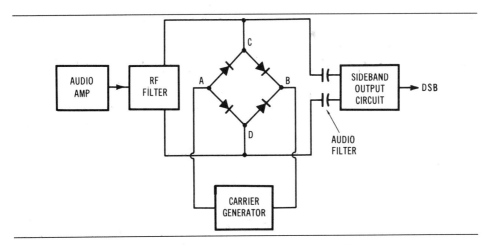

Fig. 4-26. Bridge-balanced modulator operation.

on the bridge is then negative with respect to point B. Consequently the four diodes are back-biased, and there is no current. If the four diodes have the same reverse resistance, the bridge will be balanced, and there will be no difference of potential between points C and D. Consequently, there will be no current in the output circuit.

When the radio-frequency wave swings positive, all four diodes become forward biased. Hence, their resistance is low and there will be current. However, if they all have the same resistance, the bridge will remain balanced. Therefore, no difference of potential develops between points C and D, and there will be no carrier current in the output circuit. Thus, it is apparent that neither the positive nor negative alternations of the radio-frequency wave cause an output voltage, and so the carrier is suppressed. However, the radio-frequency wave does appear across each of the four diodes, and rectifier action takes place with the diode currents being switched on and off by the alternations of the radio-frequency wave.

Diode activities differ when a modulating wave is applied simultaneously with the carrier. Inasmuch as the audio wave is made substantially lower in amplitude than the radio-frequency wave, the diode conducts only during the positive alternation of the radio-frequency carrier. The amount of current present, as in the simple diode modulator, depends on the instantaneous sum of the combined radio-frequency and audio-frequency waves. As a result, the peak radio-frequency current will vary with the modulating wave as in any form of amplitude modulation.

The influence that the audio voltage has on the bridge is important. This voltage is applied between points C and D. As a result, the bridge is unbalanced — the degree of unbalance depending on the magnitude of the audio signal. The imbalance allows side-frequency currents in the output circuit. It is apparent then that the bridge, although balanced at the carrier frequency, will be unbalanced at off-carrier frequencies. As a result, the sideband frequencies develop in the output circuit. Audio-frequency components are blocked from the output circuit by the small series capacitors and the low shunt impedance of the output tank circuit at audio frequencies.

The ring-balanced modulator shown in Fig. 4-27 delivers up to twice the output of the other diode circuits. Again, the carrier is applied in balanced fashion to appear at the same phase between points C and common and D and common. The modulating wave is applied between points A and B of the diode ring. As shown in the simplified drawing of Fig. 4-27B, radio-frequency carrier current would be present in the output circuit except that the two paths are opposing. With proper balance, the current cancels and produces no carrier output.

The presence of the audio wave unbalances the diode operation. As mentioned previously, the carrier wave does appear across each diode, and the application of audio causes a heterodyning action. The side frequencies are produced and developed across the output because of the imbalance that the audio wave introduces into the ring circuit. In the ring-balanced modulator, side frequencies are developed during both alternations of the RF wave. This is unlike the bridge circuit described previously, where current occurred only with the positive alternations and less output was available. In diode balanced-modulator circuits, carrier suppression of 40 dB and higher can be attained by careful design and adjustment.

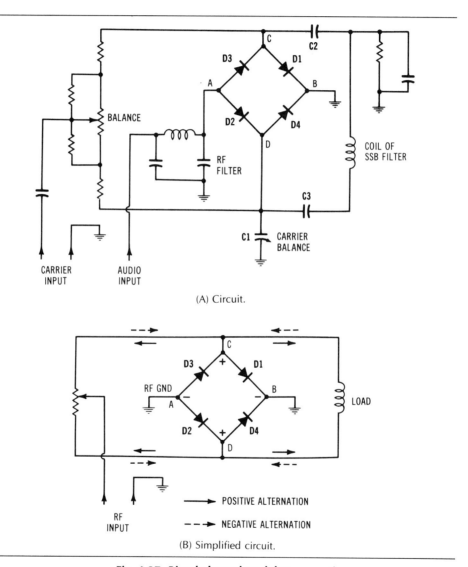

(A) Circuit.

(B) Simplified circuit.

Fig. 4-27. Ring-balanced modulator operation.

The RF carrier is introduced through a resistor network which includes a carrier-balance control. Any slight performance differentials in the ring circuit can be compensated for with this control. Thus, it is possible to adjust the circuit for a minimum carrier output. Stray and differential capacities may also disturb the ring balance. Consequently, an additional carrier-balance control is included in the form of adjustable capacitor C1.

The audio wave is introduced via a low-pass filter that blocks the radio-frequency components from entering the audio system. In the output circuit, capacitors C2 and C3 have very high reactance at audio frequencies. Consequently, the audio components are blocked from the followup sideband filter.

Integrated circuits are popular as balanced modulators because of their high level of carrier rejection. Bridge- or ring-type balanced modulators can be constructed from the popular RCA CA3019 diode array. A pinout diagram of this integrated circuit is shown in Fig. 4-28. By proper connection of diodes, either a bridge- or ring-type modulator can be constructed.

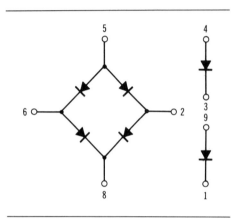

Fig. 4-28. Pinout diagram of the RCA CA-3019 diode array.

A single-sideband generator with good carrier suppression is the balanced-differential amplifier shown in Fig. 4-29. As a function of the modulating signal, sideband outputs of 0.5- to 1-volt rms can be obtained. Such a balanced modulator circuit will operate with a carrier input of about 100 millivolts and an audio drive of about 0.5-volt rms. Internal circuit configuration and external circuit plan for a double-sideband suppressed-carrier generator are shown in Fig. 4-29.

Two differential amplifier pairs are included in the integrated circuit (Fig. 4-29A) and incorporate individual transistors in their common-emitter circuits to supply constant-current bias. A second transistor is included in each leg to inject the modulating signal. The carrier is applied in a differential-mode fashion to pairs of differential transistors. Outputs of these differential pairs are out of phase; under true balance the net carrier voltage is near zero. Out-of-phase audio is applied across the bases of the two modulation-insert transistors located in the emitter legs of the differential pairs. Upper- and lower-side frequencies develop across the output while the modulating wave itself is cancelled.

Note in Fig. 4-29B that the carrier is applied between pins 8 and 7 and the modulating signal between pins 1 and 4. Bias for these two latter transistors is obtained from the negative 8-volt source connected to the arm of the carrier null potentiometer. This bias, because of its link to the emitters of the differential pairs, sets their bias level and permits an appropriate adjustment for balancing the carrier to zero.

A balanced output is available between pins 6 and 9; and single-ended output can be derived from either pin and common. The carrier rejection is excellent using the proper levels of carrier and modulating wave.

In the filter-type sideband generator, a filter follows the balanced modulator. The output of the balanced modulator, you may recall, consists of two sidebands with the carrier suppressed. The sideband filter removes the undesired sideband. Sideband filters can be made of either crystal or ceramic material. The ceramic filter, however, is commonly used.

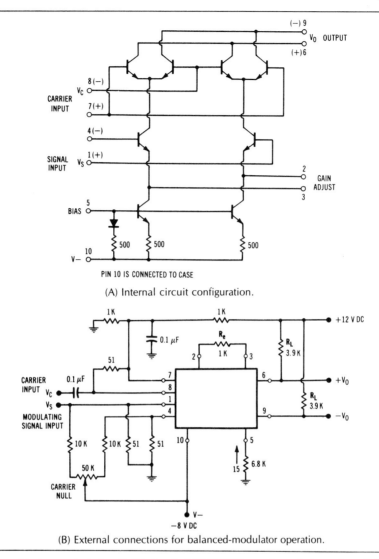

(A) Internal circuit configuration.

(B) External connections for balanced-modulator operation.

Fig. 4-29. Integrated circuit (Motorola MC-1596G) used as a balanced modulator.

A typical filter-response curve is shown in Fig. 4-30. Note that it has very steep skirts and a bandwidth of only approximately 2.5 to 3.2 kHz. A 3-kHz response is typical. This narrow-frequency response means that the filter has good frequency rejection on one side of the carrier frequency but passes with minimum attenuation the side frequencies located on the other side of the carrier frequency. Hence, if an upper-sideband signal is to be transmitted, the sideband filter will pass the frequency spectrum of the upper sideband but will reject the lower-sideband frequency components.

The sideband-product detector of a transceiver is shown in Fig. 4-31. In a product detector, two radio-frequency signals are mixed, and the output circuit develops a difference frequency. The two RF components are filtered out. The single-sideband signal is applied to the base circuit of the transistor. A demodulating carrier for the product detector is applied to the emitter circuit, developing across inductor L1. When the transceiver is set for sideband operation, diode D1 conducts and the 3.3-kΩ collector load resistor is active. The demodulated audio develops across the circuit

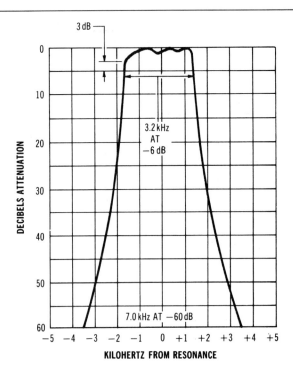

Fig. 4-30. Typical sideband-filter response.

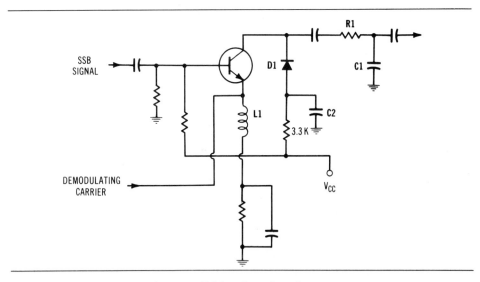

Fig. 4-31. Sideband product detector.

and is coupled through a resistor-capacitor network to the audio system. Resistor R1 and capacitors C1 and C2 filter out the radio-frequency components. These three components also have values that limit the higher audio spectrum so that frequency signals above the desired voice-frequency range are attenuated.

Additional modulation systems and circuits are covered in discussions of actual two-way radio units in the chapters that follow.

5

Digital and
Microprocessor Electronics

Digital electronics has become an important part of modern radiocommunications, augmenting the analog and linear circuits that comprise the complete two-way radio system. Digital emphasis is on control, switching, and display functions. Additional applications involve much of the test equipment used for two-way radio testing and service, such as frequency counters, voltmeters, and communications monitors. More elaborate radiocommunication systems and some test facilities incorporate microprocessors.

5-1. Digital Basics

A first step in understanding digital circuits is to learn just a bit about the binary numbering system. In a binary system, you can count with only two numerals, zero and one. In both the binary and decimal languages, *nothing* is zero or 0. Likewise, the quantity *one* is the same for both languages and is written as one or 1. From this point on, things differ. In decimal language, the quantity two is written as 2; in binary language, it is written as 10. Very often the binary code used is in the form of a 4-bit series, and the quantities zero, one, and two are set down as follows:

zero = 0000
one = 0001
two = 0010

The 4-bit expression for zero is telling us that there is no eight, no four, no two, and no one. For the quantity one, it is saying that there is no eight, no four, no two, and one one. Likewise, for the quantity two, the expression says that there is no eight, no four, one two, and no one.

In 4-bit binary language, the quanity nine is written as 1001, telling that there is one eight, no four, no two, and one one. One 8 plus one 1 equals the decimal quantity

9. Table 5-1 makes a comparison between the decimal and binary presentations. It also shows the 4-bit presentation method alone with the quantity or weight represented by each digit of the four-bit sequence. Higher-value decimal quantities can be represented in binary form by adding more bits. For example, the quantity 16 in binary form using a 5-bit sequence would be expressed as 10000; decimal 17 would be 10001; and so on.

Table 5-1. Decimal-Binary Equivalents

Decimal	4-Bit Binary	BCD	Weight 8, 4, 2, 1			
0	0000	0000	(0) 8,	(0) 4,	(0) 2,	(0) 1
1	0001	0001	(0) 8,	(0) 4,	(0) 2,	(1) 1
2	0010	0010	(0) 8,	(0) 4,	(1) 2,	(0) 1
3	0011	0011	(0) 8,	(0) 4,	(1) 2,	(1) 1
4	0100	0100	(0) 8,	(1) 4,	(0) 2,	(0) 1
5	0101	0101	(0) 8,	(1) 4,	(0) 2,	(1) 1
6	0110	0110	(0) 8,	(1) 4,	(1) 2,	(0) 1
7	0111	0111	(0) 8,	(1) 4,	(1) 2,	(1) 1
8	1000	1000	(1) 8,	(0) 4,	(0) 2,	(0) 1
9	1001	1001	(1) 8,	(0) 4,	(0) 2,	(1) 1
10	1010	0001 0000	(1) 8,	(0) 4,	(1) 2,	(0) 1
11	1011	0001 0001	(1) 8,	(0) 4,	(1) 2,	(1) 1
12	1100	0001 0010	(1) 8,	(1) 4,	(0) 2,	(0) 1
13	1101	0001 0011	(1) 8,	(1) 4,	(0) 2,	(1) 1
14	1110	0001 0100	(1) 8,	(1) 4,	(1) 2,	(0) 1
15	1111	0001 0101	(1) 8,	(1) 4,	(1) 2,	(1) 1

Various codes based on the binary 1 and 0 concept have evolved to meet the requirements of digital equipment operation and objectives. A simple code that has been extensively used is known as the binary-coded-decimal (BCD) method. Four binary bits are employed. Each digit position has a definite value (weight) in the order 8, 4, 2, 1.

In the true binary case, it is simply 8, 4, 2, 1 as shown in Table 5-1. Conversion to decimal values involves the simple addition of the weights of the digits as shown previously. In the BCD code a simple 4-bit number is used to express only decimal quantities zero through nine. Although a 4-bit binary number can designate higher numbers (up to 15 as shown in the chart), the BCD code restricts each 4-bit character to decimal numbers from zero to nine.

When a higher number is to be indicated in binary form using the BCD code, additional 4-bit characters are conveyed. For example, the number 35 in the BCD code becomes 0011 0101.

$$3 \quad 5$$
$$0011 \quad 0101$$

Note that the first 4-bit character is the binary representation of three while the second is the representation of the decimal quantity five. Thus, the number 6751 would be written:

$$0110 \quad 0111 \quad 0101 \quad 0001$$

The intriguing part of the binary presentation is that numbers can be represented by combinations of binary 0 and binary 1. Furthermore, it is very easy to understand how to use a simple switch to see a binary 1 or a binary 0. For example, a closed switch could represent a binary 1; the same switch when open, a binary 0. A sequence of switches could then be used to demonstrate a binary counting system (Fig. 5-1). The closed position of the switch in the circuit is customarily called the on position; the open position is the off position. In digital vernacular, the closed position could designate true or binary logical 1, while the off position of the switch would be designated false or logical 0. In representing the decimal quantity twelve, switches 1 and 2 would be closed, while switches 3 and 4 would be open, setting up the sequence of 1100.

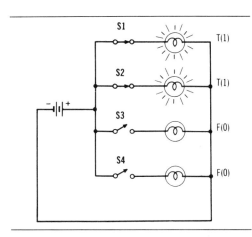

***Fig. 5-1. Binary number representation
using switches and lamps to show the
decimal number 12.***

5-1-2. Further Numbering

An 8-bit binary number is commonly used. The weighting is again related to powers of 2 or:

Digits	1	2	3	4	5	6	7	8
Powers	2^7	2^6	2^5	2^4	2^3	2^2	2^1	2^0
Decimal Equivalent	128	64	32	16	8	4	2	1

An 8-bit binary of 10010110 has a decimal value of:

$$128 + 16 + 4 + 2 = 150$$

Table 5-2 shows decimal eight-bit binary, binary-coded decimal, and hexadecimal equivalents, consecutively up to 255. The highest eight-bit binary number 11111111 is equivalent to decimal 255. This amounts to 256 combinations including zero which is 8-bit 00000000.

Hexadecimal (abbreviated hex) is a numbering system with a base 16 and employs both numbers along with letters that serve as numbers. Numbers are used from 0 through 9, letters from 10 through 15. Hex 0 through 9 is the same as decimal 0 through 9. However, in hex the decimals 10 through 15 are represented by letters A through F. Over this range hex is a single-digit number. For example 2-digit decimal 10 is represented by single-digit A. As shown in Table 5-2, hex numbering requires but two digits to count up to decimal 255. In a small control system a small 16-position

Table 5-2. Numbering Systems

Decimal	Binary	BCD	Hex
0	00000000	0000 0000	0
1	00000001	0000 0001	1
2	00000010	0000 0010	2
3	00000011	0000 0011	3
4	00000100	0000 0100	4
5	00000101	0000 0101	5
6	00000110	0000 0110	6
7	00000111	0000 0111	7
8	00001000	0000 1000	8
9	00001001	0000 1001	9
10	00001010	0001 0000	A
11	00001011	0001 0001	B
12	00001100	0001 0010	C
13	00001101	0001 0011	D
14	00001110	0001 0100	E
15	00001111	0001 0101	F
16	00010000	0001 0110	10
17	00010001	0001 0111	11
18	00010010	0001 1000	12
19	00010011	0001 1001	13
20	00010100	0010 0000	14
21	00010101	0010 0001	15
22	00010110	0010 0010	16
23	00010111	0010 0011	17
24	00011000	0010 0100	18
25	00011001	0010 0101	19
26	00011010	0010 0110	1A
27	00011011	0010 0111	1B
28	00011100	0010 1000	1C
29	00011101	0010 1001	1D
30	00011110	0011 0000	1E
31	00011111	0011 0001	1F
32	00100000	0011 0010	20
33	00100001	0011 0011	21
34	00100010	0011 0100	22
35	00100011	0011 0101	23
36	00100100	0011 0110	24
37	00100101	0011 0111	25
38	00100110	0011 1000	26
39	00100111	0011 1001	27
40	00101000	0100 0000	28
41	00101001	0100 0001	29
42	00101010	0100 0010	2A
43	00101011	0100 0011	2B
44	00101100	0100 0100	2C
45	00101101	0100 0101	2D
46	00101110	0100 0110	2E
47	00101111	0100 0111	2F

Table 5-2—cont. Numbering Systems

Decimal	Binary	BCD	Hex
48	00110000	0100 1000	30
49	00110001	0100 1001	31
50	00110010	0101 0000	32
51	00110011	0101 0001	33
52	00110100	0101 0010	34
53	00110101	0101 0011	35
54	00110110	0101 0100	36
55	00110111	0101 0101	37
56	00111000	0101 0110	38
57	00111001	0101 0111	39
58	00111010	0101 1000	3A
59	00111011	0101 1001	3B
60	00111100	0110 0000	3C
61	00111101	0110 0001	3D
62	00111110	0110 0010	3E
63	00111111	0110 0011	3F
64	01000000	0110 0100	40
65	01000001	0110 0101	41
66	01000010	0110 0110	42
67	01000011	0110 0111	43
68	01000100	0110 1000	44
69	01000101	0110 1001	45
70	01000110	0111 0000	46
71	01000111	0111 0001	47
72	01001000	0111 0010	48
73	01001001	0111 0011	49
74	01001010	0111 0100	4A
75	01001011	0111 0101	4B
76	01001100	0111 0110	4C
77	01001101	0111 0111	4D
78	01001110	0111 1000	4E
79	01001111	0111 1001	4F
80	01010000	1000 0000	50
81	01010001	1000 0001	51
82	01010010	1000 0010	52
83	01010011	1000 0011	53
84	01010100	1000 0100	54
85	01010101	1000 0101	55
86	01010110	1000 0110	56
87	01010111	1000 0111	57
88	01011000	1000 1000	58
89	01011001	1000 1001	59
90	01011010	1001 0000	5A
91	01011011	1001 0001	5B
92	01011100	1001 0010	5C
93	01011101	1001 0011	5D
94	01011110	1001 0100	5E
95	01011111	1001 0101	5F

Table 5-2—cont. Numbering Systems

Decimal	Binary	BCD	Hex
96	01100000	1001 0110	60
97	01100001	1001 0111	61
98	01100010	1001 1000	62
99	01100011	1001 1001	63
100	01100100	0001 0000 0000	64
101	01100101	0001 0000 0001	65
102	01100110	0001 0000 0010	66
103	01100111	0001 0000 0011	67
104	01101000	0001 0000 0100	68
105	01101001	0001 0000 0101	69
106	01101010	0001 0000 0110	6A
107	01101011	0001 0000 0111	6B
108	01101100	0001 0000 1000	6C
109	01101101	0001 0000 1001	6D
110	01101110	0001 0001 0000	6E
111	01101111	0001 0001 0001	6F
112	01110000	0001 0001 0010	70
113	01110001	0001 0001 0011	71
114	01110010	0001 0001 0100	72
115	01110011	0001 0001 0101	73
116	01110100	0001 0001 0110	74
117	01110101	0001 0001 0111	75
118	01110110	0001 0001 1000	76
119	01110111	0001 0001 1001	77
120	01111000	0001 0010 0000	78
121	01111001	0001 0010 0001	79
122	01111010	0001 0010 0010	7A
123	01111011	0001 0010 0011	7B
124	01111100	0001 0010 0100	7C
125	01111101	0001 0010 0101	7D
126	01111110	0001 0010 0110	7E
127	01111111	0001 0010 0111	7F
128	10000000	0001 0010 1000	80
129	10000001	0001 0010 1001	81
130	10000010	0001 0011 0000	82
131	10000011	0001 0011 0001	83
132	10000100	0001 0011 0010	84
133	10000101	0001 0011 0011	85
134	10000110	0001 0011 0100	86
135	10000111	0001 0011 0101	87
136	10001000	0001 0011 0110	88
137	10001001	0001 0011 0111	89
138	10001010	0001 0011 1000	8A
139	10001011	0001 0011 1001	8B
140	10001100	0001 0100 0000	8C
141	10001101	0001 0100 0001	8D
142	10001110	0001 0100 0010	8E
143	10001111	0001 0100 0011	8F

Table 5-2—cont. Numbering Systems

Decimal	Binary	BCD	Hex
144	10010000	0001 0100 0100	90
145	10010001	0001 0100 0101	91
146	10010010	0001 0100 0110	92
147	10010011	0001 0100 0111	93
148	10010100	0001 0100 1000	94
149	10010101	0001 0100 1001	95
150	10010110	0001 0101 0000	96
151	10010111	0001 0101 0001	97
152	10011000	0001 0101 0010	98
153	10011001	0001 0101 0011	99
154	10011010	0001 0101 0100	9A
155	10011011	0001 0101 0101	9B
156	10011100	0001 0101 0110	9C
157	10011101	0001 0101 0111	9D
158	10011110	0001 0101 1000	9E
159	10011111	0001 0101 1001	9F
160	10100000	0001 0110 0000	A0
161	10100001	0001 0110 0001	A1
162	10100010	0001 0110 0010	A2
163	10100011	0001 0110 0011	A3
164	10100100	0001 0110 0100	A4
165	10100101	0001 0110 0101	A5
166	10100110	0001 0110 0110	A6
167	10100111	0001 0110 0111	A7
168	10101000	0001 0110 1000	A8
169	10101001	0001 0110 1001	A9
170	10101010	0001 0111 0000	AA
171	10101011	0001 0111 0001	AB
172	10101100	0001 0111 0010	AC
173	10101101	0001 0111 0011	AD
174	10101110	0001 0111 0100	AE
175	10101111	0001 0111 0101	AF
176	10110000	0001 0111 0110	B0
177	10110001	0001 0111 0111	B1
178	10110010	0001 0111 1000	B2
179	10110011	0001 0111 1001	B3
180	10110100	0001 1000 0000	B4
181	10110101	0001 1000 0001	B5
182	10110110	0001 1000 0010	B6
183	10110111	0001 1000 0011	B7
184	10111000	0001 1000 0100	B8
185	10111001	0001 1000 0101	B9
186	10111010	0001 1000 0110	BA
186	10111011	0001 1000 0111	BB
188	10111100	0001 1000 1000	BC
189	10111101	0001 1000 1001	BD
190	10111110	0001 1001 0000	BE
191	10111111	0001 1001 0001	BF

Table 5-2—cont. Numbering Systems

Decimal	Binary	BCD	Hex
192	11000000	0001 1001 0010	C0
193	11000001	0001 1001 0011	C1
194	11000010	0001 1001 0100	C2
195	11000011	0001 1001 0101	C3
196	11000100	0001 1001 0110	C4
197	11000101	0001 1001 0111	C5
198	11000110	0001 1001 1000	C6
199	11000111	0001 1001 1001	C7
200	11001000	0010 0000 0000	C8
201	11001001	0010 0000 0001	C9
202	11001010	0010 0000 0010	CA
203	11001011	0010 0000 0011	CB
204	11001100	0010 0000 0100	CC
205	11001101	0010 0000 0101	CD
206	11001110	0010 0000 0110	CE
207	11001111	0010 0000 0111	CF
208	11010000	0010 0000 1000	D0
209	11010001	0010 0000 1001	D1
210	11010010	0010 0001 0000	D2
211	11010011	0010 0001 0001	D3
212	11010100	0010 0001 0010	D4
213	11010101	0010 0001 0011	D5
214	11010110	0010 0001 0100	D6
215	11010111	0010 0001 0101	D7
216	11011000	0010 0001 0110	D8
217	11011001	0010 0001 0111	D9
218	11011010	0010 0001 1000	DA
219	11011011	0010 0001 1001	DB
220	11011100	0010 0010 0000	DC
221	11011101	0010 0010 0001	DD
222	11011110	0010 0010 0010	DE
223	11011111	0010 0010 0011	DF
224	11100000	0010 0010 0100	E0
225	11100001	0010 0010 0101	E1
226	11100010	0010 0010 0110	E2
227	11100011	0010 0010 0111	E3
228	11100100	0010 0010 1000	E4
229	11100101	0010 0010 1001	E5
230	11100110	0010 0011 0000	E6
231	11100111	0010 0011 0001	E7
232	11101000	0010 0011 0010	E8
233	11101001	0010 0011 0011	E9
234	11101010	0010 0011 0100	EA
235	11101011	0010 0011 0101	EB
236	11101100	0010 0011 0110	EC
237	11101101	0010 0011 0111	ED
238	11101110	0010 0011 1000	EE
239	11101111	0010 0011 1001	EF

Table 5-2—cont. Numbering Systems

Decimal	Binary	BCD	Hex
240	11110000	0010 0100 0000	F0
241	11110001	0010 0100 0001	F1
242	11110010	0010 0100 0010	F2
243	11110011	0010 0100 0011	F3
244	11110100	0010 0100 0100	F4
245	11110101	0010 0100 0101	F5
246	11110110	0010 0100 0110	F6
247	11110111	0010 0100 0111	F7
248	11111000	0010 0100 1000	F8
249	11111001	0010 0100 1001	F9
250	11111010	0010 0101 0000	FA
251	11111011	0010 0101 0001	FB
252	11111100	0010 0101 0010	FC
253	11111101	0010 0101 0011	FD
254	11111110	0010 0101 0100	FE
255	11111111	0010 0101 0101	FF

hex keyboard permits one to put into memory an appropriate program of control and also permits one to change that program when necessary. There are as many as 256 possible combinations with 2 digits. With 4 digits you can have 65536 combinations.

In a typical operation when the hex number B is pressed the associated equipment produces a binary 1011. Simple digital integrated circuits make this conversion. Remember that memories and microprocessors respond to 1s and 0s only. If the hex number 7C were keyed the 8-bit binary number would be 01111100. Refer to Table 5-2.

A decimal number can be turned into a hex number using this simple relationship:

Power	16^3	16^2	16^1	16^0
Decimal	4096	256	16	1
Answer	?	?	?	?

Convert decimal 62 to hex. Locate the first decimal quantity that will divide into 62 an integer number of times plus a left over quantity if present. This will be 16. Determine how many times 16 can be divided into 62. This will be 3 times and 3 becomes the first hex digit. Now what is the left over number? It is 14 (62 minus 48). In hex numbering 14 is represented by the letter E. Consequently, the 2-digit hex number is 3E.

Convert decimal 200 to hex. In dividing 200 by 16 one obtains a quotient of 12 and a left over of 8. The hex number is C8. Check it out on Table 5-2. Later in this chapter a Hex/BCD counter is described.

5-2. Logic Circuits

In an actual digital system, the switches which were shown in Fig. 5-1 would be electronic and not mechanical. They operate at very high speeds causing many operations to occur simultaneously and at a high repetition rate.

Some considerable confusion exists because of the several ways of designating a logical 1 and a logical 0. In general, the terms yes and no, true and false, as well as 1 and 0, are identical. In actual circuits, logical 1s and 0s are represented by voltage levels. In a negative logic circuit the most positive voltage level (high) is 0 and the most negative level (low) is 1. Conversely, in a positive logic circuit, the most positive level (high) is defined as a logical 1, while the most negative voltage level (low) is defined as a logical 0.

It follows, then, that in a positive logic circuit, the terms 1, yes, true, and high are one and the same and that for the opposite style 0, no, false, and low are also one and the same. Conversely, for negative logic circuits 1, no, false, and low are one and the same for one state and for the opposite state, 0, yes, true and high are the same. The most common method used is positive logic.

In digital circuits using positive logic, inputs and outputs are either high (logic 1) or low (logic 0). There is no in between. Circuits act like fast switches changing over between high and low at the output in response to high and low conditions at their inputs.

The building-block of modern digital circuits is the so-called *logic* gate. Although gate circuits can be built using discrete components, they are usually in the form of multiple gates that are a part of a digital integrated circuit. The two most common families of digital integrated circuits are TTL (transistor-transistor logic) and CMOS (complementary metal-oxide semiconductors). The TTL device responds to voltages between 0 and +5 volts. Maximum supply voltage to a TTL device is +5 volts. The logic 0 voltage falls between 0 and 0.8 volt; the logic 1 between 2.4 and 5 volts. Thus a DC voltmeter or popular logic probe can be used to ascertain if input and output levels are at logic 0 or logic 1.

A CMOS digital integrated circuit will also operate at the same level as the TTL. However, supply voltages may extend between 4 and 15 volts. In most applications logic 0 would fall between 0 and 0.8 volt. The logic 1 value would be between 3 and 15 volts depending upon the supply voltage.

In addition to gates there are other digital ICs that perform a variety of functions. Some of these will also be discussed in this chapter.

5-3. Logic Probe

A key test instrument in locating faults in digital circuits is the logic probe (Fig. 5-2). The logic probe contains light-emitting diodes (LEDs) which turn on according to the logic of the point in the digital circuit to which the logic probe is connected. If it is touched to a logic 1 point the high LED will come on; at a logic 0 point, the low LED will light. The instrument can be used to check out either TTL or CMOS circuits.

A pulse LED also indicates the presence of square waves or pulses in the digital system. Each time the input changes to the logic probe, the pulse LED is activated for 0.1 second. When observing low-frequency, low duty-cycle signals, the pulse LED provides an immediate indication of the pulse activity in the circuit. Also by observing the high and low LEDs the polarity of the pulse train can be ascertained. If the high LED is on, the signal is normally high and pulsing low. If the low LED is on, the signal is normally low and pulsing high. High-frequency signals cause the pulse LED to flash at a 10-Hz rate. The incorporation of a pulse stretcher in the logic probe makes this possible.

The logic probe can be moved from circuit to circuit in a digital system and by checking the logic at key test points proper or faulty operation can be ascertained.

Measurements can be made under steady-state DC condition as well as with pulses present in the digital system.

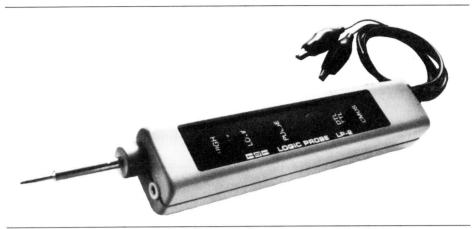

Fig. 5-2. Logic probe.

5-4. TTL and CMOS

The two most common digital integrated circuits are classified as TTL or CMOS types. A TTL digital IC incorporates bipolar transistors while the CMOS type is basically a MOSFET type. The term CMOS refers to *Complementary Metallic-Oxide Semiconductor*. The complementary designation refers to the fact that both p-channel and n-channel MOSFETs are used in the construction.

The TTL device is basically low impedance, and the supply voltage is confined to a +5 volts. The CMOS device operates over a supply voltage typical of any MOSFET device. It is a high-impedance device and requires less power than a TTL. However, it must be handled more carefully and circuit design can be a bit more critical.

A typical TTL inverter is shown in Fig. 5-3A. As many as six of these inverters may be found in a single TTL inverter integrated circuit. Usually the circuit is referred to as an inverter gate. A logic 1 applied to its input results in a logic 0 output. A logic 0 input results in a logic 1 output. Typically logic 0 corresponds to 0 volts and logic 1 to +5 volts.

The first bipolar transistor in the circuit has a low-impedance emitter input and a collector that is direct-coupled to the base of a phase inverter. The input transistor acts as a diode gate transferring the logic of the input to the base of the inverter. Inverted input logic is applied to the base of the top output-transistor pair; in-phase logic, to the base of the lower totem-pole output transistors.

In the totem-pole circuit the top transistor actually acts as the collector resistor of the bottom transistor. This connection speeds up circuit response to fast changes in input logic. The lower transistor is, of course, connected as a common-emitter type, and its output logic is inverted as compared to its input logic. Therefore, the overall device functions as a logic inverter.

A basic CMOS inverter circuit is given in Fig. 5-3B. The top FET is a p-channel type; the bottom, an n-channel. When the input logic is near ground or logic 0, the bottom n-channel type is nonconducting. However, the top p-channel does conduct, and the output at the joined drains is near the supply voltage, or logic 1.

When the input is set to logic 1, the top FET becomes nonconducting. However, the bottom FET does conduct, and the output at the joined drains is near ground, or logic 0. As in the case of a TTL as many as six of these logic gates can be mounted in a single integrated-circuit inverter.

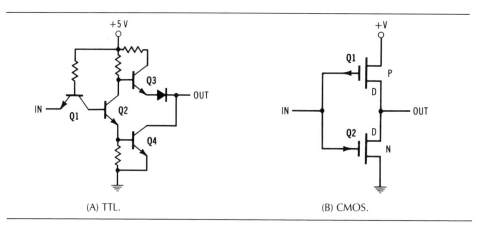

(A) TTL. (B) CMOS.

Fig. 5-3. TTL and CMOS inverter gates.

There are seven basic logic circuits that come under the general heading of logic gates. These are inverter, *AND* gate, *NAND* gate, *OR* gate, *NOR* gate, Exclusive *NOR* gate, and Exclusive *OR* gate. These gates are found built into digital integrated circuits with usually four or more gates of the same type included in the same chip.

5-4-1. Inverter

A digital inverter has an output logic which is the inverse of the input logic. Output Y is the complement of input A (Fig. 5-4A). Figs. 5-4A and B show the inverter symbol, truth table, and diagram.

It can be seen that if the input logic is 0, the output logic is 1. An input logic of 1 drives the output to logic 0. A clock pulse or other sequence of pulses applied to the input A will appear inverted at the output Y. The truth table is a manner of expressing the logic conditions of a digital circuit. It shows the logic output for every possible combination of input logic.

Data is given for the TTL 7404 hex inverter. There are six independent inverters included in this single IC chip. Note that there are twelve separate pins for the various inputs and outputs. Supply voltage is connected to pin 14, while pin 7 is grounded.

A simple demonstration circuit using just one of the inverter gates in the 7404 is given in Fig. 5-4C. The switch permits a connection of logic 1 or logic 0 to input A. If the switch were connected to the supply voltage, it would be the same as connecting a logic 1 to the input. Under this condition the output at Y would be logic 0. A logic probe like the one shown in Fig. 5-2 can be used to make the check. Also a DC voltmeter could be connected at the output (pin 2) indicating whether the output logic was 0 (approximately 0 volt) or logic 1 (approximately +5 volts). Note the supply voltage is connected to pin 14, and a ground is connected to pin 7.

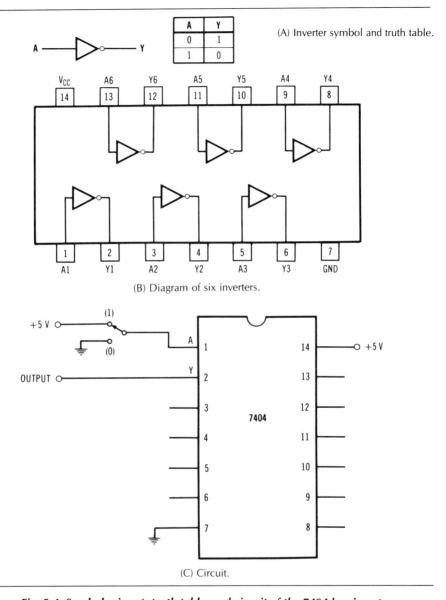

A	Y
0	1
1	0

(A) Inverter symbol and truth table.

(B) Diagram of six inverters.

(C) Circuit.

Fig. 5-4. Symbol, pinout, truth table, and circuit of the 7404 hex inverter.

If a series of positive pulses were applied to input A, they would appear at the output Y as negative pulses, showing the inversion characteristic of an inverter stage.

5-4-2. Two-Input AND Gate

The schematic diagram, symbol, and truth table of a TTL 7408 AND gate are given in Fig. 5-5. Note the symbol for the AND gate and how it differs from the triangle symbol of the inverter. In an AND circuit, input gates A *and* B must be at logic 1 before there can be a logic 1 output. If either or both of the inputs are logic 0 (low), the output Y is logic 0 (low). These facts are again given in the truth table which shows the output logic state for every possible combination of input logic states. Every possible combination of A and B is given, showing the resultant output state.

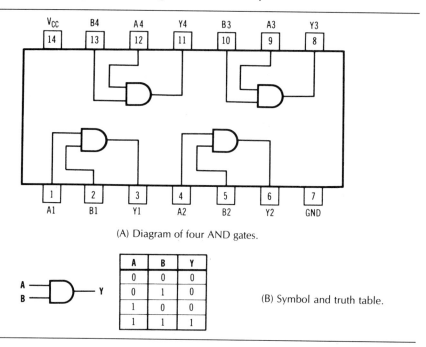

(A) Diagram of four AND gates.

A	B	Y
0	0	0
0	1	0
1	0	0
1	1	1

(B) Symbol and truth table.

Fig. 5-5. Diagram, symbol, and truth table of the 7408 AND gate.

The TTL 7408 contains four individual AND logic gates as shown in the schematic arrangement. A positive supply voltage is connected to pin 14 and pin 7 is grounded.

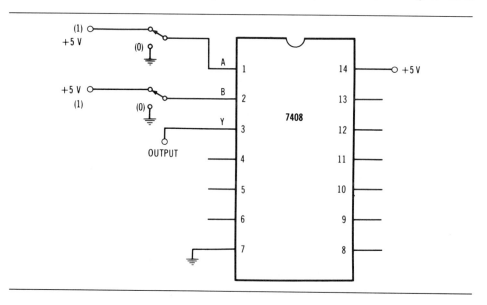

Fig. 5-6. Practical AND circuit.

Truth table verification can be obtained with the simple circuit of Fig. 5-6 using one of the AND gates in the 7408. A logic probe or DC voltmeter can be used to check the output logic at Y. When both switches are connected to logic 1 as shown, the output Y will also be logic 1. Any other combination of the two switches will result in the logic 0 at the output.

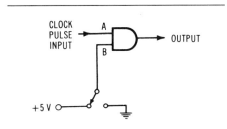

Fig. 5-7. Schematic of AND gate.

An AND gate circuit as you might find on a schematic diagram is given in Fig. 5-7. If a series of pulses, such as might be derived from a clock pulse generator, were applied to input A, their presence at the output would depend upon the setting of the logic at input B. Were the logic at input B set to logic 1, as shown, the pulses will appear at the output Y with the same polarity (no inversion). However, if the switch at B is set to logic 0 there will be no output at Y. Recall that in AND gate operation both inputs must be at logic 1 before there can be a logic 1 output.

It should be mentioned that it is customary practice in presenting diagrams of logic circuits that the supply voltages are *not* indicated. It is assumed in this case that the proper potentials are applied to pins 14 and 7 as shown previously in Fig. 5-6.

It should be stressed that the input to gate B is usually a pulse waveform too and is not the simple switch arrangement of Fig. 5-7. The waveforms of Fig. 5-8 show such a possibility. Assume that clock pulses of a particular repetition rate are applied to input A as shown. A lower-frequency and longer-duration series of pulses is applied to gate B which drives gate B between logic 1 and logic 0. Note that when gate B pulse is at logic 1, the clock pulses applied to gate A appear at the output. Conversely when gate B is set to logic 0 by the applied gating pulse, there is no output pulse present at output Y. This shows how a gate pulse can be used to gate on (enable) and off (inhibit) the AND gate, allowing or not-allowing the pulses at gate A to appear at output Y.

5-4-3. NAND Logic Gate

A schematic, symbol, and truth table for a NAND gate are given in Fig. 5-9. Again the integrated circuit houses four individual NAND gates.

In a NAND gate configuration when both or either inputs are at logic 0, the output is at logic 1. If both inputs are high at logic 1, the output is low at logic 0. In fact, the NAND gate is referred to as a Negated AND gate.

In comparing Fig. 5-9 with Fig. 5-5, note that the output logics in the Y column of the truth tables are complements. Note too that the two symbols are very similar except for the very small circle at the Y output of the NAND gate. A truth table can again be verified using the simple circuit of Fig. 5-10 and an appropriate logic probe or DC voltmeter.

When input data or a clock pulse is applied to input A, there will be no output if the gate B is at logic 0. If gate B is set to logic 1, however, there will be an output signal. However in the case of the NAND gate the output signal will be the complement of the input data. Thus the NAND gate inverts the input signal.

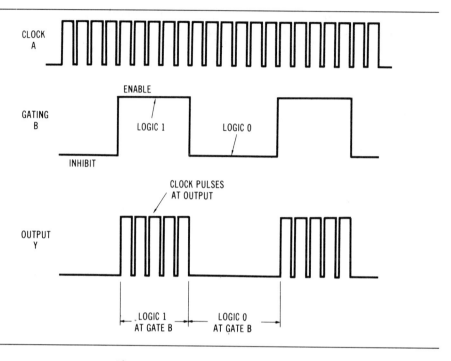

Fig. 5-8. Gated clock pulses AND gate.

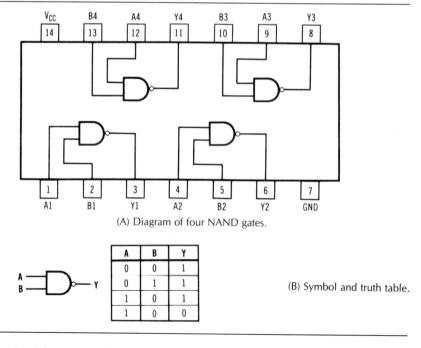

(A) Diagram of four NAND gates.

A	B	Y
0	0	1
0	1	1
1	0	1
1	0	0

(B) Symbol and truth table.

Fig. 5-9. Diagram, symbol, and truth table of the 7400 quad NAND gate.

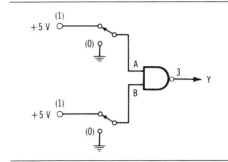

Fig. 5-10. Practical NAND circuit.

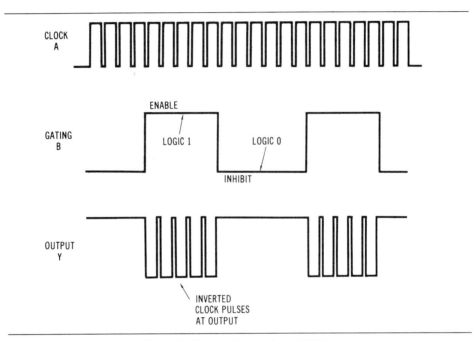

Fig. 5-11. Gated clock pulses NAND gate.

When a combination of clock and gating pulses is applied to the input as shown in Fig. 5-11, there is a different output than that obtained when using an AND gate. Note again when the gating pulse at input B is a logic 0, there is no output. However, under the logic 1 condition, there is an output. This output is a series of inverted clock pulses as shown in Fig. 5-11.

In the previous examples only two inputs were shown. However, logic gates can have more than two inputs and quite often do. An example of the symbol and truth table for a three-input NAND gate is given in Fig. 5-12. Note again that all the possible conditions for A, B, and C have been set down. The resultant output is indicated in the Y column. Again, for the NAND type of logic circuit the output is logic 0 when all inputs are logic 1. When all, two, or one input is at logic 0, the output is at logic 1.

5-4-4. Two-Input OR Gate

The diagram, symbol, and truth table for an OR gate are given in Fig. 5-13. In an OR gate circuit a logical 1 output results when a logic 1 is applied to both or either

184

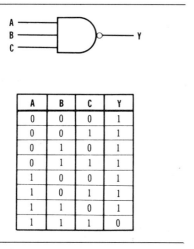

A	B	C	Y
0	0	0	1
0	0	1	1
0	1	0	1
0	1	1	1
1	0	0	1
1	0	1	1
1	1	0	1
1	1	1	0

Fig. 5-12. Three-input NAND gate.

input gates. The output is logic 0 when both inputs are logic 0. Compare the truth table of the OR gate with that of the AND gate. In the case of the AND gate the output is logic 1 when input A *and* input B are logic 1. In case of the OR gate the output is logic 1 when input A *or* input B is logic 1.

If a clock pulse or other input data is applied to input A and input B is at logic 0, the input data is transferred to the output without inversion. Likewise, when input A is at logic 0 and input B is at logic 1, or when both inputs are at logic 1, the input is transferred to the output without inversion. Only when both inputs are at 0, will the output be 0.

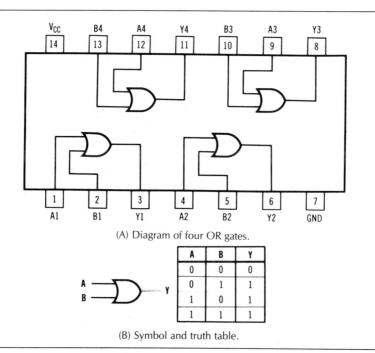

(A) Diagram of four OR gates.

A	B	Y
0	0	0
0	1	1
1	0	1
1	1	1

(B) Symbol and truth table.

Fig. 5-13. Diagram, symbol, and truth table of the 7432 OR gate.

5-4-5. Two-Input NOR Gate

The diagram, symbol, and truth table for a NOR gate are given in Fig. 5-14. Note that the NOR gate symbol is the same as that for an OR gate with the exception of the small circle at the output. In NOR gate circuit operation when either or both inputs are at logic 1, the output is logic 0. The output is logic 1 only when both inputs are at logic 0. Compare the NOR and OR gate truth tables, observing that the Y columns are complementary. The NOR is in fact referred to as a Negated OR gate, hence the name of NOR gate.

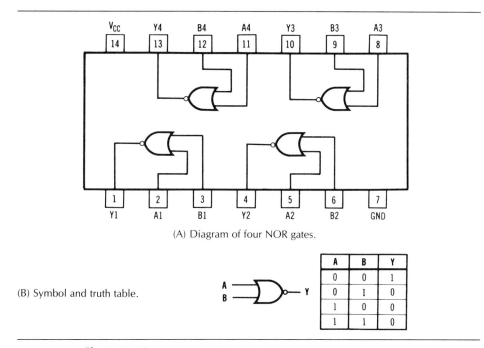

(A) Diagram of four NOR gates.

(B) Symbol and truth table.

A	B	Y
0	0	1
0	1	0
1	0	0
1	1	0

Fig. 5-14. Diagram, symbol, and truth table of the 7402 NOR gate.

If the input data or clock pulse is applied to gate A and a logic 1 to gate B, there will be no output. If a logic 0 is applied to the latter gate, however, the input signal appears in inverted form at the output. The output is, in fact, the complement of the input.

If required, a gating pulse can be applied to the gate B. In this case the output is switched on and off, and clock pulses appear in the output whenever the input gating pulse swings to logic 0. Output pulses are, of course, opposite in polarity from the input pulses applied to gate A.

5-4-6. Two-Input Exclusive/OR Gate

The Exclusive/OR gate is unique as shown in Fig. 5-15. When gates A and B are both set to logic 0 the output is logic 0. Furthermore when gates A and B are both set to logic 1, the output is also logic 0. If gate A is 0 and gate B is 1, or gate A is 1 and gate B is 0, the output is logic 1. The symbol and truth table are given in Fig. 5-15B.

The Exclusive/OR (abbreviated (XOR) gate is unusual in its response to input data or clock pulse. Assume that input data is being applied to gate input A. If gate input B is set to logic 0, the input data is transmitted directly to the output and is of the same polarity. However, if gate B is set to logic 1, the input data will also appear in the output but will be in inverted form.

It would be advisable to review all gate circuits. Pay particular attention to their symbols and truth tables. You may wish to set them down side by side and make appropriate comparisons. Memory can be aided by considering the relationships between AND and OR gates. AND and NAND gates, finally OR and NOR gates.

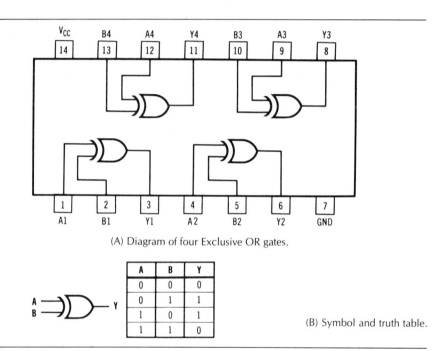

(A) Diagram of four Exclusive OR gates.

A	B	Y
0	0	0
0	1	1
1	0	1
1	1	0

(B) Symbol and truth table.

Fig. 5-15. Diagram, symbol, and truth table of the 7486 Exclusive OR gate.

5-5. LEDs and 7-Segment Digital Displays

The light-emitting diode (LED) is a semiconductor diode that emits light when forward-biased (Fig. 5-16A). A series resistor is used to limit the diode current to a safe value. The most common LED color is red; yellow and green versions are available.

LEDs are used widely in digital and analog electronic systems. They are reliable and have a long life. In TTL systems the supply voltage is usually 5 volts. An appropriate resistor must be placed between the 5-volt source and any LED that is operated in the circuit. Resistor values usually fall in the 100- to 470-ohm range. In most cases the LED current should not exceed 50 mA and an actual current of 20 to 30 mA is typical. Common series resistor values are 180, 220, 270, and 330 ohms. Of course, the lower-value resistors provide a brighter glow. CMOS circuits use higher-value supply voltages so Ohm's law can be used to calculate the higher value of series resistance required.

Fig. 5-16B, shows how an LED circuit in conjunction with a bipolar transistor can be used as a simple logic probe or lamp monitor. The LED circuit has a low impedance and could load down a particular high resistance digital or analog circuit. The purpose

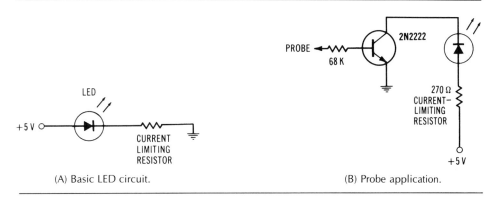

(A) Basic LED circuit.   (B) Probe application.

Fig. 5-16. LED probe.

of the bipolar transistor is to provide current amplification at the same time it presents a much reduced load to the circuit to which the probe is connected. A very low input base current will result in the significant current needed to light the LED connected in the collector circuit.

This circuit can be used as a simple probe for checking or monitoring TTL circuits. If the probe is connected to a logic 1 point (+5 volts), the LED will light. If connected to a logic 0 point (0 volts) it remains unlit.

The LED is the basis for digital number displays. A 7-segment display consists of seven LED slits, two or more of which are illuminated to display the numerals 0 through 9 (Fig. 5-17). For example, if segments f, g, b, and c are lit the number 4 will be displayed. The illumination of segments a, b, g, c, and d reproduces as the numeral 3. This typical 7-segment display plugs into a 14-pin DIP mount.

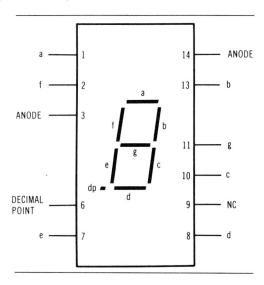

Fig. 5-17. A 7-segment display.

Anode voltage can be supplied to either pin 3 or pin 14. A specific LED slit is illuminated by connecting its associated pin to ground through the appropriate current-limiting resistor. Note in Fig. 5-17 that the individual slits are connected to pins 1, 2, 7, 8, 10, 11, and 13. Decimal point illumination is made via pin 6.

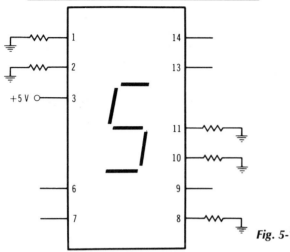

Fig. 5-18. *Wiring for displaying the numeral 5.*

The simple circuit arrangement of Fig. 5-18 shows how the number 5 is illuminated. In this case slits a, f, g, c, and d must be connected to a ground through current limiting resistors. This involves physical connections to pins 1, 2, 8, 10, and 11.

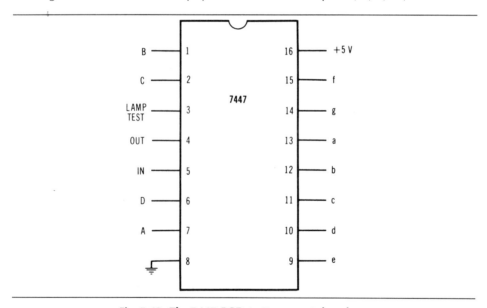

Fig. 5-19. *The 7447 BCD-to-7 segment decoder.*

To operate the 7-segment display electronically a 7-segment decoder is required. The TTL 7447 integrated circuit (Fig. 5-19) is an example of such a decoder. It is able to convert a positive logic BCD input signal to a proper sequence that lights a 7-segment display.

Recall that the BCD code is a 4-bit digital signal that represents the numerals 0 through 9 as a proper sequence of logic 0 and logic 1 bits. Refer back to Table 5-1. It is this coded signal, when supplied to pins 1, 2, 6, and 7, that provides the proper 7-segment illumination. The individual seven segments that connect to the 7-segment display involve pins 9 through 15. A schematic showing the decoder and 7-segment display properly interconnected is given in Fig. 5-20. Note the links between the decoder output and the display input by way of current-limiting resistors. If the digital logic signal applied to the 7447 is 0100 the b, c, f, and g output of the decoder will be placed at logic 0 and current will flow in the appropriate segments to illuminate the numeral 4.

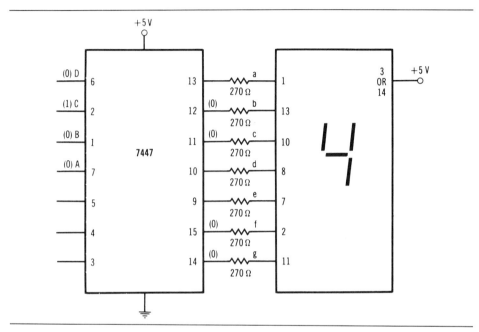

Fig. 5-20. Decoder and display connected for operation.

| | "8" | "4" | "2" | "1" | | | | | | | |
NUMBER	D	C	B	A	a	b	c	d	e	f	g
0	0	0	0	0	0	0	0	0	0	0	1
1	0	0	0	1	1	0	0	1	1	1	1
2	0	0	1	0	0	0	1	0	0	1	0
3	0	0	1	1	0	0	0	0	1	1	0
4	0	1	0	0	1	0	0	1	1	0	0
5	0	1	0	1	0	1	0	0	1	0	0
6	0	1	1	0	0	1	0	0	0	0	0
7	0	1	1	1	0	0	0	1	1	1	1
8	1	0	0	0	0	0	0	0	0	0	0
9	1	0	0	1	0	0	0	0	1	0	0

Fig. 5-21. BCD-to-decimal decoding.

The chart in Fig. 5-21 shows the operation. The first column is the actual decimal numerals. The second set of columns shows the BCD code for the various numerals. It is this code that is supplied to the input of the 7447 decoder. The final set of columns shows the individual segments of the display. When an individual segment is connected to logic 0 by the decoder, it will glow.

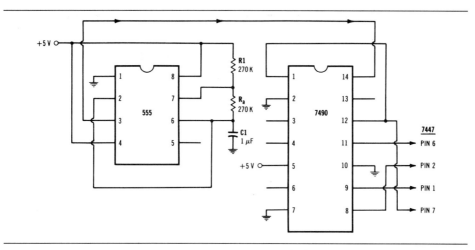

Fig. 5-22. BCD decade counter and clock generator.

Pin 3 of the decoder (Fig. 5-19) can be used to test all of the segments of the display. When it is connected to logic 0 (grounded) all the slits will glow if they are operating properly. Pins 4 and 5 are used for blanking purposes and to provide a link to other 7447 devices that are connected when a multiple readout display is required. For example, if a 4-section numeral display is desired, each individual display has its own decoder.

In a digital display system the decoder is preceded by a counter. The purpose of the counter is to convert a series of input pulses (clock) to the BCD output code. The TTL 7490 in Fig. 5-22 is an example of such a decade counter. The decade counter can be considered to have ten stable states made available at pins 8, 9, 11, and 12. These ten states match the 4 bits of the BCD code through the sequence from 0 through 9. After a complete sequence has been made, there is a return to the 4-bit 0000 that represents the numeral 0.

The purpose then of the decade counter is to count in sequence between 0 and 9 as the pulses arrive at pin 14 of the 7490. For each ten pulses coming in, in sequence, the BCD output will follow the sequence between 0000 and 1001 of the BCD code. After this sequence of ten pulses, the next arriving pulse will result in a 0000 output, and the count sequence will resume again.

The circuit in Fig. 5-22 includes a 555 clock pulse generator which is generating the sequence of pulses applied to input pin 14 of the decade counter. If you combine Figs. 5-20 and 5-22 into an actual circuit, you will come up with a demonstration counter that will continue to sequence between 0 and 9 and back to 0 and so on, as long as the clock generator is in operation.

In an actual digital display system other circuits and pulse sources are required. It may be that some analog quantity has to be measured. If so, circuits must be incorporated that will illuminate the display only for a given numeral as a function of the information being interpreted by the digital display system.

The circuit of Fig. 5-23 shows how a NAND gate can be used to control the number of clock pulses or other data that is applied to a counter. If the duration of the gate pulse is known, one can determine how many pulses are applied to the counter during this interval of time. For example, if the duration of the positive gate pulse applied to input B is one second and the counter counts up to 7 during this interval of time, it means that the pulses to be counted are arriving at a rate of 7 per second. This is the first step in understanding how a frequency counter operates.

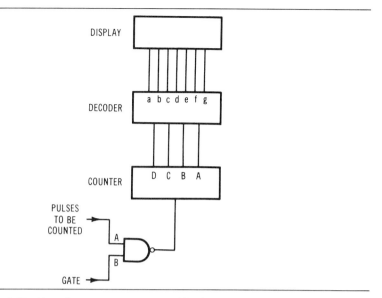

Fig. 5-23. Use of a NAND gate to enable the count sequence.

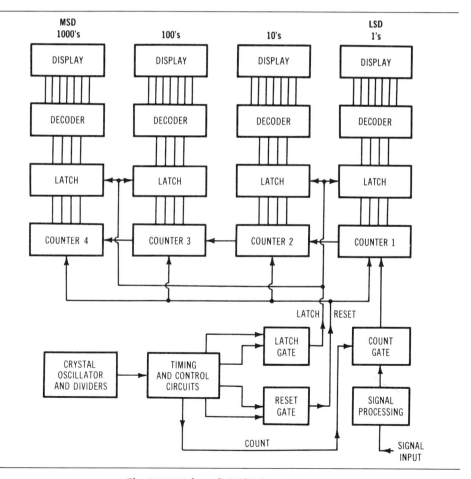

Fig. 5-24. A four-digit display system.

Recall that for the operation of a NAND gate the application of logic 1 information to gates A and B results in an output of logic 0. Refer back to the waveforms of Fig. 5-11. When the gate pulse at B is positive (logic 1) the gate is said to be *enabled* and the pulses applied to gate A will appear in the output. They will be of negative polarity which is correct for applying the information to the counter.

The sequence of pulses applied to the counter results in the generation of the BCD code signals that correspond to the number of pulses that are applied from the gate. This BCD signal is decoded and converts to the 7-segment signal that operates the LED display. When the gate B signal is at logic 0 the gate is said to be *inhibited* and no pulses applied to gate A are able to reach the counter.

This very simple counter is only capable of counting between 0 and 9 and is just a single-digit display. If a higher count is desired, individual counters can be added in series. If the series of pulses applied to the first counter exceed ten in number the excess pulses leave the first counter and are supplied to the second counter. In fact, one pulse is sent to counter 2 for each ten pulses that are applied to counter 1. The combination of the two counters in series will permit a total count of 99.

A third counter can be added to the chain and will become active if there is an excess of 99 incoming pulses. Thus with a three-digit display the total possible count jumps to 999. A fourth counter permits a maximum display 9999 and so on.

An example of such a four-digit display is given in Fig. 5-24. Note that the output of the count gate at the lower right is applied to counter No. 1. Furthermore there are interconnections that join counters 1 through 4 in series. In such an arrangement four digits will be displayed with the first counter displaying the lowest significant digit and count No. 4 the maximum significant digit.

If we assume that the count gate pulse applied to the count gate is 1 second in duration, and the signal input has a frequency of 2564 Hz, this is the number of pulses that will be applied to the counter chain in the 1 second period. Therefore, the display at counter 4 will read 2, that at counter 3 will read 5, that at counter 2 will read 6, and counter 1 will display numeral 4.

If the frequency of the signal input changes, a different number of pulses will be applied during the 1-second interval of the count gating pulse. Therefore, the display will read a new frequency, either higher or lower, depending on the direction and extent of the frequency change at the signal input.

Consider the operation of the major blocks of the 4-digit display shown in Fig. 5-24. It is important that the count gating pulse be of an exact frequency and duration. Therefore, a crystal-oscillator system is used to generate this calibrated pulse. Usually the crystal oscillates at a high frequency and a series of dividers brings down the frequency to the desired clock frequency. Timing and control circuits generate the various pulses required by the frequency counter. Three basic pulses are usually generated with specific durations and time positions. These are shown in simplified form in Fig. 5-25.

The count gating pulse was mentioned previously and is applied to the count gate along with a signal processed from the input signal. The input signal, more than likely, will be a sine wave. This sine wave is converted to a square wave by the signal processing block. The square wave has the same frequency as the input sine wave and is applied to the count gate.

The count gate permits a certain number of these pulses to pass through to its output as a function of the duration of the calibrated gating pulse. In our previous discussion we mentioned that the count gating pulse had a duration of 1 second. It could be some other known duration depending on the frequency range to be measured by the counter. A typical figure might be a duration of 100 milliseconds. At any rate it is an exact and known quantity and permits a certain number of the processed input pulses to pass through to counter 1. These pulses pass along the counter chain. They are said to *ripple* through the counter and the series connection of counters is referred to as a *ripple counter*.

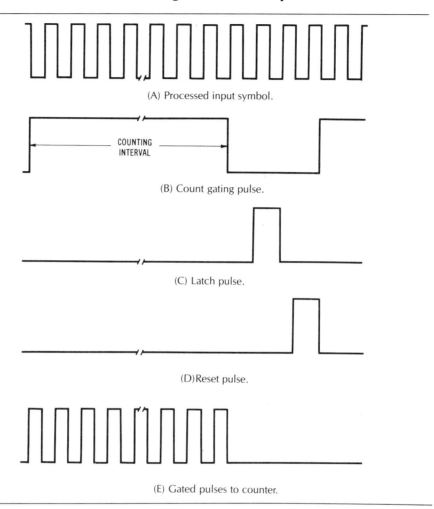

(A) Processed input symbol.

(B) Count gating pulse.

(C) Latch pulse.

(D) Reset pulse.

(E) Gated pulses to counter.

Fig. 5-25. Key digital display system waveforms.

As the pulses ripple through the counters, the entire operation would be displayed as the numbers run up on each display, finally reaching the desired final count for each individual section of the four. This would result in an annoying display, and it would be more satisfactory if the only numerals displayed would be the last ones representing the actual frequency of the incoming signal. Blanking out of the run-up of the displays is handled by a series of latches and a latching pulse as shown in Fig. 5-24. The pulse counting in each of the individual counters keeps building up to the desired value as they are applied to the individual latch circuits. However, the final number is not passed to the decoder until a latch pulse is applied to each of the individual latches. Despite fact that the ripple counters are very active during the count interval, only the final count number is seen because this data is not passed to the decoder until the latch pulse arrives. Therefore, the actual number that is displayed is the final count, and you do not see the actual counting process visually on the displays.

After the numbers are displayed for a specific interval of time, a reset pulse arrives and restores each of the individual counters to its zero, and a new cycle of activity begins. This activity repeats itself at a fast rate and a continuous display appears. At the same time, any change in the signal input frequency is recorded immediately. Thus the counter very quickly follows each change in the input frequency.

The waveforms of Fig. 5-25 tell us much about the operation of the display system. The waveform at Fig. 5-25A is the processed input signal, the frequency of which is to be measured. Fig. 5-25B shows the count gating pulse. Counting occurs when this pulse is at logic 1. After a precise interval of time the count gating pulse goes to logic 0 and the counting ceases. At this time the latching pulse (Fig. 5-25C) arrives and passes the last count number of each chain on to the decoder and to the 7-segment display. After the count has been displayed for an interval of time, the reset pulse (Fig. 5-25D) arrives and quickly returns everything to zero, ready to begin a new count.

Fig. 5-25E shows the pulses that are gated to the first counter. Note that this activity occurs during the duration of the count gating pulse. No pulses are gated to counter 1 during the times that the latching and reset pulses are active. All of these activities occur at a fast rate but the eye sees a continuous display that does not flicker or show a count run-up.

5-6. Digital IC Circuits

There are many types of digital ICs with numerous applications and functions. Several important CMOS types and associated circuits are described.

5-6-1. D-Type Flip-Flop

A flip-flop is a bistable two-element device. It has two stable states. An appropriate input signal causes a changeover from one state to the other.

In a so-called D-type flip-flop (Fig. 5-26A) the logic applied to the D input is transferred to the Q output whenever the clock makes a positive transition (edge) from

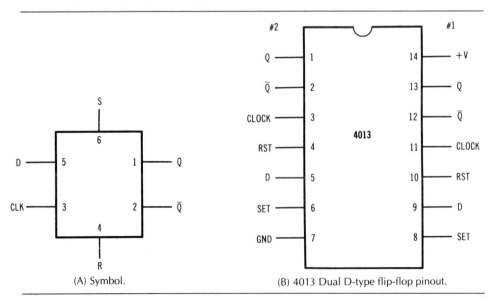

(A) Symbol. (B) 4013 Dual D-type flip-flop pinout.

Fig. 5-26. D-type flip-flop.

logic 0 to logic 1. The logic at the D input is held until the clock signal makes the positive transition. Note that the flip-flop has two outputs, Q and $\overline{Q}$ (not-Q). They are complementary outputs. When Q is logic 1, the not-Q output is logic 0 and vice versa.

Assume input D is set to logic 0. The output at Q and not-Q does not change until the clock input changes from logic 0 to logic 1. When this happens, the Q output becomes logic 0 and the not-Q output logic 1. If the D input is now set to logic 1, the circuit will flip-flop upon arrival of the next positive transition of the clock from 0 to 1. At this moment the Q output changes to logic 1; the not-Q output to logic 0.

The set and reset potentials also influence the output. A positive set results in a logic 1 at Q and a logic 0 at not-Q, regardless of previous output logics. Conversely, a positive reset results in a logic 1 at not-Q output and a logic 0 at Q output. These latter set and reset functions are dominant and overrule the output logic that has been established by the D logic.

An example of a D-type flip-flop is the 4013 digital IC (Fig. 5-26B). In fact, it contains two separate flip-flops in the same package. A test circuit for checking out the operation of the flip-flop is given in Fig. 5-27A. Four switches permit you to set the logic of the D, clock, set, and reset inputs. A transistor and LED permit you to observe the logic at the Q output.

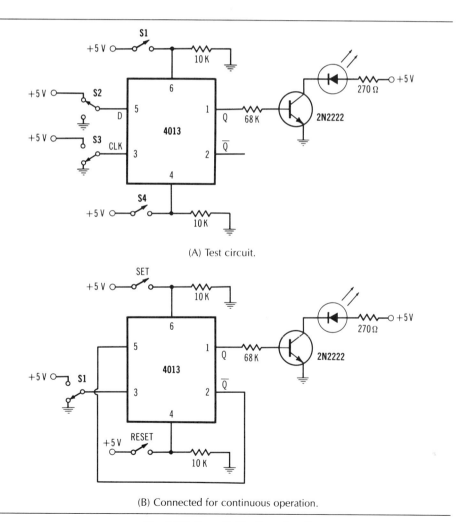

(A) Test circuit.

(B) Connected for continuous operation.

Fig. 5-27. Type-D flip-flop circuits.

As shown, a logic 1 is applied to the D input. The set and reset inputs are at logic 0 because of the link to ground through the 10 kilohm resistors. If you momentarily connect reset switch S4 to logic 1, the Q output will be logic 0 (LED off) and the not-Q output will be logic 1. Now momentarily connect the clock input to logic 1. Q output is 1 (LED on); not-Q output is 0. Connect switch S2 to ground, applying a logic 0 to the D input. The output will not change. However, if switch S3 is momentarily connected to logic 1, the output will flip and the LED will turn off. Connect switch S2 back to logic 1. Nothing will change until switch S3 is momentarily connected to logic 1. Then the output will flip again. Whenever the LED is off it can be overruled by momentarily connecting switch S1 to logic 1. This is the set function.

The basic circuit can be made to flip-flop on a continuous basis by making a feedback connection between the not-Q output and the D input as shown in Fig. 5-27B. Under this condition there will be a change in the output logic every time the clock voltage swings positive. Now the logic at the not-Q output changes the D input each time the output logics change. In other words, the not-Q output takes the place of switch S2 in circuit A. Each time switch S1 is momentarily connected to logic 1, the output logic will change.

Assume that the Q output is logic 0. The first time switch S1 is momentarily connected to logic 1, the Q output will become logic 1. The next time switch S1 is momentarily connected to logic 1, the Q output changes to logic 0. The next time switch S1 is connected momentarily to logic 1, the Q output will be back at logic 1. Note that it required two positive voltage changes of the clock input to produce a complete cycle at the Q output (1 to 0 and back to 1). There is one output cycle for each two input cycles. If a square wave were applied to the clock input, the square wave at output Q would be one half the frequency of the input square wave. The same applies for the output of the not-Q output. In this application the D-type flip-flop is dividing the input frequency by a factor of 2. It is said to be acting as a *binary counter*.

It is possible to connect the output of one flip-flop or binary counter to the clock input of the next. In this case the total division would be 4 (2×2). The combination is said to be acting as a divide-by-four counter. Four such binary counters connected in a series string would produce a total division of 16 ($2 \times 2 \times 2 \times 2$). Furthermore, by the proper choice of feedback links among the individual binary counters, it is also

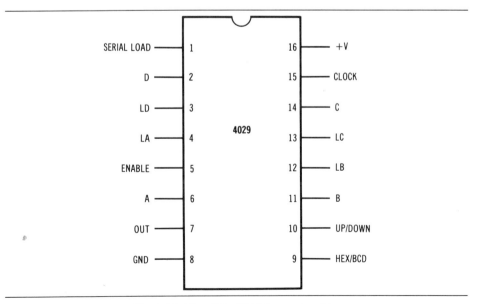

Fig. 5-28. The 4029 CMOS counter chip.

possible to establish other counts such as 5 or 10 or some other whole count. There are many applications for flip-flops and counters in digital systems.

5-6-2. Hexadecimal/BCD Counter

The CMOS 4029 is a versatile digital IC counter. The pinout diagram is given in Fig. 5-28. The package contains a series of D-type binary counters. Depending on the logic applied to pin 9, the total count can be made 16 (hexadecimal) or 10 (BCD). The logic applied to pin 10 determines whether there is an up-count or a down-count. In the case of BCD setting, then, the count can proceed 0 *up* to 9 or 9 *down* to 0.

The connections for division-by-ten counting (decade BCD) and division-by-16 (hexadecimal) counting are shown in Fig. 5-29 along with associated tables that show the DCBA binary output logic as a function of the arriving clock pulse. Circuits are connected for up-counting. If down-counting is desired, pin 10 must be connected to ground (logic 0).

There are many possible counting methods. Our accepted method is decade counting which involves numbering to the base 10. Binary counting is, of course, to the base 2 as introduced earlier in the chapter. Another popular counting method in computers and microprocessor control systems is called hexadecimal meaning counting to the base 16. For that reason the counter just described has applications in hexadecimal systems because of its division-by-sixteen capability.

In the hexadecimal system both numbers and letters are used. In counting from 0 to 16 in hexadecimal it would be 0-1-2-3-4-5-6-7-8-9-A-B-C-D-E-F. In hexadecimal all decade numbers between 0 and 15 can be represented as a single symbol. Equivalents of binary, decade, and hexadecimal counting were shown in Table 5-2.

5-6-3. CMOS Decoder/Driver

The Motorola MC14495B is a versatile driver for a 7-segment display. In fact, it is a combination latch, decoder, and driver in a single package. Furthermore the driver output can be supplied directly to the 7-segment display. No current-limiting resistors are required. Another attractive advantage is that it can be used for both BCD and hexadecimal displays. The decoding is such that the same 7 segments of the display can also be used to reproduce the hexadecimal numbers A through F. The actual display capability is shown in Fig. 5-30. The A, C, E, and F are uppercase. However, hex B and hex D are displayed as lowercase letters b and d.

The input and output are shown in the pinout diagram. A latch pulse can be applied to pin 7. Its leading edge will latch whatever binary number is being applied to the DCBA inputs. This number will be displayed so long as the latch remains high. When the latch is made low, the display will continue to count. An LED connected directly to pin 4 will turn on whenever the six numbers A, B, C, D, E, and F are displayed.

An interesting demonstration circuit is given in Fig. 5-31. The clock can be derived from a 555 timer using components that will provide a very-low-frequency output. The output should be a conventional 7-segment common-cathode display. Note that the DCBA output lines of the counter are connected to the DCBA inputs of the 4495. The three switches can be used to demonstrate the versatility of the circuit. Switch S1 permits you to switch between up-count and down-count. As connected the

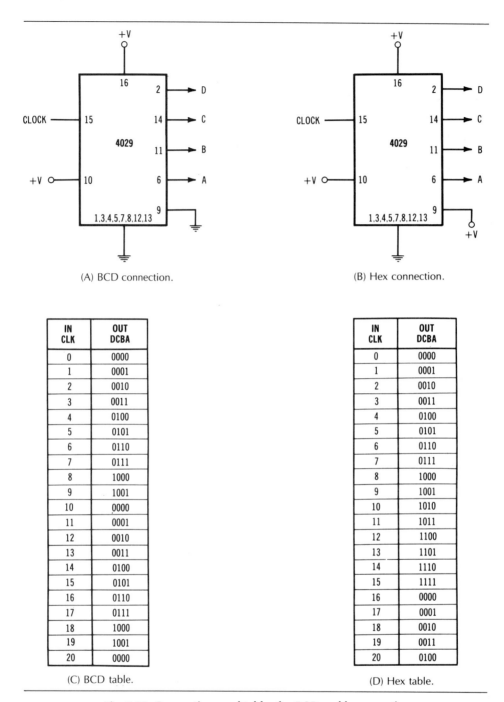

(A) BCD connection.

(B) Hex connection.

IN CLK	OUT DCBA
0	0000
1	0001
2	0010
3	0011
4	0100
5	0101
6	0110
7	0111
8	1000
9	1001
10	0000
11	0001
12	0010
13	0011
14	0100
15	0101
16	0110
17	0111
18	1000
19	1001
20	0000

(C) BCD table.

IN CLK	OUT DCBA
0	0000
1	0001
2	0010
3	0011
4	0100
5	0101
6	0110
7	0111
8	1000
9	1001
10	1010
11	1011
12	1100
13	1101
14	1110
15	1111
16	0000
17	0001
18	0010
19	0011
20	0100

(D) Hex table.

Fig. 5-29. Connections and tables for BCD and hex counting.

circuit will up-count. Switch S2 selects BCD or hex counting. As connected in the diagram it will count BCD. Switching over to logic 0 (+V) will result in hex counting and the display of the numbers A through F. Switch S3 provides a latching demonstration. As connected there is no latching. When switch S3 is connected high (+V), the binary DCBA signal applied to the 4495 input at that moment will be locked and displayed continuously. Changing switch S3 back to low will restore normal counting.

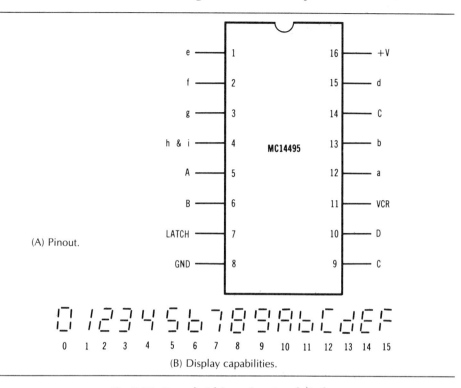

(A) Pinout.

(B) Display capabilities.

Fig. 5-30. Decoder/driver pinout and display.

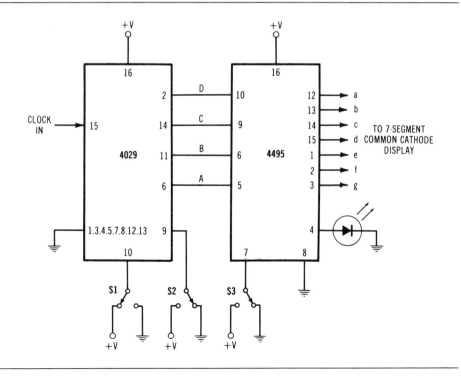

Fig. 5-31. Counter/decoder combination.

5-6-4. CMOS Data Selector

A data selector has several inputs that supply data to a single output on a scheduled basis which is determined by the binary addressing supplied to its control circuit. The 4512 chip is an example of such a selector. There are eight inputs (Fig. 5-32) that can be selected one by one according to the 3-bit binary signal applied to pins 13, 12, and 11. The highest number that can be represented by a 3-bit binary is 7, establishing proper selection for the maximum number of 8 inputs. Thus the input from 0 through 7 is selected in sequence when the 3-bit binary signal steps from 000 to 111. Of course, inputs can be selected at random according to the changing values of the CBA applied.

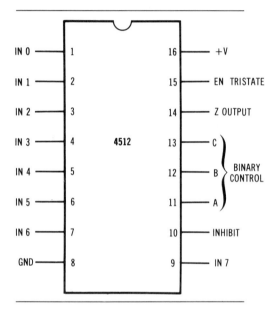

Fig. 5-32. Eight-channel data selector.

The output is removed at pin 14. If the logic at input 3 were 1 when the CBA code is 011, a logic 1 appears at output pin 14. Were the logic 0, the output would be 0. If the CBA address is changed to 110, the output at pin 14 would match the logic present at input 6.

The 4512 data selector is said to have a tristate output. Pin 15 provides tristate enabling. When pin 15 is low, the selector operates in normal fashion. However, if pin 15 is switched high, the output at pin 14 is switched to a high-impedance state. Thus the three possible outputs are 0, 1, and high-impedance disconnect. An advantage of a tristate output is that it can be connected to a bus line along with similar circuits having tristate outputs. As a result there is minimum loading and interaction among chips connected to the bus line. Only the chips which are to be activated at the moment are placed on line with the tristate enabling facility.

Circuit connections are shown in Fig. 5-33. The eight inputs are shown at the top left. With all the switches closed, a logic 0 is being applied to each input. Whenever a switch is opened for a particular channel, that input sees a logic 1 because of the connection of the input through its resistor to the supply voltage.

The output is removed at pin 14. A transistor and LED will cause the LED to turn on whenever the output is logic 1. Switches S1 through S3 can be used to provide a specific binary address. Tristate enabling can be checked with switch S4.

To transfer the logic at input 5 to the output you must use the CBA address of 101. By opening and closing the switch associated with input 5, the LED at the output will turn *on* for a logic 1 input and *off* for a logic 0 input. When the input switch of input 5 is open, the LED is on.

If you now connect switch S4 high, the LED will turn off, indicating that a disconnect has been made at the pin 14 output. For this setting of switch S4 there is really no output (neither 1 nor 0) and the transistor, and LED have been completely disconnected from the 4512.

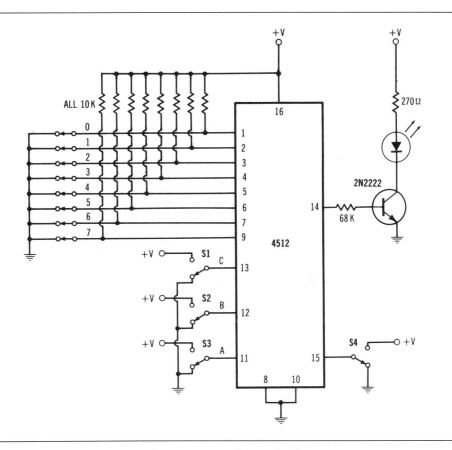

Fig. 5-33. Data selector circuit.

5-6-5. CMOS Addressable Output Latch

The performance of the output latch is complementary to the output of a data selector. In this circuit the input data is channeled to a specific output. The output selected is again determined by a binary addressing system. Furthermore the logic supplied to a specific output is latched and remains there until it is cleared by a reset pulse.

An example of an 8-output latch is the CMOS 4099 (Fig. 5-34). There are eight outputs and a single data input. The output is selected by the 3-bit binary control. Data is transferred to the output only when the Write/Disable pin 4 is low. The reset pulse is applied to pin 2.

Assume that there is a logic 1 on the data input when the binary address is 101. If at the moment pin 4 is also low a logic 1 will appear on the number 5 output (pin 14).

Once latched this output data will not change regardless of the logic applied to pin 4. Thus one or more outputs can be activated, and, in effect, serial input data is presented as parallel output data. Outputs can be deactivated by setting the chip disable or reset (pin 2) high.

A demonstrating circuit is shown in Fig. 5-35. A group of switches on the left permit setting of the data logic, CBA addressing, write/enable, and reset. The output level of the 4099 is low and is built up with the use of an amplifying inverter. In this case the output of the inverter supplies current to individual LEDs.

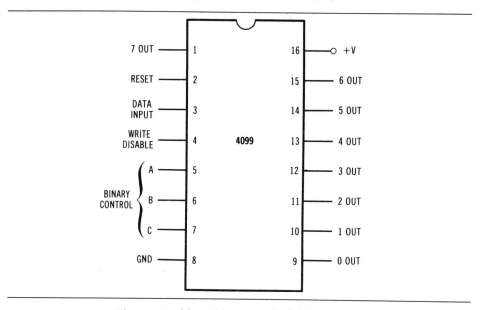

Fig. 5-34. Addressable output latch pinout.

When the circuit is connected exactly as shown the address is 000, the write activity is enabled and, therefore, the 0 output LED turns on. This output remains high even though the switch S5 is set to logic 1. If another CBA address is now used such as 111, the number 7 LED will turn on as soon as switch S5 is returned to low. Now both the 0 output and the No. 7 output LEDs are on. The output can be deactivated by setting switch S6 to high. Of course, in an actual circuit these activities would take place very quickly because of the digital signals being applied to the data and address inputs, as well as to the write and reset inputs.

5-7. Memories

A memory, as applied to control, test, and microprocessor systems is a device for storing digital 1s and 0s. This binary information can then be recalled and used again and again. There are permanent and temporary memory devices.

Memory systems abound. The three main categories are semiconductor, magnetic, and punched. Each category has a number of subdivisions. There are punched cards and tapes. There are magnetic drums, bubbles, cylinders, and cassettes. Magnetic discs are popular and include rigid and floppy types. Rigid discs are made of metal and are common in large systems. A deposited metallic film provides the

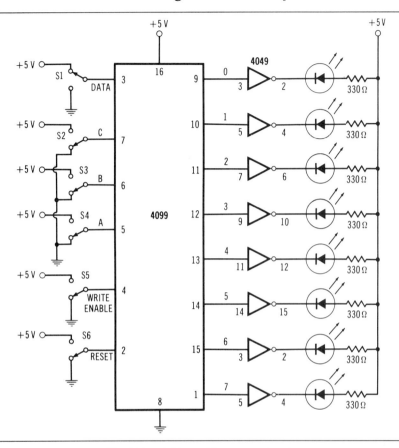

Fig. 5-35. Addressable output circuit.

magnetized material which is loaded with digital information. The floppy disc is a plastic material with an appropriate magnetic deposit. These floppy discs along with tape cassettes are popular for small systems.

Internal to the system there are a variety of permanent and temporary semiconductor memory devices. These are the subject of this section. The five major classes found in two-way radio, navigation, and test equipment are RAM, ROM, PROM, EPROM, and EAROM.

5-7-1. Random Access Memory

In a random access memory (RAM), data is stored in a series of horizontal and vertical rows which provide fast access to each storage location. The device provides facility for the entry of data (write) and for storage or removal of stored data (read) for a specific application. This stored information can be used time and time again. The RAM is said to be a volatile memory because the binary data is lost whenever the power supply is lost. Small backup batteries are often included. These switch on automatically when power is lost and hold the memory for a specified time interval.

The two basic types of RAMs are static and dynamic. The static RAM stores the 1s and 0s in flip-flop circuits. Such memory can be stored permanently so long as the supply voltage is not lost. A dynamic RAM is a MOS device that is able to close pack the 1s and 0s in a tight configuration and permits the storage of more memory in a given space than can be stored for the static type. The data is stored capacitively, however, and over a period of time the stored pattern diminishes and must be renewed by a refresh signal. Additional facilities are required to supply this refresh pattern.

5-7-2. Read Only Memory

In the read only memory (ROM) the memory 1s and 0s are stored permanently according to the program set down by a mask pattern during the manufacturing procedure. This information cannot be destroyed by the loss of supply voltage and provides a permanent program procedure for a system. However, it cannot be changed.

Once a program has been worked out for a given process, the information is supplied to the manufacturer. Hundreds or thousands of individual ROMs are then made to be used in the digested system.

5-7-3. Programmable Read Only Memories

With a programmable read only memory (PROM) the user can prepare his own ROM by the removal of fusable links in the memory pattern. Once the user programs the PROM it cannot be altered and it becomes a permanent ROM.

The erasable programmable read only memory (EPROM) incorporates a small glass window covered over by a removable metal shield. An ultraviolet light can be made to erase the EPROM when the metal shield is removed. This type of memory can be reprogrammed or corrected if a programming mistake has been made. Another version of the erasable type is the electrically alterable read only memory (EAROM). This device is similar to the EPROM but it can be erased instantly with a single electrical operation.

5-7-4. Memory Bits and Patterns

Memories are arranged in different ways. There are different output combinations. Usually a memory is referred to in terms of the number of data output lines. Often they match the number of data output lines. They may also match the number of lines in the distribution system (data bus). Typical output numbers are 1, 4, 8, 16, 32, and even 64 and up for very large computer systems. In commercial applications the most popular output selections are 4 bit, 8 bit, and 16 bit.

The number of data outputs represent the so-named word length of a memory. In the case of a 4-bit output memory, four digits comprise one word. When information is written into the memory it is written in as a complete word. If it is a 4-bit memory, the 4 bits of one word are written in simultaneously. Likewise when this information is read out, it is delivered as a complete word. Only in a memory with a single data output line is the memory coded and decoded one bit at a time. For an 8-bit memory, all 8 bits are coded and decoded simultaneously.

Another factor to point out also relates to the data lines of the memory. The very same data terminals and bus lines are often used for both input (writing) and output (reading) activities of the memory. Some memories have separate input (write) and output (read) pins. A digital pulse applied to one of the pins of the control chip does the switching between read and write.

Output terminals are usually tristate. This means when the chip is not on "write" or "read" it is deactivated. Consequently, it does not load other memories and other devices of the bus. When memories, or other types of devices on the bus line, are not being used they are digitally switched to output disconnect to prevent undue loading of the bus.

The next factor to consider is the number of words that are a part of the memory pattern. Typical values are 128, 256, 512, 1024, 4096, 8192, and 16,384. As an example consider a small 256-word by 4-bit static RAM. In simplified form it is said to be a 256 × 4 RAM. It has a storage capability of 256 words that are 4-bits wide. Thus the total number of bits that can be stored is 1024 (256 × 4). Stated loosely it is referred to as having 1K memory. A 1024 × 8 RAM is said to have a 9K memory, although the actual figure is somewhat less than this.

How are the individual memory bits accessed? In the case of the 256 × 4 RAM they are accessed 4 bits at a time. Stated another way 256 words have to be accessed. This is done with an 8-bit address code. Recall that the binary equivalent of 256 is 11111111. Thus, by supplying the appropriate binary combination to the eight address pins of the memory, any individual word space can be "addressed" for either write or read purpose.

If only part of the memory is to be used, a number of the address pins can be grounded. For example, if only sixteen words of memory are to be used, four address pins are made active while the remaining four are grounded. Thus, a 4-bit binary signal instead of an 8-bit one could be used for addressing. Often the problem is lack of memory space rather than too much. In this case additional memory chips are employed and a means must be included to activate the desired chip and tristate deactivate the other chips not being used at that specific moment.

Two pins on the chip are required for supply voltage as well as a pin to which a read/write changeover pulse can be applied. Pins are also included for chip enabling and memory expansion.

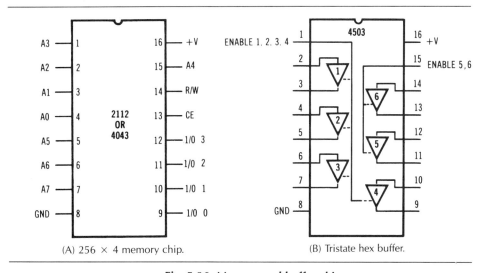

(A) 256 × 4 memory chip.   (B) Tristate hex buffer.

Fig. 5-36. Memory and buffer chips.

The 2112 chip in Fig. 5-36A, is an example of a 256 × 4 memory. This device has a 4-bit shared input/output at pins 9 through 12. There are eight address pins A0 through A7. The logics applied to these pins address a specific 4-bit word between 0 and 255. If the address logic is 00010000, the data on word 16 is chosen. In the READ position (high) of pin 14, this stored data appears on pins 9 through 12. If pin 14 is in the WRITE position (low), the data applied to pins 9 through 12 would be written into memory.

To enable the chip, pin 13 must be low. When pin 13 is high, the input/output pins (9 through 12) are set to the tristate disconnect condition.

Another chip that can be used in a simple demonstration is the tristate hex buffer of Fig. 5-36B. Each of the six buffers is a noninverting type (as indicated by the absence of a small circle at the output side), and the logic is the same at input and output. Buffers 1, 2, 3, and 4 operate in conjunction with the enable connection at pin 1. Buffers 5 and 6 are enabled by the logic applied to pin 15. Data is transferred from input to output whenever the appropriate logic pin is low. Whenever the enabling logic is high, the tristate disconnect condition is present at the outputs of the appropriate buffers so they will not load the bus lines.

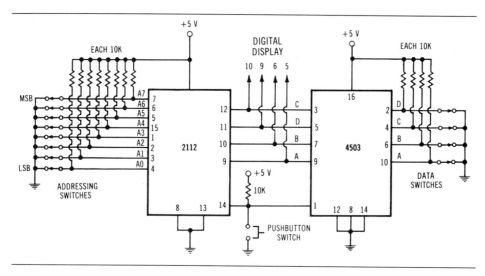

Fig. 5-37. Memory and read/write circuit.

A simple circuit arrangement is shown in Fig. 5-37. To the left of the 2112 memory chip is a set of eight switches that can be used to address any one of the 256 4-bit word positions. As shown all address pins are grounded producing 00000000. This arrangement would activate the space occupied by the first 4-bit word. If all addressing switches were set to logic 1, the address would be the last 4-bit memory word (256). The DCBA 4-bit input/output pins are 12, 11, 10, and 9 respectively. The 4-bit word on the selected memory position can be displayed on a seven-segment display chip using a proper driver.

The 4503 hex buffer facilitates the writing of a 4-bit word into the word position set up by the addressing switches. Consequently, the simple circuit permits you to both "write" into and "read" out of the memory chip.

Consider the operation of the memory circuit. The addressing switches locate the memory word to be written into or read out of. The preset data switches determine the 4 bits of data to be written into the address word position. For strictly reading out of the memory the 4503 is deactivated.

To read out of the memory, recall that pin 14 of the 2112 must be connected high. In Fig. 5-37 note that with the push-button switch open the logic at pin 14 is high. As wired the memory has been set to READ position. For a 4503 hex buffer, the individual buffers are not enabled when the logic at pin 1 is high. Thus, for read application of the memory, the 4503 outputs (pins 3, 5, 7, and 9) are disconnected, and the chip will not interfere with the read-out activitiy.

When the push-button switch is depressed, the logic on pin 14 of the 2112 will be low and the memory will be setup for the WRITE activity. At the same time the push-button switch is depressed, the logic at pin 1 of the 4503 is also low. When this logic is low, the buffers are activated and the information supplied to pins 2, 4, 6, and 10 is transferred to the output pins and on to the data lines. The 2112 has been set to receive information, and, therefore, the word that has been preset by the data switches is written into the selected memory position by the momentary push-button contact.

5-7-5. Electrically Erasable PROM

The electrically erasable programmable-type memory (E^2PROM) is destined to become a popular memory in radiocommunications and navigation equipment. One example is the 64×4 nonvolatile X2210 static RAM by Xicor. It includes a conventional RAM as well as an E^2PROM section. There is a 256-bit static RAM which is overlaid by a 256-bit E^2PROM.

A program can be evolved using the RAM. When it is verified, the entire RAM program can be transferred instantly as a complete copy to the E^2PROM. The program will be held there even though power is removed. The RAM can now be used for other assignments. Whenever the stored program is to be used, it can be transferred immediately to the RAM. If required, the stored program can be modified or corrected by first inserting the corrected program into the RAM and then transferring it to the E^2PROM.

High-voltage pulses or a special voltage supply are not required for the X2210. All operations can be accomplished with a single 5-volt supply. The device is mounted in an 18-pin DIP package. A pinout diagram is shown in Fig. 5-38. The address pins are 2, 3, 4, 5, 6, and 16; the input/output data lines are pins 12, 13, 14, and 15. When the chip-select (pin 7) is low, the chip is enabled. When it's high, the I/O terminals are in a high-impedance state. When the write-enable (pin 11) is low, data can be supplied to the RAM memory. When it's high, the memory can be read.

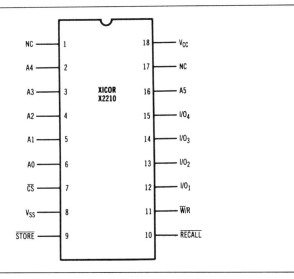

Fig. 5-38. Pinout of the X2210 E²PROM.

Whenever the store terminal (pin 9) is switched to low, the entire memory storage in the RAM is transferred instantly to the E²PROM. The RAM section is now freed for other duties. The stored program can be placed back into the RAM for use by switching the recall (pin 10) to low. The stored program will override any data presently in the RAM at this time.

The program stored in the E²PROM remains there as long as the Store input is not switched low. The stored program can be changed completely or modified by first writing the program into the RAM and using the Store low to place the new or modified program into the E²PROM.

The simple circuit of Fig. 5-39 can demonstrate the operation of the device. The 4503 tristate hex buffer is used to write a program into the RAM. In the example, a 4-bit DIP switch is used that permits 4-bit programming and displays the number with LEDs.

The 64 4-bit addresses can be selected with the six switches shown to the upper left of the X2210. Whenever the Write push button (PB3) is depressed, the binary number applied to the 4503 input is loaded into the 4-bit address selected by switches S1 through S6. The binary input number and the number on the data line are displayed on LEDs driven by 4049 inverter segments. Four-bit decoder/driver chips and 7-segment displays could be used as well.

After a program is loaded into the RAM, it can be transferred to the E²PROM simply by depressing the STORE push button (PB1). The RAM can now be used for other activities. However, the stored program can be placed back into the RAM simply by depressing the recall push button (PB2). Also power can be turned off and the program will remain stored in the E²PROM.

When power is restored, or RAM has been used in another service, one can always restore the program from the E²PROM simply by depressing the recall push button.

5-8. Microprocessor Systems

In elaborate — and not so elaborate radiocommunication systems — the microprocessor has become a popular control and organizing device. It is capable of monitoring complex facilities and making appropriate changes when necessary. Microprocessors are also found in test equipment. This section gives you a brief introduction to the major sections of microprocessor systems.

5-8-1. Microprocessing Simplified

The microprocessor unit (MPU) is the control center of a microprocessor control system or a microcomputer. Its awesome capabilities are housed within a small integrated circuit chip. Size varies from a standard 16-pin chip up to a 64-pin configuration. To carry out its activities the MPU must be surrounded by other devices, within or without, that can supply its input needs and respond to its output controls. A very simple diagram of an MCU plan is given in Fig. 5-40.

Each MPU type has its own so-called instruction set. Depending on size and power, a processor may have anywhere from sixteen, to scores, to hundreds of individual instructions that it is capable of carrying out. At a given instant a proper instruction is selected by a program stored in memory.

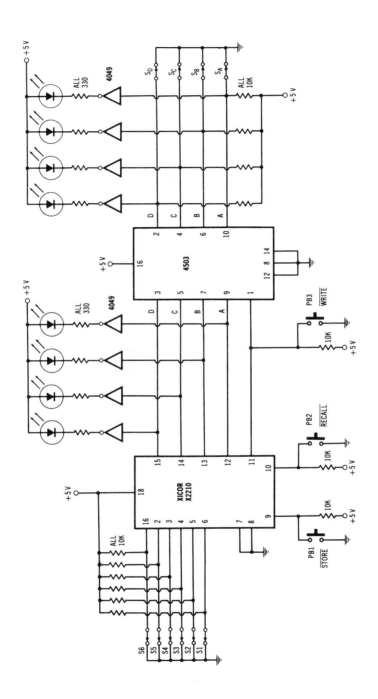

Fig. 5-39. An E²PROM demonstration circuit.

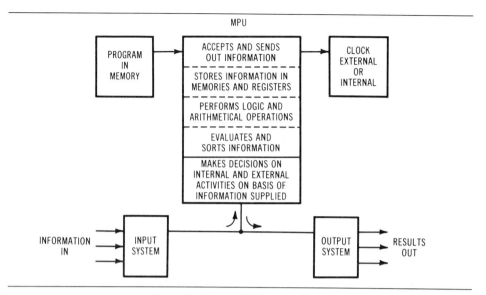

Fig. 5-40. A simplified MPU plan.

First a programmer with a knowledge of the capabilities of the MPU instructions sets down such a program which the system will fulfill in an orderly sequence to meet the needs of a microcomputer, radiocommunication, or commercial control system for which it has been designed. The program is then stored in the memory. The system can be made to run the program whenever necessary or it can be made to go through the program endlessly depending on application.

The timing or sequencing of the microprocessor activities is under control of a clock. The clock is a pulse generator that permits very fast switching of the activities of the MPU and associated chips. Clock rates may be as high as 2 million pulses per second. This gives you some idea of the speed with which a system can go through a program and the speed with which information can be evaluated and result in output activities. No human could begin to react so quickly to the vast quantity of information that can be supplied, evaluated, and responded to. It may take a long time to prepare a program and check the validity of such a program. However, once set in operation, the speed with which information can be gathered and acted upon is phenomenal.

In an MPU system there must be an input system to gather the desired information and an output system to carry out the dictates of the MPU evaluation.

In general, an MPU accepts and sends out information. Incoming information is placed in registers for short storage and immediate use. There are also memories that provide somewhat longer storage facility to allow enough time for manipulation. Each microprocessor includes an arithmetical logic unit (ALU) that solves logic functions and performs mathematical steps just like a calculator. Information must be evaluated, sorted, and distributed inside of, and outside of, the microprocessor proper. On the basis of the information supplied decisions must be made and proper internal and external activities must be initiated. No sorcerer ever matched the magic semiconductor brew in these tiny black boxes.

5-8-2. A Work Example

A simplified plan of an MPU in a work situation is shown in Fig. 5-41. In this application, the microprocessor system is to monitor, measure, and control a pro-

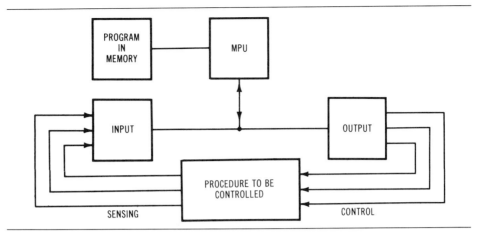

Fig. 5-41. The MPU in a work situation.

cedure. There are input sensing lines and output control lines that extend to the manufacturing machinery. The sensing devices are called sensors or transducers. They are capable of measuring the device being manufactured in various stages of assembly, monitor the operation conditions of the machinery, count the number of items being produced, as well as many other parameters as a function of the manufactured item and manufacturing procedures. There may be three sensors or scores of them or hundreds of them, depending on the complexity and exactness of the task. There can be as many controls over the manufacturing procedures as are required.

Displays can be associated with the process indicating where defects arise and what corrections are being made. Faults can be anticipated and corrections made automatically before a single bad part is produced. In the case of a serious fault a procedure or the entire process can be stopped automatically by the microprocessor system.

In a critical, or precision procedure, a tremendous advantage of a microprocessor control system is the speed with which it responds to a situation. An operating maladjustment can be identified and corrected long before a human operator would recognize that such an adjustment was needed, not even considering the time that the operator would require to react and make the necessary correction.

Sensors of many types are available. Their responsibility is to change over a reading or measurement to an electrical representation which is applied to the input of the microprocessor system. Likewise, the output of the system is an electrical one that manipulates switches and electronic controls to bring about the electrical and mechanical changes that the microprocessor has deemed necessary.

In addition to being the decision-maker of all computers, a microprocessor has many other applications. Their application in manufacturing, mentioned previously, is just one. They can operate a radiocommunication terminal, a broadcast transmitter, or a color television camera. Sublime to silly, they can control the study of Saturn's rings or be the brain of an elaborate pinball machine. They can be part of an electronic toy or an automatic pilot. Present and future applications are so many that the microprocessor is sure to stay.

5-8-3. Bits and Bytes

Microprocessors and microprocessor systems are supplied with input signals in *bits,* evaluate and act upon information in bit form, and deliver output signals in the form of bits. A bit is short for binary digit. A binary digit or bit can only be one of two quantities, a 1 or a 0. Information presented in bit form is called data. A simple example of the use of bits is in order.

Each microprocessor system has a memory which locks up the program procedure. The memory information is stored in many locations like the rows and columns of the individual compartments of an elaborate shelf. However, only two types of information are stored: these are 1s and 0s. Each storage space has a specific address. Even the address is expressed in binary form.

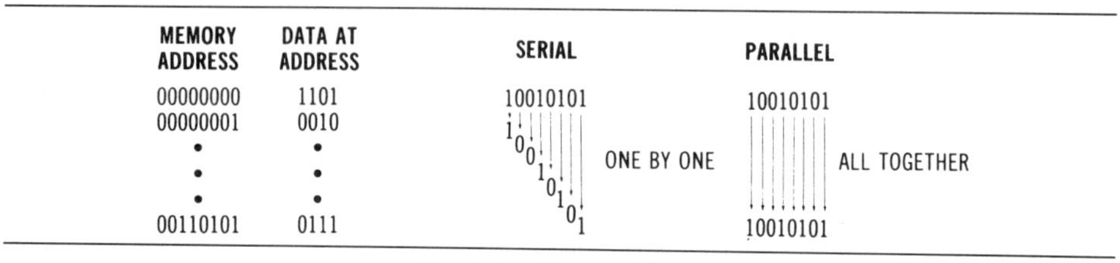

MEMORY ADDRESS	DATA AT ADDRESS	SERIAL	PARALLEL
00000000	1101	10010101	10010101
00000001	0010	ONE BY ONE	ALL TOGETHER
•	•		
•	•		
•	•		
00110101	0111		10010101

Fig. 5-42. Bits and bytes.

For example, the address of the first row in a microprocessor program may be 00000000. The second program address would be 00000001. Each one of the 0s and 1s in an address is called a bit. The 8 bits of a complete address are called a *byte*. Refer to Fig. 5-42.

Not only is the memory address given in bits but the data stored at each address is given in bits. Let's assume that the first address stores four bits of information. The data stored might be 1101. This quantity when delivered to the microprocessor might cause it to perform one of the activities of its instruction set. If the data stored were 1011, some other instruction would be performed by the microprocessor.

In the second storage place or memory address you might find the data 0010. This might cause the microprocessor to respond in a specific way to the instructions just given previously. It might pick up some incoming digital data or deliver some digital data to the output. As in the case of the memory address each 0 and 1 stored by the memory is called a bit. The 4 bits of the data together are called a byte. If you wish to be more specific, you state address bit and address byte, or data bit and data byte.

Binary information is conveyed from one circuit to another in one of two ways. These are serial and parallel. In a serial transmission system the byte is conveyed one bit at a time as shown in Fig. 5-42. For example the quantity 10010101 would be conveyed in the sequence 1-0-0-1-0-1-0-1 on one line.

If the information is to be conveyed in parallel form, the entire byte would be conveyed at one time. It is apparent that with the latter method, information can be conveyed at a much faster rate and a microprocessor will respond more quickly to operating conditions. However, the path of transmission would require eight individual conducting paths. In the serial conveyance method only a single line would be needed. Sometimes the latter is the more economical and simpler procedure when speed of action and evaluations must not be made as quickly.

5-8-4. More Essentials of a Microprocessor System

The principal activities of a microprocessor system were introduced in Figs. 5-40 and 5-41. However, additional circuits and signals are required if these activities are to be implemented. Additional essential circuits and interconnections are given in Fig. 5-43.

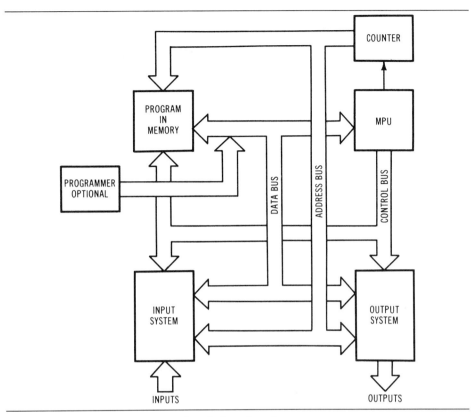

Fig. 5-43. Functional plan of a microprocessor system.

You learned previously that a memory must be addressed. There must be a means of moving the activity step by step from one memory byte position to another. This sequencing is accomplished with a counter as shown at the top right. Usually the counter is a part of the MPU proper although it is shown externally in Fig. 5-43. The counter is driven by the MPU clock which acts as the timing center for all MPU activities. If the memory has an 8-digit address, there must be eight lines connected between the counter and the memory. Such a multiconductor interconnection is called a bus. Bus lines are drawn as shown in Fig. 5-43.

Address information goes out to other parts of the system as well. In particular the input/output (I/O) system must be addressed in such a manner that a particular input is chosen at a particular time and a particular output is selected at a particular time. This important address information is said to be distributed among the sections of a microprocessor system by an *address bus*. Note the interconnections among counter, memory, input system, and output system are shown. Address information flows in a single direction out of the MPU to the various circuits where it is needed, inside of and outside of the MPU.

Data lines or the *data bus* must also interconnect the MPU with the memory and I/O systems. The data bus line is a bidirectional facility because data must be exchanged among the devices of the microprocessor system. As the program is sequenced by the step-by-step change of memory address, the information in each memory byte is released to the data bus. In Fig. 5-40 this was shown as a single line connecting the memory and the MPU. In all but the very simplest of processors a data bus interconnects the memory and MPU. Also the data bus connects to the I/O systems as well as other devices depending on the complexity of the system. Thus, there are several types of information exchanged among units of the data bus line. Instructions go out from memory to the MPU in accordance with the MPU instruction that the program selects. Another memory byte will provide the information as to where particular data can be collected and how it is to be executed by the MPU. Thus, data is delivered from the input system to the MPU. Furthermore, data must leave the MPU and go to the output system. The data bus is indeed a two-way path.

In a design microprocessor system, or in a system that permits the program to be changed, by the user, there must also be a data bus connection between the programmer and the memory. Such a facility permits programs to be programmed, changed, and checked out for performance validity. Memories are used to store the digital 1s and 0s of a program. Actually, there are three basic memory types — permanent, a temporary, and a semipermanent version that can be erased with suitable facilities and replaced with a new program. These are the ROM, RAM, and EPROM discussed previously.

Operations in a microprocessor system must be synchronized and special information must be sent out to the various segments as a function of the particular instruction activated in the MPU. This is a function of the information sent along the conductors of the control bus. One such type of information is the clock pulse which goes out to synchronize operations in other circuits with the sequencing of the program memory. A pulse must go out to select input or output operation, depending on whether data is to be delivered to the MPU from the input system or supplied to the output system. There are other special pulses sent out in accordance with the activated instruction set of the MPU.

The typical microprocessor is rated on the basis of the number of lines on the data bus. It is said to be a 1-bit, 4-bit, or even a 64-bit microprocessor. The three most common values are 4 bit, 8 bit, and 16 bit. The higher the number of bits, the higher is the so-called power of the microprocessor. What this really means is that data can be transferred and acted on faster with the parallel movement of a high number of bits. Also a system is able to respond to a greater volume of data because of the higher number of bits.

5-8-5. Simplified Program Sequence

In a microprocessor system there are two activity phases. These are known as *fetch* and *execute*. In the *fetch phase* the instructions or operational code (op code) is brought from memory and enters the MPU. In a typical microprocessor system the fetch would involve the time interval of one clock. The *execute phase* might require one or more clock periods depending on the nature of the information required to execute the instructions. In the execute activities the data must be gathered that is to be acted on. This data is known as the *operand*. In the usual programming activity the address of the operand must first be obtained from the memory. After the address is obtained then the operand must be gathered from that address. This particular type of execute then would require two clock periods. The combination fetch and execute phases in this case would equal the time interval of three clock periods. Remember that the op code is the instructions to be followed and the operand the data upon which the instructions are to be performed. All of these activities are timed and synchronized by the clock pulses.

Usually there are two clock pulses of the same frequency but differing polarity. One might be referred to as clock and the other as inverted clock. The two clock components are of the same frequency but may differ in polarity and duration.

Two clock components are shown in Fig. 5-44. The clock pulses are not square waves. Thus, in comparing the A and B clock intervals the negative portion of the B clock begins ahead of the positive portion of the A clock. The A clock has its trailing

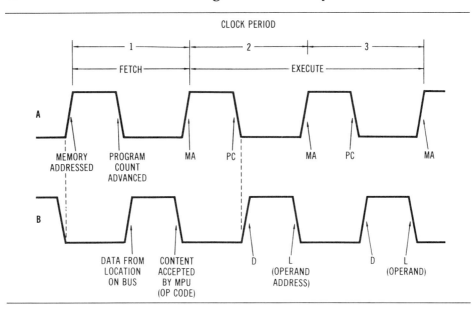

Fig. 5-44. How the clock pulses control program activities.

negative transition occur ahead of the positive transition of the B clock. These relative timings are set to properly augment the fetch and execute activities.

The activities for the three clock pulse intervals of the previous example are shown. The first positive transition of the A clock addresses the first position in the memory. The trailing transition of the A clock simply advances the count in preparation for the next memory address. The first positive transition of the B clock places the data present in the first memory address on the data bus. The negative transition of clock B causes the MPU to accept this data. The data in this case is the op code. This op code data is now latched into the MPU and causes it to evaluate what must be done and then to execute the instruction. This concludes the activity of the first clock period and the appropriate op code has been fetched.

Next the second memory position is addressed and according to op code instructions it is necessary to determine the address of the operand. The positive transition of the second B pulse causes this address to be placed on the data bus. The negative transition of the same pulse latches the operand address to the MPU.

The third line of memory is addressed by the positive transition of the third clock A pulse. As in previous cases the program count is advanced by its trailing edge. The positive transition of the B clock third pulse places the operand data on the data bus line. Its trailing edge latches the operand to the MPU and the appropriate operation is performed in response to the op code instruction supplied to the MPU, during the fetch period. Note that the execute time required two clock periods. The speed with which the instruction was fetched and executed is revealing. Assuming a clock frequency of 500 kHz or 0.5 MHz, the clock period would be 2 microseconds (1/.5). Thus the entire procedure required only 6 microseconds.

The previous instruction op code may have told the MPU to store this operand in the ALU register (sometimes called an accumulator). Other instructions are now supplied from the program asking the MPU to add this stored data to the data supplied to one of the inputs of the microprocessor system. After the addition the new result is stored in the accumulator.

Now the MPU might be provided with instructions to compare this sum with the data on some other input line. The instructions might tell the MPU to place a logic 1 on output line 2 if the two quantities are of the same value. If they are not the same, then the MPU should put a logic 1 on output line 4 and so on.

In this manner a program can be sequenced at a high rate of speed. The program can be repeated many times per second, demonstrating how quickly a microprocessor system can respond to input changes, transcribing them to output decisions.

5-8-6. Interfacing

The previous paragraphs covered the fundamental makeup of the microprocessor system. Such a system has input and output facilities that must be interfaced with a variety of input sectors. Likewise, its output must be interfaced with the systems and devices under its control.

On the input side (Fig. 5-45) there might be a mechanical or digital switching panel that is used to supply the microprocessor system with specific operational sequences. The microprocessor installation could be involved in the measurement of electrical and/or physical parameters to which the system must respond. So-named sensors or transducers are able to evaluate a variety of parameters such as voltage, temperature, current, frequency, velocity, pressure, etc. Their primary responsibility is to form an electrical output current that is a measure of the parameters to be evaluated. Since a microprocessor is a digital device, these analog signals must be converted to digital data. This changeover is handled by an analog-to-digital converter or ADC. These interfacing circuits, then, process a great variety of possible information to digital representations that can be acted on by the microprocessor system.

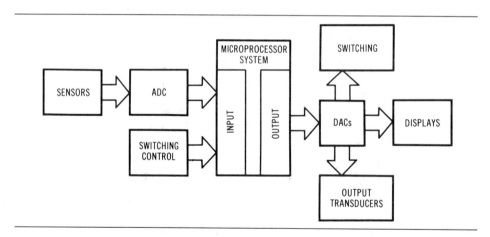

Fig. 5-45. Interfacing methods.

Digital information is also developed at the output of the microprocessor system. As a result it must often be supplied to a digital-to-analog converter, or DAC. The analog data is then used to operate a visual display, switch electrical/electronic devices on and off, change a frequency, operate an electromechanical valve, activate emergency equipment, etc. Interfacing is indeed an important segment of micro-processor control systems.

6

Test Equipment and Methods

Test instruments—both simple and complex—are needed to adjust, monitor, and troubleshoot the transmitters and receivers of two-way radio systems. For some transmitter measurements, the accuracy must be well within the two-way radio performance tolerances established by the FCC. Moreover, not only must the test equipment be of good quality, but it must be used properly as well.

The FCC is concerned primarily with the operating frequency and its stability, the power output, modulation level of the communications transmitter, and freedom from spurious radiation. The test equipment must be capable of making these measurements accurately. Otherwise, it would be difficult to determine whether the transmitter is complying with FCC technical standards.

The owner of a two-way radio system is also interested in additional performance criteria. He is concerned with reliable, intelligible, and interference-free communications. To him, transmitter and receiver performance are of equal importance. The base and mobile transmitters must convey a good signal within the area served by the installation. The transmitter power output and modulation levels must not be permitted to decline and should be held near, but not beyond, the maximum limits set by the FCC. The receiver sensitivity and stability must be maintained at a high level. It is preferable to keep the equipment in such condition that it can be used for long periods without retuning and service.

The operators of such equipment are not expected to have technical knowledge beyond turning the equipment on and off and switching from transmit to receive and back. It is imperative then that the technician in charge of the system know how to use the test equipment in a manner that will keep the system in top operating condition.

6-1. Required Test Equipment

Two or three pieces of test equipment are needed to check out a transmitter to make sure it complies with FCC technical regulations. One such instrument is an accurate frequency counter or meter, used to determine if the transmitter is set exactly

217

on the assigned frequency. Of course, such an instrument also permits the operator to tune the transmitter to its assigned frequency.

The same meter is generally used for checking the frequency stability of the transmitter. Once a transmitter is set on its assigned frequency, its frequency drift may be no more than that permitted by FCC regulations. Generally, this requirement is stated as a percentage of the assigned frequency.

Modulation meters are required for checking the percentage of modulation, to make certain it is no greater than that permitted by FCC regulations. In an FM system, 100% modulation represents a maximum frequency deviation of $\pm$ 5 kHz for most installations, and for other services a maximum deviation of $\pm$ 2 kHz or $\pm$ 15 kHz. Again, the modulation meter not only is useful in making certain that 100% modulation is not exceeded, but also permits the technician to tune the transmitter for adequate deviation.

Coverage and reliability are improved if the transmitter is made to deviate to its maximum limit on modulation peaks. Most transmitters include special circuits which prevent instantaneous modulation peaks in excess of 100%.

For AM communications systems, the modulation must not exceed 100%. A test setup can be arranged to measure the actual amplitude-modulation percentage. Here again, the modulation level should be adjusted as high as possible (average above 70%) for the greatest coverage and reliability. At the same time, modulation peaks should not exceed 100%. In AM transmitters, too, special circuits are usually incorporated to prevent modulation peaks from overmodulating the transmitter.

An accurate power-output meter is helpful in deriving the best performance from each transmitter. The assigned power output should not be exceeded. However, reliability and coverage can be improved if the transmitter operates at its assigned power output. A power-output meter is helpful in the attainment of maximum power output.

Most communications transmitters are FCC-approved and do not require an accurate power-out measurement. If the transmitter is operated according to its accompanying instructions, it can be assumed to be operating at the rated power output. Such transmitters, when operated in accordance with the tune-up instructions, are not capable of delivering more than the rated output. When the DC input power is normal, one can be reasonably certain the rated power output of such a transmitter is being obtained. The maximum permissible power is often presented in terms of power input to the final stage.

Whether this type of transmitter or the one that requires power-output measurements is employed, a power-output indicator is useful—if for no other reason than making certain the transmitter is matched to the antenna system. When the two are matched, the antenna radiates almost the total power that the transmitter is capable of delivering.

Some radio-frequency indicators can be inserted into the transmission path, between transmitter and antenna, to measure the power output and the standing-wave ratio on the transmission line. This type of instrument is very useful in measuring radiation from the line and in making certain that maximum energy is transferred between the transmitter output and the antenna.

Simpler test equipment such as radio-frequency output indicators, absorption wavemeters, dip oscillators, and others are useful in transmitter tune-up and receiver adjustments, and in the localization of trouble in the two-way radio system.

An accurate signal generator is particularly important in receiver alignment. Many of these receivers have an extraordinary sensitivity, down to 1 microvolt or less. This sensitivity is possible only if the circuits have been critically aligned and the receiver carefully tuned. Keep in mind that many of these receivers are fixed-tuned—the user has no way of tuning in the signal if it is absent or mushy.

Some standard pieces of electronic test equipment such as a VOM, DVM, capacitor checker, oscilloscope, and other component testers are helpful, too.

6

6-2. The Absorption Wavemeter

The absorption wavemeter shown in Figs. 6-1 and 6-2 is a basic radio-frequency indicator and frequency meter. It is hardly more than a calibrated resonant circuit which, when coupled near the source of radio-frequency energy, can withdraw some of the energy. This meter will absorb maximum energy when tuned to the same resonant frequency as the source.

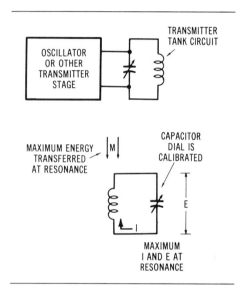

Fig. 6-1. Principle of the absorption
wavemeter.

Some form of radio-frequency indicator such as a lamp, neon bulb, or diode and DC-meter combination can be used to indicate the relative strength of the energy absorbed by the resonant circuit of the wavemeter. When the wavemeter is tuned to the frequency of the radio-frequency source, the indicator will read maximum; but if tuned to either side of the resonant-energy frequency, the meter reading or lamp brilliancy will decrease.

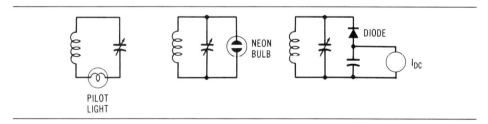

Fig. 6-2. Indicators for absorption wavemeters.

If the resonant frequency of the wavemeter tank circuit is known from the dial setting, the frequency of the radio-frequency energy can be determined. Usually the capacitor dial of the wavemeter is calibrated in frequency. Therefore, the setting of the pointer on the calibrated scale, when the capacitor is tuned for maximum RF indication, shows the frequency of the RF signal being measured. In other absorption wavemeters, the dial is calibrated from 0 to 100, and the exact resonant frequency of the absorption tank circuit is determined from a chart.

Wavemeters are usually equipped with replaceable coils so they can be made to operate on different frequency bands, with a separate dial or calibration chart for each band.

6-2-1. Using the Wavemeter

Energy from the tank circuit of the unit under test is coupled into the resonant circuit of the wavemeter. Use loose coupling to minimize loading the circuit under test, and couple the absorption wavemeter only close enough to the radio-frequency source to permit a usable RF indication (lamp glow or DC meter readings).

To provide minimum loading and additional convenience, some absorption wavemeters include a low-impedance pickup coil. The main meter coil remains part of the wavemeter proper and is not coupled close to the radio-frequency energy being measured. The small pickup loop is coupled to the source of energy and transfers the small amount needed into the absorption-wavemeter circuit (Fig. 6-3).

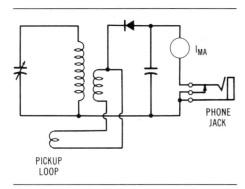

Fig. 6-3. Absorption wavemeter with pickup loop and phone jack.

The absorption wavemeter is important in making approximate frequency measurements while a transmitter is tuned, and, in particular, for checking multiplier harmonic outputs. It also serves as a good indicator of the strength of the radio-frequency energy. When set at a fixed position from the energy source, the influence of tuning on the radio-frequency output can be noticed immediately.

Some absorption wavemeters also include a phone jack into which a pair of headsets can be plugged and any AM modulation on the RF signal can be heard. Hence, when the absorption wavemeter is used to check out RF amplifiers that convey a modulated RF signal, the quality of that modulation can be tested approximately, using the detector circuit that is part of many absorption wavemeters. For proper demodulation of an FM radio-frequency signal, some form of FM detector would have to be associated with the wavemeter.

6-2-2. Wavemeter as an RF Indicator

The wavemeter principle can also be used as a sensitive radio-frequency output indicator. In fact, it is no problem to attach a small antenna to a wavemeter, as shown in Fig. 6-4, to make it even more sensitive to the radio-frequency output of a transmitter.

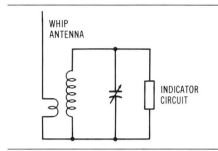

Fig. 6-4. Use of the wavemeter.

If the wavemeter is tuned to the operating frequency of the transmitter and placed somewhere in its immediate field, a strong indication can be obtained. It is in effect a *field-strength indicator*. With the meter positioned a fixed distance from a transmitter, various tuning adjustments can be made to maximize the RF output. In fact, the wavemeter, if placed in the field of the transmitter antenna, permits a rather good indication of the tuning of the antenna system and the effectiveness of energy transfer from transmitter to antenna.

6-2-3. Tuning Meter

A nonresonant RF indicator is shown in Fig. 6-5. This is a very popular instrument for making rough field checks of the power output and tuning of communications transmitters. It consists of a crystal diode and a sensitive DC meter. The indicator is a simple rectifier and filter circuit. Capacitor C1, inductor L1, and potentiometer R1 function as a filter to smooth out the unidirectional detector pulses. Thus, the steady current through the DC meter is a function of the signal strength at the input. To improve the sensitivity of the device, particularly when HF and VHF signals are being checked, a short antenna can be attached. The sensitivity can be adjusted with potentiometer R1. The amount of resistance inserted into the circuit influences the amplitude of the current through the DC meter.

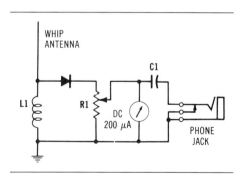

Fig. 6-5. A typical RF-field indicator.

A tuning meter of this type, when placed near the transmitter antenna, will indicate the relative power output of the transmitter, and the effect of any transmitter adjustment on the power output can then be noted.

It must be stressed that this type of RF meter, being untuned, is sensitive to an extremely wide frequency range. For this reason, it cannot be used to check the transmitter frequency.

6-3. Dip Oscillators

The dip oscillator is a useful test instrument for checking transmitter circuits. Most dip oscillators can also be used as absorption wavemeters. FET or tube dip oscillators cover the range from several hundred kilohertz up into the UHF spectrum. Plug-in coils and loops provide overlapping frequency ranges between the extremes.

The dial of the variable capacitor of the dip oscillator is calibrated in frequency. When used with the appropriate calibrated coil, the oscillator frequency can be read with reasonable accuracy.

As a dip oscillator, the test unit can be used to determine the resonant frequency of a de-energized radio-frequency tuned circuit. When a resonant circuit is brought close to the oscillating tank circuit, the tuned circuit under measurement absorbs some of the energy from the oscillator tank circuit. (Refer to Fig. 6-6A.) Inasmuch as energy is removed from the tank circuit of the oscillator, the oscillator feedback decreases. As a result, the current meter reading on the dip oscillator drops.

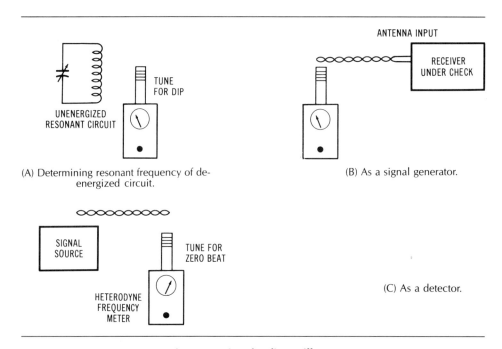

(A) Determining resonant frequency of de-energized circuit.

(B) As a signal generator.

(C) As a detector.

Fig. 6-6. Using the dip oscillator.

When the dip oscillator is set on the frequency of the resonant circuit under measurement, the meter will dip to its minimum value. This setting indicates that the dip oscillator is generating a signal of the same frequency as the resonant tuned circuit under check.

It is apparent that the dip oscillator is very helpful in determining the resonant frequency of various types of tuned circuits. Be it a small, weak-signal resonant circuit of a receiver or the larger, higher-powered resonant circuit of the transmitter final amplifier, the resonant frequency can be determined without any signal present. In transmitter circuits the dip oscillator can also be used to track down spurious resonant conditions that cause parasitic oscillations. A dip oscillator can also be utilized as a signal generator, as shown in Fig. 6-6B. Therefore, it can be used in signal-tracing a communications receiver.

The dip oscillator can also be employed as an oscillating detector, similar in action to a heterodyne-frequency meter. In this application, as shown in Fig. 6-6C, the dip oscillator is brought near the source of RF energy. A pair of headphones, inserted into the phone jack, will pick up a beat note when the frequency of the dip oscillator is brought near the signal-source frequency. If this note is zero-beat, the dip oscillator is set to the same frequency as the source of the signal. In this application the dip oscillator has been used for determining the frequency of an unknown signal source.

6-3-1. Dip Oscillator Calibration

The oscillating-detector principle of the dip oscillator can in itself be used to calibrate the meter, as shown in Fig. 6-7. In this check, it is coupled near a crystal-controlled frequency standard. Whenever the dip oscillator is tuned to the crystal frequency or to one of its harmonics, a beat note will be heard. At the beat-note position, dip calibration should be checked. Some dip oscillators provide a calibration control so the oscillator can be reset if it has drifted.

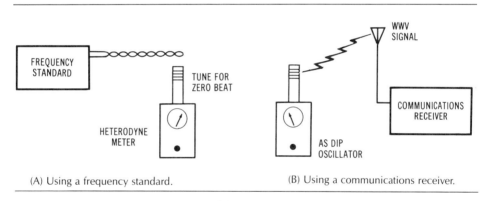

(A) Using a frequency standard.   (B) Using a communications receiver.

Fig. 6-7. Calibrating the dip oscillator.

Still another method of checking the calibration of a dip oscillator is to tune a communications receiver to a WWV frequency (2.5, 5, 10, 15, 20, and 25 MHz), as in Fig. 6-7B. The dip oscillator is then tuned to the same frequency. When a zero beat is heard *at the receiver output*, the dip oscillator has been set to the same frequency as the incoming WWV signal. The dial calibration can be checked at this point.

6-3-2. Dip Oscillator as an Absorption Wavemeter

When the oscillator is turned off, the dip oscillator becomes an absorption wavemeter. The tuned circuit and device act as a detector and the meter becomes part of the diode-load circuit. When coupled near and tuned to the frequency of an RF energy source, the meter will display a current increase. The operation is similar to that discussed for absorption wavemeters.

The dip oscillator has many applications in testing and tuning transmitter circuits. The obvious applications are for tuning tank circuits and checking the output. Other applications include use as an RF indicator in neutralizing various stages of the transmitter, or in tracking down troublesome parasitic oscillations. It is also helpful for peaking various types of resonant traps used in transmitters to prevent parasitic oscillations, or for preventing the transfer of strong harmonic components from stage to stage and from the transmitter to the antenna system. Finally, the dip oscillator is handy for checking antenna performance. It can be used in bringing an antenna system to resonance and in minimizing standing waves on the transmission line.

6-4. Power Output Meters

To minimize interference and to be fair to all users of two-way radio equipment, transmitters must adhere to certain performance standards in the form of specific FCC technical rules and regulations. These standards cover the frequency of operation, frequency stability, modulation level, and power output. Suitable test instruments are available for testing these transmitter characteristics. They must be capable of making measurements within the tolerances established by the FCC.

The maximum power output of the transmitter must comply with the maximum ratings established by the FCC for a particular service. As mentioned previously, the power output is set indirectly by the maximum power input restrictions of the FCC. Power-output measurements are not required for approved units. It is assumed that if the accompanying instructions are followed with regard to the power input, the output will not be excessive.

6-4-1. Power Meters

An RF power-output meter is helpful to the communications technician who does much work in this field. It permits him to determine if a given transmitter does function efficiently, and helps him tune up the transmitter in a manner which will give the owner as strong a signal as possible without exceeding the FCC maximum input rating.

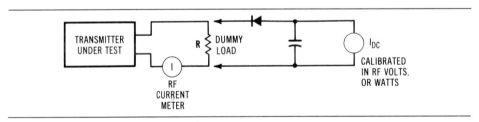

Fig. 6-8. Making RF power output measurement.

Power output can be measured by attaching a dummy load to the transmitter output. The dummy load should have the same impedance as the antenna system into which the transmitter normally works. An RF ammeter (Fig. 6-8) can be inserted into the dummy-load circuit. Power output will be:

$$P = I^2 R$$

A calibrated RF voltmeter can also be used to measure the RF voltage across the dummy load. In this case the RF power output is:

$$P = E^2 R$$

An RF voltmeter is usually made of a crystal diode rectifier and a sensitive DC meter calibrated to measure RF voltage.

6-4-2. Commerical RF Power Meters

A problem in making RF power measurements is that the circuit operating conditions change when the test instruments are inserted across the transmitter output or into the transmission-line path between the transmitter and antenna system. Commercial instruments, referred to as insertion-type RF wattmeters, provide the answer to this problem.

Courtesy Bird Electronics Corp.

Fig. 6-9. An RF wattmeter.

An insertion-type wattmeter made by Bird Electronic Corporation is shown in Fig. 6-9. Units are designed specifically for line insertion between a 50-ohm transmitter output and a 50-ohm antenna system. As shown in Fig. 6-10, it is inserted between the transmitter output and the coaxial transmission line going to the antenna system. Various plug-in termination elements are made available. By insertion of the proper elements, wattage ranges can be measured from 100 milliwatts to 10 kilowatts. Frequency ranges extend from 2 to more than 1000 MHz.

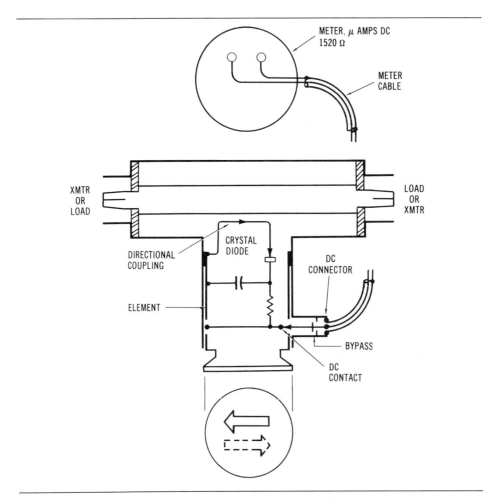

Fig. 6-10. An RF wattmeter circuit.

The instrument responds to the direction of wave travel and is capable of measuring the power in the forward wave traveling between transmitter and antenna, as well as the power lost in the reflected wave traveling back toward the transmitter because of a mismatch in the antenna system. It is apparent that the RF wattmeter is helpful not only in making power measurements, but also in tuning the transmission line and antenna system for a minimum standing-wave ratio to ensure the most efficient transfer of power from transmitter to antenna.

The wattmeter and coupling system are shown schematically in Fig. 6-10. The RF energy, passing between the transmitter and antenna, is sampled by a pickup element and applied to a crystal diode and rectifier. A rectified and filtered DC current is then linked by a meter cable to a current meter with a high sensitivity. To prevent meter and crystal damage, it is important that the proper size of plug-in element be used and that it be inserted correctly.

A complete coupling circuit which samples the traveling wave is mounted in each individual plug-in element. It consists of the pickup loop, crystal diode, and associ-

6

ated components. There are various plug-in elements corresponding to frequency and power rating. These are plugged into the front of the meter.

The pickup element of the RF wattmeter functions as a directional coupler. As shown in Fig. 6-11, the RF energy is conveyed to the crystal diode over two paths. One path is by way of capacitive coupling from the center conductor, which is part of the coaxial feedthrough arrangement. Radio-frequency energy is also inductively coupled into the pickup tube. By careful design, the two components are of equal amplitude and are either additive or subtractive.

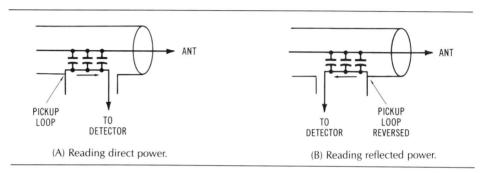

(A) Reading direct power.   (B) Reading reflected power.

Fig. 6-11. Principle of a reflectometer.

The phase of the inductive component is a function of the direction of wave travel. In the arrangement of Fig. 6-11A, the energy picked up inductively from the wave traveling between transmitter and antenna adds to the capacitive component and produces a reading on the calibrated meter. Any reflected energy returning along the transmission line induces a voltage out of phase with the direct-coupled component from the reflected wave. Consequently, the influence of the reflected wave is canceled and its strength is not recorded.

To read the reflected power, the coupling plug-in element is inserted in the opposite direction, as shown in Fig. 6-11B. The reflected power induces into the coupling circuit a voltage in phase with the capacitively coupled component. Hence, the meter will read the reflected power. Insofar as the direct wave moving from the transmitter to antenna is concerned, the coupling loop is so connected that the induced component and the capacitive components are equal and opposite in polarity. The net voltage is zero; therefore, the direct power is not recorded on the meter.

This type of power meter, usually referred to as a *reflectometer,* has the ability to measure direct and reflected power. The power delivered to the antenna or other load can be calculated by subtracting the reflected power from the direct power.

In using an RF power meter of this type, it is very important to insert a plug-in element of the proper size and in the proper direction. For example, the reflected power of a closely matched system is much lower than the direct power. To make an accurate measurement of the reflected power, therefore, requires the use of a low-power plug-in element. Moreover, if this element is inserted in the improper direction, the strong direct power will be supplied to it, and the crystal and meter could be damaged.

Bird Electronics Corp. also makes available a plug-in field-strength element for this wattmeter as well as other models. It plugs into the same position as the previous wattmeter elements. This element (Fig. 6-12) consists of a flexible receiving antenna, high-pass network, detector, and a variable-gain radio-frequency amplifier. Such capability is useful in adjusting, tuning, and positioning antennas for maximum meter indication as displayed on the wattmeter. The adjustable gain control permits accommodation for the power output level of the transmitter. A continuous-wave, one-watt output at 150 MHz supplied to a quarter-wave antenna produces full-scale meter deflection at a distance of approximately 8 feet. The frequency range is between 2 and 1000 MHz. The element is battery operated.

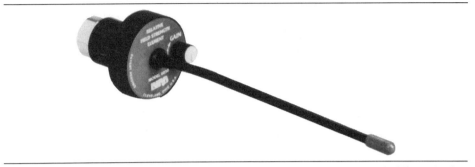

Courtesy Bird Electronics Corp.

Fig. 6-12. Field-strength meter plug-in element.

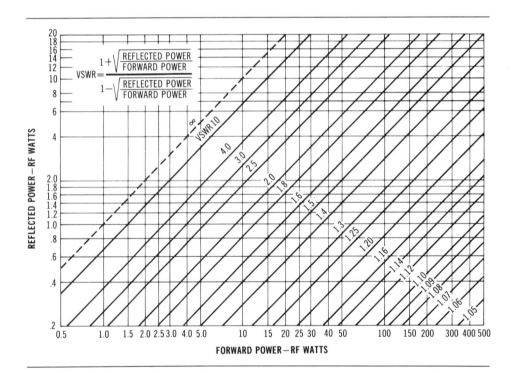

$$VSWR = \frac{1 + \sqrt{\dfrac{\text{REFLECTED POWER}}{\text{FORWARD POWER}}}}{1 - \sqrt{\dfrac{\text{REFLECTED POWER}}{\text{FORWARD POWER}}}}$$

Fig. 6-13. Conversion of power ratio to SWR.

Another Bird wattmeter, the Model 4410, provides seven overlapping power levels using the same plug-in element. In this arrangement an appropriate power switch is mounted on the wattmeter proper for power selection. For example, using a 100-watt plug-in element full-scale deflection readings of 0.1, 0.3, 1, 3, 10, 30, and 100 watts can be selected. The accuracy of the meter reading is within ± 5%. Five such plug-ins will provide frequency coverage between 25 and 1000 MHz. Elements are available for other power levels up to 10,000 watts, as well as for other frequency ranges.

Insertion wattmeters of this type measure direct and reflected powers but they do not measure the standing-wave ratio. In almost all practical applications the ratio of forward power to reflected power tells the story of proper antenna match. However, the appropriate equation can be used to convert this ratio to a standing-wave ratio (SWR). Also a nomograph can be used as shown in Fig. 6-13. The equation is also given. To check, use a forward power value of 100 watts and the reflected power of 4 watts. The horizontal and vertical coordinates of this situation intersect with the diagonal line labeled 1.5. As a result the VSWR ratio is 1.5.

6-5. Multiservice RF Wattmeters

The two RF wattmeters described previously were designed for measuring the power levels of continuous waves (CW) and frequency-modulated signals such as are common in the landmobile radio services. If your two-way radio activities involve other radio services, you may encounter other forms of modulation. Single sideband modulation (SSB) is prevalent in the HF marine bands. There are also some strictly amplitude-modulated signals in both the marine and aviation services. There are also various forms of pulse modulation used for navigation purposes in both the aviation and marine services.

The Bird model 4314 RF wattmeter in Fig. 6-14 permits the measurement of AM, sideband, and pulsed signals in addition to its CW and FM capability. It is capable of measuring the peak envelope power (PEP) so important in judging the performance of SSB and AM signals. This unit is popular in the aviation services. Appropriate plug-in elements are available for power levels between 1 and 10,000 watts and frequency bands that extend between 2 and 1000 MHz.

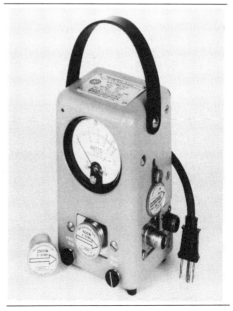

Fig. 6-14. Wattmeter with modulation measurement capability.

The basic wattmeter function is the same as that described for the previous models. In addition there is a peak-reading circuit that is activated when the peak-read button on the front panel is depressed. In this position you can read the peak power of SSB, AM, and pulse modulated RF signals. A simplified block diagram of this capability is given in Fig. 6-15. With switches S1 and S2 in the positions shown, the DC output of the wattmeter plug-in element is supplied directly to the wattmeter metering circuit. This is the connection for measuring CW and FM signals. The two switches are changed to the down positions when the peak-read button is depressed. Now the DC output of the wattmeter is applied to a differential amplifier and then to a balancing bridge used to calibrate the peak-reading capability. Resistor R1 at the input has the same resistance as the wattmeter metering circuit. Therefore, the same operating conditions are established for the peak measuring activity.

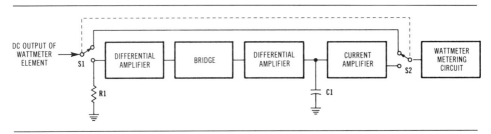

Fig. 6-15. Block diagram of peak-reading circuit.

A second differential amplifier follows the bridge and supplies a charge to capacitor C1. The charge on this capacitor represents the peak RF signal component developed across the input resistor R1. Therefore, it is a measure of the peak level of the RF signal. However, the capacitor holds a voltage charge for a long time interval. As a result the output of the current amplifier supplied to the wattmeter circuit is constant and represents the RF energy present on the modulation peaks.

Not shown in Fig. 6-15 are the power supply and additional switching required when the push button is depressed. Since the unit is battery powered, voltage is supplied to the various amplifiers only when the peak-read button is depressed. A battery charging circuit is associated with the unit and is activated when the AC power cord is plugged into the AC line.

The Bird Model 4391 power analyst shown in Fig. 6-16 is a microprocessor controlled RF wattmeter. It is referred to as a power analyst because of the various measurements it can make on CW, AM, FM, and SSB, as well as pulse and television modulation envelopes. It is capable of measuring power in milliwatts, watts, and kilowatts in nine ranges from 2.5 to 1000 full-scale forward power and 0.25 to 100 reflected power. It will also allow SWR and percentage modulation to be read directly. Various decibel readings can be taken as well.

As shown in Fig. 6-16 both a forward and reflected plug-in element is used in making a transmitter output check. To measure forward power or reflected power you need only depress the appropriate push button while equipment adjustments are made. By depressing the SWR button, conditions of the match can be evaluated. The unit not only measures peak envelope power but it is also capable of reading percentage of modulation. All the necessary switching is handled by a microprocessor control when the appropriate function button is depressed. The readings are obtained from a digital display.

A functional plan of the unit is given in Fig. 6-17. All activities are controlled from the microprocessor control capability of the single-chip computer on the lower right. The output from the directional plug-in elements is applied to the appropriate circuits

Fig. 6-16. The Bird RF power analyst.

through a complex switching system controlled by the microprocessor. The two detector blocks contain the necessary circuits for measuring modulation peaks as well as modulation percentage.

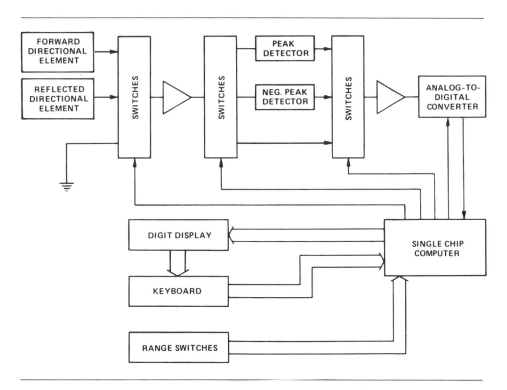

Fig. 6-17. Functional plan of RF power analyst.

The output of the wattmeter is an analog signal that is a measure of and follows the power and modulation of the transmitter signal being analyzed. As mentioned in the previous chapter digital circuits respond only to zeros and ones. As a result the analog signals must be converted to digital signals by the analog-to-digital converter. This digital information is supplied to the microprocessor control system for evaluation and distribution. A 15-bit binary number is supplied to the digital display of the instrument. Thus, a digital readout of power, modulation, or other parameter is displayed. When you depress a keyboard button, an appropriate digital signal is formed and supplied to the microprocessor which activates the requested switching and measurement activity that is a part of the microprocessor program.

6-6. Digital Frequency Counter

The digital frequency counter, because of its compactness, accuracy, and speed with which a measurement can be made, has become popular as a frequency meter in the two-way radio services. The instrument of Fig. 6-18 permits frequency measurements between 10 Hz and 1000 MHz (1 GHz). Accuracies exceed the FCC specifications for communications work up to 1 GHz. A large 8-digit display permits direct reading with automatic placement of the decimal.

Fig. 6-18. A digital frequency counter.

Courtesy Sencore, Inc.

Three separate inputs are available. One is a fuse-protected 50-ohm termination for proper reading of high-frequency signals between 10 MHz and 1000 MHz. A second input is a high-sensitivity one with 1 megohm loading to allow direct connections to lower-frequency circuits. It operates over a range of frequencies between 10 Hz and 100 MHz. A front-panel sensitivity control is included. A third input is a crystal-check facility which allows any crystal to be tested by simply inserting it into the front-panel test socket.

Two read-rate gate times of 1 second or 0.1 second are included. The fast rate provides a fast update and ability to follow a fast frequency change. The slower 1-second rate provides maximum resolution.

A 50-ohm input jack provides proper termination for a 50-ohm coaxial cable. An RF protection fuse is located inside along with two spare fuses. In addition, an adjustable antenna is provided that permits a pickup of off-the-air signals. Thus, a frequency check can be made by bringing the frequency counter close to a base or mobile transmitter.

The antenna, too, is useful because of its ability to test the output frequency of a walkie-talkie or a repeater transmitter that cannot be removed from service without causing down time. The frequency of a mobile transmitter can be measured by simply driving up next to the transmitter. There is no need to pull a good transmitter out of service.

There is a counter probe with a direct/isolate switch for use when direct connection to a signal source is desired. Also included is an RF pickup loop for making high-frequency or high-power frequency measurements when a direct connection is not desired. The pickup loop is especially useful because critical oscillator frequency measurements can be made without placing any load capacitance in the circuit. At the same time the very weak oscillator signal can be picked up and a reading obtained.

There is a 10-MHz output signal available at the rear of the counter. This signal component can be used as a reference source for calibrating less accurate counters or scopes. In addition it may be used in conjunction with the reception of a WWV signal for testing the accuracy of the counter frequency calibration.

6-7. FM Deviation Measurement

An oscilloscope and appropriate calibration system can be used to make an accurate measurement of FM deviation. Such a system is shown in Fig. 6-19. Fundamentally, it is an FM receiver that develops a deviation-calibrated output signal. A double-conversion technique is used.

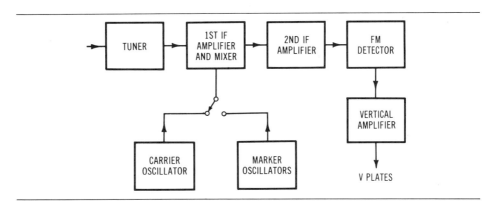

Fig. 6-19. Functional plan of a deviation meter using an oscilloscope.

The tuner must be designed to operate over the frequency range of the transmitters to be checked. In the case of the commercial FM two-way radio bands one tuner might tune between 25–55 MHz, a second between 145–175 MHz, and a third and fourth tuner to cover the 450- and 800-MHz bands.

In a typical arrangement the high IF frequency output of the tuner could be 10.7 MHz. A low intermediate frequency of 4.5 MHz could be used. In this case the carrier conversion oscillator frequency would be 6.2 MHz (10.7–4.5 MHz). At this frequency the DC output of the FM detector would be 0 volt in a typical example.

The conversion oscillator could be used to generate, depending on marker switch setting, a frequency 5000 Hz above 6.2 MHz or 5000 Hz below 6.2 MHz. By proper setting of the marker switch it is possible to supply a 4.505-MHz or 4.495-MHz signal to the low IF amplifier. By so doing, reference DC voltages are made available at the output of the detector; one voltage indicates a frequency of 5000 Hz above the center frequency and the other a frequency 5000 Hz below the center frequency.

The vertical deflection graticule of the oscilloscope can then be calibrated in terms of frequency deviation. This is shown in Fig. 6-20. In operation, the center carrier-oscillator marker line is made to coincide with the center line of the graticule (Fig. 6-20A). If the plus marker conversion oscillator is now turned on, there will be an upward movement of the calibration line. This corresponds to an upward 5000-Hz change in frequency. The vertical calibration control of the oscilloscope can be adjusted until this line coincides with, let us say, the 5th line above the center line of the graticule (Fig. 6-20B). As a result the graph is calibrated in intervals of 1000 Hz. When the minus conversion oscillator is turned on, there will be a similar calibration of the horizontal lines below the center line (Fig. 6-20C). This time it will be in steps of 1000 Hz below center frequency.

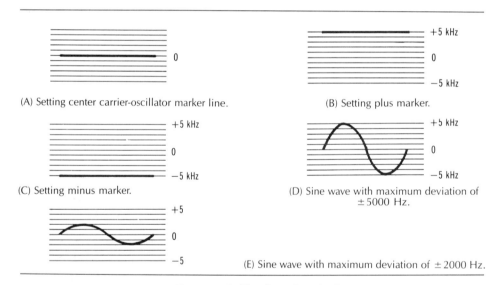

(A) Setting center carrier-oscillator marker line.

(B) Setting plus marker.

(C) Setting minus marker.

(D) Sine wave with maximum deviation of ± 5000 Hz.

(E) Sine wave with maximum deviation of ± 2000 Hz.

Fig. 6-20. Calibration of graticule.

Of course, additional marker oscillator frequencies can be made available to calibrate the oscilloscope scale for various other amounts of deviation. In so doing the scale can be calibrated for lower deviation values such as might be useful for measuring tone deviation and other special signal components.

If the incoming IF frequency were now frequency modulated by a sine wave with a maximum deviation of ± 5000 Hz, it would be displayed as a sine wave on the oscilloscope screen with the positive peaks reaching up to + 5000 Hz and down to the − 5000 Hz calibration lines as shown in Fig. 6-20D. Were the deviation only ± 2000 Hz, the sine-wave peaks would reach only to the 2000-Hz calibration lines, as in Fig. 6-20E.

In making an actual FM modulation measurement, it is necessary to supply a signal of appropriate magnitude to the input of the tuner. Off-air signals can actually be measured by picking them up on a receiving antenna. If transmitter deviation is to be measured right in the shop, it would be necessary to apply the transmitter output through an appropriate attenuator to the input of the tuner. Usually, the receiver section will include a meter that indicates when a signal of proper level is applied to the tuner input.

Such an FM deviation meter assembly not only measures the actual deviation of the transmitter but permits an observation of the actually received signal. Thus, the effects of audio processing can be evaluated. Likewise any distortion in the modulated wave will show up on the demodulated signal displayed on the oscilloscope screen. You can also check the influence of deviation limiter operation. In such a test the audio input to the transmitter can be increased somewhat above the normal level and the influence of deviation limiting action observed. The function of the deviation limiter, of course, is to prevent deviation in excess of the FCC prescribed limit for the particular FM two-way radio service.

6-8. RF Millivoltmeter

A sensitive radio-frequency voltmeter is a useful and sometimes essential piece of test equipment for the two-way radio service bench. Often the service literature will request that a level of some precise figure be applied to the antenna (or some other input point) for testing receiver performance or performing an alignment procedure. The RF voltmeter is also useful as an alignment indicator. Connected at the correct point in the circuit it will give you a reading that can be useful as you peak various alignment adjustments. Oscillator performance can also be judged.

An example of such an instrument is the Boonton RF millivoltmeter shown in Fig. 6-21. The basic voltage range of this unit extends between 200 microvolts and 3 volts. Accessory dividers are available that permit higher voltage readings if they are required. The frequency range extends between 10 kHz and 1.2 GHz. Over this frequency range a true rms response is obtained for all signals lower in level than 30 millivolts. The front panel push buttons permit choice of the most desirable full-scale voltage value.

The impedance of the RF millivoltmeter is high so there is minimal loading of circuits. A probe accessory is also available that can be used to establish an input impedance of 50 or 75 ohms for use in making transmission-line measurements and providing the proper termination for such a line. In fact, a variety of optional accessories can be purchased for all of the standard coaxial fittings including a tee-adapter that can be used to connect into a transmission line without disturbing impedance matching.

A simplified block diagram is given in Fig. 6-22. The RF signal to be measured is applied to the probe which acts as a sensor that converts the applied RF voltage to a proportional DC voltage. This DC output voltage ranges from a fraction of a millivolt to a few volts and represents the input RF voltage level.

Keep in mind that a very low level input signal is often to be measured. Thus, the immediate transfer of the signal from a radio frequency to DC is very important. To reduce the effects of drift and spurious signal components at such a low level, the DC output voltage of the sensor is applied to a solid-state chopper. The chopper converts the DC voltage to a 94-Hz square wave that has an output amplitude proportional to the DC voltage. This changeover keeps the signal clean of 60-Hz components.

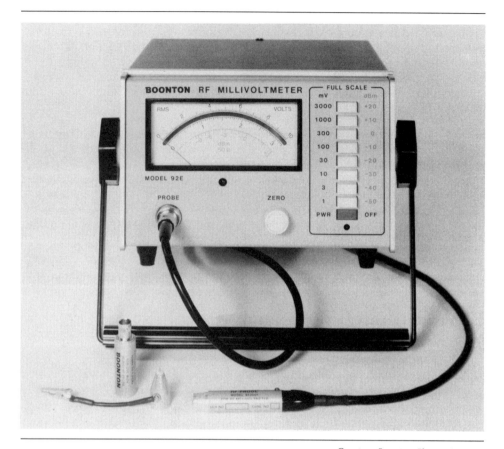

Courtesy Boonton Electronics Corp.

Fig. 6-21. An RF millivoltmeter.

Next, the 94-Hz square wave is amplified to raise the signal above interference levels. It is then demodulated back to a DC output voltage. This linear DC voltage you recall is proportional to the strength of the RF voltage applied to the input of the probe. The source of signal needed for the chopper and demodulator activities is supplied by a 752-Hz clock signal. The actual drive signal for the chopper and demodulator is generated by the frequency-divider circuits that are a part of the driver block in Fig. 6-22.

The shaping system is useful in converting the output of the demodulator to a true linear voltage for driving the meter circuit. This shaping activity also requires the presence of the clock output. Furthermore, the ranging block in response to the setting of the voltage-range push buttons on the front panel sets the amplifier gain and shaping process in accordance with the meter scale to be used. A variety of gates, flip-flops, counters, etc., and even a memory chip are a part of this instrument.

6-9. Receiver Sinad Test

The *Sinad* procedure is a standardized method of checking a communications receiver's sensitivity. Sinad is derived from *s*ignal plus *n*oise *and d*istortion. The measurement is presented as a mathematical ratio as follows:

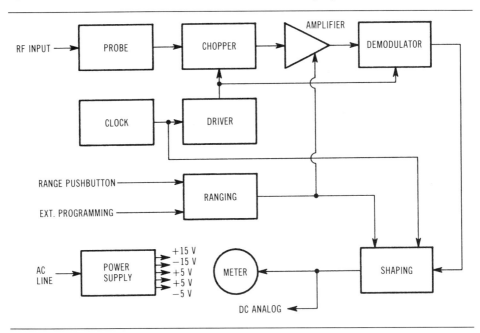

Fig. 6-22. Simple block diagram of millivoltmeter.

$$\text{Sinad (ratio)} \quad = \quad \frac{\text{Signal voltage + noise + distortion}}{\text{Noise + distortion}}$$

A second manner of presentation is in decibels:

$$\text{Sinad (dB)} \quad = \quad 20 \log_{10} \frac{\text{Signal voltage + noise + distortion}}{\text{Noise + distortion}}$$

Receiver sensitivity is measured at 12-dB Sinad. This is a standardized level and is appropriate for the two-way radio services because the incoming signal will, at that level, deliver a useful and understandable output.

The classic method of measurement is to connect an FM signal generator to the antenna input of the receiver. The generator output signal is modulated by a 1000-Hz tone, producing a deviation of plus and minus three kilohertz peak. A distortion meter is connected to the output as shown in Fig. 6-23. The receiver volume control with an applied reasonable-level input signal is adjusted for comfortable listening. The distortion meter is set to the SET position and its level control adjusted for a 100% scale reading. Then, the distortion meter is set to the READ position and the appropriate NULL controls are set for minimum reading. Next, adjust the signal generator output until a reading of 25% is obtained on the distortion meter. Adjust the level control and signal generator output until the SET reading is 100% and the READ reading is 25%. The level of signal now being applied to the receiver input from the FM signal generator represents the 12-dB Sinad sensitivity of the receiver. Note that the distortion meter reading was adjusted to the 25% level. By so doing you establish the 12-dB measurement level which is the standard Sinad value.

238

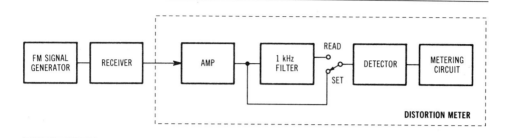

Fig. 6-23. A Sinad measuring system.

The difference between the SET and READ measurements is illustrated in Fig. 6-23. On the SET setting, the signal, noise, and distortion are read as a combined signal. On the READ setting only noise and distortion are measured. The signal component is removed by the 1-kHz filter. The follow-up adjustments given in the previous paragraph determine the 12-dB Sinad value.

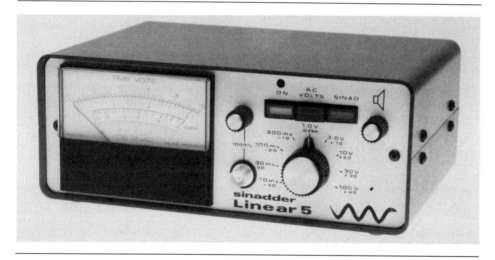

Courtesy Helper Instruments Co.

Fig. 6-24. The Sinadder Linear 5 Sinad checker.

Instruments are available that can make a direct measurement of the Sinad figure without going through the procedure outlined previously. One such instrument is the Sinadder shown in Fig. 6-24. This meter, (Fig. 6-25) takes over the assignment of the distortion meter. However, the 12-dB Sinad is displaced automatically on the meter. The loudspeaker output of the receiver is connected to the input of the Sinnader. An FM signal generator output with 1-kHz tone modulation and 3-kHz deviation is connected to the antenna input of the receiver. Apply a strong signal to the receiver input. Set the Sinadder volume control for comfortable listening. By depressing the push-in Sinad measurement button the required 12-dB reading is obtained. The microvolts output of the signal generator now corresponds to the 12-dB Sinad sensitivity of the receiver.

The Sinadder includes its own loudspeaker and volume control, and it is not necessary to hookup the loudspeaker associated with the two-way radio receiver

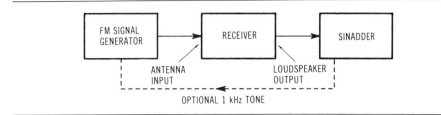

Fig. 6-25. Connections for Sinadder operation.

under test. The instrument can also be used as an rms audio voltmeter to measure the receiver output. Levels between 20 millivolts and 10 volts can be read using the voltage range switch on the front panel. A built-in 1000-Hz tone generator, which can be used to modulate the FM signal generator with a precise 1000-Hz sinewave, is also included.

In addition to Sinad measurements the Sinadder is useful for aligning the adjustments of a communications receiver. It is especially helpful in making antenna-input and radio-frequency stage adjustments. In fact, maximum gain adjustment and optimum signal-to-noise adjustment can be compared. Sometimes they do not occur on the same setting of an adjustment. Optimum signal-to-noise ratio may be a more important adjustment depending upon where the alignment adjustment is in the receiver. There are also applications for the instrument in FM transmitter tuning, AM transmitter and receiver tuning, and other wire-linked communications channels as well.

6-10. Spectrum Monitor

The spectrum monitor has become increasingly popular in checking out the performance of two-way radio transmitters and receivers. Such a monitor (Fig. 6-26) permits you to measure the relative levels of carrier, sidebands, harmonics, and other spurious signals. Components are displayed in such a manner that individual frequencies can be determined as well.

The spectrum monitor or analyzer is referred to as a frequency-domain oscilloscope because it presents an amplitude vs frequency display rather than the amplitude vs time display of a more conventional time-domain oscilloscope. The horizontal base is calibrated in terms of frequency rather than time. For example, an AM transmitter modulated by a 3000-Hz note is seen as a carrier, an upper sideband, and a lower sideband, each displayed separately along the base. The vertical deflections of the three are a true indication of their relative amplitudes.

Spurious signal components generated during the modulation process are also displayed and can be measured relative to the carrier level. As you know spurious signal components, according to FCC regulations, must be a specified number of decibels below the actual carrier level. In fact, for Citizens Band operation, these spurious components and harmonics must be at least 60 dB down relative to the desired carrier.

A functional block diagram of the Cushman's spectrum monitor is given in Fig. 6-27. In effect, it is a triple-conversion receiver which processes an incoming signal and applies it eventually to the vertical deflection plates of the oscilloscope. A sweep-frequency system makes the monitor sensitive to a selected range of frequencies on either side of the incoming signal, displaying desired sidebands as well as undesired components that appear on each side of the carrier frequency.

Fig. 6-26. Spectrum monitor.

Courtesy Cushman Electronics, Inc.

The monitor can also tune in harmonics and widely separated spurious signal components that may be emitted by the transmitter under test. Thus, the monitor actually makes a spectrum analysis of the transmitted signal to make sure that it is in compliance with FCC technical standards.

The monitor also evaluates local-oscillator radiation from the unit when the transceiver is on either the transmit or receive mode of operation. Remember that spurious signal components can be radiated even though the transceiver is set to its receive mode.

The input to the monitor is made sensitive to a specific range of frequencies because of the use of a sweep oscillator. The frequency of this local oscillator (a YIG oscillator in the case of the Cushman monitor) is swept in frequency by a ramp voltage generated in the horizontal deflection system and applied to the oscillator through the YIG driver, top left of Fig. 6-27. It is this tie-in between the horizontal deflection waveform and the local oscillator that permits accurate calibration of the horizontal sweep of the oscilloscope in terms of frequency.

The term YIG (yttrium, iron, garnet) denotes a special microwave oscillator that operates in the 2.1- to 3.1-GHz frequency range. Oscillator frequency is determined by the strength of the associated magnetic field in which it operates. This arrangement permits a smooth control of the oscillator frequency, varying the strength of the magnetic field by way of the YIG driver.

The YIG oscillator operates at this extremely high frequency to ensure that the instrument itself does not produce spurious responses and image frequencies within the measurement range of the instrument. This range extends between 1 MHz and 1000 MHz.

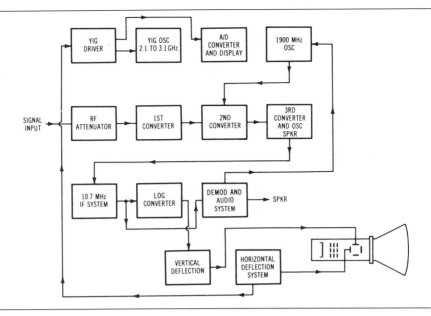

Fig. 6-27. Functional block diagram of the spectrum monitor.

The output of the first converter is applied to a second converter where the signal is reduced to the 200-MHz second IF range. Local oscillator injection is from a 1900-MHz oscillator. A third converter follows which brings the frequency of the signal down to the 10.7-MHz IF range.

Output from the third IF system is applied to the log converter and the FM demodulator. The output of the FM demodulator is applied to an audio amplifier and speaker. Additionally, a component is applied back to the 1900-MHz oscillator in the form of an AFC feedback loop.

The log converter changes the linear amplitude signals to a logarithmic output before the signal is applied to the vertical-deflection system. Thus, the resultant vertical deflection is calibrated in decibels. This permits a decibel comparison to be made between the various signal components displayed on the screen. The horizontal-deflection system, of course, generates the ramp voltage that must be applied to the horizontal-deflection plates as well as the component that is applied to the YIG driver and the followup swept YIG oscillator.

In summary, a frequency-domain display permits individual observations of carrier and sideband components of a transmitted signal. Also, the display can be used to check the transmitter final amplifier for spurious output and breakup, identify intermodulation interference, check for receiver local-oscillator radiation, measure transmitter harmonics, monitor and identify carriers with either AM or FM modulation, and do RF and IF signal tracing through a transceiver.

A typical transmitter interconnection plan for evaluating the output of a transmitter is shown in Fig. 6-28. The transmitter signal is applied through an in-line wattmeter to a 50-ohm load. Thus, the power output can be checked and preset for making the spectrum analysis. An included attenuator is needed to reduce the level of the signal for proper application to the radio-frequency input of the spectrum analyzer.

As an example of the types of troubles that can be identified refer to the patterns taken by a Cushman spectrum analyzer as shown in Fig. 6-29. The example in Fig.

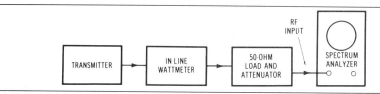

Fig. 6-28. Connection of the spectrum analyzer to the transmitter output.

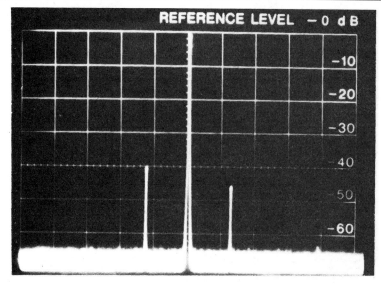

(A) FM radio transmitting at a center frequency of 158.55 MHz.

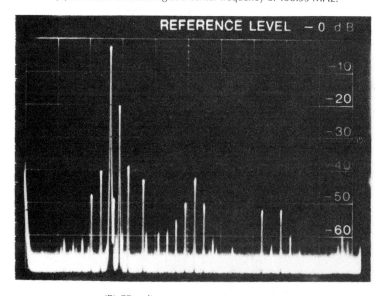

(B) CB radio transmitting on channel 13.

Fig. 6-29. Typical trouble patterns as displayed by spectrum analyzer.

6-29A shows the spectral purity of a 25-watt FM radio transmitting at a center frequency of 158.55 MHz. The vertical scale is calibrated in decibels while the horizontal scale is set for 10 MHz per division. Note that there are two spurious signals 40 and 46 dB down at about 12 MHz on each side of the carrier. According to FCC rules the spurious signals at these points should be down at least 57 dB.

The pattern of CB radio transmitting on channel 13 can be seen at the left of the illustration in Fig. 6-29B. In this case the center frequency of the analyzer is 52 MHz, and quite a bit of spurious radiation occurs at this second harmonic-frequency range. FCC rules require that second- and higher-order radiation must be suppressed by 60 dB in the Citizens Band (CB) Radio Service.

6-11. Communications Monitor

The communications monitor is an all-in-one test instrument that can be used to monitor, measure, and repair two-way radios. The Cushman CE50A (Fig. 6-30) is an example of a portable test instrument that operates in the VHF/UHF range to 1000 MHz. In the shop it can be powered by the 120-volt AC power supply or, at remote sites, by vehicular power or optional battery.

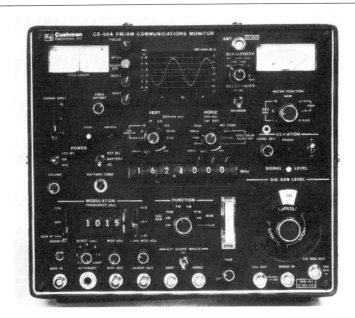

Courtesy Cushman Electronics, Inc.

Fig. 6-30. Communications monitor.

A wide variety of measurements can be made including carrier frequency and modulation characteristics of transmitted signals. Transmitted RF power measurements can be made. There is a capability for displaying demodulated audio frequencies on its internal oscilloscope for measurement or visual signal monitoring.

The receiver section of the monitor is a triple conversion superheterodyne with an adjustable sensitivity for monitoring signal levels from 2 microvolts to 500 millivolts.

Thus, transmitter testing can be made at separations from a few feet to several miles. The FM deviation as well as AM modulation percentage can be measured.

The unit also generates accurate RF signals for testing sensitivity, alignment, and performance of two-way radio receivers. The standard Sinad receiver sensitivity measurements can be made. The generated radio-frequency signal can be a continuous-wave (CW) or it can be AM or FM modulated by an audio-frequency tone synthesizer.

The signal generator is an accurate frequency synthesizer with a frequency range of 100 kHz to 999.9999 MHz. The output can be connected directly to a transceiver and includes protection from accidental transmitter keying with an automatic electronic circuit breaker. The output which is between 0.1 microvolt and 300 millivolts rms is set with precision attenuator switching.

In monitoring two-way radio signals they are picked up at the antenna input terminal at the top right (Fig 6-30). After demodulation the signal is sent to the demodulating section where the type of modulation selected is removed and displayed on the meter at the top right. The demodulated signal can also be applied to the oscilloscope for display and measurement.

A component is removed and sent to the frequency-error discriminator. The discriminator output is displayed on the meter at the top left indicating the departure of the received signal from the accurately dialed frequency of the communications monitor. The reading is the actual difference between the dialed frequency and the transmitter carrier frequency.

In summary, frequency of operation of the transmitter as well as its modulation characteristics can be observed simultaneously. In addition the demodulated wave can be displayed on the scope screen.

To measure the transmitted power up to a maximum of 100 watts power output, the transmitter signal is applied to the power meter input jack at the bottom right. Measurements are made in two ranges, 0–10 watts and 10–100 watts. Using this input connection the same transmitter characteristics mentioned previously can be measured. Customarily this is the connection procedure followed when the transmitter and communications monitor are set up on the bench. In fact, only two connections need be made between the monitor and the transceiver to make almost a complete set of transmitter and receiver measurements including the Sinad sensitivity check. Such a check provides an accurate measurement of the useful sensitivity of a receiver. The measurement even includes the receiver output stage. A special version of the CE-50A communications monitor also includes an added spectrum monitor feature.

6-12. Two-Way Radio Service Monitor

The Com-Ser Laboratories service monitor (Fig 6-31) is a versatile and easy-to-operate two-way radio service instrument. The radio-frequency generator range extends between 100 kHz and 999 MHz. An audio generator also included has a frequency range between 0.01 and 9999 Hz. The instrument includes an accurate 1000-Hz tone generator. A radio-frequency LCD display at the center of the panel, has a resolution of 100 Hz. To its right is a three-digit display that indicates power output, subaudible tone count, and AC/DC voltage up to 200 volts. The audio frequency is shown on the digital display at the lower left.

The monitor oscilloscope screen is located top center in Fig. 6-31. The frequency response of the scope extends to 5 MHz, permitting a display of AM and sideband envelope modulation patterns for IF signals that fall below this maximum. To the left of the scope screen is a meter that is used to measure frequency deviation (maximum settings of 1.5, 5, and 15 kHz), AM modulation percentage, and Sinad. To the right of the scope screen is a large frequency error meter with scales of 1.5, 5, and 15 kHz. This meter can also be used for frequency offset procedures and for calibration and measuring of transmitter frequencies.

Courtesy Com-Ser Laboratories, Inc.

Fig. 6-31. A service monitor.

The keyboard at the center is used to set the RF generator on a desired frequency. In addition it can be used to call up 64 frequencies that can be programmed into the frequency memory. Much can be learned about the service monitor and its application by reading in detail the operating instructions supplied by the manufacturer which are reported in the following:

1. Calibration

The unit may be calibrated and operated immediately after being turned on since the time base is a temperature-compensated crystal oscillator with a frequency accuracy of 0.4PPM over the temperature range of 0 to 50° C.

To calibrate, turn the function switch to Cal and set the needle of the error meter to zero using the Meter Zero knob. There are selector switches for both meters that allow the selection of 1.5, 5, or 15 kHz full-scale readings. After the error meter has been centered, the function switch should be set to FM-SG and the FM Zero knob adjusted to center the error meter needle.

Since the FM signal is generated by a voltage-controlled crystal oscillator rather than phase modulating the output of the main time base, the FM oscillator should be rezeroed from time to time.

After switching to the FM-SG function, the deviation and the frequency error of the outgoing signal may be observed on the deviation and error meters. By turning the FM Zero knob, the output frequency may be moved from the center frequency in order to see if the receiver bandpass is centered at the assigned frequency.

The subaudible frequency counter may be calibrated by setting the function switch to FM-SG and modulating the signal with a desired frequency, say 150 Hz with a deviation of at least 1 kHz. Set the Tone Switch to Lo Tone and read the 3 1/2 digit display. If the reading does not agree with the input frequency, it may be corrected by use of the Tone Adjust knob.

Every six months or so the 10-MHz time base should be checked against WWV or some other primary standard. If oscillator adjustment is needed, the bottom inner and outer covers must be removed from the instrument. On one of the PC boards near the rear of the chassis, you will see a 2 × 2 inch can. This board must be removed and replaced on an extender board so that the adjustment port on the TCXO may be reached. When the plug on the TCXO case is removed, the frequency adjustment may be made to zero beat the TCXO to the standard being used.

2. Setting RF Output Level

There are two RF jacks on the front panel. One of them, labeled RF Out gives the highest output and offers the highest monitoring sensitivity. *The maximum power allowed into this jack is 0.25 watts!!!* The other jack, labeled RF In will accept 100 watts for 10 or 15 seconds. There is 40 dB of attenuation between the jacks.

Attenuation of the signal is accomplished by a 0- to 70-dB step attenuator and two variable attenuators having a range of 10 dB. One of the variable attenuators is used at any frequency below 50 MHz and the other at 50 MHz and above. They are labeled LF and HF. The full range of the output level at the RF Out jack is 1 microvolt to 10 millivolts (80 dB). If external attenuation is applied, then the range will be lowered. For instance, a 20-dB external pad will lower the high and low levels by a factor of 10. The level at the RF In jack will range from 0.01 microvolts to 100 microvolts.

Because the step attenuator varies in 10-dB steps, it is necessary to put two scales on each of the variable attenuators. The inner scale is 1 to 3 and the outer scale is 3 to 10. The scale to be used will depend on the setting of the step attenuator. For instance, the 10- to 30-microvolt step would use the 1 to 3 scale and the 30- to 100-microvolt step would use the 3 to 10 scale.

3. Checking Transmitter Power

Connect the transceiver to the RF In jack. Set in the transmitter frequency by the use of the key-pad. If you are testing an AM transmitter, set the function switch to AM Mon. If you are testing an FM transmitter, set the function switch to FM Mon. The Meter Mode switch should be set to WATTS. When the transmitter is keyed, the transmitter output power may be read directly from the 3 1/2 digit LCD. The RF In jack connects to a power attenuator which will dissipate 100 watts for a limited time. A warning light will come on if the load attenuator becomes overheated.

4. Checking Transmitter Frequency

With the transmitter connected as in 3 above, the transmitter is keyed and the frequency error is read off the error meter which may be set to full-scale ranges of 1.5, 5, or 15 kHz.

5. Measuring Transmitter Modulation

With the transmitter connected as in 3 above and by talking or whistling into the microphone, you will be modulating the signal. The modulation level may be read on the proper scale of the modulation/Sinad meter or on the oscilloscope with the vertical gain set at "CAL". The switch under the meter must be set to the desired modulation scale. When measuring AM, the attenuators should be set for maximum modulation reading. When monitoring an FM transmitter, make certain that the step attenuator is turned up enough to quiet the FM detector system. Detected audio may be measured and observed by selecting the correct modulation range and checking the meter reading and the oscilloscope display. The oscilloscope is calibrated for deviation reading measurements when the Vertical switch is in the Dev position and the Vertical Gain is set at maximum (Cal). The speaker control may be turned up during monitoring to subjectively evaluate the quality of the transmission.

On transmitters using subaudible tone, the tone frequency may be checked by setting the Meter Mode switch to LoTone for frequencies up to 199.9 Hz and to HiTone for frequencies of 200 Hz and 1 kHz. The reading will appear on the 3 1/2 digit LCD.

If the subaudible tone from some other source is to be measured, this audio signal should be fed into the Audio In jack, the Audio Selector set to Ext, the Function switch set to FM-Gen and the level control set to about 1-kHz deviation. With these settings the frequency of the subaudible tone will be shown on the display.

The function switch should be in the SSB Mon position for the detection of SSB signals.

In some instances when attempting to monitor a frequency close to the 50-MHz point of a 100-MHz segment, an image frequency may interfere with the received signal. In this case the transmitter may be monitored by setting the monitor to an offset frequency as follows:

For frequencies below the 50-MHz dividing line subtract 1.6 MHz from the desired frequency and reverse the error meter reading, or subtract 2.0 MHz from the desired frequency in which case the error meter will read in the correct direction.

For frequencies above the 50-MHz dividing line add 2.0 MHz to the desired frequency in which case the error meter will read in the correct direction, or add 2.4 MHz in which case the error meter will read in the inverse direction. A squelch circuit quiets the audio output in the absence of any signal input. The level at which the audio system is activated is adjustable by the Squelch knob on the front panel.

6. Measuring Receiver Sensitivity

In checking a receiver first set in the proper frequency, then set the function switch to SG AM or SG FM. The output level at the RF In jack is 40 dB below the level shown by the attenuators. The output level range at this jack is 0.01 μV to 100 μV.

Modulation should be applied at the desired level. Two audio signals are available for simultaneous use. One is a fixed frequency 1-kHz tone, the level of which is controlled by the knob to the right of and above the thumb wheel switch. The other signal is the synthesized audio signal, the frequency of which may be controlled by the thumb wheel switch. This is done by setting in the proper numbers with the thumb wheels and switching to the proper multiplier. At the XI setting the decimal point is between the second and third digit, X10 between the third and fourth, and X100 after the fourth. For instance 112.1 privacy tone would have 1121 on the thumb wheels and X10 on the selector. The EXT setting on the selector switch disconnects the internal tone generator and allows you to use an external tone source plugged into the Audio In BNC jack. The Level control is also used with the external tone. If you wish to add an external audio signal to the internally generated audio, it should be connected to the Audio Out BNC jack through a resistor of at least a 1000-ohm value.

The variable frequency generator may be used to set up a subaudible tone and the 1-kHz signal may be used to simulate the voice or other signal which forms the principal information to be modulated on the carrier.

Because the unit uses direct FM rather then PM, any digital waveform within the frequency range of DC and 10 kHz which is connected to the Audio In jack will be faithfully reproduced in the output signal. The receiver volume control should be turned up so that the detected audio may be monitored and the receiver squelch should be disabled. The output level of the monitor should be adjusted until a satisfactory audio output is heard. The level of this signal may be read from the attenuators and multiplied by the proper factors depending upon the RF output jack used and any external attenuation. To obtain objective sensitivity readings it may be desirable to use quieting characteristics or Sinad readings.

To conduct Sinad tests the receiver should be connected as above. In addition, a cable is connected from the audio output on the receiver to the Vertical Sinad input of the monitor and the switch under the modulation meter is set to Sinad. The output of the monitor is deviated at a 1-kHz audio tone with the RF output set at a minimum, the receiver volume control is advanced until the meter needle reaches its maximum deflection (85 to 100% full scale). The RF level is then increased until the needle has dropped to the desired Sinad reading. Reading the RF attenuators will then give you the sensitivity for the indicated Sinad.

If the leads from the audio output of the receiver are connected to the Voltmeter jack and the Tone/Voltmeter switch is set to AC, we may determine the quieting sensitivity of the receiver. With no RF input to the receiver, and no deviation on the monitor, turn up the volume control until the voltmeter displays a convenient level. With no deviation on the signal, the RF input to the receiver is then increased until the noise output of the receiver drops to the desired quieting level. The voltage for 20 dB of quieting is 10% of the reference level. The voltage for 30 dB of quieting is 3% of the reference level.

With the receiver well quieted, modulation may be added to the generated signal and the frequency response of the receiver tested by varying the frequency of the modulation and noting the readings on the AC voltmeter.

7. Oscilloscope Operation

The oscilloscope has two functions:

1. to display recovered audio during monitor operations and
2. to act as a general-purpose 5-MHz oscilloscope.

The front panel controls are as follows:

1. POWER SWITCH For turning the AC power off and on
2. PILOT LAMP Indicates when the AC power is on
3. INTENSITY For adjusting the brightness of the CRT spot or trace
4. HORIZONTAL POSITION For adjusting the trace horizontally on the CRT
5. VERTICAL POSITION For positioning the trace vertically on the CRT
6. HORIZONTAL Four steps to set sweep frequency range from 10 Hz to 100 kHz, and EXT when an external signal is used for horizontal deflection
7. H GAIN For fine adjustment of sweep frequency between steps or width of horizontal trace amplitude when external horizontal input is used
8. METER AND OSCILLOSCOPE SELECTOR SWITCH For selecting the range for the oscilloscope and the modulation meter
9. VERT INPUT SWITCH Sets oscilloscope sensitivity for external signals or selects deviation range
10. VERT GAIN Adjusts vertical amplitude. Fully clockwise puts it into calibration
11. FOCUS Adjusts for minimum spot size
12. H IN For connection of external signals for horizontal deflection when the horizontal switch is in EXT position
13. VERTICAL SINAD IN For connection of external signals for vertical deflection when selector switch is in AC or DC position or for connection of external audio signal to Sinad circuit when switch is in Sinad position

If the CRT beam is concentrated in a spot on the screen, there is the possibility of burning that particular portion of the screen. The INTENSITY control should be adjusted during standby periods to extinguish the spot, or the spot must be kept in motion with the sweep frequency to avoid an "Ion Burn".

To begin use as a general-purpose oscilloscope set the controls as follows: Power switch on; Vertical and Horizontal positions at midposition; Vertical Gain fully clockwise; Hor. Gain fully clockwise; Vert Input at X100; Sweep Freq Hz at 10–100K; and Sweep Var at any setting. The intensity and Focus controls should be set for clear trace.

For Waveform Observation:

1. Connect the leads from Vertical/Sinad In to test point of circuit under examination.
2. For AC input, or to pick out the AC component when there is superimposed DC voltage in the input signal — set on AC. Set on DC when DC component of signal is to be observed or for DC voltage measurements.

3. Set VERT INPUT switch and adjust VERT GAIN for suitable trace amplitude.
4. Set H GAIN control for suitable trace width if external horizontal input is used.
5. Set SWEEP FREQ switch at 10–100 etc., and adjust SWEEP VARIABLE control as required for the waveform display.
6. Adjust the spot positioning controls to position the trace on the graticule as required.

Unknown frequencies may be compared with a standard frequency by the Lissajou pattern method.

1. If the unknown frequency is being received by the monitor, the waveform will appear on the oscilloscope screen when the controls are set to show the received audio. If the unknown frequency is from some external source, connect it to the Vertical Sinad In jack and adjust the vertical controls for suitable amplitude.
2. Connect the standard frequency to Horizontal In and set Horizontal switch to Ext. Adjust Horizontal Gain for suitable width. The variable audio generator may be used as the known frequency by connecting a cable from the Audio Out jack to the Horizontal jack.
3. Adjust the known or unknown frequency for a clearly defined single- or multiple-loop pattern.

8. Memory Operation

There are slots for 64 different frequencies in the memory of the unit. The liquid crystal display is used to show the address and then the frequency called forth from the address. It is very easy to enter and recall any 7-digit number from the memory. The READ-WRITE switch should be kept in the "READ" position except when a new frequency is being entered as set forth below.

To enter a frequency into the memory:

1. Clear the liquid display by pushing the # button.
2. Key in the address using the key-pad buttons. The addresses will run from 0 to 63.
3. Push the Latch button.
4. Place READ-WRITE switch in WRITE position.
5. Key in the desired frequency with the keypad. If the frequency consists of less than seven digits, leading zeros must be keyed in to result in the proper frequency being put into the memory. If an error is made in keying in a frequency, the correct frequency should be keyed in thus pushing the incorrect frequency off the left end of the display. Pushing the reset button under these conditions will necessitate starting the entry process from the beginning.
6. Push the Erase button and return the Read-Write switch to Read. The frequency is now loaded into the memory.

To recall a frequency from the memory:

1. Clear the liquid crystal display by pushing the # button.
2. Using the touch pad, key in the address for the desired frequency.
3. Push the Latch button. The desired frequency will appear on the display.

9. Voltmeter Operation

The voltmeter-tone switch should be set to AC or DC Volts. The voltage to be measured should be fed into the "Volt jack". One side of the voltmeter is connected to the monitor chassis. The meter is autoranging. The maximum input is 200 volts.

6-13. FCC Technical Standards

Technical standards for the various radio services can be found in the appropriate volumes of the FCC Rules and Regulations. For example, technical standards for the private landmobile services are found under Part 90 of Volume V. These volumes are available at FCC District Offices or can be purchased from the U.S. Government Printing Office. Such standards include requirements for standards of acceptability of equipment, frequency tolerance, modulation, emission, power, and bandwidth. The information that follows is a very abbreviated coverage of the standards as they apply to the Private Land-Mobile Radio Services. This will give you some idea of the importance of test equipment in evaluating the performance of two-way radio equipment.

6-13-1. Type Acceptance

With few exceptions only equipment which has been type-accepted by the Commission may be used in this particular radio service. Usually the manufacturer of the radio transmitting equipment requests type acceptance. At the FCC offices there is a publication entitled "Radio Equipment List, Equipment Acceptable for Licensing." This is available for public reference at the FCC field offices.

6-13-2. Power

Applications for authorizations must specify no more power than the actual power necessary for satisfactory operation. In cases of harmful interference, the Commission may order a change in power or antenna height, or both. Except where otherwise specifically provided, the maximum power that will be authorized can be usually found in chart form in the FCC Rules and Regulations.

6-13-3. Types of Emission and Bandwidth Limitations

Types of emission were covered in Section 2-2 in Chapter 2 of this book. Type of emission is a part of the station authorization. Normally operations authorized in the private landmobile services provide voice communications between stations. Although there are exceptions, the fundamental authorizations are for A3 or F3 emission. These authorizations also include the use of emissions for tone signals or signaling devices whose sole functions are to establish and maintain communications, to provide automatic station identification, and for operations in the public safety and special emergency radio services, to activate emergency warning devices used solely for the purpose of advising the general public or emergency personnel of an impending emergency situation.

F3 emissions is authorized only on frequencies above 25 MHz. The bulk of the A3 emission is sideband type A3J authorized for audio telephony systems on frequencies below 25 MHz. Emission information for other types of services can be obtained from the appropriate FCC volume.

The maximum authorized bandwidth for standard A3 emission shall be 8 kHz. However, for type A3J operation below 10 MHz the bandwidth occupied by the emission shall not exceed 3500 Hz. The frequency coinciding with the center of the authorized band of emission shall be the assigned frequency. Both the authorized carrier frequency and assigned frequency shall be specified in the authorization. The authorized carrier frequency shall be 1400 Hz lower in frequency than the assigned frequency. Only upper-sideband emission shall be used.

6-13-4. Modulation Requirements

In general, the maximum audio frequency required for satisfactory radio-telephony intelligibility in the private land-mobile radio services is considered to be 3000 Hz (2800 Hz for single-sideband operation below 25 MHz).

Each transmitter shall be equipped with a device which automatically prevents modulation in excess of that specified (which may be caused by greater than normal audio level). In most frequency ranges each transmitter must be equipped with a modulation limiter and a low-pass filter. Such a filter shall be installed between the modulation limiter and the modulated stage and shall meet specified bandwidth requirements.

When amplitude modulation is used for radiotelephony, the modulation percentage shall be sufficient to provide efficient communication and normally should be maintained above 70% on peaks, but shall not exceed 100% on negative peaks.

Regulations have been drawn up for the use of scrambling devices and digital voice modulation. Special authorization must be obtained.

6-13-5. Frequency Tolerance

A licensee in the private land-mobile radio services shall maintain carrier frequency of each authorized transmitter within a specified percentage of the assigned frequency. The abbreviated chart in Table 6-1 tabulates various key percentage values according to frequency, power, and type of station.

Table 6-1. Frequency Tolerance In Percent

Frequency Range (MHz)	Fixed and Base Stations		Mobile Stations	
	Over 200 Watts	200 Watts or less	Over 2 Watts	2 Watts or less
Below 25	0.005	0.01	0.01	0.02
25 to 50	0.002	0.002	0.002	0.005
50 to 450	0.0005	0.0005	0.0005	0.005
450 to 470	0.00025	0.00025	0.0005	0.0005
470 to 512	0.00025	0.00025	0.0005	0.0005
806 to 821	0.00015	0.00015	0.00025	0.00025
851 to 866	0.00015	0.00015	0.00025	0.00025
929 to 930	0.00015	0.00015	No Mobiles	

6-13-6. **Transmitter Measurements.**

(a) The licensee of each station shall employ a suitable procedure to determine that the carrier frequency of each transmitter authorized to operate with an output power in excess of two watts is maintained with the tolerance prescribed. This determination shall be made, and the results entered in the station records in accordance with the following:

(1) When the transmitter is initially installed;
(2) When any change is made in the transmitter which may affect the carrier frequency or its stability.

(b) The licensee of each station shall employ a suitable procedure to determine that each transmitter authorized to operate with an output power in excess of two watts does not exceed the maximum figure specified on the current station authorization. On authorizations stating only the input power to the final radio-frequency stage, the maximum permissible output power is 75% for frequencies below 25 MHz and 60% of the input power for frequencies above 25 MHz. If a non-DC final radio-frequency stage is utilized, then the output power shall not exceed 75 percent of the input power. This determination shall be made, and the results thereof entered into the station records, in accordance with the following:

(1) When the transmitter is initially installed:
(2) When any change is made in the transmitter which may increase the transmitter power input.

(c) The licensee of each station shall employ a suitable procedure to determine that the modulation of each transmitter, which is authorized to operate with an output power in excess of two watts, does not exceed the limits specified in this part. This determination shall be made and the following results entered in the station records, in accordance with the following:

(1) When the transmitter is initially installed;
(2) When any change is made in the transmitter which may affect the modulation characteristics.

(d) The determinations required by paragraphs (a), (b), and (c) of this section may, at the opinion of the licensee, be made by a qualified engineering measurement service, in which case the required record entries shall show the name and address of the engineering measurement service as well as the name of the person making the meaurements.

(e) In the case of mobile transmitters, the determinations required by paragraphs (a) and (c) of this section may be made at a test or service bench: Provided, That the measurements are made under load conditions equivalent to actual operating conditions; and provided further that after installation in the mobile unit the transmitter is given a routine check to determine that it is capable of being received satisfactorily by an appropriate receiver.

6-14. **Test Setup Summary**

Modern two-way radio test equipment usually includes two or more test functions. As described in the preceding sections, a number of all-in-one units are available to provide multiple test functions in a single instrument. The transmitter and receiver functional diagrams (Figs. 6-32 and 6-33) given in this section emphasize the more important tests that are made. Remember that many of these tests can be made by a single test instrument.

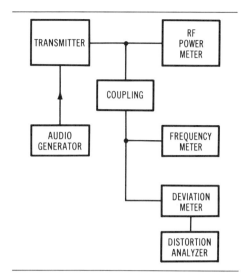

Fig. 6-32. Transmitter test setup.

6-14-1. RF Power Measurements

The RF power meter, whether it is a separate instrument or part of a composite instrument, provides a 50-ohm load at the transmitter output. A calibrated meter provides a watts-output reading. The resistive termination must be able to dissipate the power delivered by the transmitter.

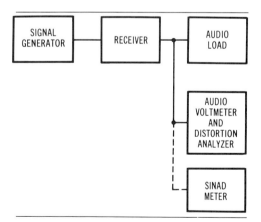

Fig. 6-33. Receiver test setup.

If the measured output is below the value suggested by the transmitter manufacturer, it may be an indication of a need for tuning or a transmitter defect. Transmitter tuning and loading can be adjusted. Some transmitters also include a power adjusting control to set the output level to the recommended value. Power output should not be adjusted higher than normal to minimize component wear.

6-14-2. Transmitter Frequency

A counter or frequency meter can be used to make a direct measurement of the transmitter frequency. When a direct connection is made between transmitter and frequency meter an attenuator coupling system is employed to prevent the application of full transmitter power to the frequency meter. Modern counters and frequency meters are usually supplied with small antennas and a good separation between transmitter and meter can be made to prevent frequency-meter damage. Also some RF power meters have a built-in coupling system that provides a weak signal takeoff for connection to a frequency meter or counter.

Frequency readings are usually expressed in one of three ways. These are specific frequency, percentage difference between transmit frequency and actual assigned frequency, or the actual frequency difference between transmit frequency and assigned frequency.

If the frequency is incorrect, be certain to follow the specific instructions given in the service manual of the particular transmitter. In fact, if incorrect readings are obtained for any of the important transmitter or receiver tests, the corrections you make should be those recommended in the instruction manual for the particular two-way radio unit.

The accuracy of the frequency meter is an extremely important consideration because of the required tight frequency tolerances of modern transmitters. Refer to the figures given in the frequency tolerance chart of Table 6-1. For best results the accuracy of the frequency meter should be 5 to 10 times better than the permissible tolerance on the particular assigned frequency. For example, if the frequency tolerance for the particular assigned frequency is ± 0.0005%, the frequency meter used to make the measurements should have an accuracy of 0.00005%.

As mentioned previously some frequency meters give an actual reading in percent frequency tolerance. If the readings are given in actual frequency or frequency error, the following equations can be used to calculate the actual frequency error in percentage:

$$(1) \ \% \ \text{error} = \frac{\text{measured frequency} - \text{assigned frequency}}{\text{assigned frequency}} \times 100$$

$$(2) \ \% \ \text{error} = \frac{\text{frequency difference}}{\text{assigned frequency}} \times 100$$

The accuracy of the frequency meter must be considered in deciding on an acceptable error percentage. Let us assume that a 150-MHz transmitter operates on a frequency with a frequency tolerance of 0.0005%. If the frequency meter itself has an accuracy of 0.00005%, an *acceptable percent error for a frequency measurement* must be less than 0.00045% (0.0005-0.00005).

Some figures will demonstrate the point. For example, according to the FCC frequency tolerance of 0.0005% on 150 MHz, a transmitter could be a theoretical 750 Hz off frequency and still be acceptable (150,000,000 × 0.000005). However, with the accuracy of the meter limiting the measurement a frequency error reading of more than 675 Hz would be *considered unacceptable* (150,000,000 × 0.0000045).

In summary then, it is important in making a frequency measurement that the actual accuracy of the frequency meter be taken into consideration. In our example any frequency error less than 675 Hz would mean that the transmitter is operating within the FCC frequency tolerance. If you had a perfect frequency meter, any frequency error less than 750 Hz would be acceptable. The latter is an impossible situation.

6-14-3. Frequency Deviation

Deviation measurements are made following the procedure given in the instruction manual. Usually a 1000-Hz signal of a specific amplitude is applied to the transmitter from the audio generator. This is the value that should produce maximum transmitter deviation. In most applications this maximum reading is normally ± 5.0 kHz. A transmitter maintenance manual may recommend a lower value for a particular transmitter making certain that the transmitter will not be overmodulated on strong voice peaks. Consideration must also be given to the deviation produced by an included tone squelch system. Thus, in some conditions the final deviation setting may be as low as 3.75 kHz. Follow the manufacturers' recommendations.

The symmetry of the deviation may be judged by comparing the positive and negative peaks. With perfect symmetry, positive and negative deviation will be identical. If a distortion analyzer and audio voltmeter are included in the test setup, the transmitter audio sensitivity as well as distortion can be measured.

6-14-4. Receiver Performance

A general interconnection plan for checking out the receiver signal of a two-way radio is shown in Fig. 6-33. The signal generator must be highly accurate and capable of being set to the precise assigned receive frequency. In fact, the frequency measuring unit for the signal generator is usually the same section of test equipment that is used to measure the transmit frequency. Thus, the signal generator can be set on frequency to the same accuracy as a transmit frequency measurement can be made. It should be possible to frequency-modulate the signal generator output with an audio tone.

The signal generator must include an accurate attenuator to permit setting of the output to some exact output level. Often an isolation pad of 6 to 20 dB is located between the signal generator output and the receiver input.

An appropriate load must be placed on the speaker output of the receiver. Across this load an accurate audio voltmeter and/or distortion analyzer is connected.

A test setup of this type permits one to measure the audio distortion and sensitivity of a given receiver. Follow the instructions given in the maintenance manual. Arrangements also permit a bandwidth and the squelch system sensitivity measure of modulation and performance. A distortion analyzer or an optional Sinad meter can be used to make the important 12-dB Sinad sensitivity measurement.

6-15. Fault Finding in Solid-State Circuits

Since extensive test equipment is needed to ensure compliance with FCC technical requirements, the very same test equipment is also available for pinpointing the general location of a fault. If there is no loss of base-station or vehicular power and no erratic operation as a result of cabling, switching, or hardware breakdown, several basic test equipment measurements are advised. Is the power output and modulation normal on transmit? How are the receiver sensitivity and the squelch performance? If operation is nonexistent, poor, or suspect on a particular mode and the installation itself is apparently normal, it is customary to remove the unit for test-bench evaluation.

Quite often a substitute unit is slipped into position. If the substitute unit performs properly, there is added assurance that the installation is okay and the trouble lies within the unit removed.

The test bench is usually set up to provide a variety of important measurements and especially those that ensure compliance with FCC technical standards. In such a test setup the faulty section or module can soon be isolated. Actual steps taken to find the defective module vary depending on the design of the specific model. Sometimes a module substitute can be made immediately and the unit placed back in service. In other cases, individual circuits must be tested and faulty components located and replaced.

Because of the great variety of circuit types and functions, it is important that you know the functions of the individual circuits that comprise the modules. This knowledge along with a good fundamental electronic background permits you to locate the faulty part with appropriate follow-up checks and measurements. The actual procedure can vary from model to model. You can save much time by following the instructions given in the manufacturer's manual for the specific model.

In commercial equipment there are often complex supply voltage and biasing systems. Thus, schematics and voltage charts are of great value in locating faults. Always set the equipment to the operating conditions that the manufacturer suggests for making these voltage measurements.

Your fundamentals knowledge comes into its own when you have found the bad stage. Inspection, parts checks, and voltage measurements will usually locate the failed component.

A high resistance voltmeter with an accurate low-voltage reading capability is of particular help in finding a bad part. Service manuals usually show typical voltage readings on schematic diagrams or include a voltage chart. In digital circuits the logic probe is essential. LEDs indicate if the logic is high or low. The typical probe accommodates both TTL and CMOS measurements. Even under signal conditions the probe can be used to indicate the presence or absence of a pulse waveform.

6-15-1. Bipolar and FET Device Voltages

Recall that for a bipolar transistor that is operating normally the base-emitter voltage is somewhere in the region of the barrier potential. Thus the voltage V_{BE} (Fig. 6-34A) will usually be between 0.5 and 0.7 volt for low-power silicons. It might range up to a volt or so for high-power types. If the bipolar transistor is a germanium type the range may be between 0.1–0.3 for low power on up to 1 volt for high-power versions.

The collector voltage is also a measurable parameter. In a linear circuit voltage V_{CE} should be less than the supply voltage depending on the voltage drop in the collector load. For a normally operating bipolar transistor, the following relationship exists:

$$V_{CE} = V_{CB} + V_{BE}$$

Fig. 6-34B shows a bipolar transistor connected in a basic common-emitter circuit. Resistors R1 and R2 set the base bias current while resistor R3 supplies stabilization. Resistor R4 is the collector load. In a linear circuit the collector voltage as measured to common is less than the supply voltage because of the voltage drop across resistors R3 and R4 (mainly R4). A typical value might fall between 4–4.5 volts.

If the collector voltage reading is 9 volts, the bipolar transistor is not conducting. The transistor is bad or the biasing system is not operating. If the collector voltage is near 0, the bipolar transistor may be drawing excessive current, indicating a transistor

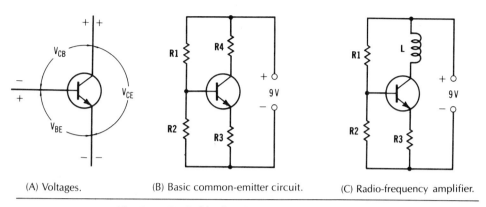

| (A) Voltages. | (B) Basic common-emitter circuit. | (C) Radio-frequency amplifier. |

Fig. 6-34. Basic bipolar circuit-voltage evaluation.

failure or a defect in the input circuit. In the resistor biasing circuit an open resistor R1 will result in no bias current. Therefore, there will be no stage operation and the collector voltage will read 9 volts.

The circuit of Fig. 6-34C relates more to the operation of a bipolar transistor in a radio-frequency amplifier with the inductor L being part of a resonant circuit or an audio power amplifier in which case inductor L would be the primary of the audio transformer. Measurements would be much the same as for Fig. 6-34B except for the influence of this inductor. Especially in the case of a radio-frequency amplifier this inductor will have a very low resistance. Thus, in normal operation the collector voltage will be quite high, approaching the supply voltage of 9 volts. In audio power amplifiers inductor L would have some resistance. This resistance would have to be considered in evaluating the normal collector voltage for the stage. Nonetheless, it will quite often be in the 6–8 volt range, assuming a 9-volt supply.

The polarities of the foregoing voltages apply to an npn transistor. The same conditions are appropriate for a pnp transistor except that a negative supply voltage would be used. Consequently, the collector-to-common and base-to-common voltages would be negative rather than positive.

Similar voltage evaluations can be made for an FET transistor. Considerations would be a bit different from those of a bipolar because the FET is basically a voltage amplifier rather than a current amplifier. Therefore, the normal gate-to-source bias is a function of the characteristics of the particular FET type. In the case of the n-channel junction FET of Fig. 6-35A the base-to-common voltage would be negative with a value depending upon the characteristics of the particular type. Hence for a normally operating n-channel JFET the drain voltage would be positive and the gate bias negative. For a p-channel type the drain voltage is negative and the gate voltage is positive. The bias voltage for MOSFET types depends on whether they are the enhancement-mode or depletion-mode devices.

In the basic common-source FET stage (Fig. 6-35B) the biasing is largely determined by resistor R3. Augmenting bias is provided by resistor R1 and R2. For linear operation the drain-to-common voltage would be 6 volts or one or two volts higher or lower depending on characteristics. The voltage measured between gain and source will be of negative value. However, a positive voltage reading between gate and common would be normal because of the presence of resistors R1 and R2. Recall that it is the positive voltage across resistor R3 between source and common that has the main influence on the negative value of the gate bias.

A high value of drain voltage would indicate a failed FET or a defect in the biasing circuit. It indicates a nonconducting situation. A very low drain voltage reading (approaching zero) shows high conduction which could also be an FET or biasing failure.

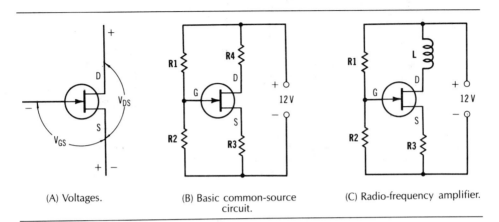

(A) Voltages.

(B) Basic common-source circuit.

(C) Radio-frequency amplifier.

Fig. 6-35. Basic FET circuit-voltage evaluation.

The influence of a drain circuit inductor as in Fig. 6-35C would be about the same as for the circuit in Fig. 6-35B. There would be only a slight voltage drop across the inductor. Therefore, it is normal when the drain voltage is the same, or only slightly less than, the supply voltage. For a p-channel FET polarities would be the complement of those shown in Fig. 6-35.

6-15-2. Digital Circuit Voltage Evaluations

Voltage measurement techniques are different in checking out digital circuits. Recall that there are only two states representing logic 1 and logic 0. In positive-logic digital circuits (by far the more common), logic 1 equals or is near to the circuit supply voltage and logic 0 near the zero volts. Transistors in general operate between saturation and cutoff. In some high-speed devices this may not be so, but, nevertheless, there are only two steady-state voltage conditions, representing logic 1 and logic 0. Thus, in most troubleshooting procedures, a logic probe does as well or better than an actual voltmeter. The voltmeter, however, is handy in checking out power sources and supply voltage lines.

A basic bipolar digital circuit is given in Fig. 6-36A. This is a very simple inverter that demonstrates the supply/saturation voltage concept basic to digital systems. Assume that the input switch is set to logic 1. The base-bias current will then be such that the transistor operates at saturation. Thus, the output voltage will drop to near zero volts (the voltage saturation point). Were the output switch set to common, or logic 0, the bipolar transistor will not conduct. As a result, the output voltage will equal the supply voltage, or be logic 1.

A logic probe connected to the input (base) would read high. Transferred to the output (collector) it would read low. If now the input is connected to ground, the logic probe would read a low input and a high at the output. These readings represent normal operation. Measurements could also have been made using a voltmeter.

The waveforms (Fig. 6-36B) show the operation with the application of 5-volt pulses. The output waveform is the complement of the input waveform. Also note that the output waveform swings between the supply voltage and the near-zero saturation voltage of the bipolar transistor.

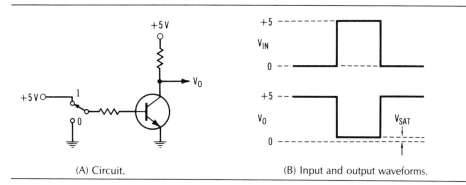

(A) Circuit.   (B) Input and output waveforms.

Fig. 6-36. Basic bipolar digital circuit.

If a low-frequency pulse is present, the actual probe attached to input or output would show the pulse changing between high and low. A higher-frequency pulse would activate the pulse LED of the logic probe and would indicate the presence of the pulse at both the input and output if the bipolar transistor and its associated circuit are operating normally.

The same conditions and measurement techniques apply for FET and MOSFET circuit operation as shown in Fig. 6-37. Normal operation swings between two definite voltage levels. In the circuit shown it is between the supply voltage and the saturation voltage as indicated by output waveform V_O, (Fig. 6-37B).

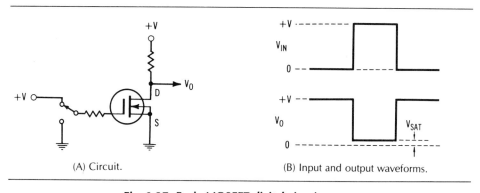

(A) Circuit.   (B) Input and output waveforms.

Fig. 6-37. Basic MOSFET digital circuit.

The logic probe must be set in accordance with the supply voltage. Usually in the bipolar TTL digital circuits it is 5 volts. In CMOS digital circuits voltage is sometimes 5 volts but can be higher. Your logic probe will have the appropriate TTL/CMOS switching. If you use a voltmeter, it must be set to the proper scale. In more specialized systems the logic levels for 1 and 0 may be somewhat different but will always be a two-level steady-state mode operation.

6-16. Schematic Evaluations

In reviewing some of the basic techniques for locating circuit faults, a number of representative circuits will be given in this section. Refresh your memory regarding the functions of various parts and try to anticipate how a specific part failure may have an adverse influence on an associated stage. In the sample schematics, parts functions and the influence of part failures are emphasized. Component values are given in these representative circuits and in a school or home-study situation they might be built up and checked out to verify results. Use low-power transistors and tubes.

Both transistor and vacuum-tube circuits are given. Although this handbook does not provide a detailed study of vacuum-tube circuits, they will sometimes be encountered.

6-16-1. Transistor Circuits

Component faults in transistor circuits produce specific operational defects. Failures affect the operating voltages and currents of a transistor stage. Such changes, in turn, cause complete signal loss, attenuation, or distortion.

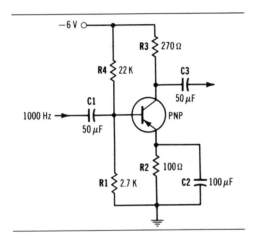

Fig. 6-38. Common-emitter stage.

A common-emitter circuit is shown in Fig. 6-38. The input signal is a 1000-Hz sine wave; its signal level is assumed to be that value which will produce a maximum nondistorted output voltage. The functions of the components are:

C1. Input capacitor that serves as a DC blocking capacitor to isolate the DC components of the input stage from the source of signal.

R1, R4. Base-bias voltage-divider resistors.

R2. Emitter stabilization resistor.

C2. Emitter bypass capacitor.

R3. Collector load resistor.

C3. Output coupling capacitor. Isolates the DC components of the collector circuit from the next stage.

Component failures will have the following influences on circuit operations:

C1 open. No signal will be applied to the input of the amplifier.

C1 shorted. Exchange of DC components that could have an adverse influence on the biasing of the stage. If an audio generator with a low impedance and no output capacitor is used, the forward bias is removed from the stage. There is no output, the collector current goes to zero, and the collector voltage rises to the potential of the supply source.

R1 shorted. Same as for C1 shorted because the bias is shorted out.

R1 open. Output distorted, collector current rises, and collector voltage falls.

An inproper operating point is established by the high forward bias applied to the base.

R4 shorted. Output falls to zero, collector voltage falls, and collector current rises. Again an improper operating point has been established.

R4 open. Bias is again removed. Output falls, collector current goes to zero, and collector voltage rises to the value of the supply voltage.

R2 or C2 shorted. Output increases, collector current rises, and collector voltage falls. There will be an adverse influence on stability.

C2 open. There is AC degeneration. DC operating conditions are unchanged.

R2 open. There is no forward biasing because of the interruption of the DC path. Output falls to zero, collector current goes to zero, and collector voltage rises to the supply value.

R3 open. Same as R2 open because of the interruption of the DC collector current path.

R3 shorted. Output falls to a low value, collector voltage and collector current both rise.

C3 open. No signal is transferred to the next stage.

C3 shorted. Interchange of DC components between stages, with possible distortion and shift of operating points.

In the common-base configuration of Fig. 6-39 the signal is applied to the emitter and removed at the collector. A 1½-volt emitter junction bias battery is needed. Recall that biasing polarity depends upon the type of transistor. For an npn type, both battery polarities would have to be reversed to those shown.

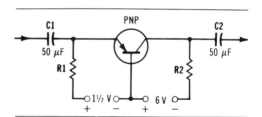

Fig. 6-39. Common-base amplifier.

The functions of the components are:

C1. Input coupling and DC blocking capacitor.
R1. Bias resistor.
R2. Collector load resistor.
C2. Coupling and DC blocking capacitor.

Component faults will have the following influence on circuit operation:

C1 open. No AC signal is applied to the input of the stage.
C1 shorted. Exchange of DC components between stages.
R1 shorted. A very high forward bias is applied. The collector current rises and the collector voltage falls. There will be no AC output.
R1 open. Stage is inoperative because of the removal of bias. There is no output, collector current falls to zero, and collector voltage rises to the supply value.
R2 open. Stage is inoperative because of the interruption of the DC path. Collector voltage and collector current fall to zero.
R2 shorted. Output decreases, while collector voltage and collector current rise.
C2 open. No AC signal is transferred to the next stage.
C2 shorted. Exchange of DC components between stages.

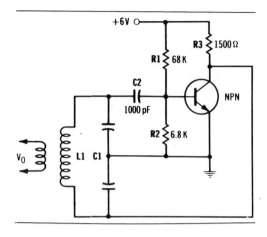

Fig. 6-40. Colpitts transistor oscillator.

A Colpitts oscillator is shown in Fig. 6-40. A small forward bias is needed to start oscillations, and, when oscillations stop in the transistor circuit, the collector current falls to zero or declines substantially. The functions of the parts are as follows:

L1, C1. Oscillator tank circuit using a split capacitor arrangement to obtain feedback of suitable magnitude and polarity.

C2. DC blocking capacitor and capacitor of the base time-constant RC combination.

R1, R2. Base-bias divider resistors.

R3. Collector-circuit resistor across which adequate RF voltage must develop for feedback use.

Component failures have the following influences on circuit operation:

L1, C1 open. When the tank circuit is disconnected, oscillations stop and the collector current falls to the low value set by the low forward bias.

L1 open. Oscillations again stop, with the collector current falling to the low forward-bias value.

L1 shorted. Same as L1 open.

C2 open. Same as L1 open.

C2 shorted. Forward biasing is disturbed causing an increase in the collector current, a decrease in the output voltage, and a shift in the oscillating frequency.

R1 open. No change in operating conditions once oscillations start. However, oscillator starting is very erratic.

R1 shorted. Collector current drops and there are no oscillations.

R2 open. Collector current falls slightly with approximately the same output voltage. However, there is poorer circuit stability.

R2 shorted. Forward biasing is removed, and there is no collector current or output voltage.

R3 open. Circuit becomes inoperative because of the breaking of the DC current path. Collector current is zero, and there is no RF output voltage.

R3 shorted. There is no feedback, and, therefore, there are no oscillations or RF output. The collector current falls to the low forward-bias value.

Two basic transmitter RF stages are given in Fig. 6-41. These are a crystal oscillator and a follow-up class-B amplifier. The functions of the components are:

R1, R2. Base-bias resistors. Crystal-oscillator starting requires the use of a small forward bias on the emitter junction.

R3. Emitter stabilization resistor.

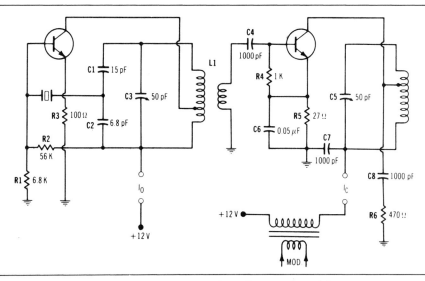

Fig. 6-41. Transistor crystal oscillator and amplifier.

C1, C2. Feedback divider capacitors that establish an optimum amount of feedback.

C3. This capacitor and the primary of transformer L1 serve as the collector tank circuit of the oscillator. The secondary of L1 serves as a low-impedance coupling link into the base circuit of the amplifier.

C4. Acts as the capacitance of the base RC combination and is also a DC blocking capacitor.

R4. Resistor of class-B amplifier base RC combination.

R5. Emitter stabilization resistor.

C6. Emitter RF bypass capacitor.

C7. Collector RF bypass capacitor.

C5. Capacitor of collector tank circuit.

C8. Coupling and DC blocking capacitor.

R6. Load for transmitter output.

The transistor oscillator and class-B amplifier differ from their vacuum-tube counterparts in that a loss of oscillations and/or RF excitation results in a decline in the collector current (either to zero or low value set by the forward bias). If the crystal stops oscillating, the collector current of the oscillator stage falls to the very low value established by forward-bias resistors R1 and R2. When the oscillator stops, no RF excitation reaches the next stage, and there can be no forward biasing. Consequently, the collector current of the class-B stage falls to zero.

Assume that the transmitter is adjusted properly and is being modulated near 95% by a 1000-Hz sine wave. Component failures will then have the following effects on the transmitter operation:

Crystal stops. There is no output. There is no class-B amplifier collector current and the crystal-oscillator current falls to the very low value established by the slight forward bias.

R1 shorted. This removes bias from the oscillator and it stops oscillating. The results are the same as for the previous condition.

R1 open. There is no great change in circuit operation. The oscillator current increases slightly and oscillator stability is impaired.

R2 shorted. There is no output and a high collector current is drawn by the oscillator stage because of the increase in the forward bias. However, it will not oscillate, and, therefore, the collector current of the class-B amplifier will fall because of the absence of RF excitation from the oscillator.

R2 open. Again there is bias removal and no output. Collector currents fall. Oscillator does not start.

R3 shorted. Spurious oscillations result because of instability. Oscillator current rises.

R3 open. The circuit becomes inoperative because of the breaking of the DC path. Oscillations stop and the collector current falls to near zero. The class-B stage draws no current.

C1 open. Oscillations stop. There are no collector currents.

C1 shorted. There is no great change in operations except that there is a loss of stability and a tendency to self-oscillations of a spurious nature.

C2 open. Same condition as for C1 shorted.

C2 shorted. Oscillations stop because of the lack of feedback. Collector current falls to near zero.

C3-L1 open. An open capacitor or inductor in the tank circuit stops oscillations and causes the collector current to drop to essentially zero.

C4 open. Oscillations continue but they are not supplied to the class-B amplifier. Therefore, the class-B current decreases to zero. However, the oscillator itself operates normally and there is collector current.

C4 shorted. The current rises and there are spurious oscillations generated in the class-B amplifier stage.

R4 open. Class-B stage is improperly biased. There is a decrease in the class-B amplifier collector current. Modulation is distorted because of the inability to follow the crest. The crystal oscillator operates in normal manner.

R4 shorted. Class-B stage is inoperative. Its collector current declines. The oscillator operates normally.

C6 open. There is RF degeneration and less gain in the class-B amplifier. Again the collector current of the class-B stage decreases. The modulation envelope is distorted because of the inability to follow modulation crests.

C6 shorted. There is a slightly greater output and the collector current rises. Stability is not good.

C5 or L2 open. Class-B stage does not function. It is possible that the class-B stage will oscillate in a self-excited manner and generate a spurious RF output.

C5 or L2 shorted. The class-B stage does not function efficiently. There is some direct feedthrough from the crystal oscillator. Output level is very low and modulation is distorted.

C7 open. No apparent change in operating conditions but the modulation system is less stable, and there could be some feedthrough of RF energy into the audio section.

C7 shorted. The modulated amplifier becomes inoperative. There is no RF output. Crystal oscillator operates in normal manner.

C8 open. No RF output is transferred to the load.

C8 shorted. A DC component also appears across the load.

R6 open. No load is placed on the output of the transmitter. Class-B amplifier may self-oscillate and draw a high collector current.

R6 shorted. Output is shorted and no pattern is seen on the scope screen. However, a somewhat greater load is placed on the class-B stage, and its collector current rises.

A radio-frequency power amplifier such as might be used at the output of a VHF or UHF FM transmitter is shown in Fig. 6-42. The output transistor is driven from the collector output of the preceding stage. Its output resonant circuit is inductor L1 and capacitor C1 which is series resonant and provides a low-impedance drive signal from across capacitor C1. This is applied to the base of the power-amplifier stage through capacitor C2 and additional input matching. Supply voltage is applied to the collector through a radio-frequency choke. Output pi-network and matching circuit supply output to a follow-up harmonic filter and antenna system. The various resonant-circuit inductors can be wire coils, microstrip lines, or part of some other type of resonant circuit.

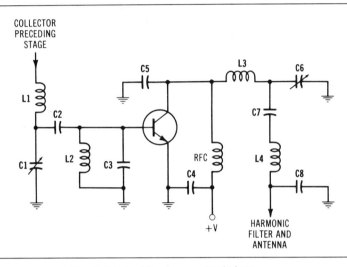

Fig. 6-42. An RF power output stage.

    Inductor L1 or capacitor C2 open would prevent the transfer of the drive signal to the base, resulting in no output or a very weak output. A shorted L1 would reduce the drive level to the output stage, and a shorted C2 would result in the transfer of an improper bias to the base of the output transistor. This bias would be positive and result in a high collector current. Shorts of inductor L2 or capacitor C3 would result in a loss of RF excitation and no or very little output. There would be a low collector current.

    An open RF choke would shut off the output stage because there would be no collector current path. A shorted capacitor C4 would also cause an inoperative stage and possible overheating or blown fuse in connection with the +V supply voltage line. An open capacitor C4 would cause instability and possibly spurious oscillations. A shorted RF choke would result in no RF output, the collector being effectively at radio-frequency ground.

    Any short or open of inductor L3 or an open capacitor C5 would upset resonant conditions in the output circuit reducing power level and causing instability. A shorted capacitor C5 would again place a very low resistance path on the supply voltage, and the effects of such a short would be felt along the supply line. This would also be the case for a shorted capacitor C6. Opens and shorts associated with capacitor C7 and C8 as well as inductor L4 would disturb the output matching and radio-frequency power level would drop off. Furthermore, a short of capacitor C7 would put the supply voltage potential on the line leading out to the harmonic filter and antenna system.

    As mentioned earlier an RF power meter connected to the antenna or dummy load is of special help in determining what influence the power amplifier stage components have on the output. After individual components are checked and changed, you can note the influence on the power meter reading after power is restored.

6-16-2. Vacuum-Tube Circuits

A triode grounded cathode amplifier is shown in Fig. 6-43. By using the component values shown, a voltage gain of approximately 50 can be obtained. That is, an input signal of one-half volt will result in a 25-volt output signal. The functions of the individual parts are:

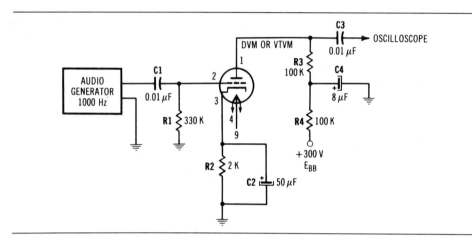

Fig. 6-43. Grounded-cathode amplifier.

C1. Coupling capacitor that provides DC isolation between input circuit and signal source.

R1. Grid resistor. The signal voltage is developed across this resistor. A secondary function of the resistor is to present a discharge path for electrons that accumulate on the control grid.

R2. Cathode resistor. The presence of plate current in this resistor develops a positive DC voltage between cathode and ground, thus developing the grid bias. The DC bias voltage acting between grid and cathode is negative.

C2. Cathode bypass filter capacitor. This capacitor prevents AC degeneration. If its filtering action were not present, an AC voltage would also develop across resistor R2 as a result of the changes in plate current with signal. The phase of such an AC voltage would be opposite to the phase of the grid signal and would subtract from the grid signal. It would reduce the effective grid signal and lower the overall gain of the stage.

R3. Plate load or plate coupling resistor. With applied signal, the changing plate current in this resistor causes a change in the plate voltage. The plate-voltage change is the useful output of the amplifier.

C3. Coupling capacitor. The coupling capacitor again isolates the DC of one stage from that of the next stage. However, such a capacitor offers a minimum reactance to the AC voltage change, and, therefore, the AC output at the stage is coupled to the next stage.

R4. This is a decoupling resistor. It isolates the AC variations of a given stage from the power supply impedance. It also blocks any AC variation that might appear across the power supply from the sensitive input stages of an audio amplifier. Often a second function of a decoupling resistor is to lower the DC voltage of the supply line to the value required by a given vacuum-tube stage.

C4. This is a decoupling capacitor. Filtering requires the joint influence of both resistor and capacitor (R4–C4) in smoothing out undesired AC variations. It is the combination that does the filtering and makes available a steady DC voltage for the individual stage.

Next consider each individual part in terms of the trouble it might cause in a circuit if it became defective. The two extremes, open or shorted, are used. It is understood that similar defects, although not as severe, can be introduced when the component value changes. In general, it introduces the same sort of defect but the degree of influence will not be as great. In considering the AC signal performance of the stage, assume that the applied signal level approximates the desired maximum signal level of operation for the stage.

C1 shorted. If the signal also contains a DC component, this DC voltage is transferred to the grid and can cause improper biasing conditions.

C1 open. This results in no applied signal. The DC operating conditions of the stage are unchanged.

R1 open. The influence of the open grid resistor depends to a great extent on the circuit arrangement and the particular tube type. In some arrangements electrons accumulate on the control grid to such an extent that the tube is cut off. In other circuit arrangements, when too high a value grid resistor is used, a grid gas current could occur to bias the grid in the positive direction which would result in excessive DC currents in the tube.

R1 shorted. No AC input or no output because the applied signal is shorted between grid and ground.

C2 open. AC degeneration results and there is less output signal for a given input signal. DC operating conditions do not change.

C2 shorted. Stage is now improperly biased and the output may become distorted. There is a drop in the DC plate voltage and a rise in the DC plate current because of the bias removal.

R2 shorted. Same defect as that which occurs when capacitor C2 is shorted.

R2 open. Tube is cut off and becomes inoperative. There is no AC output, plate current is zero, and plate voltage is maximum.

R3 open. This defect is similar to the conditions that exist when R2 is open. The tube is cut off, there is no output, and the plate current is zero. In this case the plate voltage is also zero. However, there will be maximum supply voltage at the junction of capacitor C4 and resistor R4.

R3 shorted. There is no AC output voltage. The DC plate current is higher and so is the DC plate voltage.

C3 open. No AC signal voltage is transferred to the succeeding stage.

C4 open. Output voltage may rise because of the increase in the effective AC load resistance with the removal of the decoupling circuit and the addition of resistor R4 to the load. Output voltage may be distorted because of the nonlinear operating conditions. If the stage were associated with an amplifier chain, there would be a danger of self-oscillation, motorboating, or other disturbances that arise from improper decoupling.

C4 shorted. When C4 is shorted, there is no supply voltage applied to the stage. Output is zero, plate current is zero, and plate voltage is zero. In many circuits there could be excessive current in the decoupling resistor R4 and it would overheat.

R4 open. The supply voltage would again be removed from the stage. Output voltage, plate current, and plate voltage would all be zero.

R4 shorted. Supply voltage increases as do the DC plate current and DC plate voltage. Output voltage may increase slightly. Again, if the stage were associated with a multistage amplifier, low-frequency feedback disturbances could arise.

A pentode grounded-cathode amplifier is shown in Fig. 6-44. Except that a screen-grid tube is used, note its similarity to the circuit of Fig. 6-43. A major advantage of the pentode stage, in addition to the better isolation between output and input, is the fact that the plate voltage has much less of an influence on the plate current. The screen grid takes over in the control of electron flow between cathode and plate. As a result the pentode has a greater voltage-amplification capability. That is to say, an output voltage of a given magnitude can be obtained with a much lower input voltage in comparison to a comparable triode circuit. The circuit is itself identical to that of a triode with the exception that a screen resistor R5 and a screen capacitor C5 are required. An input signal of one-half volt will result in a 40-volt output for the circuit of Fig. 6-44.

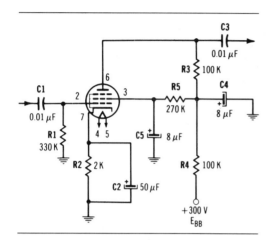

Fig. 6-44. Pentode grounded-cathode amplifier circuit.

The function of screen resistor R5 is to reduce the supply voltage to a value appropriate for the desired operating conditions. The screen capacitor C5 is a bypass or filter capacitor. It prevents degeneration in the screen-grid circuit. It does so by preventing the variations in the screen grid current from causing a change in the screen-grid voltage. It holds the screen-grid voltage constant in the same manner that the cathode filter capacitor holds the cathode bias constant. The remainder of the components of the stage have functions identical to their like components in the triode circuit in Fig. 6-43.

Except for the screen resistor and screen capacitor combination, component defects produce the same faults as those covered in conjunction with Fig. 6-43. If screen-grid resistor R5 opens, there is no screen-grid voltage and the stage reverts to triode operation. The output voltage is low and distorted. There is also a change in the DC operating conditions, plate current falls, and plate voltage rises. If resistor R5 were to short, there would be a higher than normal screen grid voltage. The screen and plate current would rise, and there could be excessive screen-grid and/or plate dissipation.

If the screen-grid capacitor were to open, the screen-grid voltage would also vary with the applied signal. The stage would become degenerative, and there would be a reduction in the output voltage. A shorted screen-grid capacitor would also remove screen grid voltage, and the same circuit faults would develop that result when the screen-resistor is open.

In troubleshooting one should always remember that a shorted capacitor, more than likely, will also result in an overheated resistor. Thus, what often appears to be a resistor defect is, in fact, being caused by a shorted or leaky capacitor. Thus, in the foregoing example the shorted capacitor might also cause an overheated screen-grid resistor.

A single-tube phase splitter is shown in Fig. 6-45. Such a stage provides a means of obtaining opposite-polarity and a nearly equal-amplitude output signal for driving the input of a push-pull stage. One output is removed across resistor R3; the other output is taken across resistor R4. Inasmuch as the stage has both plate and cathode outputs, it functions in part as a cathode-follower, and, therefore, the gain is very low. For example with a 5-volt input signal there is approximately 4.9 volts output at the plate. Considering the two outputs as being connected in series, there would be a net overall gain approaching 2. It is most important to recognize that the two output voltages are of opposite polarity and almost equal in amplitude.

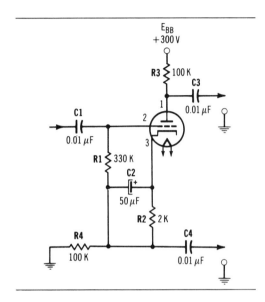

Fig. 6-45. Single-tube phase splitter.

The functions of the parts are:

C1. Coupling capacitor. Function is the same as capacitor C1 of Fig. 6-43.

R1. Grid resistor. Function is the same as resistor R1 of Fig. 6-43. Note that the low end of resistor R1 is connected to the junction of resistors R2 and R4. This connection makes certain that the grid-cathode bias equals the DC charge placed on capacitor C2.

R2. Cathode bias resistor. The DC plate current in this resistor develops the DC bias voltage for the stage.

C2. The cathode bypass filter capacitor. The DC charge on this capacitor is the bias for the stage.

R3. Plate load resistor. The AC plate current variation in this resistor develops the output voltage change at the plate of the tube.

C3. Coupling capacitor. It has the same function as C3 of Fig. 6-43.

C4. Also a coupling capacitor for the opposite polarity output of the stage.

R4. This is a cathode output resistor. The cathode-current variation (same as plate-current variation) in this resistor develops the AC output voltage that is made available in the cathode circuit. The AC voltage across this resistor is less than the applied AC voltage because it is a cathode-circuit load. A similar but opposite polarity voltage is made available at the plate.

The influence of component faults is as follows:

C1 open. Loss of grid signal.

C1 shorted. Possible change in operating conditions through the exchange of DC components. In this case the high DC voltage across R4 is transferred to the preceding stage or signal source.

R1 open. This open resistor results in an improper bias which causes a fall in the DC plate current and a rise in the DC plate voltage. Under certain circumstances, a distorted AC output also occurs.

R1 shorted. There is a reduction in the magnitude of the output signal that is made available by the basic design. The input signal is in effect applied across resistor R4.

R2 open. Circuit becomes inoperative because of the interruption of the DC current path. Plate current is zero and the plate voltage high.

R2 shorted. No bias is applied to the stage and improper operating conditions reestablished. There could be some distortion of the output voltage. Plate voltage falls and plate current rises.

C2 shorted. Same effects as R2 shorted.

C2 open. The influence would be limited although there would be some additional inequality in the output magnitudes.

R3 shorted. The plate voltage and plate current both increase. The stage itself reverts to a cathode-follower with no output made available at the plate.

R3 open. The stage becomes inoperative because of the interruption of the DC current path. The plate current and the plate voltage both fall to zero.

C3 open. No transfer of AC signal to next stage.

C3 shorted. Undesired exchange of DC components betweeen stages.

C4 shorted. Likewise, an undesired exchange of DC components between stages.

C4 open. No transfer of AC signal to next stage.

R4 open. Stage becomes inoperative because of the interruption of the DC current path. Plate current is zero and plate voltage is maximum.

A crystal oscillator is shown in Fig. 6-46. This oscillator crystal acts as the grid resonant circuit. The cathode and plate currents are one and the same, and, therefore, the plate current can be measured with a meter inserted in the cathode circuit.

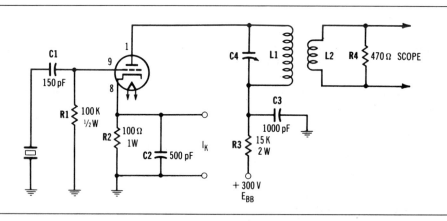

Fig. 6-46. Crystal oscillator.

A popular metering method is shown in Fig. 6-46. A low-value cathode resistor is used, and the oscillator-circuit operation will remain essentially the same whether the meter is in or out of the circuit. This technique is adaptable to meter-switching arrangements because the meter can be switched in and out of the cathode circuit and among other circuits of the transmitters at will without affecting operation. The functions of the parts are as follows:

C1. Capacitor of grid RC combination. In some crystal circuits this capacitor is not used because the crystal and its holder can provide the capacitance of the grid RC combination.

R1. Resistor of grid RC combination.

R2. Metering resistor.

C2. Metering circuit bypass.

C3. Decoupling RF filter capacitor.

R3. Decoupling resistor and plate voltage-dropping resistor.

C4. Capacitor of plate tank circuit.

L1. Inductor of plate tank circuit.

L2. Low-impedance secondary coil.

R4. Output load of the oscillator.

It is important to know the tuning characteristics of a crystal oscillator. The plate current rises when the crystal stops oscillating or other defects develop. Likewise, detuning capacitor C4 from crystal resonance stops oscillations and causes a plate current rise. As the plate-tank capacitor is tuned to resonance, oscillations are indicated by a dip in the plate-current meter reading. The oscillator kicks out of resonance very quickly when the tank is tuned to the low side of the crystal frequency. Oscillations fall off more slowly when capacitor C4 is tuned to the high-frequency side of resonance. For best circuit stability it is customary to tune tank-circuit capacitor C4 slightly to the minimum-capacitance (high-frequency) side of maximum plate-current dip. The output can be displayed on a scope screen. Be certain the scope can accommodate crystal frequency.

Component faults will have the following influence on stage operation:

C1 open. Oscillations cease, RF output falls to zero, and plate current rises.

C1 shorted. There will be no great change in operation because the crystal capacitance takes over.

R1 open. The RF output drops as does the DC plate current.

R1 shorted. No oscillations, no RF output, and plate current rises.

R2 or C2 shorted. No change in circuit conditions. However, metering circuit will not function.

R2 open. Stage becomes inoperative because of the breaking of the DC path to the supply line. There will be no oscillations and the plate current will fall to zero.

C2 open. No significant change in circuit operation except perhaps some slight detuning.

C4 or L1 shorted. No oscillations, no output, plate current rises.

C4 open. No oscillations, no output, and plate current rises.

L1 open. Circuit becomes inoperative because of the interruption of the supply voltage. There will be no oscillations, no output, and the plate current falls to zero.

R3 shorted. There is a somewhat greater output as well as a higher plate current. When the supply voltage is too high and/or the feedback current too great, the crystal can be fractured.

R3 open. Circuit again becomes inoperative because of the interruption of the supply voltage. There will be no oscillations, and the plate current will fall to zero.

C3 open. No oscillations because of the interruption of the RF path. The plate-current meter reading rises.

C3 shorted. The stage becomes operative because of the removal of the plate voltage. However, the current drawn through R3 can be excessive and the resistor overheats.

272

R4 shorted. A heavier load will be placed on the oscillator output and the plate-current meter reading rises. Too severe a load on a crystal stage may cause the circuit to stop oscillating completely.

R4 open. A very light load will be placed on the oscillator, and the dip in the plate current will be very decided. Output voltage as displayed on the oscilloscope will increase because of the lighter load.

A basic, simple, and low-power AM transmitter circuit is shown in Fig. 6-47. The RF circuit consists of a triode Pierce crystal oscillator and follow-up class-C amplifier. The audio section consists of a triode voltage amplifier and a pentode class-A modulator. Only four receiving-type tube sections are needed.

The functions of the parts are as follows:

X1. Crystal.
C1. DC blocking capacitor that keeps the DC plate voltage from the crystal. It is also a part of the grid RC combination.
R1. Resistor of grid RC combination.
C2. Capacitor that provides easier starting and a more favorable feedback division for the Pierce crystal oscillator.
R2. Plate-load resistor of the Pierce crystal oscillator.
R3. Metering resistor.
C3. Interstage coupling capacitor and capacitance of grid RC combination.
R4. Resistor of grid bias RC combination for the class-C amplifier.
R5. Metering resistor.
C4. Screen-grid RF bypass capacitor.
R6. Screen-grid voltage-dropping resistor.
C5. RF plate-circuit filter capacitor. It is made high enough in value that it also filters out the high audio frequencies above 3000 Hz.
C6-L1. Plate tank circuit.
R7. Metering resistor.
B1. No. 46 pilot-bulb load.
C7. Input coupling capacitor of the audio amplifier.
R8. Grid resistor.
R9. Cathode-bias resistor.
C8. Cathode-filter capacitor.
R10. Plate-load resistor of the voltage amplifier.
C9. Interstage coupling capacitor.
P1. Audio gain control.
R11. Cathode-bias resistor.
C10. Cathode-filter capacitor.
C11. Decoupling and audio filter capacitor.
R12. Voltage dropping and decoupling resistor.
R13. Isolation resistor for supplying signal from an audio generator.
C12. RF filter capacitor.
T1. Transceiver modulation transformer or audio choke.

The RF section of the transmitter has only a single control; this is the plate tank capacitor of the class-C amplifier. At resonance there will be a dip in plate current. The capacitor is adjusted for maximum glow of the bulb. The RF waveform can be observed by connecting an oscilloscope probe across the output.

The audio generator can now be connected to the transmitter, and the gain control advanced until the modulation envelope appears. Almost 100% modulation can be obtained. The modulating-frequency range extends from several hundred hertz up to 3000 or 4000 Hz.

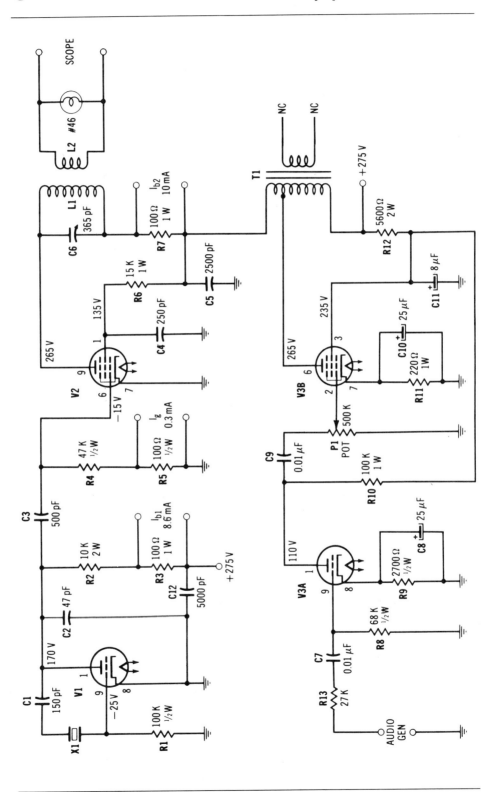

Fig. 6-47. An AM transmitter.

The effects of RF excitation loss on an AM transmitter can be checked by removing the crystal from its holder. Both the oscillator and RF amplifier plate currents rise. The grid current falls to zero, and there is no RF output.

The influence of modulation on the plate current and output can also be observed. The plate current of the class-C amplifier remains essentially constant as the percentage of modulation is increased slowly. The bulb also increases in brightness, indicating that with modulation more power is being delivered to the load. In effect the pilot bulb is functioning as an RF antenna meter which normally reads higher with modulation. At percentages near 100% the modulation becomes nonlinear, and there is a slight drop in the plate-current reading (negative carrier shift).

Component failures influence circuit operation in the following manner:

X1 inoperative. Crystal stopping results in no output and no class-C amplifier grid current. Both DC plate currents rise.

R1 shorted. Oscillations stop, producing the same events as X1 inoperative.

C1 open. Same as X1 inoperative.

C1 shorted. No significant change.

C2 open. Oscillator is sluggish in starting.

C2 shorted. Oscillations stop and crystal-stage plate current rises. Class-C amplifier grid current falls, class-C plate current increases, and there is no RF output.

R2 shorted. Oscillations stop and a high plate current is drawn by the oscillator tube. Grid current falls to zero for the class-C stage, and its plate current increases. There is no RF output.

R2 open. Oscillator stage becomes inoperative. Grid current falls to zero and class-C plate current rises.

R3 open. Same conditions as with R2 open.

R3 shorted. No influence on circuit operation but metering circuit will not function.

C12 open. Possible RF feedback and instability.

C12 shorted. Complete transmitter becomes inoperative because of the short across the supply line. Could damage power supply.

C3 open. No RF excitation to class-C stage. Grid current goes to zero, plate current rises, and there is no RF output. Oscillator stage will operate in normal fashion.

C3 shorted. Output falls to zero and grid-meter current direction is opposite because of the plus DC grid voltage. Class-C plate current rises.

R4 shorted. Output falls and plate current rises. Oscillator operates normally.

R4 open. Grid current goes to zero, plate current falls, and output drops substantially. Modulation becomes nonlinear.

R5 open. Same conditions as with R4 open.

R5 shorted. No circuit effect. Metering position will be inoperative.

C4 open. RF output declines.

C4 shorted. Output falls and plate current rises. Screen-grid voltage goes to zero.

R6 shorted. Plate current rises and output increases slightly. In some cases screen-grid dissipation would be exceeded.

R6 open. Screen-grid voltage goes to zero causing the output to drop and plate current to fall.

C5 open. RF energy can feed into the modulator causing instability. Modulation frequency response can be affected adversely.

C6 or L1 shorted. Output falls to zero and plate current rises.

L1 open. Circuit becomes inoperative because of the removal of plate voltage.

C6 open. Tank circuit seriously mistuned and plate current rises as the RF output falls to zero.

R7 open. Circuit becomes inoperative because of removal of supply voltage.

R7 shorted. Circuit operations unaffected. Metering position will not function.

Failures in the audio section will result in the removal of modulation or the application of a distorted modulating wave to the class-C amplifier. The first stage is a triode grounded-cathode circuit. The influence of part failure on the operation of a voltage amplifier was covered in conjunction with Fig. 6-43. Failures in the audio-output stage have the following effects:

C9 open. No audio is conveyed to the output stage and the transmitter is not modulated.

C9 shorted. Modulating wave is distorted because of the application of a positive voltage to the grid of the output tube. Output-tube plate current rises.

P1 fault. Improper operation of potentiometer can result in modulation instability and the introduction of noise into the modulating system.

R11 open. Output stage becomes inoperative because of the interruption of the DC current path.

R11 shorted. Improper biasing and a distorted modulating wave.

C10 shorted. Same as R11 shorted.

C10 open. Decrease in modulation because the degenerative feedback reduces the amplitude of the modulating signal.

C11 shorted. No screen-grid voltage with a resultant reduction in plate current and audio power output.

C11 open. Screen-grid degeneration and a reduction in the magnitude of the modulating wave and degree of modulation.

R12 open. Removal of screen-grid voltage and a resultant decrease in plate current and audio power output.

R12 shorted. An increase in the screen-grid voltage and, in the circuit arrangement of Fig. 6-47, an increase in the plate-supply voltage of the triode voltage amplifier. Some small increase in audio output will result but safe dissipation powers may be exceeded.

T1 open. No modulation and no RF output because of the removal of the supply voltage from the class-C stage.

T1 shorted. No modulation, but there is RF output because the supply voltage to the class-C stage is not interrupted.

Some transmitters use a combination of solid-state and vacuum-tube devices. Fig. 6-48 shows a typical circuit. Note that there are two separate supply voltage points: a low-voltage one for the MOSFET; and a high-voltage source for the vacuum tube. In this case a MOSFET stage is driving a vacuum-tube RF amplifier. The vacuum tube has a high-impedance input. Therefore, a simple resonant circuit can be used to supply the drive signal.

Biasing of the input stage is handled by the two fixed resistors, while the RF signal is applied to the second gate. Any failures in the biasing or input stage would result in a loss of RF output and drive to the vacuum tube. An open radio-frequency choke would shut off the input stage. A shorted radio-frequency choke would result in instability and loss of neutralization because it would place a radio-frequency short across the 820-pF capacitor which is a part of the neutralization network along with capacitor C_N.

The bias for the vacuum-tube output stage is set by the grid resistor-capacitor combination and the safety cathode resistor. A loss of a component in the input system would result in a loss of drive and no, or very weak, radio-frequency signal at the

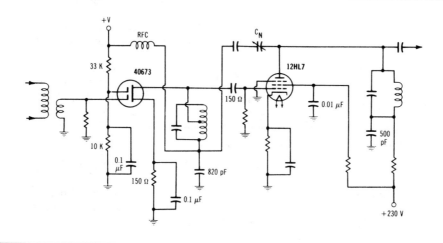

Fig. 6-48. A MOSFET driving a vacuum-tube amplifier.

vacuum-tube plate. However, the tube itself is protected from a loss of excitation by the cathode resistor-capacitor combination.

The screen-grid resistor and capacitor combination will influence the RF power output in the manner that was described previously for vacuum tube stages. Likewise, the plate circuit components would have the same influence on operation as covered previously.

7

Antenna Systems and Interference

The antenna system is an important essential in a landmobile or marine two-way system. Antennas must be of good design and properly installed. The transmitter and its output system must be designed and tuned to transfer power efficiently from transmitter to antenna.

Since the landmobile and marine spectra are well used and crowded with signals, interference among stations is prevalent. Special considerations must be given to reducing interference. These reductions involve the antenna system itself as well as the transmitter output and the receiver input systems. This chapter will serve as an introduction to antenna systems and interference reduction techniques.

7-1. Antenna Basics

The prime responsibility of the antenna system is to make the most effective use of the radio-frequency power provided by the transmitter. The antenna system comprises the output system of the transmitter, the transmission line, and the antenna proper. The radio-frequency energy must be transferred to the transmission line, and the line must convey that energy to the antenna as shown in Fig. 7-1. The antenna, in turn, must radiate it. Infrequently, there may be a tuning unit at the antenna in the form of matching hardware or LC tuner.

There is a great variety of basic antenna styles and modifications. However, most antennas stem from the fundamental Hertz and Marconi types shown in Fig. 7-2. These antennas are said to be "resonant" because their physical lengths are related to the wavelength of the RF energy they radiate. The Hertz antenna is usually called a half-wavelength or half-wave antenna because its physical length corresponds to that dimension of a radio wave. Thus the actual physical length depends on the frequency.

The radio-frequency energy is most often supplied to the center of the Hertz antenna as shown in Fig. 7-2A. Such an antenna is referred to as a half-wave dipole. However, it can be supplied at the end as shown in Fig. 7-2B or at some other position along its length.

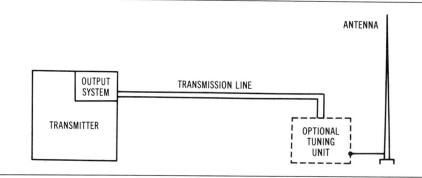

Fig. 7-1. Major segments of an antenna.

Physically, a Marconi antenna is one-quarter wave long. Electrically, it acts like a half-wavelength antenna because the ground beneath it forms a mirror quarter-wavelength segment as shown in Fig. 7-2C. The characteristics and quality of the mirror segment are related to ground conditions. A network of conductors or large area metallic surface is often laid out beneath the antenna to provide a more uniform and lower resistance ground system.

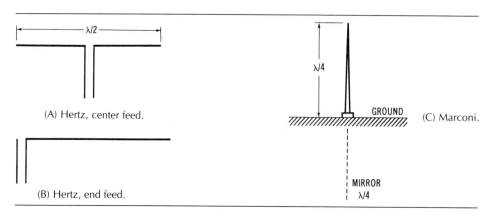

Fig. 7-2. Basic antenna types.

The quarter-wave element can be mounted on a base insulator or grounded directly. In practice, the former is more common because the results are more uniform and matching is less of a problem.

A horizontal antenna radiates a horizontally polarized wave (electric vector is horizontal); a vertical antenna, a vertically polarized wave (electric vector is vertical). If a vertically polarized wave is desired, it is possible to mount a half-wave dipole vertically. However, the Marconi is not used as a horizontal antenna because it needs a mirror-ground.

A very practical formula for calculating a half wavelength is:

$$\frac{\lambda}{2} = \frac{492}{f}$$

where,
$\lambda/2$ is the length of a half-wavelength in feet,
f is the frequency in megahertz.

The free-space dimension calculated from this formula represents the half-wavelength separation of radio waves traveling in free space. Inasmuch as a radio wave travels slower in most other media than in air, the half-wavelength separation would be shorter than the free-space calculation. This means a radio wave travels slower in a transmission line or antenna than in free space; therefore the separation between adjacent waves is less than in free space.

A similar relationship exists for a radio wave on an antenna — a half-wave antenna is physically from 1% to 6% shorter than its free-space measurement. A point of discontinuity between the antenna conductor and space exists at the ends of the antenna. To a degree, space acts as a dielectric material, and the capacitive effect links the two ends of the antenna. This end effect lowers the resonant frequency of the antenna. For this reason, it must be cut shorter than the free-space calculation to obtain resonance at a given frequency. In other words, an antenna must be cut to an *electrical half wavelength* which is physically shorter than a free-space half wavelength.

A thin antenna element must be cut only slightly shorter than its free-space value, whereas a large-diameter antenna must be made significantly shorter. Since a shorter physical length is required at the higher frequencies, the length is much more critical at these frequencies.

The formula most often used for calculating antenna resonant length for operation in the high-frequency spectrum is:

$$\frac{\lambda}{2} = \frac{468}{f}$$

where,

$\lambda/2$ is the half wavelength in feet,

f is the frequency in megahertz.

The voltage and current distribution on a basic half-wave antenna is shown in Fig. 7-3A. The voltage maxima are at the ends and are of opposite polarity because the ends are one-half wavelength apart. The difference in polarity is comparable to that between the peaks of adjacent sine-wave alterations. The magnitude of the voltage is related to the strength of the radio wave supplied by the transmitter.

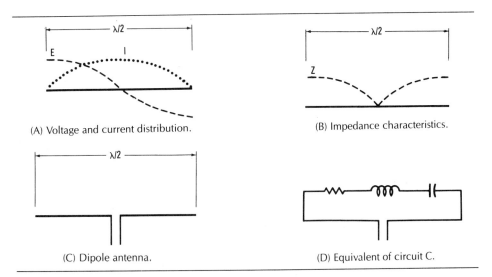

(A) Voltage and current distribution.

(B) Impedance characteristics.

(C) Dipole antenna.

(D) Equivalent of circuit C.

Fig. 7-3. Characteristics of a half-wave antenna.

The current is maximum at the center of the antenna and falls away to zero at both ends. Since impedance is the ratio of voltage to current, the high-voltage ends display maximum impedance, and the high-current center, minimum impedance. Fig. 7-3B shows the impedance variation along the length of an antenna.

Impedance is a very important consideration in connecting an antenna to a transmission line. With a center-feed system, the line must match a low impedance. Conversely, an end-feeding arrangement calls for a high-impedance line.

A half-wave antenna fed at the center (Fig. 7-3C) has inductance, resistance, and capacitance; in this respect, it resembles a series-resonant circuit as shown in Fig. 7-3D. When the antenna is cut to the proper length for the applied frequency, the inductive and capacitive reactances are equal, and the antenna is said to be resonant. At resonance the impedance is resistive and minimum, just as it is in a series-resonant circuit. This resistive impedance is called the radiation or antenna resistance (R_A).

The radiation resistance of a center-fed half-wave antenna is approximately 72 ohms; this value is influenced to some extent by the height of the antenna above ground. The radiation resistance of a base-fed quarter-wave Marconi is 36 ohms; this value is affected by ground conductivity beneath the antenna.

Antenna resistance is also affected by the shape and area of the antenna element, the location of the feedpoint, and the proximity of other elements. For example, as the element is made larger, the antenna resistance rises. This effect is similar to increasing the resistance of a series-resonant circuit — the antenna has a lower Q and a lower ratio of reactance to series resistance. Likewise its bandwidth increases. Thus larger-diameter and specially shaped elements permit the antenna to operate over a wider span of frequencies. Also the length to which it is cut is less critical. The capacitive end effect is somewhat greater; therefore such an antenna must usually be cut shorter than a thin dipole operating on the same center frequency.

7-2. Radiation Patterns

If an antenna could be isolated in space and operated as a point source, its electromagnetic radiation pattern would be perfectly spherical. However, antennas are of a finite dimension and are operated near ground or other objects. Consequently the electromagnetic energy travels from the antenna at differing intensities — both horizontally and vertically.

Where a uniform horizontal radiation in all directions is desired, the pattern can be represented by a perfect circle, as shown in Fig. 7-4A. In other cases one may want to concentrate the radiation in a given direction in order to transmit the maximum signal between two fixed stations. A typical directional pattern is shown in Fig. 7-4B.

There are also reasons why one must be concerned with the vertical angle at which the electromagnetic energy leaves the antenna. Is the energy to be directed skyward or toward the horizon? For short-range communication one would prefer to direct the energy at a low vertical angle, as shown in Fig. 7-5A.

In establishing a contact over a long-range path at a certain time and season of the year, it may be necessary to direct the signal skyward at a specific angle, as shown in Fig. 7-5B. The signal can be bounced off one of the ionized layers and returned to earth at the desired receiving point.

The horizontal and vertical radiation patterns of the two basic antennas — the Marconi vertical quarter-wave and the Hertz horizontal half-wave — are given in Fig.

7-6. The basic vertical antenna has an omnidirectional (i.e., circular) horizontal pattern. Approximately the same level is sent out in all directions. The vertical antenna above a good conductive ground has a low-angle vertical radiation pattern. In other words, more radiated energy is directed over the surface of the earth, toward the horizon, instead of skyward. (Of course, there is some skyward radiation.) Special antennas are used to further concentrate the vertical radiation at low angles.

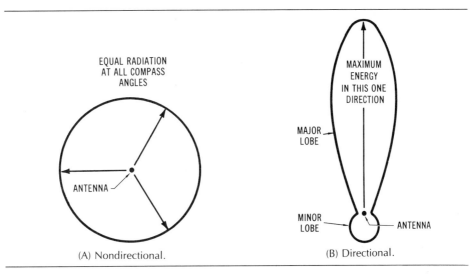

Fig. 7-4. Horizontal radiation patterns.

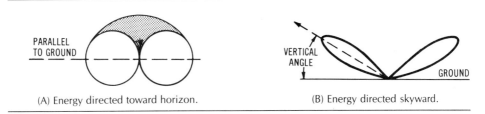

Fig. 7-5. Vertical radiation patterns.

The radiation pattern of a half-wave horizontal antenna is shown in Fig. 7-6B. The doughnut-like emission has been shifted through 90°. Now the vertical radiation pattern is circular and an equally strong signal is transmitted up, down, and to the sides. Even though the vertical free-space pattern is circular, the presence of ground does influence the vertical radiation for a horizontal antenna. In fact, the angular magnitudes vary in relation to height above ground. The actual pattern results from the addition and subtraction of radiation from the antenna itself and components reflected from ground.

The horizontal radiation pattern is a figure 8 with most of the energy moving out perpendicular or broadside to the direction of the antenna element. There is minimum signal radiation horizontally off the ends of the antenna. If such an antenna is to send out the strongest signal in a given direction, it must be positioned at right angles to the desired direction.

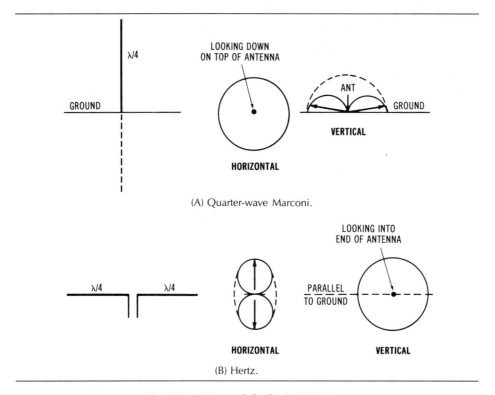

(A) Quarter-wave Marconi.

(B) Hertz.

Fig. 7-6. Patterns of the basic antenna.

7-3. The Vertical Antenna

In most communication services the vertical antenna is king. Particularly in vehicular communications, the vertical antenna presents fewer installation problems. In general, vertical polarization provides more reliability when the antenna must be mounted close to ground (in mobile installations). Furthermore, the radiation patterns are more appropriate. In general the horizontal radiation pattern of a vertical antenna is circular. Consequently, the same level of signal is sent out at all angles, a preferred condition in maintaining contact with cruising mobile units. The vertical antenna also has a low-angle vertical radiation pattern. Such a pattern is preferred in sending out signals over the countryside toward the horizon. In other words, the power supplied to the vertical antenna is used more effectively (with respect to the radio service to be rendered) than for a horizontal antenna.

Most dipole antennas, along with the various higher gain and directive combinations, can be made to radiate and receive vertically polarized signals. One of the most common radiocommunications antennas is the simple quarter-wave vertical, with or without modification. Basically, it is a quarter-wave Marconi.

The most common antenna for two-way mobile radio systems is the simple quarter-wave whip shown in Fig. 7-7A. The antenna has a low enough resistance that it can be fed directly via a 50-ohm coaxial line. Its attractions are ease of mounting, limited length, plus a simple feed system that can take advantage of the shielding provided by a coaxial cable. Shielding is, of course, important in vehicular installations because of ignition and other electrical noise problems.

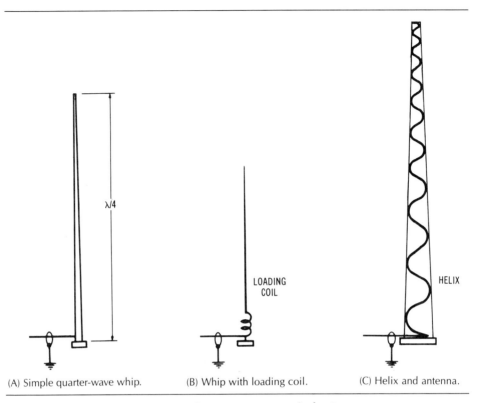

(A) Simple quarter-wave whip.   (B) Whip with loading coil.   (C) Helix and antenna.

Fig. 7-7. Basic quarter-wave vertical antennas.

At some frequencies, even a quarter-wavelength antenna is too cumbersome for vehicular installation. There are ways of physically shortening quarter-wavelength antennas. However, there is some sacrifice in gain and performance. A popular method is to use a loading coil at the base of the antenna, as shown in Fig. 7-7B. When an antenna is cut shorter than a quarter wavelength at the desired frequency, the antenna becomes capacitive. If we now insert a reactance of opposite sign (inductive reactance of a coil), the antenna can still be brought into resonance, even though its overall length is shorter than a quarter wave.

An antenna has two important parameters — the overall length it occupies in space, and its resonant frequency. When the two factors are optimized, the antenna system gives peak performance. Use of the loading coil does permit the antenna to be tuned to resonance; therefore performance is improved over that of a short antenna that is not tuned. However, the performance does not attain the level possible with both proper overall length and resonant tuning.

Overall antenna length can also be reduced with the coil-like antenna structure as shown in Fig. 7-7C. This antenna usually takes the form of a helical conductor supported by an insulator such as fiberglass. In fact, the conductor is often mounted inside the insulator to protect it from the environment.

Although the simple quarter-wave whip (Fig. 7-8A) is used, more elaborate vertical antennas are usually employed at the base stations of two-way radio systems. Often associated with a quarter-wave whip is a ground plane such as that shown in Fig. 7-8B. The presence of a ground plane makes the performance of the antenna more uniform with relation to its mounting position above actual ground. Furthermore, the ground plane is so positioned that the low angles of the vertical radiation pattern are emphasized. The signal coming off the antenna is radiated across the surface of the earth toward the horizon, an ideal condition for communicating with mobile units and their relatively low antennas. Because of this concentration, an antenna of this type has more gain than a simple quarter-wave whip.

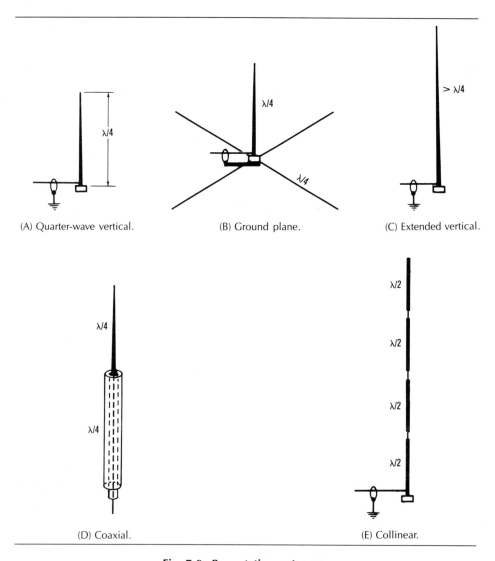

(A) Quarter-wave vertical.   (B) Ground plane.   (C) Extended vertical.

(D) Coaxial.   (E) Collinear.

Fig. 7-8. Base station antennas.

Three other popular vertical antennas are shown in Fig. 7-8. The overall length of the vertical whip can be extended to more than a quarter wavelength (Fig. 7-8C). If such an antenna is suitably matched, it will also have gain because of its ability to concentrate the vertical radiation at low angles. The overall length of the coaxial antenna, (Fig. 7-8D) is approximately a half wave. This arrangement also provides a means of matching when feeding the transmission line up through the center of the larger-diameter lower section. It has a gain and an improved vertical radiation pattern.

In the UHF and VHF spectra, collinear verticals (Fig. 7-8E) have become increasingly popular. They provide a substantial gain and concentration of the vertical pattern to low angles as compared to a single quarter-wave element.

7-4. Phased Arrays

The use of additional antenna elements permits the energy transmitted or received to be concentrated at more narrow horizontal and/or vertical angles. Such an antenna is said to have gain because more of the power is directed into specific angles of radiation. Thus, antenna gain does not mean that the antenna operates like an amplifier; instead, it means that the antenna concentrates the power into preferred horizontal and/or vertical radiation patterns.

In the measurement of antenna gain, a half-wave dipole or a quarter-wave vertical can be used as a reference antenna, and its gain is assigned a value of 0 dB. At other times the 0-dB reference is a theoretical point referred to as an *isotropic* source. If an antenna is said to have a gain of 3 dB, this means that if this antenna is directed toward a specific receiving location, it will deliver 3 dB more signal than the reference antenna.

There are three ways to interconnect antenna elements into an array, as shown in Fig. 7-9. These are broadside, end-fire, and collinear. A collinear involves stacking one antenna immediately above the other, as shown in Fig. 7-9A. Note that both antennas are fed from the transmission line. This antenna has a circular horizontal radiation pattern. Its gain comes from the fact that its vertical radiation pattern is concentrated at very low angles and the signals are sprayed out toward the horizon. Only a minimum amount of energy is sent skyward. Fig. 7-9B is an end-fire arrangement in which one element is placed in front of the other. The transmission line is connected to the first (rear) antenna, and then a second small piece of transmission line, only one-quarter wavelength long, is connected to the front antenna element. This style of antenna is directed horizontally, and maximum signal is sent out along the line from the back antenna element toward the front antenna element.

The third type is known as a broadside array. The two antenna elements in Fig. 7-9C are positioned side by side approximately one-half wavelength apart. The feed system divides and over the same distance connects to the two antenna elements. Thus the elements are fed in phase. Maximum radiation from this antenna is broadside to the plane of the two elements. There is minimum radiation off the sides.

A common version of the broadside array is the popular phased vertical array shown in Fig. 7-9D. In a mobile installation these elements might be quarter-wavelength types fed by coaxial transmission lines using a centrally located T-joint.

Antenna gain can also be obtained by using antenna elements of various lengths that are not electrically connected to the driven element to which the transmission line is attached. These elements are called parasitic elements. An element longer than the driven element acts as a reflector. A parasitic element shorter than the driven element is called a director. A popular version of this antenna is the Yagi shown in Fig. 7-10A. In the example there is one reflector and three directors. Maximum signal is sent out along the line of the elements. A typical radiation pattern is shown in Fig. 7-10B. Note how sharp it is, indicating that the antenna has a very high gain. However, the signal is radiated very strongly in a single direction. Very little radiation goes out at other angles. It is said to have a very small beamwidth. This beamwidth is usually given as the angle between the half-power positions on the directional pattern as shown. Yagi antennas are most often used at first locations from which a very strong signal is to be directed toward another fixed location.

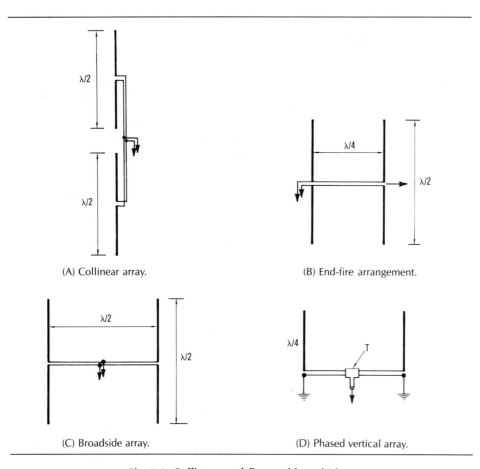

(A) Collinear array.

(B) End-fire arrangement.

(C) Broadside array.

(D) Phased vertical array.

Fig. 7-9. Collinear, end-fire, and broadside arrays.

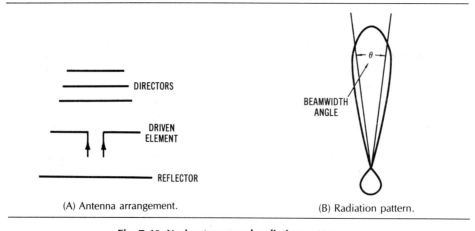

(A) Antenna arrangement.

(B) Radiation pattern.

Fig. 7-10. Yagi antenna and radiation pattern.

7-5. The Transmission Line

The transmission line (Fig. 7-11A) serves as the link between the transmitter and antenna. When the transmission line is suitably matched at the input and output, maximum energy is transferred. The equivalent circuit of a transmission line is shown in Fig. 7-11B. Even though the line is made up of continuous wires, these conductors have a very small inductance. The space between the wires, whether air or some other insulating material, inserts a small but definite capacitance between conductors. This distributed capacitance, as well as the inherent inductance, is uniform along the entire length of the line. In effect, the transmission line is an LC (inductance-capacitance) network. A radio wave requires a finite time to travel the length of the line, because capacitance opposes any voltage change, and inductance opposes any current change. There is also a small but significant opposition to current flow by the actual resistance (R) of the line.

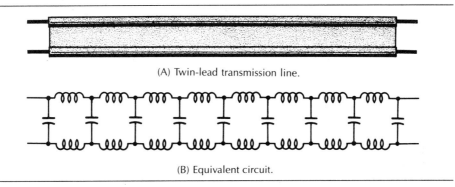

(A) Twin-lead transmission line.

(B) Equivalent circuit.

Fig. 7-11. A transmission line and its equivalent circuit.

Three important transmission-line parameters are associated with the LCR values of a practical line. The line displays a definite resistive impedance called its characteristic, or surge, impedance. It has an approximate value of:

$$Z_o = \sqrt{\frac{L}{C}}$$

where,
    Z_o is the characteristic impedance,
    L is the inductance per unit length,
    C is the capacitance per unit length.

Usually L and C are stated as so much inductance and capacitance per foot.
    The surge impedance is related directly to the diameter and spacing of the conductors. The larger the diameter, the lower the inductance per unit length. Likewise, the closer their spacing, the greater the capacitive effect per unit length.
    The foregoing factors apply to both parallel and coaxial lines, in accordance with the following formulas:
    For parallel lines:

$$Z_o = \frac{276}{\sqrt{k}} \log \frac{b}{a}$$

where,

Z_o is the characteristic impedance,
k is the dielectric constant of the insulating material,
b is the center-to-center spacing between conductors,
a is the radius of the conductors.

For coaxial lines:

$$Z_o = \frac{138}{\sqrt{k}} \log \frac{b}{a}$$

where,

Z_o is the characteristic impedance,
k is the dielectric constant of the insulating material,
b is the inside diameter of the outer conductor,
a is the outside diameter of the inner conductor.

Of course, for open-wire line where air serves as the dielectric material, the k factors are omitted and the formulas become:

$$Z_o = 276 \log \frac{b}{a}$$

and

$$Z_o = 138 \log \frac{b}{a}$$

The characteristic-impedance values are the figures you state when you purchase transmission line. When you ask for 50-ohm line, you are stating the characteristic impedance. Again, this is not a value you can measure with an ohmmeter; it is a resistive impedance.

Another important transmission-line parameter is its velocity factor. Because of the finite inductance and capacitance of a line, a radio wave travels more slowly along a transmission line than in air. The velocity factor is the ratio of the velocity along the line to the velocity in air or free space. The velocity of propagation along a line is computed by the formula:

$$\text{Velocity} = \frac{1}{\sqrt{LC}}$$

A third important parameter is the electrical length of a line, which is stated in wavelengths or fractions of a wavelength. For example, a one-wavelength section of transmission line has a physical length that corresponds to the separation between positive peaks of the radio wave on the line. A half-wavelength section corresponds to the separation between adjacent positive and negative peaks.

In determining physical length, we must consider the velocity factor. If the radio wave traveled along the transmission line at the same velocity it traveled in space, the regular half-wave free-space wavelength formula given previously could be used.

However, the velocity of propagation along a practical transmission line is slower than the free-space velocity. Consequently the half-wave section of line will be shorter than the free-space dimension according to the velocity factor of the transmission line.

$$\frac{\lambda}{2} = \frac{492}{f} \times V$$

where,
$\lambda/2$ is the half-wavelength of the line in feet,
f is the frequency in megahertz,
V is the velocity factor.

The electrical length of a transmission line is often given in electrical degrees, 360° being equal to one wavelength. Thus a half-wavelength section is often called a 180° line; a quarter-wavelength section, a 90° line.

Line attenuation refers to the losses a radio wave encounters in traveling from input to output. It is the result of I^2R (current squared times resistance) heat loss in the conductors and the heating of the dielectric material between them. The dielectric loss is insignificant for an air dielectric line and is much higher in lines with a dielectric material.

The lower the surge impedance of the line is, the higher the conductor loss becomes, because more current flows for a given output power. On the other hand, the dielectric loss increases as the surge impedance rises, because of the voltage stress placed across the conductors.

Conductor and dielectric losses both increase with frequency because of skin effect and decreasing dielectric reactance. Thus, the attenuation of practical lines increases with frequency.

In the radiocommunications services, the coaxial line is the most common transmission line, even though it has a higher loss than open-wire and twin-lead types. A coaxial line has better shielding because of its grounded outer conductor. The performance of the line thus remains more uniform with environmental changes and is less affected by nearby metallic objects.

7-5-1. Lines in Operation

A theoretically perfect line has no power loss. In fact, if the surge impedance of the line matches the internal impedance of the generator (radio-frequency source), maximum power will be transferred to the line. This is a basic electrical law — maximum power is delivered to any load, when it has the same impedance as the source.

If the line were infinitely long, radio-wave energy would travel along it indefinitely with no loss and would not return to the source. Likewise, if the line were broken at some point, as shown in Fig. 7-12, and a pure resistance of the same ohmic value as the surge impedance were placed across the line, all the power fed to its input would be dissipated across the resistive termination. Here, too, none of the energy impressed at the input would ever return to the source because it would all be dissipated across the termination. This means that a properly terminated line displays the same characteristics as an infinitely long line. Furthermore, a properly terminated line will operate effectively, regardless of its length.

No lines can be theoretically perfect. However, under reasonably ideal conditions, the only signal loss will be due to line attenuation. In other words, when properly

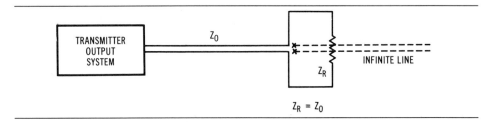

Fig. 7-12. The untuned transmission line.

matched, the line will act as an efficient means of transferring the output of the RF power amplifier to its antenna termination.

A transmission line that is so matched is called an untuned line because its length is unimportant to the matching. The untuned line can be matched by designing the antenna with an antenna feedpoint impedance that matches the surge impedance of the line. Matching sections can be used when the antenna feedpoint impedance and the line impedance differ.

When an untuned line is matched exactly, the current is the same at any point along the conductor. The voltage will show only a gradual and usually insignificant decline (as a result of attenuation) from the input to the termination.

7-5-2. Influence of Termination

Let us now consider the characteristics of a line terminated in other than its surge impedance. Fig. 7-13A shows the far end of the line short-circuited. Here the energy will move down the line until it reaches the short. There is no load to absorb the energy and only one way for it to travel — so back it goes along the line, over the same path. The RF power traveling down the line to its termination is called the *incident power*; the power reflected from the termination and moving back toward the source is the *reflected power*.

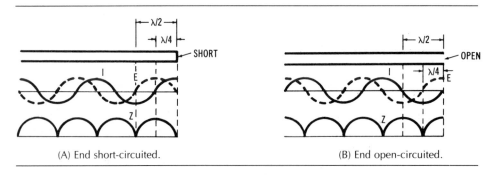

(A) End short-circuited.　　　　(B) End open-circuited.

Fig. 7-13. Standing waves on transmission lines.

Since the termination in Fig. 7-13A is a short circuit, there is maximum current flow and no voltage at this point. Inasmuch as the reflected current now moves back along the line at the same velocity it came down the line, the instantaneous magnitude and phase of the incident and reflected currents will differ everywhere along the line. At some points their phase will be the same and their amplitude almost double. At other points, the two currents will be out of phase, producing almost no current. Their amplitudes will be between minimum and maximum at still other points, as shown by the waveforms.

At the short, the two currents are in phase, and there is a maximum reading. Exactly one-quarter wavelength back from here, the two currents will be out of phase, and the net current will be minimum. One-half wavelength back from the short, the two currents will be back in phase and there will be another maximum, and so on, back to the source.

A similar relationship exists for the voltage; it is zero at the short circuit and maximum one-quarter wavelength back (at the same point where the current is minimum). One-half wavelength back the voltage is back to minimum (at a maximum current point).

The variation of current and voltage along the line is referred to as a *standing wave*. Maximum current or voltage points are called loops or antinodes and minimum points are nodes. Thus a voltage loop occurs at the current node and vice versa.

Similar but opposite relationships exist for an open-circuited line as shown in Fig. 7-13B. As before, the RF wave traveling down the line meets a termination that cannot dissipate the energy; again it turns back toward the source. Since the termination is an open circuit, the current flow is zero and the incident and reflected currents, although equal in value, are opposite in phase. However, the two voltage components are in phase and combine to form a maximum. Standing waves again form on the line, but the positioning of the loops and nodes is opposite that of the short-circuit distribution.

7-6. Standing-Wave Ratio

When a line is matched by a resistive impedance equal to its surge impedance, no standing waves are set up on the line because the termination absorbs all the energy. If the resistive termination has an ohmic value higher than the surge impedance, the standing-wave pattern set up on the line will resemble that of an open-circuit condition, as shown in Fig. 7-14A. The higher this ohmic value is, the more closely the standing-wave condition approaches that of an open-circuit condition. Moreover the voltage loop is always maximum at the termination, just as it is in an open circuit.

As the resistance of the termination is increased further and further from the surge impedance, less power is absorbed by the termination and more is reflected down the line. Hence, the standing waves are of higher magnitude in lines terminated in high resistance, as shown in Fig. 7-14B.

A similar relationship exists when the ohmic value of the termination is less than the surge impedance (Figs. 7-14C and D). Now, however, the termination acts more like a short circuit — the standing-wave magnitude increases as the ohmic value of the termination decreases. As the value of resistive termination is decreased, more power is reflected. In a short-circuit condition (zero resistance), all the incident power is reflected. But when the ohmic value of the termination is only slightly less than the surge impedance, more of the incident power is absorbed, and what little power is reflected sets up a weak standing wave on the line as shown in Fig. 7-14C.

A measure of the magnitude of the standing wave on the line is called the standing-wave ratio, or SWR. It can be determined from the following formulas:

where the current is known:

$$SWR = \frac{I_{max}}{I_{min}}$$

292

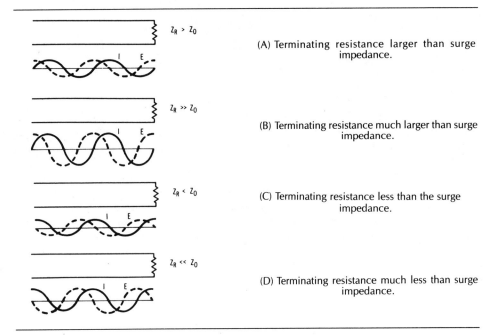

(A) Terminating resistance larger than surge impedance.

(B) Terminating resistance much larger than surge impedance.

(C) Terminating resistance less than the surge impedance.

(D) Terminating resistance much less than surge impedance.

Fig. 7-14. Influence of termination on standing waves.

where the voltage is known:

$$SWR = \frac{E_{max}}{E_{min}}$$

The SWR can be determined by measuring the voltage at a loop and a node with an RF voltmeter, or the current magnitudes at a loop and node with an RF current meter.

Impedance measurements can also be used. The larger quantity is always the numerator:

$$SWR = \frac{Z_{load}}{Z_o} \text{ or } \frac{Z_o}{Z_{load}}$$

Commercial instruments are available that can directly measure standing-wave ratio in the transmission lines. These were considered in Chapter 6.

The SWR reading tells much about the operation of an antenna system — the higher it is, the greater is the mismatch. Consequently, the less power reaches the termination.

A useful chart that depicts percent of reflected power in terms of VSWR is given in Fig. 7-15. Note for an SWR of 2.0 the reflected power is 10%. This indicates that with a power output capability of 20 watts only 18 of those watts would reach the antenna load [20 − (0.1 × 20)].

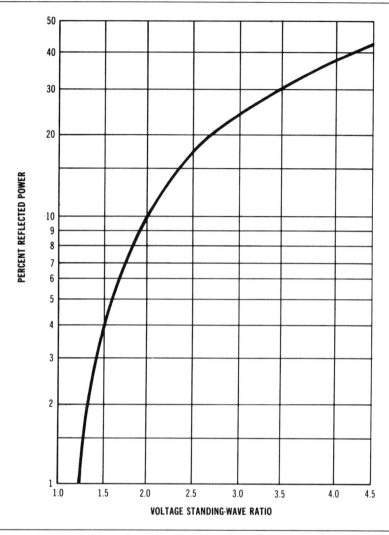

Fig. 7-15. Reflected power versus standing-wave ratio.

7-7. Typical Mobile and Base Antennas

Three basic antenna types designed mainly for mobile use are shown in Fig. 7-16. Fig. 7-16A is a coaxial type that can be employed where there is an inadequate ground plane such as a large metallic surface or radials. The antenna is center fed with the upper quarter-wave section being a continuation of the inner conductor of the coaxial transmission line. The outer conductor of the coaxial line attaches to the quarter-wavelength sleeve that is immediately beneath the center insulator. This acts as a transformer and isolating section that permits an effective coaxial feed system up through the center of the sleeve. The section of tubing beneath the coaxial sleeve is a support mast for the antenna. Mounting options would be a snap-on bumper mount, vehicular side mount, or a trunk/body mount.

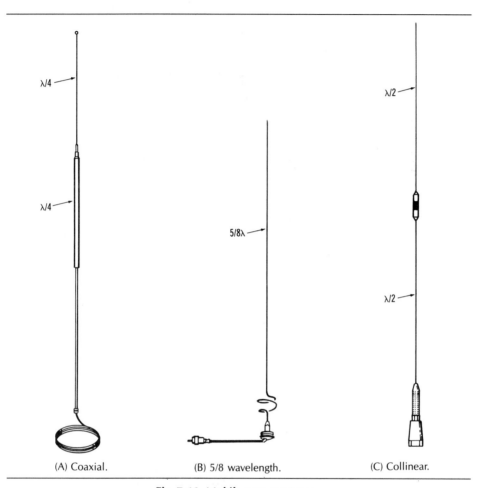

(A) Coaxial.   (B) 5/8 wavelength.   (C) Collinear.

Fig. 7-16. Mobile antenna types.

Fig. 7-16B is a 5/8-wavelength antenna which has a good low vertical angle of radiation. As a result the gain of the antenna is 2.5 dB at those angles which best favor vehicular radiocommunications. The coil at the bottom of the antenna serves as a combination base loading coil and spring. Thus an appropriate match can be made to a 50-ohm coaxial line. The coil provides loading and proper matching.

Fig. 7-16C is a collinear gain antenna comprised of two half-wave sections. Gain is 5.2 dB. There is a loading coil at the base of the antenna which permits a properly matched end-fed array. A phasing coil is located at the center and permits the proper in-phase feed of the two collinear elements.

Base station antenna types are shown in Fig. 7-17. The driven element is a vertical folded dipole. The presence of the mounting mast in Fig. 7-17A provides some directivity in the direction away from the mast toward the driven element. Thus the antenna can be mounted in such a manner that a somewhat stronger signal is radiated in some favored direction. If an additional director rod is included as in Fig. 7-17B, there will be additional antenna gain in a favored direction.

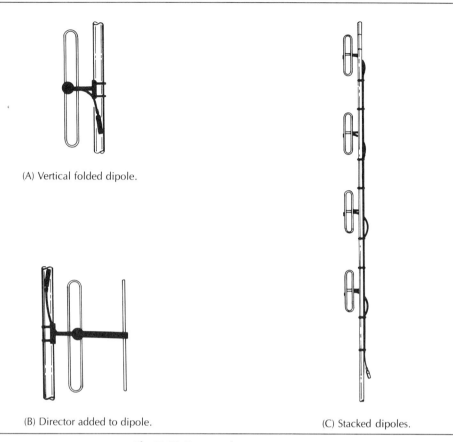

(A) Vertical folded dipole.

(B) Director added to dipole.   (C) Stacked dipoles.

Fig. 7-17. Base station antenna types.

Additional antenna gain can be obtained by stacking a group of driven elements on the mast as shown in Fig. 7-17C. A gain of 9 dB is possible when each of the driven elements is mounted one beneath the other. A directional pattern results. If an omnidirectional pattern is desired, the elements can be staggered and not all facing the same direction. Possible gain is 6 dB.

Each of the elements is fed with a separate 50-ohm line. These four feedlines are cut to the proper length to provide equal power and in-phase energy excitation of the elements. The four lines are combined in a four-way matching assembly.

Antenna-mounting guidance recommended for a remotely controlled base station is given in Fig. 7-18. Proper construction and grounding is important in terms of lightning protection. Note that a lightning rod extends above the mast and it is suggested that the top of the antenna support be positioned below the top of the tower. To obtain a low resistance to ground, a No. 4 (or larger) copper conductor, extends from the top of the mast down through the center of the tower. This copper conductor serves as an appropriate ground for the transmission line, bandpass cavity, and base station cabinet.

Guy wires, if used, are also bonded to the mast and when necessary the individual guys are broken up with insulators to minimize their influence on the loading and pattern characteristics of the antenna. A bandpass cavity blocks off-frequency signals from being radiated by the transmitter and also prevents off-frequency signals that are picked up from the antenna system from being supplied to the base station receiver. Surge suppressors are used across both the tower and phone line inputs to the base station.

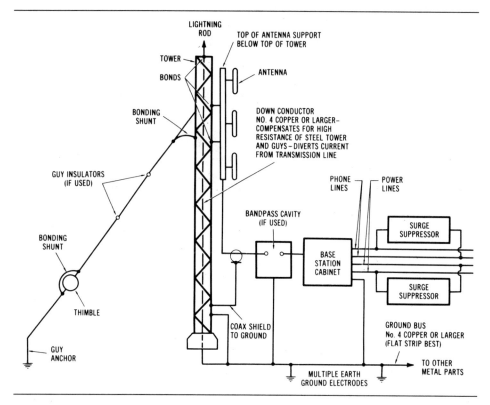

Fig. 7-18. Antenna system recommendations.

7-8. 800-MHz Antennas

In the 800-MHz band gain antennas can be made physically short because of the very short wavelength. In this frequency spectrum, for example, one-quarter wavelength corresponds to a physical length of only 3.5 inches. One of the most common antennas is the vertical collinear, the basics of which are shown in Fig. 7-19. The vertical collinear has gain accompanied with an omnidirectional horizontal radiation pattern and a low-angle vertical radiation pattern. To obtain such a pattern the half-wavelength segments must be fed in phase.

Fig. 7-19A is not a collinear antenna. It is true that it comprises two half-wavelength segments. However, note the voltage polarity indicates that the two segments are out of phase. Fig. 7-19B shows how the two half-wave segments can be brought into phase. A quarter-wave stub is attached at the center. A quarter-wave stub has a high impedance at its open end acting as a parallel resonant circuit. The opposite ends of a parallel-resonant circuit are out of phase, setting up the collinear in-phase relationship of Fig. 7-19B. At VHF and UHF frequencies a similar effect can be accomplished using a small wide-spaced coil as shown in Fig. 7-19C. This coil along with its distributed capacitance performs the same function as the quarter-wave stub.

Basic antennas for the 800-MHz region are illustrated in Fig. 7-20. The bottom section of the antenna in Fig. 7-20A is simply a quarter-wave vertical antenna. When mounted on an auto, the metal roof, hood, or side panel acts as the ground segment.

Atop of the quarter-wave segment is a small coil and then a full half-wavelength segment of antenna rod.

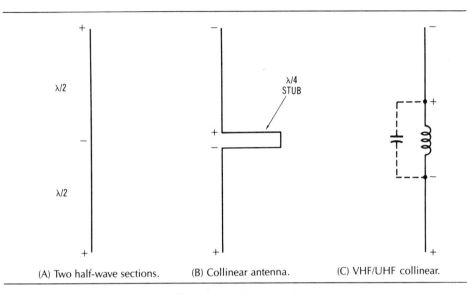

(A) Two half-wave sections.   (B) Collinear antenna.   (C) VHF/UHF collinear.

Fig. 7-19. Collinear basics.

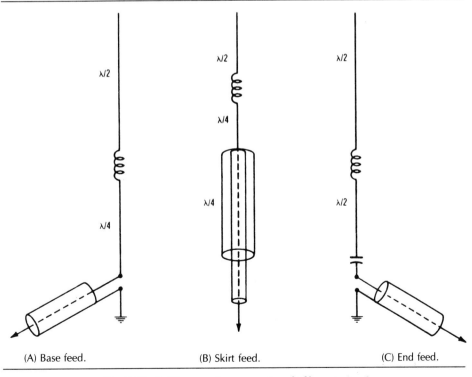

(A) Base feed.   (B) Skirt feed.   (C) End feed.

Fig. 7-20. Collinear antennas — two half waves in phase.

Fig. 7-20B is similar to Fig. 7-20A with the exception that the feed method includes a quarter-wave skirt for optimum matching at the center of the bottom half-wavelength segment. Fig. 7-20C shows an end-fed arrangement. It is said to be high-impedance or voltage fed from the transmission line.

Two popular collinear antennas for trunked and cellular band operation are shown in the photographs of Fig. 7-21. The antenna in Fig. 7-21A has a gain of 3 dB and consists of a 5/8-wavelength upper segment and quarter-wavelength lower segment separated by an air-wound phasing coil. It is mounted on the roof of an auto.

(A) Roof mounted.	(B) Windshield mounted.

Courtesy Antenna Specialists, Inc.

Fig. 7-21. Collinear antennas.

Fig. 7-21B shows an unusual collinear antenna because it is mounted on-glass. The antenna attaches at the top of the windshield. In such an arrangement it is unnecessary to drill a hole anywhere in the car to mount the antenna. At these ultrahigh frequencies the windshield glass itself acts as a capacitor to couple the radio-frequency energy efficiently between the antenna and a coaxial cable attached inside of the glass. An appropriate coupler box mounted on the inner surface of the wind-shield in proximity to the antenna mount couples the radiator element to the transceiver and provides a 50-ohm impedance match. In effect one end of the bottom half-wavelength segment is capacitively end fed. It is possible to use the same mount at the top of the rear window as well.

Even longer collinear antennas can be used at the base station to obtain a higher gain. Several collinear segments can be used instead of just two. Furthermore, reflectors can be incorporated as shown in Fig. 7-22. As a result more gain and a good

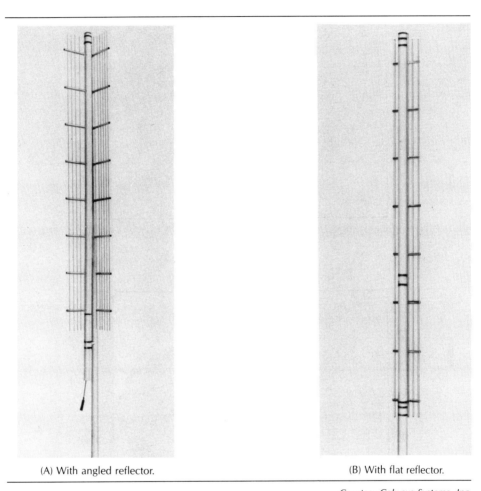

(A) With angled reflector.   (B) With flat reflector.

Courtesy Celwave Systems, Inc.

Fig. 7-22. Collinear unidirectional antennas.

directional pattern can be obtained. The antenna in Fig. 7-22A has a gain of 17 dB and the one in Fig. 7-22B has a gain of 10.5 dB over a frequency range between 806 and 896 MHz. Their directional patterns are shown in Fig. 7-23. The directional pattern is chosen to be most suitable for your radio service. If the pattern must be omnidirectional, a collinear antenna without a reflector should be chosen. The overall length of the antennas in Fig. 7-22 is approximately 8 feet.

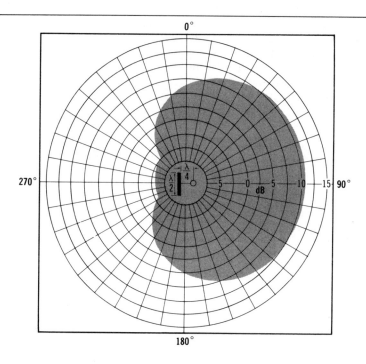

(A) Pattern for antenna of Fig. 7-22A.

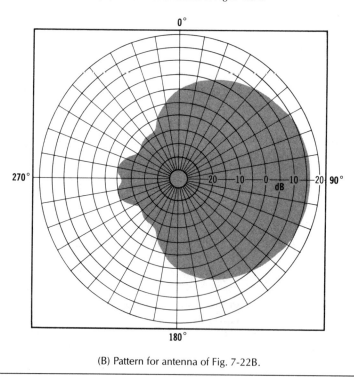

(B) Pattern for antenna of Fig. 7-22B.

Fig. 7-23. Horizontal radiation patterns.

The antenna of Fig. 7-24A is known as a corner reflector. It consists of a dipole and a reflector that concentrates the energy in the sharp directional pattern of Fig. 7-24B.

The gain of this antenna is 9 dB although each reflector plate is only 13 inches by 16 inches. Highly directional antennas of this type can be used to radiate signals between a fixed base station and the repeater.

(A) Antenna.

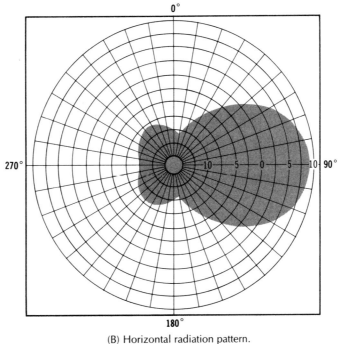

(B) Horizontal radiation pattern.

Fig. 7-24. Corner reflector antenna.

7-9. Radio Interference and Electronic Equipment

In the last two decades the growth of the two-way radio services has been phenomenal. Millions of transmitters are in operation. The Citizens Band Radio Service in particular has brought the radio transmitter into home and car, business, and truck. Significantly, transmitters have been brought in close proximity to home entertainment devices such as television receivers, radios, audio amplifiers, tape recorders, electronic organs, etc. Radio interference problems have become more prevalent due to the very nearness of transmitter and home electronic equipment.

The FCC has technical standards for transmitters and compliance is mandatory. Despite this fact, the very closeness of a source of radiation to electronic equipment means the interference problem can prevail. The characteristics and performance of home electronic devices, other than transmitters, do not come under the jurisdiction of the FCC. Providing thorough shielding for such devices is also a cost consideration. Nevertheless many radio interference problems can be eliminated or reduced. The transmitter and its antenna system must be properly installed and adjusted. The same applies to the home electronic equipment. The use of simple low-cost filters, capacitors, and other components (most connected externally) can do much to reduce interference. Some examples follow.

Sources of radiation from a transmitter and/or antenna are the desired signal; undesired harmonics of the transmitted signal; and undesired spurious radiation from multipliers, oscillators, and mixers. Small as these components might be, they can cause problems because of their very nearness to other electronic equipment. The undesired harmonics and spurious components are kept at very low levels by design and transmitter shielding. They must be kept below levels specified in the FCC technical standards for the particular radio service.

However, more ideal suppression of undesired components is attained with proper grounding and proper antenna match. Use a good earth ground for the transmitter via a large diameter wire or copper strap. This precaution minimizes radiation from the transmitter proper.

The typical transmitting antenna is mounted high and clear, and usually some distance away from the home electronic equipment. However, the transmission line itself originates at the transmitter and can be very near to television receivers, radios, etc. Therefore it is important to keep the line from radiating a strong signal by holding down the standing-wave ratio. Install the antenna system wisely and properly and keep the SWR to a very minimum.

The harmonic output of a CB transmitter can be troublesome. The second harmonic of the 27-MHz output of a CB transmitter falls on channel 2 of the television band. Third harmonic components fall on channels 5 and 6. To prevent this type of interference, it is important to keep the harmonic output of the transmitter low and, at the same time, reduce the pickup of the radio interference by the television receiver. Quite often the installation of a low-pass filter (Fig. 7-25) at the output of the CB transmitter will solve the problem. These filters are low cost and connect between the antenna transmission line and the transmitter. They have no adverse influence on the operation of the CB transmitter. However, they do offer high attenuation on frequencies above the 27-MHz band. Consequently the harmonics are suppressed and do not reach the transmission line and the antenna system.

On occasion, harmonic and other spurious frequency components feed into the power line. An appropriate filter can be connected in the power line circuit (Fig. 7-25). Such a radio-frequency filter can also be added to the power line circuit of the receiver or other home electronic equipment that is troubled with radio interference.

Low-cost high-pass filters are available for receivers. These connect between the transmission line and the television receiver (Fig. 7-26). They are effective in blocking the fundamental frequency of a CB or other transmitter or any other low-frequency radio-frequency interference. At the same time there is little or no attenuation of the desired television signal components.

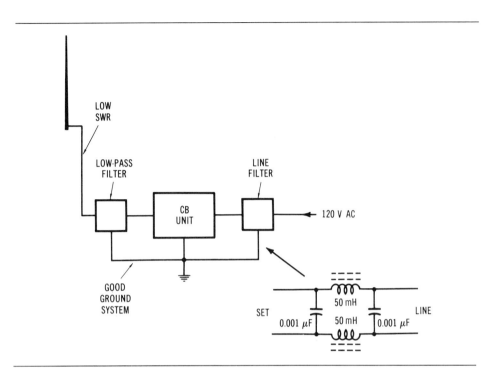

Fig. 7-25. Reduction of undesired radiation at transmitter.

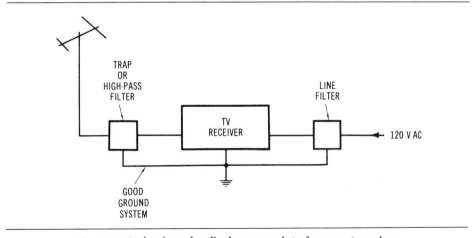

Fig. 7-26. Reduction of radio-frequency interference at receiver.

Resonant traps are also useful in blocking interference when the frequency of that interference is known. These are connected across or in series with sensitive inputs of a television receiver, radio, or audio amplifier (Fig. 7-27). A parallel-resonant circuit is placed in series with the signal path, while a series-resonant circuit is connected directly across the input of the device. An adjustable trimmer capacitor can be used to tune the resonant circuit for maximum rejection of the undesired signal.

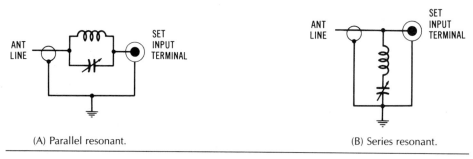

(A) Parallel resonant.　　　　　　　　　　　　(B) Series resonant.

Fig. 7-27. Use of resonant traps.

Radio-frequency signals can cause trouble even in an audio system. The RF energy can be rectified by any such nonlinear device as a transistor, integrated circuit, diode, etc. Proper grounding of transmitter as well as the electronic device being interfered with is important. Use large-diameter and as short as possible grounding leads. Power line filters can be of help.

In the case of rectification in an audio amplifier, a series inductor or a shunt capacitor can be of help in blocking the radio-frequency interference from a sensitive input (Fig. 7-28). A 0.001-microfarad capacitor would be a typical value. The value of the radio-frequency choke depends on the frequency of the interference. Typical values would be 1.5 millihenry up to 20 MHz, 500 microhenry for a range of frequencies between 20 and 50 MHz, and a value of 100 microhenry for a frequency range between 50 and 500 MHz.

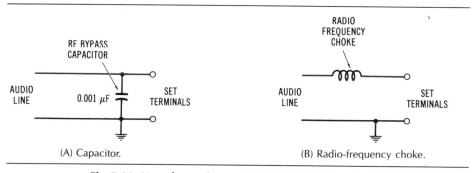

(A) Capacitor.　　　　　　　　　　　　(B) Radio-frequency choke.

Fig. 7-28. Use of capacitor or RFC to block RF interference.

7-10. Intermodulation Interference

Intermodulation interference has become a significant problem in areas crowded with two-way radio systems. These interference components can be generated by the transmitter or the receiver. Intermodulation components are generated when two or more signals are applied to a nonlinear device. These components are on differing frequencies and can cause interference with reception on other channels. If the interference is comparable to or greater than the desired signal, the on-channel signal is interfered with severely. If the interference is weaker than the desired signal, the interference will only be heard when the desired signal is not present.

When two or more transmitters are in close proximity to each other, there is coupling between each transmitter and the others, usually by way of the antenna system. Radiation from each transmitter enters the final amplifier and transmission system of the others. Intermodulation products are formed, and those falling within the bandpass of the final amplifier and its output are radiated. This radiation can be on channels other than those to which the transmitters have been assigned.

Intermodulation products can also be formed at the receiver. Two or more strong off-channel signals may drive the RF amplifier into nonlinear operation or even intermodulate in the first mixer. These components can interfere with an incoming desired signal or can be heard in the output when no signal is arriving on the operating channel.

The example of Fig. 7-29 can be used to demonstrate the influence of inter-modulation products. Normal operation exists between transmitter C and the receiver. Both are tuned to the desired channel of 160.35 MHz. Transmitters A and B are in close proximity to each other and transmit on the frequency assignments indicated. Even though their transmit frequencies are not the same as that of transmitter C, they can cause interference at the receiver if they generate intermodulation components.

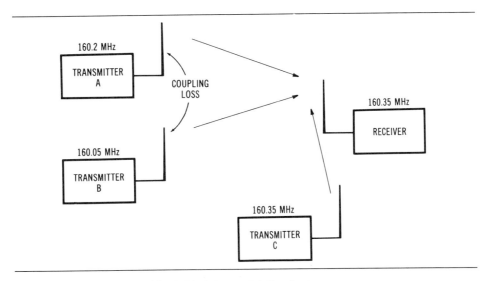

Fig. 7-29. Intermodulation basics.

Let us assume that there is a low coupling loss between the two transmitters. As a result some of the output from transmitter B enters the power output stage and antenna system of transmitter A. Likewise, some of the output of transmitter A enters transmitter B. Intermodulation components are generated in both transmitters. The difference frequency between the two transmitters is 0.150 MHz (160.200 − 160.050). This difference frequency subtracted from the carrier frequency of transmitter B produces an intermodulation frequency component of 159.900 MHz. This is radiated along with the desired 160.05-MHz signal whenever the two transmitters are operating simultaneously.

The difference frequency added to the frequency of transmitter A produces an output at 160.350 MHz. This component is transmitted along with the 160.2 MHz whenever the two transmitters are operating simultaneously. However, it should be noted that 160.35 MHz is the same frequency as transmitter C and is also the frequency to which the receiver is tuned. Thus it can be picked up by the receiving antenna and cause interference on the channel being used by transmitter C and the receiver.

It is important, if intermodulation components are to be eliminated, that there must be no significant coupling (high-coupling loss) between the two transmitters in close proximity to each other. Thus, in the installation of transmitters that are near to each other, every attempt must be made to obtain as high as possible a coupling loss between the transmitters and antenna systems.

Intermodulation components can also be generated at the receiver. Assume that there is no exchange of signals between transmitters A and B. Therefore the inter-modulation components are not generated. However, the transmit frequencies of 160.05 and 160.02 MHz are transmitted and can possibly enter the receiver. If the two signals arrive simultaneously and reach the receiver in such strength that they can produce nonlinear operation of the receiver RF amplifier or reach the first mixer, they will interact with each other and generate the very same intermodulation frequency components. Thus, there will be the same interference with the desired 160.35-MHz signal from transmitter C. This time the interference is the result of intermodulation products being formed at the receiver. This receiver intermodulation distortion can occur even though transmitters A and B are separated a great distance. If A and B come on the air simultaneously and are able to get into the receiver, the receiver will generate the intermodulation components.

It must be stressed that a variety of intermodulation frequency components can be generated. Most significant are the odd-order products. The even-order products (second, fourth, etc.) are so far removed in frequency that interfering effects do not occur. Most significant are the third- and fifth-order products. Although higher-order products can be generated, they are usually of insignificant level.

The equations for the third- and fifth-order intermodulation products can be set down. Assume that A is the transmit frequency of transmitter A and B is the transmit frequency of transmitter B:

- Second order = $2A - B = 320.4 - 160.05 = 160.35$ MHz.
- Second order = $2B - A = 320.1 - 160.2 = 159.9$ MHz.
- Third order = $3A - 2B = 480.6 - 320.1 = 160.5$ MHz.
- Third order = $3B - 2A = 480.15 - 320.4 = 159.75$ MHz.

Of course, if there are three or more transmitters in close proximity to each other, there will be additional third- and fifth-order intermodulation products generated.

The relationships among the two carrier frequencies and the intermodulation products are shown in Fig. 7-30. Note that they are all separated from each other by 0.15 MHz, which is the difference frequency between the carrier frequencies of the two transmitters. In other words the distortion products appear periodically above and below the frequencies of transmitter A and transmitter B.

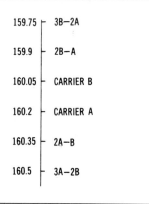

159.75	3B−2A
159.9	2B−A
160.05	CARRIER B
160.2	CARRIER A
160.35	2A−B
160.5	3A−2B

Fig. 7-30. Carriers and frequency location of third- and fifth-order intermodulation products.

7-11. Intermodulation Reduction

Transmitter intermodulation is reduced by increasing the coupling loss among transmitters. Refer to Fig. 7-31. A major step that can be taken is to separate the antenna systems as far as is practicable. The influence of antenna spacing is shown in Fig. 7-32. For example, if two antennas are vertically separated by 30 feet on the 160-MHz band, there is an isolation of 55 dB. A horizontal separation of the same 30 feet results in an isolation of something more than 30 dB. This indicates that you can obtain a higher coupling loss by separating the antennas vertically rather than horizontally.

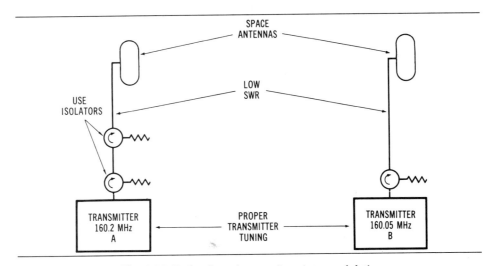

Fig. 7-31. Reduction of transmitter intermodulation.

Isolators are often used to increase the coupling loss as shown in Fig. 7-31. An isolator is usually a ferrite device that has a low impedance for the transfer of signal in one direction, but an exceedingly high opposition to the transfer of signal in the opposite direction. Consequently the cross-coupling of frequencies is reduced without impeding the desired transmit signal on its way along the transmission line to the radiating antenna. Isolators usually include a terminating resistor across which the energy traveling in the wrong direction is dissipated. Thus the two isolators in the transmission-line system of transmitter A in Fig. 7-31 will allow a frequency of 160.2 MHz to reach the antenna, while the coupling component of transmitter B on 160.05 MHz will not pass through the two isolators to transmitter A. In a similar manner the isolator in the antenna system of transmitter B will block any pickup of transmitter A signal and keep it from reaching transmitter B.

Intermodulation components can be reduced by proper tuning of both transmitters and antenna systems. Poor tuning and bad joints usually result in high SWR readings. Thus matching and tuning are very important in maintaining a low SWR on the transmission lines.

The generation of intermodulation products in the receiver is pretty much a matter of receiver design. Suppression filters connected between the antenna system and the receiver are a definite aid in blocking out those frequencies that are producing intermodulation components in the receiver. To set up such a filter arrangement, it is of course necessary to first determine the incoming frequencies that are causing the

308

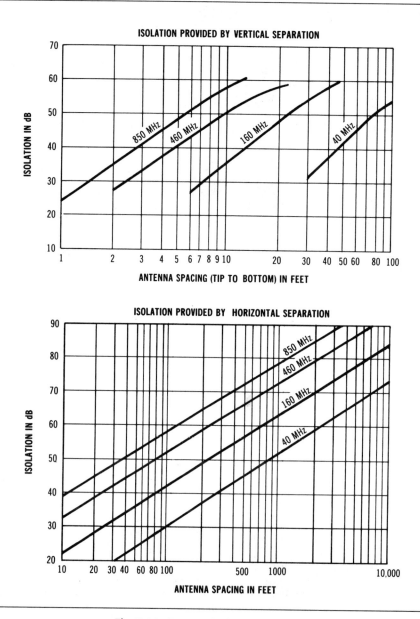

Fig. 7-32. Antenna isolation curves.

receiver to generate intermodulation components. For example, two filters ahead of the receiver of Fig. 7-29, which are tuned to 160.05 MHz, would reduce the inter-modulation components generated by the receiver. Of course, the filters must be tuned shaply and must not result in any serious attenution of the desired 160.35-MHz incoming signal.

In addition to isolator/circulator combinations, there are a variety of components that can be used to reduce interference at shared radio sites and shared repeater installations, conventional and trunked. In many instances an isolator attached to the output of a transmitter should also have a harmonic filter between it and the antenna to prevent the radiation of undesired harmonics. Three devices used extensively in shared repeater systems are transmitter combiners, receiver multicouplers, and duplexers. The transmitter combiners combine the outputs of the various transmitters and supply them to a single antenna. Receiver multicouplers permit a single receive antenna to supply signals to the various receivers of a shared installation. Usually a multicoupler includes a wideband amplifier to compensate for signal losses in the division process.

Duplexers are used to maintain a high level of transmitter/receiver isolation particularly at frequencies between, and adjacent to, the operating frequencies. These devices must be tuned according to the frequency assignments and exact frequencies must be specified in ordering duplexers. Smaller duplexers are also available for mobile installations to reduce interference when they are operated in a very active two-way radio area.

There are various types of resonators or resonant cavities that are of help at multitransmitter locations and in busy two-way radio areas. Three common types are bandpass, pass reject, and notch filters. Again, in ordering filters exact frequencies must be specified to match the interference problems of the site and area. Some are adjustable in terms of insertion loss and selectivity. Most are quarter-wave resonant cavities. Two or more can be used to improve selectivity. Similar cavities are available for use in receiver multicoupling systems in high radio-frequency density environ-

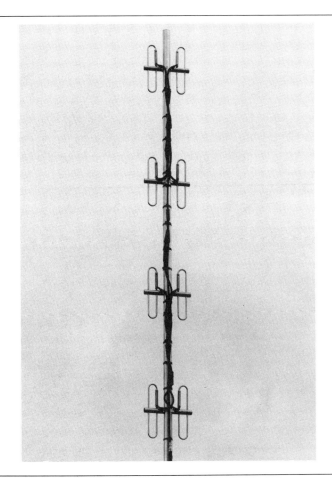

Courtesy Cushcraft Corp.

Fig. 7-33. Omnidirectional base station antenna.

ments. They can be purchased in four, six, or eight cavity models according to the selectivity or rejection that is required. Coaxial, stripline, and helical resonators are used.

The notch cavities are designed to reject one narrow band of frequencies while passing all others in the operating band. These can be useful at transmitter sites because of their ability to cope with a specific interferring frequency. A pass-reject cavity passes one frequency and rejects another on either side of their frequency passband. Thus a close-in frequency of interference can be notched out on the troublesome side of a bandpass. It is a useful filter in duplex operations.

Two base station antennas for 450-MHz operation are shown in Figs. 7-33 and 7-34. The vertically stacked folded-dipole pairs in Fig. 7-33 produce an omnidirectional horizontal pattern and a sharp vertical pattern at low angles. The operating range extends between 450–470 MHz and the gain is 6.8 dB. The overall height of the array is 9.5 feet. The sleeve-like feed arrangement acts as an impedance transformer to present an antenna resistance of 50 ohms despite the folded dipole configuration.

A high-gain directional antenna for a 450-MHz base station is shown in Fig. 7-34. This is a 6-element Yagi with a forward gain of 10 dB. Its front-to-back ratio is 18 dB, indicating how well it concentrates the radio-frequency energy in the desired direction. At the same time there is less pickup from the back which may be the direction of a possible source of interference. The vertical mounting of the Yagi results in a signal with vertical polarization corresponding to the polarization of the mobile antennas. Such an antenna can also be used at both ends of a base station to repeater air link.

Courtesy Cushcraft Corp.

Fig. 7-34. Directional base station antenna.

8

Landmobile Radio

The landmobile two-way radio bands are busy segments of the radio spectrum. Tune in almost any time and you will hear action. The most active bands are 50, 150, and 450 MHz with increasing operations above 800 MHz. Many transceiver models are available. Some typical circuits are described in this chapter.

As for most electronic equipment, improper adjustment results in faulty or less efficient operation. Circuits do drift, or their operating characteristics change with shifts in the supply voltage. Faulty connections can cause problems in radio frequency and digital circuits. Sometimes when components must be replaced, their characteristics differ from those used originally. Environmental changes such as temperature or humidity can also alter operating conditions over a period of time.

The foregoing variables require that a transceiver be retuned periodically if peak performance is to be maintained. Base station and mobile units must occasionally be brought into the shop and checked out in accordance with a definite preventive-maintenance schedule. To do so, it is important that you have a knowledge of circuits and systems. Some typical circuits along with test and tune-up procedures are presented in this chapter. A sound bit of advice for any technician is to make certain you study the maintenance manual in detail for the particular equipment to which you are assigned.

8-1. 450-MHz Transceiver Circuitry

The GE transceiver shown in Fig. 8-1 will be used as an opening example. Circuit detail, alignment procedures, and other information are treated at length. Additional circuit and system discussions follow this detailed presentation. The transmitter power output is 25 watts and receiver 12-dB Sinad sensitivity is 0.25 microvolt. Aligned and tuned properly it will operate over a 25-MHz span of frequencies on the 450-MHz band. The transmit and receive frequencies over this range can be programmed for operation on 16 individual channels. Furthermore, erasures can be made by the user that will permit frequency changes to be made. Frequencies are controlled by a synthesizer and no frequency-control crystals are required.

Fig. 8-1. 450-MHz mobile radio.

Courtesy General Electric Co.,
Mobile Communications Div.

The maximum voice deviation is ± 3.75 kHz. An additional deviation of ± 0.75 kHz is assigned to channel-guard modulation. Channel-guard circuits activate the receiver audio output of the transceiver only when that particular unit is being called. As a result, the operator is not annoyed by transmissions that are not intended for him. The channel-guard activity is under control of a subtone audio frequency conveyed by the received signal. When your particular subtone is received, the channel-guard circuit will turn on the audio output of your receiver and your message can be heard. Channel-guard activity can also be under the control of a received digital code that performs the same operation. If desired, the channel-guard activity can be turned off. An arrangement can be installed that will deactivate channel guard whenever the microphone is removed from its hook.

The receiver also includes a squelch system which can be service preset in such a manner that annoying background noises are reduced and receiver output activated only when a reasonably strong signal is received. The frequency response of transmitter and receiver is such that its curve is within + 1 dB to − 3 dB of a standard 6-dB-per-octave preemphasisis and deemphasis between 300 and 3,000 Hz.

An optional scan unit is also available. In this arrangement automatic scanning of any or all of the 16 available channels can be programmed. Thus, on a routine basis, the unit will change frequency to allow momentary listening to programmed channels according to an established schedule. Two priority capabilities are provided. Priority one locks in a particularly important channel whenever a signal is present. In fact, this channel is scanned every half second. Priority two establishes a lock on a second chosen channel, except when there is a signal present on the priority one channel. Priority two scan is accomplished every two seconds. The scan activity can be turned on and off by the operator.

8-1-1. Block Analysis

Internally the mobile radio consists of two circuit boards — one for the transmitter and receiver and the other for the synthesizer and interconnect. The boards plug into each other, eliminating the need for interconnecting wires. All external connectors, controls, and indicators are mounted directly on the two boards. The only wires used in the radio are the plug-in leads for the panel-mounted speaker.

The speaker is to the right on the front panel. The monitor and mode buttons, along with volume control and on-off switch, are on the left. The channel selector push button and the channel-number LED indicator are at the top center. There are also transmitter-on and busy-channel indicator lights. Power on is indicated when the channel-number LED comes on.

Functional block diagrams of the two boards are given in Figs. 8-2 and 8-3. The injection voltages for the transmitter (top left) and the receiver (left center) in Fig. 8-2, originate from the synthesizer (U101) which is located at the center of Fig. 8-3. These transmit and receive injection voltages are taken off at the transmit/receive switch on the far right of Fig. 8-3. You can follow the path of the signal from the microphone preamplifier block at the bottom center of Fig. 8-3 through the audio processor and audio modulator to the frequency modulated VCO. A buffer follows the VCO and then with the T/R switch on transmit, a frequency-modulated signal in the 150-MHz range is applied to the transmitter input RF amplifier at the top left of Fig. 8-2. A tripler stage multiplies the signal to the 450-MHz band. A succession of RF amplifiers then build up the signal to the nominal 25-watt output. A power adjust control is associated with the first power amplifier. This circuit will be discussed in detail later.

In the receive position of the T/R antenna switch (Fig. 8-2), the signal from the antenna is applied to a two-pole filter (L401, L402) at the receiver input. An amplifier (Q401) follows and then a mixer which reduces the incoming frequency to an intermediate frequency of 45 MHz. As mentioned previously the source of the injection voltage for the first mixer is the synthesizer of the other board. This injection signal is applied to the LO buffer (Q351) at the left center of Fig. 8-2. This injection voltage is also in the 150-MHz range and must be tripled before it is applied to the first mixer.

The 45-MHz signal output of the mixer is the difference frequency between the received signal frequency and the injection voltage. After amplification the signal is applied to the second mixer at the lower left in Fig. 8-2 which reduces the frequency to the standard 455-kHz range. The source of the injection voltage for this mixer is a crystal oscillator and frequency-adjust circuit (Y501 and L501). The stages that follow are a quadrature detector, audio buffer, audio deemphasizer, and loudspeaker audio amplifier.

Several additional functional sections should be pointed out. Integrated circuit U501 at the lower left of Fig. 8-2 also includes the receiver squelch system. It segregates and evaluates the noise component in the audio output and develops the necessary DC control voltage to squelch the audio output when there is no signal present. The squelch adjustment is set in such a manner that annoying background noise is cut off; at the same time a practical-level incoming signal can break the squelch so it can be heard at the audio output.

The channel-guard block is to the right of integrated circuit U501. As mentioned previously, this circuit activates the audio output whenever a proper tone or digital signal is present for your receiver. Otherwise, the output remains cut off. Monitor switch S602, which is on the front panel, causes the channel-guard activity to be bypassed when it is depressed. Consequently, it is possible for the operator to listen in on a channel at any time he wishes. Also, a CAS component is derived for the computer-assisted squelch. This turns on a yellow indicator light whenever the channel is in use. You will refer to this block again when the circuits are described in more detail.

Some additional functional sections should be pointed out on the synthesizer/ interconnect board of Fig. 8-3. The synthesizer area is in the center. Some of the key blocks are the frequency dividers, phase detector, prescaler, etc. Under the control of microprocessor U801, the outputs of the necessary transmit injection and receive injection frequencies are generated for the particular channel chosen by the channel-select switch (S1) and the receive mode A/B switch (S601) shown at the left center of Fig. 8-3.

314

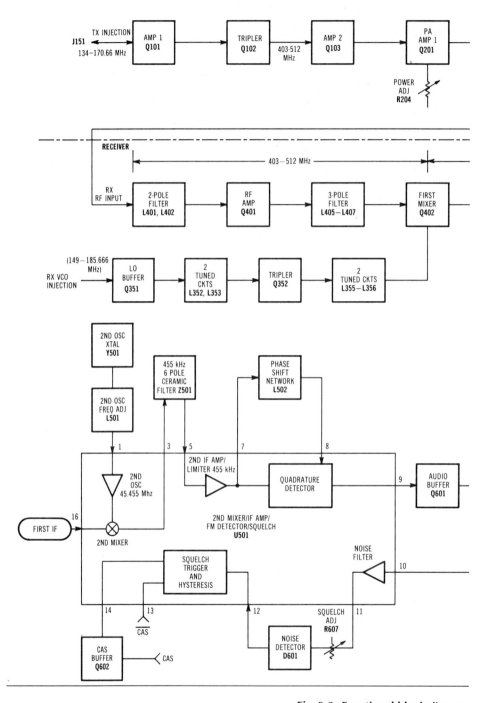

Fig. 8-2. Functional block diagram

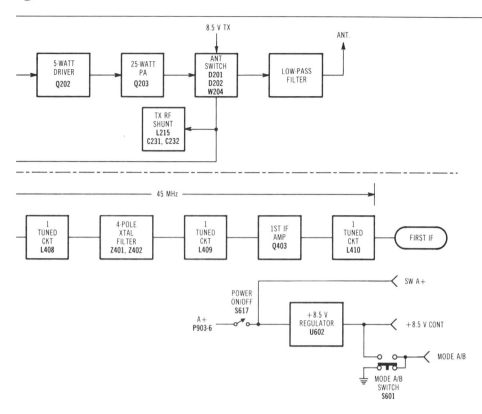

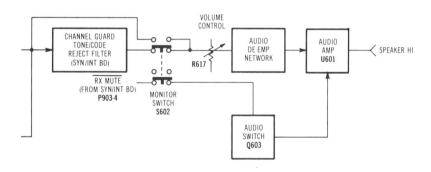

of 450-MHz mobile radio.

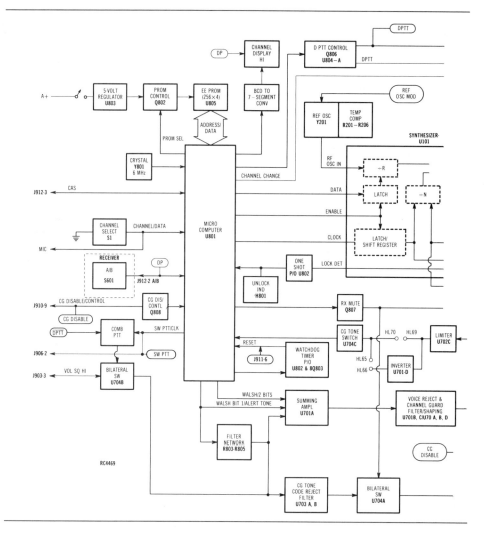

Fig. 8-3. Block diagram of

The memory system for the microprocessor includes the circuits shown at the top left. As mentioned previously, all of the channel data is stored in a PROM. An address and data bus line join the PROM to the microprocessor. Remember the PROM is an eraseable type and can be programmed by the user. This type of PROM was discussed in Chapter 5.

The clock for the microprocessor is a 6-MHz crystal circuit. The microprocessor also supplies the necessary digital signals to a seven-segment LED channel display.

The channel-guard operation is also under control of the microprocessor and through a group of blocks near the bottom center of the illustration the channel-guard modulation is applied to the audio processor (U301) for application to the frequency-modulated signal being formed. Channel-guard information is also stored in the PROM memory. Carrier-on timing is also controlled by the microcomputer system.

The 16 operating channels are selected with the aid of the mode A/B switch and the channel selector (Fig. 8-4). Mode A permits a choice of 8 channels while mode B permits a choice of 8 additional channels to obtain a total of 16. In mode B the decimal point to the right of the LED number turns on. In effect, 16 independent transmit and receive frequencies can be selected. In a typical application the mode A/B switch can

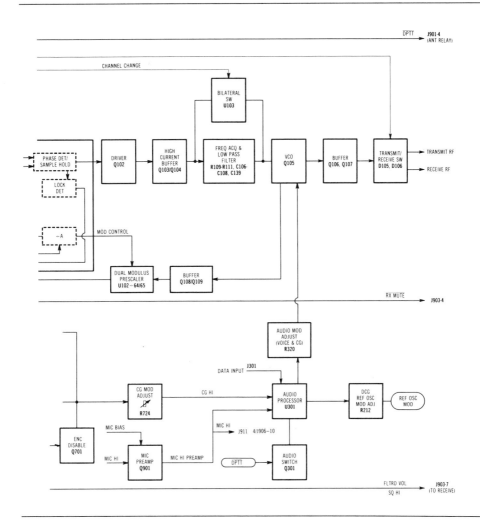

synthesizer/interconnect board.

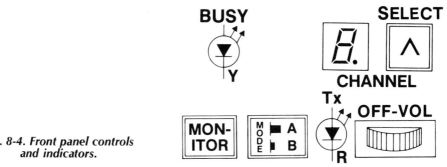

Fig. 8-4. Front panel controls and indicators.

be programmed to provide mobile-to-mobile communications through an intermediate repeater or by direct contact between two mobiles. In this application as an example, Channel 1 mode A may be programmed for the repeater frequency path while Channel 1 mode B is programmed for the mobile-to-mobile path. Either path can be selected on Channel 1 by proper setting of the mode switch. A variety of useful combinations can be established. Also shown in Fig. 8-4 are the channel-busy and transmitter-on indicators, as well as the channel monitor push-in button and on/off volume control. These are the only controls needed by the operator except the handswitch on the microphone.

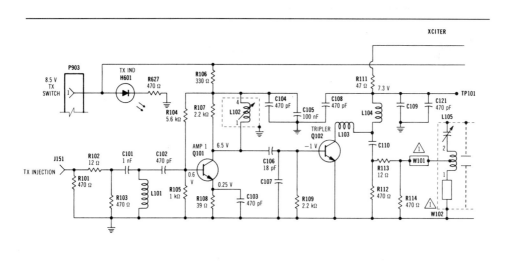

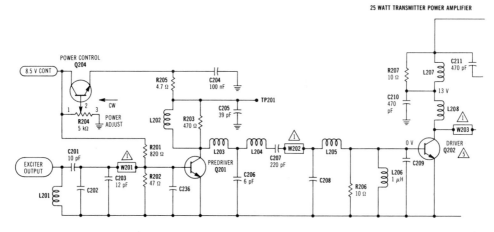

Fig. 8-5. Transmitter schematic

8-1-2. Circuit Descriptions

A schematic of the transmitter is given in Fig. 8-5. At the top is the three-stage exciter consisting of input amplifier, tripler, and follow-up second amplifier. Its output is supplied to the input of the three-stage transmitter power amplifier at the bottom. The input level to the exciter is approximately 5 milliwatts supplied by the voltage-controlled oscillator that is a part of the synthesizer mounted on the second board. The

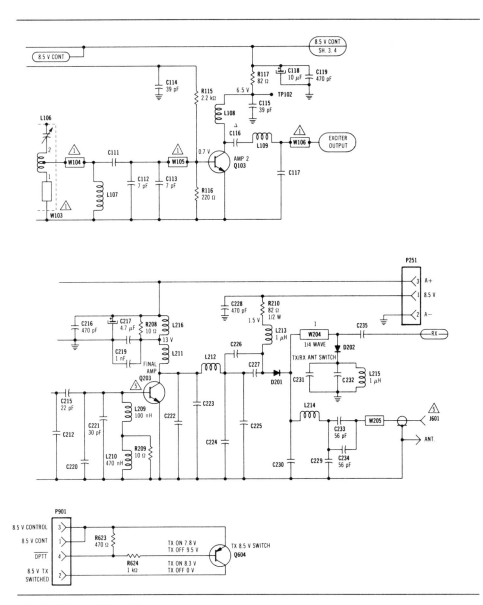

of 450-MHz mobile radio.

output of the exciter is 60 milliwatts minimum, which drives the input to the power amplifier. Transistor Q101 operates as a class-A amplifier. Input resistors R101, R102, and R103 operate as a 2-dB resistive pad that presents a constant load for the VCO output in order to maintain frequency stability when switching between the transmit or receive modes. This input pad is followed by an impedance-matching network composed of C101, C102, and L101 which matches the base of Q101 to 50 ohms.

In the transmit mode of the transceiver, the 8.5 volts applied to the exciter at the top left supplies voltage to the collector circuit of Q101, placing this stage in operation. The same path also applies bias to the base circuit of amplifier 2. This supply-voltage switching turns on the exciter. The removal of this voltage turns off the transmitter. When voltage is applied, the LED at top left comes on. This LED is the transmitter indicator on the front panel. Resistor R627 is a current-limiting device for the LED.

Base bias for Q101 is supplied by resistors R104 and R105. The power source is decoupled by resistor R106 and capacitors C104 and C105. Often two capacitors are used for decoupling to obtain uniform decoupling over a span of frequencies. A wideband output resonant circuit is assured by inductor L102 and resistor R107.

Capacitors C106 and C107 provide matching into the input circuit of the tripler. The tripler obtains supply voltage from the 8.5-volt continuous source. It is not necessary to switch voltage to this circuit when switching between transmit and receive. The group of collector inductor L104, capacitors C108, C109, and C121 and resistor R111 provides decoupling isolation as well as minimizes the loading of the tripler output. Resistor network R112, R113, and R114 provides matching of the tripler output circuit to a helical two-pole filter through a 50-ohm impedance strip W101. There are a number of such 50-ohm segments in the transmitter that can serve as points for monitoring or injecting of signals for locating faults and testing using 50-ohm sources and terminations. The helical filter transfers only the tripled-frequency output of the tripler. Other frequency components are rejected, minimizing the development of spurious signal components and intermodulation distortion.

The helical filter is followed by another impedance-matching circuit for driving the class-B output stage (Q103) of the exciter. The 50-ohm output of the exciter is supplied to the base of the input stage of the 25-watt power amplifier at the bottom left in Fig. 8-5. The signals are matched by the network composed of L201, C201–C203, and 50-ohm microstrip W201.

Helical filters and resonators are popular in modern VHF/UHF transceivers because of their very high values of unloaded Q and exceptional selectivity. In receiver application, such resonant circuits offer protection from images, spurious signals, and intermodulation distortion components. In transmitter application, they are able to select desired harmonics in a frequency-multiplier system and are a big assist in radiating a pure signal on the desired channel. In addition, they are physically compact and sturdy.

Basically the helical resonant circuit is a quarter-wave section of transmission line housed in a circular or square container (Fig. 8-6). The container acts as a shield with a nearly lossless dielectric. The bottom of the helix is connected to the shield. The top of the helix is connected to the shield through a low-loss variable capacitor that can be used for tuning the resonator. Coupling can be made in various ways with inductive loops or capacitive probes. However, the direct tap on the coil, as shown in Fig. 8-6, is the most common.

A two-section or two-pole helical filter can be formed by using two sections in a single shield, setting up a double-tuned transformer arrangement. Input and output connections are made by taps on the input and output coils. Each section has its own tuning capacitor (Fig. 8-7). Coupling from one tuned circuit to the other is by way of an aperture; the location and size of the aperture has a decided influence on the characteristics of the two-pole filter.

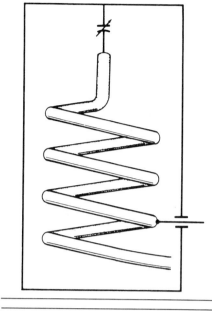

Fig. 8-6. Basic helical resonator circuit.

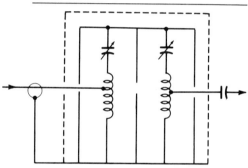

Fig. 8-7. Two-section helical filter.

Sections of stripline serve as excellent resonant circuits and inductors in UHF transmitter amplifier circuits. Striplines are printed-circuit board pads especially shaped to provide a characteristic impedance similar to a transmission line. Electrically they are transmission lines with series inductance and parallel capacitances distributed along the line. The width of the line, the circuit-board thickness, and the dielectric of the circuit-board material are all physical characteristics that determine the impedance of a stripline. Since the circuit board thickness and material cannot be changed readily, the method used to set impedance is to alter the width of the pad. Actually, the wider the pad, the lower the characteristic impedance.

The power output of the transmitter can be adjusted with power-adjust control R204 in the predriver circuit. This adjustment, in association with the transistor connected to its rotor, regulates the supply voltage to the collector, permitting a fine adjustment of transmitter output power.

Additional amplification is supplied by the driver (Q202) which then feeds the signal through the usual impedance-matching network to the final 25-watt power amplifier, Q203. Matching into the antenna system is by way of a pi network composed of inductor L212 and capacitors C222 through C227.

The remaining components have to do with antenna matching and switching. The antenna switching activity is controlled by the 8.5-volt TX voltage that is present when the push-to-talk switch of the microphone is pressed. When this happens, this voltage not only turns on the transmitter but connects the power amplifier output to the

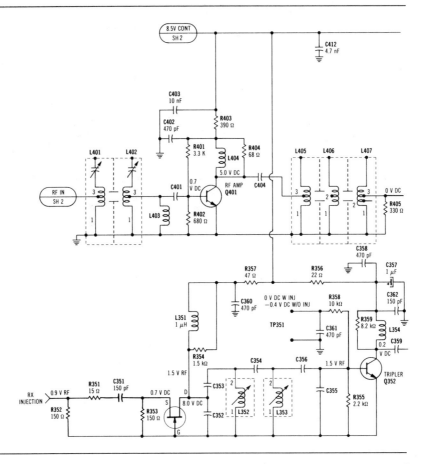

Fig. 8-8. RF and IF sections of

antenna. The antenna is switched electronically by diode 201, quarter-wave strip stub W204, diode D202, C231, C232, and inductor L215. When the transmitter is keyed on by the microphone switch, 8.5-volts TX is applied to D201 through R210 and L213. As a result D201 and D202 are forward biased and pass the power amplifier output directly to the antenna through the low-pass filter composed of inductor L214, as well as capacitors C229 and C230, W205, and C233 and C234. At the same time, the quarter-wave stub segment W204 and forward biased diode D202 present an open circuit to the receiver preventing any possible damage to the receiver input circuit. Actually, a short is placed on the output side of the quarter-wave line segment by the conduction of D202. Consequently, a high impedance is reflected at the opposite end of the line and the transmitter signal cannot enter.

In the receive mode D201 and D202 are turned off by removal of the 8.5-volt TX voltage. As a result the radio-frequency short at the output of the quarter-wave stub is removed and a 50-ohm impedance is present which allows the received signal to pass through a low-pass filter to the receiver.

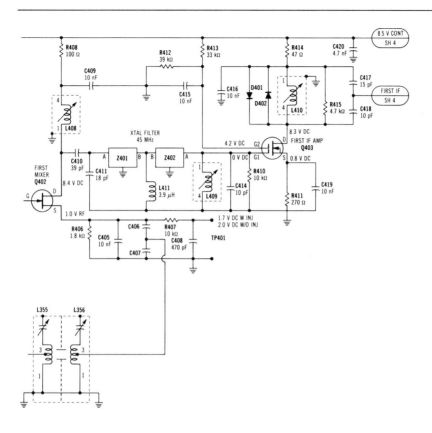

450-MHz mobile radio.

8-1-3. Receiver Circuit

Schematics of the receiver are given in Figs. 8-8 and 8-9. The received signal arrives by way of the low-pass filter and antenna switch described previously, passing through the first two-pole helical resonator, L401 and L402, to the base of the RF amplifier Q401. Three more helical resonators that follow transfer the signal to the gate of the FET mixer Q402. The five helical resonators set the selectivity of the RF section.

An FET mixer provides a high input impedance, a high power gain, and an output relatively free of intermodulation products. The signal is applied to the gate and local oscillator injection is made at the source.

Injection voltage comes from the synthesizer and is applied to J351 at the lower left of Fig. 8-8. The injection power level is approximately 5–15 milliwatts. A resistor-capacitor combination makes the necessary match to the source input of a common-

324

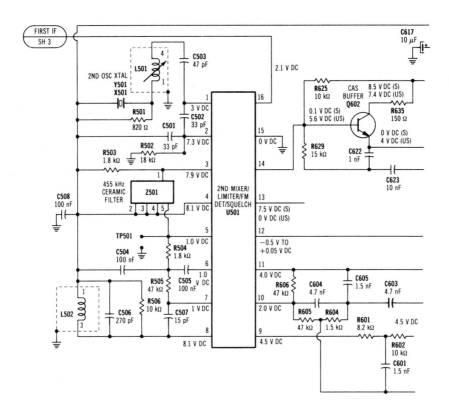

Fig. 8-9. Low IF and audio sections

gate buffer amplifier (Q351). This FET configuration has a low input impedance and a high output impedance. It is a radio-frequency gain stage that does not require neutralization and has the low input impedance for matching. Details on the various configurations of bipolar and FET transistors were given previously in Chapter 3.

An inductor-capacitor filter follows, passing only the injection voltage frequency range between 149–185 MHz. Other frequencies are shunted to ground. Tripler Q352 now multiplies the injection frequency by a factor of three. By so doing the mixer injection frequency range is such that a 45-MHz difference frequency is produced at the output of the mixer. Initially, however, the output passes through a two-section

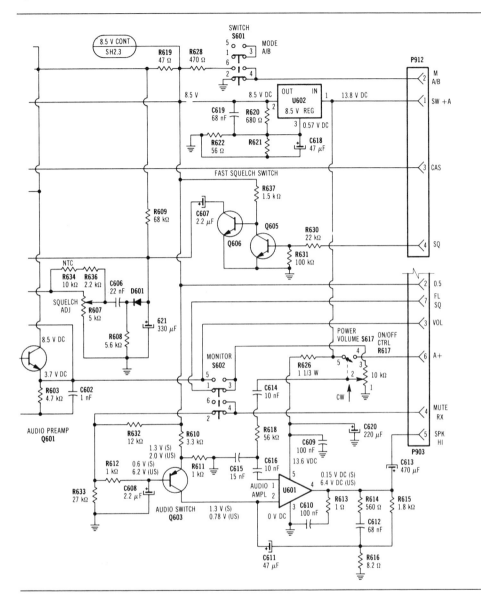

of 450-MHz mobile radio.

helical filter consisting of L355 and L356 which is tuned to pass frequencies in the 447- to 555-MHz range.

The 45-MHz mixer output is coupled from the drain of mixer Q402 through an impedance-matching network and applied to a four-pole crystal filter Z401 and Z402. This filter is highly selective and sets the first intermediate-frequency (IF) selectivity of the receiver. Through another matching network the signal is then applied to the first IF amplifier Q403. This amplifier is a dual-gate MOSFET. This type of transistor was also discussed in detail in Chapter 3. Note that the output of the crystal filter is applied to gate one of the MOSFET. The biasing potential applied to gate 2 determines the stage gain. This amplifier provides approximately 20 dB of IF gain. The drain resonant circuit and an impedance-matching network follow, transferring the signal to the multipurpose integrated circuit U501, pin 16 (Fig. 8-9). Diodes D401 and D402 provide limiting for the 45-MHz IF signal to 1.4 volts peak-to-peak, preventing high-level overload of U501.

The integrated circuit provides four separate functions — second mixer, limiter, FM detector, and squelch. The integrated circuit includes a crystal oscillator that operates on exactly 45.455 MHz. This frequency can be set precisely with inductor L501. After mixing with the incoming first IF signal in the integrated circuit, a precise 455-kHz difference signal is produced, amplified, and supplied at the output (pin 4). A six-pole ceramic filter Z501 follows. This filter provides the second IF selectivity.

The second IF signal is now amplified and limited in the integrated circuit. An inductor L502 shifts one component of this IF signal by 90° and reapplies it to the internal FM detector. The combination of the direct component and the 90° shifted component results in quadrature detection. The comparison of the two components permits a recovery of the original audio modulation. The audio output of the integrated circuit at pin 9 is applied to the base of the audio preamplifier Q601. The emitter output is applied to the monitor keyswitch S602 and channel-guard filter circuit that is a part of the synthesizer board, as well as the squelch circuit input of the integrated circuit U501, (pin 10).

First consider the operation of the squelch circuit. Circuits internal to U501 provide filtering and apply received noise in the 6- to 8-kHz frequency band at pin 11 to potentiometer R607. The output of this squelch-adjust control is connected to the noise detector consisting of R608, C606, C607, C621, and diode D601. As the noise increases in magnitude in a negative direction, negative spikes cause D601 to conduct and charge capacitors C607 and C621 to a DC level proportional to the noise power. This component is applied to the squelch trigger (pin 12) of the integrated circuit.

Squelch activity takes place within the integrated circuit, and, with no received signal, the audio output at pin 9 has been squelched to prevent a high noise level at the output of the speaker. When a signal is received, the circuit is unsquelched because the signal dominates the noise by so much that noise is not present at pin 11. As a result, a normal audio output is present at pin 9 and will be reproduced by the audio amplifier and loudspeaker.

A squelch DC component is also present at pin 14 of the integrated circuit and is applied to the CAS buffer, making available sufficient drive for operating an optional channel busy light or an external relay control. CAS squelch is used in the computer activities associated with the scan option.

The second component from the output of the audio preamp Q601 is applied (via plug P903, pin 3) to the channel-guard filtering section U703 on the synthesizer/interconnect board. If the code is valid, the audio component is returned to the receiver board passing through the monitor switch S602 to the volume control R617. Through capacitor C614 the audio is applied to the audio amplifier output stage U601, and on to the loudspeaker after amplification. Resistor R618 and capacitor C615 serve as the deemphasis network.

The actual switching of the audio output is handled by Q603. The RX mute line, pin 4 of P903 is high when a message is received and accompanied by the correct channel-guard tone or code. As a result, the audio switch Q603 is turned off. This enables the audio amplifier, and there is loudspeaker output. Under this condition, there is a normal bias applied to pin 2 of the operational audio amplifier (U601). When the mute line is low, as it is when no signal is received, the audio switch Q603 turns on. Additional bias current is applied to pin 2 of the audio amplifier and U601 is turned off.

The third component at the output of the audio preamp Q601 is applied to the monitor switch S602. The monitor switch is pressed and the channel-guard activity is bypassed. At the same time the RX mute line to Q603 is high, and the audio amplifier goes into operation. This facility permits the operator to listen in on the channel to determine if it is active or not. If the channel is busy, the operator can then delay his transmissions until communications on the channel have been completed. You may like to review the functional block diagrams (Figs. 8-2 and 8-3) to gain a better understanding of how the functional sections are interconnected between the two transceiver boards.

8-1-4. Audio Processing and the VCO System

The audio processor circuit is shown in Fig. 8-10. A hand-held electret microphone is used. Its output is applied to the base of a common-emitter bipolar transistor stage (Q901). Electret microphone biasing is from the 8.5-volt supply line. Amplified audio is linked through capacitor C312 and resistor R301 to pin 6 of the operational amplifier (U301B) that is a part of the processor proper. Details on operational amplifiers are given in Chapter 3.

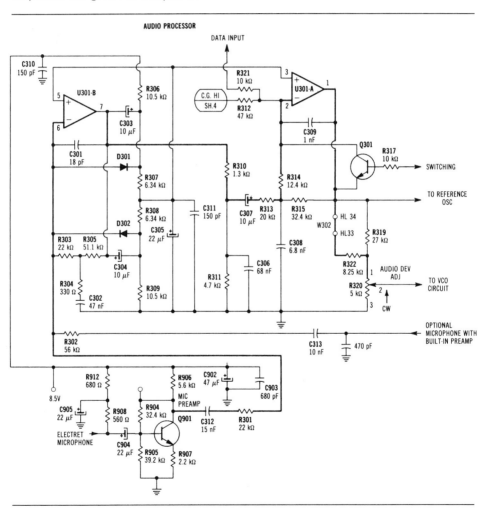

Fig. 8-10. Audio processor section of 450-MHz mobile radio.

The operational amplifier provides a gain of 24 dB. It is also powered by the 8.5-volt source. However, there are a series of voltage divider resistors R306 through

R309. At the junction of resistor R307 and R308, there is a potential of 4.25 volts, which acts as the operating reference point for the operational amplifiers. Capacitor C305 stabilizes this voltage providing an AC ground at the junction point.

When the input audio signal from the microphone preamp is such that the output present at pin 7 of U301B does not exceed 4 volts, the amplifier provides a nominal 20-dB gain. If the audio signal exceeds 4 volts, the peak-to-peak diodes D301 and D302 conduct, reducing the amplifier gain. Consequently, the audio amplitude is limited at 5 volts peak to peak, and, within reason, the operator cannot speak too loudly into the microphone. This limiting, of course, prevents over deviation of the transmitter. Resistors R303, R304, R305, and capacitor C302 form a preemphasis network that improves the signal-to-noise ratio of an FM system.

A major advantage of FM transmission is its ability to reject the amplitude-varying noise and interference components. However, an FM system is not completely noise free because there are some FM noise components to contend with. The fact that such interference has less effect at low modulating frequencies than at higher ones is characteristic of the FM system. An improved signal-to-noise ratio is obtained when the FM deviation is made greater for higher-frequency components than for lower ones. The application of this principle is called preemphasis.

In the example of Fig. 8-11, there is a simple series resistor-capacitor combination that can be used to obtain preemphasis. Since the capacitance of C1 is low, its capacitive reactance is quite high at low- and mid-range audio frequencies, decreasing to a rather low value at high modulating frequencies. Hence, for a comparable input to the preemphasis network, the higher-frequency components will be present at the input of the amplifier stage with approximately the same amplitude as existed at the input to the preemphasis network. However, with a decrease in frequency the reactance of the capacitor increases, and, as a result, the amplitude of the signal delivered to the next stage is decreased. The typical preemphasis response is shown in the curve of Fig. 8-11.

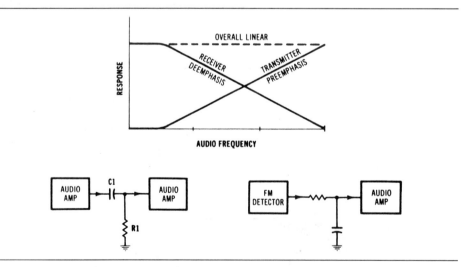

Fig. 8-11. Preemphasis and deemphasis in an FM system.

Because preemphasis is used, the high-frequency components of the audio signal at the receiver output will appear at a greater relative level than the middle and low ones. Now it is necessary to equalize the curve. The audio-frequency components are restored to their initial relative value with the use of a deemphasis network at the output of the receiver detector. The deemphasis curve is of opposite slope to that of preemphasis. That is, the higher frequencies are attenuated more than the lower ones but in exactly the same proportion as the highs were initially preemphasized at the transmitter. Consequently, the overall frequency response is made more linear, and, at the same time, the overall signal-to-noise and signal-to-interference ratios have been improved. The deemphasis network in the receiver was mentioned previously. However, this discussion ties together the functions preemphasis at the transmitter and deemphasis at the receiver.

Note that the preeemphasis network is connected between pin 6 of U301B and output pin 7. Consequently, it is in effect a feedback network between output and input. At higher frequencies the feedback is less, and consequently the gain of U301B is more. The highs in effect are preemphasized.

The audio output of the first operational amplifier is transferred to the input gate of the second amplifier U301A through a suitable resistor-capacitor coupling combination. Channel-guard information (tone or digital) is supplied to the same input. This information also modulates the FM transmitter and will activate the receiver with which communication is desired. In a tone channel-guard system the activating frequency falls between 71.9 and 210.7 Hz. There are 83 standard programmable digital codes. These codes are programmed previously using a hex keyboard and hex numbers. The hex numbering system was discussed in Chapter 5.

There is a post limiting filter at the output of the operational amplifier composed of resistors R314, R313, R315, C308, and C309, providing a 12 dB per octave rolloff. Rolloffs of this type are used to establish a frequency-modulating signal that does not modulate the transmitter with components above the voice-frequency limit of 3,000 Hz. Potentiometer R320 sets the level of transmitter deviation to a maximum of approximately 4.5 kHz (3.75 kHz voice plus 0.75 kHz channel-guard modulations). There is also an output path to the reference oscillator which is a part of the frequency synthesis process. Transistor Q301 is an electronic switch that shorts out operational amplifier U301A and prevents receiver interference when the transmit section of the transceiver is in operation.

The output of the audio processor is applied to the varactor-diode modulator through the capacitor C138 and resistor R116 coupling combination at the center left of Fig. 8-12. The VCO is a FET oscillator (Q105) with the varactor frequency modulator positioned in its gate circuit. Its operating frequency range is between 134.33–185.66 MHz. The presence of audio changes the capacitance of varactor diode D104, deviating the frequency of the oscillator. The center frequency of operation is controlled by a DC control voltage from the synthesizer which determines the capacitance of varactor diode D102. Note that both diodes shunt the gate resonant circuit. One is controlled by a DC voltage; the other is controlled by the audio modulation. Frequency centering is controlled by preset inductor L102.

The VCO FET is connected as a source-follower, and the output across inductor L104 is applied to two bipolar output transistors Q106 and Q107. These buffers provide drive signal for receiver injection and transmitter excitation. Refer to Figs. 8-5 and 8-8.

Pin diodes D105 and D106 direct the output to the transmitter or the receiver. When switching is high from the microcomputer, D105 conducts and a frequency-modulated RF signal is supplied to the transmitter. When switching is low, diode D106 conducts, and injection voltage is fed to the receiver.

The DC frequency-control voltage is applied from the synthesizer to the base of the input driver Q102 at the top left of Fig. 8-12. This stage is followed by the high-current buffers Q104 and Q103. The control voltage output passes through a low-pass filter consisting of resistors R109–R111 and capacitors C106–C108 through the coupling network to varactor diode D102. This filter eliminates any undesired pulses that may be present on the error control line.

Device U103 is an electronic switch that permits the low-pass filter to be bypassed whenever the channel change pulse is present. This operation increases the band-

330

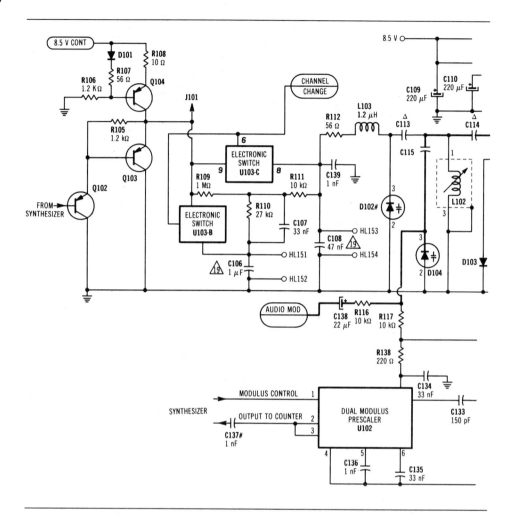

Fig. 8-12. VCO and associated

width and improves the acquisition time when switching to a different channel.

The reference oscillator of the synthesizer circuit operates on 13.2 MHz and is held on frequency by a temperature-compensating network that was shown in Fig. 8-3. This oscillator is also frequency modulated by the same audio that frequency modulates the VCO. The resultant reference signal is applied to divider R of the group of three located in the synthesizer chip. When the transmit/receive switch (PTT) is changed over or a different channel is selected, new logic is present on the data, enable, and clock lines from the microprocessor. This serial data determines the new frequency of the VCO as well as the ratio by which the reference oscillator is divided. Both the VCO and the reference components are divided down to the proper comparison frequency before application to the phase detector. The VCO output is reduced to this correct comparison frequency by the dual modulus prescaler and the N divider. Division is either by 64 or 65 as a function of the logic on the modulus control line. The final comparison frequency is 4.1667 kHz.

If the phase of the two compared frequencies differs, a DC error voltage develops that corrects the VCO frequency by way of the voltage-variable capacitor D102. The frequency control process associated with the VCO was discussed previously. All of these significant frequencies are controlled by the microprocessor logic which in turn responds to the logic preprogrammed into the memory.

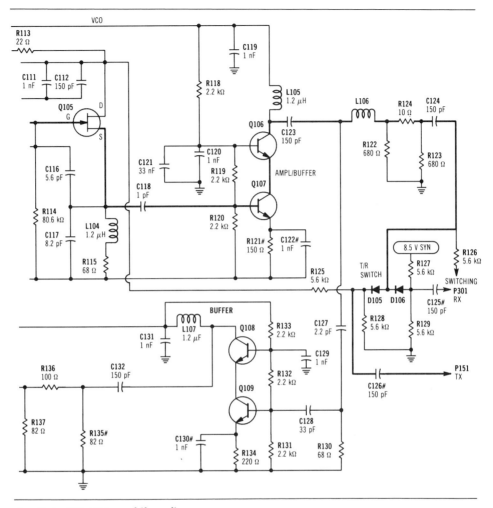

circuits in 450-MHz mobile radio.

8-2. 450-MHz Transceiver Service Procedures

Test, alignment, and troubleshooting procedures vary greatly from manufacturer to manufacturer and from model to model. Study and follow the instructions contained in the service or maintenance manuals supplied with the equipment. A detailed but not entirely complete coverage of the service data for the unit just described follows. Its purpose is to give you some idea of just what is involved in tuning and repairing two-way radio sets. Test equipment and procedures were covered in Chapter 6 along with additional fault-locating guidance.

Recall that the frequency of operation, power output, and modulation level are of principal concern to the FCC. Equipment used to make these measurements was detailed in Chapter 6. Portable test equipment is available that can make these measurements even as the equipment is installed in a mobile station. An advantage of the in-service check of a mobile radio is that with the use of a directional coupler output meter the standing-wave ratio on the antenna line can be measured. Consequently, you also have a check of antenna performance at the same time you test the mobile radio. Typically, the average voice level should produce approximately 75% modulation (deviation).

Of course, such tests can be made in the service shop or at the base station using the simple interconnection plan of Fig. 8-13. Receiver performance can be checked with a Sinadder or appropriate sensitivity/distortion meter combination. These checks should be performed periodically and appropriate records kept. A good preventive maintenance schedule is the answer to high system reliability. General Electric suggests the maintenance checks in Chart 8-1 on a scheduled basis. Set up your time system according to operating environment and usage. Visual and mechanical checks should be done often because of the vibrations of a mobile environment. Modern radios are inherently subject to microphonics and static noises. Consequently, it is most important to keep watch on the tightness of mounting screws, support structures, etc.

A number of servicing aids are a part of this transceiver. There are six convenient test points — three for the transmitter and three for the receiver. They are as follows:

Receiver

TP351   Tripler Input (Q352)
TP401   Receiver First Oscillator Injection
TP501   455-kHz IF

Transmitter

TP101   Tripler (Q102)
TP102   Amplifier 2 Collector (Q103)
TP201   Predriver (Q201)

The local oscillator injection voltage for the receiver first mixer is present at test point TP401 in Fig. 8-8. The operating conditions at the input of the tripler Q352 can be judged with the test position TP351 located in its base circuit. Locate the third test point of the receiver. If you did not locate it, try Fig. 8-9. Often you must search among several schematics. Locate the three transmitter test points.

In testing and servicing, the radio signal and voltage paths can be evaluated at the connectors that are a part of the plug-in design, especially those on the synthesizer/interconnect board.

The microcomputer circuits are checked out with the self-diagnostic programming that is a part of the microprocessor. Since the radio cannot function with a defective microcomputer, these tests include internal and input/output observations to verify the proper operation of the computer. The internal tests include a ROM test to make sure the proper program is in the chip and a RAM test procedure to check the transfer data to and from all memory locations. The input/output tests include procedures which ground one pin at a time on port 1 and the data bus. Tests evaluate the data bus logic, push-to-talk activity, mode A/B switch, channel select, and channel-guard disable, etc. The operation of the ports and data bus are verified. There is a check made on the input/output instructions of the microcomputer. Step-by-step sequence is not given here because it is not a generalized procedure that can be applied to all microprocessor-controlled radios. You must use the exact procedure given by the manufacturer for the particular model. Refer to the appropriate instruction manual.

The transmitter is factory preset and requires no adjustment. When installed, the antenna length should be adjusted for optimum VSWR. The power output, frequency, and modulation should be measured and appropriate records kept according to FCC requirements. No initial receiver adjustments are required. The transmit and receive frequencies and operating modes are set by the microcomputer system. These, as well as tone and digital channel-guard signals, are stored in memory. Since the radio uses PROM facilities, the operating conditions can be changed with an appropriate program.

Chart 8-1. Preventive Maintenance Checks

Connections

Ground connections and connections to the voltage source should be periodically checked for tightness. Loose or poor connections to the power source will cause excessive voltage drops and faulty operation. When ground connections are not made directly to the battery, the connection from the battery to the vehicle chassis must be checked for low impedance. A high impedance may cause excessive voltage drops and alternator noise problems.

Electrical System

Check the voltage regulator and alternator or generator periodically to keep the electrical system within safe and economical operating limits. Overvoltage is indicated when the battery loses water rapidly. Usage of 1 or 2 ounces of water per cell per week is acceptable for batteries in continuous operation. A weak battery will often cause excessive noise or faulty operation.

Mechanical Inspection

Since mobile units are subject to constant shock and vibration, check for loose plugs, nuts, screws, and parts to make sure that nothing is working loose. Be sure that all screws are properly torqued.

Antenna

The antenna, antenna base, and all contacts should be kept clean and free from dirt or corrosion. If the antenna or its base should become coated or poorly grounded, loss of radiation and a weak signal will result.

Alignment

The transmitter and receiver meter readings should be checked periodically, and the alignment "touched up" when necessary. Refer to applicable alignment procedure and troubleshooting sheet for typical voltage readings.

Frequency Check

Check transmitter frequency and deviation, as required by the FCC. Normally, these checks are made when the unit is first put into operation, after the first six months, and once a year thereafter.

Supply voltages are indicated on schematics. In addition voltage charts are often available in the maintenance manuals that are a help in checking individual circuits and individual transistor stages. Follow the manufacturer's instructions. For example, it may indicate that measurements were made with a 20,000 ohms-per-volt meter. Also, in checking transmitter RF stages, the instructions may indicate that a 10 microhenry RF choke be used in series with the hot meter lead. This step prevents detuning of RF circuits.

8-2-1. Transmitter Alignment

The transmitter has been aligned at the factory and requires no realignment. The following procedure is followed when there is a component replacement on the transmit/receive board. Use the test setup of Fig. 8-13. Preliminary to the procedure set the helical cores L105 and L106 (Fig. 8-5) to the position suggested by the manufacturer's manual. Set the power control R204 to maximum. Follow the alignment procedure given in Table 8-1. The frequencies selected depend upon the span of frequencies served by the particular radio. For example, if the span of frequencies extends between 450–470 MHz, the center frequency is approximately 460 MHz. In performing the transmitter alignment, choose the program transmit frequency that is nearest to 460 MHz. The highest frequency used in alignment would be a program transmit frequency nearest to 470 MHz; the lowest frequency is the one nearest to 450 MHz. In performing the alignment the 20,000 ohms-per-volt meter is connected to the monitor positions indicated in the chart. The power output is measured at antenna output jack J601.

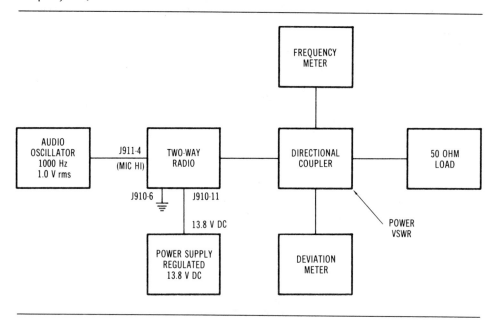

Fig. 8-13. Transmitter test hookup.

Table 8-1. Transmitter Alignment Procedure

Step	Monitor	Tuning Controls	Adjust For	Remarks
1.	TP101	L102	Minimum	Select center frequency
2.	TP201	L105	Minimum	Select highest frequency
3.	TP201	L106	Minimum	Select lowest frequency
				NOTE
				Repeat steps 1–3 until no further change in core setting of L102, L105, and L106 occurs.
4.	Antenna Jack J601	R204	25-Watts Output Power	If output power exceeds 25 watts, adjust to 25 watts. Check all channels. RF output power should be between 22 and 25 watts.

Inductor L102 in the VCO circuit (Fig. 8-12) is adjusted for correct transmit frequency using the transmit frequency nearest to the center frequency of the spectrum covered by the particular radio. The modulation adjustment control (R320 in Fig. 8-10) is factory preset to obtain 75% modulation for the average voice level. However, the modulation level control associated with channel-guard modulation must be checked each time the tone frequency is changed.

8-2-2. Receiver Test Procedures

The following test procedures are designed to help you to service a receiver that is operating — but not properly. The problems encountered could be low power, poor sensitivity, distortion, limiter not operating properly, and low gain. By following the sequence of test steps starting with Step 1, the defect can be quickly localized. Once the defective stage is pin pointed, refer to the "Service Check" listed to correct the problem. Additional corrective measures are included in the troubleshooting procedures which follow. Before starting with the receiver test procedures, be sure the receiver is tuned and aligned to the proper operating frequency. Disable the squelch with R607 (Fig. 7-9).

Step 1 — Audio Power Output and Distortion

Measure the Audio Power Output as follows:
1. Apply a 1000-microvolt, on-frequency test signal modulated by 1000 Hz with a ±3.0-kHz deviation to antenna jack J601 (Fig. 8-5).
2. *With a 3-Watt Speaker*
   Disconnect speaker from jack. Use a Sinadder or a 4.0-ohm load resistor (5 watts) which is paralleled with the Distortion Analyzer across the speaker jack. Either method can be used to measure the output.
3. Adjust the Volume control for a 3-watt output (3.46 volts across 4 ohms). Use distortion analyzer as a voltmeter.
4. Make distortion measurements. The reading should be less than 5%. If the receiver sensitivity is to be measured, leave all controls and equipment as they are.

Service Check — If the distortion is more than 5%, or maximum audio output is less than 3 watts, make the following checks:

5. Battery and regulator voltage—low voltage will cause distortion.
6. Audio gain (Refer to Receiver Troubleshooting Procedure in Section 8-2-4).
7. FM detector alignment (Refer to Receiver Alignment in Section 8-2-3).

Step 2 — Usable Sensitivity (12-dB Sinad)

If Step 1 checks out properly, measure the receiver sensitivity as follows:
1. Apply a 1000-microvolt, on-frequency signal, modulated by a 1000-Hz with a 3.0-kHz deviation to J601. Use Sinadder or distortion meter across output.
2. Place the Range switch on the Distortion Analyzer in the 200- to 2000-Hz distortion range position (1000-Hz filter in the circuit). Tune the filter for minimum reading or null on the lowest possible scale (100%, 30%, etc.)
3. Place the Range switch to the Set Level position (filter out of the circuit) and adjust the input Level control for a +2-dB reading on a midrange (30%).
4. Set the signal generator output to a 0.4-microvolt output. Switch the Range control from Set Level to the distortion range. Readjust the Distortion Analyzer Set Level as required until a 12-dB difference (+2 dB to −10 dB) is obtained

between the Set Level and distortion range positions (filter out and filter in).

5. The 12-dB difference (Signal plus Noise and Distortion to Noise plus Distortion ratio) is the "usable" sensitivity level. The sensitivity should be less than rated 12-dB Sinad specifications with an audio output of at least 1.5 watts.

6. Leave all controls as they are and all equipment connected if the Modulation Acceptance Bandwidth test is to be performed.

Service Check — If the sensitivity level is more than rated 12-dB Sinad, check the alignment of the RF stages as directed in the Alignment Procedure (Section 8-2-3).

Step 3 — Modulation Acceptance Bandwidth (IF Bandwidth)

If Steps 1 and 2 check out properly, measure the bandwidth as follows:

1. Set the signal generator output for twice the microvolt reading obtained in the 12-dB Sinad measurement.

2. Set the Range control on the Distortion Analyzer in the Set Level position (1000-Hz filter out of the circuit), and adjust the input Level control for a + 2-dB reading on the 30% range.

3. While increasing the deviation of the Signal Generator, switch the Range control from Set Level to distortion range until a 12-dB difference is obtained between the Set Level and distortion range readings (from + 2 dB to − 10 dB).

4. The deviation control reading for the 12-dB difference is the Modulation Acceptance Bandwidth of the receiver. It should be more than ± 7 kHz.

Service Check — If the Modulation Acceptance Bandwidth test does not indicate the proper width, refer to the receiver Troubleshooting Procedure (Section 8-2-4).

8-2-3. Receiver Alignment

Receiver alignment procedures vary from model to model and manufacturer to manufacturer. Again, it is important that you follow the instructions given in the maintenance manual. However, you can gain a good knowledge of alignment procedures following the alignment charts of Table 8-2. Place yourself in the position that it is your responsibility to align this receiver. Try to understand each step and, if possible, locate the various test points, signal injection positions, and components that must be adjusted. In the book all of them are not shown in the schematic diagrams associated with the circuit descriptions. However, many of them are. Certainly you will gain a fundamental understanding of what is involved, and you will be better prepared when the first instruction manual and radio are placed before you for alignment.

The first step is to gather together the necessary test equipment. In the case of the GE radio, it would be a UHF signal generator, high-impedance AC voltmeter, DC voltmeter, various alignment tools, as well as the programming information for a microprocessor-controlled radio. Various preliminary checks and adjustments may be necessary. Switch positions must be set correctly. Certain coils and other controls must be preset properly. It is most important that you follow all of these preparation instructions exactly as they appear in the maintenance manual if you are to avoid improper results.

Table 8-2. Receiver Alignment Procedure

Step	Monitor	Tuning Control	Adjust For	Remarks
1.	TP501		Less than 50 millivolts AC	Connect RF Generator to antenna jack and set to center frequency corresponding to EE PROM center frequency. Adjust output level for 25–50 millivolts AC at TP501. Maintain this level throughout Alignment Procedure when monitoring TP501.

LOCAL OSCILLATOR FILTER INITIAL ALIGNMENT

Step	Monitor	Tuning Control	Adjust For	Remarks
2.	TP351 (DC Meter)	L352, L353	Negative Peak	Tune L352 and L353 for maximum negative voltage at TP351.
3.	TP401 (DC Meter)	L355, L356	Peak	Tune L355 and L356 for a positive peak.

45-MHz ALIGNMENT

Step	Monitor	Tuning Control	Adjust For	Remarks
4.	TP501 (AC Meter)	L408-L410	Peak	Set RF Generator to center frequency corresponding to EE PROM center frequency. Peak L408, L409, L410 in sequence. Reduce output level of generator as necessary to prevent limiting level at TP501. This should be less than 50 millivolts AC.

LOCAL OSCILLATOR FILTER FINAL ALIGNMENT

Step	Monitor	Tuning Control	Adjust For	Remarks
5.	TP351 (DC Meter)	L353	Negative Voltage	Set RF generator to center frequency corresponding to EE PROM center frequency. Detune L353 to obtain the minimum negative voltage.
6.	TP351	L353, L352	Peak	Peak L352 and then L353.

NOTE
The purpose of Step 7 is to balance the frequency response curve for the segment tuned by equalizing the voltages on the band edges. When these voltages are equal, the total response will be satisfactory.

Table 8-2—cont. Receiver Alignment Procedure

Step	Monitor	Tuning Control	Adjust For	Remarks
7.	TP351	L353, L352	Balance Response	Alternately select band edge frequencies noting the voltage at TP351. Slightly adjust L353 for equal voltage readings at both band edges.
8.	TP501	L356	Peak	Remove the core in L355 and replace with the detuning tool (banana plug). Set RF Generator to center frequency corresponding to EE PROM frequency. Tune L356 for peak indication.
9.	TP401	L355	Peak	Remove test core from L355 and replace it with original core. Peak L355.
10.	TP401	L355	Balance	Alternately select the band edge frequencies and slightly adjust L355 to equalize the voltage readings at the band edges.

PRESELECTOR ALIGNMENT

Step	Monitor	Tuning Control	Adjust For	Remarks
11.	TP501	L402	Peak	Remove the core in L401 and replace with the detuning tool. Set the generator to the center frequency corresponding to EE PROM center frequency and peak L402.
12.	TP501	L401	Peak	Remove detuning tool from L401 and replace it with original core. Peak L401.
13.	TP501	L405, L407	Peak	Remove the core in L406 and replace it with the detuning tool. Peak L405 and L407.
14.	TP501	L406	Peak	Remove the detuning tool from L406 and replace it with the original core. Peak L406.
15.	TP501	L406	Balance	Alternately select the band edge frequencies, each time setting the RF Generator to the center frequency corresponding to EE PROM center frequency and slightly adjust L406 to obtain maximum but equal voltages at the band edges.

8-2-4. Troubleshooting

Chapter 6 supplied details on using test equipment and how they can be of help in locating defects. Also there is considerable detail about fault-finding in individual circuits. The troubleshooting chart in Table 8-3 will augment your knowledge about procedures to be followed in locating defects. It is a particularly good chart and presents considerable detail. Most of the circuits, test points, and components can be found in the schematics used for circuit description. Certain others you may not find exactly but you can gain a good idea of their locations by referring to the functional block diagrams. You become familiar with the problems of locating controls and parts when you have to work with a number of reasonably complex schematics.

Table 8-3. Troubleshooting Procedures

SYMPTOM	PROCEDURE
No. 13.8-volt Supply Voltage	Check power connections and continuity of supply leads. Check On/Off switch. Check radio for shorts. Check fuse in power line.
Low 13.8-volt Supply Voltage	Check for low or discharged battery possibly with bad cell in vehicle. Check radio for shorts or high resistance at A+ paths.
No. 8.5-volt Regulated Supply	Check 13.8-volt supply at pin 1 or regulator U602. If 8.5-volt supply is low, check for short on output of U602.

No Audio Output	1. <u>Receiver may be squelched</u>
	  • Rotate R607 (squelch potentiometer) fully counterclockwise to unsquelch the receiver.
	  • Measure the DC voltage on pin 2 of U601 (audio amp.). If this voltage is greater than 0.8 volt, the audio is being squelched. Check Q603 and RX Mute voltage at P912-4. This input voltage should be approximately 6.2 volts to unsquelch the audio. Note operation of S602 (monitor switch) opens the input to Q603 which should always result in Q603 being biased off, thereby insuring that U601 is unsquelched.
	2. <u>No audio to U601</u>
	  • Check for audio at P902-7 (Filtered Volume/Sq. High).
	  • Check for audio at P902-3 (Volume/Sq. High).
	If audio is present at either of these points but does not reach pin 1 of U601 (audio amp.), check for loss of signal in channel-guard reject filter on synthesizer/interconnect board or through monitor switch (S602) and volume potentiometer (R617). Check for open in volume control and deemphasis circuits. Check DC voltages around U601 according to schematic.

Low Audio	Check the supply voltage at pin 5 of U602. Verify correct audio levels at:
	  P903-3 300 millivolts +100 −50 millivolts
	  P903-7 270 millivolts +100 −50 millivolts
	  U602 pin 1 37.5 ±10 millivolts at maximum volume
	(NOTE: 1-kHz modulation at ±3-kHz deviation)
	If audio levels are low, tune L501 for maximum level.
	If low level at pin 1 of U601, check for defective components, shorts, or opens, between U601 and volume control.

Table 8-3—cont. Troubleshooting Procedures

SYMPTOM	PROCEDURE
Distorted Audio Output	Apply a strong RF signal with standard test modulation and measure audio distortion into a 4-ohm dummy load. Distortion should be less than 5% at 3.46 volts rms audio output. Check for 13.8 volts at pin 5 of U601. Check DC voltages around U601 per schematic. Tune L501 slightly to note any improvement. Tune L410, L409, and L408 slightly and note any improvement. (They may be detuned.) Check frequency of second oscillator at U501-2 with high impedance counter. Should be 29.945 MHz ± 200 Hz. If no improvement, check for defective filters (Z401, Z402, and Z501).
Poor or No Sensitivity	Verify that proper injection power is present and at the correct frequency, (f_c + 21.4 MHz). This can be done by a high impedance probe from the junction of C406 and C407 to ground. The power seen should be approximately 10 dBm. If OK, then use a 50-ohm probe with a signal generator to inject signal into various portions of the radio to isolate the bad section. Set the generator with standard modulation to the level and frequency indicated on the large service schematic and probe those points starting with IC (U501) and moving forward to the antenna jack. In some cases parts must be adjusted for best sensitivity while probing. This is indicated on the schematic. Once the faulty stage is isolated, measure bias voltages.
No or Low Injection Power	Monitor the Local Oscillator input with a high impedance probe at J351, synthesizer input. This level should be approximately +10 dBm at the injection frequency. Check the bias levels on Q301 with a DC voltmeter.
Frequency Won't Adjust Properly	Check reference oscillator frequency at U101-2 and set to 13.2 MHz. Check VCO control line voltage at TP101 for 6.5 volts using a high impedance probe. Select the highest frequency in the radio and tune L104 for 6.5 volts.
No Transmit 8.5 V	Check the switching transistor Q604.
Radio Won't go into Transmit Mode	Check Q604. If OK, check pin 4 P901. There should be no voltage between pin 4 and ground when PTT is depressed.
Low or No Transmit Power	Check the voltage at TP101. When PTT is depressed, the DC voltage should decrease by about 1 volt. If not, then check J151. Make sure the feedthrough pin from Interconnect board is making good contact with J151. If everything is OK, then check voltage at TP102. When keyed, this voltage should be approximately 6.5 volts. If not, refer to the Transmitter Alignment Procedure and tune L102, L105, and L106.
Oscillator Frequency Will Not Adjust Properly	Check circuitry associated with reference oscillator Q101. Verify part values and check crystal Y101 and L101. Oscillator frequency should adjust to 13.2 MHz.

Table 8-3—cont. Troubleshooting Procedures

SYMPTOM	PROCEDURE
No Transmitter Deviation	Check audio processor U301 and its associated circuitry. If OK, check Q301 and audio levels at output of potentiometers R320 and R316. If potentiometers OK, check C122 and C101.
No or Incorrect Detector Output	Check audio level at P903-3, (Volume/Squelch High). Should be 300 millivolts (+ 100, − 50 millivolts) under standard test conditions. Tune L501 and note improvement, if any. Check for shorts or opens around L501 circuitry. Check DC bias levels around U501 and Q601 under high RF input level (1 millivolt or more) per schematic. Check limiter output at pin 7 of U501 with scope; should be square wave at 455 kHz at 0.4 volt peak-to-peak.
No Second Oscillator Activity	Substitute a known good crystal for Y501. Check voltages on U501 pins 1 and 2.
Radio Permanently Squelched	1. Squelch Circuit Apply an on channel RF signal of 1 millivolt with standard modulation. Measure the AC audio level at Volume/Squelch High (P903-3). The level should be 300-millivolt rms (+ 100, − 50 millivolt). If this level is not met, follow the detector troubleshooting procedure. *If* the audio level is correct, measure the DC level at CAS (P912-4). The reading should be 0 volt. Remove the RF signal from the receiver input and the reading should change to 7.5 volts DC. If both measurements are correct, the squelch circuit is working and the audio switch circuit should be checked next. If not, measure the bias voltages on U501 pin 10-14. With no RF input signal, the voltage on pin 12 of U501 should vary as R607 is varied (see schematic). If not, check the noise detector diode D601 and its associated circuitry (C606, C607, C621, R608, and R609) and the noise filter circuitry (R604 –R606 and C603–C605). Otherwise, U501 is probably defective and should be replaced. 2. Audio Switch Circuit Apply an on-channel RF signal of 1 millivolt and standard modulation. Depress Monitor switch (S602) momentarily. If audio is heard from the speaker, the audio switch and audio amplifier are working and the problem is on the systems interconnect board. (Check the operation of the channel guard, audio gate, and microprocessor sections on the systems interconnect board.) If audio is not heard from the speaker, measure the voltages on Q603 and on pins 2 and 4 of U501. Remove the RF signal from the receiver input and measure these voltages for the squelched condition (see schematic). If the voltages are correct, follow the procedure for "No Audio Output."
Radio Won't Squelch	1. Squelch Circuit Without a signal applied to the receiver input, ground RX MUTE (P903-4). If the receiver does not squelch, follow the audio switch circuit troubleshooting procedure. If the receiver does squelch, remove the ground from RX MUTE and turn R607 (Squelch Adj) maximum clockwise. If the receiver now squelches, R607 was misadjusted. If the receiver remains un-squelched, apply an on channel RF signal of 1 millivolt and standard modulation. Measure the AC audio level at Volume/

Table 8-3—cont. Troubleshooting Procedures

SYMPTOM	PROCEDURE
	Squelch High (P903-3). The level should be 300 millivolts rms (+100, −50 millivolts). If this level is not met, follow the detector troubleshooting procedure. If the audio level is correct, measure the DC level at CAS (P912-4). The reading should be 0 volt. Remove the RF signal from the receiver input and the reading should change to 7.5 volts DC. If both measurements are correct, check the operation of the microprocessor section on the systems interconnect board. If the $\overline{CAS}$ readings don't change, measure the bias voltages on U501 pins 10–14. With no RF input signal, the voltage on pin 12 of U501 should vary as R607 is varied (see schematic). If not, check the noise detector diode D601 and its associated circuitry (C606, C607, C621, R608, and R609) and the noise filter circuitry (R604–R606 and C603–C605). Otherwise, U501 is probably defective and should be replaced.

2. Audio Switch Circuit

Ground $\overline{RX\ MUTE}$ (P903-4) and measure the voltages at Q603 and pins 2 and 4 of U601 for the squelched condition (see schematic).

Courtesy General Electric Co.,
Mobile Communications Div.

Fig. 8-14. A personal radio.

8-3. Personal Transceiver

An example of a hand-held personal radio is shown in Fig. 8-14. GE has units available for the 150- and 450-MHz bands with 2- and 4-watt outputs. A switch selects operation on one of two channels. The unit illustrated is also equipped with an encoder dialing pad that permits it to serve as a simplex portable telephone. The power source is a rechargeable nickle-cadium battery. Battery drain is 17 millamperes on standby. With the transmitter and receiver in operation the current draw is 150 milliamperes on receive and 750 milliamperes on transmit for the 2-watt model.

The transmitter as depicted in the block diagram of Fig. 8-15, is a crystal-controlled, frequency-modulated model for one or two frequency operation in the 136 to 174-MHz band. It consists of two assemblies — the audio board and the transmit/receive board.

The transmitter is shown at the bottom of the block diagram. The microphone is at the far right and supplies its output through a preemphasis network and an optional microphone mute switch to the post limiter. As detailed in the previous discussion, the post limiter prevents over deviation of the transmitter. It also includes an auxiliary input as well as a channel-guard input.

The transmitter crystal oscillator, Fig. 8-16, uses a bipolar transistor connected in a Colpitts circuit. Note capacitors C82 and C83. Resonant tuning is accomplished in its collector circuit.

Fine tuning to the precise frequency of transmission is accomplished with inductors L36 and L37 in the two separate varactor diode circuits. Refer to the circuits associated with diodes D6 and D7 along with crystals Y4 and Y5. Switch S2 at the top selects one of two channels.

A temperature compensating circuit provides an automatic frequency correction at low operating temperature. This DC component establishes a correcting charge on capacitor C14 and has an influence on the center-frequency capacitances of varactor diodes D6, D7, and D10. The microphone audio is applied to the tops of the individual channel potentiometers R69 and R70. The adjustable voltage at the arm of the potentiometer determines the extent of the frequency deviation of the oscillator because it sets the amount of capacitance change introduced by an individual varactor diode.

The frequency-modulated output of the oscillator is supplied to a multiplier/buffer combination that multiplies the frequency by a factor of three up to the transmit frequency. The three succeeding stages increase the power level of the signal and also include a power level adjustment. A solid-state antenna changeover switch follows, and from there the signal passes through a low-pass filter to the unit-mounted antenna rod.

The receiver is a dual conversion type with intermediate frequencies of 10.7 MHz and 455 kHz. When the push-to-talk switch is not depressed, the solid-state antenna switch connects the antenna to the input RF amplifier Q1 of the receiver, at the top left of Fig. 8-15. This amplifier stage is followed by the mixer which receives its injection signal from the receive crystal oscillator Q3. Separate receive crystals Y1 or Y2 determine the appropriate receive frequency. The first mixer is followed by a two-pole crystal filter which along with the 455-kHz ceramic filter of the second IF system determines the selectivity of the receiver.

After amplification by the 10.7-MHz IF amplifier (Q5), the signal is supplied to an integrated circuit composed of second mixer/oscillator, IF amplifier/limiter, quadrature detector and squelch system. The demodulated audio is recovered at the output of the integrated circuit and supplied to the volume control. The audio signal is built up in level and supplied to the loudspeaker. Squelch, channel-guard, and deemphasis capabilities are a part of this small transmitter/receiver personal radio.

344

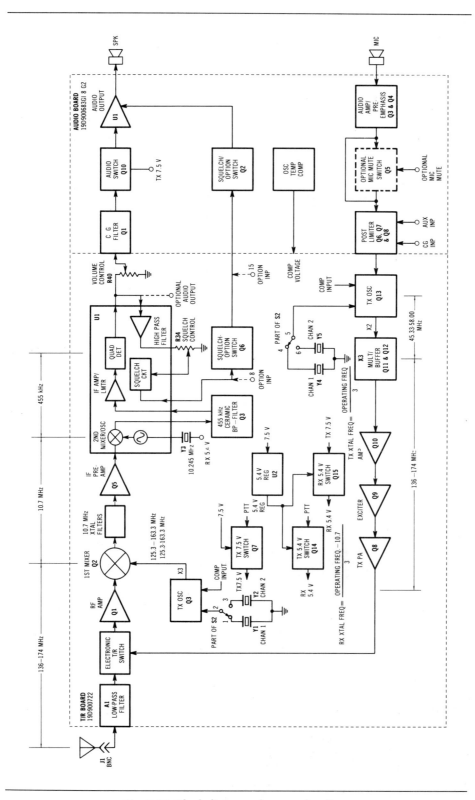

Fig. 8-15. Block diagram of personal radio.

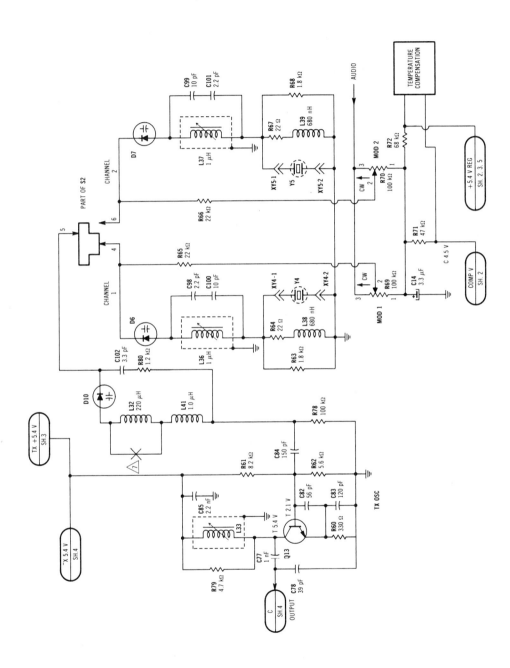

Fig. 8-16. Varactor frequency modulator.

8-4. High-Powered Transmitter

Base-station, high-powered transmitters are used to extend the reliable operating range of two-way radio systems. In association with a gain antenna and a tall tower, the combination delivers strong signals to the mobiles. In addition, the high gain antenna delivers a strong signal to the base-station receiver from each mobile.

The single-channel Quintron transmitter of Fig. 8-17 has a power output of 250 watts between 450–475 MHz and 200 watts between 475–512 MHz. The three major sections of the transmitter are exciter, power amplifier, and power supply. The FM-modulated exciter output of 200-milliwatts is built up to the 200- to 250-watt range in three stages by the power amplifier.

Courtesy Quintron Corp.

Fig. 8-17. High-powered base-station transmitter.

The simplified block diagram of the exciter (Fig. 8-18) shows the five major boards — audio, phase detector, voltage-controlled oscillator (VCO), oscillator, and amplifier. These are all modules that are a part of the master board. Associated with the major function of each board are the necessary control circuits, protection circuits, and troubleshooting aids.

The oscillator board generates the reference signal for the phase detector. Here it is compared with the divided-down frequency from the VCO board. The output of the phase detector provides a voltage which is proportional to the phase difference between oscillator and VCO. The phase detector output is filtered and supplied as a DC frequency control voltage to the VCO which generates the center frequency of the transmitted FM signal. The VCO output is increased in level by RF amplifier Q3 and then passed to the amplifier board. Further amplification builds up the signal to the 200-milliwatt level.

The source of the modulating audio for the VCO is the audio board. The audio board provides facilities for three separate audio inputs. The signal supplied between terminals 6 and 7 of the input terminal strip is supplied to a preemphasis network and succeeding amplifiers and filters. If desired, a flat response rather than a pre-emphasis response, can be obtained by applying a signal between terminals 8 and

9. The CTCSS subtone squelch signal is supplied to terminal 10. Note in the phase detector block that the audio signal is divided. One part goes to frequency modulate the VCO while the second component modulates the phase detector output.

Exciter operation occurs when there is a low at terminal 5 of TB1. The exciter can also be turned on by depressing switch S1. If no faults are detected, the exciter comes on. The AC input voltage is supplied to the transformer shown at the bottom left. However, if AC fails, the exciter will switch over automatically to a battery voltage source.

The diagram of Fig. 8-19 shows the transmitter power amplifier blocks. The output of the exciter is supplied to the input of the intermediate power amplifier at the left. The IPA increases the power level of the signal to 10 watts. The succeeding RF driver steps up the power to 50 watts and the power amplifier increases it to 250 watts. Before application to the antenna, the signal passes through a low-pass filter and directional coupler. The directional coupler provides voltage samples that are proportional to forward power and reflected power. These samples are used to operate the transmitter power meter and the power control circuits.

The monitoring segment of the control and monitoring block can be used to display the standing-wave ratio and RF power output when supplied to the transmitter metering system. Additional control and monitoring logic is used to key the transmitter on, operate at a low test power F_o, indicate faults, and supply exciter key logic.

8-4-1. Circuit Description

In the circuit description that follows, the emphasis will be on the transmitter rather than the exciter. The audio sections and FM modulation systems were covered in previous discussions of two-way radio equipment. However, the VCO and the RF amplifier segment of the exciter will be treated briefly. The VCO circuit is shown in Fig. 8-20. It consists of an FET oscillator (Q1) whose frequency can be changed by either a DC or an audio voltage. The oscillator output is supplied to two buffers (Q2 and Q3) that supply output to the phase detector and exciter RF amplifier respectively.

A quarter-wave stripline along with various end capacitors form the drain resonant circuit of the VCO in Fig. 8-20. The various capacitors are C28, C29 along with capacitor C26, and the varactor diode CR2. On the other side there are capacitors C6, C7, and the varactor diode CR1. Also, two capacitors C8 and C9 are connected in series at the end of the line serving as the feedback pair for the Colpitts oscillator connection.

The audio signal varies the capacitance of CR1 determining the deviation of the oscillator frequency. The center frequency of the oscillator is held precisely on the 450-MHz band frequency by the DC voltage that appears on varactor diode CR2. The source of this DC control voltage is the phase detector circuit. Precise tuning to the center frequency is accomplished with capacitors C26 and C29. The DC supply voltage to the FET is connected at the center of the resonant-line strip.

Inductive coupling to a second segment of the stripline conveys the frequency-modulated signal to the bases of the two output transistors (Q2 and Q3). Stripline resonant circuits are located in the collector circuit of each transistor. The drive signals for the RF amplifier and phase detector are removed from their low impedance ends.

The output of the VCO is supplied to the exciter RF amplifier located center left in Fig. 8-21. Two broadband amplifiers, bipolar transistors Q5 and Q6, build up the signal to the 200-milliwatt level. There is a stripline resonant circuit at the input of Q5 and an interstage stripline coupling circuit between Q5 and Q6. Transistor Q5 is the gain stage while Q6 provides a low-impedance output for matching the cable that connects to the input of the power amplifier section of the transmitter. Resistors R21, R22, and R23 are responsible for isolation and stabilization. A small portion of the RF

348

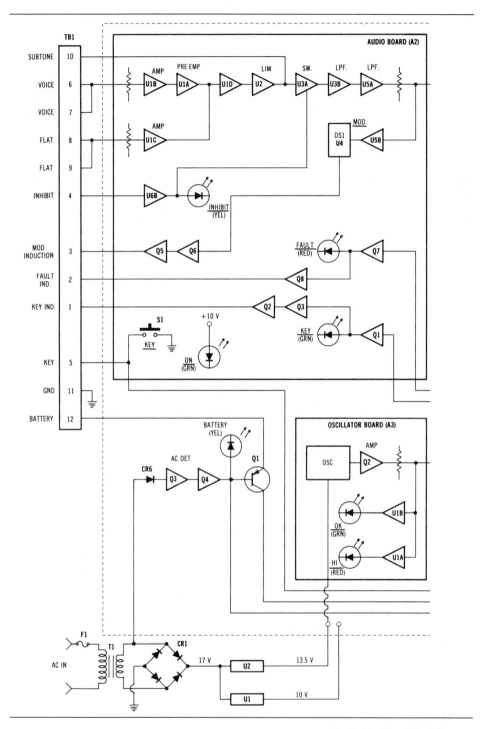

Fig. 8-18. Simplified diagram

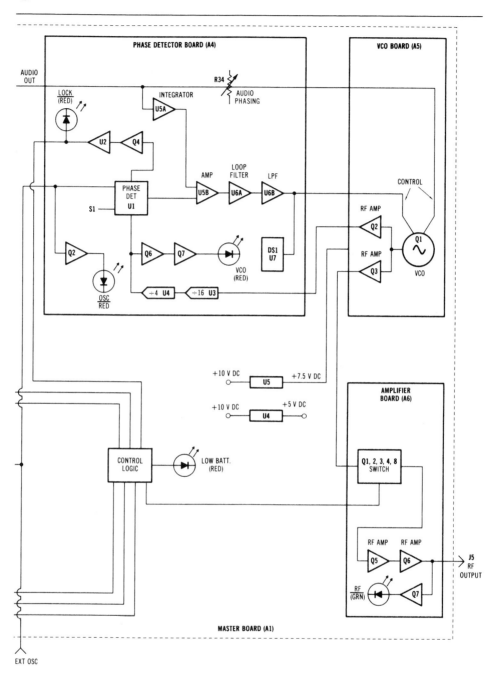

of exciter circuit.

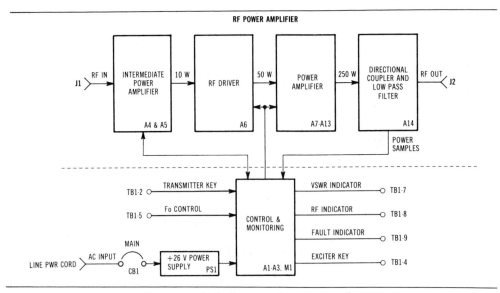

Fig. 8-19. Block diagram of power amplifier unit.

energy in the collector circuit of Q6 is supplied through C26 to a diode rectifier and filter followed by transistor Q7. The charge on C23 is present when there is RF energy in the collector circuit of Q6. This charge turns on the green LED, indicating that the exciter has been keyed on and is supplying signal to the input of the power amplifier.

The diodes CR1 through CR4 in the input circuit of Q5 function as an electronic switch. When the transmitter is to be keyed on, diodes CR2 and CR3 are biased off. However, CR1 and CR4 conduct and the RF voltage at the input terminals (J1-B) passes on to amplifier Q5. If the exciter is unkeyed, CR1 and CR4 switch off and CR2 and CR3 conduct. Diode CR2 places a 51-ohm termination across the input terminals providing a proper load on the VCO. CR3 places an RF short across the input of Q5.

The voltages for turning the diodes on and off are handled by the five bipolar transistors below the diodes in Fig. 8-21. When the exciter is to be keyed off, a low is placed on the keyline at terminal 2 located at the lower left in Fig. 8-21. The net result is to turn off transistor Q1 and turn on transistor Q2. As a result diode CR3 is switched on while diodes CR1 and CR4 are switched off. Transistor Q4 is also switched off when the exciter is keyed off, turning on diode CR2.

When the low is removed from the keyline (terminal 2), transistors Q1 and Q4 are turned on while Q2 is turned off. As a result, diodes CR1 and CR4 conduct, and the path is closed between the RF input terminal and the base circuit of Q5.

The output of the exciter supplies the 200-milliwatt FM carrier to the input of the power amplifier. Refer to the lower right-hand corner of Fig. 8-22. The interconnection plan of Fig. 8-22 shows the modular makeup of the transmitter and how the modules are joined together. On the right is the group of modules that make up the RF section of the transmitter. The transmitter control board and power supply are located at the bottom left. At the top left is the metering board and the meter and LED display assembly. The transmitter operation, monitoring, and fault-location activities are performed by the circuits of the control board. The transmitter can be keyed on or off and, if desired, operated at ultralow power F_o. Sensitive circuits monitor and protect the power amplifier. This is done by circuits that monitor critical parts of the power amplifier to ensure proper operation, maintain the transmitter output power at the rated power level, or reduce the power to a safe level if a fault occurs. Various local and

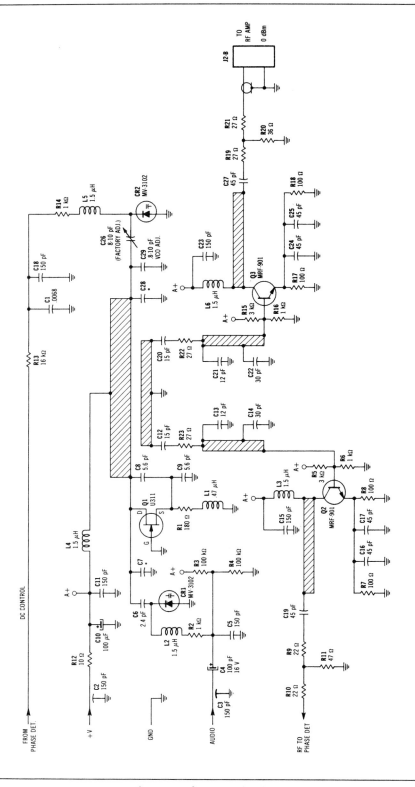

Fig. 8-20. The VCO circuit.

352

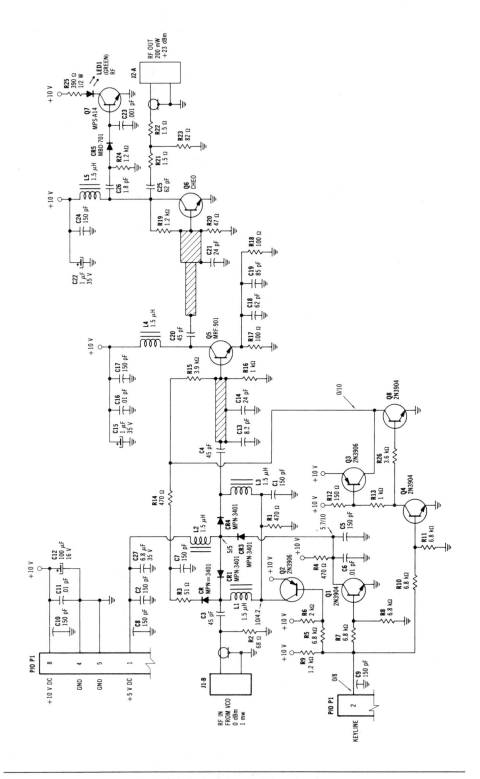

Fig. 8-21. Exciter RF amplifier circuit.

remote fault indicators are monitored and LEDs operate on or off to identify the fault location.

Automatic shut down of the transmitter occurs if the output power drops below the 50- to 100-watt level. For example, should one of nine faults occur, the output from an associated fault detector would gain control. This activity shuts down and holds the transmitter output power to zero even though the transmitter is keyed. Each of the nine fault circuits also turn on its associated fault location LED. The transmitter will also shut down for either a low voltage, high voltage, high temperature, or door interlock fault. The transmitter also has facilities for maintaining a constant output level with normal changes in operating conditions. Actually, the automatic power control either maintains the transmitter power output at the level set by adjustment or shuts down the transmitter completely when certain faults occur. The transmitter can be operated at any chosen power level between its rated power and the shut down value.

The front panel meter is selected by switch S1 to provide an analog indication of forward power, reflected power, or one of nine multimeter functions. The latter include the IPA driver and the series of power amplifiers in the transmitter. The metering board itself contains the circuits used to measure and limit the current to the IPA driver and five RF modules. Also included are the components that respond to multimeter switching for any one of the nine measurement functions that can be displayed on the front panel meter.

The incoming RF signal is first increased in level by amplifier-module A4 and IPA A5 located at the lower right of Fig. 8-22. A driver module (A6) follows which has its output divided by A7 into five equal-level values that supply a signal to the five RF modules A8 through A12 connected with paralleled outputs. All outputs are combined on the combiner board A13. From there the high-power level signal passes to the directional coupler and on to the antenna.

8-4-2. Radio-Frequency Modules

The two IPA modules are shown in Fig. 8-23. Actually the two modules (A4 and A5) combine to form the complete intermediate power amplifier. The power output is 13 watts with a minimum input level of 150 milliwatts and an input/output impedance of 50 ohms. The IPA module provides the necessary interface connections for the Motorola UHF power amplifier module A4 at the lower left. It is only necessary to connect the required external striplines and components to complete the amplifier.

The RF drive from the exciter is supplied to a matching stripline at the right center of Fig. 8-23. The signal continues through a transmission-line strip that eventually applies the signal to the input of the amplifier by way of terminal 7. The horizontal section of line acts as an adjustable attenuator and provides a means of controlling the output power of the transmitter.

Pin diodes CR1–CR3 are spaced at quarter-wavelength intervals. They are biased by the changeable voltage that arrives by way of the AGC terminal at the top right. This DC control voltage changes the pin diode resistance. The spacing and circuit arrangement permits the attenuation offered by CR1 and CR3 to vary the line losses in such a manner that the transmitter output power can be controlled within the power range of 100 to 250 watts. At the same time, the impedance is held at the required 50 ohms. When the amplifier A4 is operational, the amplified signal is available at terminal 1.

When a fault or operating condition requires that the transmitter output power drop to zero, all three diodes are biased high enough to attentuate the input signal to

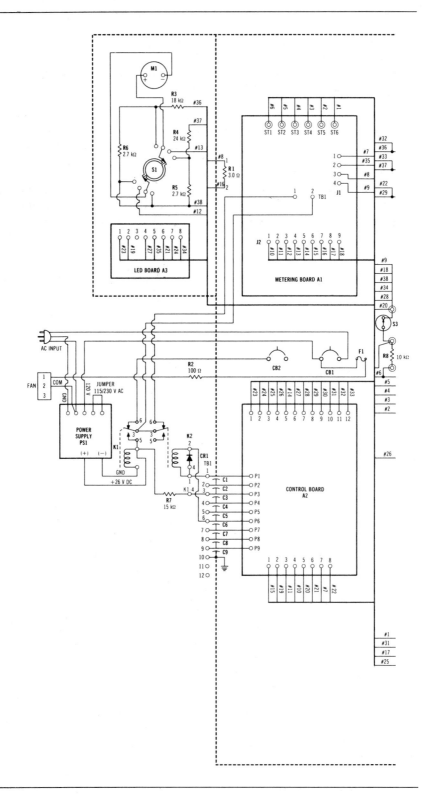

Fig. 8-22. Power amplifier

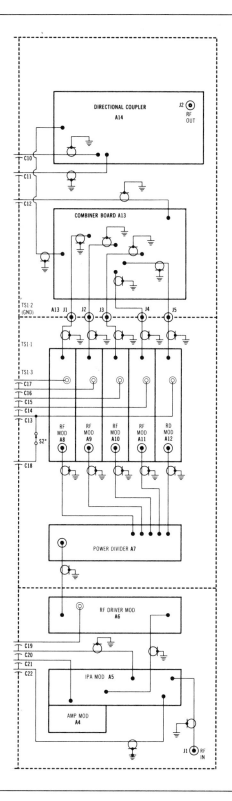

interconnection plan.

356

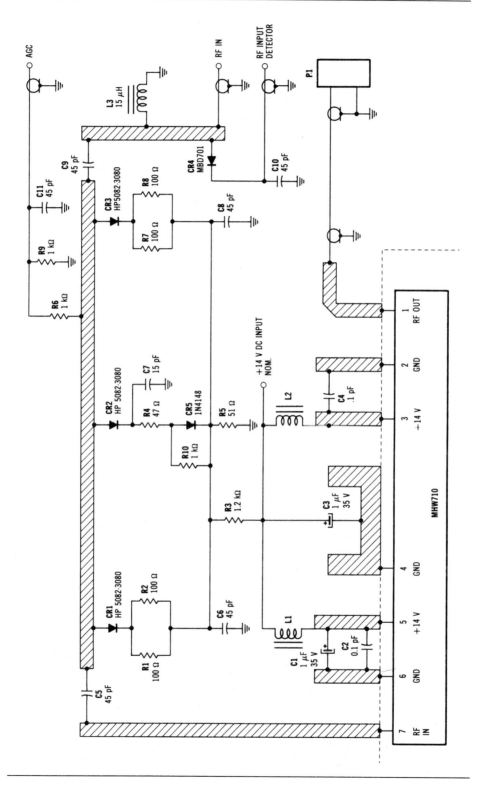

Fig. 8-23. Intermediate power amplifier modules.

zero. Whenever the power output drops below 100 watts, CR2 aided by CR5 increases the line attenuation to drop the signal level at terminal 7 of A4 to zero level.

There are two decoupling filters connected between terminals 5 and 6 as well as terminals 2 and 3. They decouple the supply voltage below 5 MHz and, in conjunction with an internal capacitor, the frequency range between 5 and 512 MHz as well. A hot-carrier diode (CR4) is connected slightly up on the input line on the right side of Fig. 8-23. It produces a rectified output voltage on capacitor C10. This component is conveyed to the input RF sensing circuit on the control board. When the input signal reaches a predetermined level, the RF input indicator on the power amplifier front panel lights.

A schematic of each power amplifier module (A6 and A8 through A12) is given in Fig. 8-24A. One module of this type (A6) acts as the driver while five more identical modules (A8–A12) are connected in parallel to form the main RF power amplifier. Refer back to Fig. 8-22. Each module is a single-stage stripline amplifier with a gain of 7 dB. The values of capacitors C4 and C7 are determined by the operating frequency. Variable capacitor C8 serves as fine tuning and is adjusted for maximum output during transmitter alignment. The input and output impedance is 50 ohms.

The striplines as they are mounted on the circuit board are shown in Fig. 8-24B. Note the input connector and series capacitor C1 at the far right. Almost at the opposite end of the line near capacitor C4 there is another segment attached. The length is such that stripline matching is maintained, and RF energy is not shunted to ground by loading. On the left side you can find fixed capacitors C5, C6, C7, and adjustable capacitor C8. Two output capacitors (C9 and C10) as well as the RF output connector are at the opposite end of the line. Near capacitor C6 there is another added section of stripline that permits the connection of the supply voltage to the collector of the transistor. Again, it is a decoupling stripline section that provides a means of connecting external components without causing a loss of the amplified RF signal. In normal operation, this module will supply 65 watts of output when the input signal level is 13 watts.

Refer to Fig. 8-22 again. Notice there is a power divider located between the driver module and the power amplifier module. This is also made of a stripline section as shown in Fig. 8-25. In this operation, the section of stripline suitably segmented can be used as a power divider. The input of the line is the 65 watts from the driver, and there are five individual outputs each with a signal level of 13 watts. Capacitor C1 is used to tune the divider. During transmitter alignment it is set for maximum output power.

The total power output for the transmitter is obtained by combining the five outputs of the final power amplifier modules. Again, sections of stripline are used as shown in Fig. 8-26. Each of the five power amplifiers drives one of the five in-phase ports through its coaxial connector output. The strip sections provide isolation between the PA modules, making the power addition with very low loss. The combined RF outputs appear across 50 ohms at the output port.

To the right of each connector from the driver, there is an RF isolation and attenuator section of line that extends back to five individual fault protection circuits. A minute amount of power appears across resistors R6 through R10. This power is rectified by diodes CR1 through CR5 and is applied to the combiner overload sensing circuit that can take control of the automatic gain control line to hold the transmitter power output to a safe level.

A list of controls and indicators is given in Table 8-4. Inasmuch as location and function are also given, the listing acts as a summary of the high-powered transmitter design plan. Many of the controls and indicators were not mentioned in the copy. Block diagrams and schematics will help you locate them and also give you some idea about the circuits in which they function.

358

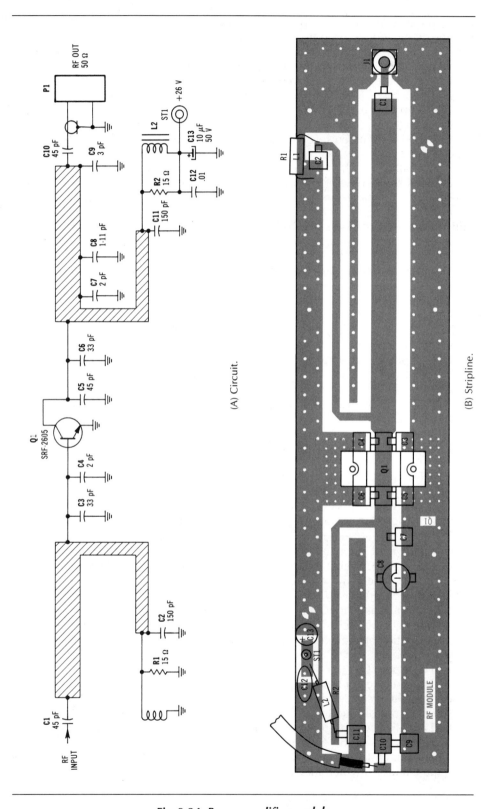

(A) Circuit.

(B) Stripline.

Fig. 8-24. Power amplifier module.

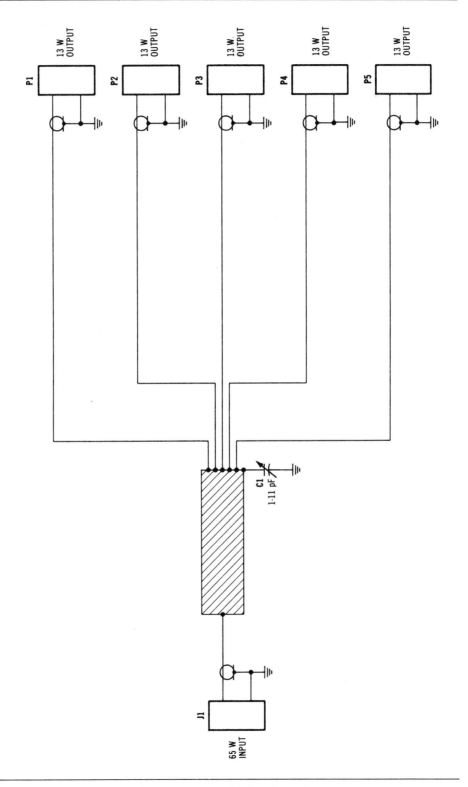

Fig. 8-25. Power divider schematic.

360

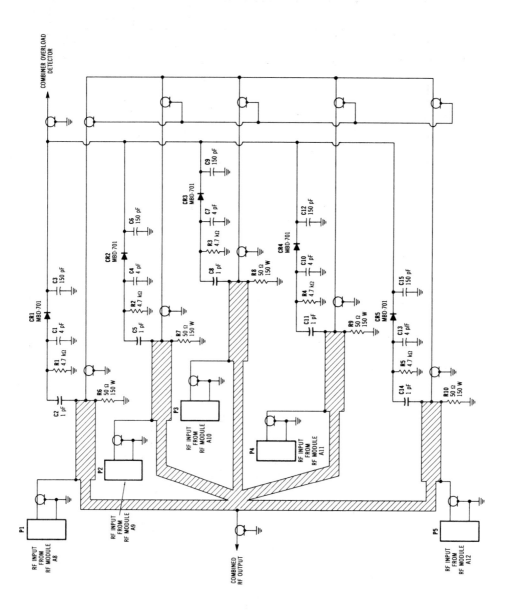

Fig. 8-26. Output combiner schematic.

Table 8-4. Transmitter Controls and Indicators

Control/ Indicator	Location	Function
Selector switch (S1)	PA front panel	Selects forward power, multimeter functions, or reflected power for display on meter M1.
Meter (M1)	PA front panel	Provides front panel analog display of forward or reflected power in watts, or multimeter voltage and current functions.
Multimeter Selector (S1, S2)	PA metering board (A1)	Selects one of nine multimeter input functions: PS-V, PA1-A, PA2-A, PA3-A, PA4-A, PA5-A, DRV-A, IPA-A, and IPA-V.
Keying Switch PA (S1)	Control board (A2)	Provides alternate transmitter keying. Up (ON), center (OFF), down (MOMENTARY ON).
KEY switch (A2S1)	Exciter audio board A2	Momentary push-button switch. Keys exciter when pressed.
Status Indicators	PA front panel (LED Bd A3)	Six LEDs that provide the following status indications:
ON (Green)		Indicates the DC output of power supply PS1 is sufficient to energize power supply relay K1.
RF IN (Green)		Indicates RF drive from exciter is above the predetermined level, not necessarily enough to cause PA to reach rated output power.
RF OUT (Green)		Indicates that output power is above level preset by customer (0 to 100% of rated output power, 100–250 watts).
F_o MODE (Yellow)		Indicates that ultralow output power mode of operation is selected (0.5 to 2.5 watts, adjustable).
FAULT (Red)		Indicates that one or more of nine PA protective circuits has sensed an overload condition.
SHUT DOWN (Red)		Indicates that transmitter output power is forced and held to zero (FAULT indicator should also be on).
AC POWER switch (CB1)	PA chassis (internal)	15-ampere circuit breaker switch that controls application of AC power to PA unit.
BATTERY switch (CB2)	PA chassis (internal)	30-ampere circuit breaker switch (toggle) that controls battery power (when installed) to normally closed contacts of power control relay K1.

Table 8-4. — cont. Transmitter Controls and Indicators

Control/Indicator	Location	Function
AGC indicator (Green)	PA control board A2	Indicates that forward power sample is exceeding the level set by HI PWR ADJ R54 and AGC amplifier U1D. Output is switching high. This normally indicates that U1D is controlling transmitter output power.
PA internal fault indicators	PA control board A2	Nine LEDs (red) that provide overload or out-of-normal indications as follows: INTERLOCK (door), COMBINER, TEMP, HI VOLT, LO VOLT, High VSWR, IPA current, DRV current, and PA current.
Exciter format panel indicators	Exciter audio board A2	Five front panel indications are provided for the exciter as follows:
ON (Green)		Power on indicator LED, powered from +10-volt regulator U2 on exciter chassis. Should be on when AC line cord is connected.
MODULATION		Modulation level indication is provided by a 10-segment bar graph indicator.
KEYED (Green)		An LED indicates exciter is keyed either by a low EXCITER KEYLINE from PA or alternately from KEY switch (S1) on audio board A2.
FAULT (Red)		An LED indicates an exciter fault for either an out-of-lock condition, or loss of AC line power with backup battery power employed.
Audio inhibited (Yellow)		An LED indicates when audio is inhibited from modulating exciter as a result of a logic low being placed on the MODULATION INHIBIT line exciter TB1-4.
Internal exciter indicators		Eight LEDs and a bar graph indicator provide indications of the operating status of the exciter circuits when the front panel is removed as follows:
Oscillator HI (red) OK (green)	Exciter oscillator A3	These two LEDs are used as tuning aids when setting the oscillator level during the preoperational check and adjustment procedures.
Fault indicators (three, red)	Phase detector pcb A4	Three LEDs provide indications of problems on the phase detector board. These include lost VCO, OUT OF LOCK, and lost OSC from top to bottom.

Table 8-4. — cont. Transmitter Controls and Indicators

Control/ Indicator	Location	Function
VCO control level indicator	Phase detector pcb A4	A ten-segment bar graph indicator is used to set the VCO rest frequency during alignment. Should have one of two center bars lighted.
Battery indicators (yellow, red)	Exciter master board	Two LEDs provide battery indications when backup battery power is employed. Yellow LED indicates exciter operating on battery power (exciter fault indicator should also be on indicating loss of AC power). Red LED indicates that battery voltage is below a predetermined level, nominally 16 volts DC.
RF output indicator (green)	Exciter RF amplifier	An LED provides an indication that the RF output of the exciter is above the predetermined level.

8-5. Landmobile Sideband Transceiver

A special sideband form of modulation for the landmobile services has been pioneered by Stephens Engineering Associates (SEA). It is referred to as amplitude compandered sideband (ACSB). The big advantage of a sideband signal as compared to FM is the very narrow band of frequencies the signal occupies. The ACSB signal would require only a 5-kHz channel as compared to the 15- and 30-kHz FM channel. Also, it is possible that two ACSB channels could share the spectrum space between existing FM channels.

Typical spectrum utilization for an ACSB signal is given in Fig. 8-27. Upper sideband transmission is used and the carrier-frequency assignment is approximately 1 kHz above the low frequency end of the channel. The voice band extends between 300 Hz and 2600 Hz. In the ACSB system there is a pilot frequency at 3.1 kHz. In this respect the ACSB mode of operation differs from that of conventional single sideband transmission. Before covering the ACSB system, it would be helpful to review the sideband discussions of Chapter 4 (Sections 4-7 and 4-8).

In the ACSB transmitter (Fig. 8-28), the microphone audio is increased in level by an appropriate amplifier. This amplifier also includes an audio filter that establishes the correct audio frequency limits permissible. Next, there is a compressor circuit that reduces the amplitude range by a specific ratio called the compression ratio. In the ACSB transmitter that ratio is 4 to 1. In such a circuit, a 40-dB change at the input would be reduced to a 10-dB change in the output. This compression has influence on what is known as the dynamic range of the audio, and it is not to be confused with the activity of a limiter circuit. Dynamic range is related to the voltage change between the weakest voice frequency components and the strongest voice frequency components. The entire amplitude range of the voice frequencies is compressed but the voice frequencies are still conveyed in a linear matter.

The modulation efficiency and signal-to-noise ratio are improved. It is possible to obtain maximum usable RF power output over widely varying microphone levels. The original dynamic range of the audio is restored by the receiver, and, in the process,

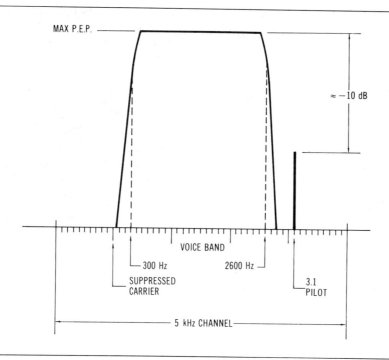

Fig. 8-27. The ACSB channel layout.

there is an improvement in signal-to-noise ratio. The compressed dynamic range is also of benefit in the amplification process that takes place throughout the later stages of the transmitter because good linearity can be retained more readily.

The audio output now passes through a controllable attenuator that responds to a DC control voltage that is developed by the automatic level control (ALC) system of the transmitter. Next the pilot tone frequency of 3100 Hz is added. At the receiver its function will be to hold the incoming signal on a precise frequency for final demodulation. Thus a good-quality audio will be reproduced. The first three waveforms shown at the top of Fig. 8-28 show the activities that have occurred. The first waveform shows the initial amplification of the audio signal; next, the compression is shown. This is followed by the addition of the pilot tone.

The pilot tone is conveyed continuously with all transmissions and is set approximately 10 dB below the rated PEP output power level. It is stable in amplitude and frequency and serves as a useful reference signal at the receiver.

Next, the signal is sent to the balanced modulator which suppresses the injected carrier component so it does not appear in the output. The balanced modulator output consists of the upper and lower sidebands which are now present above and below the suppressed carrier frequency of 10.240 MHz. In the ACSB system the lower sideband is removed, and the upper sideband passes through a very narrow bandpass crystal filter that has a very flat linear characteristic over the passband.

Amplitude linearity is an important consideration in sideband transmission. Good linearity is necessary to follow the amplitude changes in the signal faithfully so as not to produce distortion. The stages of sideband equipment are designed to pass a certain range of amplitudes without overloading or distorting. Balanced linear operation of stages is important. As a result the balanced modulators, RF mixers, and IF and RF amplifiers all operate in a linear fashion.

The output of the upper sideband filter is next converted to the operating channel by the RF mixer. It is designed for linear operation and usually is a balanced circuit so as to prevent the injected local oscillator frequency from appearing in the output and

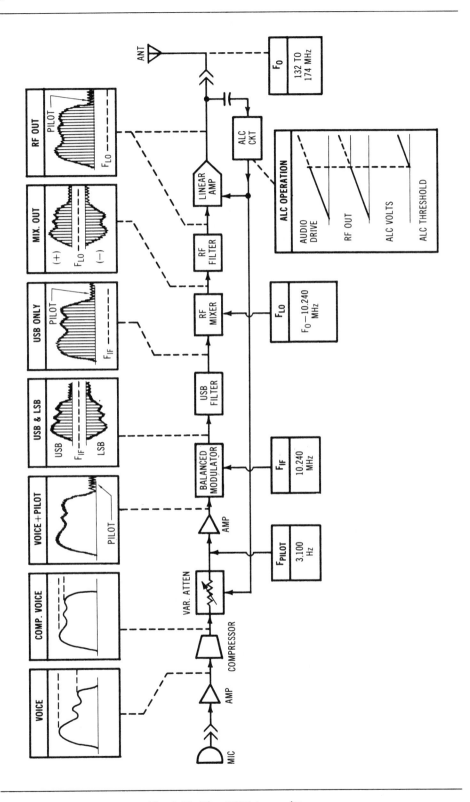

Fig. 8-28. The ACSB transmitter.

entering the next stage. The injection local oscillator frequency has a value which is the desired output frequency minus the 10.240 MHz IF value. For example, if the desired output frequency is 150.24 MHz, the local oscillator injection frequency needs to be 140 (150.24 − 10.24) MHz.

The output of the RF mixer contains the sum and differences of the modulated upper sideband and the injection local oscillator frequency. A follow-up RF filter removes the difference band (LSB) and passes the sum upper sideband frequencies (USB) to the linear amplifier. The linear amplifier builds up the signal to the final transmit power. These amplifiers are designed for extremely linear operation and low distortion. A low-pass filter is used at its output to reduce any harmonic radiation before the linear amplifier output is applied to the antenna.

Momentary voice peaks, extraneous noises, or other disturbances such as misadjustment may cause a transmitter to exceed its rated output and/or operate in a nolinear fashion that produces distortion. The automatic level control (ALC) circuit minimizes such faults by evaluating the RF output and reducing the gain of one or more stages in the transmitter. The ALC circuit develops a DC control voltage that is sent back to prevent any RF output that exceeds a preset level. As a result this voltage can be supplied to the linear amplifier and the variable attenuator acting as an automatic gain control which reduces gain in proportion to the amount of ALC voltage present. Its operation is fast enough to catch and correct voice frequency transients.

As in other landmobile equipment the key frequencies are generated and made stable by PLL synthesizer systems. Such systems are essential in maintaining frequency stability and voice clarity.

An incoming signal at the receiver (Fig. 8-29) is applied to a broadband RF amplifier that will accommodate the complete receive frequency range of a given band. In the balanced mixer the incoming signal is down converted to the IF frequency. The mixer does pass sum and difference frequency spectra. However, it is the upper frequency spectra that carries the desired information that is passed by the succeeding upper sideband filter. The receiver selectivity is determined primarily by the characteristics of this filter. Note that there is an intervening noise blanker that reduces noise bursts and transients. An IF amplifier follows the sideband filter.

The product detector recovers the audio frequencies and the pilot tone as well. As in all sideband detectors it is necessary to reinsert the reference carrier in the demodulation process. In the example this frequency is 10.240 MHz. The output of the product detector follows two paths. Voice frequencies pass through the audio filter (which blocks the pilot tone) to the gate circuit associated with the squelch and AGC systems of the receiver.

Voice frequencies are then passed to an expander, audio amplifier, and loudspeaker. In the expander, the audio levels are expanded by the same ratio as they were compressed by the compressor in the transmitter. Its ratio is also 4 to 1. In effect the dynamic range that was compressed at the transmitter is now restored to its original level at the receiver. In the process the signal-to-noise ratio is also improved.

The voice and tone frequency components are also passed to a bandpass filter which rejects voice frequencies and passes only the tone component to the phase detector. Here the tone is compared with a 3100-Hz reference generated within the receiver. The output of the phase detector is a DC voltage that varies in magnitude and polarity in relation to the difference between pilot and reference tones. Its action is similar to any phase-locked loop system. The output of the phase detector is supplied to the injection local-oscillator frequency generator. Therefore the receiver is locked to the incoming transmitter frequency. Thus the voice clarity is good; the problem of intermittently difficult to understand audio output of some conventional single-sideband receivers has been eliminated.

As is customary in single-sideband systems many of the transmitter and receiver circuits of a sideband transceiver can be used in both the transmit and receive mode, as shown in Fig. 8-30.

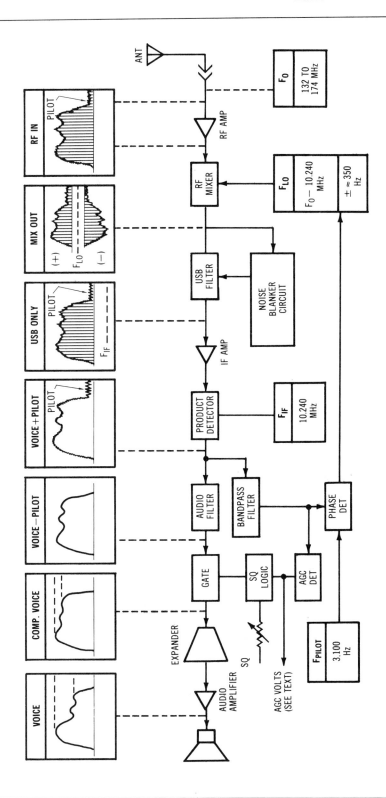

Fig. 8-29. The ACSB receiver.

368

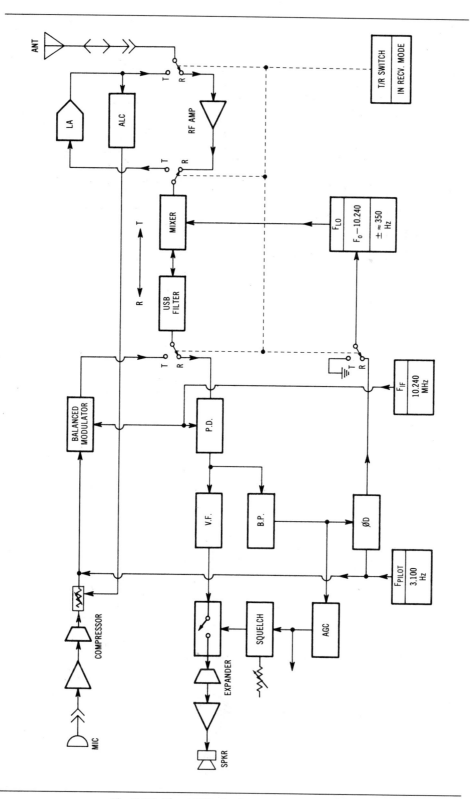

Fig. 8-30. The ACSB simplex transceiver layout.

Relay contacts in the diagram are used to represent the switching positions. Ordinarily this is accomplished by switching the DC supply voltage among the various circuits or by solid-state switches. Many of the tuned circuits in the sideband transceiver are also arranged for bidirectional operation. The contacts at the lower center show how the output of the phase detector associated with the pilot tone reaches the injection local oscillator. On transmit, this path to the phase detector is disconnected, and the input to the local oscillator is grounded. The contacts at top center connect the output of the upper sideband filter to the product detector on receive. On transmit, the output of the balanced modulator is supplied to the upper sideband filter and passes on to the mixer. Note that the signal is now traveling in the opposite direction. The two sets of contacts at the top right handle antenna switching between receiver and transmitter section. Also, the output of the RF amplifier on receive supplies a signal to the first mixer. On transmit, a signal leaves the mixer and passes through the linear amplifier to the antenna system.

A SEA ACSB mobile transceiver is shown in Fig. 8-31. The unit is designed to operate on 16 simplex or half-duplex channels. In half-duplex operation the separation between the transmit and receive frequencies can be as much as 6 MHz. The frequency range of the unit extends between 132–174 MHz.

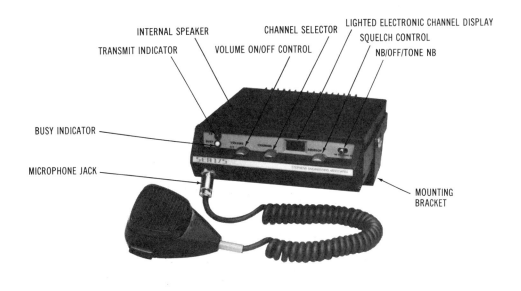

Courtesy Stephens Engineering Associates

Fig. 8-31. The ACSB transceiver controls and indicators.

The transmitter power output is 25 watts PEP and the receiver sensitivity 12-dB Sinad at 0.25 microvolt. Transmission is on the upper sideband. The lower sideband and carrier suppression are at least 60 and 45 dB respectively.

SEA also makes available a hand-held unit and a repeater. The hand-held unit (Fig. 8-32A) operates on 12 selected channels with a PEP output of 5 watts. The pilot tone is at the 600-milliwatt level. The repeater (Fig. 8-32B) operates between 132–174 MHz with 16 available channels. Again, the transmit and receive frequency separations can be up to 6 MHz. The power output is 25 watts PEP, and the required input power from the power lines is less than 100 watts. The repeater operation is economical and the unit could be powered readily with a solar panel, if required.

Fig. 8-32. Handheld transceiver and repeater.

8-6. System Plans

Two-way radio installations can be arranged in various ways to meet the needs of the user. Several basic plans are illustrated in Fig. 8-33. In the simple arrangement of Fig. 8-33A the base station equipment can be identical to the units installed in each of the mobiles except that a 110-volt AC power supply is required. The antenna can be mounted on the roof or along the side of the building occupied by the user's business or other activity which requires the two-way radio service. The power outputs are the same and base and mobiles operate on the same frequency. Such is the lowest cost system. Additional mobile installations can be made as the needs of the business increase.

If improved range and reliability are required, one or more of three possibilities exist as shown in Fig. 8-33B. One possibility is to use a higher-gain antenna mounted at the same site. An increase in antenna height can also provide significant help in extending range. It can be in the form of a higher mounting mast or an antenna tower. The third possibility is to increase the transmitter power.

In busy two-way radio areas more than one radio service can be assigned the same channel. In other words, frequencies are shared. Consequently, your base and mobiles when they are turned on and not squelched can hear the signals from these other services. Likewise, the other installations can hear your signals when they are on the air. The process of using tone or digital-coded transmissions alleviates some of the channel chatter. In the basic coded system of Fig. 8-33C, the base and mobile radios are only turned on when the signal they pick up contains the decided-upon tone or digital information. At other times, the receivers remain quiet. Details on coding were covered in Section 8-1.

Coded systems can be made more complex than the basic plan just described. For example, in the arrangement of Fig. 8-33C the base station can transmit four separate codes, one for each of the four mobiles. Thus, when a specific mobile is to be contacted, the base station can do so without activating the other three mobiles. Each

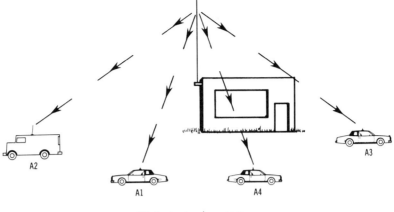

(A) Basic simple system.

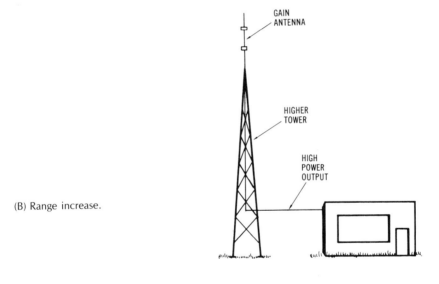

(B) Range increase.

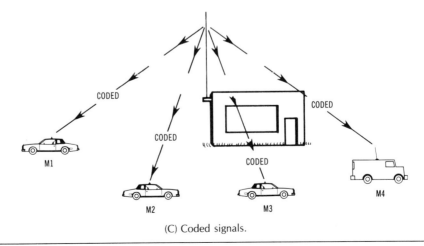

(C) Coded signals.

Fig. 8-33. System plans.

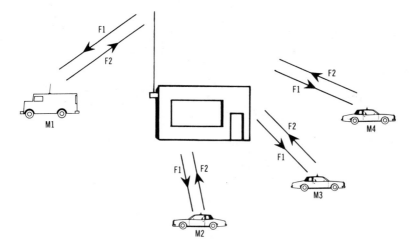

(A) Two frequencies.

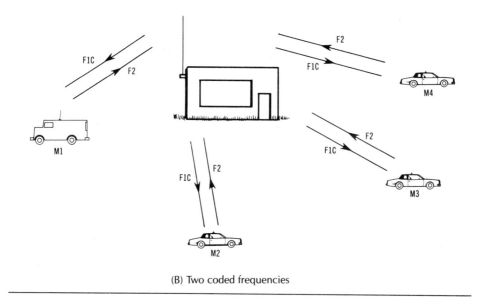

(B) Two coded frequencies

Fig. 8-34. Additional

of the transmit mobiles will have a code that will only activate the base station, and even the transmissions from the specific mobiles will not be heard by the other three. You can understand that coding is an important transmission advantage when there are many mobiles on a system. For example, a system may have thirty mobiles and you can well understand the chatter on the frequency if it were not possible for the base station to choose the mobiles selectively.

Assume that a system has thirty mobiles, plus three supervisory mobiles. A coded system could be set up to have a group of ten of the mobiles assigned as a responsibility

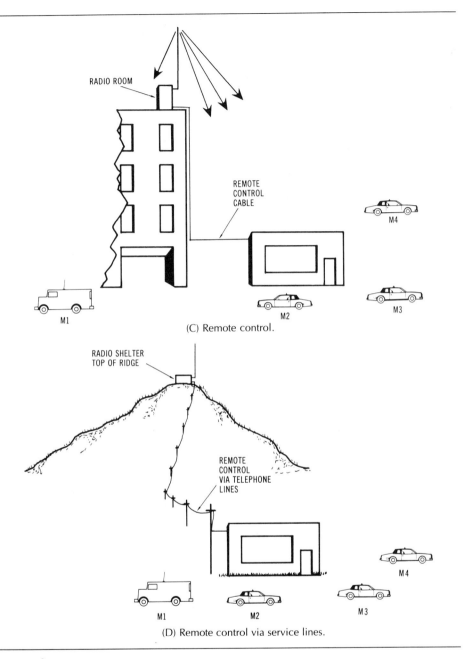

(C) Remote control.

(D) Remote control via service lines.

system plans.

to each supervisor. Consequently, a coded system could be arranged to keep each supervisor in coded contact with the base station. At other times it may be necessary to contact one of the supervisors and each of the ten mobiles under his supervision. Perhaps at certain times it is an advantage to be able to contact all thirty-three at the same time. You can now understand the importance of the rather complex microprocessor and PROM coding capabilities used in the equipment described in Section 8-1.

Some two-way radio services are assigned two frequencies, one to the base station and a second frequency to all of the mobiles. Refer to Fig. 8-34A. The system base station transmits on frequency F1 and receives on frequency F2. Each of the mobiles transmits on frequency F2 and receives on frequency F1. Such systems can be coded in many combinations. In the arrangement of Fig. 8-34B, assume a proper code is transmitted by the base station. When received, this coded signal will activate the four mobiles. However, other systems operating on the same frequency but using a different code will not activate any one of the mobile receivers.

Again, the coding has many possibilities, depending upon the needs and desires of the user. For example, four separate codes can be transmitted by the base station on F1. Consequently, only one of the mobile units of the group of four can be activated selectively. The same coding versatility as mentioned previously can be built into the mobiles, and coding can be arranged to activate units in groups along with supervisor and manager mobiles. Often the coding is planned to match the activities of the mobiles of a business. For example, the mobiles can be segregated into supervisory, sales, and service. Each group, according to activity, can then be selectively called using tone and digital coding techniques.

After considering the various coding arrangements, it is apparent that a method for overriding the decoding circuits at each receiver becomes obvious. The receiver is activated only when you are called. At other times the channel may be busy and you do not know it, particularly if the channel is shared by other similar two-way radio services. Thus, if you grab your microphone and call some other station, you may interfere with a conversation that is taking place on channel. In many installations the procedure of removing the microphone from its hanger automatically activates the receiver so you can listen to the activities on channel before you turn on your transmitter with the push-to-talk switch. In some installations you must depress an appropriate switch to override coding.

Remote control facilities are often a part of two-way radio installations. Fig. 8-34C shows a typical case. In this installation the actual radio is mounted on the top floor of a tall building or in a small radio enclosure mounted on the roof. The control center for the system is located at the place of business and a remote control cable interconnects this dispatch point with the remotely controlled radio equipment. Many installations have several dispatch points throughout a business location. In some installations there is one remote control center and then one or more additional dispatch points that are usually placed into operation by taking an ordinary telephone off its hanger. By depressing appropriate pad buttons, you can place the transmitter on the air with its appropriate code signal and establish communications with a mobile or, perhaps, some other fixed station that is a part of the business establishment.

Another plan, illustrated in Fig. 8-34D, is used quite often in small town and rural installations; the radio is located in a radio shelter atop a high ridge. If the ridge is in back of your business place and on your property or if willing landowners own the intervening property, you can run the cable up the side of the ridge to the radio shelter. Often the high location will be some distance away, and you would have to cross many property lines with your cable. Thus, instead of running your own line, a line pair is rented from the local telephone company, and the remote control switching signals and voice communications are carried between the radio shelter and the business place over a rented telephone line.

9

Repeater, Trunked, and Cellular Radio Systems

A repeater transmitter-receiver combination is used to increase the coverage area of a two-way radio system or to insure more reliable performance in areas where signals are reflected or attenuated by buildings or terrain. Repeater systems are common in metropolitan and suburban areas to obtain coverage to all mobile units in the area. In hilly and mountainous regions, repeaters are used for more reliable coverage in low areas and valleys. Also, they are a necessity in remote areas where a large coverage is required.

Cellular radio is a radiotelephone system that has a direct tie-in with your local telephone company. With cellular radio, you can carry on a phone conversation with family, friend, neighbor, or business associate from your car, golf links, beach, or anywhere else a cellular system is in operation. Presently, they are in operation in a number of large cities, and, eventually, you should be able to travel across the country and tie in from just about anyplace along the way.

9-1. Conventional Repeaters

Normally, repeaters are mounted at a high site, such as on a tall building, a tower, an area of high average terrain, or on a ridge or mountaintop. The transmitter may have an output of several hundred watts. The antenna provides gain by using a low-angle omnidirectional vertical pattern. Height, power, and gain permit delivery of the strongest possible signal to the mobile receivers. At the same time the high location of the repeater antenna permits better pickup of the mobile signals.

In some instances, the repeater site can be located on the edge of the coverage area. For example, it may be on a ridge on the west side of a small city. In this case, the antennas can be designed with a horizontal directional pattern toward the east so additional transmitter gain and receiver pick-up sensitivity are provided in the area of coverage. A basic repeater system is shown in Fig. 9-1A. The repeater is located atop a

376

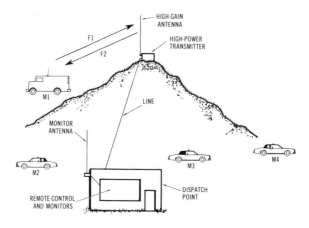

(A) With wired link.

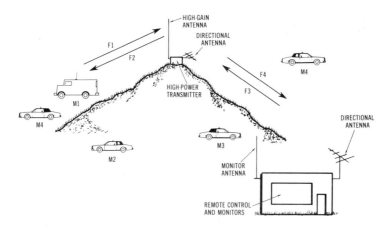

(B) With radio link.

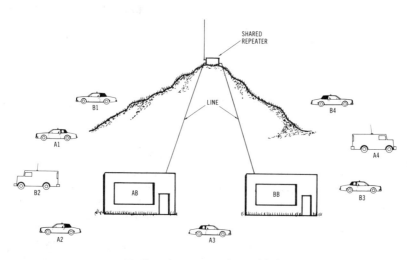

(C) Shared repeater with wired link.

Fig. 9-1. Basic repeater systems.

ridge. Usually two frequencies are used, one between mobile and repeater and the other for the path between repeater and mobile. A private telephone line or a user's wire line interconnect the repeater with the master-control dispatch point at the business, industrial, or service establishment. Transmitters are monitored at the master control to keep a continuous check on the repeater operation. Information can be exchanged over the control line. Often a monitor antenna is included to permit an on-the-air pickup of the repeater transmission. Usually the repeater itself includes an operating position. Thus, the repeater can also be checked out at the repeater site.

Quite often more than one repeater is installed at the high location. When such is the case, it is necessary to make the right choice of frequencies to minimize interference and intermodulation components. There must be cooperation among the individual owners, and often local advisory boards are formed to insure minimum interference and fair treatment for the owners of the systems. Even proper antenna mounting is a consideration in reducing technical problems.

In remote areas or in any location where there are no telephone lines running up to the repeater site, or if there is a great distance between the users and the repeater site, a radio link can be established between the control points and the repeater. As shown in Fig. 9-1B, the efficiency of operation can be improved with the use of directional antennas at the control point and at the repeater. Sometimes power is not available at a mountain-top repeater site. In this case remotely controlled gasoline- or diesel-driven power generators can be used. They are often augmented with a solar panel power supply. Control and monitoring data can be exchanged over the radio link.

9-1-1. Shared Repeaters

In a shared repeater facility more than one two-way radio system shares a repeater (or repeaters) in terms of operation, initial cost, and continuing service costs. In its simplest form (Fig. 9-1C) two, three, or four operational systems may share a single repeater mounted at a high location. The example depicts two companies with four mobiles each. It should be understood that the number of mobiles can be fewer or more than four. Also, such a basic system could accommodate more than two businesses. Each business has its own base control facility and the usual listening and monitoring equipment. The mobiles from each system can operate freely within the range of the repeater signal. Each system has its own dispatcher who is responsible for monitoring the repeater frequency so as not to cause interference when another member of the system is using the repeater for radiocommunications.

Large repeater installations may serve hundreds of mobiles and their base stations. The smaller of these large systems may be operated by user associations formed by the members of two-way radio systems the repeaters serve. There are also private businesses that operate repeater systems and rent the repeater services to users. Often these companies are also a part of a two-way radio sales and service business. Distributors associated with manufacturers of two-way radio equipment also operate large repeater systems especially in large metropolitan areas.

A large shared repeater system is illustrated in Fig. 9-2. Here five repeaters are assumed — it could be more or less. These repeaters along with a shared antenna system are housed at a high site. Sometimes all of the repeaters are housed in a large rack and panel arrangement. The number of repeaters chosen depends upon the number of two-way radio systems and their mobiles that must be served, plus some capability for adding users. In the Fig. 9-2, family 1 is assigned to repeater 1. This family is assumed to have five separate two-way radio systems with their individual mobiles and individual dispatch/control point connected by lines to repeater 1. The system plan may be such that approximately 50 mobiles can be handled per family or an average of 10 for each two-way radio system.

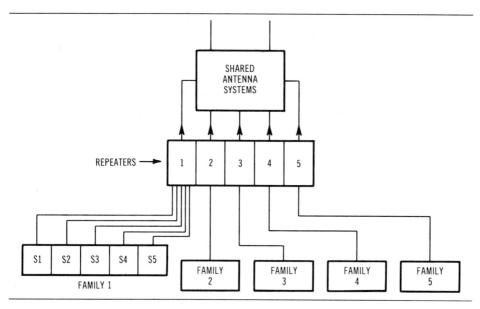

Fig. 9-2. Conventional shared repeater system.

The number of systems that can be handled by each repeater is related to the number of mobiles that each system uses. For an average of 50 mobiles per family the conventional shared repeater system could possibly handle a total of 250 mobiles.

In the conventional shared repeater system, it is necessary that each mobile operator monitor his repeater before transmission to make certain there is no interference to a conversation in process. In the large shared repeater systems the mobiles have separate transmit and receive frequencies, and, with proper receiver design and system arrangement, full duplex operation is possible. This means that a conversation can be telephone-like rather than the push-to-talk simplex operation of simple two-way radio communications. For example, on the 450-MHz band there is a 45-MHz frequency separation between the repeater and mobile transmission frequencies. Excellent duplex operation is possible.

One of the limitations of an active conventional shared repeater system is the fact that one repeater can become clogged with calls while certain other repeaters are at that moment inactive. Hence, it is necessary for some of the systems to wait until their particular repeater is free of traffic. A much better chance of finding an inactive slot is possible using the so-called "trunked" repeater arrangement. This system will be discussed later in this chapter.

The basic essentials of a three-transmitter repeater setup are given in Fig. 9-3. There are three transmitters that supply signals to a single transmit antenna through a combiner system. A single receive antenna picks up signals from the mobiles and, through a multicoupler, supplies them to the appropriate receiver. The audio signals come and go over a hard-wire line (telephone or owned) that links the various dispatch points to the repeater. Digital and tone signals are also exchanged over the lines along with control and monitoring data. If 20 users are assigned to each transmitter, the repeater in Fig. 9-3 would be serving 60 systems. The general plan is valid for conventional and some trunked repeaters. However, the distribution and control segment would be more elaborate and complex for most trunking installations. There are a variety of other components that are a part of a repeater setup. These are involved mainly in the reduction of interference and interaction among the transmitter and receiver facilities. Coverage on these devices was given at the end of the antenna chapter; additional information appears later in this chapter.

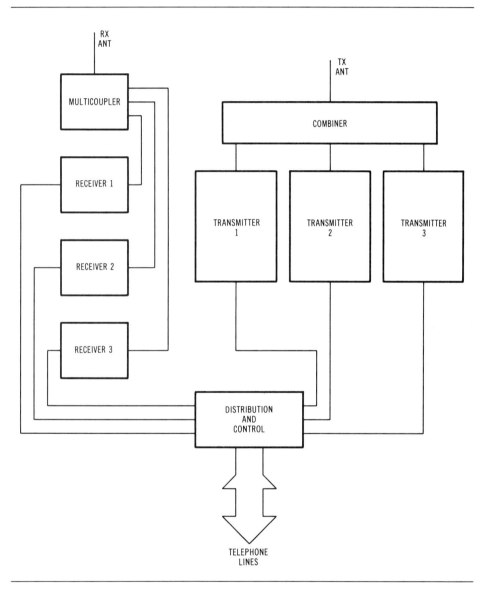

Fig. 9-3. Simplified conventional repeater setup.

9-2. Trunked Repeater Systems

As mentioned previously, in a conventional repeater system, one repeater can become overloaded and the other repeaters in the same system are inactive. This causes some of the systems to wait until their particular repeater is free, while other repeaters are not being used. To better utilize the facilities, the *trunked repeater* system is used. Although the electronics is considerably more complicated than for the conventional system, the basic plan of the trunked system does not differ greatly from that of the conventional system. Each of the families is still assigned an individual repeater. However, if a system assigned to repeater 1, for example, finds that repeater active, the trunking system will seek out an inactive repeater to carry the communications. This requires an involved electronic priority and digital switching system to continuously monitor the communication activities and to make the necessary switchovers instantly.

The electronics of trunked systems reduces to four major techniques. The dashed segments of the basic three-transmitter arrangement of Fig. 9-4 illustrate the basic differences. All of the systems conserve radio spectrum and improve two-way radio service.

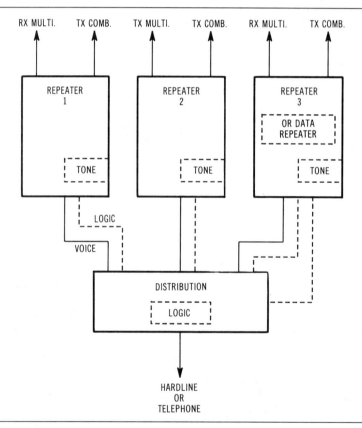

Fig. 9-4. Basic trunking techniques.

One popular system assigns the trunking electronics to the receiver. Appropriate tones must be transmitted by the repeater. However, the sources of these tones are from the user mobile and base stations. This is hardly a change from the conventional shared system because these systems often transmit tones for selective calling and other functions. The solid blocks of Fig. 9-4 depict such a repeater system.

In operation each receiver scans the assigned repeater-channel frequencies looking for incoming calls. A mobile unit desiring service locates an idle channel electronically and accesses its repeater. The mobile sends its call through the repeater to the desired base or mobile stations to be contacted. Scanning stations pick up their identification tone (ID) as it has been sent out from the calling station. A lock-in is then made. Channel selection and assignment is done by the logic circuits in each transceiver. Only about 4 seconds are required to place a call on a 20-channel system. After a lock-in has been made among the stations involved in the conversation, the other receivers of the system continue to scan and await calls. After the conversation has been completed the receivers of the stations involved begin to scan again.

In a second system an idle channel is indicated by a continuous tone from its repeater. In this arrangement mobile and base units scan until they find a tone and, then, wait there for a call. If the channel becomes busy, any listening receiver not called moves on to the next idle tone. A mobile unit desiring service activates an idle channel, and its call and appropriate ID are sent out to the base and/or mobiles to be contacted. Other stations are listening electronically on the idle channel, and those with the correct ID make the connect. Other mobile receivers scan on to the tone of the next idle channel.

The final two trunking systems use a central switching and logic system at the repeater. Interrogation from a station desiring service goes into the central system. Here the traffic is directed electronically and the eventual voice connection is made.

Data communications in these systems must be conveyed between central system and subscribers. In one of the two systems it is transmitted over a separate carrier. One of the repeater transmitters is used full time for transmitting data. In this system, each mobile monitors a fixed data channel. When called, they are directed away from this position electronically to make the connect. The fourth technique conveys the data on each voice channel as a continuous stream of low-frequency tones. In this system each transceiver monitors a "home" repeater and makes a call through it. When the home repeater is busy, logic directs the units to an idle one.

FCC frequency allocations for the 800-MHz band are shown in Table 9-1. Note that the trunked allocations for base and repeater transmit extend between approximately 854 and 866 MHz. The mobile transmit frequencies fall between 809 and 821 MHz approximately. A segment of the these two frequency spans also includes some conventional repeater allocations. Observe the variety of additional allocations on the 800-MHz band including paging, medical, conventional, cellular, and others. The frequency separation between the base and mobile transmit frequencies is 45 MHz. Consequently, 45 MHz is the high IF frequency of trunk mobile radios.

Table 9-1. 800-MHz Frequency Assignments

Frequency MHz	Usage	
806		
	Conventional Mobile 150 Channels	Mobile Transmit
809.750		
	Conventional and Trunked Mobile 250 Channels	Mobile Transmit
816		
	Trunked Mobile 200 Channels	Mobile Transmit
821		
	Cellular Reserve Mobile 133 Channels	

Table 9-1. — cont. 800-MHz Frequency Assignments

Frequency MHz	Usage	
825		
	Cellular Nonwire Line Mobile 333 Channels	
835		
	Cellular Wire Line Mobile 333 Channels	
845		
	Cellular Reserve Mobile 200 Channels	
851		
	Conventional Base 150 Channels	Base Transmit
854.750		
	Conventional and Trunked Base 250 Channels	Base Transmit
861		
	Trunked Base 200 Channels	Base Transmit
866		
	Cellular Reserve Base 133 Channels	
870		
	Cellular Nonwire Line Base 333 Channels	
880		
	Cellular Wire Line Base 200 Channels	
890		
	Cellular Reserve Base 200 Channels	
896		
	Unpaired Reserve	
902		
	Industrial/Scientific/Medical	
928		
	Unpaired Reserve	
929		
	Private Radio Paging	
930		
	New Technology Paging	
931		
	Common Carrier Paging	
932		
	Unpaired Reserve	
947		

9-3. Johnson LTR System

The Johnson repeater is automatic and is similar to a conventional repeater except for control logic addition. There is one repeater for each RF channel, and each repeater contains a logic module. These modules share information among the repeaters of the system by way of a high-speed coaxial data bus (Fig. 9-5).

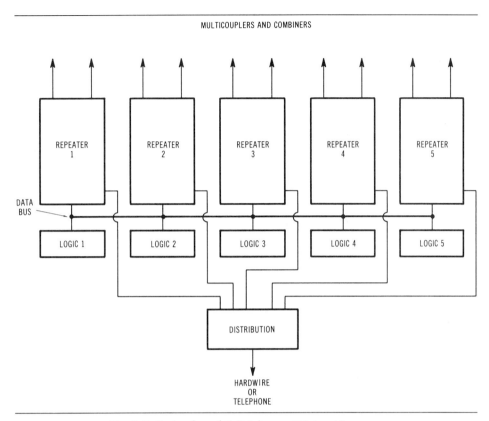

Fig. 9-5. Basic plan of E. F. Johnson LTR trunking system.

Each repeater in the system, therefore, is responsible for the data signaling on its channel. Subaudible digital data is applied continuously to its RF carrier and occurs simultaneously with voice modulation. When a repeater is in use, it transmits the channel number of a free repeater as part of its data signal. This information is used when a given mobile initiates a call and finds the home repeater active. When a repeater is not in use, it sends a 150-millisecond data burst every 10 seconds to update the mobiles and control dispatch stations.

The foregoing logic control technique is referred to as distributive processing. Since a small logic unit performs the signaling on each channel, no system control facility or separate data repeater are required. If a repeater should fail, the remainder of the repeaters in the system remain operational.

Mobiles in the system are assigned a home repeater from which they receive system commands. These commands include information as to which repeater in the system is free and which mobile is receiving a call. A mobile always uses its home channel to make a call unless that repeater is busy. If busy, the mobile is guided to an inactive repeater. As many as 250 IDs can be assigned to each home channel. This permits up to 1250 different addresses in a 5-channel system and 5000 in a 20-channel system. Only mobiles programmed with the same ID can be accessed. A number of IDs can be made selectable by an appropriate front panel switch.

The Johnson mobile transceiver of Fig. 9-6 operates on up to any 20 of the 600 channels allocated for trunk use. These channels are from 809.7625- to 820.9875-

MHz transmit, and 854.7625- to 865.9875-MHz receive. On each channel the transmit-receive spacing is 45 MHz. The transceiver is logic controlled, which eliminates the need for the operator to select channels, monitor before transmitting, or adjust the squelch. It has only power, transmit, volume set, and call indicators on the front panel, and a push-to-talk switch on the microphone.

Courtesy E. F. Johnson Co.

Fig. 9-6. The E. F. Johnson LTR receiver.

The call indicator turns on if any of the receive ID codes are decoded, and it remains on until the volume set or push-to-talk switch is pressed.

Inasmuch as a digital synthesizer generates all the required frequencies, no crystals are required except one reference crystal. Channel frequencies, ID codes, and other operating conditions are determined by the digital synthesize program. The transceiver power output is 15 watts, and the bandwidth occupies a span of 250 channels.

The system-group select switch is an optional capability for the transceiver of Fig. 9-6. This switch mounts above the volume set switch and selects one of two individually programmed code PROMS. When such an option is included, the operator can select different ID codes to be used in such a manner that permits transmission to mobiles with different home repeaters, operation in different LTR systems, and other operational facilities that may be of benefit to the user.

9-3-1. Functional Description

A functional block diagram of the transceiver is given in Fig. 9-7. It includes the transmitter, receiver, and synthesizer. The VCO is located at the center. The audio and data modulation for the VCO come from an associated audio/logic board. The capacitance of varactor diode CR901 is varied by the audio/data signal and results in frequency modulation of the oscillator. The frequency-control DC voltage for the VCO is removed from the loop filter circuit at the lower right. The voltage across varactor diode CR902 is a DC component that maintains the center frequency of the FM signal precisely on the assigned channel.

The output of the VCO oscillator is supplied to a buffer (Q852) and a follow-up frequency doubler (Q853). Actually, the oscillator operates at one half of the transmit frequency, with the output of the doubler being the transmit frequency. This output is supplied to a series of RF amplifiers Q601, Q602, Q501, Q502, and Q503, at the lower left. From here the transmit signal goes to the antenna through the antenna switch. A power control circuit maintains a constant output by sensing the current drawn by the final amplifier Q503. Through transistors Q101, Q102, and Q103 the supply voltage to Q501 and Q602 is regulated. If the output current is too high, the power control circuit reduces the supply voltage to the second amplifier and predriver pair to establish the desired output from the transmitter.

The output of the doubler Q853 not only serves as the transmit frequency but is also the first mixer IF injection frequency for the receiver. When the unit is on receive, the incoming signal passes through the antenna switch and a helical filter to the receiver RF amplifier (Q201). It arrives at the first mixer (Q202) through a second helical filter. The first IF frequency of the mixer is 45 MHz. Consequently, the synthesizer supplies only one frequency for a given channel that permits the operation of both the transmitter and the receiver on correct frequency.

On FCC channel 300 of the 800-MHz band, the transmit frequency is 813.4875 MHz while the receive frequency is 858.4875 MHz. Note if you subtract the transmit frequency from the receiver frequency, you will have a difference frequency of 45 MHz. If the transceiver of Fig. 9-7 is set on channel 300, the output of doubler Q853 will be the transmit frequency of 813.4875. This will be the transmitter output frequency supplied to the antenna after amplification by the transmitter. When the transceiver is on receive, it will pick up the receive signal on a frequency of 858.4875. This is the frequency supplied to first mixer Q202. Also applied to the same mixer is a frequency that is the same as the transmit frequency, or 813.4875. The difference between the incoming signal frequency and the injection frequency is, of course, 45 MHz (858.4875 − 813.4875).

The output of the first mixer is supplied to a crystal filter and then on to the second mixer. The injection frequency for the second mixer is 34.300 MHz. The source of this injection frequency is the reference frequency crystal oscillator (U300). It is shown at the top right. Its operating frequency is 17.150 MHz. This frequency is doubled to 34.300 MHz for application to the second mixer. The difference frequency between the 45-MHz signal frequency applied to the mixer and the injection frequency is 10.7 MHz. This, too, is the frequency of a succeeding crystal filter. The 45- and 10.7-MHz crystal filters of the receiver determine the selectivity of the receiver. A second IF amplifier and a second 10.7-MHz crystal filter follow. Next is the limiter-discriminator of the receiver, which demodulates the incoming audio signal. The audio/data output is applied to the audio/logic board.

The reference frequency oscillator (U300) is crystal controlled on a frequency of 17.150 MHz. It operates in a temperature-compensated circuit to insure stability because of its importance in maintaining the frequency stability of the synthesizer and, therefore, the transceiver on both transmit and receive. Its output is supplied to the phase detector integrated circuit U803 at the lower right of Fig. 9-7. This component is present at the OSC-IN terminal of the chip. In the chip it is divided down by a factor of 1372, producing an output of 12.5 kHz. This 12.5-kHz component is supplied as the reference frequency to the phase detector portion of the chip where it is compared with a divided-down component from the VCO. The signal derived from the VCO is applied to the prescaler buffer and to a succeeding dual-modulus prescaler. The total

386

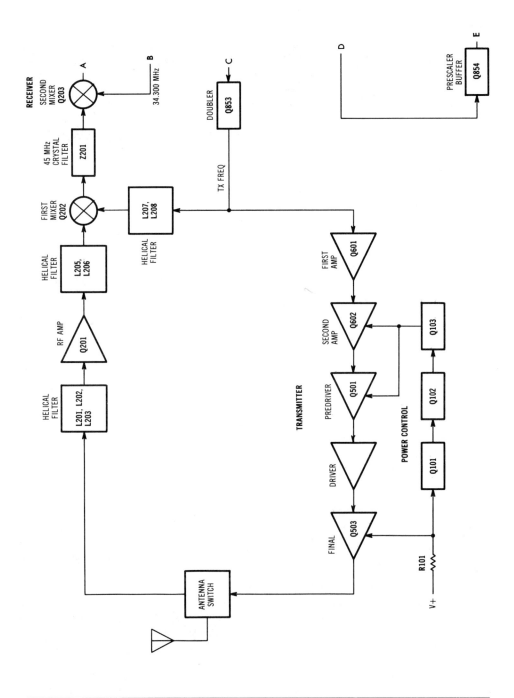

Fig. 9-7. Block diagram

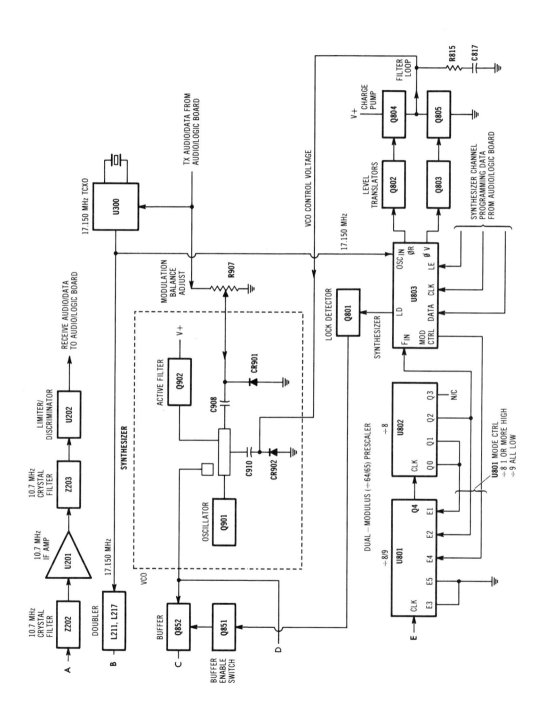

of the transceiver.

division is such that a 12.5-kHz comparison component is applied to the F-IN terminal of synthesizer chip U803.

The DC control voltage at the output of the phase detector is supplied to two level translators Q802 and Q803, which compensate for supply voltage potentials. A charge pump follows. The charge pump responds to any changes in the phase relationship between the reference and signal-derived component supplied to U803. It charges and discharges the DC voltage charge on capacitor C817 in response to the phase differentials. This changing DC voltage is applied to varactor diode CR902 in the VCO circuit and maintains the oscillator on assigned frequency. Resistor R815 along with additional capacitors in the charge pump serve as a loop filter, which has an influence on the synthesizer stability and the time required to produce a locked-up frequency condition.

Lock detector Q801 is associated with phase detector chip U803. Through the buffer enable switch (Q851), it disables the transmitter and receiver when the synthesizer is not locked on frequency by removing the power supply to buffer Q852. This

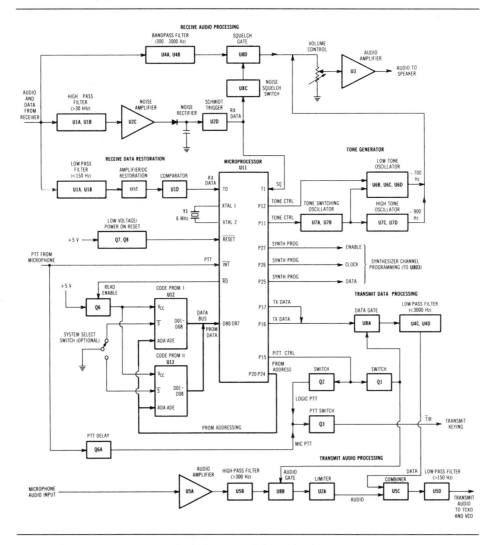

Fig. 9-8. Block diagram of the audio/logic board.

prevents the VCO frequency from arriving at the input of the doubler. It should also be noted that not only is the VCO modulated, but a component of the applied modulation at the center right is also supplied to the reference crystal oscillator (U300). Consequently, the reference frequency is also modulated. If only the VCO were frequency modulated, phase detector U803 would sense the frequency change that is a result of the desired frequency modulation of the VCO. Thus, the synthesizer system does not respond falsely to the desired applied modulating signal. Potentiometer R907 can be used to precisely balance these two modulation components.

The dual-modulus prescaler and the divider built into synthesizer chip U803 (Fig. 9-7) form an exciting circuit. The three chips divide the 400-MHz range VCO output down to 12.5 kHz, a total division in excess of 32,000. The combination of chips U801 and U802 divide by either 64 or 65 depending upon the logic on the modulus control line coming from the synthesizer. The output of this pair of chips is in the 6-MHz range and is applied to the F-IN terminal of the synthesizer. An additional division in the 500 range is accomplished by the activities of synthesizer chip Q803. The prescaler and synthesizer division activities are under control of the programming data supplied from the audio/logic board. This has been previously programmed for the particular operating frequency of the transceiver.

An example will demonstrate the general operation of the divider system. Assume again that the transceiver has been programmed to operate on channel 300. The transmit frequency is 813.4875 MHz. This means the VCO output frequency is one half of that value or 406.74375 MHz. This must be divided down to 12.5 kHz. In the transceiver the N counter is programmed to divide by 508 for this frequency. As a result the input to the N counter must be 6.35 MHz (0.0125×508). Thus, the output of the prescaler must be 6.35 MHz. If you divide the 406.74375 VCO frequency by 64, you will obtain a value of 6.3553711. A division by 65 would produce a frequency that is too low. Consequently, the prescaler is programmed to divide by 64 for the channel 300 operation. Dividing this latter quantity by the N divider value of 508 would produce a frequency at the output of the N counter which is exactly 12.5106 kHz. It is apparent that the division is not exactly 12.5 kHz. This is no problem because the frequency of reference crystal oscillator U300 can be adjusted precisely for minimum frequency error. Its frequency is shifted ever so slightly to guarantee the proper frequency of operation over the span of frequencies on which the transceiver has been programmed to operate. A programmer is used to supply data to the transceiver PROM that will result in the proper division activities for the reference, N, and prescaler counters for each assigned channel.

9-3-2. Audio/Logic Board

The major functions of the chips and components mounted on the audio/logic board are receive audio processing, receive data restoration, microprocessor control and memory, tone generation, transmit audio processing, and transmit data processing. Refer to the functional block diagram of Fig. 9-8. The initial consideration is the receive and transmit audio processing. The audio output of the receiver of Fig. 9-7 is supplied to the receive audio and data circuits at the top left of the logic board (Fig. 9-8). The three paths taken by the signal are to the receive audio processing, squelch circuit, and receive data restoration. In the receive audio processing path the signal is first supplied to a bandpass filter with a frequency range between 300 and 3000 Hz. This filter attenuates the low-frequency data tone and high-frequency harmonics. It also provides some deemphasis.

The bandpass filter output is applied to squelch gate U8D. This gate is influenced by both the noise squelch circuit and the microprocessor. The microprocessor system permits the audio to pass only if that particular mobile is to be the recipient of a message. Communications on the channel intended for other mobiles are not allowed to pass.

Squelch operation is controlled by the noise level present in the detector output. When no signal or a weak signal is received, there is a significant noise level present. For a normal signal, there is very little noise. In this path the signal is first applied to a high-pass filter which detects the noise components above 30 kHz. As a result, the audio and data signals do not pass into the squelch system. The noise signal is amplified and rectified to develop a DC component that operates a trigger circuit (U2D). When a high level of noise is present, the trigger output of the squelch gate blocks the audio signal in the audio processing circuit. As a result the background noise is not heard in the loudspeaker output when there is no signal present or when there is a very weak incoming signal.

The output of the squelch gate is applied to the volume control circuit and on to the audio amplifier. There are resistor-capacitor combinations that set the relative levels of the audio and tone signals as well as reduce the high-frequency harmonics of the tone generator. Five watts of audio power is available to drive the speaker. The circuits associated with the receive data restoration will be covered in the discussion of the logic circuits of the board.

The microphone audio input is shown at the lower left of Fig. 9-8. The microphone signal is applied to audio amplifier U5A which also includes some high-frequency peaking (preemphasis). From here the signal goes to a high-pass filter which passes frequency components above 300 Hz. Consequently, any frequency components below 300 Hz do not pass on to audio gate U8B. This minimizes interference with the low-frequency data band. The audio gate of the transmit audio processing circuit functions in a similar manner to the squelch gate of the receive audio processing system. When the gate closes (under control of the microprocessor), the microphone audio passes on to the succeeding stage. Actually, the audio signal is only passed when the microprocessor and logic circuits indicate that a logic connection (handshake) has been made with the appropriate repeater.

The next stage after the audio gate is a limiter that sets the level of the audio between specified values and prevents overmodulation when the input levels from the microphone are excessive. The audio is next applied to a combiner circuit. Here the audio and data logic are combined. Separate potentiometer adjustments are included to maintain the proper levels of audio and data. The signal next passes through a low-pass filter, which attenuates frequencies above approximately 3000 Hz. As a result the audio signal is limited to the voice range, and spurious frequencies generated in the modulation processing system are removed. The transmit audio output is applied to the transceiver at the point shown center right of Fig. 9-7.

There are two tone generators that produce the busy and intercept tones heard in the speaker. When the channel is busy, a busy tone is heard in the loudspeaker. It is produced by combining a 700-Hz and a 900-Hz tone and switching them on and off at a 2-Hz rate. This operation is under control of the microprocessor. Note the connection to terminals P11 and P12 of U11 in Fig. 9-8.

An intercept tone is produced when there is an out-of-range condition between mobile and repeater. This condition is indicated when there is no data handshake between the two. The intercept tone results from a switching between the 700-Hz and 900-Hz tone at a 2-Hz rate. This is different than the tone heard when the 700-Hz and 900-Hz tones are transmitted in a combined fashion as they are for the busy tone. A busy signal combines the two tone oscillator outputs while an intercept tone is the switching of the two oscillators on and off.

The microprocessor located at the center of Fig. 9-8 controls most of the transmit and receive functions of the transceiver such as channel selection, squelch, transmitter keying, tone operation, etc. The data that is conveyed between the mobile and the repeater is encoded and decoded by the microprocessor system. Data from the microprocessor programs the synthesizer chip of Fig. 9-7 with the data needed to select a specific operating channel. Note that the three lines from terminals P25, P26, and P27 in Fig. 9-8 connect to the transceiver synthesizer.

The microprocessor operates according to the instructions stored in an internal preprogrammed ROM (read-only memory). In addition to the internal ROM, there is an external PROM (U12) to the lower left of the microprocessor in Fig. 9-8. This PROM stores information unique to each mobile or LTR system such as channels used, home repeater number, ID codes, etc. The memory chip is field programmed by the user or can be programmed at the factory. When the transceiver has an optional system select switch, a second PROM (U13) is required.

The operating speed of the microprocessor is controlled by a 6-MHz crystal (Y1). An adjustable capacitor is available to pull the crystal frequency exactly on frequency. Internal dividers reduce this frequency to 400 kHz to obtain a 2.5-microsecond instruction cycle. Note the various input and output ports of the microprocessor. Mentioned already were the squelch port (T1), the two tone-control ports (P11 and P12), as well as the three synthesizer programming ports (P25, P26, and P27). When data is to be read from the memory, ports P20 through P24 are active. Five lines are required to address 32 locations in binary code. The system select switch to the left of the code PROMs makes the selection of one or the other. When the $\overline{RD}$ output of the micro-processor goes low, Q6 turns on and power is applied to the appropriate PROM. The addressed data then appears on the D01 through D08 data bus and is conveyed to microprocessor terminals DB0 through DB7.

When the microphone push-to-talk switch is pressed, a logic low is applied to the interrupt ($\overline{INT}$) terminal of the microprocessor as well as the PTT delay. The low applied to the interrupt input asks the microprocessor to initiate a call to an available repeater. The output of Q6A goes high and turns on Q3 provided Q2 is turned off by a low from the PTT control terminal (P15) of the microprocessor. When Q3 turns on, the transmitter is keyed on. The combination of Q2 and Q3 acts as an interlock that prevents the transmitter from being keyed on by a logic failure. To operate, the PTT switch must be pressed momentarily and the output of P15 of the microprocessor must be low. Now the PTT switch is released. However, the microprocessor has sent out a data message via the transmitter. Note too that the T1 input of the microprocessor is connected to the squelch circuit. If this input goes high, a carrier is being received that tells the microprocessor that information appearing on the T0 input is valid data from the repeater and contact has been established. The call can now be made to another mobile by closing the PTT switch and speaking. When this mobile answers, voice communication is established between the two mobiles.

If in the calling process a busy or an intercept tone is heard, it indicates the channel is busy or the mobile is out of range of the repeater. Also, in the interrogation process if the transmitter is keyed continuously for over three minutes, the logic automatically disables the transmitter. This prevents transmitter damage or extended channel blockage. Don't forget, if the home repeater is busy, the repeater logic switches over to an inactive repeater. The busy tone is heard only if all repeaters are active at the interrogating time.

The receive data restoration blocks are shown at the top left of Fig. 9-8. The incoming audio and data signal is applied to low-pass filter U1A and B. The filter passes frequencies below 150 Hz and rejects those above. Consequently, only the low-frequency data signal is applied to the amplifier and DC restoration circuit (U1C). In association with U1D the data signal is restored to digital levels by these two sections of U1. The reconstructed digital signal applied to the data input terminal (T0) of the microprocessor swings between 0 and 4.5 volts.

The blocks associated with the transmit data processing are shown at the lower right of Fig. 9-8. The transmit data circuits gate and filter the transmit data generated by the microprocessor. The data output is shaped properly to minimize interference when the information is band-limited by low-pass filter (U4C and D). Digital signals contain high-frequency components which are not to be transmitted because they would produce noise in the voice-frequency range. In effect, the low-pass filter rounds off the digital information and assigns it to a frequency band that is below 150 Hz. However, as covered in the previous paragraph, the digital pulse shape is restored in the receive data restoration circuits. The properly shaped output is applied to the combiner (U5C), where it is combined at proper level with the voice signal.

9-4. General Electric MARC V System

In the General Electric MARC V system a logic module is a part of each transceiver. The repeater requires no logic system. In fact the only signal that needs to be transmitted by the repeater is a 1962.9-Hz tone that is sent out by the repeater transmitter to acknowledge (handshake) with a calling unit. This tone indicates that the repeater has been accessed by the mobile or base transceiver. Data logic is used within each individual transceiver only. Even the exchange of information between and among the transceivers of a system is in the form of tones rather than data logic. A fault in a logic module only takes out its associated transceiver. Thus, the possibility of problem with a logic unit in the repeater station which could take some or all of the transceivers out of service has been eliminated.

The basic MARC V transceiver has but few controls. There is a power-on switch, volume control, earpiece or external speaker selection, along with push-to-talk and clear switching. There are three indicators — transmit, wait/ready, and call — that illuminate to signal conditions. There are also several alert tones that sound to indicate various operating conditions such as busy, channel acquisition, call received, carrier control, and warning tone.

Operation is very simple. To send a message, press the power on button. Lift the handset from its hanger and press the PTT switch momentarily. The wait/ready indicator flashes indicating that your transceiver is trying to access a repeater. Do not transmit during this interval. When the wait/ready indicator lights continously, you can again close the PTT switch and begin your call. You will also hear appropriate tones indicating whether the repeater has been acquired or if all channels are busy. There is a tone that alerts the operator when the microphone has been keyed continuously in excess of a preset time. Another warning tone sounds when the channel has been used in excess of a preset time provided all channels of the system are busy.

To receive a message, of course, the power must be on. Also set the volume level by using the control buttons and listening to the loudness of beeps. When you have an incoming call, the call indicator illuminates. You will also hear the call received tone. When the wait/ready indicator illuminates continuously, lift the handset and press the PTT switch. You can now answer the call.

There are a number of options available that can be selected according to the needs of a user system. Additional control(s) may be needed.

Several GE MARC V trunked mobile radios are shown in Fig. 9-9. The one on the left is discussed in the coverage that follows. It includes several additional controls. The mobile radio enables the user to share up to 29 communication channels. A logic board in each mobile and control base station accesses and controls all communications channels through a repeater and alerts the user to incoming calls. An area expander option permits the radio to be programmed for up to 20 channels in each of seven areas and up to 100 different radio frequencies. An area select option permits the user to operate his system on more than one GE MARC V trunked radio system. A group select option permits the user to select up to five different encode/decode tone combinations. They can be used for select calling that permits individual mobiles or groups of mobiles to communicate for special needs. Another option permits individual mobiles to receive calls from the control base station over a personal line. Another arrangement activates the auto horn or lights when a call is received. Of course, a transceiver with special options of this type requires additional controls. For example, there are controls to select the proper group and the proper area repeater system. Also a switch is needed to select the proper selective calling combinations.

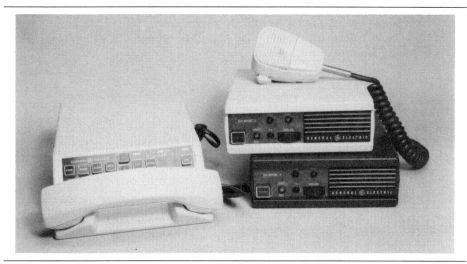

Courtesy General Electric Co., Mobile Communications Div.

Fig. 9-9. General Electric MARC V trunked mobile radios.

When a call is originated, the mobile identifies an idle repeater channel and interrogates with a single burst of busy tone. Upon receipt of the first busy tone, the repeater keys its transmitter and sends a burst of acquisition tone back to the mobile unit. Upon reception, the mobile transmits a select tone and group tone which the repeater passes to all idle mobile units in the system. These idle mobiles have been scanning all channels continously and will stop on the active channel if they recognize the select tone, and wait for the group tone. If all matches, the scanning mobiles stopped on frequency open their audio circuits and alert the operator of an incoming call. If the tones are not recognized, the idle transceivers resume their scan of the channels. Once a mobile is locked on a channel, it will remain there until the repeater times out or the operator hangs up the microphone.

Actually, the three operational modes of the radio are idle, wait, and ready. The radio enters the idle mode when power is turned on and begins scanning channels for incoming calls. The wait mode is entered when the user wishes to place a call. The radio remains in the wait mode until a channel is acquired or it determines that all channels are busy. The final ready mode or conversation mode is indicated by an alert tone and the constant illumination of the wait/ready indicator.

A functional plan of the transceiver is given in Fig. 9-10. The receiver and transmitter blocks are shown at the lower right. At the left is the logic circuitry block which includes the microprocessor and other chips. All the decisions that permit a simple operating procedure in a complicated repeater system are made in the logic circuitry. The responsibilities of the logic circuits are system timing, frequency selection, mode selection, tone selection and sequencing, transmit/receive control, alert tone sequencing, status display, audio routing and mute control, volume control, response to operator controls, integration of tone detector output, and maintenance functions.

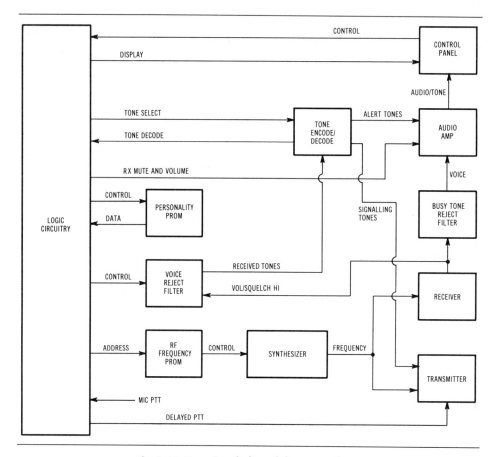

Fig. 9-10. Functional plan of the transceiver.

There are two PROMs — RF frequency and personality. The frequency PROM stores a total of 32 8-bit locations — the binary frequency code for up to 29 user frequencies and 3 test frequencies. The 29 channels may be assigned and programmed to operate in up to 5 areas with a maximum of 15 channels assigned to an area. The personality PROM also contains 32 8-bit locations of the operating parameters and other required information. Typical stored information includes tone signaling frequencies, main system timing, fade margin timing, external alarm option, call light option, alert tone format, group selection format, area selection format, call monitor option, RF channel addresses, carrier control timer, model identification, compatibility option, and control station operation. All of the PROM activities, of course, are under control of the microprocessor as it makes use of the stored information.

There are filters that segregate received tones and audio. This permits only the voice frequencies to be heard on the speaker. Of course, voice frequencies are removed from the signal applied to the tone decoder.

The tone encoder/decoder generates all the signaling and alert tones as well as detecting the incoming tones carried by the incoming signal. For example, the burst of unattenuated busy tone originates here and is transmitted on an idle channel to acquire the repeater. The tone deviation for this operation is approximately 2–5 kHz. When a channel is acquired as a result of the reception of the acquisition tone from the repeater, an attenuated busy tone and other signaling tones accompany the mobile transmission. Alert tones are also generated in this block and are supplied to the audio amplifier. The synthesizer block is located at the lower center of Fig. 9-10. Here the radio frequency for transmission, as well as the receive injection frequency, are generated under control of the logic circuits and frequency PROM. The microprocessor must also provide a data interface with the various control and display functions on the control panel.

9-4-1. Functional Discussion

Additional details on the operation of the GE trunked radio are aided with the discussion of the synthesizer block and sources diagram of Fig. 9-11. The two legs of the signal-forming blocks supply signal to a combiner at the right center. The combiner functions as an adder to produce an output frequency that is one half the final transmit frequency. A doubler stage follows to obtain the final transmit/injection frequency that is needed for the transmitter and receiver proper.

The leg that is derived from the synthesizer at the top center of Fig. 9-11, is in the 42-MHz range. Its precise frequency of operation is determined by frequency PROM U2 to its left. The signal in the second leg is derived from the ICOM at the bottom center. This is an FM crystal oscillator that operates on an approximate frequency of 122 MHz. This FM signal is amplified by Q2608 and multiplied by a factor of three by Q2609 to produce an approximate 366-MHz component for application to the combiner.

The synthesizer is very much like those described previously. Note the reference oscillator that operates on 12.8 MHz and an associated divide by 1024 counter which is a part of the synthesizer chip. The frequency is reduced to 12.5 kHz and then applied to the phase detector. The synthesizer uses an N counter and a dual modulus that counts 15 or 16 rather than the 64 or 65 count of the transceivers discussed previously. There is one other difference in the synthesizer system in that the VCO is not frequency modulated. The function of the leg is to insure proper center-frequency stability on the frequency of operation as designated by the PROM. Should the synthesizer go out of lock, its lock detector and the frequency lock detector will shut down the ICOM, which is generating the FM component.

The ICOM circuit shown in Fig. 9-12 includes a cyrstal-controlled Colpitts oscillator. This is a third-overtone-type oscillator with the output frequency three times the cyrstal frequency. The frequency control (L2) provides a fine adjustment of oscillator frequency while the level control (L3) adjusts the collector output circuit for maximum output. Frequency modulation is accomplished by applying the audio signal to varactor diode D2.

The audio and tone signals are applied to the audio processor at the lower left in Fig. 9-11. From here the signal goes to the modulation switch which closes the circuit to the ICOM on transmit and blocks it on receive.

The power control switch and antenna relay switch area are also shown at the lower left in Fig. 9-11. Some delay is a part of the circuit activity to accommodate the signaling requirements of the transceiver. An alarm relay control block is also shown. The user supplies an external relay that can be used to perform such functions as sounding a horn, turning on a light flasher, etc., when a call comes through.

Along the left side of Fig. 9-11 are the interconnections made to other sections of the transceiver providing the necessary links to power sources, logic circuits, and transmitter/receiver. At the top left is the input/output (I/O) expander. Such an expander provides the interface between the microprocessor on the logic board and the operator controlled functions on the control panel as well as transfers the frequency address codes from the logic board to the frequency PROM. Basic input/output devices were described in Chapter 5.

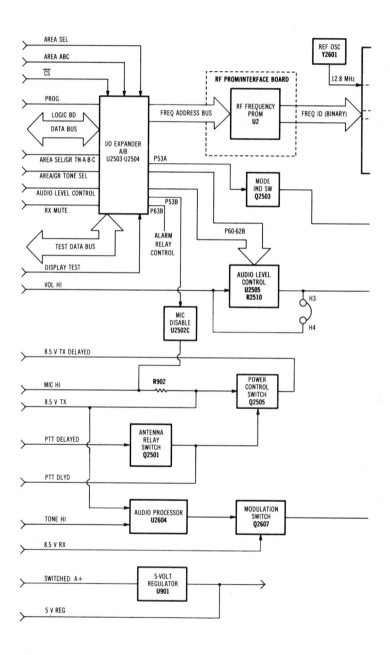

Fig. 9-11. Block diagram of

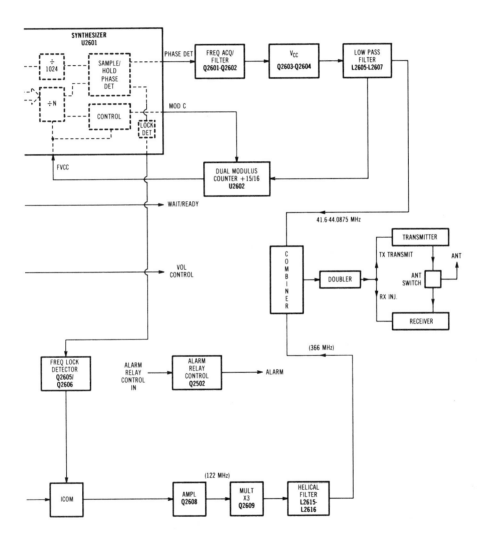

synthesizer and sources.

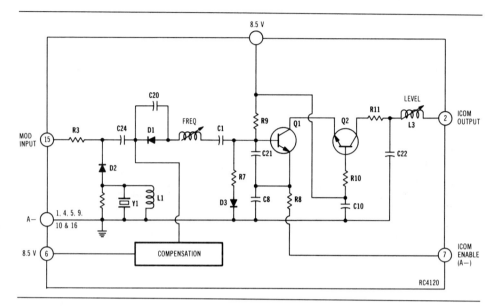

Fig. 9-12. The ICOM circuit.

Various I/O ports provide an electronically controlled audio level adjustment, an operation of the mode indicator, a receiver mute interface to the radio, and a means for transferring the address code to the frequency PROM. Additional ports permit an operational testing mode. A port makes certain the indicator shows the wait mode by flashing and the ready mode by illuminating continously. The idle mode is active when the indicator does not light.

9-5. Cellular Radio

Unlike the trunked radio systems described previously, cellular radio relies on your local phone company for interconnection. In a cellular system a local area is subdivided into groups of operational radio cells as shown in Fig. 9-13. Each cell has its own low-power transmitter that reaches out to the mobiles that cruise the limited area of its cell. Each of the mobiles operates at much lower power (3 watts or less) than the ones described earlier in this chapter. In the older radiophone systems there was one high-powered transmitter that reached out to the mobiles of the system. However, the cellular arrangement using microprocessor control can serve many more mobiles with less erratic communications conditions, less interference, and simple operating procedures.

Cellular radio systems operate in the 800-MHz band, as was shown in Table 9-1. Like the trunk radio systems there is a 45-MHz frequency separation. Consequently, full-duplex operation is possible. Over 600 such duplex channels are available using a frequency separation of 30 kHz. A small number of these channels are assigned to signaling and supervisory responsibilities in each system. A small cellular system is capable of supplying the needs of hundreds of subscribers; larger systems, tens of thousands of subscribers, and more. It has been determined that the hexagon-shaped cellular arrangement of Fig. 9-13 provides the most uniform coverage without the gaps present in circular and other configurations.

The three basic units as shown in Fig. 9-13 consist of the cell-site transceiver and antenna, the mobile switching office, which is wire-linked to each cell as well as the main telephone office. The mobile switching unit is known officially as the Mobile Telephone Switching Office or MTSO. This is the master computer control center of the system.

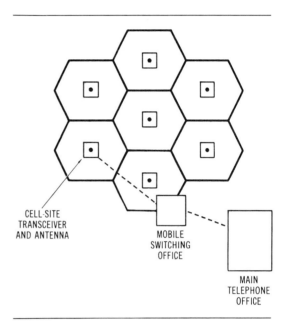

CELL-SITE
TRANSCEIVER
AND ANTENNA

MOBILE
SWITCHING
OFFICE

MAIN
TELEPHONE
OFFICE

Fig. 9-13. The basic cellular radio plan.

Each cell site also has a computer system that, in effect, not only controls the receiver but the transmitter of each mobile operating in the cell. The receiver of the cell-site transceiver continuously monitors, awaiting a digital call from one of the user mobiles. When one is intercepted, it sends back a digital recognition to the mobile and proceeds to assign a frequency pair for the connection. If the connection is to be a telephone link or a mobile operating in another cell, the connection must be handled through the MTSO and the local telephone office as required. This complex operation is handled by the MTSO.

Another complexity arises when a mobile cruises from cell to cell. In a properly operating cellular system this transition is barely recognized by the two parties of the conversation. Again, it is handled with microprocessor and digital techniques. It is the MTSO that monitors continually all of the digital signals being picked up by the cell sites. It knows when the mobile is to make a cellular crossover, and there is a quick reassignment of channels and cell-site transceivers that sustains the contact unbeknown to the users. Even within the cell itself there are often separate directional receiving antennas that cover the area. For a given connection, the antenna performs as a diversity system that automatically chooses the antenna that will deliver maximum signal with regard to the position of the mobile in the cell.

Typical antennas are shown in Fig. 9-14. A low-density cell (limited number of users) would use the simple structure of Fig. 9-14A, which includes an omnidirectional transmit antenna and two receiving antennas for diversity operation. Figs. 9-14B and C are representative of high-density cellular antennas. The transmit antenna again is omnidirectional and sends out a signal of the appropriate power level to cover the confines of the entire cell. However, to derive the best signal possible from the mobiles, there are three separate dual, unidirectional collinear antennas. Each antenna provides dual and independent directional coverage. Actually, it consists of

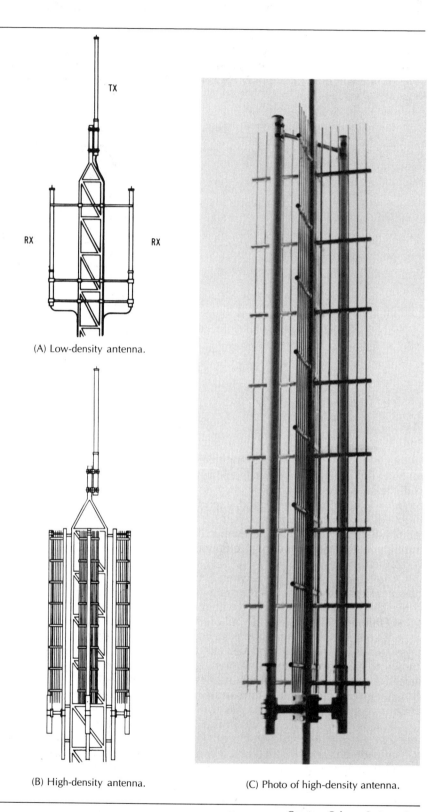

(A) Low-density antenna.

(B) High-density antenna.

(C) Photo of high-density antenna.

Courtesy Celwave Systems, Inc.

Fig. 9-14. Cellular radio antennas.

two separate directional antennas welded to a common support that is capable of receiving signals from exactly opposite directions. When three of these antennas are supported on a signal tower, there are six directional antennas with a 60° spacing. The signal picked up from a single mobile delivers a signal to each antenna and the diversity system of the cell-site installation sorts out the stronger signal for use in making the connection. As the mobile cruises about the cell it will automatically choose the antenna section that delivers the strongest signal to the cell-site receiver. In fact, it will do the same for each user mobile in the cell that is active at the moment.

Another responsibility of the cell-site equipment is to use a direction-finding process to keep check on the position of each active mobile in the cell. This is accomplished with digital signals that are supplied to the MTSO. It is this exchange between cell site and MTSO that permits the smooth transition of operations from one cell to another when the mobile moves into the area of an adjacent cell. The MTSO must data contact this new cell-site transceiver, making an instant and unrecognizable transfer. The MTSO must also log the operations of the entire system, sending along billing and other data to the main telephone office.

Of course, the entire system must be monitored continuously for faults and appropriate bypasses or corrections made. Power levels are checked continuously, and it is possible to maintain the minimum power level needed to maintain an excellent connection. Actually, each cell site contains a high number of transmit and receive frequencies and their appropriate generators. Hence it is possible to bypass electronically under microprocessor control, equipment that may develop an operating fault. Even a fault that develops with an established connection can usually be bypassed instantly.

9-5-1. Cell-Site Equipment

The major components of cell-site equipment have been mounted in the Quintron assembly of Fig. 9-15. The cell-site controller and reference generator are mounted at the top. The cell-site controller employs an MC6800 microprocessor. In the Quintron installation it is able to control cell-site activity for up to 96 channels and provide communications with the systems switch. The reference generator produces the common electrical signals utilized by the transmitter and receiver radio frame equipment. All of this is stabilized by a high-stability reference oscillator. It also generates the data clock as well as the supervisory audio tones (SAT).

The radio frame at the center supports the necessary units and interconnect facilities for up to eight radio-channel sets. A signal channel consists of four plug-in units, the exciter, receiver, channel controller, and channel audio card. The channel controller oversees all channel-specific activities and communicates with the cell-site controller. The channel audio card processes the incoming and outgoing audio signals. Companding and preemphasis are accomplished with appropriate filters. Manual tuning along with level setting are virtually eliminated by the installation.

The amplifier frame at the bottom supports the eight channel power amplifiers. Their responsibility is to increase the signal level delivered by the exciter. The output power level is adjustable continuously from 1 to 60 watts.

A functional block diagram of a small eight-channel cell-site system is given in Fig. 9-16. The reference generator at the lower left generates an 860.16-MHz component for use in signal generation and mixing. It also supplies the 8-kHz data clock as well as the supervisory audio tones of 5970, 600, and 6030 Hz. All are derived from a single high-stability crystal oscillator.

A series of eight audio processing cards are shown at the left. The cards convey audio to their own exciter and also accept audio from their associated receiver.

Each receiver module consists of two individual receivers sharing a common

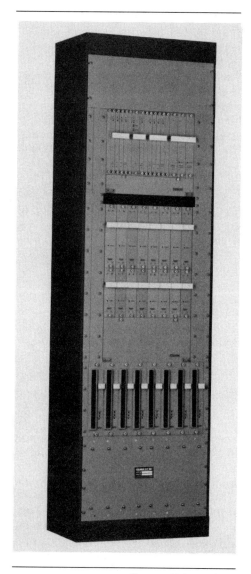

Fig. 9-15. Cell-site equipment.

Courtesy Quintron Corp.

synthesized local oscillator system. In addition to recovering the audio, the receiver includes a signal strength level output that is needed in making proper antenna selection. Note that each receiver picks up its two signals from the multicoupler at the lower right. This multicoupler functions as a duplexer and permits the reception of the many signals on the two receiving antennas that are a part of the small system.

The exciter picks up its audio, encoded data, and supervisory tones from its associated audio card. Its varactor-controlled oscillator is locked to the component from the reference generator and produces a frequency-modulated output that is supplied to the power amplifier.

The power amplifier consists of several stages that build up the signal level and then apply it to a circulator/filter stage at the output. It also supplies information to the channel controller such as power-in detection, power-out detection, output level, reflected power level, heat-sink temperature, and automatic level-control sample.

An optional redundant channel relay can be included. If a primary channel fails

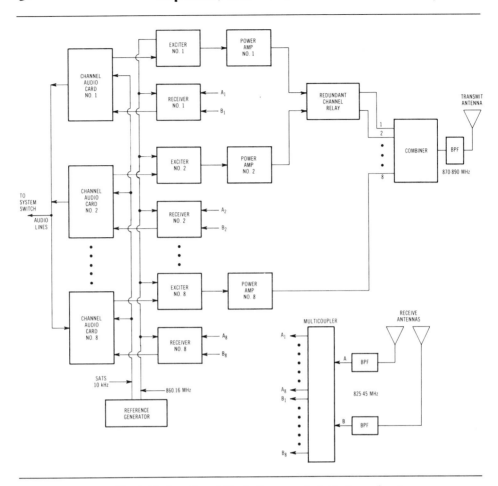

Fig. 9-16. Functional block diagram of eight-channel system.

such a relay switches the back-up channel into the proper combiner cavity. The combiner just like the combiners used in trunked relay systems permits many transmitters to feed signal to a common antenna without interaction.

9-5-2. Mobile Radiophones

The E.F. Johnson Company produces equipment for cell-site and mobile use. Their mobile equipment carries the Western Union label (Fig. 9-17). This photograph shows a mobile transceiver and loudspeaker as well as several telephone handsets and their keyboard pads. The radio transceiver is usually mounted in the trunk or under the seat while the telephone set is mounted on the dashboard or console.

The transceiver contains a radio-frequency section and a logic section. A receiver front-end, receiver IF, power amplifier, and synthesizer comprise the receiver section. A microprocessor system, signaling circuits, and power supply make up the logic section. Interfaced with the transceiver is the telephone-style control unit, which contains the numbered keyboard or dial, status indicators, and level controls.

The mobile transceiver has two antenna ports. One is connected to an antenna that is used for both transmit and receive while the other connects to a receive-only antenna. The two receive antennas permit space diversity reception, which helps the

Fig. 9-17. Cellular transceiver and handsets.

receiver to consistently maintain a maximum receive signal. The maximum power output of the transmitter is only 3 watts. A power control circuit is included that can increase or decrease the transmitter power in 4-dB steps. Recall that cell site and mobile power levels are logic controlled and hold down interference by restraining transmit powers to the level that maintains a good voice contact.

The events that take place in establishing a radiophone contact are many and complex, and the speed with which contact is established is almost unbelievable. When a call is to be made to a mobile, the call is routed from the calling party's central office by standard wire-line connection to the mobile telephone switching office (MTSO) serving the desired mobile. The MTSO collects the digits, converts them to the mobile ID number, and instructs the cell sites to page the mobile over the paging channels. This is not voice paging but it is handled by digital data logic. This paging signal is broadcast over the entire cellular service areas. The mobile unit, after recognizing its page, scans the paging channels for access into the mobile service. The strongest cell site (usually the nearest one) is then chosen. The mobile then responds over the paging channel to the cell site selected. The selected cell site then reports the reply to the MTSO over its dedicated landline data link.

The MTSO then selects an idle voice channel and associated landline trunk to the cell site that handled the paged reply. The cell site, in turn, informs the mobile of its channel designation over the paging channel. The mobile automatically tunes to this channel designation and transmits the appropriate supervisory audio tone (SAT) over the voice channel. Upon recognition, the cell site places the associated landline trunk connection in off-hook state which the MTSO intreprets as successful voice channel communications.

After all of these activities a message is transmitted over the voice channel to an alerting device in the mobile radiophone which signals the customer that there is an incoming call. An audible ringing is then conveyed. When the customer answers, the cell site recognizes removal of the signaling tone by the mobile and restores the landline trunk to an off-hook state. This is noted by the MTSO, the audible ringing is removed, and the voice connection can begin.

In originating a call from a mobile unit, a process for cell-site selection begins as soon as the send key on the mobile unit is pressed. The logic procedure is similar to that described for an outside originated call. The stored digits along with the mobile ID are transmitted over the mobile-selected paging channel. Its associated cell site receives the information and relays it to the MTSO over landline link. The MTSO designates a voice channel and contact is made with the mobile; the MTSO then completes the call through an appropriate wire-line network or through an appropriate cell site if a mobile-to-mobile contact is to be established.

9-5-3. Indicators and Controls

A further understanding of the operation of the mobile radio phone can be gained by considering the function of the various controls and indicators:

HSET — Sets the volume to the handset.

On/Off Spkr — Turns the unit on or off and sets the volume for the speaker.

Roam Indicator — Lit when the mobile is in a system other than its home system. Flashes when it is not in the preferred system (Option).

Lock Indicator — Lit when the control unit is in locked-out condition to prevent unauthorized use. Flashes when an attempt to answer a call has been made while in hard lock (Option).

No Svc Indicator — Lights when out of range.

In Use Indicator — Lit when a call has been originated or when incoming call is answered.

Alert Volume — Three position rocker switch to set volume of the ringing tone.

Horn Alert —Momentary rocker switch to allow the vehicle horn to sound when the unit rings. This allows the unit to stay on if the ignition is off.

Horn Alert Indicator — Lit when the horn alert is activated.

Digital Display — A visual display of phone numbers, elapsed time, and other information.

Key Pad — Positive action keypad to help eliminate dialing errors.

Store Functions — Stores up to 10 numbers, with a maximum of 16 digits for recall and automatic dialing.

Recall — Retrieves numbers stored in memory. Restores display of last number dialed (option). Enables certain option key sequences.

Clear — Will clear the display and option functions when applicable.

Send — Will send the number shown on the display or answer an incoming call.

Auxiliary — Used with certain options.

End — Terminates a call the same as the switch hook.

9-5-4. Basic Operation

The following procedures should be followed when placing or receiving a call over a cellular system.

To place an automatic call:

1. Turn the ON/OFF SPKR thumbwheel clockwise past the click.
2. Lift the handset. It is also possible to place a call with the handset in the cradle.
3. If dial tone is heard, touch dial the number. If a reorder tone is present, there is no channel available and you must try to place the call again later. If you make a dialing error, press CLR and redial.
4. Press SND; the number will be dialed.
5. When the party answers, speak in a normal tone of voice.
6. When the call is completed, replace the handset or press END.

Receiving a call:

1. Be sure power is on.
2. Upon receipt of a call, the alert will sound and the IN USE light will be lit when the handset is taken off hook.
3. Lift the handset or press SND. The call may be monitored with the handset on hook by pressing SEND.
4. Answer in a normal tone of voice.
5. When the call is completed, replace the handset or press END.

9-5-5. Functional Block Description

Some functions, circuits, and components of the mobile radiophone are similar or identical to those discussed in connection with regular and trunked radio services described previously in this chapter. This is especially so for the 800-MHz transceivers discussed previously. In the paragraphs that follow some of the points of difference are covered beginning with the transceiver's front end (Fig. 9-18).

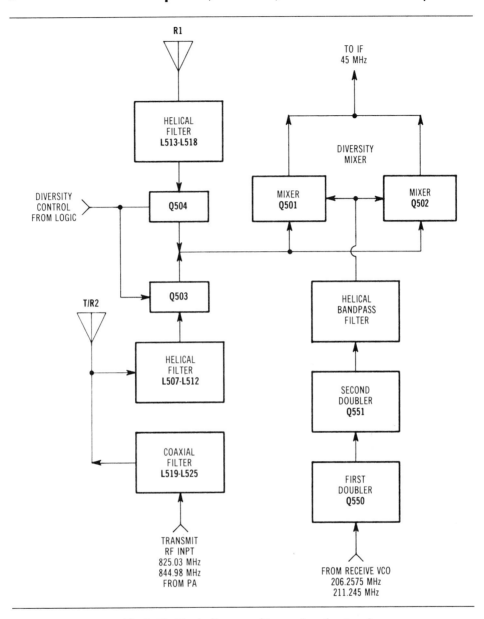

Fig. 9-18. Block diagram of transceiver front end.

The cellular radio uses two antennas, one for transmit/receive application and the other for receive only. There is a helical filter attached to the output of receive antenna R1. It has a bandpass between 870 to 890 MHz. A similar filter is connected to the output of transmit/receive antenna T/R2. The transmit signal reaches this same antenna through a coaxial filter that has a bandpass range extending between 825–845 MHz.

The logic diversity switches (Q503 and Q504) display either a minimum or maximum series attenuation to the signal transfer depending upon which antenna is delivering the most signal at that moment. At a later position in the receiver, the level of the incoming signal is monitored continuously and information is passed to the logic board of the receiver. Here the diversity switching logic is developed and applied

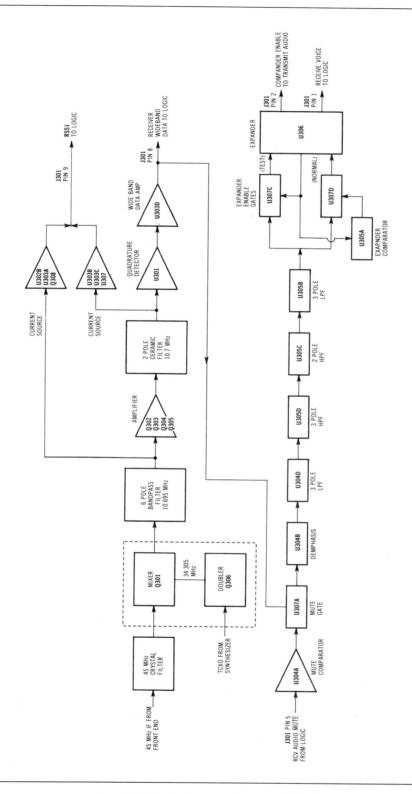

Fig. 9-19. Block diagram of receiver IF block.

to Q503 and Q504, which select the antenna with the stronger received signal as the mobile unit cruises within the cell site.

The output is then applied to the mixer stage (Q501 and Q502). Local oscillator injection for the mixer is derived from the synthesizer section of the receiver. This component passes through two doubler stages and a helical bandpass filter prior to its application to the mixer. The difference frequency of 45 MHz is applied to the receiver IF system.

The 45-MHz IF signal is applied through a crystal filter to the second mixer-oscillator combination in Fig. 9-19 which results in a 10.7-MHz IF output. Follow the signal through the ceramic filter onto the quadrature detector and follow-up amplifier. Note that ahead of the amplifier and the quadrature detector current source signals are applied to stages that evaluate the incoming signal level to develop the receive signal strength output. These stages provide the control logic that is used for diversity operation as well as providing monitor and test capabilities.

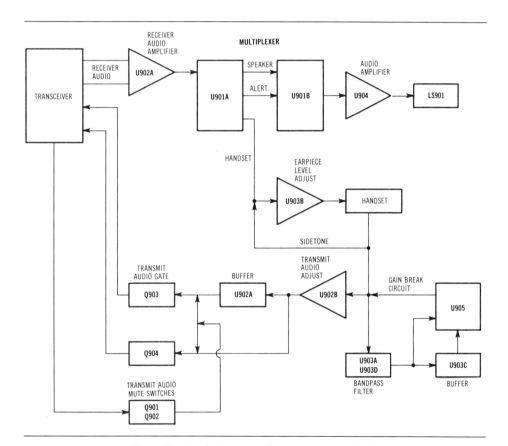

Fig. 9-20. Block diagram of control unit audio block.

A wideband amplifier following the quadrature detector provides two outputs. One of them is the SAT wideband and high-speed data signals to the control logic. Recall that these are the components that permit so much control over the mobile radio by the MTSO instructions transmitted from the cell-site transmitter. The second output is the received voice signal that is applied to U307A at the lower left.

The received audio can be muted from the logic board. After the deemphasis stage, the speech signals are passed through a voice-range filter series and then on to the expander circuitry. Here the amplitude range (dynamic range) is restored to

410

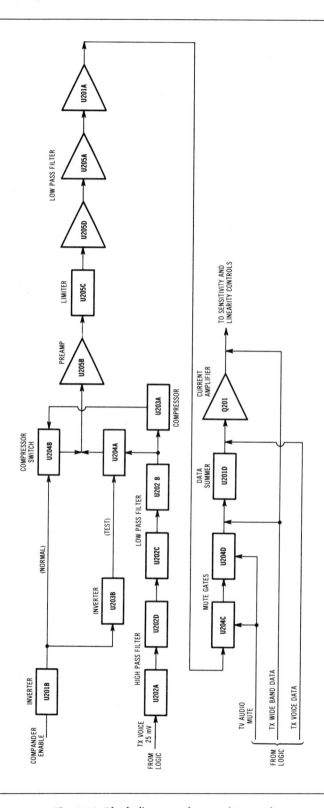

Fig. 9-21. Block diagram of transmitter exciter.

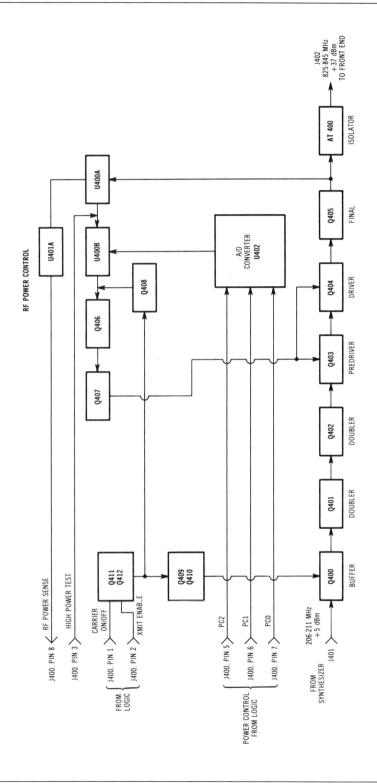

Fig. 9-22. Block diagram of transmitter power amplifier.

compensate for the speech compression that is a part of the transmission process. The actual expansion ratio is controlled by a comparator. The expander operates only on voice-frequency components because the preceding filters have removed wideband data information and noise.

The received voice ouput provides the audio for the remotely located headset or handset. The expansion circuits of the receiver and the compression circuits of the transmitter can both be bypassed for making tests and adjustments in the mobile radiophone.

The control unit audio block is shown in Fig. 9-20. The receive audio output is applied to the receive audio amplifier at the top left and then to a multiplexer. Here the signal can be passed to the loudspeaker system or to the handset by way of a level adjustment.

The transmit audio originates at the handset and is passed through the appropriate audio stages and audio gate to the transceiver. As required the transmit audio can be muted at this point.

The transmit audio is applied to the transmitter exciter (Fig. 9-21) at a 25-millivolt level. Sets of low- and high-pass filters limit the voice frequency range between 300 and 3000 Hz. After filtering, the signal passes to a compressor (U203A). Its responsibility is to compress the audio magnitude without any limiting or clipping. This circuit makes the high- and low-amplitude voice components come out nearer to each other in amplitude, without introducing distortion. Consequently, the transmitter accommodates those who speak loudly or softly into the microphone. A secondary benefit is an improved signal-to-noise ratio for the entire system. As mentioned previously the true amplitude ranges are restored by the expander circuit of the receiver, restoring voice fidelity.

The preemphasis and limiting that is a part of an FM system follows the compressor. The limiting handles high-level noise and voice peaks thereby avoiding overmodulation of the transmitter.

The voice audio is now applied to the mute gates and on to the data summer stages where data signals from the logic board are added to the signal that is to be transmitted. This information can be carried above and below the voice frequency range. The combined voice and data components are then applied to the frequency synthesizer, where the signal is used to phase-modulate the transmit RF signal generated by the synthesizer circuitry.

The various injection frequencies for the receiver set are also generated by the synthesizer circuitry. Synthesizer details are not given because of its similarity to those described previously. All frequency components are stabilized by a temperature-compensated crystal oscillator operating on 17.125 MHz. As a function of channel selection and the logic memory of the system, the output frequency of the synthesizer is an FM component that falls somewhere between 206–211 MHz. This output is applied to the input of the power amplifier in Fig. 9-22. The power amplifier assembly consists of the necessary frequency multipliers and a power-amplifier chain. The maximum transmitter power output is 3 watts. Through an isolator the transmit signal is applied to the input coaxial filter shown in Fig. 9-18. The transmitter carrier frequency falls between 825–845 MHz.

There are various power control circuits that are a part of this block of circuits. Output samples are taken out and used to maintain a constant power output level as a function of the setting of the automatic power control. An automatic change of power occurs when it is so designated by a command from the control logic. This control comes from the MTSO by way of the cell-site transmitter. It can be regulated in 4-dB steps from 3 watts down to approximately 7 milliwatts. Special filters are included to suppress high-order multiplier harmonics that could cause an incorrect interpretation of the RF level in the power control circuitry. Such filters also ensure that spurious outputs are not transmitted.

10

Marine Radio and Navigational Systems for Small Craft

The marine radio services serve many needs but the most important are distress communications, safety at sea, and rescue services. Boats carrying more than six passengers for hire, as well as many other commercial craft, are required to carry radio equipment. However, a marine radio is a safety and utilitarian asset on even the smallest boat that plies the coastal and inland waters.

10-1. Radio Applications

The two major distress, safety, and calling frequencies are 156.8 MHz (channel 16) and 2182 kHz. Distress frequencies are also designated as calling frequencies to insure that a maximum number of stations will be listening at any given time. Thus, if you have a distress situation, it is more likely that you will be heard immediately. The success of this arrangement depends on the cooperation of all users to maintain a listening watch on these two frequencies and, at the same time, keep them clear of all unnecessary communications.

Other applications for your marine radio are to communicate between your vessel and local and federal agencies, such as the United States Coast Guard, to exchange information pertaining to navigation movement or management of vessels and for communications among stations and vessels engaged in commerce. There are frequencies available for vessels to communicate via shore telephones (public correspondence stations), and others for the special needs of recreational boating people.

The VHF-FM marine radio band between 156–158 MHz is a very active segment of the marine spectrum. There are 48 channels assigned to a variety of applications for coastal, inland waters and lake communications, and navigation. The reliable range of operation is no more than 20 miles. This means that communications can be depended upon up to this limit although, as a function of propagation conditions, the range can be greater than 20 miles. For distances greater than 20 miles the 2–3 MHz marine band can be used.

There are additional marine bands near 4, 6, 8, 12, 16, and 22 MHz. For example, on the marine segments of the 4–6 MHz spectrum, the noon range is 100 miles and becomes 600 miles at night. On 8 MHz the noon range is 500 miles; this may extend out to 2000–3000 miles at night. These figures are average ones and do vary with changes in propagation. Higher frequencies are used for greater range and on some of the bands the range of operation can be in excess of 10,000 miles at certain times of the day.

Marine radio operators and marine radio technicians require proper FCC license grades varying from a simple permit granted upon application to a higher-level general radiotelephone license that requires an FCC examination. The general license is required for those persons who install, adjust, and repair marine two-way radios. Refer to Chapter 14.

The various marine channels and their uses for the VHF-FM band are listed in Table 10-1 according to channel number and frequency. Allocations and usage are determined by the FCC and the Radio Technical Commission for Maritime Services. Note that there are two frequencies given, one for transmit and the other for receive. Note also that transmit and receive frequencies are the same on some channels while they differ on others.

When a marine radio includes a synthesizer, you can usually tune to any one of the channels. If your unit does not have a synthesizer, you can only tune to the channels preset in your equipment. In this latter type of radio the number of channels and frequencies are set up when the unit is installed depending upon the channels used in your particular operation area. Of course, the more channels available, the better is the communications capability.

Table 10-1.   Marine Channel Assignments

	Frequencies (MHz)		
Channel Number	Ship Transmit	Ship Receive	Intended Use
1A	156.050	156.050	Port Operations and Commercial (Intership and Ship-to-Coast).
63A	156.175	156.175	Available for use within the U.S.C.G. designated Vessel Traffic Services (VTS) area of New Orleans, and the Lower Mississippi River.
5A	156.250	156.250	Port Operations (Intership and Ship-to-Coast). Available for use within the U.S.C.G. Vessel Traffic Services radio protection areas of New Orleans and Houston.
6	156.300	156.300	Intership Safety. Required for all VHF-FM equipped vessels. For intership safety purposes and search and rescue (SAR) communications with ships and aircraft of the U.S. Coast Guard. Must not be used for nonsafety communications.
7	156.350	160.950	International Use.
7A	156.350	156.350	Commercial (Intership and Ship-to-Coast). A working channel for commercial vessels to fulfill a wide scope of business and operational needs.
8	156.400	156.400	Commercial (Intership). Same as channel 7A except limited to intership communications

Table 10-1—cont. Marine Channel Assignments

Channel Number	Frequencies (MHz) Ship Transmit	Ship Receive	Intended Use
9	156.450	156.450	Commercial and Noncommercial (Intership and Ship-to-Coast). Some examples of use are communications with commercial marinas and public docks to obtain supplies or schedule repairs and contacting commercial vessels about matters of common concern.
10	156.500	156.500	Commercial (Intership and Ship-to-Coast). Same as channel 7A.
11	156.550	156.550	Commercial (Intership and Ship-to-Coast). Same as channel 7A. It should be noted, however, in certain ports channels 11, 12, and 14 are used selectively on the U.S.C.G. Vessel Traffic Service.
12	156.600	156.600	Port Operations (Intership and Ship-to-Coast). Available to all vessels. This is a traffic advisory channel for use by agencies directing the movement of vessels in or near ports, locks, or waterways. Messages are restricted to the operational handling, movement and safety of ships and, in emergency, to the safety of persons. It should be noted, however, in certain ports 11, 12, and 14 are used selectively for the U.S.C.G. Vessel Traffic Service.
13	156.650	156.650	Navigational. (Ship's) Bridge to (Ship's) Bridge. This channel is available to all vessels and is required on large passenger and commercial vessels (including many tugs). Use is limited to navigational communications such as in meeting and passing situations. Abbreviated operating procedures (call signs omitted) and 1-watt maximum power (except in certain special instances) are used on this channel for both calling and working. For recreational vessels, this channel should be used for listening to determine the intentions of large vessels. This is also the primary channel used at locks and bridges.
14	156.700	156.700	Port Operations (Intership and Ship-to-Coast). Same as channel 12.
15	——	156.750	Environmental (Receive Only). A receive-only channel used to broadcast environmental information to ships such as weather, sea conditions, time signals for navigation, notices to mariners, etc. Most of this information is also broadcast on the weather (WX) channels and EPIRB.
16	156.800	156.800	Distress, Safety, and Calling (Intership and Ship-to-Coast), Also EPIRB's. Required channel for all VHF-FM equipped vessels. Must be monitored at all times station is in operation (except when actually communicating on another channel). This channel is monitored also by the Coast Guard, public coast stations, and many limited coast stations. Calls to other vessels are normally initiated on this channel. Then, except in an emergency, you must switch to a working channel.

Table 10-1—cont. Marine Channel Assignments

Channel Number	Frequencies (MHz) Ship Transmit	Ship Receive	Intended Use
17	156.850	156.850	State Control. Available to all vessels to communicate with ships and coast stations operated by state or local governments. Messages are restricted to regulation and control, or rendering assistance. Use of low-power (1-watt) setting is required by international treaty.
18	156.900	161.500	International Use.
18A	156.900	156.900	Commercial (Intership and Ship-to-Coast). Same as channel 7A.
19	156.950	161.550	International Use.
19A	156.950	156.950	Commercial (Intership and Ship-to-Coast). Same as channel 7A.
20	157.000	161.600	Port Operations (Intership and Ship-to-Coast). Available to all vessels. This is a traffic advisory channel for use by agencies directing the movement of vessels in or near ports, locks, or waterways. Messages are restricted to the operational handling, movement and safety of ships and, in emergency, to the safety of persons.
21	157.050	156.050 (or 161.650)	International Use.
21A	157.050	157.050	U.S. Government Only.
22	157.100	161.700	International Use.
22A	157.100	157.100	Coast Guard Liaison. This channel is used for communications with U.S. Coast Guard ship, coast, and aircraft stations after first establishing communications on channel 16. Navigational warnings and, where not available on WX channels, Marine Weather forecasts are made on this frequency. *It is strongly recommended that every VHF radiotelephone include this channel.*
23	157.150	156.150 (or 161.750)	International Use.
23A	157.150	157.150	U.S. Government Only.
24	157.200	161.800	Public Correspondence (Ship-to-Coast). Available to all vessels to communicate with public coast stations. Channels 26 and 28 are the primary public correspondence channels and therefore become the first choice for the cruising vessel having limited channel capacity.
25	157.250	161.850	Public Correspondence (Ship-to-Coast). Same as channel 24.
26	157.300	161.900	Public Correspondence (Ship-to-Coast). Same as channel 24.
27	157.350	161.950	Public Correspondence (Ship-to-Coast). Same as channel 24.
28	157.400	162.000	Public Correspondence (Ship-to-Coast). Same as channel 24.

Table 10-1—cont. Marine Channel Assignments

Channel Number	Frequencies (MHz) Ship Transmit	Ship Receive	Intended Use
65	156.275	160.875	International Use.
65A	156.275	156.275	Port Operations (Intership and Ship-to-Coast). Same as channel 12.
66	156.325	160.925	International Use.
66A	156.325	156.325	Port Operations (Intership and Ship-to-Coast). Same as channel 12.
67	156.375	156.375	Commercial (Intership). Same as channel 7A except limited to intership communications. In the New Orleans U.S.C.G. Vessel Traffic Service protection area, use is limited to navigational bridge-to-bridge intership purposes.
68	156.425	156.425	Noncommercial (Intership and Ship-to-Coast). A working channel for noncommercial vessels. May be used for obtaining supplies, scheduling repairs, berthing and accommodations, etc. from yacht clubs or marinas, and intership operational communications such as piloting or arranging for rendezvous with other vessels. It should be noted that channel 68 (and channel 70 for intership only) is the most popular noncommercial channel and therefore is the first choice for vessels having limited channel capacity.
69	156.475	156.475	Noncommercial (Intership and Ship-to-Coast). Same as channel 68.
70	156.525	156.525	Noncommercial (Intership). Same as channel 68, except limited to intership communications.
71	156.575	156.575	Noncommercial (Intership and Ship-to-Coast). Same as channel 68.
72	156.625	156.625	Noncommercial (Intership). Same as channel 68, except limited to intership communications.
73	156.675	156.675	Port Operations (Intership and Ship-to-Coast). Same as channel 12.
74	156.725	156.725	Port Operations (Intership and Ship-to-Coast). Same as channel 12.
77	156.875	156.875	Port Operations (Intership). Limited to intership communications to and from pilots concerning the docking of ships.
78	156.925	161.525	International Use.
78A	156.925	156.925	Noncommercial (Intership and Ship-to-Coast). Same as channel 68.
79	156.975	161.575	International Use.
79A	156.975	156.975	Commercial (Intership and Ship-to-Coast). Same as channel 7A.
80	157.025	161.625	International Use.
80A	157.025	157.025	Commercial (Intership and Ship-to-Coast). Same as channel 7A.

Table 10-1—cont. Marine Channel Assignments

Channel Number	Frequencies (MHz) Ship Transmit	Ship Receive	Intended Use
81	157.075	161.675	International Use.
81A	157.075	157.075	U.S. Government Only.
82	157.125	161.725	International Use.
82A	157.125	157.125	U.S. Government Only.
83	157.175	156.175 (or 161.775)	International Use.
83A	157.175	157.175	U.S. Government Only.
84	157.225	161.825	Public Correspondence (Ship-to-Coast). Same as channel 24.
85	157.275	161.875	Public Correspondence (Ship-to-Coast). Same as channel 24.
86	157.325	161.925	Public Correspondence. (Ship-to-Coast). Same as channel 24.
87	157.375	161.975	Public Correspondence. (Ship-to-Coast). Same as channel 24.
88	157.425	162.025	In areas of the Puget Sound and of the Great Lakes except Lake Michigan and along the St. Lawrence Seaway available for use by ship stations for public correspondence. Same as Channel 24.
88A	157.425	157.425	Commercial (Intership). Except in Lakes Erie, Huron, Ontario, and Superior and along the St. Lawrence Seaway. Same as Channel 7A except limited to intership communications and between commercial fishing vessels and associated aircraft while engaged in commercial fishing.
WX1	——	162.550	Weather (Receive Only). To receive weather broadcasts of the Department of Commerce, National Oceanic and Atmospheric Administration (NOAA).
WX2	——	162.400	Weather (Receive Only). Same as WX1.
WX3	——	162.475	Weather (Receive Only). Same as WX1.

All marine radios in this band must be equipped to operate on channel 6, channel 16, and at least one working frequency. Channel 6 is the intership safety channel that permits ship-to-ship communications as indicated for its channel usage in the table. At least a 12-channel capability is recommended. If you have a radio scanner and live near the shore, you can listen to the activities on this marine band.

Some coastal, inland waters, and lake boats are equipped with radios that operate on the landmobile bands. They are assigned to communicate with land-based mobile and base stations. This is to be anticipated because many shore businesses involve both land and water business or industrial activities. Citizens Band units are often installed on boats to provide personal or business communications over a short range. As on land, CB channel 9 is designated as the emergency channel. Communications can be established with land-based and motor vehicle stations. Although CB is a convenience, it is by no means a substitute for a marine radio distress unit although in certain areas there is some Coast Guard monitoring of CB activities.

The safety channels on the VHF-FM marine band were mentioned previously. However, there are a number of other important channel allocations. Refer to channel 22A. On this frequency and other frequencies you can establish contact with the Coast Guard, and you can obtain a variety of navigational and weather information. Take a look at channel 24, which is used for public correspondence. You can call such a station to receive telephone calls to and from any telephone with access to the nationwide telephone network.

If you glance over the other channels on the list, you will also note that they are used widely by shipping companies (cargo or passenger), port operations, government services as well as international use when you are in the coastal region of other countries. The last three are weather-only receive channels. You can tune in these channels on a continuous basis to obtain local weather information.

On the higher-frequency marine bands, single-sideband transmission is used for radiotelephone communications. When communications must extend beyond 20 miles for coastal, inland waters, or lake communications the 2–3 MHz medium-frequency marine band is used. It provides a range of 50–150 miles in the daytime. If your transmission requirements extend beyond 20 miles, this type of equipment should be aboard. However, you cannot obtain a marine station license for a single, sideband (SSB) installation unless you also have a licensed VHF-FM radiotelephone station. This is a requirement to prevent congestion on the important 2–3 MHz band.

When your operations extend beyond this range into the open seas, your SSB equipment must be able to operate on some of the higher-frequency marine bands or you can purchase a separate unit for operating on these higher frequency bands. Of course, any marine radio for operation on the 2–3 MHz band must be capable of operating on 2182 kHz, the international distress and calling frequency, and at least two other frequencies. United States Coast Guard and public correspondence stations also operate on key frequencies on all of these bands. For example, the public coast stations provide service for ships 20–50 miles away on the VHF/FM band and also provide a medium-frequency service for 100 to over 1000 miles from shore. Finally, in the high-frequency service, there are public coast stations that provide long-range service to anywhere in the world. The four major US public coast stations are WLO Alabama, KMI California, WOO New Jersey, and WOM Florida. They operate on a variety of frequencies on the high-frequency bands to provide their ship-to-shore radio services.

There are also many code (CW) assignments on the high-frequency marine bands. Most ocean-going vessels include both radiotelephone and radiotelegraph capability. In fact, if a ship does not have an appropriate radiotelephone installation, it is mandatory that it have a radiotelegraph station aboard. When a ship has an approved radiotelephone installation, it is not necessary that it have a radiotelegraph capability. However, most high-seas radiotelephone installations do include radiotelegraph capability whether it is used or not.

Radiotelegraph equipment is usually available for operating on the long-wave marine band for long-distance code communications. An installation must be capable of keeping a watch on the radiotelegraph distress frequency of 500 kHz. Automatic alarm systems and radioteletype equipment are common aboard the larger ocean-going vessels. Radionavigational equipment of various types is used aboard ship. This can range from a simple direction finder for operating on the VHF or medium-wave radio bands to precision Loran-C receivers that permit very accurate direction finding. Loran-C shore stations operate on 100 kHz. Depending upon ship size, small or large radar units can be purchased. A small short-range unit is particularly helpful in navigating coastal, inland waters, and lakes at nighttime or during bad weather conditions. Larger, longer-range radar units can be used on the high seas. Satellite systems may be the eventual ultimate for direction finding at sea. Various types of marine radiocommunications and navigational equipment are covered in the three chapters that follow.

10-2. FM Marine Radios

The Raytheon Model Ray-78 shown in Fig. 10-1A is a versatile and compact VHF-FM marine radio. It weighs only 5 lbs 11 oz and the dimensions are height 3.1 inches, width 9.4 inches, and depth 10 inches. A convenient mounting position can be found on even the smallest of boats. It operates on all of the U.S., International, and Canadian channels. There are a total of 55 transmit/receive channels and an additional number of receive-only channels including eight weather channels and four special Canadian channels. It is a synthesized unit with an appropriate LCD channel display and provides various forms of automatic scanning of all channels.

(A) Photo of unit.

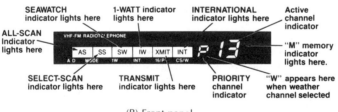

(B) Front panel.

Courtesy Raytheon Marine Co.

Fig. 10-1. A VHF-FM marine radio.

There are a number of quick-select buttons on the front panel as well as associated indicator lights as shown in Fig. 10-18. Below this front panel are the jack for inserting the PTT microphone, on-off switch, volume control, squelch control, and indicator light dimmer, as well as the large channel select switch.

Along the center is a group of six select buttons. The A/D (add and delete button) at the far left is used to place in memory or remove from memory the channel indicated on the LCD (in this case, channel 13). When the switch is depressed for approximately 3 seconds, the channel on display will be entered into the select scan memory of the radio and the letter M will appear next to the channel numerical display. If this channel has already been programmed, depressing the switch for approximately 3 seconds will delete the channel from memory and the M will not appear. If the channels stored in memory are to be displayed sequentially, the A/D and mode buttons (second button along row) are depressed simultaneously. The radio is then set to receive on the channel selected by the rotary switch during this operation.

The mode switch selects the scanning modes sequentially in the order SW, SS, or AS. In the sea watch (SW) mode there is automatic alternate monitoring of channel 16 and the channel displayed at the time the sea watch mode was selected. If a signal is received on the alternate channel, the receiver will lock on and monitor that channel. However, the priority channel 16 is scanned every 3 seconds while the alternate is busy. If a carrier is detected on the emergency channel 16, the radio immediately goes to that channel.

In the select scan (SS) mode the unit monitors whatever channel is selected as priority (13 in the photograph) and all other channels are stored in memory for scan. If a signal appears on any scanned channel, the radio will stop on the channel until the carrier is removed. When the carrier is removed, it remains on that channel for 5 seconds, and, if the carrier does not reappear, scanning continues. Even though the program channel is busy, the priority channel is scanned every 3 seconds, and if a carrier appears on the priority channel, the radio immediately reverts to the channel. Of course, the priority channel can be changed at any time by locating the channel selector control to a different channel.

On all scan (AS) mode the radio will scan all of the U.S. or International channels depending on which is selected. The particular mode that is active results in an associated indicator light display (AS, SS, or SW) that lights up above the buttons on the panel.

The third button chooses either 1- or 25-watt power output to the antenna. For 1-watt operation an associated indicator comes on. If the indicator is dark, the unit is operating with the full 25-watt power. The fourth push button along the row chooses either U.S. or International channel operations.

The fifth push button permits a quick select of channel 16 (emergency) operation. The final button permits the changeover from scan to manual channel select operation using the rotary channel selector. Once returned to manual operation, this switch also permits an alternate choice between regular channels or weather channels.

The second-to-last indicator light shines red whenever the transmitter is keyed by depressing the microphone PTT switch. It comes on whenever there is RF energy at the antenna output jack. The final indicator illuminates green when the radio is in the International mode. When dark, the radio is operating on the U.S. channels. In Fig. 10-1 the LCD indicators are showing P13. This indicates that the priority channel is 13. If the unit were set to receive a weather channel, the P would change over to a W. Canadian channels are indicated when a letter C appears to the right of the channel indicator. Any channel in memory will be so indicated by an M to the right of the channel indicator display.

When radiocommunication is to be established, the unit is taken out of scan. The rotary channel selector is set to the desired channel. Either 1-watt or 25-watt power must be chosen. The FCC rules require that no more than 1-watt transmitter power be used for close-in harbor communications. To transmit all you need do is press the push-to-talk switch.

Circuit details are not given for the various VHF-FM marine radios because they are similar to those used in landmobile radios discussed in previous chapters. Some newer and most of the older marine radios operate on a limited number of channels. Usually, the older radios are crystal-controlled types, and the appropriate crystals are installed during installation as a function of the areas in which the boat travels.

10-3. Hand-Held Marine Radio

The Ray Jefferson Company hand-held unit of Fig. 10-2 can communicate on 78 of the U.S. and International marine radio channels. In addition it receives four weather channels. The switch on the bottom left in Fig. 10-2B permits a choice of either a 1- or 3-watt output. The radio can be used as the primary radio for a small craft or as an invaluable backup on larger boats. The 1-watt output is useful for communicating on channels 13 and 17 because the maximum permissible power on these two channels is 1-watt. Refer to Table 10-1. Communications on these two channels are related mainly to close in and passing situations and, for establishing contact with ships and coast stations operated by state or local governments. On these and other channels the unit is ideal for ship-to-ship or ship-to-shore communications in harbors and marinas. High power is not necessary, and, therefore, interference to other shore and ship transmissions is reduced.

The second switch along the bottom row permits a selection of either U.S. or International channels. The channel selector is in the form of a knurled thumbwheel digital selector. There is a three-position switch to the right of the channel selector. The center position is for the priority selection of emergency channel 16. The two other positions are weather and normal communications. The two top knobs are for squelch and volume control. The on-off switch is associated with the volume control. This model is equipped with a built-in microphone. There is a push-to-talk switch on the left side of the set.

The radio is powered by rechargeable batteries. A battery-level indicator is at the lower left in Fig. 10-2A. On transmit the LED lights. If the LED is only dimly lit, it is an indication that the batteries should be recharged. A battery charger is supplied with the transceiver. Proper nickel-cadmium battery care permits more than 300 charging cycles and a life of 3 to 5 years.

The radio can be operated with the supplied short antenna or a larger fixed-position one can be used with the proper adapter. In addition there is an external speaker/microphone with PTT switch available. This unit can be inserted into the appropriate jack to obtain normal push-to-talk switching.

A block diagram of the radio is given in Fig. 10-3. The receiver is depicted by the blocks along the top row. The second and third rows are for the transmitter. The bottom two rows show the basic circuit blocks associated with the phase-locked loop (PLL) and microcomputer frequency selection. Two blocks at right center represent the power supply. The power source for the PLL and receiver are regulated. The transmit power supply and another supply for the audio amplifier are unregulated. These circuits are switched during normal transmit/receive operations. During transmit, and when a high-level squelch noise is developed, the audio amplifier power supply is turned off to conserve battery life.

IC5 at the lower left is the phase detector of the PLL system. The crystal reference oscillator frequency is 12.8 MHz which is divided by 1024 to obtain the 12.5-kHz PLL comparison frequency. As a function of the channel selector, the proper channel code is supplied to microcomputer chip IC7. A program divider (IC8) establishes the proper division ratio for that particular channel. The source of the signal to be divided is transistor Q21 which carries a component derived from the VCO output. A 12.5-kHz component is supplied from the divider as a second 12.5-kHz comparison signal to the phase detector.

The DC frequency-control voltage at the output of the phase detector is supplied to the frequency-controlled varactor diode D18 through a low-pass filter. In turn, a sample of the output of the VCO is applied through an amplifier, mixer, and finally IF amplifier to the program divider, completing the PLL loop. Transistor Q25 provides a crystal-controlled, 67.3-MHz injection signal for the loop mixer.

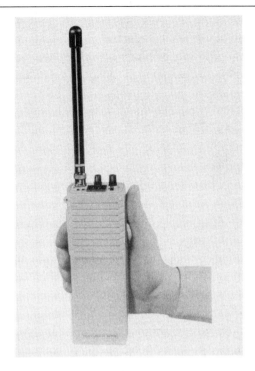

(A) Photo of unit.

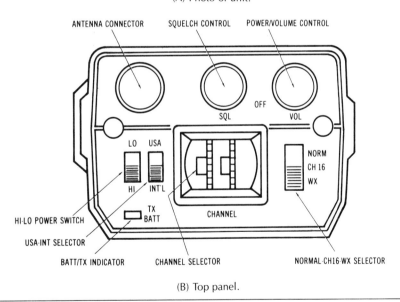

(B) Top panel.

Courtesy Ray Jefferson Co.

Fig. 10-2. A hand-held marine transceiver.

A third connection for the phase detector links it with unlock switch Q20. If for some reason the phase-locked loop unlocks, an inhibit signal is developed by the phase detector which prevents the radio from transmitting a signal on an undesirable frequency. The transmitter is also inhibited when the unit is set to one of the weather channels. Thus, if the PTT switch is depressed inadvertently, no undesirable signal will be transmitted.

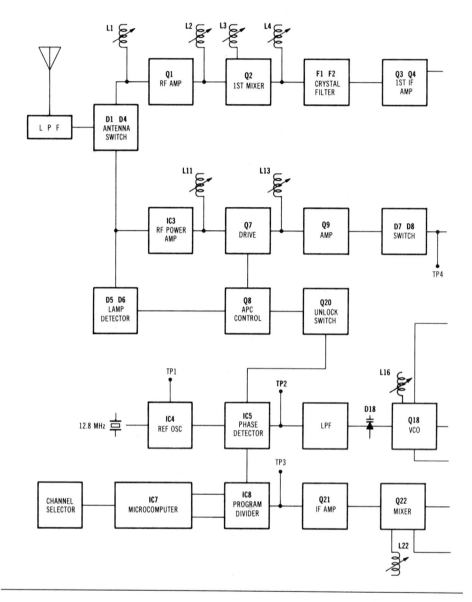

Fig. 10-3. Functional plan

An incoming signal is picked up by the antenna and passes through a low-pass filter and electronic antenna switch to the RF amplifier (Q1) at the input of the receiver. The local-oscillator component for the first mixer (Q2) is derived from the VCO and a 10.7-MHz first mixer output signal is passed through an appropriate crystal filter to the first IF amplifier. The first IF crystal filter and second IF ceramic filter determine the selectivity of the receiver.

Integrated circuit IC1 contains the second mixer, second IF amplifier, and detector. In addition it houses the second local oscillator and provides connecting pins for the external 10.245-MHz crystal. As a result the second IF frequency is 455 kHz. After the

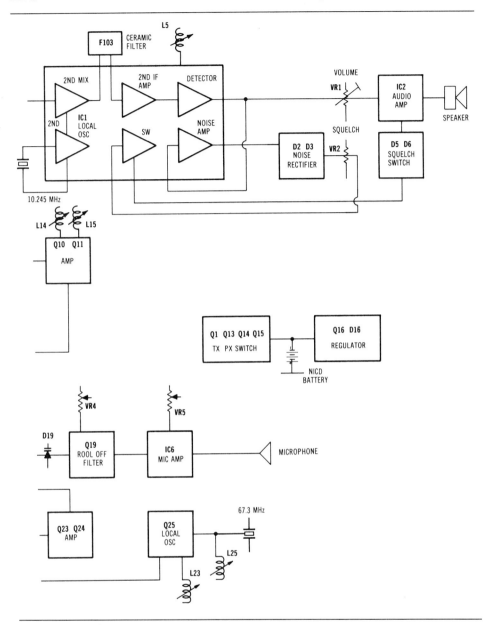

of hand-held radio.

second IF amplifier, the signal is demodulated and supplied to audio power amplifier IC2, the output of which drives the built-in loudspeaker. The squelch system consists of an external noise rectifier and squelch switch as well as the internal noise amplifier and switch in IC1.

In the transmit mode, the output of the VCO is amplified and passed to the transmit/receive switching arrangement of D7 and D8. On transmit, the signal passes to amplifier transistor Q9 followed by drive stage Q7. The integrated circuit RF power amplifier (IC3) builds up the signal level for application to the antenna switch. A portion of the transmitter output is sampled and rectified. The resultant DC output controls the power output of driver FET Q7. In this circuit the high/low switch is active and permits a choice of either high- or low-power output. The transmitter feedback path also provides automatic power control and turns on the transmit LED.

The built-in microphone is a sensitive electret type, which supplies a voice signal to microphone amplifier chip IC6. Associated with the audio system is a low-pass filter and limiter. The final output frequency modulates the VCO using varactor diode D19. Controls adjust for proper microphone signal level and maximum specified frequency deviation of the transmitter.

10-3-1. Alignment

In the alignment of the hand-held radio four test points are of value. As shown in Fig. 10-3, TP1 carries the 12.8-MHz reference frequency. A DC component is present at TP2 and represents the DC control voltage from the phase detector that keeps the VCO on frequency. TP3 carries an RF component, which is the output of the feedback loop from the VCO as it is applied to the frequency divider. This component is divided down in accordance with the operating channel and is supplied as a comparison signal to the phase detector. TP4 also contains an RF signal, which is supplied originally by the VCO and then amplified before it is supplied to the switching arrangement that supplied RF drive to the transmitter. This component is also supplied to the first mixer of the receive section.

The alignment procedure for the unit suggests that a frequency counter be attached to TP1. Set the channel selector switch to channel 06 and make certain that the frequency indicator indicates 12.8 MHz ± 50 Hz. All the alignment procedures are performed with the unit on receive except for the final transmit tuneup. In the second alignment procedure connect a DC voltmeter to TP2. Adjust inductor L16 in the VCO circuit to obtain a DC voltage reading of 2 volts ± 0.2 volt. This sets the frequency of the VCO for proper control by the PLL loop.

In the third procedure an oscilloscope is connected to TP3 to observe the RF signal applied to the program divider by way of the PLL feedback loop. A frequency counter and RF voltmeter are connected to TP4. Inductors L22 and L23 are adjusted for maximum amplitude on the oscilloscope display to make certain that the amplifier, mixer, and local oscillator in the feedback loop are adjusted properly. Next adjust inductor L25 to obtain a frequency reading of 145.1 MHz ± 200 Hz. This is done as in the previous procedures with the channel selector set on channel 06. A feedback signal of the proper frequency is now being applied to the frequency divider from the feedback loop. Inductors L14 and L15 in the Q10-Q11 amplifier are now adjusted for maximum output on the RF voltmeter connected to TP4. In these procedures the PLL and input amplifiers to the transmitter and receiver local oscillator circuits have been adjusted.

The next adjustments will peak the receiver operation. The receiver is aligned by connecting an FM signal generator to the antenna connector and adjusting it to the 156.8-MHz (channel 16) frequency. Modulate the generated signal with a 1000-Hz tone and apply a 1-millivolt signal with a frequency deviation of ± 3 kHz. Connect an 8-ohm dummy load across the speaker output circuit. Attach a distortion analyzer meter. Adjust the radio-frequency tuning controls for interstage transformers L1, L2, L3, and L4 alternately to obtain the lowest distortion. Adjust inductor L5 in the demodulation chip circuit to obtain maximum audio output power. Now set the channel selector to channel 28. Adjust inductor L3 to obtain the lowest distortion.

The next procedures tune up the transmitter. In these procedures a 50-ohm wattmeter is connected to the antenna output. The channel selector is set to channel 18. In these steps the transmitter is set to the transmit mode with the power switch connected to high. Adjust inductors L11 and L13 to obtain a power reading of 2.5 watts on the wattmeter.

Now apply a 1000-Hz 30-millivolt signal to the microphone input circuit. Connect a 50-ohm FM deviation meter to the antenna connector. Adjust control VR4 at the output of the audio amplifier to obtain a $\pm$ 5-kHz deviation. Now reduce the modulating signal level at the microphone input to 3 millivolts. Adjust VR5 at the integrated-circuit microphone amplifier to obtain a frequency deviation of $\pm$ 3 kHz. These adjustments make certain that the transmitter will not be overdeviated and, at the same time, that the proper deviation level will be obtained when speaking into the microphone at normal voice level.

10-4. Marine Radio With Direction Finder

The Regency Polaris (Fig 10-4) is an example of a versatile marine radio that also includes a direction finder. The direction-finding segment shown at the left consists of 36 yellow light-emitting diodes (LED), which are capable of displaying directions with an accuracy of $\pm$ 5°. The bearing indicated is relative to the bow of the boat to which it is attached.

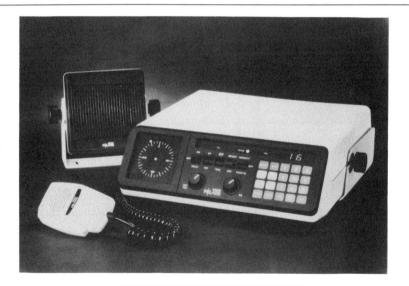

Courtesy Regency Electronics, Inc.

Fig. 10-4. Marine radio with direction finder.

10-4-1. Transceiver

The receiver can be programmed to operate on any of 55 allocated channels. It can also scan a minimum of 2 channels or as many as 55. The transmitter power output is 25 watts, with a capability of switching to 1 watt. Channel selection is made by touching keyboard pressure pads (Fig. 10-5). A beep is heard each time a key is pressed to indicate an action has taken place. The channel in operation is displayed above the keyboard.

428

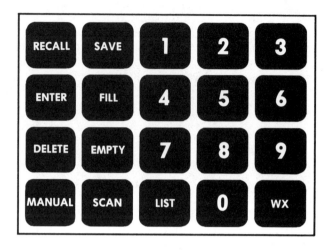

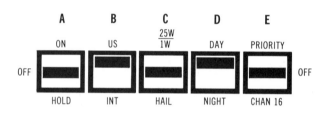

Courtesy Regency Electronics, Inc.

Fig. 10-5. Keyboard, switches, and indicators for the Regency marine radio.

The volume and squelch controls are located to the left of the keyboard. Above these controls is a row of five switches with the applications shown in Fig. 10-5. To the left of the channel digital display, there are three LED indicators as shown at the bottom of Fig. 10-5. One comes on when the radio is on transmit while the other two indicate when the radio is scanning or a weather channel is being monitored.

An understanding of the operations and capabilities of the radio can be obtained by considering the functions of the various keyboard pads and the switches. The transmitter and receiver circuit details will not be given. However, there is a considerable technical discussion of the direction-finding section of the radio.

First, consider the functions of each of the five switches. Switch A is used for direction-finding operation. When the switch is on center position, the direction finder is off and the normal antenna is in operation to obtain higher receive sensitivity. Throwing the switch up operates the direction finder using the DF antenna. When the switch is set to hold, the DF display will continue to hold the last bearing. This capability is of advantage when the received DF signal fades out.

Switch B permits the selection of either U.S. or International frequencies.

Switch C allows 25-watt operation when up and 1-watt operation when centered. The hail position permits the audio amplifier to be operated as a hailer using the microphone, audio amplifier, and an external speaker.

Switch D is a day-night switch that controls the brightness of the digital display and the illumination of the keyboard.

Switch E has a center off position. When it is set to channel 16, the transmitter and receiver lock for manual operation on the emergency channel. You can transmit and receive on this channel immediately. The keyboard becomes inoperative while the unit is locked on channel 16. When the radio is set to another channel and this switch is set to the priority position, channel 16 is sampled once per second for activity. In an emergency you can lock directly back on channel 16 simply by setting this switch back to channel 16.

Two-way communications can be initiated most readily by selecting a specific channel using a two-stroke entry. The radio is now in the manual mode on that channel until a subsequent change is made. You may use the channel to transmit by pressing and holding the PTT switch. The red transmit LED comes on when the transmitter operates. However, the transmitter will not come on unless you have stroked in a valid channel, and it will not operate if you are on the scan or list mode of the keyboard. You can quickly switch out of either of these two modes by depressing the keyboard manual button. Then, you can go directly to the keyboard to input the desired channel on which you wish to communicate.

A weather channel is received by depressing the WX button followed by the weather station channel number. The scan function permits the radio to step through two or more channels looking for activity. You go out of scan simply by depressing the manual keyboard button. The recall, enter, delete, save, fill, and empty buttons are used for placing channels in memory and establishing a desired scanning sequence. Any such established sequence can be reviewed by depressing the list button. On this mode you cannot transmit or receive.

10-4-2. Direction Finder

The direction finder display that is a part of the Regency Marine Radio in Fig. 10-4, consists of 36 LEDs mounted in a circle as shown in Fig. 10-6. The antenna array (Fig.

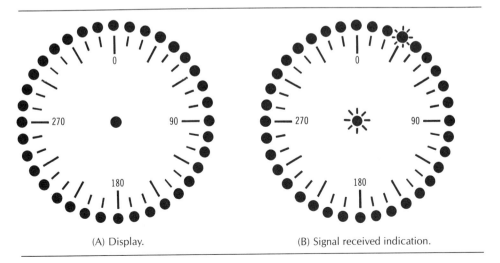

(A) Display.   (B) Signal received indication.

Fig. 10-6. Direction finder LED display.

10-7) consists of four vertical dipole elements mounted physically at 90° intervals around a circle. The direction-finding circuits switch these antennas in two pairs. Each pair consists of the two dipoles that are directly across from each other. One of the dipoles is marked with a black dot. It is this dipole that must point to the bow of the vessel as shown in Fig. 10-7B. Two leads from the antenna must be connected to the radio. When the radio is operated on its direction-finding position, it is this antenna that is connected to the radio. When the direction finder is switched off, the radio immediately switches over to the main antenna because of its added sensitivity and transmit capability.

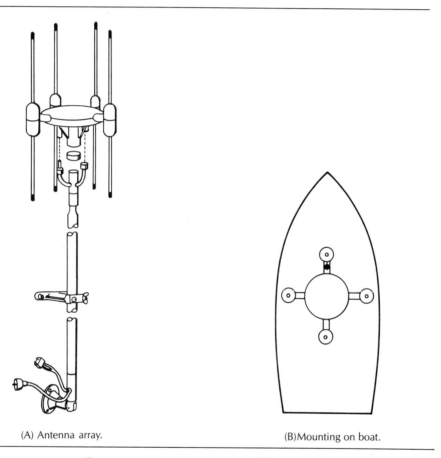

(A) Antenna array.

(B)Mounting on boat.

Fig. 10-7. Antenna arrangement and mounting.

To operate the direction finder, set the direction finder switch (Switch A in Fig. 10-5) to the ON position. As soon as this happens, the LEDs in Fig. 10-6 flash, each in turn, giving the appearance that they are circling clockwise. Note that the numbers around the perimeter indicate degrees, which will display the direction of incoming signal arrival with respect to the bow of the ship. When a signal is received, the circling stops, and one of the LEDs remains lighted. Also, the center LED comes on and the line between the center LED and the LED on the circle perimeter sets up the bearing of the station from the boat. This may be a coastal station or another boat. Fig. 10-6B shows the two LEDs on and indicates a bearing of 30°.

To steer the boat in the direction of the arriving signal, change the direction of travel until the 0° LED comes on, indicating that the bow of the boat now faces the direction of signal arrival. If you take bearings on two or more fixed-position stations, you can use triangulation practices to determine your own position on a chart.

If a received signal fades out, the LED continues to indicate direction for approximately 2 seconds, after which circling resumes. In some cases you may not have the opportunity to observe the direction before circling begins. However, the direction-finding switch has a hold feature. By depressing this switch you can get a hold on the direction as soon as you pick up the signal. When the signal fades out, the center LED disappears, but the outer LED will remain on to indicate direction. It will hold as long as the switch is not moved from hold or until the mode of operation is changed. The operator can also put the desired channel on manual and get updated direction information from subsequent transmissions as a given signal fades in and out. When a signal is received while the direction finder is in operation, you will also hear a low 1200-Hz tone in the background.

In the operation of the direction-finding circuits, the bearing information is derived from the phase relationships of the signal being received on the pairs of dipoles. Fig. 10-8A shows the dipole switching circuit. The signal from each dipole is

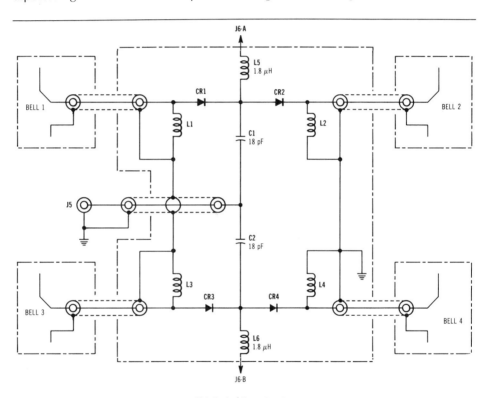

(A) Switching circuit.

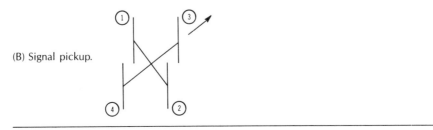

(B) Signal pickup.

Fig. 10-8. Dipole switching and signal pickup.

sampled by applying a forward conduction bias (through RF chokes L5 and L6) to its associated diode that connects the signal from the dipole to the receiver input. The sampling pulses applied through L5 switch on CR1 and CR2 alternately, depending upon the sampling pulse polarity. The same applies to diodes CR3 and CR4. The sampled information then passes through capacitors C1 or C2 on their way to the direction-finder input by way of J5.

One pair of dipoles is sampled 25 times and then the second pair at the same rate. Each time the signal from a dipole is sampled, the phase change between it and the other dipole in the pair is interpreted as a frequency change by the FM detector in the transceiver. The result is a pulse output from the detector. The amplitude of the pulse at the output of the detector is determined by the amount of phase change between the signal arriving at one dipole as compared to the other dipole. Recall that in FM fundamentals the greater the phase change, the greater the resultant frequency change. Furthermore, the greater the frequency deviation of an incoming signal, the higher the amplitude of the demodulated output.

Maximum pulse amplitude results when a signal is received from a direction in line with the two dipoles. For example, in Fig. 10-8B a signal from the direction indicated by the arrow produces maximum output because the distance of signal travel between dipole 3 and dipole 4 is greatest, producing the highest amplitude output. Insofar as dipoles 1 and 2 are concerned, they are broadside to the arriving signal. Consequently, signals arrive at dipoles 1 and 2 in phase and result in zero output. It is significant that a signal arriving from some other angle will activate both dipole pairs and the maximum amplitude pulse output occurs at some angle between the planes of the two dipole pairs. For example, in Fig. 10-6B the two dipole pairs are producing a maximum for an angle of 30°.

The cycling of the LED display is synchronized with the sampling of the dipole pairs. Therefore, the angular direction of the dipole sampling process matches the bearing rotation of the LEDs. When a signal arrives from a given direction, it will illuminate a specific LED. The frequency of the pulses that occur in the audio output as a result of the antenna switching and sampling is approximately 1200 Hz.

The audio amplifier response in a typical marine radio is such that frequencies above the audio range are rolled off. This may affect the amplitude and shape of the pulses. So, the audio is passed through an equalizer amplifier inserted to correct the pulse distortion. The pulses are applied to a tone bandpass filter shown at the top left of Fig. 10-9. This filter produces an output that is proportional to the amplitude of the pulses that result from antenna sampling. The audio signal is eliminated.

After amplification and level setting, the signal is applied to two amplitude detectors. These are synchronized detectors under control of the X and Y synchronizer. The controlled signals are so timed that one detector responds to the signals from one pair of antennas and the other from the other pair. The polarity and amplitude of the output voltage is determined by the phase relationship of the received signal from the appropriate pair of dipoles. The amplitude detector outputs are passed through individual buffers to two commutators, which are gated by the output of the phase reference generator. Recall that signal processing must be synchronized to the circling LED display. The summed output is passed through a low-pass filter and phase-shift network (which can be adjusted for proper phase calibration) and on to a crossover detector. The output of this group of circuits will be a squared wave with a phase determined by the direction of the received signal. In fact, its output will light the center LED of the display and through appropriate circuits the correct directional LED.

Note that the crossover detector output is applied to a switching block that is controlled from the divide-by-36 counter. A narrow pulse is produced and passed to two latches. They will latch on at the phase determined by the phase of the pulses. Through a buffer they are applied to the LED display circuits and will turn on the proper LED in the directional circle.

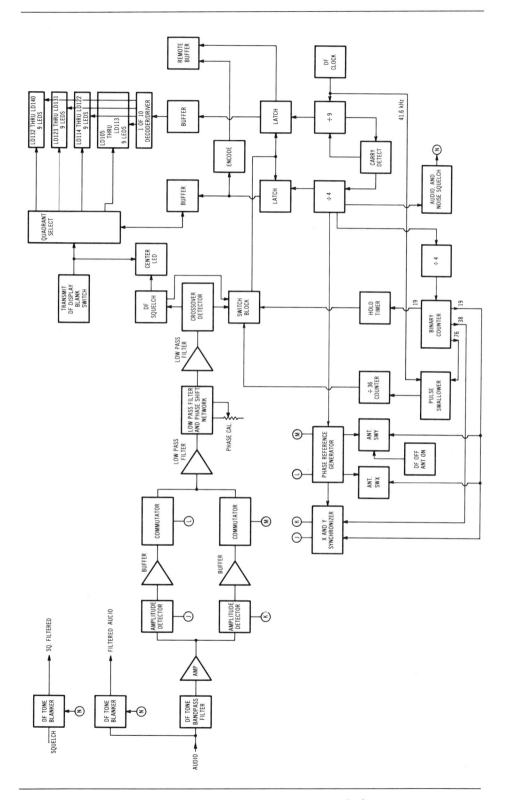

Fig. 10-9. Functional plan of direction finder.

The DF clock at the lower right of Fig. 10-9 consists of a ceramic-resonator oscillator along with a divider that generates the basic clock frequency of 41.6 kHz. All activities are timed and synchronized by this clock output. It is first applied to a divide-by-nine counter that generates a component applied to the latch that can enable one of the nine LEDs in a specific nine-LED quadrant of the directional display. This activity is accomplished through a one-of-ten decoder when an incoming pulse of a specific timing is applied to the latch. Through a carry circuit, a divide-by-four counter is also driven. Its output is applied to an associated latch and buffer and then on to the quadrant selector. By so doing the correct quadrant of nine LEDs can be chosen according to the pulse applied to its associated latch. In summary, the timing system permits the selection of the proper individual LED in the proper directional quadrant. When there are no latching signal pulses, the LEDs will come on in rotation.

The clock output is also supplied to a pulse swallower and a following divide-by-36 counter. Through the switch block these components are also applied to the latches. In the pulse swallower, every 36th pulse of the clock signal is removed. The resultant signal is then divided by 36. The output then applied to the latch is such that the latches move the circular display one light which is equivalent to 10°. The display makes a complete circle in approximately 1 second, the LEDs coming on at 10° intervals. When a signal is received, these pulses are shorted out and the latches respond to the timing of the incoming pulse to illuminate the proper directional LED. There is a hold timer beneath the switch block. Its purpose, as mentioned previously, is to hold the directional LED on if the operator desires.

The clock signal through the series of counters also reaches the binary counter at the lower center. Its output is needed to operate the pulse swallower. In addition, one of its outputs is applied to the antenna sampling blocks which do the switching of the diodes in the antenna system. These are the diodes discussed previously in connection with Fig. 10-8A. Binary counter outputs are also applied to the synchronizer, which has the responsibility of operating the amplitude detectors in step with the antenna switching. The phase reference generator is also supplied with clock pulses from the divider chain. Its responsibility is to correct phasing of the antenna switching activity with the commutating switch gates.

Two DF tone blanker blocks are shown at the top left of Fig. 10-9. They are connected to the audio and noise squelch block at the lower right, which is driven by the output of one of the counters. Each time a DF pulse occurs in the audio, the blanker stage blocks it from the audio signal that is transferred into the receiver audio amplifier. Thus, loud DF pulses will not be heard in the loudspeaker. The second blanker prevents the DF pulses from affecting operation of the squelch system in the radio. The squelch, of course, must respond to an incoming signal and not the DF component.

10-5. High-Frequency Sideband Transceiver

Stephens Engineering Associates (SEA) produces a synthesized high-frequency single-sideband transceiver. This unit (Fig. 10-10) operates between 2–9 MHz and supplies 150 watts of peak envelope power (PEP). Transmission is on upper sideband with the channel frequencies under control of a precision crystal mounted in an appropriate oven.

The unit can be supplied with up to 1024 channels in memory. These are arranged in 32 groups called pages of memory. A single memory page provides 32 channels (8 each on the 2-, 4-, 6-, and 8-MHz bands). Chosen channels may be either simplex

(A) Photo of unit.

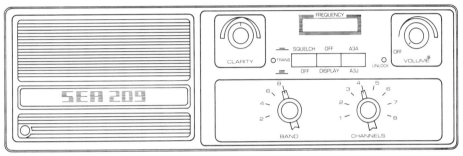

(B) Front panel controls.

Courtesy Stephens Engineering Associates, Inc.

Fig. 10-10. A synthesized HF/SSB transceiver.

(transmit and receive on the same frequency) or semiduplex (transmit and receive on differing frequencies). Internal switching permits the selection of other pages.

Each page of 32 frequencies is programmed for a certain area such as East Coast U.S.A., Gulf Coast, Caribbean, Mexico, West Coast U.S.A., etc. Twenty-four such pages are put into preprogrammed EPROMS which cannot be erased with accidental loss of power. There are eight additional pages that can be custom programmed for special user requirements. There are adequate pages for world-wide cruising.

The unit is supplied with an internal preset antenna coupler. An optional, fully automatic coupler which is mounted externally is also available.

The front panel controls are shown in Fig. 10-10B. At the bottom there is a bandswitch for selecting the 2-, 4-, 6-, or 8-MHz marine band. For each band setting there are eight channels available as selected by the channels switch. At the top right is a combination on/off switch and volume control. To its left is a clarity control that permits adjustment of an off-frequency signal for optimum intelligibility. An LED frequency display is located at the top center between the two controls. This display can be turned on or off by the middle push-button switch located below the display.

The first push-button switch turns the squelch on or off while the third one adjusts the sideband transmission for either FCC A3J or FCC A3A transmission. The A3J is the true sideband mode with at least 40 dB of carrier suppression. The A3A mode provides a pilot carrier which is 16 dB below peak envelope power. This mode is used primarily in contacting public correspondence channels, permitting the shore station to make a lock on the pilot carrier with an autotune receiver.

To the left of the set of three switches is a transmit indicator lamp which comes on when power is applied to the transmitter. To the right of the set of switches is the unlock indicator lamp that turns on when the transmitter is disabled either through the program in memory (unit set to a channel that does not permit transmission) or failure of the two phase detectors to lock.

Operation of the sideband transceiver is very simple. First select the desired band and channel frequency. Before speaking, listen on channel to make certain it is not in service. There is no need to shout into the microphone as it may decrease intelligibility. Remember that in the sideband mode no signal is transmitted until you speak or there is some other nearby noise that is picked up by the microphone.

A typical installation is shown in Fig. 10-11. Usually, a whip antenna that covers the range between 2–9 MHz is used. This antenna is single-wire fed from the single-wire output terminal J2. A low-impedance output terminal that permits a coaxial line feed is supplied at J1. This output can be used to feed a coaxial line, a 50-ohm coupler, or a low-impedance antenna. The mounting bracket fits underneath or on top of the transceiver for bulkhead, overhead, or shelf locations. Try not to choose a mounting position that is directly over a heater or one that lacks adequate ventilation. Avoid blocking airflow that should carry heat away from the heat sink fins on the rear panel.

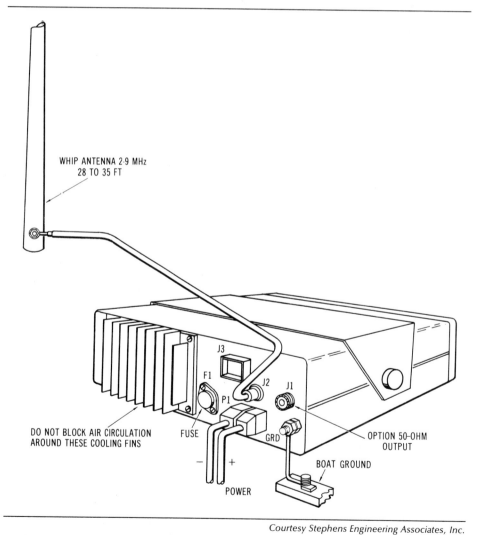

Courtesy Stephens Engineering Associates, Inc.

Fig. 10-11. Rear connection terminals of transceiver.

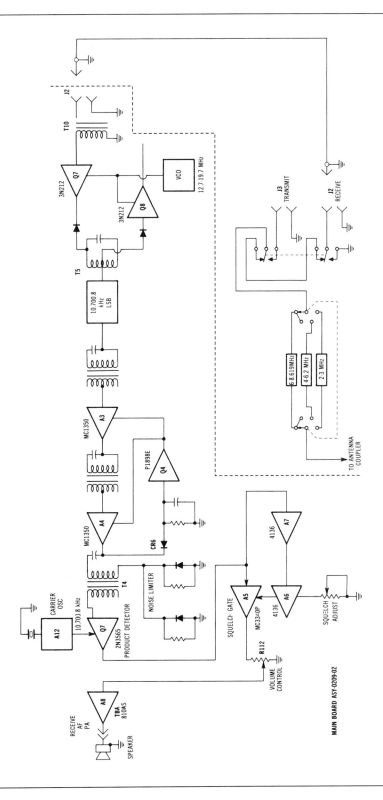

Fig. 10-12. Block diagram of receiver.

Also, avoid mounting the transceiver near an open window or in any position where it could be sprayed with water. Be certain to provide an adequate ground connection on wooden or fiberglass boats. A copper ground plate or metal keel is necessary. An improper ground may make it impossible to obtain efficient loading of the antenna.

The SEA model 209 is a single-conversion sideband transceiver. As in most sideband equipment some circuits perform the same function in receive and transmit (bilateral operation). The intermediate frequency is 10.7008 MHz. A broadband design results in a minimum of tuned circuits. Low-pass filters provide excellent image, spurious, and harmonic rejection.

10-5-1. Receiver Operation

A receive block diagram is given in Fig. 10-12. The incoming RF signal is routed through the three switchable low-pass filters to the antenna relay system and on to the RF input transformer T10. Transistor Q7 is a MOSFET mixer. Local oscillator injection is supplied by the 12.7- to 19.7-MHz voltage-controlled oscillator (VCO). The frequency of operation depends upon the settings of the band and channel switches. The resultant IF signal is 10.7008 MHz.

A simple schematic of the mixer circuit is given in Fig. 10-13. Note that the signal and local-oscillator injection are supplied to gates 1 and 2 respectively of the MOSFET. The drain output is supplied to transformer T5. The influence of transmit/receive switching on mixer operation can be seen. When the radio is on receive, a positive voltage is applied to diode D1 via transformer T5. The mixer operation is now normal, and the signal is transferred to the input of the SSB filter by way of T5. On transmit, this positive voltage is removed, and diode D1 is not conducting. However, on transmit a positive voltage is applied to D2 and consequently an RF short is placed across the output of the mixer. Later this circuit will be added to and discussed in conjunction with transmit mixer operation.

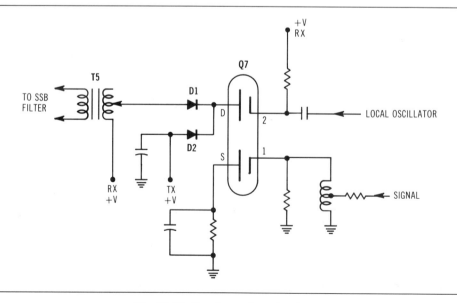

Fig. 10-13. Receiver mixer circuit.

The output of transformer T5 is connected to the sideband filter. This filter is a crystal ladder network that selects and passes the upper sideband of the incoming signal. At the same time it rejects any spurious low sideband signal or noise components. Two IF stages (A3 and A4) follow as shown in Fig. 10-12. Diode CR6 and transistor Q4 function as an automatic gain control circuit. In operation an increasing signal level increases the AGC voltage, the gain falls, and a more constant output voice level is maintained with changes of incoming signal level. A two-diode noise-limiter circuit is also a part of the IF output circuit.

A product detector is used to demodulate the IF sideband signal. Local carrier injection is supplied by a crystal oscillator.

A schematic of the product detector is given in Fig. 10-14. The IF sideband signal is applied to the base of Q6 while the demodulating clock component is applied to the emitter. The difference in frequency is the voice component that is removed at the collector and applied through a low-pass filter to a squelch gate and on to the audio amplifier and follow-up loudspeaker. The resistor-capacitor combination in the output circuit rejects the frequencies above the high-frequency limit of the voice range, preventing the IF sideband and clock frequencies from appearing in the output.

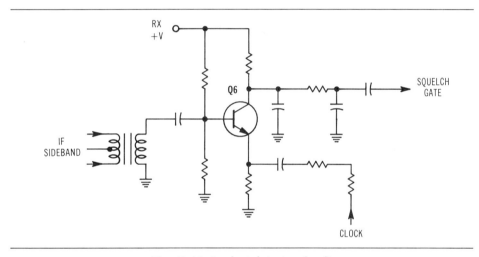

Fig. 10-14. Product detector circuit.

The signal level is adjusted by the volume control. The audio power output (A8) produces 4–5 watts of audio at less than 10% distortion. This output is also determined by the bias applied to the squelch-gate preamplifier A6 by a voice-operated squelch system.

The SEA voice-operated squelch system makes use of the fact that the human voice contains low-frequency voice components which vary in frequency at a syllabic rate. In the squelch operation, demodulated audio is also applied to integrated circuit A7. Three successive stages of amplification in the integrated circuit provide strong limiting which removes all amplitude variations. The output is next detected and filtered to extract the very low frequency components. The resultant low-frequency signal is then applied to a full-wave detector that responds to the instantaneous variation in syllabic frequency. This output is further amplified and compared with the reference level set by the squelch control. The output from the last stage is a DC level that is high with no signal present and low when a voice signal is detected. This component opens and closes the squelch gate, closing the path to the volume control only when a voice signal is present in the output of the product detector.

10-5-2. Transmitter Operation

A block diagram of the transmitter is given in Fig. 10-15. At the upper left, the microphone signal passes through a microphone gain control potentiometer to a two-stage amplifier (Q1 and Q2). The output of Q2 plus the 10.7008-MHz signal from the carrier oscillator is applied to a balanced modulator for processing. In the balanced modulator a double-sideband suppressed-carrier signal is formed. The balanced modulator is an integrated circuit and requires no external balance control to attain at least 40 dB of carrier suppression.

Let us assume the signal coming to the balanced modulator from the microphone amplifier is a pure tone of 1000 Hz. In the balanced modulator two sideband components will be generated — one 1000 Hz above and the other 1000 Hz below the 10.7008-MHz carrier. The carrier will not be present because it is suppressed in the balanced modulator. However, there will be two sideband components at 10.6998 and 10.7018 MHz.

Of course, the voice-frequency components generated in a microphone have many differing frequencies depending upon voice content. In this case, an upper sideband and a lower sideband spectra of these voice frequencies will be generated by the balanced modulator.

The double-sideband suppressed-carrier signal is then applied to a follow-up IF amplifier (A2). The gain of this amplifier is regulated by an automatic level control (ALC) system. This feedback arrangement makes certain that the drive signal to the final RF power amplifier does not become excessive, thereby avoiding distortion and, at the same time, making sure there is efficient transmission of a sideband signal.

The output of the transmit IF amplifier is applied to a sideband filter. In the filter the high-frequency sideband is suppressed, and there is additional attenuation of any carrier that might have gotten through. Thus, the only output of the sideband filter is the lower sideband. In our hypothetical example of 1000-Hz modulation this lower-frequency sideband would have a frequency of 10.6998 MHz. It is this component that is supplied to the second transmit mixer (MOSFET Q8). Here the sideband signal is down converted to the transmit frequency with the application of an appropriate injection frequency from the VCO which operates between 12.7–19.7 MHz. The frequency selected depends upon information supplied from the memory circuit with regard to the frequency of the selected channel. If we assume that operation is to be on 2182 MHz, the VCO frequency would set to 12.8828 MHz. Hence, the output of the mixer would be 2.182 MHz (12.8828 − 10.7008), if the carrier were present.

In our example of 1000-Hz tone modulation, the only signal being applied to the mixer is the 10.6998-MHz lower sideband. In this case, the mixing process produces an output frequency of 2.183 MHz (12.8828 − 10.6998) component. Note that this sideband is 1000 Hz above the 2.182-MHz carrier frequency. An upper sideband signal has been generated. Recall that for marine sideband transmission it is standard to transmit on upper sideband. Of course, in practice this would be the entire range of voice frequencies that would occupy the upper sideband spectrum while there would be no carrier or lower-frequency sideband spectrum transmitted.

The transmit and receive mixers are shown in abbreviated form in Fig. 10-16 to demonstrate their relationship in the bilateral operation of the transceiver in this section. MOSFET Q7 is the receive mixer described previously in conjunction with Fig. 10-13. The sideband filter is bilateral in operation and is used for both receive and transmit. Its operation for receive was mentioned previously.

The balanced modulator block is shown at the top left along with the transmit IF amplifier. Note diodes D3 and D4. In the transmit mode diode D3 conducts and the output of the transmit IF amplifier is applied to the sideband filter. Diode D4 is cut off so the transmit signal does not pass into the receive circuits. Conversely, with the change over from transmit to receive diode D3 cuts off the diode D4 turns on.

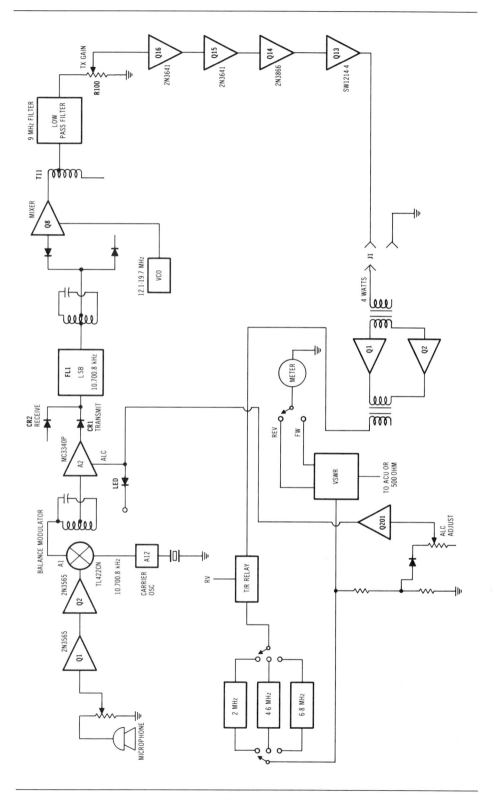

Fig. 10-15. Block diagram of transmitter.

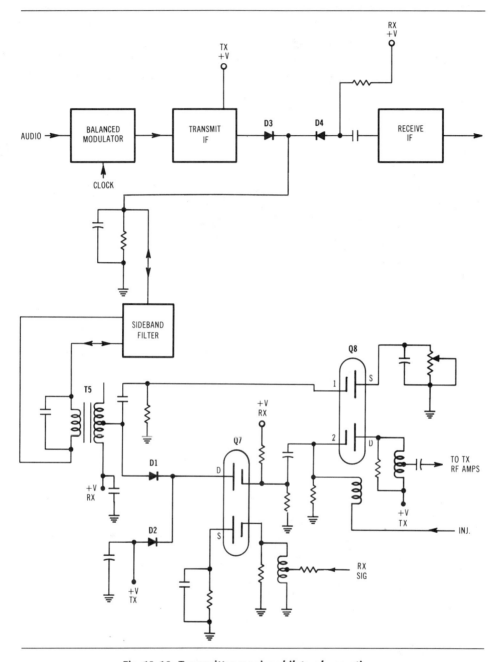

Fig. 10-16. Transmitter-receiver bilateral operations.

Consequently, an incoming receive signal will pass into the receive circuits of the transceiver.

In the transmit mode, the output of the sideband filter passes through transformer T5 to gate 1 of transmit mixer Q8. The path to receive mixer Q7 is blocked because of the nonconduction of diode D1. The proper injection frequency for generating an output on the selected channel is applied to gate 2 of transmit mixer Q8. The sideband signal is removed at the drain output and supplied to a succession of transmit RF amplifiers that follow.

The single-sideband signal at the output of the mixer (Fig. 10-15) is first applied to a 9-MHz low-pass filter that removes any spurious frequency components that may have been generated above 9 MHz. They could be sideband or intermodulation components. From here the signal passes through a power output gain control to a series of four RF amplifiers that build up the signal level to 4–5 watts PEP. There follows a push-pull final amplifier that increases the power level of the signal to 150-watts PEP. The input and output transformers are of unique design using ferrite-loaded tubular windings. These are low impedance windings, which have the higher impedance sides of the transformer threaded through the tubular members. This technique provides excellent balance as well as good frequency response and power handling capabilities. The power output stages are biased class-B for good operating efficiency and low distortion. Output is supplied to the transmit/receive relay and on to the bandpass filters which are used on both transmit and receive. Proper filters are selected by the front panel bandswitch. Output is applied to an antenna coupling unit (ACU) through a standing-wave bridge which, along with an appropriate meter, can be used to measure the forward and reflected power on the antenna system. The antenna coupling unit is discussed later.

A low-level sample is removed at the VSWR bridge to obtain feedback for the automatic level control circuit. A small component is rectified and changed over to a DC potential that is a measure of the maximum power output. It is this component that is fed back to the transmit IF amplifier integrated-circuit A2. DC voltage controls the gain of the IF amplifier and prevents the maximum power output of the transmitter from becoming excessive.

The synthesizer block diagram is given in Fig. 10-17. The system employs a phase-locked loop (PLL) in the form of a double loop. First there is a high-frequency loop that operates with a 3.2-kHz reference frequency. The second loop of the two-loop system operates with a 100-Hz reference frequency. The combination of the two loops provides a 100-Hz resolving power over the high-frequency spectrum on which the radio operates. By so doing the radio has high-frequency stability and an optimum switching and settling time.

Double-loop operation is established with the use of a VCXO that operates crystal-controlled on 11.52 MHz (top center of block diagram), and a 10.7008-MHz crystal-controlled clock (lower left).

The high-frequency loop starts with the voltage-controlled oscillator (VCO) that supplies injection voltages to the Q7 and Q8 mixers discussed previously in conjunction with Fig. 10-16. This oscillator operates between 12.7–19.7 MHz and is varactor tuned by the voltage applied to the varactor diode D1, located at the upper right in Fig. 10-17.

An additional sample of the VCO output is buffered by transistor Q12 and applied to the synthesizer down-converter mixer Q9. The output of the VCXO is also supplied to the same converter. The output of Q9 is in turn passed through a low-pass filter and reaches the divide-by-N input of chip A10. The divider reduces the reference frequency to 3200 Hz. The actual division count is determined by the logic supplied from the memory PROM for the desired frequency of operation of the radio.

The 3200-Hz signal is compared in the phase detector portion of A10 with a stable 3200-Hz reference derived from the master clock. Any phase difference between the two signals is detected and converted to an appropriate DC error voltage which is applied to the varactor diode of the VCO. This completes the high-frequency loop.

The low-frequency loop begins with the VCXO at top center. This oscillator operates over the range of 11.520–11.5231 kHz in 100-Hz increments and is varactor tuned by a DC control voltage applied to its varactor diode D2. This oscillator output is applied along with a signal from the master clock oscillator to integrated circuit mixer Q10. After comparison with the clock frequency, an output of approximately 820 kHz is supplied to the divide-by-N input of the frequency synthesizer chip A11. The function of the divider is to divide down this signal to 100 Hz. The 100-Hz signal is then

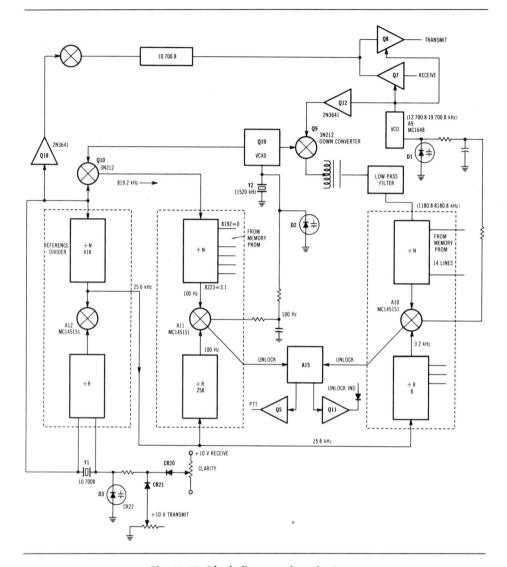

Fig. 10-17. Block diagram of synthesizer.

compared to a stable 100-Hz signal derived from the master clock oscillator. The phase difference between the two develops an error DC voltage that sets the frequency of the VCXO. Proper division is accomplished by the divider in response to the logic applied from the memory PROM. This logic is used to set the radio on the desired operating frequency.

This master clock oscillator is a part of integrated chip A12 at the left. Its output is applied to down converter Q10 and also the divide by N in the chip. As a result an output frequency of 25.6 kHz is made available for application as a reference to both the A10 and A11 loop circuits. Such a reference frequency is necessary for proper operation of both the high-frequency (3.2-kHz) loop and the low-frequency (100-Hz) loop. In effect both corrected frequencies are applied to down converter Q9 providing an accurate and quickly corrected frequency of operation.

The clock crystal oscillator can be varied slightly in frequency with a DC voltage applied to its varactor diode D3 (lower left). The variable resistor shown here is the clarity control on the radio front panel. A slight variation of the clock frequency can be used to clarify the received voice frequency when the incoming signal is slightly off frequency. The clock frequency is also applied through buffer Q18 for application to the transmit mixer on transmit, and the second receive mixer on receive.

The memory address block is given in Fig. 10-18. Two PROMs (A and B) apply logic to the high and low loop dividers respectively. Frequency selection is made by the *band* and *channel* switches shown at the left. The four-position band switch is connected by a two-wire line to the A3 and A4 logic positions of the two PROMs. Although not shown, the A0 to A10 terminals of PROM A are parallel with the same terminals of PROM B. Therefore, the two leads at the output of the bandswitch are also connected to terminals A3 and A4 of PROM A. In terms of the four-position band-switch and its two output leads, there are four possibilities from logic 00 to logic 11. Stated another way, the two lines could be set to logic 1 or both set to logic 0. The other two possibilities are the top line at logic 1 and the lower line at logic 0 or vice versa.

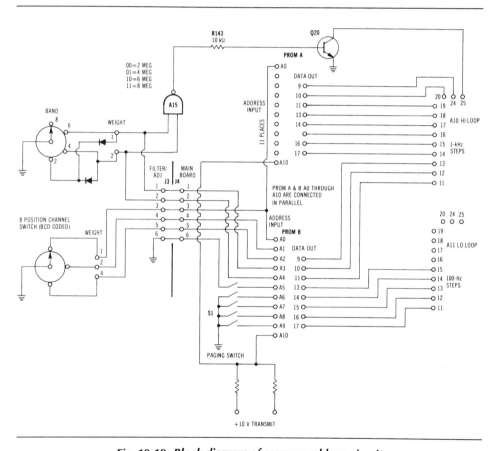

Fig. 10-18. Block diagram of memory address circuit.

The channel switch has eight positions; it is referred to as BCD-coded switch. These eight positions correspond to the binary logic code extending between 000 and 111. The three output terminals of this switch connect to the A0, A1, and A2 terminals of both PROMs.

In the arrangement of Fig. 10-18 five lines interconnect to the low-frequency N divider and 14 lines interconnect the second PROM to the high-frequency N divider. There is no problem at all accommodating the 32 discrete frequencies of one memory page (four band positions and eight channel positions for a total of 32). The interconnecting lines can accommodate many more — up to a total 1024 receive/transmit pairs. Other pages of memory can be selected by the main board dip switch S1. This switch can be set to accommodate 31 additional selectable program pages. (32 pages times 32 discrete numbers equals 1024.) Hence it is possible to make available nearly all of the U.S. and internationally established marine frequencies without any reprogramming. Also, it is possible to prepare a wide variety of custom programs for other marine use or for special applications.

10-5-3. Antenna Coupler and Tuner

The basic plan of the built-in antenna tuner is shown in Fig. 10-19A. All of the possible interconnections among matching transformer taps, loading coil taps, and fixed capacitors are not shown in interest of clarity. Recall that the power amplifier output is untuned. According to the setting of the bandswitch, the output is passed through an appropriate bandpass filter to the tuner. The first inductor the signal sees is a toroid matching transformer and, then, a series loading coil, Fig. 10-19B. If required, a capacitor (C) of proper value can be switched across the loading coil output ahead of the antenna.

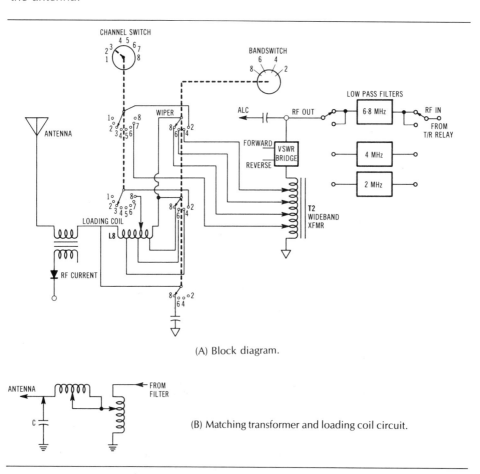

(A) Block diagram.

(B) Matching transformer and loading coil circuit.

Fig. 10-19. The antenna tuner.

In the radio signal path through the antenna coupling system, there is also a standing-wave bridge that will provide either a measure of the forward or the reverse power to the antenna system. There is an appropriate metering circuit connected to the bridge, and the meter itself is mounted inside of the radio case. A small amount of signal power is also removed and linked to the automatic level control (ALC) circuit described previously. At the output end of the loading coil, there is a small transformer that removes a small amount of RF energy that can be applied to the meter to give an indication of the relative antenna current. Also, there is a convenient transmitter switch that can apply 20–25 watts of carrier power as an aid in tuning up the antenna coupling unit.

Matching the transmitter to the antenna on the 2–3 MHz band is critical because bandwidths tend to be quite narrow. Therefore, proper tune-up on each of the channel frequencies used on this band is usually necessary. On the other three bands a single setting of taps permits efficient operation on all eight of the channels assigned to each band.

The recommended tune-up procedure follows. When the antenna is short (less than 1/4 wavelength), the tune-up generally requires a low-impedance tap point on toroid transformer T2, a critical adjustment of loading coil L8 and no output shunt capacitor. First set the tap on T2 at approximately 12.5 ohms. Switch the meter to read reflected power and adjust the series inductor tap for minimum reflected power. Readjust the tap on T2 for minimum reflected power.

If the antenna is longer than one-quarter wavelength, it is usually advisable to use a high impedance tap point on T2, a critical adjustment of series loading coil L8, and a proper selection of the output capacitance. The first step is to position the tap on

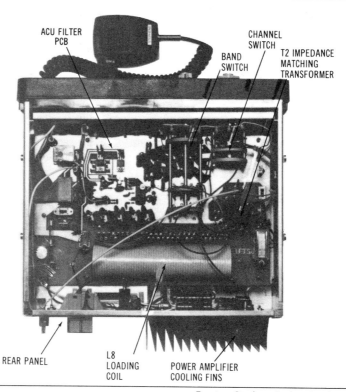

Courtesy Stephens Engineering Associates, Inc.

Fig. 10-20. Bottom view of marine radio.

448

transformer T2 at the 50-ohm point. Switch the meter to read reflected power and select an appropriate output shunt capacitor. Now adjust the tap on series loading inductor L8 for minimum reflected power. If there is no decided drop in reflected power, select an alternate output capacitor and try again. Next, set the tap on for minimum reflected power. Finally, fine tune the series inductor tap to obtain a very minimum reflected power.

The logic behind these adjustments is discussed in more detail in the marine antenna topic that follows.

The underside view of the SEA marine radio (Fig. 10-20) shows the key antenna coupler components T2 and L8 along with the band and channel switches as well as the antenna coupling-unit filter board. The top view in Fig. 10-21, shows the modular printed circuit board construction and additional components.

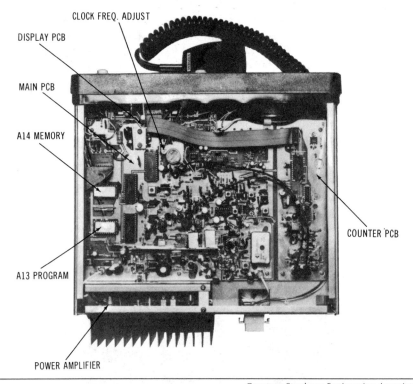

Courtesy Stephens Engineering Associates, Inc.

Fig. 10-21. Top view of marine radio.

10-6. Marine Antennas

Antenna types for the VHF/FM marine band are the same basic types that are employed in the landmobile VHF service. These were discussed in a previous chapter. In almost all situations they are matched antennas and do not require an antenna tuner/coupler. The story is quite different for operation on the MF/HF marine bands which are spotted at various positions in the frequency spectrum between 2 and 22 MHz. Usually, a single antenna is employed for operation on all bands with the aid of a tunable or preset antenna coupler. The SEA marine radio just described operates on the 2-, 4-, 6- and 8-MHz marine bands.

The basic concepts of operating a single-antenna/coupler combination over a wide span of frequencies is illustrated in Fig. 10-22. The fundamental antenna is a quarter-wave Marconi. This is a quarter-wave vertical operated against ground as shown in Fig. 10-22A. Such an antenna displays a purely resistive impedance of approximately 35–40 ohms at its feed point if the antenna is an exact electrical quarter wavelength and if the RF ground system approximates the ideal lossless condition. If these requirements are met, a 50-ohm coaxial line can be used to match the transmitter to the Marconi antenna and an antenna coupler/tuner is not required. However, these ideal conditions cannot exist over the marine bands for a single antenna. Therefore, a coupler is indeed required.

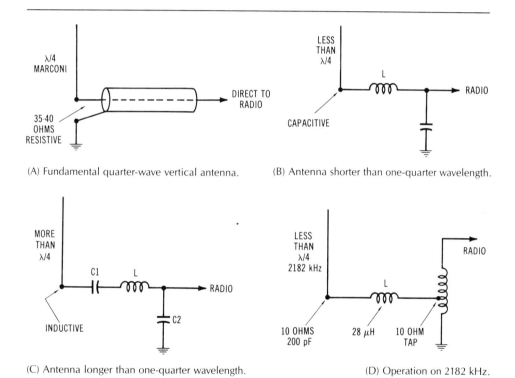

(A) Fundamental quarter-wave vertical antenna.   (B) Antenna shorter than one-quarter wavelength.

(C) Antenna longer than one-quarter wavelength.   (D) Operation on 2182 kHz.

Fig. 10-22. Basic MF and HF marine radio antenna concepts.

An antenna cut for operation as a quarter-wave vertical on 6.2 MHz of the 6-MHz band would have a length of approximately 37 feet (234/6.2). However, on the 2- and 4-MHz bands it would be too short and on the 8-MHz band too long. A proper antenna coupler permits this same antenna to be loaded and matched on the 2-, 4-, and 8-MHz bands as well as the 6-MHz band.

What happens to the antenna characteristics on the off-frequency bands is shown in Figs. 10-22B and C. When the vertical antenna is shorter than a quarter wavelength, as it is on the 2- and 4-MHz bands, the resistive component of the feed-point inpedance becomes smaller, approaching as little as 5 ohms when the length is only 0.1 wavelength. Also, the capacitance of the antenna increases. To obtain an efficient transfer of power to the antenna, the coupler must provide a match in resistance and an equal but opposite reactance. In Fig. 10-22B inductor L has an inductive reactance that cancels the capacitive reactance displayed by the short antenna. The combination of L and C also provides the proper resistive match between the transmitter output and the antenna.

On the 8-MHz band the technique of Fig. 10-22C can be used. When the antenna length is greater than a quarter wavelength, the antenna resistance rises and displays an inductive reactance. This inductive reactance may approximate 200 ohms at 0.4 wavelength. To reduce the effect of the inductive reactance, capacitor C1 is made to have an equal but opposite reactance. Again, inductor L and capacitor C2 provide the proper resistive match between the transmitter and the antenna.

The matching technique employed in the SEA marine radio is depicted in Fig. 10-22D. Consider operation on 2182 kHz where an antenna may display a resistance of 10 ohms and a capacitance of 20 picofarads. In a typical match case, inductor L would have a value of 28 microhenrys. If you calculate its inductive reactance at 2181 kHz, it will match the capacitive reactance of the antenna on the same frequency. Resistive impedance matching of the antenna is handled by the tap on the inductor connected to the output of the radio. You learned this radio uses inductors with numerous taps plus switchable capacitors that permit matching of the antenna over the frequency range employed by the radio. Adjustment procedures were described in the Section 8-5-3.

One of the major problems of shipboard mounting of antenna systems is the often limited ground capability. If the RF ground has any resistance or reactance, these

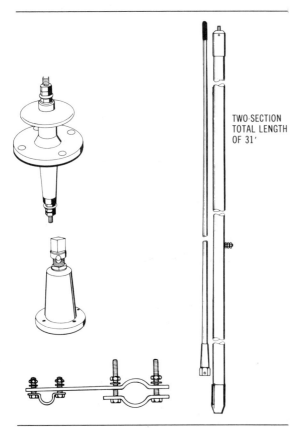

TWO-SECTION
TOTAL LENGTH
OF 31'

Fig. 10-23. MF/HF marine antenna and mounts.

Courtesy Celwave Systems, Inc.

quantities are added to the characteristics of the feed-point impedance at the antenna base. Any power dissipated in the ground system represents loss. In fact, if the ground impedance is not extremely low, the overall antenna efficiency can be such that more power is lost in the ground than is radiated by the antenna. Connection to the ground system is extremely important. In fact, ground runs of over a few inches should be made using four-inch wide copper strapping. An extensive ground system with screening embedded in decks or roofs, and bonding at all rails, stack shrouds, water and fuel tanks, engine mounts, etc. should be used.

A two-section MF/HF marine antenna by Celwave is shown in Fig. 10-23. The total length of the antenna is 31 feet. Two basic insulator mounts are shown at the left. The

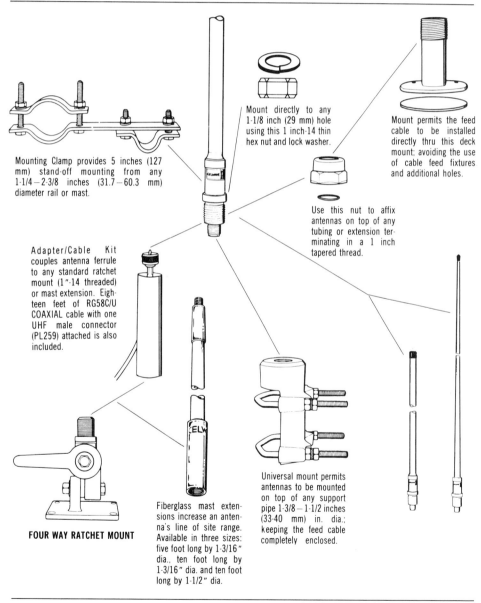

Mounting Clamp provides 5 inches (127 mm) stand-off mounting from any 1-1/4 – 2-3/8 inches (31.7 – 60.3 mm) diameter rail or mast.

Mount directly to any 1-1/8 inch (29 mm) hole using this 1 inch-14 thin hex nut and lock washer.

Mount permits the feed cable to be installed directly thru this deck mount; avoiding the use of cable feed fixtures and additional holes.

Use this nut to affix antennas on top of any tubing or extension terminating in a 1 inch tapered thread.

Adapter/Cable Kit couples antenna ferrule to any standard ratchet mount (1"-14 threaded) or mast extension. Eighteen feet of RG58C/U COAXIAL cable with one UHF male connector (PL259) attached is also included.

FOUR WAY RATCHET MOUNT

Fiberglass mast extensions increase an antenna's line of site range. Available in three sizes: five foot long by 1-3/16" dia., ten foot long by 1-3/16" dia. and ten foot long by 1-1/2" dia.

Universal mount permits antennas to be mounted on top of any support pipe 1-3/8 – 1-1/2 inches (33-40 mm) in. dia.; keeping the feed cable completely enclosed.

Courtesy Celwave Systems, Inc.

Fig. 10-24. VHF FM antennas and mounts.

top one is a feedthrough arrangement that permits the antenna transmission line connection point to be protected. A stand-off mount can be used or double-clamp arrangements that permit the antenna to be attached to a support mast. Also available are ratchet mounts that permit the antenna to be angled between vertical and horizontal positions as required by the boat structure.

Two VHF/FM marine band antennas and appropriate hardware by Celwave are shown in Fig. 10-24. The longer antenna is a 5/8-wave model with a total length of 8½ feet. The gain is 6 dB. The shorter 3-dB gain antenna has a length of 4 feet. Various mounts include a deck mount, mounting clamps, ratchet mount, and U-bolt assembly. A special fiberglass mast permits higher antenna erection if required. The transmission line feeds down through the mast extenstion. Side mounting clamps are also available that can be welded directly to a support structure.

11

Marine Radio System for Larger Craft

Vessels to be navigated on the open sea outside a harbor or port, passenger ships (irrespective of size), and cargo vessels of 1600 gross tons and upward must be equipped with a radiotelegraph station complying with the appropriate provisions of the Communications Act of 1934. Cargo ships of 300 gross tons and upward but less than 1600 gross tons, unless equipped with a radiotelegraph station complying with the provisions, must be equipped with a radiotelephone station in compliance with the same act.

Operators, installers, and technicians must be appropriately licensed by the FCC. If a radiotelegraph station is aboard ship, the operators must have an appropriate radiotelegraph license which requires that they know the Morse Code. Additional licensing details are given in Chapter 14. The operator requirements also depend upon whether or not the ship is equipped with an autoalarm. A compulsory frequency band for ocean-going vessels that employ radiotelegraphy extends between 450–535 kHz. This low-frequency compulsory band includes the 500-kHz (600-meter) international distress frequency.

11-1. Radiotelegraph Shipboard Station

Many shipboard installations are in the form of a complete package including an operating desk. The ITT Mackay Marine radiotelegraph console (Fig. 11-1) is a complete installation including main transmitter and receiver as well as the reserve battery-operated receiver and transmitter.

11-1-1. System Components

The main transmitter is housed at the center of the console and includes the antenna and keying relay as well as an approved clock. Two compulsory silent periods are distinctively marked on the clock face. During these periods, there must be a listening "watch" on the distress frequency.

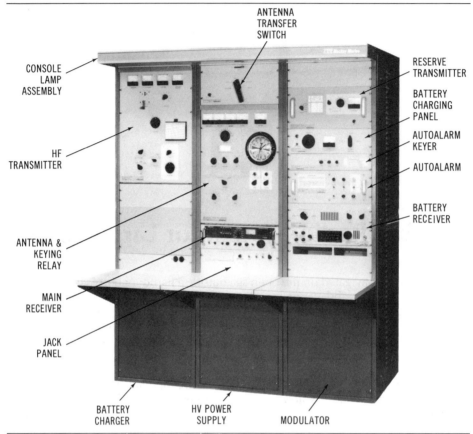

Courtesy ITT Telcom Products Corp., ITT Mackay Div.

Fig. 11-1. A shipboard radiotelegraph console.

The main transmitter operates over the 400- to 535-kHz frequency band and has an output of 500 watts. The A2 modulator for the transmitter is located at the lower right beneath the desk.

The main receiver is located at the bottom of the middle tier. It is a solid-state unit that covers a frequency range extending between 15 kHz and 30 MHz. It is capable of receiving CW and MCW radiotelegraph signals as well as FSK (frequency-shift keying) signals. Radiotelephone AM and single-sideband signals are also receivable.

The autoalarm keyer is located in the third tier to the right center of the main transmitter. The receive autoalarm is located beneath it. The autoalarm keyer is an emergency device that can be used to key either the main or reserve transmitter with the automatic alarm-signal sequence (dashes 4 seconds in length and breaks between dashes 1 second in length). This keying device is placed in operation upon receipt of orders from the captain or other authorized officer of the vessel. It sends out an alarm signal to alert other stations prior to the transmission of a distress signal.

The autoalarm device mounted beneath the alarm keyer operates in conjunction with the receiving system of the console. Whenever an autoalarm signal is received, the autoalarm unit operates warning bells and lights. It alerts the bridge and the operator in the radio room that an alarm signal has been transmitted by another ship. The radio operator aboard ship must respond to the warning and listen for the possible reception of a distress signal. The autoalarm is automatic and operates even though the radio operator may not be on watch.

The antenna transfer switch is located above the main transmitter. It has six positions. On the main-transmitter setting, it can be used to connect either the main or reserve antenna to the main transmitter. On its reserve-transmitter position, either antenna can be connected to the reserve transmitter. Its ground position permits the connection of either antenna to ground. On its direction-finder position, both antenna circuits are open, and an interlock is closed which allows the direction finder to be used. On the direction-finder and autoalarm position, the main antenna connects to the autoalarm receiver. Also on this position AC power is applied to the autoalarm receiver, and an interlock is closed to allow the direction finder to be used. The final position of the switch permits the connection of the appropriate antenna to the output of the high-frequency transmitter.

The high-voltage power supply and the battery charger are mounted in the second tier beneath the desk. The actual battery-charging control panel is positioned to the right of the clock. The battery-charging system permits the 12-volt reserve battery to be charged from the 115-volt AC line. Either the normal maximum charge or the trickle charge rate can be established with the switch on the charging panel. The metering facility permits the battery charge to be monitored. For lead-acid cells, the normal charging rate is 15 amperes, and the trickle charge rate is 200 milliamperes. For nickel-cadmium cells the charge rate is 12 amperes, and the trickle rate is 500 milliamperes.

The reserve transmitter is located at the top of the third tier. It is an all solid-state unit which has five crystal-controlled channels. Its output is 40 watts (A2 emission). The reserve receiver is also solid state and can receive A1, A2, and A3 (AM or SSB) signals.

The high-frequency transmitter is located at the top of the first tier. It provides a 500-watt output (A1 emission) over a frequency range of 2–24 MHz.

11-1-2. Antenna System

Three or more antennas are sometimes associated with a shipboard radiotelegraph station. The main antenna is usually an electrical quarter wavelength in the 500-kHz band. This antenna length usually includes the lead-in wire as well as the flat-top section (Fig. 11-2). For fine tuning of the antenna and compensating for the fact that the antenna wire may not be a full quarter wavelength physically, a variometer is included at the transmitter end of the antenna. The insertion of inductance at one end of a quarter-wavelength antenna is equivalent to adding physical length to the antenna wire. The fact that this inductance is tunable permits the antenna to be tuned to exactly the desired transmitting frequency.

The shipboard installation also includes a reserve antenna which may not be more than half the length of the main antenna. This, too, can be tuned with a variometer and by additional loading shunt capacitances. Thus, the combination of shunt capacitance and series variometer inductance resonates the shorter antenna to the desired frequency.

If a high-frequency transmitter is incorporated in the console, a third antenna would be a high-frequency half-wave doublet or some other form of antenna that operates efficiently at shortwave frequencies. Occasionally, a broadcast receiving antenna and an additional short emergency antenna may be a part of the installation. The latter antenna may occasionally be used for receiving purposes; although in some cases, it can even be loaded by one of the transmitters.

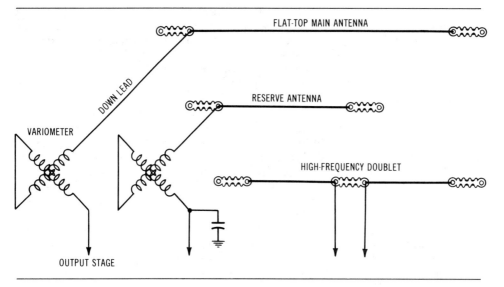

Fig. 11-2. Basic shipboard antennas.

The final antenna (or antennas) is associated with the direction-finding equipment. Such an antenna is usually mounted well away from the other antennas in a clear area where nearby metallic obstacles will not interfere with its directional characteristics. A direction-finding antenna must be calibrated only after the other antennas have been installed in their final mounting positions. Furthermore, the direction finder is usually calibrated when the other antennas are disconnected at the radiotelegraph installation by the antenna transfer switch. Hence, when the directional equipment is used on the bridge, facilities are included to deactivate the other antennas while the measurements are being made. Thus full calibration accuracy can be obtained. This safety arrangment also prevents the transmitters from being put on the air; they could deliver a damaging signal to the input of the direction-finding equipment.

11-1-3. Reserve Transmitter

A functional plan of the 405- to 535-kHz reserve transmitter is given in Fig. 11-3. The transmitter is solid-state with a 40-watt output (A2 emission). The formation of the low-frequency signal is interesting; it begins with a crystal oscillator operating in the 2-MHz frequency range. This is in the form of a Butler crystal oscillator using two bipolar transistors (Fig. 11-4). Five separate switchable crystals are employed, permitting five-channel capability. The emitter-to-emitter feedback between two stages provides an easy means of generating stable oscillations. Note that no resonant circuit is required. The output of the crystal oscillator is supplied to an integrated-circuit four-to-one frequency divider. For example, with the crystal-oscillator frequency set on 2 MHz, the frequency at the output of the divider would be 2000/4, or 500 kHz. The keying circuit operates in conjunction with the divider and a follow-up phase detector. This arrangement prevents any harmonic frequency components from feeding through to the amplifier. The phase detector is keyed so as to permit only the 500-kHz component to pass through. Resonant circuits are associated with the amplifier and the power amplifier to develop an amplified and good-quality low-frequency RF sine wave.

The tone oscillator generates a 500-Hz component. This low-frequency tone is increased in amplitude by a follow-up amplifier and applied to the modulator. The modulator output high level modulates the power amplifier.

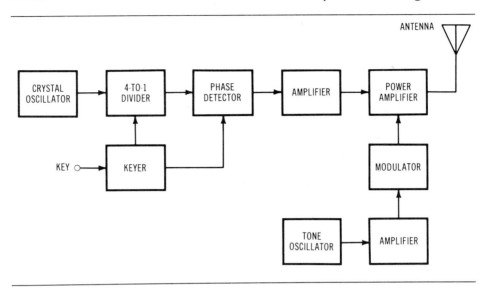

Fig. 11-3. Functional plan of reserve transmitter.

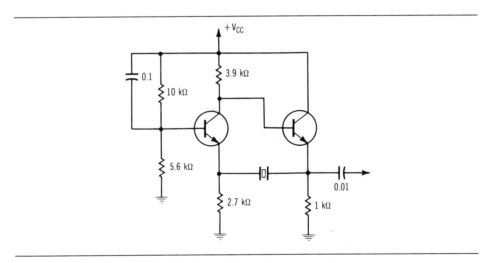

Fig. 11-4. Butler crystal oscillator using npn bipolar transistors.

The power amplifier (Fig. 11-5) employs three power transistors in parallel. The CW input is applied to the paralleled bases. The collectors are also paralleled and receive the DC component of collector voltage (which has been modulated by the tone frequency) by way of a radio-frequency choke. A T-network matches the low-impedance output of the power transistors to the antenna system. The output circuit includes the antenna RF ammeter and the break-in antenna changeover relay. In the relay position shown, the antenna is connected to the receiver. However, when the key is down, relay K1 is energized, and the relay contacts connect the output of the power amplifier to the antenna through the variometer system. There is a two-position tap on the variometer coil that provides coarse antenna tuning. The variometer itself provides tuning and exact match to the antenna.

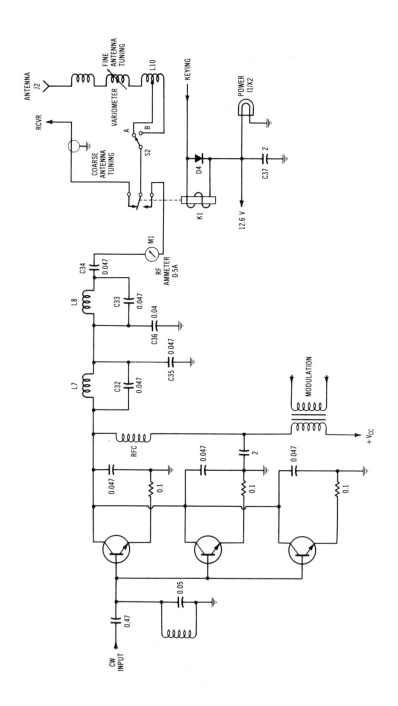

Fig. 11-5. The power output stage (40 watts).

11-1-4. Receiver

The solid-state receiver (Fig. 11-6) employs a regenerative detector. It includes a two-stage RF amplifier, followed by the detector and an audio amplifier, and an integrated-circuit audio output system. This receiver employs four transistors and two integrated circuits. Its regenerative detector provides high sensitivity and the capability of receiving both A1 and A2 emissions. The receiver operates in four bands as follows: 15–41, 37–105, 95–260, and 240–560 kHz.

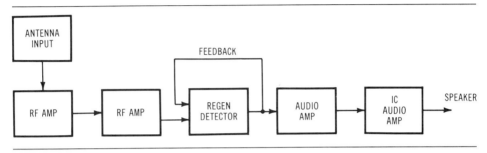

Fig. 11-6. Functional plan of solid-state reserve receiver.

The receiver can be operated from the power mains or from the console battery system. As mentioned previously, a battery charger and battery control panel are part of the shipboard console.

The radio-frequency amplifier and detector sections of the receiver (Fig. 11-7) use MOSFET and junction FET transistors. The signal is first applied to a tuned input transformer which is connected to one of the input gates. The second stage employs a tuned output circuit that links the signal to the detector. Radio-frequency gain is controlled with the potentiometer that sets the bias on the second gate of both transistors. Two low-noise and stable high-gain RF stages result. The detector uses a junction FET connected in a regenerative detector circuit. Feedback is supplied to the input circuit from the source by way of a coupling capacitor and the feedback coil. The regeneration control is associated with the source circuit. This control is advanced just slightly beyond the oscillation point for the reception of A1 signals; it is adjusted slightly below this setting for A2 signals. Audio is removed from the drain output circuit by way of an audio transformer.

11-1-5. Autoalarm Receiver

The autoalarm receiver (Fig. 11-8) is a part of the radiotelegraph console and can be operated, tested, and adjusted from the operating position. This compulsory piece of equipment monitors the international distress channel (492–508 kHz) automatically while the radio officer is off watch. If it intercepts the international alarm signal, it causes alarm bells to ring in the radio room, on the bridge, and in the radio officer's cabin. The device also sets off the alarm bells when there is a low mains voltage or a failure in the internal power supply of the autoalarm receiver.

Whenever the bridge autoalarm warning bell rings, the radio officer should be notified immediately. It is the responsibility of the radio officer to go to the radio room

460

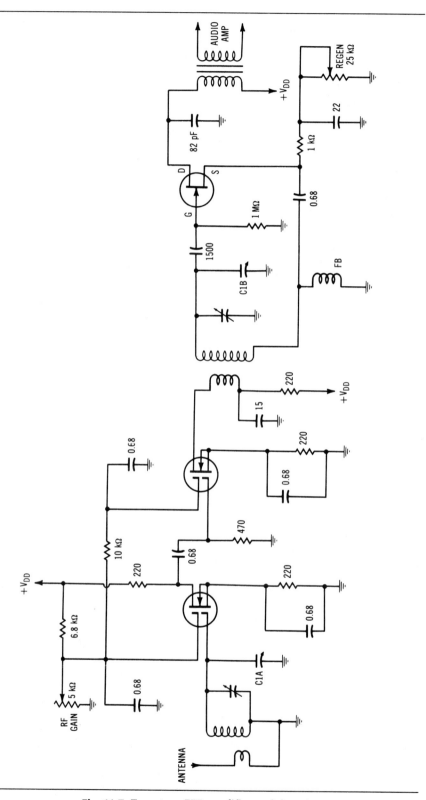

Fig. 11-7. Two-stage FET amplifier and detector.

Courtesy ITT Telcom Products Corp., ITT Mackay Div.

Fig. 11-8. The autoalarm unit.

if he is not already there; this is the only location from which the alarm bells can be shut off.

Alarm bells indicate one of the following conditions: reception of a true alarm, reception of a false alarm, or a power failure. With the reception of a true alarm, the bells can be silenced by depressing the normal-reset button momentarily. The operator must then listen on the 500-kHz distress band for a distress signal.

Occasionally, an alarm can be set off as the result of interference, static, or atmospherics. Modern autoalarm receivers respond only occasionally in such a way that a false alarm results. Nevertheless, the operator must momentarily depress the normal-reset switch and monitor the distress frequency.

If the alarm bells continue to ring after the normal-reset switch has been depressed momentarily, an equipment failure is indicated. In this condition, the bells can be silenced only by taking the autoalarm off watch until the failure has been corrected.

Although it will not set off the alarm, it is possible that severe interference, in the form of a more or less continuous signal, can reduce the effectiveness of the receiver in being able to respond to an actual alarm signal. Autoalarm receivers also include facilities that indicate improper receiver adjustment or other failures in the equipment. Such a warning light is often installed on the bridge. When this condition exists, the radio officer must make the necessary receiver adjustments to reach an optimum setting for receiving a possible alarm signal under adverse reception conditions. Modern autoalarm receivers include special AGC systems that help in maintaining the utmost sensitivity to any received alarm signal while rejecting interference and static as much as possible.

The standard autoalarm signal involves the transmission of 4-second pulses with intervening 1-second spaces for a period of 1 minute. Thus, 12 pulses are transmitted in a 1-minute period. Autoalarm receivers must respond to four successive pulses of this type, setting off the alarm bells.

When an automatic alarm keyer is used, the alarm signal is sent in a precise manner. However, when the alarm signal must be keyed by a radio operator, the timing may not be as exact. Consequently, the autoalarm receivers have certain limits of operation. For example, an ITT Mackay Marine unit responds to pulse durations between 3.5 and 6 seconds and spacings of 0.01 to 1.5 seconds.

A functional block diagram of the solid-state model is shown in Fig. 11-9. The input circuit consists of two ceramic filters (MFL1 and MFL2) connected in cascade;

these provide passage of signals transmitted in the distress band but reject off-channel signals and interference. There are four cascaded single-tuned RF stages (A1 through A4) using dual-gate FETs; these permit the autoalarm system to be actuated even though the input autoalarm signal is less than 100 microvolts. An emitter-follower stage (A5) provides proper drive to the diode detector.

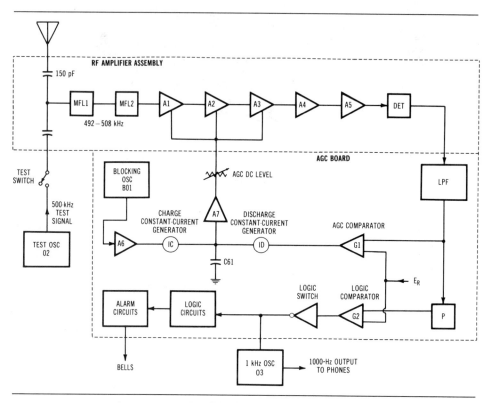

Fig. 11-9. Functional diagram of the autoalarm receiver.

Note that an AGC voltage is applied to the first three RF stages. This AGC system is unique in its operation in maintaining the receiver operating condition such that it most readily responds to an alarm signal. Thus, frequent manual adjustment is not required.

When there is steady, severe atmospheric noise or telegraphic interference, the AGC system reduces the receiver gain slowly. It also prevents impulse interference from building up an AGC voltage that will lower the receiver sensitivity too much. When there is dense interference, the gain is only reduced slowly until gaps appear in the interference. The sensitivity is restored quickly. Because of this action, an arriving alarm signal can be intercepted. A level setting control sets the AGC bias for zero-signal conditions. This bias results from the constant-current pulses placed on capacitor C61 by the output of the blocking oscillator. The AGC adds bias to this capacitor when necessary.

In operation, the receiver threshold sensitivity is held above the average noise level, preventing the noise from locking up the succeeding logic circuits.

The 500-kHz test oscillator can be used to check the operation of the autoalarm circuits. When an incoming signal exceeds the receiver threshold level by 6 dB, the logic comparator operates and drives the logic switch to a 1 level. It is the function of the logic circuits that follow to respond to the time duration for which the logic switch is at 1 and to the duration that it is switched back and held at zero as the incoming signal switches the logic output between 1 and 0, and 0 and 1.

When the logic section interprets four correctly timed and correctly spaced pulses, it sets off an alarm system, indicating that a ship may be about to send a distress signal. The logic system must be designed to make an appropriate response to the following conditions: when it has been determined that a dash is too long, when it has been determined that a dash is too short, when it has been determined that a dash is valid, when it has been determined that a space is too long, when it has been determined that a space is too short, and when it has been determined that a space is valid. When valid dashes and spaces occur in the proper sequence, the alarm indicator is activated and a relay system turns on the bells.

11-2. Portable Lifeboat Radio

Portable distress transmitter-receivers are available for use in lifeboats and liferafts. They are small in size and compact. Some equipment is not battery operated but receives its power from a hand-cranked generator. Thus, they can be operated continously for an indefinite length of time until help is forthcoming. The units are easy to operate and have both automatic and manual operating modes. When set up properly for automatic operation, one need only to turn the crank at a speed of 50 to 70 revolutions per minute. Turning the crank faster is of no help and is likely to tire the operator unnecessarily. Batteries can be used for some units if available.

The ITT model described here operates on the three distress frequencies of 500, 2182, and 8364 kHz. It can be operated on your lap or from a flat surface as shown in Fig. 11-10A. On 500 kHz and 8364 kHz it will transmit the radiotelegraph alarm and distress signals. On 2182 kHz it transmits the radiotelephone two-tone alarm signal on transmit; however, voice messages can also be conveyed.

The unit is portable and self contained except for the headset with microphone and the antenna items. It is supplied with a 40-foot long-wire antenna, and a 20-foot folded vertical whip antenna, along with ground cable and nylon rope. Fig. 11-10B shows how the long-wire antenna can be used if the lifeboat has a mast, Fig. 11-10C demonstrates the use of the vertical whip antenna on a life raft.

Telegraphy is transmitted and received on 500 kHz and 8364 kHz while speech is transmitted and received on 2182 kHz.

The usefulness and versatility of the radio can be gained by reading the short operating and set-up procedures:

Operating Instructions

1. Read the General Instructions and Assembly Instructions first. You cannot transmit and receive without the antenna and ground assembled correctly.

2. Use emergency frequencies in the following manner for best results.
   a. Use 500 kHz in all areas, particularly at 15–18 and 45–48 minutes past each hour, when stations listen for distress calls.
   b. Use 2182 kHz in coastal areas, particularly at 0–3 and 30–33 minutes past each hour, when stations listen for distress calls.
   c. Use 8364 kHz at intervals in ocean areas away from shipping lanes. There are no distress listening periods, but shore stations regularly monitor this frequency for distress calls.

464

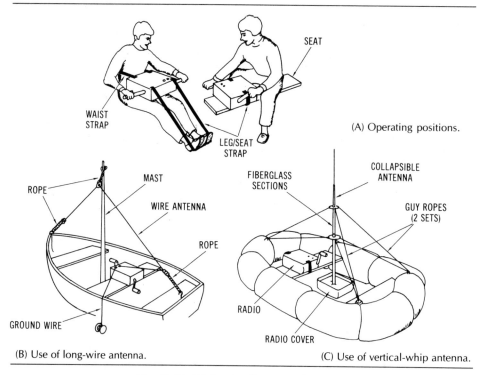

(A) Operating positions.

(B) Use of long-wire antenna.

(C) Use of vertical-whip antenna.

Fig. 11-10. Lifeboat radio use and antennas.

3. You can use the radio to:
   a. Transmit automatically an alarm signal on 500 kHz, a telegraph distress signal on 500 kHz, and a telegraph distress on 8364 kHz. This is the simplest mode of operation. You transmit only, and you can hear the transmitter working, but you cannot receive in this mode.
   b. Transmit an emergency alarm and to transmit and receive speech on 2182 kHz.
   c. Transmit and receive morse code on 500 kHz. The code is printed on the radio front panel.
   d. Transmit and receive morse code on 8364 kHz.

4. Now read the Setup Procedures.

Setup Procedures

1. Follow these setup procedures each time before transmitting or receiving in any mode.

2. Check that antenna and ground are connected.

3. The hand cranks are to be used for power. Crank the handles, in either direction, about 60 to 70 times a minute.

4. Maintain cranking speed fast enough to produce a steady light in the Test Lamp. Overcranking will not produce more power.

5. *You must keep cranking to tune the radio, to transmit, and to receive. When you stop cranking, the radio turns off.*

6. Select the mode which you require and read the relevant Transmit Instructions.

   To Set Up And Transmit Automatic Distress Call
1. Read detailed assembly and operating instructions on plate in lid.

2. Check that antenna and ground are connected correctly.

3. Fasten hand cranks to shaft. Tighten end screws.

4. Crank handles in either direction about 60 times a minute. It is not necessary to crank faster; you cannot generate extra power by overcranking.

5. Maintain cranking speed fast enough to produce steady light in test lamp. If you crank too slowly and the test lamp does not glow steadily, the distress call may not be transmitted.

6. Keep cranking to generate voltage. You must keep cranking during tuning and transmission.

7. Set the Mode switch to Tune 1 position.

8. Slowly tune 8364 knob for maximum meter reading.

9. Set the Mode switch to Tune 2 position.

10. Slowly tune 500/2182 knob for maximum meter reading.

11. Set Mode switch to Auto Xmit. You are now transmitting a distress call. Do not stop cranking until the distress signal has completed its entire 2-minute cycle.

Detailed operating steps for the four operating modes is given in Chart 11-1.

Chart 11-1. Detailed Operating Procedures for Lifeboat Radio

To Transmit an Automatic Distress Call

---

1. Check that Set-Up Procedures have been followed correctly. Ensure that the antenna and ground are connected. Do not attach dummy load.
2. Set the control marked Mode to TUNE 1.
3. Slowly tune 8364-kHz knob for maximum meter reading.
4. Set the Mode control to TUNE 2.
5. Slowly tune 500/2182-kHz knob for maximum meter reading.
6. Set the Mode control to AUTO XMIT. You are transmitting an automatic alarm signal on 500 kHz and a telegraph distress signal on 8364 kHz, in turn. *Do not* stop cranking until the distress signal has completed its entire 2-minute cycle.
7. Check for the signals in your earphones. Adjust Volume control to the desired level. You are transmitting only in this mode. You cannot receive.
8. The meter indication should fluctuate as the automatic distress call is transmitted.
9. Learn to use the other modes of operation.

To Transmit an Alarm and to Transmit and Receive Speech on 2182 kHz

---

1. Check that Set-Up Procedures have been followed correctly. Ensure that the antenna and ground are connected. Do not attach dummy load.
2. Set the control marked Mode to XMIT ALARM.
3. Slowly tune 500/2182-kHz knob for maximum meter reading.

Chart 11-1—cont. Detailed Operating Procedures for Lifeboat Radio

4. You are transmitting an alarm on 2182 kHz. You can hear the alarm in your earphones. Adjust Volume for listening level.
5. Transmit ALARM for about 30 seconds.
6. Set the Mode control to XMIT SPEECH.
7. Talk in a normal voice into the mouthpiece and give the distress message:

"MAYDAY, MAYDAY, MAYDAY, THIS IS . . . (name of ship) repeat 3 times"

"ESTIMATED POSITION IS . . ." and state nature of distress.

8. The meter indication should fluctuate as you speak and is an indication that a signal is being transmitted.
9. Set the Mode control to RECEIVE. You are now receiving signals on 2182 kHz. Adjust Volume control for listening level.
10. Repeat steps 2 through 9 at 5-minute intervals.

To Transmit and Receive Morse Code on 500 kHz

1. Check that Set-Up Procedures have been followed correctly. Ensure that the antenna and ground are connected. Do not attach dummy load.
2. Set the control marked Mode to TUNE 2.
3. Slowly tune 500/2182-kHz knob for maximum meter reading.
4. Set the Mode control to 500 kHz TELEGRAPH. You are receiving signals on 500 kHz. Adjust Volume control for listening level in your earphones.
5. Operate the Telegraph Key to send a message in Morse code. Whenever the key is down, you are transmitting. Whenever the key is up, you are receiving.
6. Send the Morse code distress signal:

"SOS, SOS, SOS."

. . . — — — . . .   . . . — — — . . .   . . . — — — . . .

7. Listen for replies.
8. Repeat the message at 5-minute intervals.
9. The meter should show an indication when the key is down and should fluctuate as a Morse-code message is transmitted.

To Transmit and Receive Morse Code on 8364 kHz

1. Check that Set-Up Procedures have been followed correctly. Ensure that the antenna and ground are connected. Do not attach dummy load.
2. Set the control marked Mode to TUNE 1.
3. Slowly tune 8364-kHz knob for maximum meter reading.
4. Set the Mode control to 8364 kHz TELEGRAPH. You are receiving signals on 8364 kHz. Adjust Volume control for listening level in your earphones.
5. Operate the Telegraph Key to send a message in Morse code. Whenever the key is down, you are transmitting. Whenever the key is up, you are receiving.
6. Send the Morse code distress signal:

"SOS, SOS, SOS."

. . . — — — . . .   . . . — — — . . .   . . . — — — . . .

7. Listen for replies. Slowly turn knob marked Receiver Tuning, searching between 8200 kHz and 8800 kHz for replies.
8. Repeat the message at 5-minute intervals.
9. The meter should show an indication when the key is down and should fluctuate as a Morse-code message is transmitted.

Courtesy ITT Telcom Products Corp., ITT Mackay Div.

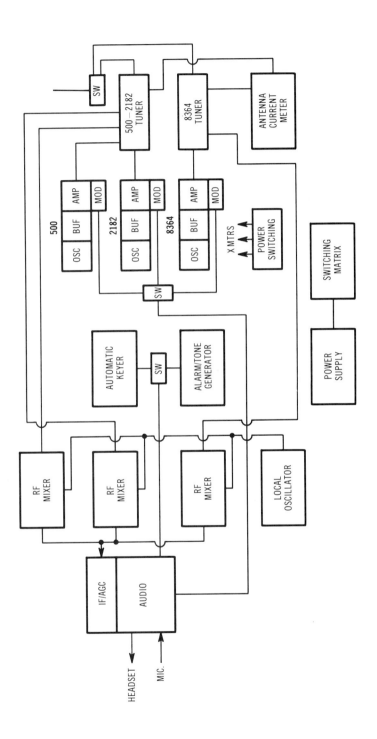

Fig. 11-11. Block diagram of lifeboat radio circuits.

The radio contains three separate transmitters, one for each band as shown in Fig. 11-11. The 2182-kHz and 8364-kHz transmitters each consist of a crystal-controlled Colpitts oscillator, a buffer-driver and a class-B push-pull power amplifier.

The generation of the 500-kHz output is interesting. It begins with a 2-MHz oscillator, the output of which is shaped and applied to a CMOS divide-by-four counter. The resultant 500-kHz square wave is attenuated and filtered to remove harmonics. This signal is then amplified by a tuned amplifier and a 500-kHz sine wave is formed for application to buffer-driver and RF power amplifier.

The output of the 500- and 2182-kHz transmitters is supplied to a joint tuner and then on to the antenna. A single control permits this output circuit to be tuned to either of the two frequencies. There is a second tuner that resonates the antenna system for 8364 operation.

An included antenna current meter is a definite aid in tuning the transmitter output circuits. A complex switching matrix is used for power switching among the various transmitters, receiver sections, etc. according to the mode of operation. Also switching (SW) facilities are included for antenna, transmitter, modulation etc. for various operating modes. These changeovers although quite extensive take place with the simple mode control switch.

The automatic keyer section of the radio sets up the time sequences required to generate the radiotelegraph alarm and distress signals. The sequence begins with an alarm signal consisting of 12 4-second dashes with 1-second spacing. There follows the SOS distress signal three times. Now a frequency changeover between 500 kHz and 8364 kHz is made because the alarm and distress signals are transmitted alternately on the 500-kHz and 8364-kHz frequencies. Finally, there is a 42-second dash transmitted that is useful when direction finders are being used to locate the position of the lifeboat or life raft.

The alarm/tone generator forms the radiotelephone alarm signal for 2182-kHz transmission. The signal consists of alternating 2200- and 1300-kHz tones along with a 700-Hz tone for modulated telegraphy. These tones are generated by a Hartley oscillator. Follow-up multivibrators set the spacing times and key the individual tones on and off.

The receiver section in Fig. 11-11 has three separate RF amplifier/mixer sections for the three distress frequencies. There are also three separate local oscillators. There are two crystal-controlled local oscillators that operate on 11.2 and 12.882 MHz. The 11.2-MHz oscillator provides an injection frequency for the 500-kHz receiver. The resultant difference frequency is 10.7 (11.2 − 0.5) MHz. This is the IF frequency for the receiver. The 12.822-MHz local injection frequency is applied to the 2182-kHz mixer. Again the difference frequency is 10.7 MHz.

The variable-frequency local oscillator produces an output frequency that is variable between 18.9 and 19.5 MHz. As a result the 8364-kHz receiver is tunable between 8200–8800 kHz. The difference frequency is again 10.7 MHz.

The mixer outputs are supplied to the IF/AGC/audio system which first builds up the level of the IF input signal. The AGC system rectifies an IF component and develops a DC voltage that corresponds to the incoming signal level. This AGC voltage is used to control the gain of the RF and IF amplifiers of the receiver. A beat-frequency oscillator (BFO) mixes with an incoming CW signal to produce an audible 1-kHz difference frequency. This circuit demodulates any incoming radiotelegraph signal.

An audio amplifier builds up the demodulated signal prior to its application to the headset. The audio system also takes the microphone signal and builds it up to the proper level for modulating the transmitter.

11-3. Radiotelephone Shipboard Station

The ITT Mackay Marine Radio console in Fig. 11-12, provides five operating modes. The single-sideband modes are A3J for reception on single-sideband receivers, A3A with a low-level transmitted carrier for contact with autotune public coast stations, and A3H for reception on conventional AM receivers. The other two modes are radioteletype and A1 radiotelegraphy.

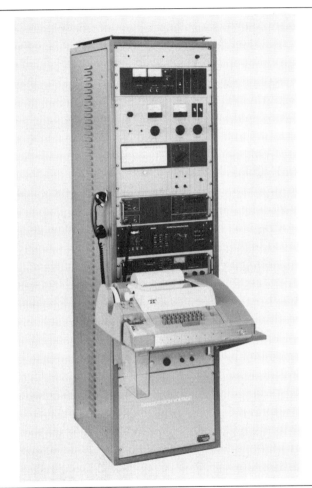

Courtesy ITT Telcom Products Corp., ITT Mackay Div.

Fig. 11-12. A shipboard SSB, CW, and radioteletype console.

Starting at top of rack (Fig. 11-12) and moving down, the sections are the harmonic filter, antenna coupler control unit, linear amplifier, exciter, radioteletype modem, receiver, and radioteletype. The console also houses the various power supplies and an optional alarm generator.

The recommended transmitting antenna is a 35-foot vertical whip. The same antenna can be used with receive when there is appropriate switching or a separate long-wire antenna. When separate antennas are used for transmit and receive, it is recommended that they be separated by a minimum of 50 feet.

11-4. Marine Transmitter-Receiver Combination

The usual coastal station or shipboard console is made up of a separate transmitter and receiver. The ITT Mackay Radio units of Fig. 11-13 consist of a separate transmitter exciter and receiver. The exciter itself can be used as a transmitter with 125-watts (PEP) output. More often it is used to drive a linear power amplifier (Fig. 11-14), which can step up the power to 1000-watts PEP. The frequency range of the units extends

(A) Exciter/transmitter.

(B) Receiver.

Courtesy ITT Telcom Products Corp., ITT Mackay Div.

Fig. 11-13. Marine radio exciter/transmitter and receiver.

between 1.6–30 MHz. The major application mode of operation is single-sideband (USB) voice communications. Other exciter modes are CW, radioteletype, frequency-shift keying data, facsimile, AM with inserted carrier (AME), and independent side-band (ISB). The receiver has the same reception modes but its frequency range extends between 10 kHz and 30 MHz.

The exciter can be operated from its front panel controls, by remote control, or computer control. For some coastal radio applications, the transmitter and receive centers are often separated. The frequency and mode of transmission are selected directly using a keypad, or appropriate information may be stored in memory for instant recall. Tuning is in 10-Hz increments, and a readout of the frequency is given on an LED digital display. Keypad entry can be made by either frequency or channel number. In appropriate situations the exciter can be operated with only 20-watts PEP output.

The linear amplifier is in two sections — the high-frequency power amplifier and the power supply. Despite the high level of output, the linear amplifier is strictly solid state and no vacuum tubes or motor-driven tuning devices are required. To obtain the rated power output, four parallel-connected 300-watt broadband solid-state amplifiers are used. Should any one of the 300-watt modules fail, the amplifier continues to operate at reduced power. An RF power output of 1000-watts PEP is obtained with an input power of 125-watts maximum PEP. Actually, maximum power output can be obtained with a substantially lower level than 125 watts. The input and output impedances are 50 ohms.

The transmitter output is untuned and in almost all marine applications an external antenna coupling unit matches the output to the antenna system. Typically, the antenna would be a 35-foot vertical or a 30- to 100-foot long wire.

The receiver permits direct frequency selection or sweep tuning. As many as 99 easily programmed channels can be scanned, either sequentially or in groups. In addition to the usual marine applications, it can be used as a versatile receiver for monitoring and surveillance applications. It can also be used as an integrated part of a high-frequency communications system where isolated receiver sites operate by remote control. Computer control is also possible. Even narrow-band FM signals can be received. The three units along with an appropriate antenna coupling unit make a complete high-frequency communications system which includes a receiver that can tune all the way down to 10 kHz.

11-4-1. Exciter Description

An ITT Mackay radio exciter and receiver are shown in Fig. 11-13. The exciter design facilitates efficient field service and repair. Modular construction is used. The front panel, rear panel, and power amplifier assemblies are removable with only a screwdriver, and the printed-circuit boards simply unplug from the motherboard. The exciter is composed of eight major subassemblies.

The chassis-motherboard design is so arranged that all subassemblies in the exciter are electrically or mechanically connected to the board. It houses all plug-in printed-circuit boards and provides shielding. It also supports all interconnecting wiring in the exciter. All controls, the air filter, and the LED indicators and displays, (and their associated circuitry) are all mounted on the front panel board.

The logic board contains the microprocessor, memory, and exciter-control logic. The exciter channel memory is a CMOS type kept alive by a lithium battery with a 10-year typical life. Signals from the logic board provide frequency information to the synthesizer, and band and mode information to the exciter modules.

The five printed circuit boards that are a part of the exciter signal path are the transmit modulator, IF filter, mixer, high-pass filter, and half-octave filter. When transmitting, the exciter accepts and amplifies inputs from the microphone or other source. A synthesizer generates the proper signals for mixing. A double-conversion system is used with a first intermediate frequency of 59.53 MHz and a second IF of 5 MHz. The two sets of associated crystal filters determine the exciter bandwidth. A signal compressor on the transmit modulator board improves the peak-to-average power output ratio.

Three PLL printed circuit boards and a reference board are a part of the synthesizer. Two provide the exciter with the first local oscillator and second local oscillator frequencies; the third local oscillator component comes from the reference board. All frequencies are derived from a temperature-compensated crystal oscillator on the reference board. A sidetone of 1000 Hz is also furnished by the reference board. If a fault causes any of the loops to lose lock, the loss-of-lock LED comes on and transmission is inhibited.

The sixth module supports the power supply which is a switching type developing +5 and +26 volts DC from an input voltage of 115 or 230 volts DC.

The rear panel assembly is of aluminum and supports the PA assembly and various connectors.

The eighth and final assembly is the power amplifier. It is a solid-state broadband amplifier rated at 125 watts of peak envelope power (PEP) and 125 watts average into a 50-ohm load. This power amplifier is cooled by a heat-sink and fan mounted on the rear panel.

The ratio exciter output can be used to drive a linear amplifier (Fig. 11-14) to raise the power level to 1000 watts PEP.

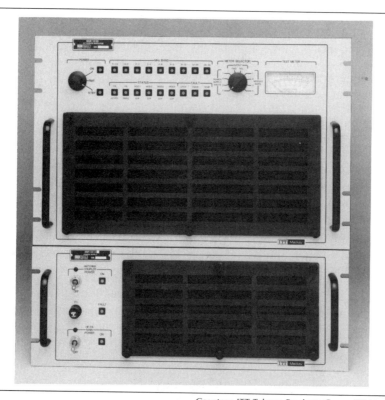

Courtesy ITT Telcom Products Corp., ITT Mackay Div.

Fig. 11-14. A 1-kilowatt linear amplifier.

11-4-2. Receiver

The receiver is also modular in construction and is composed of six major subassemblies. All subassemblies are electrically or mechanically connected to the chassis motherboard. The chassis houses all plug-in printed-circuit boards and contains all the interconnecting wiring in the receiver.

All controls and the speaker are mounted on the front panel assembly. Included are the LED indicators and associated circuitry which is mounted on the display and keypad boards attached to the panel.

The logic board contains the microprocessor, memory, and receiver control logic. The memory is a CMOS type which is kept alive by a lithium battery with a ten-year typical life. Signals from the logic board provide frequency information to the synthesizer, and band filter, AGC, and mode information to the receiver modules.

The receiver signal path assembly consists of six individual printed circuit boards. These are low-pass filter, high-pass filter, mixer, IF filter, audio and squelch, and speaker amplifier. These boards provide the signal path from the antenna to the speaker, using inputs from the synthesizer. The double conversion frequencies are 59.53 and 5.00 MHz. Two sets of crystal filters determine the radio bandwidth.

The synthesizer is composed of four PC boards. These are the major loop, translator loop, minor loop, and reference board. The synthesizer is a three-loop design which provides the receiver with the first local oscillator, the second local oscillator, and the third local oscillator frequencies. All frequencies are derived from a temperature-compensated crystal oscillator on the reference board. If a fault causes any of the loops to lose lock, the loss-of-lock LED lights. As a result reception is also inhibited and appropriate fault display results.

The rear panel assembly supports the power supply and various external interface connectors.

A modularized plan of the receiver is given in Fig. 11-15. The signal from the antenna is applied to a pair of filters (low-pass and high-pass) at the top left. These filters act together to produce an octave bandpass response that covers the 30-MHz tuning range in eight bands. Each band setup is switched automatically by microprocessor control. The low-pass filter contains a 10-watt input protection circuit, a 30-MHz low-pass filter, and a parallel bank of eight selectable low-pass filters with cut-off frequencies of 2, 3, 4, 6, 13, and 30 MHz. The companion high-pass filter board has a parallel bank of eight filters with cut-off frequencies of 1.6, 2, 3, 4, 6, 9, 13, and 20 MHz. These are also selected automatically. Also included is a broadcast filter which provides attenuation of greater than 70 dB to broadcast signals (below 1.6 MHz) to reduce possible interference. The assembly also mounts a low-noise RF amplifier.

The signal from the filter board is applied to the mixer along with local-oscillator injection from the major loop of the synthesizer. The local oscillator frequency is tuned between 59.63 and 89.53 MHz to produce an IF frequency of 59.53 MHz. A crystal filter, a low-noise FET amplifier, and a second filter follow before it reaches a second double-balanced mixer. In this mixer the 54.53-MHz second local oscillator component from the translator loop board of the synthesizer is mixed to produce the 5-MHz second IF signal.

A pair of IF filters follow along with associated squelch circuits depending upon the options of the particular receiver. In fact there are a number of 5-MHz filters as related to the reception of USB, LSB, and AM modes. The appropriate filter is selected by diode switching as a result of filter or mode control signals from the follow-up interface board. Various filters that allow up to six bandwidths or optional ISB mode capability can be chosen.

In effect the 5-MHz second IF signal from the mixer board is passed through the appropriate IF filter combination and further amplified in three stages. The IF gain is adjustable, and, in addition, there is appropriate AGC circuitry.

474

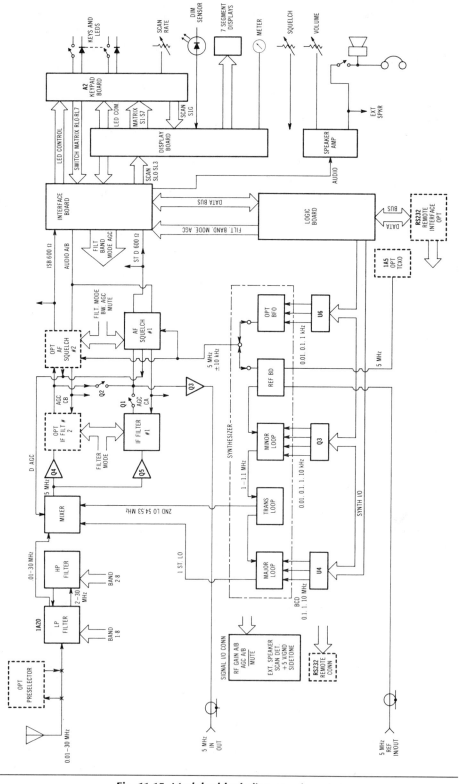

Fig. 11-15. Modular block diagram of receiver.

The logic board is located below the interface board in Fig. 11-15. It contains the microprocessor and supporting circuitry to supply frequency, band, mode, filter, AGC action, BFO offset, and channel information to assemblies in the receiver. Similar functions are so controlled in the exciter. Logic capability is provided to interface the microprocessor with external control inputs and outputs in the system. Just like the companion exciter the receiver can be remotely controlled or controlled by a computer.

All controls and indicators are a part of the front panel assembly. The displays that indicate channel, frequency, emission mode, faults, and other indications are mounted on the display board. There are also the meter and associated switching circuitry to indicate RF and audio signal levels, and the tuning control is attached to this board. The keypad arrangement consists of numeric push buttons plus lettered ones up to a total of 34. The output from the interface board also drives the speaker amplifier and output arrangement. It will provide 4 watts to drive the speaker.

The major and translator loops of the synthesizer were mentioned previously. The minor loop board supplies the 1.0- to 1.09999-MHz signal to the translator loop board. This component determines the 10-Hz, 100-Hz, 1-kHz, and 10-kHz digits of the receiver frequency. Reference signals for the operation of the minor phase-locked loop circuit come from the logic board and the reference board. The frequency accuracy is dependent only on the 5-MHz TCXO oscillator on the reference board.

If the optional BFO board is included, its output replaces the output of the reference board for the third local oscillator component. As an aid in copying some signal modes, it provides a $\pm$ 7.99-kHz offset in 10-Hz steps by varying the output above and below 5 MHz.

11-4-3. Ground and Antenna Systems

Both the receiver and the exciter should be securely grounded. Improper grounding can degrade performance and make tuning difficult. The units can be grounded directly to the vessel's structure when it has a metal hull. When the hull is fiberglass or wood, an adequate ground-counterpoise is recommended. The counterpoise should have as much surface area as possible. In fact, for 2-MHz operation, 100 square feet is recommended. A reasonably good ground can be obtained by bonding together large metal objects. Grounds should be bonded together with two or three copper straps running as far as possible fore and aft along with a number of cross members. A typical ground-counterpoise system is shown in Fig. 11-16.

If the exciter is to be operated as a 125-watt PEP transmitter to form a transmitter-receiver combination, an appropriate coupler and antenna system is required for marine operation. The exciter should drive a resistive antenna system with a 2 to 1 maximum permissible VSWR. Typical marine couplers can operate with a 16- to 35-foot whip antenna over a frequency range of 1.6–30 MHz or a 50- to 150-foot long-wire antenna over the same frequency range.

Mount the antenna as high as possible using one that is at least one-eighth wavelength long at the lowest operating frequency. Short antennas are not efficient radiators. Short antennas, as mentioned previously, are also most sensitive to ground loss. Consequently, use as an extensive a ground-counterpoise system that is possible. Make use of large metal objects, copper screens, the propeller shaft, and the recommended bonded copper straps.

Two typical coastal station antennas are shown in Figs. 11-17 and 11-18. In both installations notice that the antenna coupler is mounted outside of the building; therefore, it must be protected by a weatherproofed housing. An excellent ground is obtained by using as many radial wires as possible and making them at least the same length as the antenna. If the antenna coupling unit is controlled remotely, there must also be a control cable run between the transmitter-receiver and the antenna coupler.

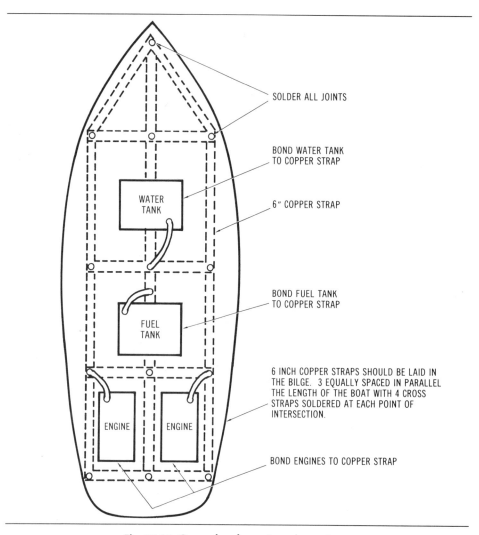

SOLDER ALL JOINTS

BOND WATER TANK TO COPPER STRAP

6" COPPER STRAP

BOND FUEL TANK TO COPPER STRAP

6 INCH COPPER STRAPS SHOULD BE LAID IN THE BILGE. 3 EQUALLY SPACED IN PARALLEL THE LENGTH OF THE BOAT WITH 4 CROSS STRAPS SOLDERED AT EACH POINT OF INTERSECTION.

BOND ENGINES TO COPPER STRAP

WATER TANK

FUEL TANK

ENGINE   ENGINE

Fig. 11-16. Ground and counterpoise system.

Usually an automatic antenna coupler is used with shipboard and coastal marine installations. When set up properly, all the operator need do when changing frequency is to depress the tune button. Antenna-coupling tuning now takes place automatically. A typical automatic tuner plan is given in Fig. 11-19. At the center, transformer T1 provides a proper tap for coupling into the tuner from the 50-ohm output of the transmitter. Capacitor C1 and inductor L1 are motor tuned. Parallel capacitors C2 and C3 are usually needed to tune a long-wire antenna on the higher frequency bands. In this case the jumper is removed. Otherwise, a jumper takes them out of the circuit to the antenna. When a long-wire antenna is used, checks must be made at the time of installation to determine if the capacitors are necessary. Capacitors are not required when the antenna coupler is connected to a standard marine whip antenna.

The tuning procedure is simple when an appropriate automatic antenna coupler is connected to the output of the exciter being used as a transmitter, or a coupler (with a

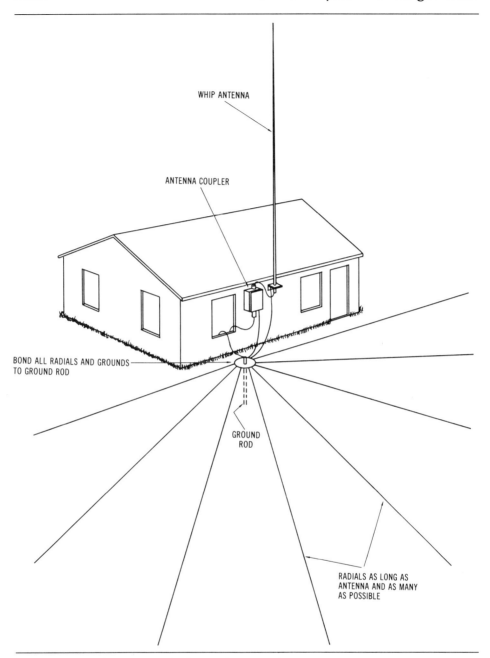

Fig. 11-17. Typical coastal station whip antenna installation.

higher power rating) is connected to the output of the linear amplifier. After a frequency change has been made, depress the tune button. Only a momentary depression of this button is required. When the exciter is turned on initially, a steady, nonblinking light comes on. When the time delay runs out (approximately 30 seconds after initiation of a tune command), the light will blink. Anytime the VSWR exceeds 2 to 1 the light will blink except during a tuning cycle. There is also a *not-tuned light* which illuminates only during the tuning cycle. A *ready light* illuminates after a tuning cycle has been completed, and the coupler has tuned automatically to a VSWR of less than 2 to 1.

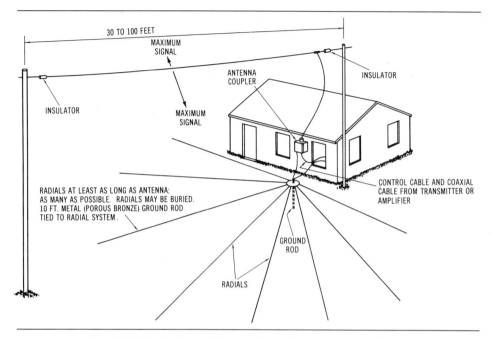

Fig. 11-18. Typical coastal station long-wire antenna installation.

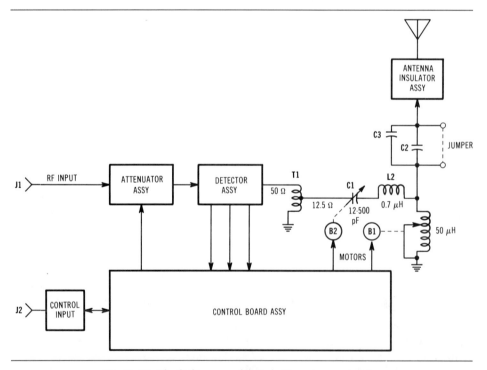

Fig. 11-19. Block diagram of automatic antenna coupler.

A VSWR metering system measures the forward and reflected ratios. A no- or a low-reflected reading when transmitting indicates that the antenna has been correctly matched to the transmitter. The attenuator assembly at the top left in Fig. 11-19 provides an attenuator pad and switching relay that limits impedance variations during the tuning cycle. A relay keeps this pad inserted during the portion of the tuning cycle when the VSWR can be high.

The detector assembly employs a phase discriminator, magnitude discriminator, and a forward-reflected power detector. The function of the phase discriminator is to sense the reactive component of the antenna impedance. The discriminator DC output is applied to the servo that drives the variable capacitor to a setting that will corrrect the condition. The function of the magnitude discriminator is to sense the resistive component of the line impedance. It develops a proportional DC output for the servo system that will drive the variable inductor to attain a resistive component of 50 ohms. The forward and reflective power detectors also provide the voltage samples of forward and reflected power on the line for metering purposes.

The control board assembly contains the active coupler logic circuits, the servo amplifiers, and the required power supply elements. These include the circuits associated with the tune initiate request and the series of automatic procedures that follow. Circuits in this assembly evaluate information from the detector assembly. The attenuator operation is also initiated from the control board. Appropriate information must be sent back to the display indicators. The control input block supplies the interconnections for applying DC power and the control interconnections to the transmitter.

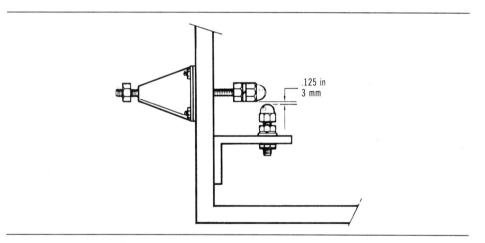

Fig. 11-20. Antenna terminal and internal ball gap.

A ball gap (Fig. 11-20) is a part of the antenna terminal of the antenna coupling unit. It discharges any high-voltage charges that accumulate on the antenna. Customarily, the gap separation is set to 0.125 inch.

11-4-3. Linear Amplifier

The linear amplifier is a two-unit package consisting of the linear power amplifier and its associated switching-type power supply. The amplifier covers the frequency range between 1.6–30 MHz. It is fully automatic and amplifies a nominal 50-watt RF output from the exciter to a 1-kilowatt peak or average power output. The amplifier and the appropriate external antenna coupler are fully automatic and can be con-

480

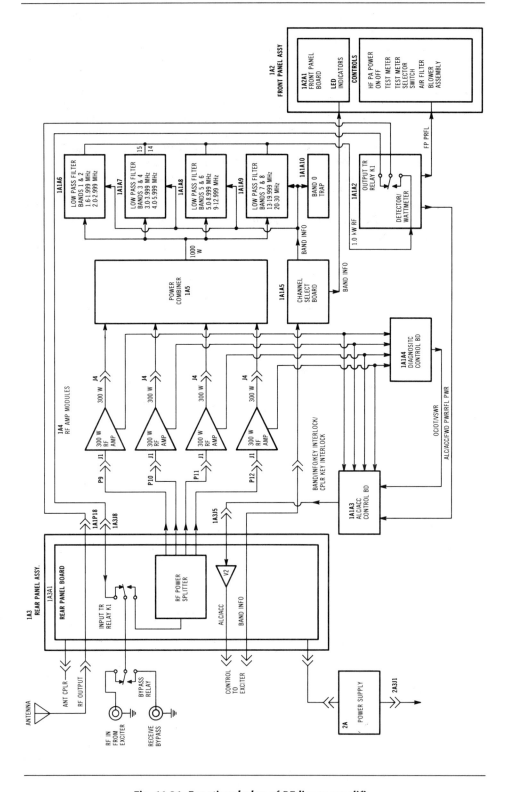

Fig. 11-21. Functional plan of RF linear amplifier.

trolled from the exciter described previously. Like the exciter all subassemblies of the modular construction are electrically or mechanically connected to the chassis motherboard. The 1-kilowatt output is obtained by using four 300-watt amplifier modules along with a power output combiner. The functional block plan is given in Fig. 11-21.

The rear panel assembly contains all connectors for interfacing with the exciter, power supply, and antenna coupler. Also present, as shown at the top left, are the transmit-receive relay and input power splitter. This power splitter consists of transformers T1 through T5 and resistors R1 through R4 as shown in Fig. 11-22. The splitter receives the input power from the exciter and divides it equally four ways with minimum phase shift. The input of 50 ohms to T5 is divided down to 12.5 ohms for driving the remaining four transformers. The four 28-ohm resistors provide isolation between the outputs and absorb power if one of the outputs becomes open or shorted. Physically, these transformers are made of lengths of coaxial line loaded with ferrite beads. The outputs of the splitter connect to the individual inputs of the power amplifier modules.

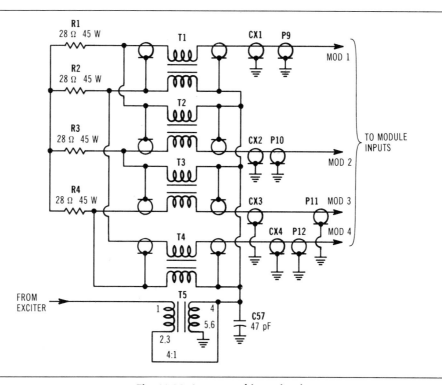

Fig. 11-22. Input combiner circuit.

The rear panel assembly also contains detector circuits that supply a DC potential to the automatic level control board. Another component is used to drive a front panel indicator that is illuminated when RF drive is present. There are various other relays and fault lines included on the rear panel board.

A block diagram and partial schematic of a 300-watt module is given in Fig. 11-23. Each 300-watt power amplifier is designed to give approximately an 11-dB gain over the frequency range 1.6–30 MHz. On each module there is protection to prevent damage in case of excessive VSWR, temperature, or output power. The module also

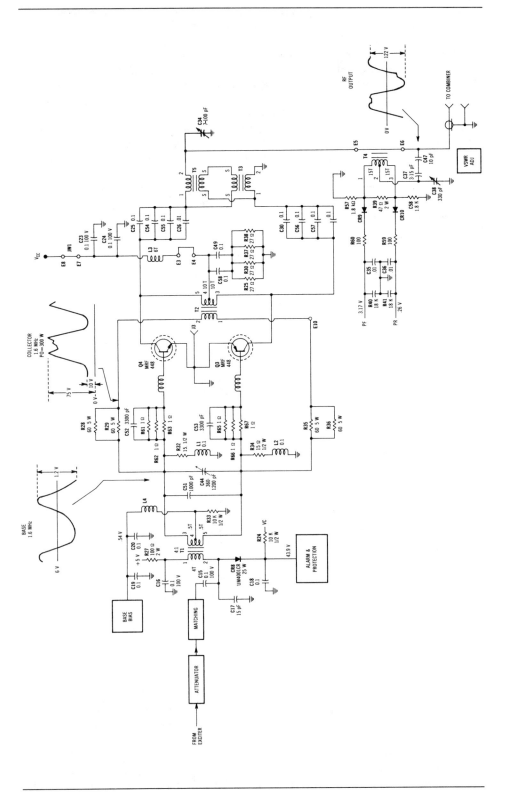

Fig. 11-23. Power module circuit.

provides logic outputs to indicate the presence of faults in any of these areas. Also, a logic output indicates that the module is supplying power. The arriving RF drive signal is first applied to an attenuator, with selectable values of 0, 0.5, 1.0, and 1.5 dB. Individual attenuators for each module permit a precise matching of module gain and balance.

A rather elaborate impedance matching network follows. Its function is to ensure proper match over the wide frequency range without any necessity for making matching adjustments when changing frequencies.

From the matching network the signal passes into the power amplifier stage proper. The power amplifier stage operates push-pull class B. Proper biasing is obtained from an adjustable bias supply. Transformer T1 (with a reduction ratio of 36 to 1) is used to transform the higher-impedance drive signal applied to its primary to the low base impedance of the two power transistors. Capacitors C17 and C44 compensate for the leakage inductance of T1 and aid with impedance matching over the 20- to 30-MHz range. Output transformer T2 is used as a balanced power feed and also provides feedback to the transistor bases through two pairs of resistors. This feedback along with the series leakage of the transformer stabilize gain over the wide bandwidth of the amplifier. Transformers T3 and T5 are transmission-line type transformers and transform the 50-ohm output impedance to a 12-ohm collector load for the power transistors.

A network associated with transformer T4 supplies output for direct and reflected power VSWR measurements. Capacitor C37 provides a VSWR adjustment.

A base bias block develops proper bias for the power transistors. Bias power is also switched off by this circuit during receive. Thus, the power amplifier does not transmit extraneous signals on receive.

There is an alarm and protection block. A thermally coupled device is mounted near the power transistors. If the temperature becomes excessive, it will remove the drive to the transmitter and shut down the module.

There is a circuit that monitors the reflected power output and, if excessive, shuts down the module. A third circuit monitors the power amplifier current and will also shut down the module if current is excessive.

The individual outputs of the four power amplifiers are supplied to the combiner (Fig. 11-21). Here they are combined to produce the 1-kilowatt output. The inputs from each module are equal in magnitude and phase. If the voltages applied to each end of the balancing resistors R1 and R2 in Fig. 11-24 are equal, the resistors dissipate no power.

Assume identical module outputs of 345 volts peak-to-peak (corresponding to 300 watts). The outputs of transformers T1 and T2 also will be 345 volts but at 25 ohms rather than 50 ohms for a combined output of 600 watts. Since these outputs are balanced, the 600-watt outputs are also matched and no power is dissipated in the balancing resistor pair R3 and R4. Transformer T3 transforms the two 600-watt components at 25 ohms into an output of 12.5 ohms (1200 watts). The final transformer T4 changes this signal over the 692 volts peak-to-peak at 50 ohms corresponding to 1200 watts.

Recall that the linear amplifier continues to operate at reduced power if one or more modules fail. For example, if module 1 fails and each of the remaining ones continue to produce 300 watts, resistor R1 would dissipate 150 watts and pass 150 watts on to T3. The voltages on each side of R3–R4 are also no longer balanced and the resistor pair dissipates 75 watts. Now the total output power is 675 watts (900 − 50 − 75). Under this condition the automatic level control circuitry takes over and makes certain that the remaining good modules do not operate at excessive power.

The combiner output is now applied to a set of low-pass filters (Fig. 11-21) that pass the desired range of frequencies corresponding to the channel selection made. They are switched properly with a relay control circuit. On receive mode these filters are bypassed.

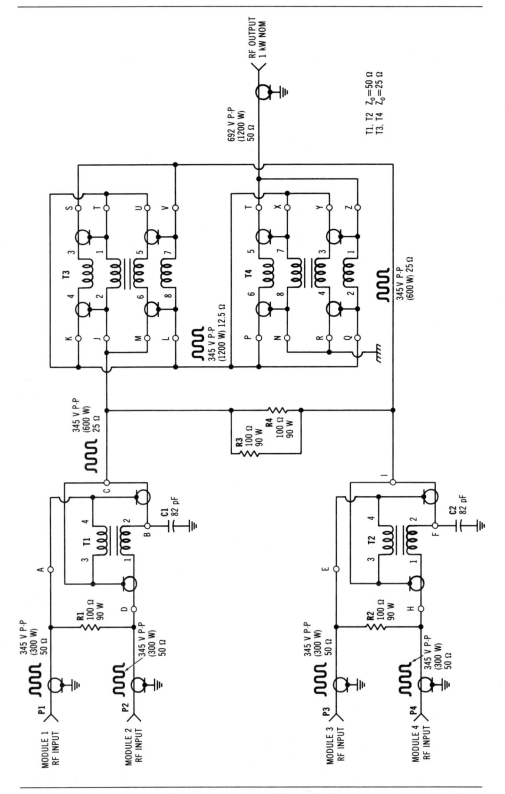

Fig. 11-24. Power combiner circuit.

The special band-O trap below the filters acts as an oscillation suppressor when the transmitter is operating between 9 and 30 MHz. The termination provided prevents the modules from breaking into a low-frequency oscillation. This trap is also energized by a channel select switch.

The detector/wattmeter block supports the forward power detector, reflected power detector, ALC/ACC detectors, and the RF transfer relay.

Note the signal path to the ALC/ACC board at the lower left. ALC refers to automatic level control which controls the power level in single sideband and other modes. Thus, output is maintained at a level which produces efficient operation with no distortion. The ACC circuit is referred to as automatic carrier control and does the job of maintaining proper power level when AM modulation with inserted carrier (AME) is used.

The diagnostic block at the lower center is used to monitor the linear amplifier operation and to provide a visual indication of its status. Light-emitting diodes associated with the board can be observed to isolate fault conditions such as standing-wave ratio, over current, and over temperature. The operation of the antenna coupler can also be monitored. Circuits are also included to reduce the RF drive under fault conditions. Even ALC and ACC line monitoring takes place.

The front panel of the linear amplifier contains the various LED indicators, high-frequency power-amplifier power switch, test meter, meter-select switch, air filter, and blower assembly. Fault indicators and indicators of proper operation are of significant help to the operator and technician. This is particularly the case when the linear amplifier is controlled remotely or from the RF exciter described previously.

11-5. Marine Satellite Communications

Satellite radiocommunications is on the rise in the maritime services. Worldwide coverage can be provided, and, since transmissions are at microwave frequencies, the transmission path is essentially unaffected by atmospheric and propagation conditions. The result is superior communications quality, speed, and security. One such satellite communications system operated by Telesystems (a Comsat company) is illustrated in Fig. 11-25. The shipboard terminal is but one unit in a three-unit system. The other two units are a shore station and an INMARSAT satellite. All communications to and from the shipboard terminal pass through the satellite and shore station. Operations are controlled by the shore station.

The satellite is in geostationary position about 22,300 miles above the equator. There are three such satellites, one each over the Atlantic, Pacific, and Indian oceans as shown in Fig. 11-26. On the map the 10° and 5° patterns define the 10° and 5° elevation angles of the satellite above the horizon. If your position is nearer to a given satellite, the elevation angle needs to be positioned higher. The satellites are served by earth stations at various locations around the world.

A shipboard terminal is capable of communications with the shore in four basic modes.

1. Duplex voice mode in which a normal telephone conversation can take place. Both parties can talk at will. There is no need to instruct the calling party when to start talking by saying "over," or "go ahead," etc.
2. Telex (duplex TTY mode) allows the terminal to send or receive a telex message. The message is sent with a keyboard or tape reader and is received on a teleprinter.

486

3. Telex (simplex TTY mode) allows one-way transmission of telex from ship to shore or from shore to ship.
4. Duplex data mode permits the sending of data or facsimile transmissions to and from the shore that can be carried out simultaneously.

The satellite transponders employ antennas with an almost circular radiation pattern as set off by the limits shown in Fig. 11-26. The terminal antenna is kept pointed at the appropriate satellite by an automatic stabilizing system. When the shipboard operator desires to send a message, he must first transmit a request message through the satellite to the shore station. The shore station then, by return transmission, assigns a channel to the terminal and stands by to receive the message.

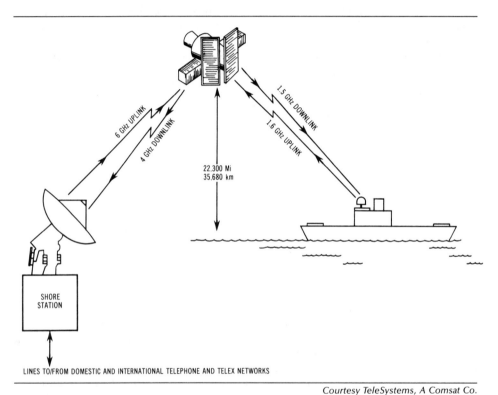

Courtesy TeleSystems, A Comsat Co.

Fig. 11-25. TeleSystems maritime satellite communications system.

Once the shore connection has been made for either telex or telephone, the shore station itself is out of the communications. It serves only to maintain the connection and make the disconnect when the call is completed. Terminal identification and location information is transmitted automatically; the operator is only required to press a button to request a channel and identify the terminal.

The shore station can call any terminal in much the same manner, except that the terminal takes no part in the assignment of the selected calls or broadcasts. Selected calls or broadcasts can be made through the shore station to a specific terminal, a group of terminals, a group of terminals in a particular geographical area, all terminals served by a satellite, or combinations of the above. Selective calls or broadcasts are automatic and even allow a terminal to receive a telex message at any time of day or night whether the shipboard terminal is attended or not. These messages are recorded automatically on a teleprinter or a punched paper tape.

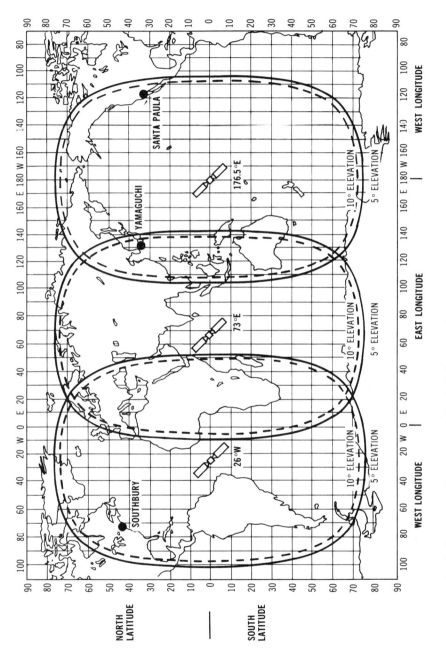

Fig. 11-26. Nominal coverage areas of the INMARSAT satellites.

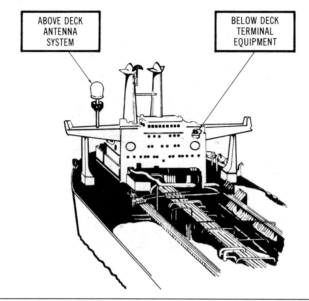

ABOVE DECK
ANTENNA
SYSTEM

BELOW DECK
TERMINAL
EQUIPMENT

Courtesy TeleSystems, A Comsat Co.

Fig. 11-27. The two major sections of the shipboard terminal.

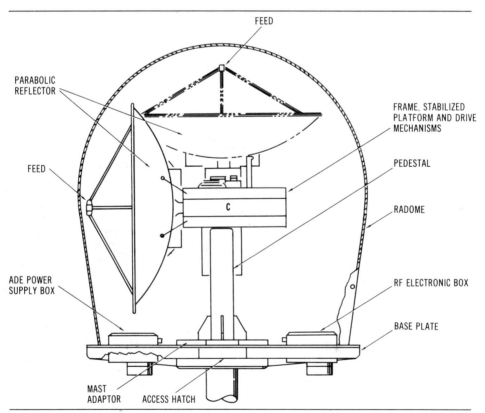

FEED

PARABOLIC
REFLECTOR

FRAME, STABILIZED
PLATFORM AND DRIVE
MECHANISMS

FEED

PEDESTAL

C

RADOME

ADE POWER
SUPPLY BOX

RF ELECTRONIC BOX

BASE PLATE

MAST
ADAPTOR

ACCESS HATCH

Courtesy TeleSystems, A Comsat Co.

Fig. 11-28. The antenna assembly.

11-5-1. System Description

The shipboard terminal has two major units — the antenna and the terminal control unit — as shown in Fig. 11-27. The antenna system is completely protected by a weatherproof radome and is controlled remotely from the terminal control unit. The two units are electrically connected by a single interface cable. The terminal control is used to orient the antenna to the proper satellite. It also handles the transmission and reception of voice, data, and teletype information.

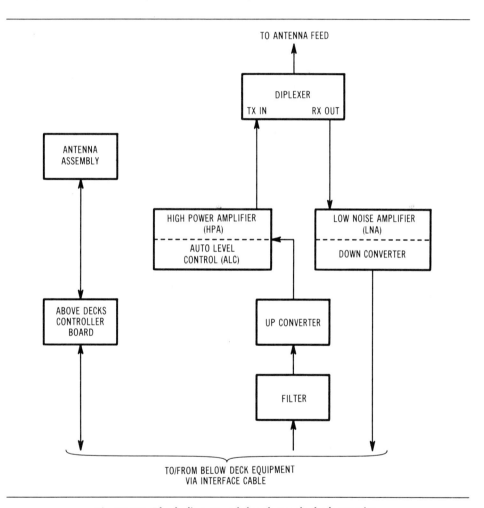

Fig. 11-29. Block diagram of the above-deck electronics.

The antenna assembly is shown in Fig. 11-28. The antenna proper consists of a parabolic reflector with a centrally positioned circular feed. It is mounted on a platform that permits changes in elevation and azimuth. The platform is gyrostabilized with the platform driven through a mechanical universal joint from a pedestal.

The major blocks of electronic equipment in the antenna assembly are shown in Fig. 11-29. In the receive mode the signal is passed through a diplexer to a low-noise amplifier and on to a down converter that steps down the frequency from microwaves to one suitable for conveyance over a coaxial cable to the terminal control unit. In the transmit mode the signal from the control unit passes through a filter to the up

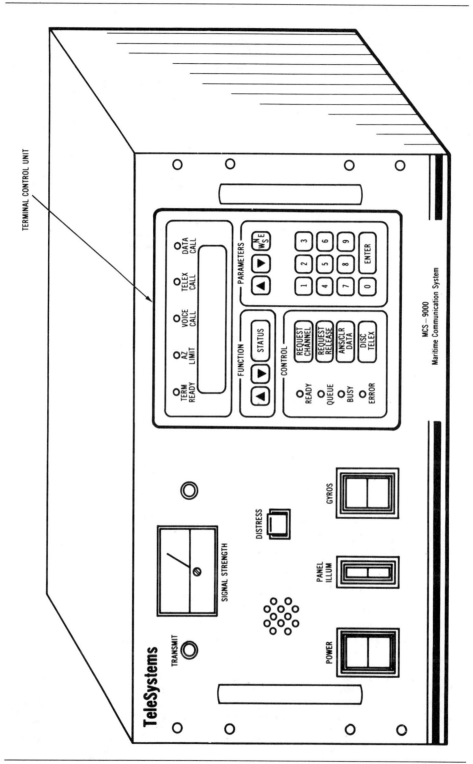

Fig. 11-30. The below-deck equipment.

converter that changes the lower frequency to a microwave frequency. The signal is built up in level by a high-power amplifier and passes through the diplexer to the parabolic antenna system. The diplexer permits the same antenna to be used on transmit and receive.

Signal components generated by the ship gyro are processed in the control unit and conveyed to the above deck controller. Information from the controller is passed to the antenna assembly to compensate for errors in antenna orientation that might result from ship yaws, pitches, and rolls, as well as ship course changes.

The below-deck terminal equipment and a basic modular diagram are shown in Figs. 11-30 and 11-31. The terminal control unit proper is an operator-controlled block used to orient the antenna to the proper satellite and perform necessary operational procedures. There is a central processing unit which is a solid-state microprocessor system that completes most of the communication systems' functions. Signals from the ship's gyro sent to the processing unit are programmed and then processed to the appropriate antenna-system control board. Regulation of the transmission and reception of voice and teletype data is also controlled here along with additional exchanges of information between the control unit proper and the microprocessor.

The RF card module processes voice, telex, and other data to and from the antenna system assemblies. The voice card processes and interfaces the transmission and reception of voice and teleprinter data. It also interfaces the CPU with the gyro input.

11-5-2. Basic Operation

A basic understanding of the operation and capabilities of the Telesystems shipboard satellite station can be gathered by examining the list of front panel controls and indicators in Table 11-1. Read the function of each as you go down the list.

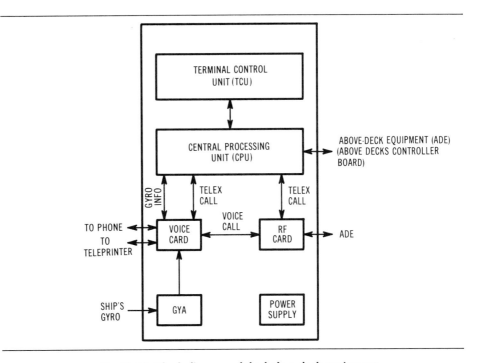

Fig. 11-31. Block diagram of the below-deck equipment.

Table 11-1.   Satellite Station Controls and Indicators

Control/Indicator	Function
POWER	When set to "on" (light position), this combination rocker-type power switch and circuit breaker applies primary power to the entire terminal, except the gyros in the antenna assembly.
PANEL ILLUMINATION	When set to "on" (light position), this rocker-type switch turns on the Signal Strength meter backlight, Distress switch backlight, and the shaded night light (to the right of the meter). Used for providing illumination at night or in dimly lit areas.
GYROS	When set to "on" (lighted position), this rocker-type switch applies power to the gyros in the antenna assembly.
DISTRESS	A guarded push-button switch that, when depressed, immediately sets up a distress call request to the shore station. Call type will be that previously set into the terminal.
SIGNAL STRENGTH	This meter provides an indication of the strength of the signals received from the satellite.
TRANSMIT	This light comes on only during actual transmission to the satellite. It may blink momentarily during a request burst and during telex transmission and will remain on when a voice or data call is in progress.
TERM READY	A green light that indicates the satellite has been acquired by the system and that the terminal is ready to receive or initiate calls.
AZ LIMIT	A red light that indicates the antenna is approaching an azimuth limit (within 45°). Red light will come on only when making or receiving a call. During a call, if the red light comes on, you are reaching a limit and the call may be interrupted. To avoid interruption terminate the call to allow the antenna to rewrap. NOTE: The antenna rewraps automatically during silent periods. The red AZ limit light does not illuminate during this process.
VOICE CALL	A steady yellow light indicates that a voice call is in progress. When flashing, it indicates the shore station has assigned a voice channel to the terminal.
TELEX CALL	A yellow light indicates that a Telex call is incoming or in progress.
DATA CALL	A yellow light indicates that a data call is incoming or in progress.
REQUEST CHANNEL	This key is pressed to request a channel for communications. The terminal will use the specific call information already in memory (entered by Function and Parameter

Table 11-1 — cont. Satellite Station Controls and Indicators

Control/Indicator	Function
	keys) to format a request message which is then transmitted to the shore station.
REQUEST RELEASE	This key cancels a call request if an automatic release does not occur.
ANS/CLR DATA	When a data call is received, it may sometimes be inappropriate to answer the call by lifting the telephone handset. This may interfere with the flow of modem data and signaling. The answer/clear key is used to answer and also must be used to "hang-up," or disconnect from data calls.
DISC TELEX	This key is used as an alternative means for disconnecting a Telex call. Normally the operator can disconnect by sending a disconnect code from the keyboard at the end of transmission. Ocassionally, it is convenient to send canned messages which may not have integral disconnect codes.
READY	A green light indicates that the request has been granted and that the channel is ready. (Voice Call, Telex Call, or Data Call light should also come on, depending on which was selected.)
QUEUE (Not used in the INMARSAT System)	A yellow light indicates that the request is valid but, due to heavy call traffic, the request has been placed on queue and will be granted a channel in order. (The operator should wait for ready light before making call.)
BUSY	A yellow light indicates that the system has all channels busy. The operator should try again later. Wait at least 6 seconds.
ERROR light	A red light indicates that some parameter of the call is in error and that the request cannot be granted.
N W E key S	Used to enter Longitude (East or West) and Latitude (North or South).
ENTER key	Used to confirm data entry to CPU.
▲ ▼	Directional keys used to scroll the display up or down.
STATUS key	Each time the status key is pressed, one of five different status messages will appear.
DIRECTIONAL keys	Rotates display to show CPU information and to allow call data to be entered.
NUMERICAL keys	Numbered buttons on pad, located in lower Parameter section, used to make numerical entries of Function or Parameter data.
FUNCTION	With the use of the directional keys will display and rotate or scroll the display to various call functions.
PARAMETER	With the use of directional keys will display the various parameters of a call function via a number of display lines.

There are two major steps in the operation of the terminal. First, the antenna is pointed at the satellite, and then a message is sent or received. When the station is placed in operation after a shut-down interval the antenna pointing requires a moderately long step-by-step procedure. Once this is accomplished the sending and receiving of messages is relatively simple. The operating procedure for establishing voice duplex operation for ship-to-shore and shore-to-ship communications follows. For other modes of transmission other procedures must be used.

Voice (Duplex) Ship to Shore

This mode of operation will allow a voice message to be sent to shore.

1. Set the Priority by scrolling the Function directional keys of the Terminal Control Unit (TCU). Scroll the Parameter directional keys to select a parameter of Routine, Urgent, Safety, or Distress.
2. Set the Ocean Area by scrolling the Function directional keys of the TCU. Scroll to numbers corresponding to Ocean Area on the Parameter directional keys.
3. Scroll Network on the Function directional keys. Scroll the Network number in the Parameter directional keys.
4. Scroll the Shore station on the Function directional keys. Scroll the shore station number on the Parameter directional keys.
5. Set the service to Voice by scrolling the Function directional keys.

Note: The terminal is now ready to operate in the voice (duplex) mode. The Ready light on the TCU *must* be illuminated.

6. Remove the telephone handset from the hookswitch and press the Request Channel push button on the TCU panel. The establishment of a transmission circuit to the shore is automatic, and the TCU panel indicators will display the status of the call as follows:
   a. Under normal conditions, a circuit will be made available in a few seconds and the automatic call sequence will start.
   b. If the circuits are busy, and queue space is available, the yellow Queue indicator will illuminate. This means that you have been placed in a queue (waiting line) by the shore station and will be called when your turn comes. (Queue is not used in the IMARSAT system).
   c. If the circuits are busy and queue space is not available, the yellow Busy indicator will illuminate for about 5 seconds, then extinguish. You must wait at least 6 seconds and try the call again by pressing the Request Channel push button.

Note: To terminate the call replace the telephone handset on the hookswitch.

   d. If the red Error indicator illuminates, an error was made in the format of the request message that was entered. For example, if you had requested a network that does not have a certain capbility, this would be an invalid request.
   e. If no indication is received in about 10 seconds, press the Request Channel push button again.

Note: When the circuit is assigned by the shore station, the green Ready indicator and the yellow Voice indicator will illuminate. Check to see that the red AZ Limit indicator on the TCU panel is extinguished. If it is illuminated, the antenna may be approaching a travel limit. In this case the antenna will lock, and the transmission circuit may be interrupted.

7. You will hear the sound of ringing in the telephone. The operator will come on the line and ask you for the number you want and other information pertinent to the call. (If the operator has not answered in 60 seconds, the circuit will be disconnected. Replace the telephone handset on the hookswitch. Then request a circuit again by pressing the Request Channel push button.)

   Note: The shore operator will complete the call for you, verify that the called party is on the line, and then exit from the call. The telephone call can now proceed as for a conventional shore-side call.

8. When you are finished with the call, hang the telephone handset back on the hookswitch. This will signal the shore station that you no longer require the circuit.

9. If you want to place another call, you must first terminate (hangup) this call, then start the calling procedure over again at Step 1.

10. After replacing the handset on the hookswitch, it may take from 3 to 15 seconds for the green Ready and yellow Voice indicators to extinguish. The green Term Ready indicator should still be illuminated, and another call can be placed immediately.

Voice (Duplex) Shore to Ship

The telephone handset must be hanging on the hookswitch to receive an incoming call.

1. An intermittent audio tone will be heard from the audio annunciator on the TCU panel. The yellow Voice indicator will be flashing, and the green Ready indicator will be illuminated.

2. Pick up the telephone handset. The audio tone from the TCU panel will stop. The yellow Voice indicator will illuminate steady. Acknowledge the call.

3. When you have finished with the call, hang the telephone handset back on the hookswitch. This will signal the shore station that you no longer require the circuit.

4. If you want to place a call, you must first terminate (hangup) this call. Then start the calling procedure outlined previously (Ship-to-Shore Call).

5. After replacing the handset on the hookswitch, it may take 3 to 15 seconds for the green Ready and yellow Voice indicators to extinguish. The green Ready indicator should still be illuminated, and another call can be placed immediately.

12

Marine Direction Finders

Marine navigational equipment consists primarily of directional finders and radar (the subject of the following chapter). Direction finders aboard modern ships are of two basic types — radio compass and loran. A radio compass operated in the medium-frequency band, 285–320 kHz, has good accuracy up to 100 miles, and useful bearings can be taken in the daytime up to nearly 200 miles. In its nighttime range, it is less reliable beyond 100 miles because of the interaction between the ground wave and sky wave. Under some circumstances, the adverse influence of the nighttime skywave can be felt at distances even less than 100 miles. Nevertheless, the radio compass is very reliable and is used extensively in sailing coastal waters.

High-accuracy, longer-range readings are possible with the *LO*ng *RA*nge Navigational equipment known as loran. Its range can be greater than a thousand miles.

When using a radio compass, the operator takes bearings on radio beacon coastal stations, the exact positions of which are known. Similar coastal stations transmit loran signals on approximately 100 kHz. The loran receiver on shipboard evaluates the time delay in the reception of various signals from two pairs of loran coastal stations. This information is processed by the loran receiver, and a readout bearing can be obtained.

12-1. Direction Finder Principles

Modern ships use a marine radio compass to determine their positions exactly. The basic principle of direction finding is based on the fact that radio waves travel in a straight line, particularly over water where there are no objects that can distort their passage. If a receiving system can determine the direction of signal arrival, one has a means of obtaining bearings.

A radio or other navigational officer uses his radio compass to obtain an exact bearing on each of three or more shore stations. The operating conditions and locations of the shore stations are known. Once the required bearings have been obtained, a navigation chart can be used to obtain the exact position of the ship relative to the shore stations or in geographic coordinates (degrees of latitude and longitude).

A radio compass requires the use of a directional antenna system. Such a directional antenna system can be in the form of a rotatable loop, or it may be a fixed-position antenna with its directivity changed by a rotating coil assembly or other electronic means.

A half-wave dipole or horizontal Hertz antenna has a figure-eight directional pattern (Fig. 12-1A). This antenna is most sensitive when the plane of the antenna is broadside to the direction of signal arrival. It displays minimum sensitivity, or *nulls,* off the antenna ends. Consequently, as such an antenna is rotated, there will be two positions in which it will receive maximum signal and two positions which will be null points. If such an antenna is made into a loop of approximately one wavelength in circumference, it will also display a similar figure-eight pattern (Fig. 12-1B); there will be maxima perpendicular to the plane of the loop and minima in the plane of the loop.

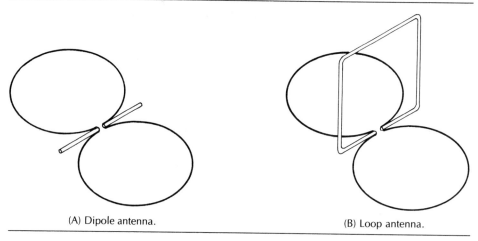

(A) Dipole antenna.   (B) Loop antenna.

Fig. 12-1.   Figure-eight directional antenna patterns.

A converse situation exists when the size of the loop is made very small in comparison to the wavelength of the received signal. The coastal radio-beacon stations transmit at very low frequencies. Therefore, they have very long wavelengths. A loop approximately 3 feet in diameter consisting of multiple turns of wire has a very short physical dimension in comparison to the wavelength of the radio-beacon signals. Observe the directional characteristics of a small loop in Fig. 12-2. Its sensitivity pattern is also a figure eight. However, the two null points are perpendicular to the plane of the loop, and the maxima occur in the end-on directions.

It should be noted that the two null points are sharp and deep and not nearly as broad in angular width as are the two maxima. Thus, it is customary in the operation of a radio compass to take bearings within the null positions because a more distinct and accurate reading can be obtained. Since there are two null points, such a directive system is said to be *bilateral.*

The reason for the particular directional pattern of a loop antenna with an electrical diameter that is many times shorter than the wavelength of the received signal is shown in Fig. 12-3. When the loop is in the position shown in Fig. 12-3A, the voltages induced into the sides are equal, resulting in equal currents that have the same direction. The net current is zero. With the loop positioned end-on (Fig. 12-3B), the instantaneous induced voltages are not equal. A differential current is present in the loop, and a signal voltage appears at the output.

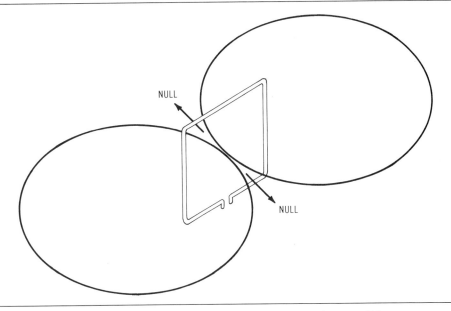

Fig. 12-2. Figure-eight directional antenna pattern for a small loop.

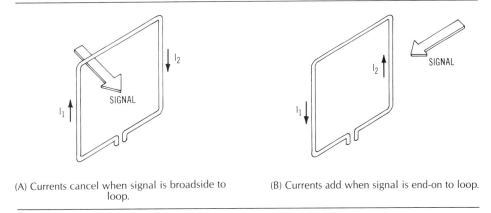

(A) Currents cancel when signal is broadside to loop.

(B) Currents add when signal is end-on to loop.

Fig. 12-3. Directivity of a small loop.

The quality and accuracy of the figure-eight pattern of a loop antenna depends on how well the loop is constructed, how well it is shielded, and the exactness of the balance in the two sides of the loop. To ensure bearing accuracy and to minimize the influence of nearby metallic surfaces, such a loop antenna is completely shielded from antenna to radio-compass receiver input. The loop shielding is continuous from the top of the loop, along the transmission line, and into the receiver input circuit. Only a small noninsulated aperture is located at the very top of the loop; it is here that the signal enters. This is a small entrance area, and it is necessary that the receiver be a highly sensitive one. The high powers used by the beacon transmitters are an aid in delivering an adequate signal to the radio compass.

The input circuit to the receiver is also balanced so as to equalize leg currents. Furthermore, balancing capacitors are included and can be set for sharp and properly positioned nulls. Also, to ensure a high degree of bearing accuracy, compensations can be made for nearby metallic surfaces when the radio compass is installed. This is the reason that the ship radio-station antennas should be in position and the antenna transfer switch set to its bearing-reading position prior to the calibration of the ship's radio direction finder.

12-1-1. Unilateral Sense Indication

As mentioned previously, a direction-finding loop has a bilateral pattern. Thus the arriving signal could be from either side of a null setting. Such a loop alone indicates only the line along which the ship is located relative to the transmission point of the received signal (shore station). Usually the operator does know the approximate bearing of the shore station being received, and it is not necessary to take a sense reading. For example, in sailing along the eastern coast, one would know that the shore station would be to the west.

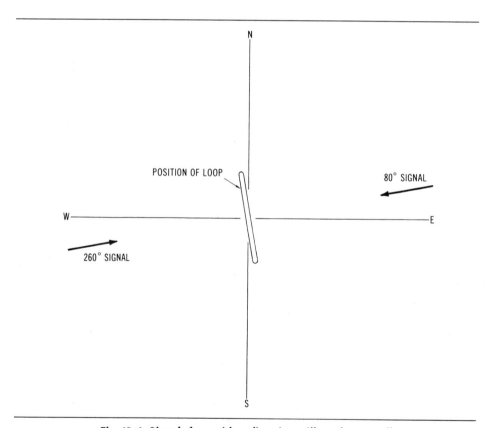

Fig. 12-4. Signals from either direction will produce a null.

However, there might be situations in which a null-signal position would raise a doubt. For example, is the bearing 80° or 260° in Fig. 12-4? When this situation arises, a vertical *sense* antenna is used along with the loop. The pattern of a vertical antenna is circular, as shown in Fig.12-5A. The net effect of the vertical and loop antennas is to obtain a composite pattern called a *cardioid* pattern (Fig. 12-5C). Such a vertical sense antenna is usually located near the direction finder, and it can be switched in and out of the circuit as an aid in obtaining a sense reading. Notice that the cardioid pattern has only one maximum and one minimum.

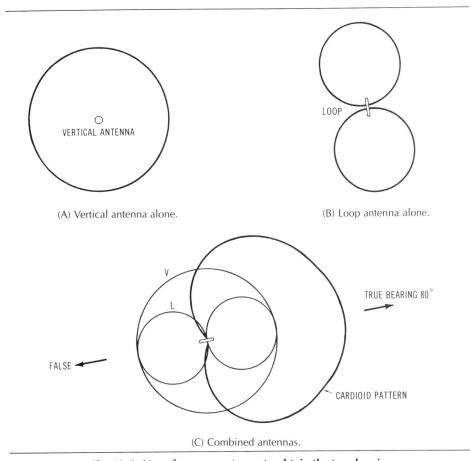

(A) Vertical antenna alone.

(B) Loop antenna alone.

(C) Combined antennas.

Fig. 12-5. Use of a sense antenna to obtain the true bearing.

In taking an actual bearing, the loop antenna is first used alone to obtain a sharp bidirectional minimum. Then the sense antenna can be switched into the circuit and the loop rotated for maximum to determine the sense of the bearing and the true direction of signal arrival. Finally, the sense antenna is switched out, and the loop is readjusted for a null to obtain the exact reading. The use of the sense antenna permits one to select the true bearing rather than the reciprocal one. An exact fix is obtained by taking bearings on two or more beacons and plotting them on a navigation chart.

12-1-2. Bellini-Tosi Radio Compass

A direction finder can use two fixed antennas instead of a rotatable loop. In such an arrangement (Fig. 12-6), two loops are mounted at right angles to each other. Shielded leads then connect each loop to the corresponding fixed coil of a *goniometer.* Inside of the two fixed coils is a rotatable coil. This coil develops an output voltage that corresponds to the relative signal levels in the two fixed coils. The shaft of the rotor is connected to a calibrated scale.

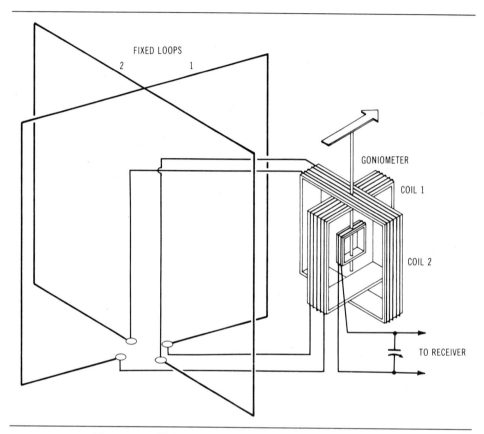

FIXED LOOPS

2   1

GONIOMETER

COIL 1

COIL 2

TO RECEIVER

Fig. 12-6. Bellini-Tosi goniometer direction-finder system.

Actually, the rotating coil is similar to a rotating loop and is used for determining the direction of arrival of received signals. The entire assembly must be shielded and balanced just as the rotatable loop assembly described previously. Balancing capacitors as well as loop-tuning capacitors are included.

Each loop has a figure-eight sensitivity pattern with maximum voltage being induced when the signal arrives in the plane of the loop. If we assume that the signal is arriving in the plane of loop 1, there will be maximum current present in coil 1 of the goniometer. Conversely, with minimum induced voltage in loop 2, there will be minimum current in fixed coil 2. If the rotating coil is now moved in such a manner that its plane is parallel with the plane of coil 1, there will be maximum voltage induced into the rotor. If the rotor is positioned where it is perpendicular to coil 1 and parallel to coil 2, there will be minimum induced voltage.

Assume that the radio wave arrives at a 45° angle relative to both loops. In this case the amplitudes of the currents in the fixed coils are the same. However, the phasing is such that there will be maximum induced voltage in the rotor when it is positioned in a plane midway between the planes of coil 1 and coil 2.

In summary, a complete rotation of the rotor will result in a response that is identical to that obtained by the rotation of a loop antenna, despite the fact that the antenna actually consists of two fixed loops mounted at right angles.

12-2. Automatic Direction Finder

An advantage of the combination of fixed loop and goniometer is that it is adaptable to automatic direction finding. In such an arrangement, the goniometer rotor is rotated by a servo system. An example of this type of direction finder is the ITT Mackay Marine Model in Fig. 12-7. The operator sets the direction-finder receiver on the frequency of the radio beacon to be received. In two seconds, the bearing is indicated automatically. The true bearing is indicated directly on the circular bearing scale if a suitable coupling is made to the ship's gyrocompass. A simple fixed card bearing scale provides a bearing reading that is relative to the ship's heading.

Courtesy ITT Telcom Products Corp., ITT Mackay Div.

Fig. 12-7. *An automatic direction finder.*

The automatic direction finder (ADF) has three operating modes. In the automatic mode, the incoming signals are picked up by the loop and sense antennas. By suitable combining and processing, the bearing information is displayed automatically. The second mode is receiver only; in this mode the loop-antenna circuits and servo system are disabled. The signal picked up on the sense antenna can be demodulated to obtain audio output information. The third mode is manual; the sense antenna is disconnected, and the receiver picks up a directional signal from the loop antenna. It is now possible to rotate the bearing pointer manually to obtain an aural null after sensing has been determined in the automatic mode. This manual function is used only when heavy noise and interference conditions make it impossible to obtain a precise automatic bearing.

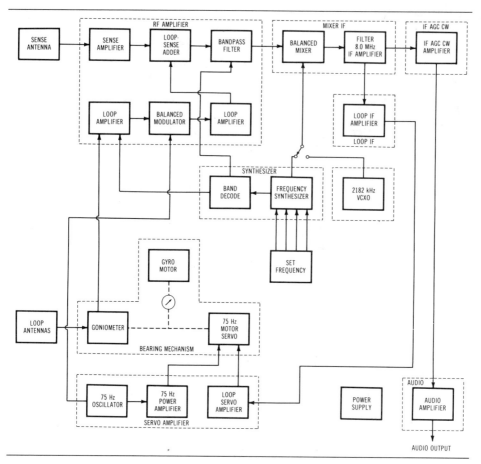

Fig. 12-8. Block diagram of automatic direction finder.

A block diagram of the system is given in Fig. 12-8. Note that the goniometer has a mechanical connection to a 75-Hz servomotor. This is the mechanical link to the goniometer rotor. The power for the servomotor and servo system is generated by a solid-state power oscillator. A succeeding power amplifier has an output that is applied to the fixed-phase winding of the servo induction motor. The oscillator also supplies a switching voltage to the balanced modulator located in the RF amplifier chain. The servoloop is completed from the loop IF amplifier to the loop servoamplifier, which supplies the error signal to the servomotor.

The output of the rotary coil of the goniometer is applied to the loop amplifier, the output of which is then applied to the balanced modulator. In the balanced modulator, the RF signal is modulated by the output of the 75-Hz oscillator. In effect, a double-sideband signal with suppressed carrier is formed. This results in the generation of two 75-Hz sidebands. The magnitude of these sidebands depends on the position of the goniometer rotor relative to the level of the loop signals in the two fixed coils of the goniometer. The output of the balanced modulator becomes zero after the goniometer rotor hunts and finds its null position.

The output of the loop amplifier is applied to the loop-sense adder. Here it combines with the signal delivered from the sense antenna. The adder, too, is in the form of a modulator and produces amplitude modulation of the incoming sense signal. The depth of the modulation is proportional to the angular difference between the goniometer rotor and the null position it is seeking. The 75-Hz modulation changes in polarity from one side of the null to the other, causing the phase of the modulation envelope to be determined by the displacement direction away from the null position. Thus, the output produced contains information relative to angular position and phase. The output of the adder goes to zero on a null position because of the absence of loop signal.

A bandpass filter and then an up-conversion mixer follow. Note that the output of the frequency synthesizer is applied to this mixer as well, resulting in an 8-MHz output which is supplied to a succeeding IF amplifier. The IF signal contains the error-signal modulation as well as the modulation from the received station. After amplification and detection, the AC component of the error-signal modulation is used as an error signal which is applied to the loop servoamplifier. It is this component, after being shifted in phase by 90°, that is supplied to the changing-phase winding of the servomotor. This causes the motor to rotate the goniometer rotor until the true null position is found.

The frequency synthesizer generates the highly stable local-oscillator components that permit tuning the automatic direction finder over the 190–550-kHz frequency range. In the receiver-only mode, the unit can be operated on these frequencies or on the 2182-kHz distress band by switching the 2182-kHz VCXO circuit into operation. The local oscillator which is center tuned to 10.182 MHz (to obtain the 8.0-MHz difference frequency) can be varied approximately ± 15 kHz, and the receiver is tunable between 2167 and 2198 kilohertz.

12-3. Loran Principles

As mentioned at the beginning of this chapter, a loran system evaluates the time difference between signals arriving from the coastal loran stations instead of the direction of signal arrival as interpreted by a radio compass. Radio waves travel at a constant velocity. If a unit is aboard the ship shown in Fig. 12-9, one can determine the difference in signal arrival time from stations A and B. For example, if the signals at A and B are sent out simultaneously and arrive at exactly the same time at the ship, it is an indication that the ship is traveling along a line that is exactly halfway between stations A and B. If the A signal arrives before the B signal, the ship is at some point between the center line and station A. Conversely, if the A signal arrives after the B signal, it means the ship is somewhere between the center line and station B. In fact, a series of hyperbolic lines showing the time positions can be drawn on a map. Line calibrations indicate differences in arrival times (Fig. 12-10).

There are some problems with this basic plan. The main problem is the difficulty of determining which of the two pulses arrives first. There is also a possibility, at certain locations, that one pulse will not conclude before a pulse arrives from the other station, producing an overlap condition. To avoid these difficulties, a practical loran system delays the transmission of the pulse from one station a specific amount. This fact can be taken care of by the processing circuits in the loran receiver aboard the ship. Calibrations for the previous example would be as shown in Fig. 12-11.

The greater the separation between the two stations M and S, the higher is the maximum possible time difference. In a practical system the time differences are calibrated in tens of thousands of microseconds because the separations among stations can be hundreds of miles. The following brief introduction to Loran operation is derived from a small book published by the U.S. Coast Guard. The U.S. Coast Guard is responsible for the operation of the Loran-C transmitter stations.

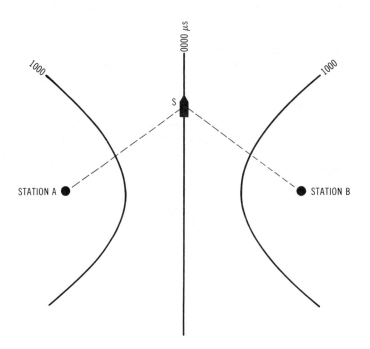

(A) Ship equidistant from stations.

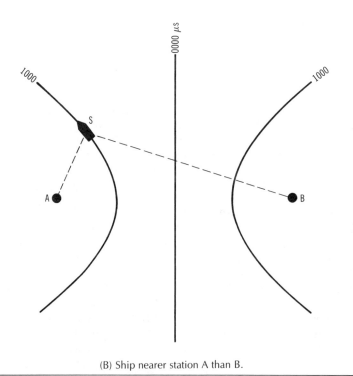

(B) Ship nearer station A than B.

Fig. 12-9. Basic principles of loran.

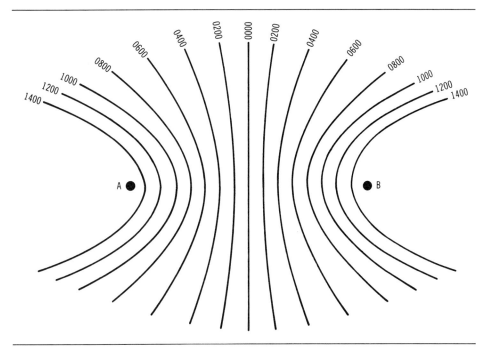

Fig. 12-10. Loran lines of equal delay.

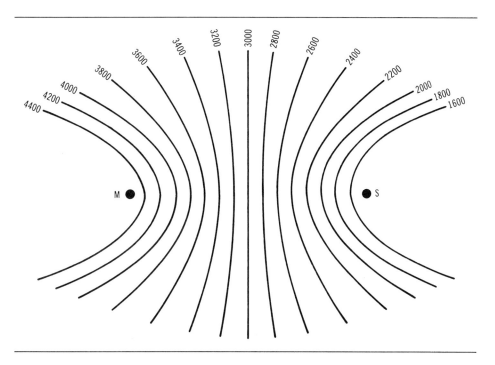

Fig. 12-11. Hyperbolic equal-delay lines of a loran.

508

12-3-1. Loran-C at Work

One station in a *chain* of three to five land-based transmitting stations (Fig. 12-12) separated by several hundred miles is designated as the *master station* (M), and the other stations are designated as *secondary stations*, Whiskey (W), Xray (X), Yankee (Y), and Zulu (Z). The signals transmitted from the secondaries are synchronized with the master signal. In Fig. 12-12B the master station (M) and the secondary station (W) transmit synchronized pulses at precise time intervals. The on-board Loran-C receiver measures the slight difference in time that it takes for these pulsed signals to reach the ship from this pair of transmitters.

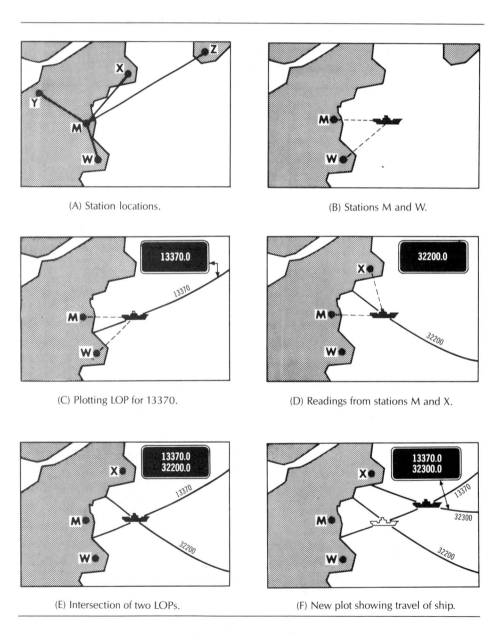

(A) Station locations.

(B) Stations M and W.

(C) Plotting LOP for 13370.

(D) Readings from stations M and X.

(E) Intersection of two LOPs.

(F) New plot showing travel of ship.

Fig. 12-12. Basic operation of loran system.

This *time difference* (TD) is measured in microseconds (millionths of a second) and is then displayed as one readout on the receiver. In the example the time difference displayed is 13,370.0 microseconds. This time difference can be plotted on a Loran-C chart as a *line-of-position* (LOP). The vessel position is located somewhere along the 13,370 line-of-position as illustrated in Fig. 12-12C.

Next, a time difference measurement is taken from the master station (M) and another of the secondary stations (in this case X of Fig. 12-12D). The Loran-C receiver then displays the time difference between M and X. In this example, the time difference displayed is 32,200.0 microseconds. Again, this time difference is plotted on a Loran-C chart as a line-of-position (LOP) and the vessel position is located somewhere along the 32,200.0 line-of-position. The second LOP intersects the first LOP, so the ship's exact position is where the two LOPs — 13,370.0 and 32,200.0 — intersect as shown in Fig. 12-12E.

If the ship were to sail for some distance and another reading were taken, the receiver might display 13,370.0 and 32,300.0 microseconds. This would mean that the ship was following the 13,370 LOP and was now at the intersection of 13,370.0 and 32,300.0 as shown in Fig. 12-12F.

12-3-2. Loran Charts

A much simplified loran chart is given in Fig. 12-13. Observe how the LOP lines overlap as signals are radiated by the master station and slave 1 and the master station and slave 2. A TD calibration has been assigned on one LOP of each pair. The center line between master and slave 1 is calibrated 22,200; between master and slave is 44,900. These numbers refer to the TD in microseconds. For example, 22,200 indicates that along its line the signal from slave 1 is delayed that many microseconds

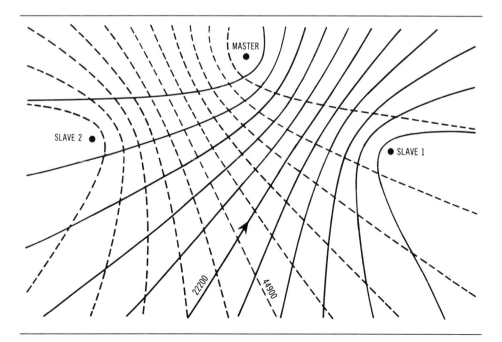

Fig. 12-13. Simplified loran chart.

with respect to the signal from the master. The exact positioning of a ship passing through the area is determined by interpreting the pairs of delays as it proceeds on its course. If the ship were passing the intersection of the two calibrated lines as shown, its position would be 22,200.0/44,900.0

The calibration lines on Fig. 12-13 are very coarse considering that the master and slave stations may be separated by hundreds of miles. Of course, there are a host of possible bearings in between the calibration lines shown that are interpreted by a loran receiver. The loran charts that are superimposed upon navigation charts are also much more finely calibrated. A chart covering only the operating area and with a higher density of LOPs is used to allow more accurate interpolation when the measured TDs fall between the lines on the chart. Such an example is given in Fig. 12-14. This chart shows an expanded section of Fig. 12-13 with some position fixes between the lines detailed.

The foregoing charts do indicate in general terms the loran navigation technique. An actual loran chart has the hyperbolic patterns in different colors overprinted on a navigation chart on which the geographic and topographic information are shown. In addition, the loran chart contains specific repetition rate information and, in some cases, the pattern of overlapping chain areas.

A loran receiver picks up and interprets the incoming signals and actually displays the two TD values. Furthermore, by proper switching, the loran receiver is capable of converting the TD values to geographic positions and will display both the longitude and latitude of the ship. These readings will change continuously as the ship traverses the area a given loran system serves.

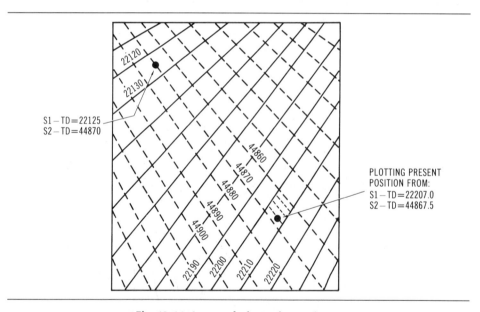

Fig. 12-14. Low scale factor loran chart.

12-3-1. Loran-C at Work

A loran receiver is able to make use of signals transmitted by any one of several transmitter chains. Such a chain consists of from three to six transmitters, usually located hundreds of miles apart. In operation the loran receiver must always be set to receive the particular chain that matches the area through which the ship is traveling. Each transmitter chain is identified by a four-digit number referred to as the group repetition interval (GRI) of the chain in tenths of microseconds.

The GRI is a measure of how often the group of Loran pulses are transmitted. This information is found on the Loran-C chart for the desired area. For example the GRI of the northeast United States chain is 9960, indicating that the transmission is repeated

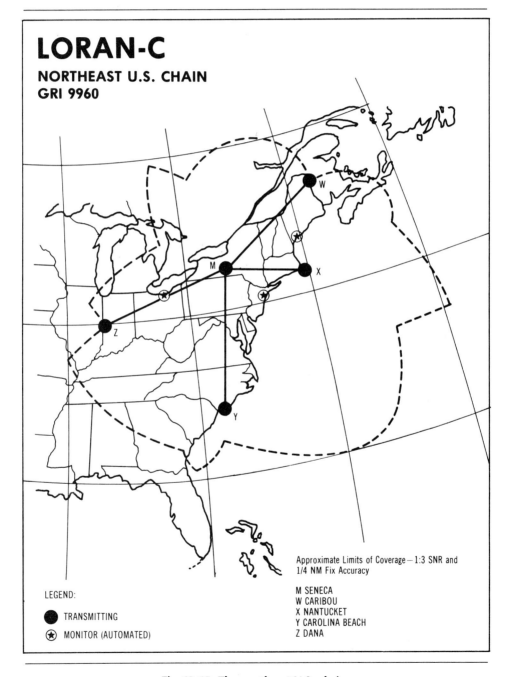

LORAN-C

NORTHEAST U.S. CHAIN
GRI 9960

Approximate Limits of Coverage — 1:3 SNR and
1/4 NM Fix Accuracy

LEGEND:

● TRANSMITTING

✪ MONITOR (AUTOMATED)

M SENECA
W CARIBOU
X NANTUCKET
Y CAROLINA BEACH
Z DANA

Fig. 12-15. The northeast U.S. chain.

at intervals of 99,600 microseconds. You would set your receiver to 9960 to receive this chain. A table of GRI designations for active loran chains is given in Table 12-1.

Slave transmitters are designated in several ways on the chart. Each is officially designated by one of the letters W, X, Y, or Z. Each master and slave combination is also shown by different colored lines on a navigation chart.

The northeast U.S. chain has four slave stations as shown in Fig. 12-15. They extend from Caribou, Maine, to Carolina Beach, North Carolina, and as far west as Dana, Indiana. The pattern extends hundreds of miles out into the ocean and also provides coverage of the St. Lawrence Seaway. If you are sailing a great distance, you can traverse from one chain to another by appropriate receiver switching. Chains overlap and in some areas you can choose the chain that best meets your immediate navigational need. The chain also includes monitoring stations that check on the operation of the master and slave stations. When defects are discovered, warnings are broadcast over Coast Guard radio and they are listed on local notices to mariners. Sometimes a station continues operation with minor errors. When this happens, a special blink signal is sent out that produces a blinking light warning on the loran receiver front panel.

Table 12-1. Active Loran Chains

Chain	GRI Designation
Central Pacific	4990
Canadian East Coast	5930
Commando Lion (Korea)	5970
Canadian West Coast	5990
Labrador Sea	7930
U.S.S.R. Far East	7950
Gulf of Alaska	7960
Norwegian Sea	7970
U.S. East Coast	7980
Mediterranean Sea	7990
Great Lakes	8970
U.S. West Coast	9940
U.S. North East	9960
Northwest Pacific	9970
Icelandic	9980
North Pacific	9990

If possible, choose a chain that you can use for an entire voyage. By doing so you can lock on the signal prior to departure and keep it in the track position for the entire trip. Selection of the secondary station is also a consideration. Choose the master-secondary pair that offers the most accurate navigation. This choice involves selecting the pairs that provide the lower TD gradient. Some receivers have the capability of tracking more than two secondary transmitters.

12-3-4. Loran Signal

The loran transmit carrier frequency is 100 kHz and the loran signal occupies a frequency bandwidth that extends between 19–110 kHz. Each loran transmit burst or pulse (Fig. 12-16) consists of approximately 20 cycles. At a 100-kHz carrier frequency the duration of the burst is approximately 200 microseconds. The separation between the burst transmitted by each loran transmitter is approximately 1000 microseconds, and they are transmitted in groups of eight.

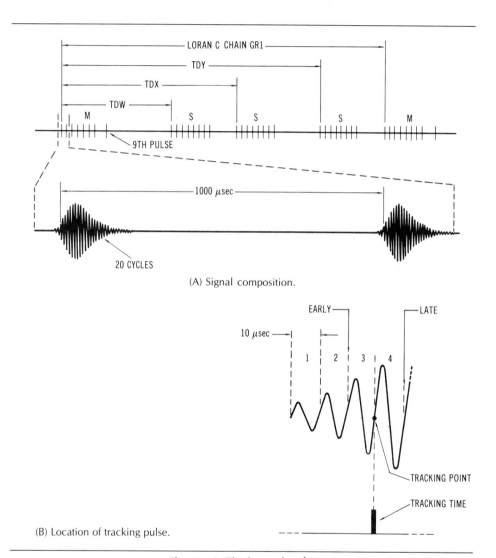

(A) Signal composition.

(B) Location of tracking pulse.

Fig. 12-16. The loran signal.

After the master station transmission, the two or more slave transmitters take turns transmitting their own pulses in groups of eight. There are set time delays between the transmission of the pulse from a master and the first slave (W) and between the first slave burst (W) and the second slave burst (X), etc. The actual time separation between the master and the first slave and between the individual slaves is at least 10,000 microseconds.

The total transmission time required to convey the master and all the slave signals is known as the group rate interval (GRI). It is this group rate that identifies a specific loran transmitter group. As mentioned previously the total time of the northeast United States chain is 99,600 microseconds, and its identification is GRI 9960.

A very important part of the loran transmission occurs at the zero crossing of the third cycle of the master and slave pulse as shown in Fig. 12-16B. At this very moment the signal is strobed and a timing pulse is developed by the receiver. Later, a pulse comes in from the W slave transmitter and is strobed at the very same crossover and a resultant timing pulse is produced. It is the time difference (TD) between the master and slave that establishes the LOP. In the simplified example of Fig. 12-13 the TD between the master and slave 1 was measured by the receiver as 22,200 microseconds, indicating that the ship was on this contour of the navigation chart. A second measurement of the time difference between the master and slave 2 indicated a time difference of 44,900. The example of Fig. 12-13 indicates that the ship is positioned at the 22,200-44,900 intersection.

Several additional examples are given in Fig. 12-14. Additional information on the signal format and functions derived from the Coast Guard Loran-C handbook follow:

Pulsed and coded signals are used to minimize the effects of skywave interference. (Skywaves are echoes of the transmitted pulses which are reflected from the ionosphere.) Skywave conditions vary from day to night and in different parts of the world. A skywave may arrive at a receiver as little as 35 microseconds or as much as 1000 microseconds after the groundwave. In the first case, the skywave will overlap its own groundwave, while in the second case, the skywave will overlap the groundwave of the succeeding pulse. Either situation will cause distortion of the received signal in the form of fading and pulse shape changes. Large positional errors would result if these conditions were not minimized by the selection of a proper Loran-C signal format, and the careful design of the receiver. Pulse groups improve signal to noise without the antenna requiring an increase in peak radiated power.

The problem caused by early arriving skywaves can be overcome by making the time of arrival measurements on the first part of the pulse. This ability is enhanced by the fast rising pulse, achieving high power prior to the arrival of skywaves. The shape of the pulse also allows the receiver to identify one particular cycle of the 100-kHz carrier. This is essential to prevent ambiguities in the time difference measurement and allows the high accuracy of the phase measurement system to be achieved.

To prevent the late-arriving skywaves from affecting the time difference measurements, the phase of the 100-kHz carrier is changed in each pulse of a group in accordance with a predetermined pattern. The phase codes for Loran-C are shown in Table 12-2. Additionally, the phase code is different for the master and secondary signals so that automatic receivers may use the code for station identification. The master ninth pulse, Fig. 12-16A, is used for master signal identification and for blink purposes. The master ninth pulse is normally continuously on; however, sometimes the ninth pulse is blinked. Blinking of the ninth pulse is reserved for internal (Coast Guard) use and is sometimes used to establish communications with secondary stations in the loran chain by transmitting predetermined codes. The code can be used by properly designed receivers to determine extent of errors in the transmissions.

Secondary station blink is employed to notify the user that navigational information from the concerned baseline of the system may be absent or inaccurate. Secondary station blink is accomplished by turning on and off the first two pulses of the eight-pulse group. The duration of the "on" period is between 0.2 and 0.35 seconds and repeats every 4 seconds. To summarize:

1. Master station functions include the following:

    a. Transmit signals of the proper format within a prescribed tolerance.
    b. Set the epoch time, repetition rate, and carrier frequency for the chain.
    c. Monitor the signals of the secondary stations.
    d. Blink when directed by the station in control.

2. Secondary stations are also transmitting stations, but their functions differ somewhat from those of the master station. Secondary station functions include the following:

     a. Transmit signals of the proper format within a prescribed tolerance.
     b. Maintain the proper emission delay.
     c. Blink when directed.
     d. Monitor the master-secondary time differences of stations as required.

12-4. Loran Navigator

The Raytheon Loran-C navigator of Fig. 12-17 is a keyboard-operated unit that displays lines of position (LOPs) or latitude and longitude fixes on an LCD frontpanel display. Two microcomputers take care of navigational calculations and signal measurements. Once the operator selects the GRI of a specific Loran-C chain, the unit automatically locks on to the station and tracks continuously its master signal and up to four slaves simultaneously. The computer then makes the necessary calculations and displays the bearing as well as other factors such as present position, steering to destination, time-to-go, and distance-to-go. In addition to the 16-pad keyboard there is a rotary function switch, and the power on/off and dim keys. Some additional capabilities of the unit include up to 50 waypoints, range and bearing to each successive waypoints, and anchor watch.

Table 12-2. Loran-C Phase Codes

GRI	Master*	Each Secondary*
A	+ + − − + − + − +	+ + + + + − − +
B	+ − − + + + + + −	+ − + − + + − −

* A + indicates zero phase shift and a − indicates 180° shift in carrier phase.
   Loran-C intervals A and B alternate in time.

The loran receiver is a two-unit installation. The receiver contains all electronic circuitry for signal amplification, signal processing, computer functions, display, and control. The second unit is an antenna coupler containing an RF preamplifier and impedance-matching circuits. A whip antenna screws into the antenna coupler.

The antenna and coupler arrangement is shown in Fig. 12-18A. A 96- to 108-inch fiberglass whip antenna is suitable. A coaxial cable links the coupler to the receiver. Mount the antenna assembly high and clear in such a manner that it is not shielded by stacks, masts, bridge structures, or vertical stays as shown in Fig. 12-18B. It should not be placed under horizontal wire antennas such as HF or MF communications antennas. Keep clear of heat and smoke. The antenna should be mounted vertically and separated as much as possible from the other antennas on the vessel.

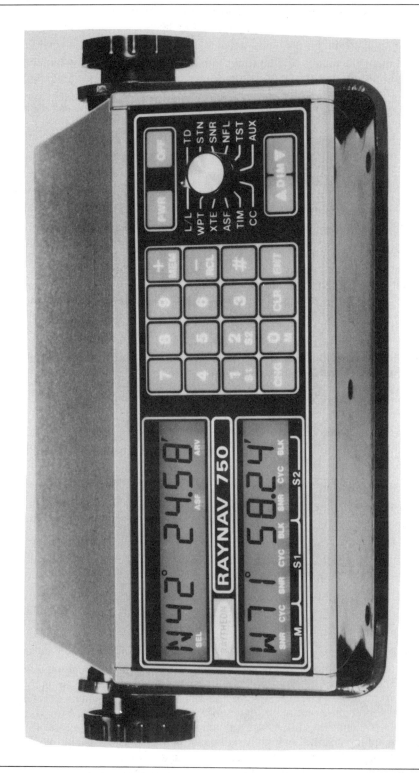

Fig. 12-17. The Raynav 750 Loran-C navigator.

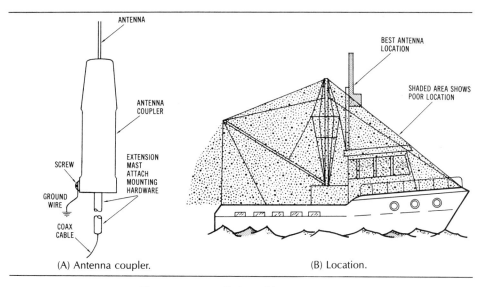

(A) Antenna coupler.   (B) Location.

Fig. 12-18. Installation of loran antenna.

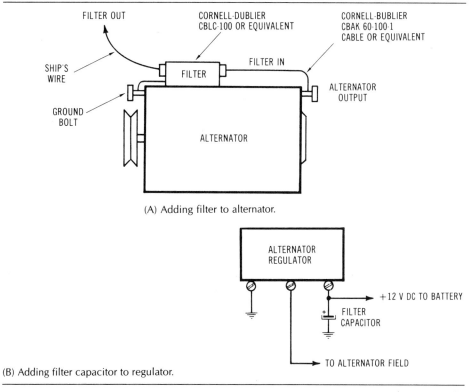

(A) Adding filter to alternator.

(B) Adding filter capacitor to regulator.

Courtesy Raytheon Marine Co.

Fig. 12-19. Alternator noise reduction techniques.

Mount the receiver away from excessive heat, dampness, salt spray, and vibration. Keep the receiver mounted at least 15 feet away from other antennas and in close proximity to a satisfactory electrical ground.

A good ground is important for the receiver, and it is critical that a good ground exist for both the antenna coupler and the receiver. Factors and methods of grounding were covered in detail in Chapter 11.

The minimization of RF interference and noise is of great significance to increase the range of operation that will produce accurate readings. Other nearby receivers can generate components that mask the loran signal. Horizontal oscillators in conventional television sets aboard ship are strong sources of carrier interference. Electrical noises from the variety of electronic and electrical devices aboard ship can be a source of trouble.

When connecting power lines, take the shortest possible route to the ship's battery, but keep away from noise-generating equipment such as the engine, pumps, motors, and radar equipment. Alternator noise can be reduced with an appropriate L-C filter (Fig. 12-19A). Make certain that the filter itself is grounded firmly. The alternator regulator can be a source of radio noise; adding an appropriate good-quality filter capacitor (Fig. 12-19B) is advisable. Keep the leads as short as possible.

The receiver should be grounded carefully with a copper strap if at all possible. The bonding of all metal masses (as in Fig. 11-16) is an important aid in reducing RF interference aboard ship.

The best way to look for the presence of interference is to turn the receiver on, allow it to settle, and watch the signal-to-noise ratio (SNR) readings on one or two moderately weak loran signals. These readings rise as interference is reduced and drop off when there is more interference. You can watch the reading as various checks are made aboard ship in your attempt to improve the range and accuracy of your loran installation. You can turn other electronic devices on and off and note the influence on the SNR readings. The SNR checks should be made with the engine operating at cruising rpm.

12-4-1. Operation

After the loran receiver has been installed properly, routine measurements are easy. However, it is a very complicated device and, after you acquire operating skill, many additional complex measurements can be made following the operating procedure given by the manufacturer. These procedures vary from manufacturer to manufacturer and model to model so you must refer to the specific manual. In the material that follows the ease of making routine measurements is covered. Refer to the front panel of the receiver in Fig. 12-17.

There are two ways to display your position. These are by TDs or latitude and longitude. The TD readings are transferred to your navigation chart and show your exact position. The latitude and longitude readings are not as precise because they are subject to electronic conversion errors. They are useful but not always exact. Simply set the function switch to the one you wish to be displayed (L/L or TD).

A loran transmitter chain is identified by its group repetition interval (GRI) as covered previously. This GRI is marked on the Loran-C chart of the area. To select a transmitter chain, turn the function switch to STN (station select), and then press O/M followed by its four-digit GRI code, and then press ENT on the keypad.

To display the course and speed of the vessel, as averaged over several minutes, turn the function switch to L/L and press CHG. The date and time are displayed by setting the function switch to TIM. (This assumes that the proper time functions were entered in when the set was turned on.)

Steering to a given destination can also be displayed assuming that the memory has been told initially where you wish to go. The receiver displays the distance to go (and the time to go) to the destination, as well as the crosstrack error. The latter factor is the computed distance to the left or right from the desired path of travel.

The quality of the received signals is extremely important for safe and reliable loran navigation. This quality is expressed by a display of the signal-to-noise (SNR) ratio. You can obtain this reading by setting the function switch to SNR. The SNRs of the master and two selected secondaries will be displayed. The readings will range from zero to 99. Good readings extend between 70 and 99, fair between 40 and 70, and poor between 15 and 40. When the signal quality drops to approximately 10, a warning indicator is activated.

In addition to the low SNR alarm, there are various other warnings and alarms. There is a cycle alarm that flashes until the signal processor has sufficient confidence that the correct cycle of the incoming signal from the desired GRI signal is being tracked. When tracking is established, the flashing stops and does not flash again unless the receiver lacks confidence that the correct cycle is being tracked.

There is a blink alarm mentioned previously that indicates when the Coast Guard is warning that there may be a problem with a particular station.

There is another warning activated when the vessel approaches an assigned waypoint that has been stored in memory. A waypoint is a point of reference or location of interest that has been chosen by the user. This can be in terms of LOPs or latitude and longitude. As many as 50 waypoints can be stored in memory as you make a trip to a specific destination or destinations. To set up a waypoint all you need are two bits of information, the direction to steer, and the distance to the waypoint. This information can be gathered from the appropriate chart and entered before you leave. An off-course alarm can be activated when the extent of the crosstrack error reaches a preset value.

The loran receiver has anchor watch capability. When in operation, it monitors the position of the vessel while at anchor. If the vessel's line of drift extends substantially beyond the area encompassed by the circular area of its anchor chain, an alarm sounds.

The envelope of the transmitted loran-C burst or pulse has a carefully controlled shape from the beginning to the peak. It is related uniquely in time to the particular 100-kHz carrier that is tracked. This envelope can be changed as a result of propagation or other disturbances and can affect the ability of the receiver to select the proper sampling point. This relationship can be observed by setting the function switch to SNR and pressing CHG. There are numerous other applications for a loran receiver that can be put to work depending upon the skill of the operator or navigator and his knowledge of his particular loran receiver.

12-4-2. Functional Block Diagram

A simplified block of the loran receiver is given in Fig. 12-20. As shown at the top left, the preamplifier is a part of the antenna mount. It is an impedance-matching amplifier that permits the development of adequate signal current from the short antenna before it is transferred by coaxial cable to the receiver. In so doing it raises the incoming signal level above much of the noise that may be picked up by the transmission line.

Bandpass filters open the receiver to a range of frequencies between about 85 kHz and 115 kHz only. Off-band signals are rejected as much as possible. Next, there are notch filters in the receiver that remove interfering signals that can lower the SNR value. Notch filters are selected for the individual GRIs according to possible sources of interference with the signals of the individual chain. The data processing unit does the filter selection through the notch control interconnection shown in Fig. 12-20. The receiver does considerable limiting and changes the incoming signal over to a switching-level type signal, called a "hard-limited" signal, that can be sampled in the

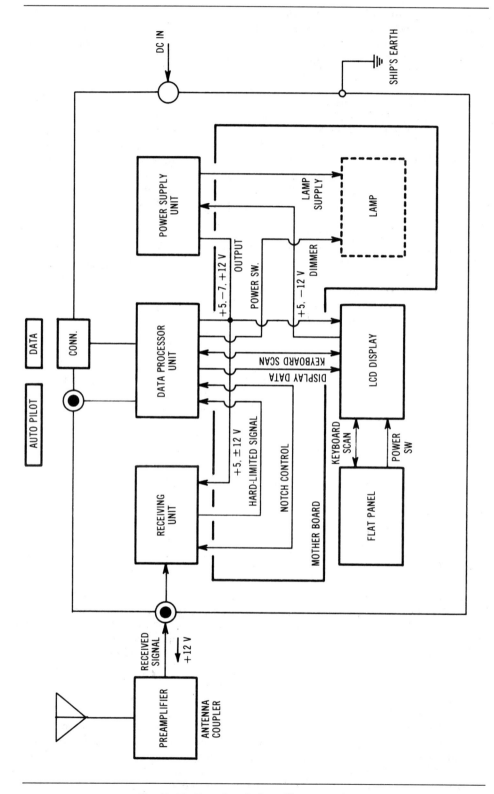

Fig. 12-20. Functional plan of loran receiver.

data processor. By so doing the exact timing of the zero-crossover tracking can be preserved. A component that is derived from the complete envelope is also developed and changed into a pulse that helps in the selection of the proper tracking point. This component can also be used in adjusting the receiver gain to maintain a constant amplitude.

In the data processor unit the loran signals from the receiver are sampled at proper times for correct operation. All operations are under the control of a temperature-compensated crystal oscillator to precisely set the correct timing. The microprocessors control all functions including the commands from the control panel. Therefore, they control the readouts of the LCD as the signal is acquired and the TDs computed. Instructions are contained in program memory and the microprocessor has a capability of about one million instructions per second.

The unit also has output data connections and an available link to an automatic pilot. The remaining blocks in Fig. 12-20 are the power supply and the operational lamp.

13

Marine Radar

Radar is used principally as a navigation guide. It is a self-contained system and requires no coastal station. It sends out its own transmission in the form of a microwave pulse. When this pulse strikes a reflecting surface, a return signal is picked up by the radar receiver. By evaluating the time needed for a pulse to go out and come back, and knowing the angle from which the return pulse has come, the radar display is able to determine the distance and direction of obstacles in the path of navigation. In fact, a radar unit displays on a CRT screen a simple relief map that shows the various other ships, obstacles, and shore outline. It is a definite aid in navigating busy waters near shore and for traveling in fog and other adverse weather, day or night.

13-1. Radar Principles

Radar is fundamentally a distance-measuring system using the principle of radio-echoing. You have heard an echo of your own voice as it has been bounced off a cliff or a distant large-area reflecting surface. Equipped with an accurate timing device plus a knowledge of the speed at which sound travels, you can determine just how far away the point of sound reflection is located. You have heard that bats in their nocturnal and cave travels use supersonic sounds for obstacle avoidance and for locating swarms of insects. The porpoise uses similar audio soundings in his underwater travel.

A radio wave travels many times faster than a sound wave. Nevertheless, with suitable instrumentation, radar can be used to measure the distance, or range, to a surface that reflects radio waves. In fact, the word "radar" is a contraction of its definition — RAdio Detection And Ranging.

Radio waves travel at the speed of 300 million meters per second, or approximately 186 thousand miles per second. These figures can be brought down accurately to any number of practical rule-of-thumb distance constants. The most common of these constants are given in Chart 13-1.

Chart 13-1. Radar Wave Propagation

Radio Wave Travel

186,000	Miles per Second
162,000	Nautical Miles per Second
3×10^8	Meters per Second
3.28×10^8	Yards per Second
0.186	Statute Mile per Microsecond
0.162	Nautical Mile per Microsecond
328	Yards per Microsecond

Radar Timing

10.75	Microseconds per Mile
12.35	Microseconds per Nautical Mile
164	Yards per Microsecond
0.081	Nautical Mile per Microsecond

It must be stressed that radar ranging is a two-way process. As shown in Fig. 13-1, the radio wave must travel out and back, and therefore the distance that the wave travels is twice the distance between the radar and the reflecting obstacle. In terms of nautical measurement, a radio wave travels 162,000 nautical miles per second. This corresponds to 0.162 nautical mile per microsecond (one microsecond equals one millionth of a second).

Because the radio wave must travel out and back, the actual radar-range velocity is usually stated as 0.081 nautical mile per microsecond. In other words, an obstacle 0.081 nautical mile away from the radar would require a total radar wave travel time of one microsecond (one-half microsecond out and one-half microsecond back).

Since a nautical mile is equal to 2027 yards, the velocity of radio-wave travel is equivalent to 328 yards per microsecond. However, effective radar velocity for range measurement purposes is again one half of this true radio-wave velocity; it is 164 yards per microsecond.

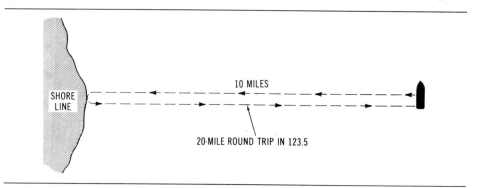

Fig. 13-1. Using radar to determine the distance to land.

In the example of Fig. 13-1, the distance to the shore line is to be determined. The radar instrumentation indicates that the radar wave in traveling out and back requires an elapsed time of 123.5 microseconds. This indicates that the range to the nearest land is approximately 10 nautical miles (0.081 × 123.5)

In using a radar set, it is not necessary to clock how many microseconds (μs) it takes the radio wave to travel out and back or to make any sort of calculation using radar range velocity and elapsed time. The radar set as such is calibrated in terms of range. The radar display directly indicates the distance to a reflecting surface.

The radar display may indicate the typical ranges shown in Fig. 13-2. If it is indicating that your position is 1000 yards to the left bank and 800 yards to the right bank, the actual radar signals are making round-trip excursions in 6.1 (1000/164) and 4.88 (800/164) microseconds, respectively. Up ahead there is another vessel some 500 yards on the left, and 2000 yards ahead is a pair of buoys. These correspond to elapsed times of 3.05 and 12.2 microseconds, respectively.

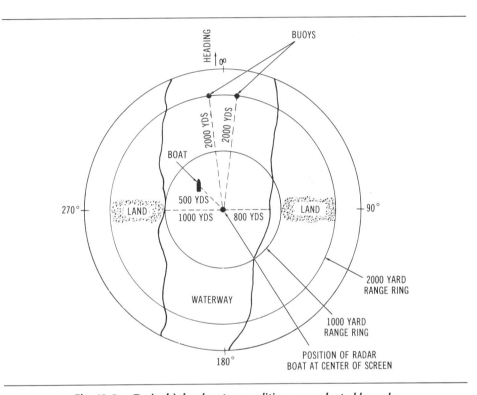

Fig. 13-2. Typical inland water conditions as evaluated by radar.

The display of information shown in Fig. 13-2 is quite similar to what you would see on the most common type of radar display. However, the background would be dark, and the actual targets would be illuminated. In addition, there would be several concentric illuminated rings which are called *range rings* or *range marks*. They calibrate the display in terms of distance from the radar set. In the example, calibrations are in terms of thousands of yards.

A radar set is not only able to determine the range to a point of reflection, but it also determines the bearing of the point of reflection with relation to the position of the radar or with respect to some reference direction such as true north. For the usual shipboard radar, the ship heading is often established as the 0° reference angle, as depicted in Fig. 13-2.

Radar signals are transmitted on an extremely high frequency. Therefore, the wavelength is very short, and it is possible to build highly directional antennas with practical dimensions. Microwave signals travel in straight-light-beam fashion. These characteristics make it possible to concentrate the radar energy into a small-diameter, pencil-like beam. Thus, the direction from which a reflection returns to the radar set is indicated by the angular position of the radar antenna at that instant. This fact is illustrated in Fig. 13-3. If the antenna is pointing directly north, there will be a reflection from obstacle 1. Since the reflection occurs when the antenna is pointing in the direction of the ship's heading, it is indicated that the obstacle is at 0°, or dead ahead. Likewise, with the antenna directed at an angle 30° or 135° relative to the ship's heading, there will be a return echo indicating that there are obstacles in these directions.

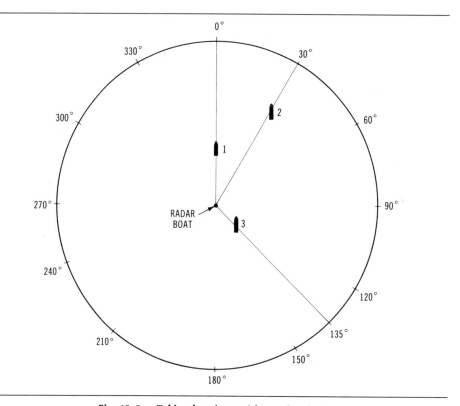

Fig. 13-3. Taking bearings with a radar display.

In summary, a radar is able to determine the range to an obstacle or target by evaluating the time needed for a signal to go out to the target and return. The bearing of the target is shown by the angle of the antenna when the target signal returns. These two factors are of particular importance in using radar for marine navigation and safety.

Radar can be used to evaluate additional attributes of a target that is returning echoes to the set. The size of the image as it appears on the radar display tube gives some inkling of the dimensions of the target. A large vessel produces a larger mark or "blip" than a smaller vessel produces; a buoy appears smaller than a vessel. The shore line illuminates a much larger segment of the display, indicating a large land mass. A large island illuminates a larger area on the radar display tube than does a smaller island.

The greater the range to a target of a given size, the smaller its corresponding blip on the display screen. A stationary target appears stationary on the display. The faster the target moves, the faster it moves across the display tube as compared to a slower moving target. There are radar systems that can accurately determine the actual velocity and direction of motion of a moving target.

The strength of a return signal from a given range can also give a clue to the makeup of the target. A metallic surface reflects a strong signal. A large target made of wood or other material that does not reflect radio waves well returns a much weaker echo, or no echo signal at all.

The ability to "read" a radar display separates the good radar operator from the mediocre one. Interpretive skill comes with practice. Practice when vision is good so that you can "see" the object and its corresponding blip.

To summarize again, radar can be used to determine target range, target bearing, and something about the physical attributes and motion of the target.

13-2. Pulse Radar

There are various forms of radar transmission. The most common type is called *pulse radar*. Pulse radar sets are widely installed on small boats and ocean-going vessels. A pulse radar set sends out a strong pulse of microwave energy. The transmitter then shuts down, and the radar receiver listens for returning echos from this burst of energy. Radar pulses vary in duration from considerably less than 1 microsecond up to 4 or more microseconds. Depending on the range and type of radar service to be rendered, from 60 pulses up to several thousand pulses are sent out per second.

Under all circumstances, the transmit time is very much shorter than the receive time. This is a necessity because the receiver must listen for an elapsed time equal to the time of travel out to a target at the maximum range and back again to the receiver. Recall that a radar nautical mile corresponds to an excursion time of 12.35 microseconds. If the maximum range of a particular radar set is 12 miles and there is a target at that distance, the total elapsed time will be 148.2 (12 × 12.35) microseconds. Remember that the receiver listens for a much greater time than the transmitter transmits, as shown in Fig. 13-4.

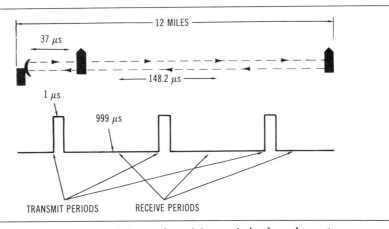

Fig. 13-4.   Transmitting and receiving periods of a radar system.

In Fig. 13-4 it has been assumed that the duration of the transmit pulse is 1 microsecond. The time spacing between the end of one pulse and the beginning of the next has been assigned a value of 999 microseconds. Thus, the radar pulse and its reflected return pulse have adequate time to travel 12 miles and return. Of course, there is more than adequate return time to obtain a reflected pulse before the next transmit pulse is sent out.

If the conditions just mentioned apply to a maximum 12-mile range, what is the maximum number of 1-microsecond pulses that are transmitted per second? The time interval between the start of one pulse and the start of the next corresponds to 1000 (1 + 999) microseconds. This is the pulse period. What would be the number of pulses transmitted per second or pulse repetition rate? The answer is found by dividing the pulse period into one million microseconds or:

$$\text{Pulses Per Second (PPS)} = \frac{1 \text{ second}}{\text{period}} = \frac{1{,}000{,}000 \text{ } \mu s}{1000} = 1000$$

The answer is the number of times that a transmit pulse is sent out each second.

Note that another earlier pulse is being received in the example of Fig. 13-4. For this target the pulse goes out and back in 37 microseconds. How many miles away is this ship? All you need do is divide 37 by 12.35 to obtain a range of approximately 3 miles. On the radar screen it would appear much nearer to the ship position as represented by the center of the screen than the second ship which is at 12 miles and would be near the edge of the screen.

It is apparent that the radar transmitter functions for only a small portion of each second. During these intervals of transmission, a high peak power is radiated. However, if the power is averaged over an entire second, it is found to be much lower. Radar transmitters have a high peak-power output but a low average power output. Peak powers for small to moderate-sized vessels fall between 1–50 kilowatts. For large ocean-going vessels it is higher.

The average power output of a radar transmitter can be calculated in a simple manner. First you need to determine for what fraction of a second radar power is being transmitted. In the example of Fig. 13-4, the pulse duration was 1 microsecond, and 1000 of these pulses were transmitted each second. Consequently, the transmit time averaged over a second is:

$$\text{Transmit Time} = 1 \text{ } \mu s \times 1000 = 1000 \text{ } \mu s$$

In the example the transmitter transmits for 1000 microseconds out of each one million microseconds. This quotient is referred to as the duty cycle of the radar:

$$\text{Duty Cycle} = \frac{\text{Transmit Time}}{10^6} = \frac{1000}{1{,}000{,}000} = 0.001$$

Furthermore, if the peak power of the radar is known to be 3000 watts, the average power can be determined by multiplying the peak power by the duty cycle. Thus, in the previous example, the average power can be calculated to be:

$$\text{Average Power} = \text{Duty Cycle} \times \text{Peak Power}$$
$$\text{Average Power} = 0.001 \times 3000 = 3 \text{ watts}$$

The higher the duty cycle, the greater is the average power output. The duty cycle is increased by increasing pulse duration and/or the pulse repetition rate.

13

13-3. Basic Functional Blocks

The block diagrams that follow give you some basic concepts of how radar operates. In modern radar sets many of the operations to be discussed are handled electronically resulting in smaller, less costly, more precise, and higher definition display. An array of memories, microprocessors, and digital techniques are employed. Even the incoming reflected pulses (video) are digitized to obtain a brighter and higher definition presentation.

The major units are shown in the block diagram in Fig. 13-5. The timing center of a radar set is called the *timer*. It generates a basic set of timing pulses that trigger and control the generation of the pulses that turn on the radar *transmitter*. In effect, the timer decides the pulse-repetition rate of the radar system.

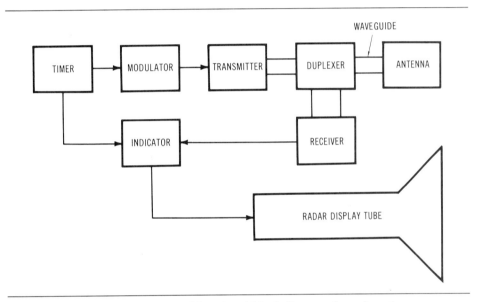

Fig. 13-5. General functional block diagram of a radar set.

The transmitter contains the high-powered microwave generator. It is usually a magnetron power oscillator. The function of the magnetron is to generate a high-powered RF pulse of proper duration and repetition rate. The power pulses that turn on the magnetron are generated in the *modulator*. The modulator pulse generator is always under the control of timing pulses from the timer.

The oscillator operates only during the power pulse and sends out a burst of microwave energy through the *duplexer* and *waveguide* to the antenna. Then the transmitter shuts down, and the *receiver* listens. The return echoes from a distant object strike the same antenna, and through the waveguide and duplexer, the return signals enter the receiver. Here they are increased in level and demodulated. The signals are next applied to an *indicator* and are observed on a special cathode-ray *display tube*. The scope display and associated circuits are calibrated by the timer so that any actual time measurement can be made between the time of pulse transmission and the time of echo arrival. In so doing, a conversion is made between time and distance.

The indicator display also takes into consideration the direction to which the antenna is pointed when the echo returns. Consequently, the radar display can also be calibrated in terms of bearing.

On transmit the duplexer places a short circuit across the receiver input. Consequently, the high-powered transmit pulse does not injure or delay the operation of the radar receiver. On receive the path opens to the receiver and the weak returning echo can be recovered. The duplexer now prevents the transmitter output circuit from loading down the receiver input.

The receiver is very sensitive and to maintain the best signal-to-noise ratio it converts the high-frequency microwave signal to a lower intermediate frequency before amplification. Usually the magnetron, duplexer, and oscillator-mixer are mounted near to the microwave antenna. After some IF amplification the signal is routed to the receiver proper. Local oscillator injection is supplied by either a klystron or a gunn oscillator. The signal is then amplified and demodulated in preparation for its application to the indicator section. In the indicator section there is further signal processing along with the introduction of the calibration signals and other useful display arrangements that simplify the operation of the radar set. Also, under control of the timer, the indicator section develops the necessary sweep waveforms used to deflect the beam of the cathode-ray display tube.

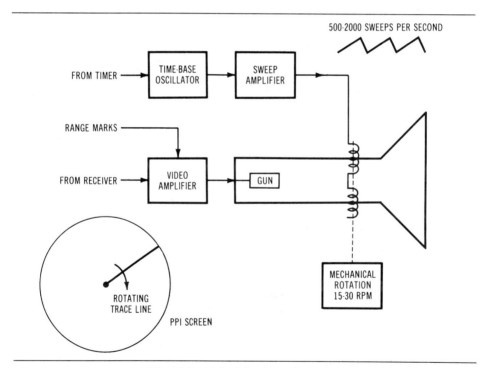

Fig. 13-6. Principle of PPI display.

13-4. Radar Display

The range and bearing are displayed on the plan-position indicator (PPI) screen. The basic PPI presentation is a circular one that is traced out by a rotating sweep line, as shown in Fig. 13-6. The center of the round screen is the origin of the trace and corresponds to the position of the radar installation.

As the antenna rotates in a PPI radar installation, the angular position of the sweep line indicates the azimuth angle of the antenna. In fact, the PPI trace line rotates (15 to 30 rpm) in synchronism with the antenna, always indicating the azimuth angle or bearing of the antenna relative to a zero reference angle. The reference angle can be the ship's heading or it can be true north.

As it rotates, the trace line causes some illumination of the screen. An arriving target signal causes a brighter illumination of the screen. The return target signals are applied to the electron gun of the radar cathode-ray tube and cause intensity modulation of the beam. This process can be compared to the influence of a video signal applied to the grid of a television picture tube.

If a target is "painted" on the screen by the rotating trace line, as in Fig. 13-7A, its angular position on the display tube shows the target bearing. Often a mechanical or electronic cursor is included. It can be rotated until its hairline, as shown in Fig. 13-7B, crosses the target and sets off the bearing on the azimuth scale that surrounds the periphery of the display tube.

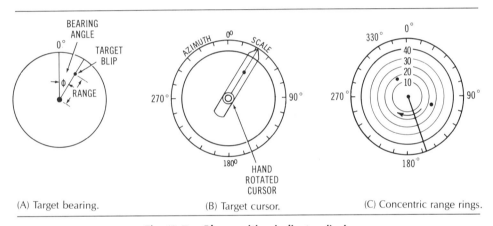

(A) Target bearing.   (B) Target cursor.   (C) Concentric range rings.

Fig. 13-7.   Plan-position indicator display.

The range of the target is disclosed by the distance between the target and the center of the display. A target at maximum range would appear at the edge of the display. A nearer target would appear on the screen at a point nearer to the origin.

The PPI display can be range calibrated. The range calibrations are set off by concentric circles referred to as range rings. Assuming a 40-mile range, it is possible that there would be four concentric rings, as in Fig. 13-7C, setting off the 10-, 20-, 30-, and 40-mile ranges.

In the example of Fig. 13-7C, there are two targets. One appears at a bearing of 330° and is approximately 18 miles away. A second target at 25 miles has a bearing of approximately 110°.

The PPI radar system does not just pick out a few isolated targets; rather, it picks up any target capable of returning a signal, so long as that target is within the useful range of the radar set. The targets are painted on the screen regardless of their bearing. In fact, a PPI presentation is almost map-like.

A radar picture of New York harbor is shown in Fig. 13-8. Make a comparison between what is seen on the radar screen and the map of the same area shown beside the radar display. Your location, at the center of the radar screen, corresponds to a position on the East River. In fact, you have just passed under the Manhattan and

Brooklyn bridges and are moving between the edge of Manhattan and Governor's Island. Notice how the radar sets off the land masses with a large area of illumination. The water area is dark. The docks can be distinguished along the shore lines.

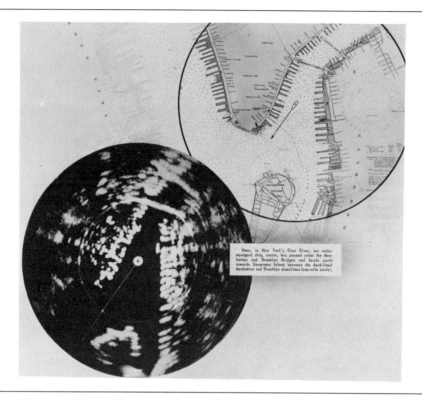

Courtesy Raytheon Marine Co.

Fig. 13-8. Radar display of New York Harbor.

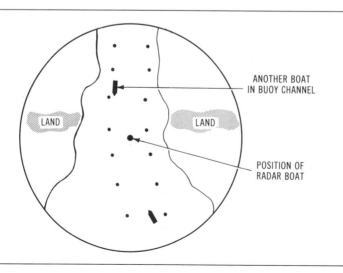

Fig. 13-9. Buoy-channel display.

Another type PPI presentation is shown in Fig. 13-9. This type of pattern can be seen in moving along a bay or inland waterway. The actual buoys along the channel can be seen. The radar shows other small boats moving along the channel; shore lines and bridges stand out clearly.

In summary, the PPI screen is ideal for shipboard radar because of its map-like type of display. Aircraft radars use the PPI display for the same reason. Likewise, land-based radar that must keep watch on aircraft traffic in all directions can make good use of the circular display. Although the PPI is by far the most common type of display, there are specific uses for other types in such applications as weather radar, aircraft landing, and missile tracking.

13-5. Waveguides and Antennas

A particular advantage of microwave transmission is that the microwave energy can be concentrated into a pencil-like beam with an antenna of practical dimensions. A highly directional beam is important in obtaining an accurate bearing and a bearing resolution that will permit the radar operator to delineate closely spaced targets.

A problem of microwave transmission is that the signal must be handled carefully to minimize losses. The attenuation and radiation losses of a conventional coaxial or flat-type transmission line are excessive above 1000 megahertz. These losses increase with frequency. Occasionally, for short spans, very high-quality coaxial lines are used on operating frequencies up into the medium-microwave range. However, by far the most efficient transmission line is the waveguide, which is a single hollow metal conductor (Fig. 13-10). Waveguides may be rectangular, round, or oval; the rectangular type is the most common.

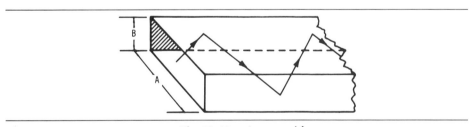

Fig. 13-10.   A waveguide.

13-5-1. Waveguides

Microwave energy travels within the metal enclosure of a waveguide by bouncing off the inner walls. There is no significant penetration of the walls and, consequently, no radiation loss. In fact, the waves are reflected off the inner walls with little attenuation loss. Thus the waves propagate along the guide with very little loss, even as compared to the current losses encountered by a lower-frequency wave traveling along a conventional transmission line.

The transmission of microwave energy along a waveguide is in the form of electromagnetic propagation, just as a wave is propagated through space, except that the radiation is confined within the guide. In considering the operation of a waveguide, therefore, we are concerned with magnetic and electric lines of force. These hold the same significance as the RF current and voltage distribution along a regular transmission line.

There are *electric lines of force* between the plates of an operating capacitor, as in Fig. 13-11. There are *magnetic lines of force* about a current-carrying conductor. In the case of an actual coaxial transmission line, there are electrostatic lines of force between the inner and outer conductors, and a magnetic field is set up about the current-carrying wire. In this case, the magnetic lines are confined within the outer conductor.

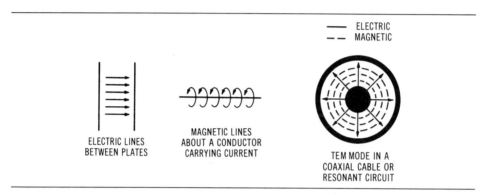

Fig. 13-11.   *Electric and magnetic fields.*

From the preceding, it is apparent that there are both electric and magnetic lines of force in the air or other dielectric material between the inner and outer conductors of a coaxial line. These lines of force are perpendicular to each other and are perpendicular to the direction of current flow in the line, as shown in Fig. 13-11. The electrostatic field configuration for such a coaxial line is said to be *transverse electromagnetic* (TEM), because both fields are normal to the direction of wave travel. The transverse electromagnetic mode of operation is common to all types of transmission lines except waveguides.

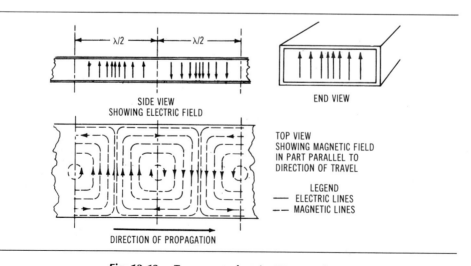

Fig. 13-12.   *Transverse electric (TE$_{10}$) mode.*

In the transmission line, the two conductors provide a return path for field energy. A waveguide has only one conductor. There is no physical return path for the RF energy. The changing lines of force must provide the continuous movement and completed loops within the guide. Either the electric or the magnetic field must be oriented in part in the direction of propagation. Since the electric and magnetic fields are always perpendicular to each other, both fields cannot be perpendicular to the direction of propagation. Thus, the TEM mode is impossible in a waveguide.

There are two basic modes of waveguide propagation. One is called *transverse electric* (TE) because the electric field is perpendicular to the direction of propagation (Fig. 13-12). The magnetic field in this case is parallel to the direction of propagation. In the *transverse magnetic* (TM) mode, the magnetic field is perpendicular to the direction of propagation, while the electric field parallels the direction of propagation.

There are various subdivisions of the basic TE and TM modes. These are indicated by two subnumerals which indicate the number of amplitude peaks that fall along the long or short walls of the waveguide. The first subnumeral indicates the number of patterns or half periods that fall along the long walls of the rectangular guide (side-to-side *A* dimension of Fig. 13-10). The second subscript indicates the number of patterns or half periods that fall along the short walls from top to bottom (*B* dimension in Fig. 13-10).

In the case of the TE mode, these patterns are electric field patterns; for the TM mode, they are magnetic field patterns. In the example of Fig. 13-12, the mode is TE_{10}, indicating that the electric field pattern shows one pattern from side to side and is uniform from top to bottom.

13-5-2. Waveguide Accessories

Waveguides present various mechanical problems. Bends, turns, and joints can be made, but they must be planned carefully to provide a gradual and smooth transition along the path of propagation. Bends should be beveled or have a large radius of curvature. In this way, discontinuities and harmonics are not introduced into the particular mode configuration. Flange joints are common; they must be smooth and tight fitting.

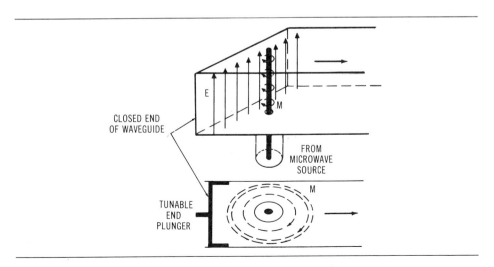

Fig. 13-13.   Probe used to excite TE_{10} mode in a waveguide.

There must also be a means of transferring energy from a signal source to the guide. In such a transfer, the waveguide must be excited at the proper mode.

Most microwave tubes, such as magnetrons and klystrons, have waveguide inputs and outputs. Hence, it is possible to use a flange joint. Some microwave tubes employ coaxial input and/or output. In this case, it is necessary to use a probe excitation arrangement, as in Fig. 13-13. An extension of the inner conductor of the coaxial segment extends probe-like into the waveguide. Its electric field is parallel to the probe. Consequently, the electric vector in the waveguide becomes parallel with its short sides and transverse to the long side and the direction of propagation. Oppositely, the magnetic lines of force from the probe, although normal to the electric lines, are parallel to the direction of propagation. In this arrangement, therefore, the waveguide is excited in the TE_{10} mode.

Choke joints, such as that shown in Fig. 13-14A, provide a smooth, tight fit. A choke joint has a flat and a slotted flange. The entire length of the section, from the aperture in the wall of the waveguide to the shorted end in the slotted flange, is exactly one-half wavelength. Since a shorted half-wavelength section of line reflects a short to its opposite end, the aperture between the two sections at the waveguide wall is an electrical short circuit which maintains near-perfect electrical continuity along the waveguide wall at the radar microwave frequency.

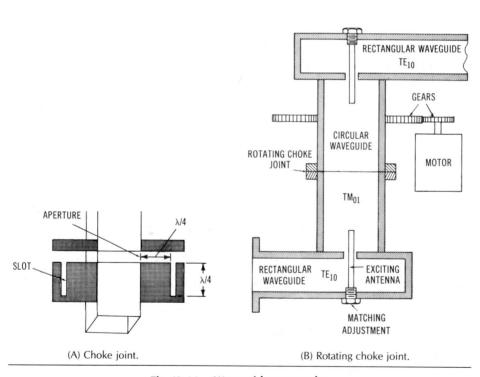

(A) Choke joint.

(B) Rotating choke joint.

Fig. 13-14. Waveguide accessories.

A rotating choke joint is shown in Fig. 13-14B. The rotating joint is again a choke type having a flat and a slotted section; one is fixed and the other rotates. In the arrangement, despite some slight mechanical separation between the two flanges, the electrical continuity is sustained by the choke-joint arrangement. In fact, separations up to several millimeters can be used without a serious disturbance of the energy being propagated along the guide. Two probe arrangements make the necessary transfers between rectangular and circular waveguide segments. The TE_{10} mode transfer can be made with the simple arrangement of Fig. 13-13.

Appropriate accessories can be used to match impedances. Typical arrangements are shown in Fig. 13-15B. Tabs or diaphragms can be inserted into the waveguide. When dimensioned correctly and inserted at the proper positions, these tabs or diaphragms provide an impedance transformation.

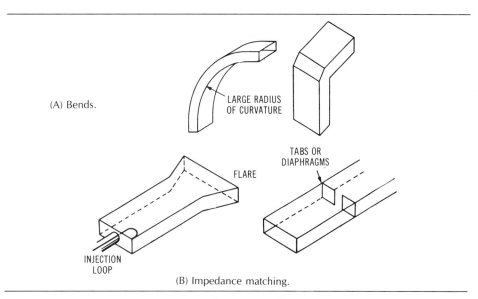

(A) Bends.

LARGE RADIUS OF CURVATURE

TABS OR DIAPHRAGMS

FLARE

INJECTION LOOP

(B) Impedance matching.

Fig. 13-15. Other waveguide accessories.

Waveguides must also transfer signals to the radar antenna. Sometimes the open end of the waveguide is a source of radiated signal for a parabolic reflector. A better match and proper excitation or *illumination* of the reflector can be accomplished by tapering the end of the waveguide into a horn. Even a coaxial line can be used to excite such a waveguide horn. In this case, the inner conductor of the coaxial line extends as a loop into the waveguide radiator.

Waveguides can be cut at specific lengths to serve as open or short circuits, or they can be made to display capacitive or inductive reactances. In association with diaphragms or external sections, waveguides can be made to have the characteristics of traps, bandpass filters, or band-rejection filters. In fact, a properly dimensioned waveguide section can be made to operate as a series or parallel resonant circuit, just as transmission-line sections can be made to serve similar functions.

As shown in Fig. 13-16, waveguide segments can be closed off into various shapes and forms. These are all called *resonant cavities*. The simplest resonant cavity can be made by closing off both ends of a half-wavelength section of a rectangular or circular waveguide. In such a cavity, there will be a circulating magnetic field similar to the circulating RF current in a conventional tuned circuit. Such a waveguide cavity can be excited by an inductance loop coming from a coaxial line or by a waveguide coupling system through a slot or iris. A waveguide cavity can be tuned by using either a plunger arrangement or capacitive slugs.

A waveguide cavity can be made to have an exceptionally high Q (often in excess of 10,000), and it is inherently stable and well shielded. When carefully calibrated in

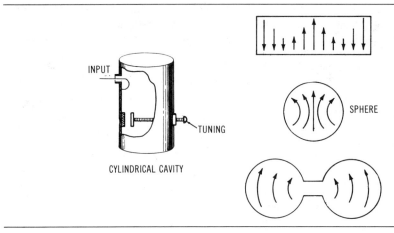

Fig. 13-16. Resonant cavities.

association with an accurate micrometer movement and scale, the waveguide cavity can serve as an effective wavemeter for checking microwave frequencies and other parameters.

13-5-3. Radar Antennas

The parabolic reflector and waveguide horn (Fig. 13-17) constitute the basic radar antenna. The microwave pulse is directed onto a parabolic reflector from the expanding aperture (horn) at the end of the waveguide. The horn taper matches the small waveguide to the surrounding space; its length and flare angle influence the radiation and gain characteristics of the antenna system.

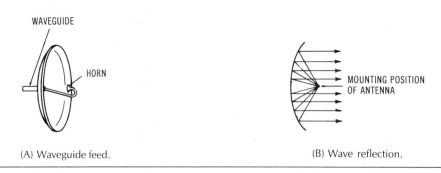

(A) Waveguide feed.　　　　　(B) Wave reflection.

Fig. 13-17. Parabolic antennas.

The shape of the parabolic reflector is controlled in a manner that concentrates the RF energy into a single source of radiation that can then be sent out in a single direction. As shown in Fig. 13-16, there are equal angles of wave incidence and reflection at the parabolic surface. Thus, the rays coming off the reflecting surface flow outward in parallel paths. The energy coming off a full parabolic surface of this type is

concentrated into a small-diameter pencil-like beam. The larger the parabolic antenna in terms of wavelength, the smaller the diameter of the beam is and the greater the antenna gain.

Parabolic-reflector diameters are at least several wavelengths and often ten or more wavelengths. Power gains of several thousand are practical.

Sectionalized parabolic reflectors are often employed if a circular beam is not required. Such sectionalized types generate beams of specific vertical and horizontal angles of radiation. At the same time, the physical dimensions of a sectionalized type can be made such that the sections are less awkward in terms of erection space and the need for rotation or scanning.

In many radar services, the horizontal radiation angle should be very narrow so as to have a good bearing resolution. However, it is often preferable for the vertical radiation angle to be substantially broader so as to minimize the vertical stability problem. For example, there is considerable vertical motion of a ship because of the waves. Hence, it is very likely that a radar beam would swing above and below the target as the boat "rode the waves." However, this would not be so if the vertical beam from the antenna were rather wide. Hence, a common antenna for shipboard radar would be a sectionalized parabola, as shown in Fig. 13-18. In terms of the horizontal beam width, the parabolic section has a large diameter in terms of wavelength; therefore the beam is quite narrow. The height dimension of the reflector is limited,

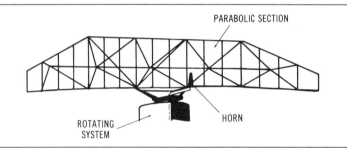

Fig. 13-18.   Parabolic section and rectangular horn illuminator.

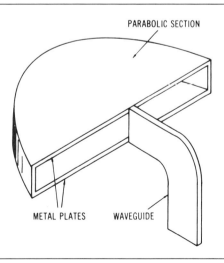

Fig. 13-19.   Basic pillbox antenna.

and therefore the vertical radiation angle is rather broad. Even the illuminating horn is an upright rectangle that helps establish a narrow horizontal angle and a wider vertical angle.

The antenna style of Fig. 13-19 is adaptable to marine radar, and it is referred to as a *pillbox*. The pillbox ia a parabolic section positioned between two metal plates. The separation between the two plates can be somewhat less than one wavelength. The waveguide directs energy into the pillbox slot; the energy is then reflected from the parabolically shaped rear wall into a narrow horizontal beam. The vertical beam is rather broad, as is required for many practical radar applications.

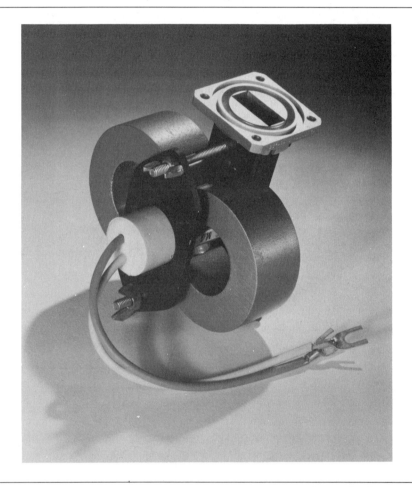

Courtesy Raytheon Marine Co.

Fig. 13-20.   *Low-powered magnetron for small plane or boat radar.*

13-6. Magnetrons

The magnetron is the most common radar transmitting tube. It is used almost exclusively in marine radar installations. Klystrons are sometimes used for extremely

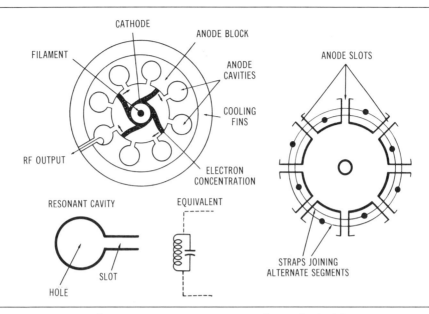

Fig. 13-21. Magnetron construction and principles.

high-powered search-radar installations. The magnetron is a self-contained oscillator and requires only a means of input power application and RF microwave energy removal. The essential parts (Figs. 13-20 and 13-21) are the anode block and cathode mounted in an evacuated envelope, external magnet, and means for applying filament power and removing microwave energy. Following are some typical electrical data:

Heater Voltage	5.0 Volts
Heater Current	0.65 Ampere
Pulse Duration	0.2 Microsecond
Duty Cycle	0.0003
Peak Anode Voltage	5.0 Kilovolts
Peak Anode Current	3.5 Amperes
Peak Power Output	5.0 Kilowatts
Frequency	9410 ± 50 MHz
Life	500 Hrs Min.

The anode block consists of a series of resonant cavities, each of which has the characteristics of a parallel resonant circuit. In approximation, the holes function as inductances, and the slots function as capacitances. The cavities operate as individual resonant circuits connected in parallel. Therefore the total capacitance of the magnetron oscillator is nC (n = number of cavities), while the total inductance is L/n. Inasmuch as the resonant frequency of the magnetron varies inversely with the square root of the LC product, the frequency of the magnetron oscillator is the same as the resonant frequency of each individual cavity.

The multicavity arrangement and the unavoidable mutual coupling between cavities means that there are other resonant modes. Thus the magnetron has stability problems, and it is possible that it may oscillate at other than the desired mode. This lack of stability and the tendency to oscillate at spurious modes are reduced with the technique of strapping, as shown in Fig. 13-21. In this arrangement, every other resonant section is joined together with a segment of a circular ring. A second strap then joins the alternate set.

The cathode is positioned at the center of the magnetron structure. Between the cathode and the anode block is the *interaction space*. In this area, there is interaction between the electrons moving from cathode to anode and the magnetic lines of force generated by a powerful external fixed magnet.

As shown in Fig. 13-22, heater power is supplied through a pulse transformer. The anode block forms the major portion of the outside area of the tube. For safety reasons, it is usually grounded. Therefore, in pulsing the magnetron oscillator, it is necessary to use a pulse of a high negative amplitude which is applied to the cathode. Inasmuch as the anode operates at ground potential, the cathode and filament circuits must be designed to withstand a high negative potential. The filament chokes and transformer isolate the filament source from the pulse circuit.

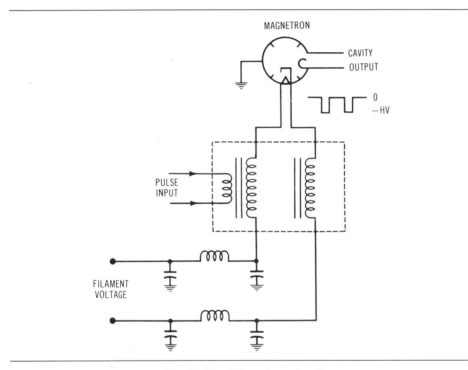

Fig. 13-22. Magnetron circuit.

Most magnetrons are fixed-tuned, with the frequency being determined by the physical dimensions of the cavity. Some slight change in frequency can be accomplished by varying the load into which the magnetron operates. Magnetrons can be tuned by mechanical means with the use of a bellows or a threaded arrangement. A frequency-changing inductive element can be made to move into the individual cavities, or a capacitive element can be inserted into the individual slots.

Fundamentally, the magnetron oscillator is a transit-time or velocity-modulated type. The electrons released from the cathode come under the influence of various fields during the time that they are in transit between cathode and anode. These various fields cause a change in velocity among electrons and cause them to bunch as they come closer to the anode.

In understanding magnetron operation, it is necessary to consider the influence of three fields. When the anode is positive with respect to the cathode, there is an electric field that draws the electrons in a straight-line path between the cylindrical cathode and the anode block (Fig. 13-23A).

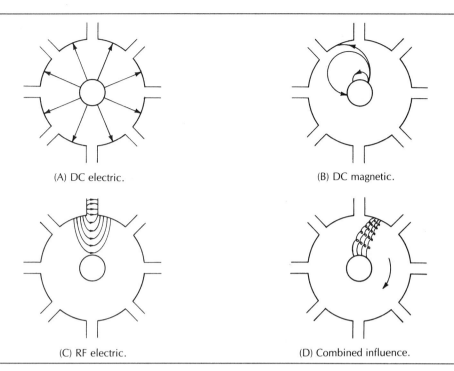

(A) DC electric.   (B) DC magnetic.

(C) RF electric.   (D) Combined influence.

Fig. 13-23.   Influence of three fields on electron motion.

In addition to the electric field, there is a DC magnetic field established by the magnet. The influence of a magnetic field on an electron is to cause the electron to move in a direction normal to the magnetic field and its own surrounding magnetic field. (When any electron is in motion, it has a surrounding magnetic field). Thus, the electron would have a tendency to revolve in a circle were it not for the combined influence of the electric and magnetic fields, as shown in Fig. 13-23. When the magnetic field is strong, it is dominant; thus when the electron leaves the cathode, it is turned around in a rather tight circle, returning to the cathode surface. For a somewhat weaker magnetic field, the electron would continue to return to the cathode, but over a longer path. With a magnetic field of proper magnitude, the electron has sufficient velocity, under the influence of the combined fields, to reach the anode block over a curved path.

In addition to the DC electric and DC magnetic fields, there is a radio-frequency (microwave) field which extends outward from the cavity slot, as shown in Fig. 13-23C. This is a fast-changing oscillating field that corresponds to the resonant frequency of the cavities.

As in the start of any type of oscillator, a finite time is required for the buildup. In the case of the magnetron oscillator, any slight discontinuity in electron flow becomes the catalyst that initiates the buildup of oscillations. The influence of the resultant RF field is pronounced; it causes the electron velocities to build up and slow down. The relative influence the field exerts depends on the position from which a given electron leaves the cathode surface relative to the phase of the changing field. Thus, the RF field does not influence each electron to the same extent. As shown in Fig. 13-23D, the electrons are made to loop in transit between cathode and anode. The relative influence is such that the differing electron velocities cause the electrons to bunch together prior to their striking the anode, setting up the spoking action shown in Fig. 13-21.

Furthermore, as the RF field varies, the bunching activity revolves around the anode block like the spokes of a wheel. As the spokes revolve past the slots in the resonant cavities, bursts of energy are released, setting each cavity into oscillation. As you recall, in a vacuum-tube or transistor oscillator the bursts of current (plate and collector current, respectively) cause the output tuned circuit to oscillate. Similarly, in the case of the magnetron, it is the cyclic bursts of energy delivered to the resonant cavities that sustain continuous oscillations.

In the case of a radar pulsed magnetron, these oscillations continue for the duration of the high-powered negative trigger pulse applied to the cathode from the modulator. Between pulses, there is no difference of potential between magnetron anode and cathode, and oscillations cease.

In normal magnetron operation, a substantial number of electrons never reach the anode but are returned to the cathode surface. The bombardment of the cathode by these electrons produces additional heating and augments the filament power. In some magnetron circuits, the filament power is actually removed once the electrons have taken over the heating of the cathode surface.

13-7. Small Boat Radar

The Raytheon Mariners Pathfinder® Radar in Fig. 13-24 is an example of a modern compact and lightweight radar that operates with less than 50 watts of total supply power. It is a two-part arrangement consisting of a radome housing antenna and tranceiver called a scanner unit and a control and display unit. The latter weighs but 15 lbs and can be mounted at the helm or at any other viewable location. An alternative is a cabin mount where it would be better protected from the weather. Mounting on a swivel-arm shelf is a good idea. Such a mounting allows the display to be moved into any desired position.

On many small ships the scanner unit can be installed directly on the top deck of the wheelhouse near the ship's center line. Mount as high as possible and remember that its scanning beam should not be obstructed by nearby large objects. If sufficient height or clearance cannot be obtained, a radar mast or pedestal may be necessary.

The Raytheon small-boat radar uses digital technology which translates conventional radar signals to digital levels that can be compared for interference rejection and stored memory. The raster-scan system updates the cathode-ray tube display continuously with the most current signals stored in the memory to produce a sharp and bright image. A bright picture is of particular help in viewing the radar image from a distance. The image is displayed in bright green on a black background.

There are seven scanning ranges (from 1/4 to 12 nautical miles) and a full range of controls. Controls permit the display of range scale, range rings, heading markers, and other navigation aids. There is a hold switch to freeze a given image. Rain clutter and interference controls aid in adjusting for the clearest display.

The rotation speed of the antenna is 27 revolutions per minute. Consequently, the PPI screen is updated every 2.2 seconds with a scanning sweep on its 9-inch diagonal screen. A bearing scale is illuminated around the screen and is used to determine the relative bearing to a target. Bearing accuracy is better than ± 1°. Range scales of 0.25, 0.5, 1.0, 2.0, 4.0, 8.0, and 12.0 nautical miles are available. The following controls and switches are mounted along the bottom of the indicator in Fig. 13-24. From left to right they are operate, tune, sea-clutter adjustment, gain, and hold switch. The ones along the right (from top to bottom) are rain-clutter switch, marker switch, interference rejection switch, brilliance switch, and the five range buttons. Details on control functions and operating procedures are given in the following discussions.

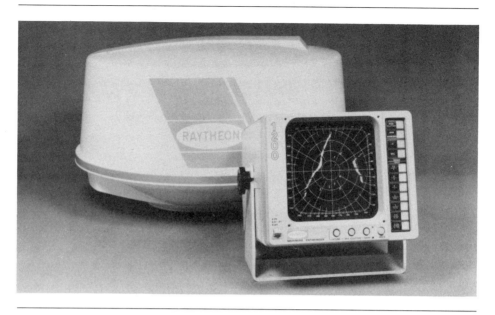

Courtesy Raytheon Marine Co.

Fig. 13-24.   Raytheon Marine Pathfinder^R Radar.

13-7-1. Functions of Controls

OFF–ST-BY–ON

The operator switch is labeled OFF-ST-BY, and ON. In OFF position there is no power supplied to the scanner unit or the display unit. In ST-BY position, power is supplied to both units, but radio waves are not being transmitted. Approximately 90 seconds after switched to ST-BY, the Ready light will glow, meaning the radar is available for operation. In the ON position, (with the Ready light glowing) the system is transmitting, and any echoes from targets received are amplified and displayed on the screen.

TUNE

The TUNE control allows you to maximize target echoes by "fine" tuning of the local oscillator which is located in the scanner unit.

GAIN

The GAIN control varies the amplification in the receiver, and thus the strength of echoes as they will appear on the screen.

SEA CLUTTER

The SEA CLUTTER control reduces the gain level at short range only.

RAIN CLUTTER

The primary use of RAIN CLUTTER is to break up the returns from rain or snow, thus allowing weaker targets to become visible.

SHM, MARKERS

The SHM MARKERS switch is a four position switch which selects the ship heading, markers, both, or none for the display.

BRIL

The BRIL controls four levels of the screen brilliance (brightness).

IR

The IR switch turns the interference rejector "on" to eliminate interference from other ship radars.

HOLD

The HOLD switch is used to temporarily "freeze" the picture on the screen to assist the operator in determining bearing and ranges. Pushing the HOLD switch stops the transmission of RF power; releasing the switch restores normal operation.

RANGE

The seven RANGE switches select the scale which you wish the radar to display. The range selected automatically determines the proper number and calibrated distance between the range rings and the proper transmission pulse length as shown in Table 13-1.

13-7-2. Operating Procedure

TO SWITCH ON

To switch on the radar, proceed as follows:

1. Set the Operate switch to ST-BY.

2. After the READY light glows (approximately 90 seconds), set the Operate switch to ON.

3. Set the BRIL switch to obtain the desired brightness of the screen.

4. Set range scale to the 4-, 8-, or 12-mile range.

5. Assure that the RAIN CLUTTER, IR, and SEA CLUTTER switches are off.

6. Adjust the TUNE control for maximum echoes on the screen. If there is no target available (that is, in the open sea) adjust for the maximum strength of sea clutter.

7. Push the RANGE switch of the scale you wish to cover.

8. Adjust RAIN CLUTTER and SEA CLUTTER as necessary.

9. If necessary, press IR to reduce radar interference. When the radar is no longer required, set the Operate switch to OFF. If you want to keep the radar in a state of immediate readiness, the Operate switch should be set to ST-BY position.

Table 13-1. Relation of Range, Rings, and Pulse Length

Range (nautical miles)	Range Rings Interval (nautical miles)	Number of Rings	Pulse Length (microseconds)
0.25	0.125	2	0.12
0.5	0.25	2	0.12
1.0	0.25	4	0.12
2.0	0.5	4	0.12
4.0	1.0	4	0.5
8.0	2.0	4	0.5
12.0	3.0	4	0.5

RANGE AND BEARING MEASUREMENTS

The picture on the screen (Fig. 13-25), shows a plan view of the possible positions of targets around the vessel. In effect, your ship is at the center of the screen and targets are presented in polar coordinates (or maplike) throughout 360°. The display is referred to as the PPI (Plan Position Indicator).

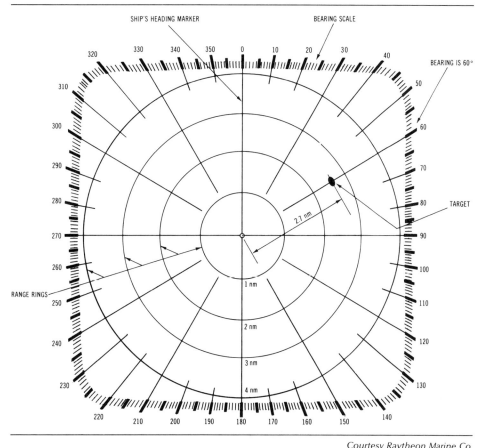

Courtesy Raytheon Marine Co.

Fig. 13-25. PPI presentation.

548

Range Measurement

To measure a target's range proceed as follows:

1. Note the range scale in use and the distance between rings.

2. Count the number of rings between the center of the screen and the target, and visually estimate the distance between the inner edge of the target and inner edge of the nearest ring. There is a target 2.7 nautical miles away in Fig. 13-25.

Bearing Measurement

Using the bearing scale engraved on the screen filter, read the bearing where the radial line passes through the center of the target. The reading you obtain will show the target's relative bearing in degrees. Target is at 60° in Fig. 13-25.

13-7-3. Using the Controls

TUNE Control

The magnetron and the gunn oscillator may take about 10 minutes to completely stabilize on frequency. So after switching on and tuning initially, the tuning should be rechecked after the first 10 minutes.

Symptoms that the equipment may be out of tune are a lack of distant echoes or the appearance of double echoes (one echo behind another). Normally, it is possible to fine tune the radar by selecting a comparatively weak echo and then rotating the TUNE control until the strongest echo and best definition are combined.

GAIN Control

The correct setting of the GAIN control is for a light background speckle to be just visible on the screen. The equipment is then in its most sensitive condition. Objects will be detected at the greatest possible range. With too little gain, weak targets may be missed, and there can be a decrease in detection range. With excessive gain (a few) extra targets may be brought in, but the contrast between echoes and background noise will be substantially reduced, making target observation more difficult.

In crowded regions, the gain can be temporarily reduced to clarify the picture. This must be done with care since important marks may be missed. With the gain at its normal setting, clutter from rain or snow may obscure the echo from a ship inside a squall or storm. A temporary reduction in gain will usually permit the stronger and more distinct ship echo to be distinguished.

Detection of targets beyond the storm may, however, require slightly higher gain than normal, since the clutter may have attenuated, but not completely obscured, echoes from the targets. The GAIN control should always be returned to its normal position as soon as any temporary alteration is no longer required.

SEA CLUTTER Control

Whereas the GAIN control affects the strength of echoes at all ranges, the effect of the SEA CLUTTER control is greatest on short-range echoes, becoming progressively less as range increases. The SEA CLUTTER control is only effective up to a maximum of about three miles.

In particular, the SEA CLUTTER control reduces the strength of the mass of random signals received from waves at short range. The setting used should be sufficient to reduce the strength of signals until clutter appears only as small dots, and until small targets can be distinguished, the setting should never be advanced so far as to blank out all clutter.

The sensitivity of the SEA CLUTTER control is fully variable, thus enabling an optimum picture to be obtained under adverse weather conditions.

Maximum reduction in the strength of close-range echoes takes place when the control is turned fully clockwise. When it is turned counterclockwise, there is no reduction in the strength of echoes.

The SEA CLUTTER control may be used to reduce some rain or snow clutter, as well as strong sea clutter, in the immediate vicinity of the vessel. A temporary increase in the setting will usually permit strong echoes from ships, and most navigational marks inside storms or squalls, to be distinguished.

At close range in crowded regions the control may be temporarily advanced to clear the picture. This should be done with care, so as to avoid missing important echoes. The SEA CLUTTER control should be always returned to its optimum position after any temporary alteration.

RAIN CLUTTER Switch

During heavy rain or snow which may clutter the picture, use RAIN CLUTTER to give better contrast between echoes and the clutter. Under some conditions of sea return, both RAIN CLUTTER and SEA CLUTTER will help to clarify the picture. When viewing large masses of land, coastlines, etc. RAIN CLUTTER reduces the background and will cause promontories to stand out more clearly.

IR Switch

When a radar on another ship is using the same frequency band as your radar, an interference which typically appears arranged in curved spokes may occur. Radar interference is mainly noticeable on longer range scales.

Using the IR switch will eliminate this form of interference as well as any other form of a synchronous noise.

13-7-4. Navigation with the Radar

Obtaining a Position Fix

The radar set is an accurate and reliable navigational aid for determining your ship's position. A position fix based on two or more navigational points will furnish a more accurate fix, especially when the points approach 90° apart from your ship's position.

Avoiding Collision

The moment a target appears on the screen, its range and relative bearing should be noted. This is best done on a plotting sheet or chart.

As in visual observation, "a constant bearing indicates a collision course."

As soon as a series of plots indicates a closing range and no significant change in successive bearings, positive action should be considered mandatory and "The Regulations for Preventing Collisions at Sea" should be observed.

Determining Your Radar Line-of-Sight Range

When searching for distant targets, your radar line-of-sight range to the target can be a limiting factor. Radar waves behave like light waves but they are refracted slightly more, increasing the distance to the radar horizon slightly more than that to the optical horizon. As Fig. 13-26 shows, the radar line-of-sight range is a combination of the radar horizon of your ship's radar scanner and the radar horizon of the target.

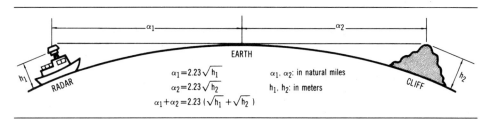

Fig. 13-26. The radar horizon.

The distance to the radar horizon from the radar scanner under standard conditions, may be calculated from the formula

$$\text{Distance} = 2.23 \ \sqrt{h}$$

where,
   Distance is in nautical sites,
   h is the height of scanner in meters.

For example, a scanner at a height of 5 meters has a radar horizon of 5 nautical miles (nm).
   A cliff 5-meters high also has a radar horizon of 5 nm. Therefore, under standard conditions, the cliff should begin to appear on the screen when the ship closes nearer than 5 + 5 or 10 nautical miles.

13-7-5. False Echoes

Occasionally, signals appear on the screen at positions where there is no target. They are false echoes. The following are known as most common false echoes.

Side Echoes

Some radiation escapes on each side of the main beam in side lobes. If they are reflected by a target, they will be displayed on the screen as an echo. (See Fig. 13-27A) These echoes appear as arc echoes on each side of the true echo. They will sometimes be joined together if the side echoes are strong.

Multiple Echoes

Multiple echoes may appear if there is a large target having a wide vertical surface parallel to your own ship at a comparatively short range. The signal will be reflected by

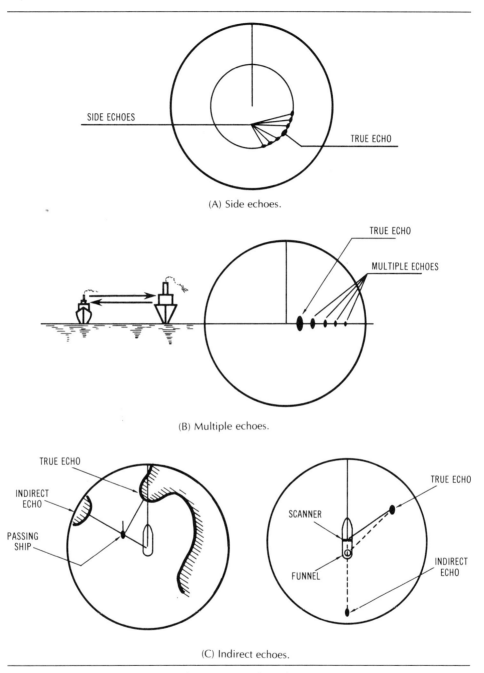

(A) Side echoes.

(B) Multiple echoes.

(C) Indirect echoes.

Fig. 13-27. False echoes.

the wide vertical surface. Then the reflected signal strikes your own ship, and it will return along the same paths to the target. This will be repeated. Thus, the multiple echoes will appear beyond the true target echo on the same bearing as shown in Fig. 13-27B.

552

Indirect Echoes

As shown in Fig. 13-27C indirect echoes may appear if there is a large target (such as a passing ship) at a short range, or a reflecting surface (such as a funnel) on your own ship. The signal, on first striking the smooth side of the large target, will be deflected. Then when it encounters a second target, the echo will return along the same paths to the scanner. Thus, the echo from the second target will appear beyond that of the large target but on the same bearing. The indirect echoes will also appear when the signal is deflected by the reflecting surface.

13-7-6. Block Diagram Description

A simplified block diagram of the radar set is given in Fig. 13-28. The scanner and the associated transmit-receive equipment is on the right; the indicator circuits and cathode-ray tube are on the left. The antenna or radiator is horizontally polarized and consists of a resonant center-fed slotted-waveguide array mounted with an appropriate flare. Approximately 2 feet in length it is coupled to the transmitter and receiver by way of a short waveguide, rotary joint, and circulator. At half-power points the horizontal beam width is only 5°. The vertical beam width is 25°. A 12-volt DC motor rotates the antenna at seven rpm.

An associated encoder produces the bearing pulses for the rotation synchronization. One pulse is generated each 0.176° of rotation (2048 pulses per rotation). The ship heading marker (SHM) switch produces a signal that corresponds to the heading position when a permanent magnet fitted on the main gear passes across a reed switch. This once-each-rotation pulse is conveyed to the clear pulse generator in the display unit. The pulse from the encoder is conveyed to the bearing pulse generator in the display unit. These two components are used to synchronize the bearing of the radar display, display timing, and transmit triggering. Thus, the radio scanning motion on the display is synchronized with the direction toward which the antenna is pointed at a given moment. The triggering of the transmitter and the receiver display timing is also synchronized with the firing of the magnetron and the follow-up listening period.

A properly timed trigger pulse from the transmitter trigger generator of the indicator circuitry is applied to the modulator. The modulator is a line-type pulser which uses an SCR as a high power switch. This rectifier is pulsed on by the incoming trigger pulse. Short pulses are generated when the 0.25-, 0.5-, 1-, or 2-nautical-mile range switches are selected. Longer pulses result for operation on the 4-, 8-, or 12-nautical-mile ranges. The pulse repetition frequency is 920 Hz. This pulse of proper width is supplied to the magnetron which generates a high-energy oscillation on approximately 9445 MHz for the duration of the input pulse. This pulse is sent out and the receiver now listens for echoes.

A ferrite circulator serves as the duplexer. In addition a diode limiter offers additional protection to the receive section when the high-level microwave pulse is transmitted or when an excessively high-level signal is received. Two small diodes fitted inside the mixer waveguide assembly form a balanced mixer which supplies a 38-MHz frequency signal to the IF amplifier. The local injection voltage is supplied from a gunn oscillator that is tuned 38 MHz higher than the transmit frequency.

The IF amplifier consists of a low-noise transistor amplifier followed by an integrated-circuit chip amplifier. The second stage is controlled by a gain-control sea-clutter signal from the display unit. The IF signal is demodulated to obtain video rate signals for display. It is followed by an emitter-follower that provides an impedance match to the coaxial cable that conveys the video signal down to the display unit.

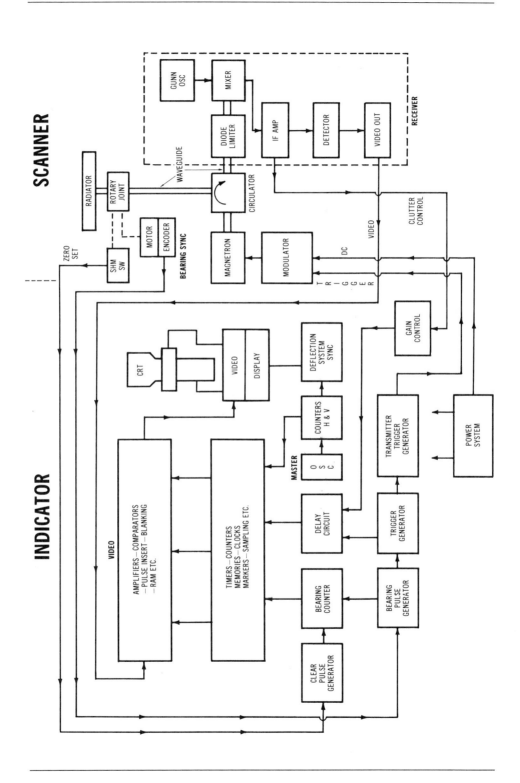

Fig. 13-28. Simple block diagram.

There is an array of circuits in the video section of the display unit. There are circuits that amplify, shape, and control the pulse duration according to the selected range. There is a memory that stores the video data of three successive transmissions in 112 memory cells and a video RAM containing 65,536 memory cells that is the main memory for the display. The CRT screen consists of 224 by 224 dots that are the responsibility of the main memory. There are interference rejection circuits as well as stages in which appropriate pulses are inserted that establish the ship heading marker and range markers as well.

All of these activities are initiated and processed by a variety of circuits represented in the large block below the video block in Fig. 13-28. Operations are synchronized by information from the encoder and SHM of the scanner, as well as the 6-MHz clock pulse from the master oscillator of the indicator. This oscillator output is also applied to the horizontal and vertical counters which supply signal synchronizing information to the CRT synchronizing and deflection circuits.

The bearing pulse generator synchronizes the display timing with the signal from the motor encoder. The output from the motor encoder is applied to both the bearing counter and the main trigger generator. The latter generator produces the trigger pulse for the transmitter and display control timing. The trigger generator output is also passed through a delay circuit that permits a variable delay time for adjusting the PPI center to exact zero nautical mile as compensation for transmitter firing delays. The clear pulse generator produces an output used for resetting the bearing counter to zero. This is the generator that is triggered by the SHM pulse from the antenna system.

14

FCC Licensing, Operating Practices, and Examination Requirements

This chapter covers FCC licensing procedures and requirements. Types of licenses, including station and operator licenses, are discussed in relation to the various radio services. Guidance in obtaining proper licenses and in preparing for the examinations associated with some license grades are included. Topic listings for various FCC element examinations help you orient your examination preparations. This handbook along with various key publications available from the Government Printing Office are a definite aid. Additional helpful publications are mentioned.

14-1. The Federal Communications Commission

The FCC was created by the Communications Act of 1934 for the purpose of regulating communications. Among the general powers given to the Commission is the authority to classify radio stations, prescribe the qualifications of operators, and to issue radio station and radio operator license.

14-2. Radio Station Licenses

Radio stations come in many shapes and sizes. When the FCC talks about a "radio station," they don't just mean the local broadcast stations that transmit entertainment and news. A radio station from the FCC's point of view can be anything from a million-watt television station to the two-way radio in your small boat or plane. One thing most radio stations have in common is a station license issued by the FCC. With this station license the FCC gives the station authority to transmit. A CB station requires no station or operator license.

In many ways a station license is like an automobile registration. Almost anyone may own a car but it may be used on a public road only after a registration has been issued by the state. This registration assigns a unique combination of letters and numbers to the vehicle, defines the purpose for which the vehicle is to be used (personal transportation, farming, commercial, etc.), and imposes a requirement that the vehicle be used only in accordance with a set of regulations, called a motor vehicle code.

Similarly, a radio station license assigns a unique station identification, states the purpose for which the station is being used (broadcasting, business, aviation, etc.) and requires that the licensee comply with the Federal Communications Commission Rules and Regulations. Except for certain low-power stations which are clearly labeled as not requiring a license, all radio stations must be licensed before they are operated. Operators should check to be sure that the station they wish to operate has a valid station license before making any transmissions.

The FCC station license application forms are:

Form 574 Land Mobile Services

Form 506 Small-Boat and Ocean-Going Vessels

Form 404 Private and Commercial Aviation

14.3. Operator Licenses

14-3-1. Who Needs a Commercial Radio Operator License?

You need a commercial radio operator license if you operate, maintain, or repair radio transmitters in the maritime, aviation, broadcast, or international fixed public radio services. This includes:

- Ship radio and radar stations on all types of vessels from small motor boats to large cargo ships
- Coast stations of all classes
- Hand-carried portable units used to communicate with ships and coast stations on marine frequencies
- Radios on all types of aircraft from small private planes to large airliners
- Aeronautical ground stations (including hand-carried portable units) used to communicate with aircraft
- AM, FM, and TV broadcast stations including international broadcast stations.
- Transmitters operated in the Experimental Television Broadcast, Experimental Facsimile Broadcast, Developmental Broadcast, Low-Power Television, Television Broadcast Translator, FM Broadcast Translator, or FM Broadcast Booster radio services.
- International fixed public radiotelephone and radiotelegraph stations.

The FCC does *not* require you to obtain a commercial radio operator license for operation, maintenance, or repair of:

- Two-way landmobile radio equipment, such as that used by taxicabs, police and fire departments, businesses, and local government agencies (effective 11/11/84)

- Personal radio transceivers used in the Citizens Band, Radio Control, and General Mobile Radio services (effective 11/11/84)

- Auxiliary broadcast stations such as remote pickup stations and others except as mentioned previously.

- Stations operated in the Domestic Public Fixed and Mobile Radio Services. This includes mobile telephone systems, point-to-point microwave services, Multipoint Distribution Service, etc.

- Stations operated in the Cable Television Relay Service.

14-3-2. **Types of Licenses, Permits, and Endorsements**

The FCC currently issues six types of commercial radio operator licenses and two types of endorsements, which are described briefly below:

1. **Restricted Radiotelephone Operator Permit**

A Restricted Radiotelephone Operator Permit allows operation of most aircraft and aeronautical ground stations, marine radiotelephone stations on pleasure vessels (other than those carrying more than six passengers for hire), and most VHF marine coast and marine utility stations. It is the only type of license required for transmitter operation, repair, and maintenance (including acting as chief operator) at all types of AM, FM, TV, and International broadcast stations.

There is no examination for this license, but to be eligible for it, you must meet all of the following requirements.

- Be at least 14 years old

- Be a legal resident (eligible for employment) in the United States or, if not so eligible, hold an aircraft pilot certificate valid in the United States or an FCC radio station license in your name (see limitation on validity in the following)

- Be able to speak and hear,

- Be able to keep at least a rough written log

- Be familiar with provisions of applicable treaties, laws, and rules which govern the radio station you will operate.

A Restricted Radiotelephone Operator Permit is normally valid for the lifetime of the holder.

If you are a nonresident alien applying for a Restricted Radiotelephone Operator Permit, you must hold one of the following:

- A valid United States pilot certificate issued by the Federal Aviation Administration or a foreign aircraft pilot certificate which is valid in the United States on the basis of reciprocal agreements entered into with foreign governments

- A valid radio station license issued by the FCC in your own name.

If you claim eligibility on the basis of possession of the FCC issued station license, the Restricted Radiotelephone Operator Permit issued on the basis of that eligibility will authorize operation of only your own station.

2. Marine Radio Operator Permit

A Marine Radio Operator Permit is required to operate radiotelephone stations on board certain vessels sailing the Great Lakes, any tidewater, or the open sea. It is also required to operate certain aviation radiotelephone stations, and certain maritime coast radiotelephone stations. It does *not* authorize the operation of AM, FM, or TV Broadcast stations.

To be eligible for this license, you must meet all of the following requirements:

- Be a legal resident of (eligible for employment in) the United States
- Be able to receive and transmit spoken messages in English
- Pass a written examination covering basic radio law and operating procedures

Marine Radio Operator Permits are normally valid for a five-year term. They can be renewed at any time during the last year of the license term or up to five years following expiration. An expired permit is not valid.

3. General Radiotelephone Operator License

A General Radiotelephone Operator License is required for persons responsible for internal repairs, maintenance, and adjustment of FCC licensed radiotelephone transmitters in the Aviation, Maritime, and International Public Fixed radio services. It is also required for operation of maritime land radio transmitters operating with more than 1500 watts of peak envelope power and maritime mobile (ship) and aeronautical transmitters with more than 1000 watts of peak envelope power.

To be eligible for this license, you must meet all of the following requirements:

- Be a legal resident of (eligible for employment in) the United States
- Be able to receive and transmit spoken messages in English
- Pass a written examination covering basic radio law, operating procedures, and basic electronics

The General Radiotelephone Operator License is normally valid for the lifetime of the operator.

4. Third-Class Radiotelegraph Operator Certificate

The Third-Class Radiotelegraph Operator Certificate is required to operate certain coast radiotelegraph stations. It also conveys all of the authority of both the Restricted Radiotelephone Operator Permit and the Marine Radio Operator Permit.

To be eligible for this license, you must meet the following requirements:

- Be a legal resident of (eligible for employment in) the United States
- Be able to receive and transmit spoken messages in English
- Pass Morse code examinations at 16 code groups per minute and 20 words per minute plain language (receive and transmit by hand)

- Pass written examinations covering basic radio law, basic operating procedures (telephony), and basic operating procedures (telegraphy).

Third-Class Radiotelegraph Operator Certificates are normally valid for a renewable five-year term. They can be renewed at any time during the last year of the license term or up to five years following expiration. An expired certificate is not valid.

5. Second-Class Radiotelegraph Operator Certificate

A Second-Class Radiotelegraph Operator Certificate is required to operate ship and coast radiotelegraph stations in the maritime services and to take responsibility for internal repairs, maintenance, and adjustment of any FCC licensed radiotelegraph transmitter other than an amateur radio transmitter. It also conveys all of the authority of the Third-Class Radiotelegraph Operator Certificate.

To be eligible for this license, you must meet the following requirements:

- Be a legal resident of (eligible for employment in) the United States

- Be able to receive and transmit spoken messages in English

- Pass Morse code examinations at 16 code groups per minute and 20 words per minute plain language (receive and transmit by hand)

- Pass written examinations covering basic radio law, basic operating procedures (telephony), basic operating procedures (telegraphy), and electronics technology as applicable to radiotelegraph stations.

Second-Class Radiotelegraph Operator Certificates are normally valid for a renewable five-year term. They can be renewed at any time during the last year of the license term or up to five years following expiration. An expired certificate is not valid.

6. First-Class Radiotelegraph Operator Certificate

A First-Class Radiotelegraph Operator Certificate is required only for those who serve as the chief radio operator on U.S. passenger ships. It also conveys all of the authority of the Second-Class Radiotelegraph Operator Certificate.

To be eligible for this license, you must meet the following requirements:

- Be at least 21 years old

- Have at least one year of experience in sending and receiving public correspondence by radiotelegraph at ship stations, coast stations, or both

- Be a legal resident of (eligible for employment in) the United States

- Be able to receive and transmit spoken messages in English

- Pass Morse code examinations at 20 code groups per minute and 25 words per minute plain language (receive and transmit by hand)

- Pass written examinations covering basic radio law, basic operating procedures (telephony), basic operating procedures (telegraphy), and electronics technology as applicable to radiotelegraph stations.

First-Class Radiotelegraph Operator Certificates are normally valid for a renewable five-year term. They can be renewed at any time during the last year of the license term and up to five years following expiration. An expired certificate is not valid.

Ship Radar Endorsement

The Ship Radar Endorsement is required to service and maintain ship radar equipment.
To be eligible for this endorsement, you must meet the following requirements:

- Hold a valid First- or Second-Class Radiotelegraph Operator Certificate or a General Radiotelephone Operator License

- Pass a written examination covering the technical fundamentals of radar and radar maintenance techniques.

Six-Month Service Endorsement

The Six-Month Service Endorsement is required to permit the holder to serve as the sole radio operator on board large U.S. cargo ships.
To be eligible for this endorsement, you must meet the following requirements:

- Hold a valid First-Class or Second-Class Radiotelegraph Operator Certificate

- Have at least six months of satisfactory service as a radio officer on board a ship (or ships) of the United States equipped with a radiotelegraph station in compliance with Part II of Title III of the Communications Act of 1934

- Have held a valid First-Class or Second-Class Radiotelegraph Operator Certificate while obtaining the six months of service

- Have been licensed as a radio officer by the U.S. Coast Guard, in accordance with the Act of May 12, 1948 (46 U.S.C. 229 a-h), while obtaining the six months of service.

14-3-2. Written Examinations

There are five written examinations in the commercial radio operator series. They are as follows:

Elements 1 and 2 (Marine Radio Operator Examination) — Basic Marine Radio Law and Basic Marine Radio Operating Practice. Provisions of laws, treaties, and regulations with which every radio operator in the maritime radio services should be familiar. Radio operating procedures and practices generally followed or required in communicating by radiotelephone in the maritime radio services.

Element 3 (General Radiotelephone Examination) — Provisions of laws, treaties, and regulations with which every radio operator in the maritime radio services should be familiar. Radio operating procedures and practices generally followed or required in communicating by radiotelephone in the maritime radio services. Technical matters including fundamentals of electronics technology and maintenance techniques as necessary for repair and maintenance of radio transmitters and receivers.

Element 5 (Radiotelegraph Operating Practice) — Radio operating procedures and practices generally followed or required in operation of shipboard radiotelegraph stations.

Element 6 (Advanced Radiotelegraph) — Technical, legal, and other matters, including electronics technology and radio maintenance and repair techniques applicable to all classes of radiotelegraph stations.

Element 8 (Ship Radar Techniques) — Specialized theory and practice applicable to proper installation, servicing, and maintenance of ship radar equipment.

14-3-3. Telegraphy Examinations

The telegraphy tests for commercial radio operators consist of both transmitting and receiving tests. To pass them, you must copy by ear and send by hand plain text and code groups in the International Morse code, at the required speeds, for one continuous minute, without making any errors. Each test will last approximately five minutes.

Code speeds are computed using five letters per word or code group. Punctuation symbols and numerals count as two letters each.

You may use your own typewriter to copy the 25 words-per-minute receiving test, but you must copy tests at lower speeds by hand. Likewise, you may use your own semiautomatic key ("bug") to send the 25-words-per-minute sending test, but you must send tests at lower speeds using a hand key. The failing of any code test automatically terminates the examination.

14-3-4. Application Forms and Licensing Procedures

You must use the following FCC forms to apply for commercial radio operator licenses, permits, and endorsements:

FCC Form 753 — Use this form to apply for a Restricted Radiotelephone Operator Permit if you are legally eligible for employment in the United States (citizen or resident alien). It incorporates a temporary permit for immediate operating authority.

FCC Form 755 — Use this form to apply for a Restricted Radiotelephone Operator Permit if you are *not* legally eligible for employment in the United States (nonresident alien, foreign aircraft pilot, etc.). It incorporates a temporary permit for immediate operating authority.

FCC Form 756 — Use this form to apply for any of the commercial radio operator licenses other than the Restricted Radiotelephone Operator Permit. Also use it to apply for renewal of a license which requires renewal, replacement of a lost or multilated license, and for a verification card, when necessary.

14-3-5. Passing Scores and Waiting Period for Reexamination

To pass a written examination, you must answer at least 75% of the questions correctly. Each written examination consists of multiple-choice type questions. Element 6 also contains several schematic diagram completion questions.

If you fail any element of an examination (including a code test), you must wait two-months before reapplying for examination. If you attempt to be re-examined before the two-month waiting period has elapsed, you will be in violation of FCC Rules and subject to penalties which could jeopardize your eligibility to hold FCC licenses. Under conditions of unusual hardship, the FCC may waive the two-month waiting period. When such conditions warrant, you may apply for such waiver at the FCC field office which administered the failed examination.

14-3-6. Photographs Required for Radiotelegraph Licenses

If you are applying for a *radiotelegraph* operator license or permit, you must send in, with your completed application, two identical, signed photographs of yourself. The photographs may be in color or black and white, but they must have been taken within six months of the date of the application. The photographs must be clear, front view, full-face and include not more than the head and shoulders, or upper torso. Newspaper, magazine, or photocopied photographs are not acceptable. The background in the photographs should be light and plain. The photographs must be no smaller than 2 inches by 2 inches (51 mm) and no larger than 3 inches by 3 inches (76 mm). You must sign each photograph along the left-hand side using ink. Do not mar the facial features in the photographs when you sign them. Your signature on the photographs must agree with your signature on the application. Do not tape or staple the photographs to your application.

14-3-7. Commercial Radio Operator Applications Processing

Applications for Restricted Radiotelephone Operator Permits are processed in Gettysburg, Pennsylvania. If you need assistance with these, contact:

Consumer Assistance Branch
Federal Communications Commission
Gettysburg, Pennsylvania 17325

Phone: (717) 337-1212

Applications for radiotelegraph licenses are processed in Washington, DC. If you need assistance with these, contact:

Public Service Division
Radio Operator Branch
Federal Communications Commission
Washington, DC 20554

Phone: (202) 632-7240

Applications for the General Radiotelephone Operator License and the Marine Radio Operator Permit are processed locally by the FCC Field Offices. Also, all examinations are conducted by the Field Offices. They are listed in the next section of this bulletin. Examinations are conducted quarterly in the cities where the FCC has offices. Additionally, the offices periodically conduct examinations in certain cities where the FCC does not have offices. Advance appointments are required for all examinations. Contact your nearest FCC field office or FCC Washington, DC 20554 for a copy of the latest printed examination schedule.

14-4. FCC Rules and Regulations

It is necessary that a radio operator or prospective radio operator (Restricted Radio Operator Permit, Marine Radio Operator Permit, and Third-Class Radiotelegraph Operator Certificate) be familiar with appropriate FCC laws and operating practices. He should have a copy of the FCC no-charge publication "Study Guide and Reference Material for the Marine Radio Operator Permit." Additionally, the radiotelegraph operator or prospective radiotelegraph operator should have a personal copy or ready access to FCC Part 83. More advanced operator grades should be familiar with these publications plus additional information related to technical information and more advanced operating practices.

The radio operator/technician or prospective radio operator/technician (General or more advanced Radiotelegraph Operator) should have personal copies or easy access to the FCC Parts that apply to his active radio service be it Land Mobile, Aviation, Marine Radiotelephone, or Marine Radiotelegraph. These Parts are also helpful in preparing for the license examinations. Questions related to FCC Rules and Regulations are frequent.

FCC Volumes and Parts can be obtained from the U.S. Government Printing Office, Department of Documents, Washington DC 20402. Contact the Government Printing Office at this address for the latest prices.

Volume I: Part 0 — Commission Organization
                Part 1 — Practice and Procedure
                Part 19 — Employee Responsibilities and Conduct
                S/N 004-000-00409-4

Volume II: Part 2 — Frequency Allocations and Radio Treaty Matters,
                          General Rules and Regulations
                Part 5 — Experimental Radio Services (Other than Broadcast)
                Part 15 — Radio Frequency Devices
                Part 18 — Industrial, Scientific, and Medical Equipment
                S/N 004-000-00410-8

Volume III: Part 73 — Radio Broadcast Services
                Part 74 — Experimental Auxiliary, Special Broadcast, and
                          Other Program Distributional Services
                S/N 004-000-00411-6

Volume IV: Part 81 — Stations on Land in the Maritime Services
                Part 83 — Services on Shipboard in the Maritime Services
                Part 87 — Aviation Services (Formerly in Volume V)
                S/N 004-000-00408-6

Volume V: Part 90 — Private Land Mobile Radio Services
                Part 94 — Private Operational-Fixed Microwave Service
                S/N 004-000-00412-4

Volume VII: Part 21 — Domestic Public Fixed Radio Services
                Part 22 — Public Mobile Radio Services
                Part 23 — International Fixed Public Radiocommunications
                Part 25 — Satellite Communications
                S/N 004-000-00401-9

Volume VIII: <u>Part 31</u> —Uniform System of Accounts for Class A and
Class B Telephone Companies
<u>Part 33</u> —Uniform System of Accounts for Class C
Telephone Companies
<u>Part 34</u> —Uniform System of Accounts for Radiotelegraph
Carriers (Formerly in Volume IX)
<u>Part 35</u> —Uniform System of Accounts for Wire-Telegraph and
Ocean-Cable Carriers (Formerly in Volume IX)
S/N 004-000-00413-2

The following Parts are available as separate items:

<u>Part 13</u> —Commercial Radio Operators (Formerly in Volume I)
S/N 004-000-00415-9

<u>Part 17</u> —Construction, Marking, and Lighting of Antenna
Structures (Formerly in Volume I)
S/N 004-000-00416-7

<u>Part 95</u> —Subpart E (Technical Regulations) (Formerly in
Volume VI)
S/N 004-000-00414-1

<u>Part 97</u> —Amateur Radio Service (Formerly in Volume VI)
S/N 004-000-00424-8

14-5. Element Examinations

Elements 1 and 2 cover basic radio laws and operating practices. These elements must be passed by all prospective radiotelephone or radiotelegraph, license holders, except for the Restricted Radiotelephone Operator Permit which requires no examination. To prepare for Elements 1 and 2 examination send for the latest edition of the free FCC publication, "Study Guide and Reference Material for the Marine Radio Operators Permit." This publication contains all the information needed to pass Elements 1 and 2.

To obtain a General Radiotelephone License, you must also pass Element 3. To obtain a Third-Class Radiotelegraph Operator Certificate, you must pass Elements 1, 2, and 5. A license for Second-Class Radiotelegraph Operator Certificate requires that you pass Elements 1, 2, 5, and 6. A Radar Endorsement for your license requires that you also pass Element 8.

As an assist in preparing for the Element 3 examination the Federal Communications Commission makes available "A Study Guide for the General Radiotelephone Operator License Examination." Write to the FCC Regional Services Division, Washington DC 20554. This publication is a series of questions only, that can be of assistance in orienting your examination studies. At one time the FCC also produced similar study guides for the radiotelegraph license Elements 3, 5, 6, and 8 but they are no longer available.

The author has available copy-machine study guides for these elements. They include expanded answers to the various questions in the Element 3 guide. Certainly they do not guarantee passage of the examination but they can be of assistance. The author also has available the original questions of the study guide that one time was available from the FCC for Elements 3, 5, 6, and 8. Study answers to these questions are also available. For information about availability and prices send a self-addressed, stamped long envelope to the following address:

Edward Noll
P.O. Box 75
Chalfont, PA 18914

14-6. FCC Field Offices

The following addresses and telephone numbers can be used to contact the FCC field office for your area.

Alaska
Room 240, 1011 E. Tudor Rd.
P.O. Box 102955
Anchorage, AK 99510
Examination Information (Recording)
Phone: (907) 561-1550
Other Information
Phone: (907) 563-3899

California
Room 501, 3711 Long Beach Blvd.
Long Beach, CA 90807
Examination Information (Recording)
Phone: (213) 426-7886
Other Information:
Phone: (213) 426-4551

(San Diego)
Room 405, 7840 El Cajon Blvd.
La Mesa, CA 92041
Examination Information (Recording)
Phone: (714) 293-5460
Other Information:
Phone: (714) 293-5478

Room 424, 555 Battery St.
San Francisco, CA 94111
Examination Information (Recording)
Phone: (415) 556-7700
Other Information:
Phone: (415) 556-7701/2

Colorado
12477 West Cedar Dr.
Denver, CO 80228
Examination Information (Recording)
Phone: (303) 234-6979
Other Information:
Phone: (303) 234-6977

Florida
Koger Bldg.
8675 NW 53rd St.
Miami, FL 33166
Examination Information (Recording)
Phone: (305) 593-0399
Other Information:
Phone: (305) 350-5542

Room 601, Interstate Bldg.
1211 N. Westshore Blvd.
Tampa, FL 33607
Examination Information (Recording)
Phone: (813) 228-2605
Other Information:
Phone: (813) 228-2872

Georgia
Room 440, Massell Bldg.
1365 Peachtree St., NE
Atlanta, GA 30309
Examination Information (Recording)
Phone: (404) 881-7381
Other Information:
Phone: (404) 881-3084/5

Hawaii
Room 7304, Prince Kuhio Federal Bldg.
300 Ala Moana Blvd.
P.O. Box 50023
Honolulu, HI 96850
Phone: (808) 546-5640

Illinois
Room 3940, 230 S. Dearborn St.
Chicago, IL 60604
Examination Information (Recording)
Phone: (312) 353-0197
Other Information:
Phone: (312) 353-0195

Louisiana
1009 F. Edward Hebert Federal Bldg.
600 South St.
New Orleans, LA 70130
Examination Information (Recording)
    Phone: (504) 589-2094
Other Information:
    Phone: (504) 589-2095

Maryland
1017 Federal Bldg.
31 Hopkins Plaza
Baltimore, MD 21201
Examination Information (Recording)
    Phone: (301) 962-2727
Other Information:
    Phone: (301) 962-2729

Massachusetts
1600 Customhouse
165 State St.
Boston, MA 02109
Examination Information (Recording)
    Phone: (617) 223-6607
Other Information:
    Phone: (617) 223-6609

Michigan
(Detroit)
24897 Hathaway St.
Farmington Hills, MI 48018-1398
Examination Information (Recording)
    Phone: (313) 471-0052
Other Information:
    Phone: (313) 226-6078

Minnesota
691 Federal Bldg & U.S. Courthouse
316 North Robert St.
St. Paul, MN 55101
Examination Information (Recording)
    Phone: (612) 725-7819
Other Information:
    Phone: (612) 725-7810

Missouri
Room 320, Brywood Office Tower
8800 East 63rd St.
Kansas City, MO 64133
Examination Information (Recording)
    Phone: (816) 356-4050
Other Information:
    Phone: (816) 926-5111

New York
1307 Federal Bldg.
111 West Huron St.
Buffalo, NY 14202
Examination Information (Recording)
    Phone: (716) 856-5950
Other Information:
    Phone: (716) 846-4511/2

202 Varick St.
New York, NY 10014
Examination Information (Recording)
    Phone: (212) 620-3436
Other Information:
    Phone: (212) 620-3437/8

Oregon
1782 Federal Bldg.
1220 S.W. Third Ave.
Portland, OR 97204
Examination Information (Recording)
    Phone: (503) 221-3097

Pennsylvania
(Philadelphia)
Room 404, One Oxford Valley Office Bldg.
2300 East Lincoln Highway
Langhorne, PA 19047
Examination Information (Recording)
    Phone: (215) 752-1323
Other Information:
    Phone: (215) 752-1324

Puerto Rico
(San Juan)
747 Federal Bldg.
Hato Rey, PR 00918–2251
Examination Information (Recording)
    Phone: (809) 753-4008
Other Information:
    Phone: (809) 753-4567

Texas
Room 13E7, U.S. Courthouse
Earle Cabell Federal Bldg.
1100 Commerce St.
Examination Information (Recording)
    Phone: (214) 767-0764
Other Information:
    Phone: (214) 767-0761

Room 5636, New Federal Office Bldg.
515 Rusk Ave.
Houston, TX 77002
Examination Information (Recording)
    Phone: (713) 229-2750
Other Information:
    Phone: (713) 229-2748

Virginia
Military Circle
870 Military Highway
Norfolk, VA 23502
Examination Information (Recording)
  Phone: (804) 461-4000
Other Information:
  Phone: (804) 441-6472

Washington
3256 Federal Bldg.
915 Second Ave.
Seattle, WA 98174
Examination Information (Recording)
  Phone: (206) 442-7610
Other Information:
  Phone: (206) 442-7653

Index

C